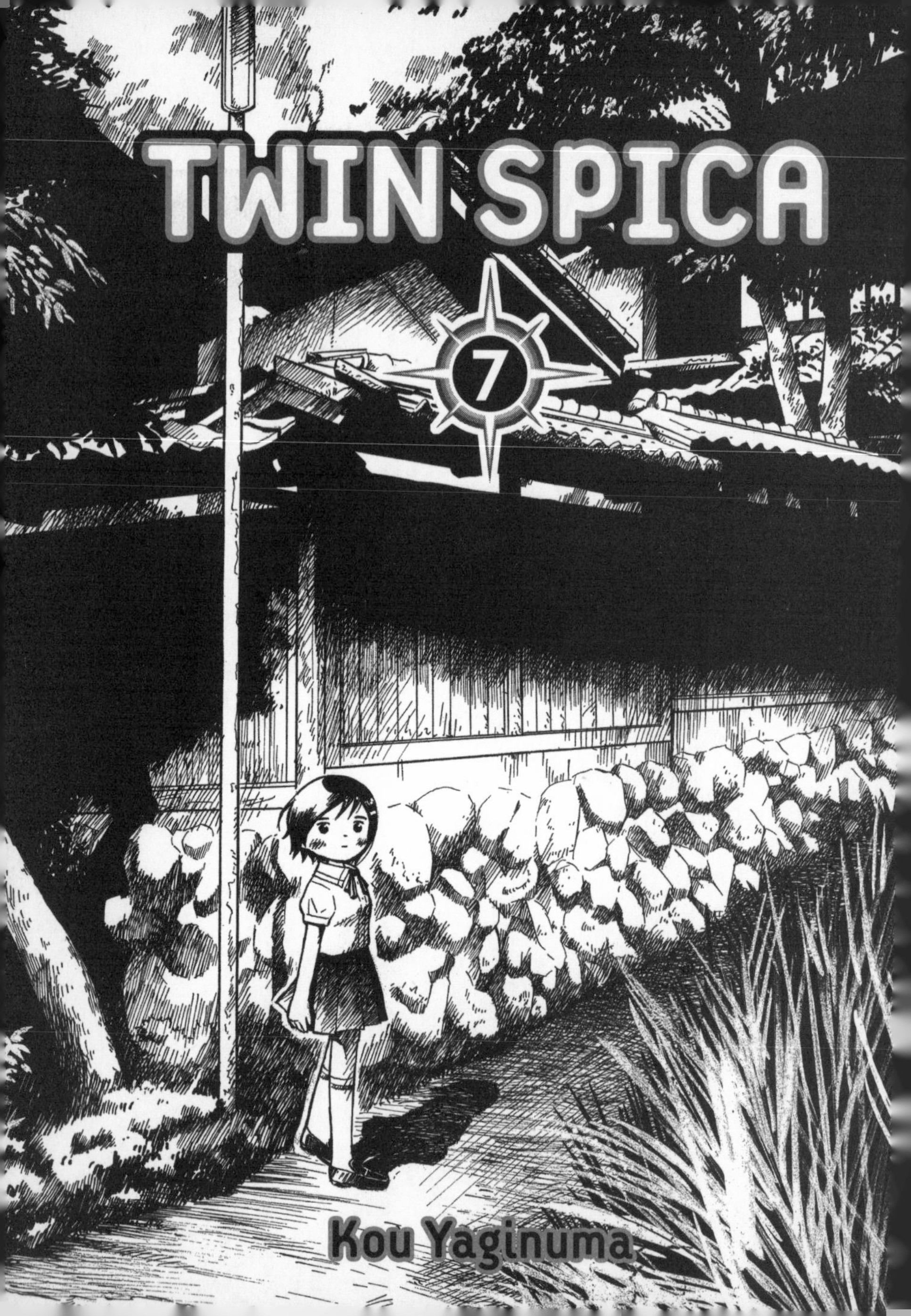
TWIN SPICA
7
Kou Yaginuma

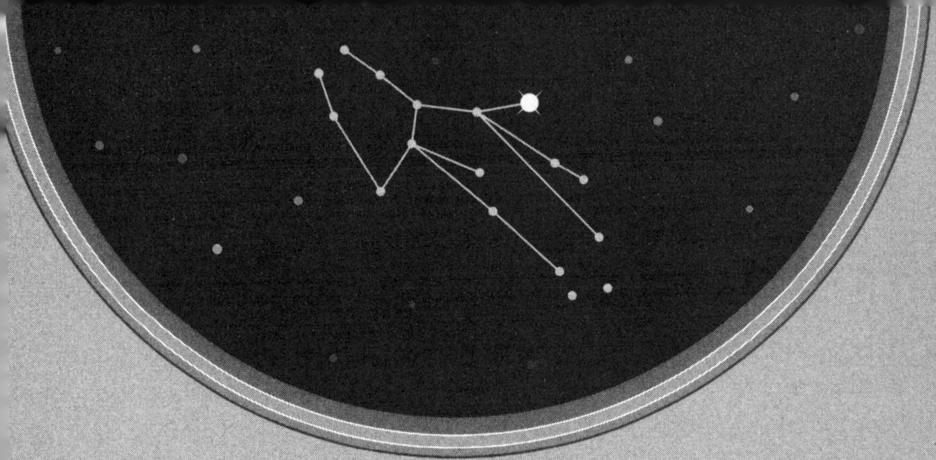

CONTENTS

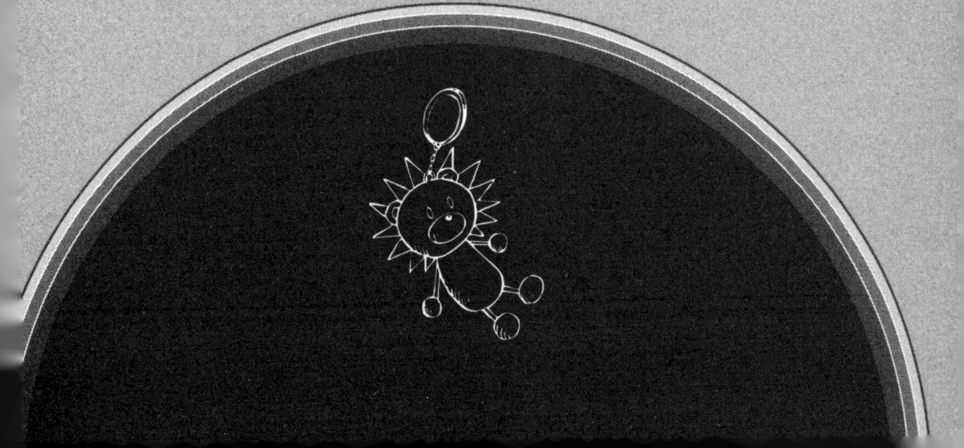

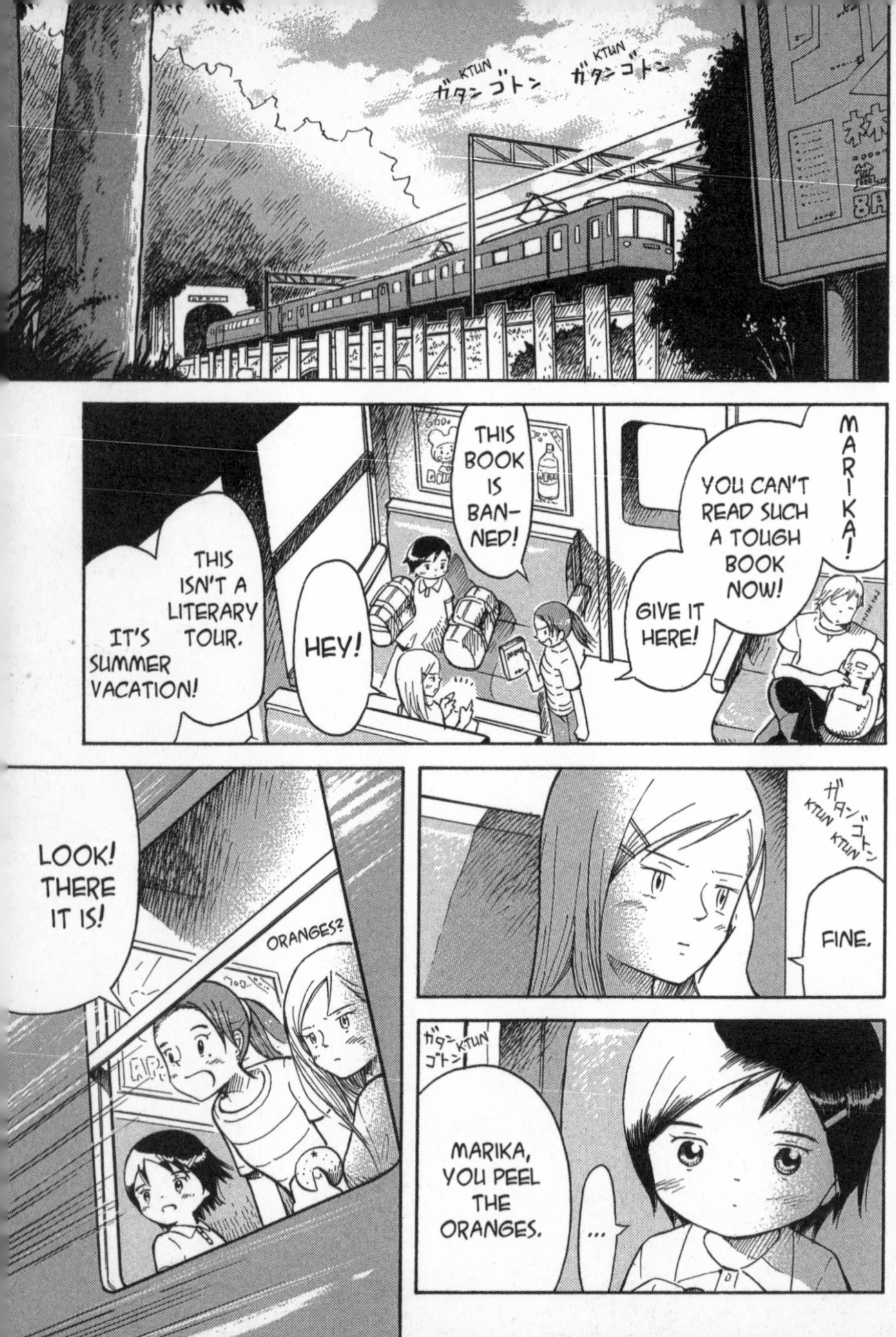
KTUN ガタンゴトン
KTUN ガタンゴトン
MARIKA!
YOU CAN'T READ SUCH A TOUGH BOOK NOW!
GIVE IT HERE!
THIS BOOK IS BAN-NED!
HEY!
THIS ISN'T A LITERARY TOUR. IT'S SUMMER VACATION!
ガタンゴトン KTUN KTUN
FINE.
ガタンゴトン KTUN
MARIKA, YOU PEEL THE ORANGES.
...
LOOK! THERE IT IS!
ORANGES?

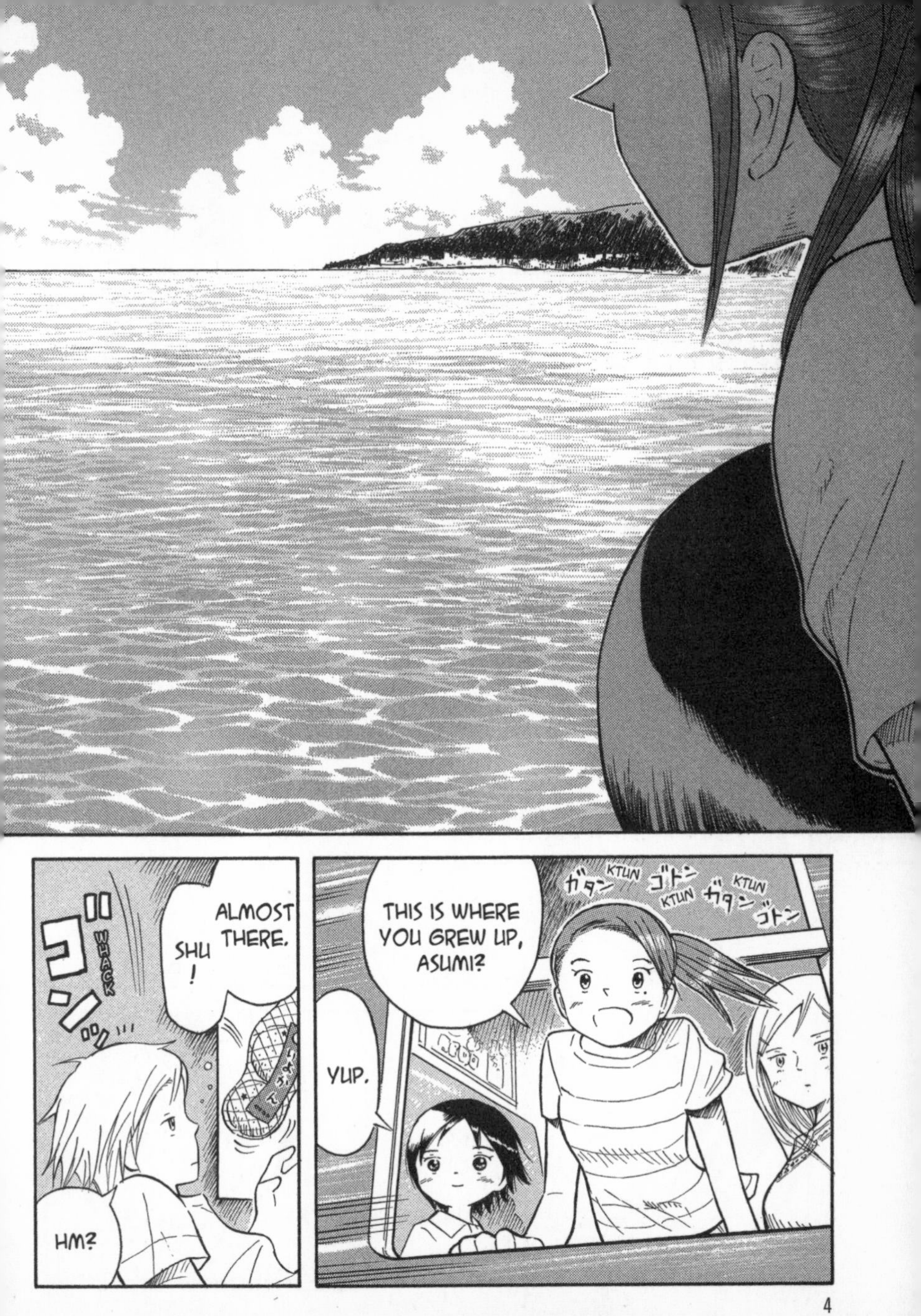
ガタン
KTUN
ゴトン
KTUN
ガタン
KTUN
ゴトン
THIS IS WHERE YOU GREW UP, ASUMI?
YUP.
ALMOST THERE.
SHU!
WHACK
HM?

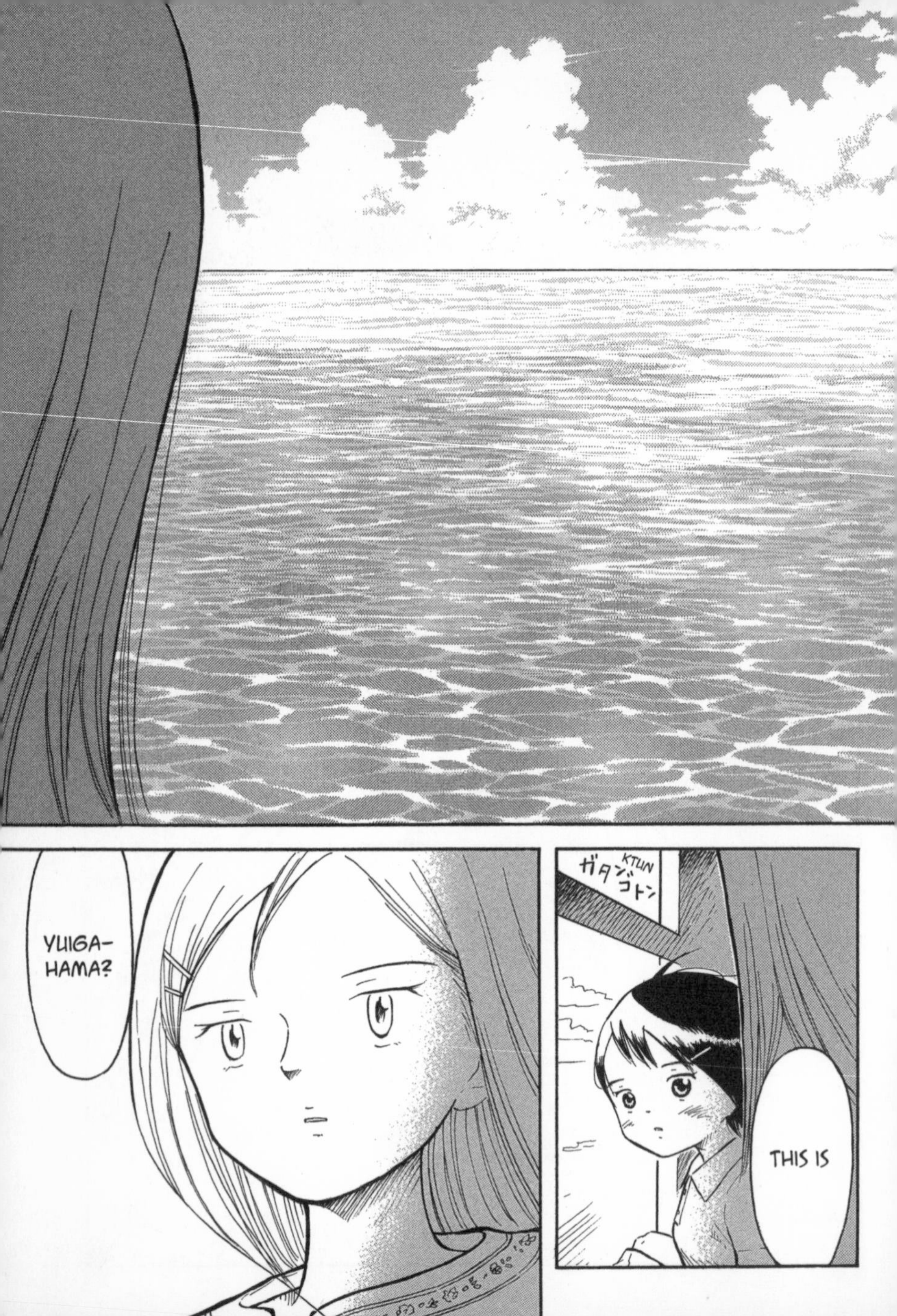
KTUN
ガタンゴトン
THIS IS
YUIGA-HAMA?

MISSION:30

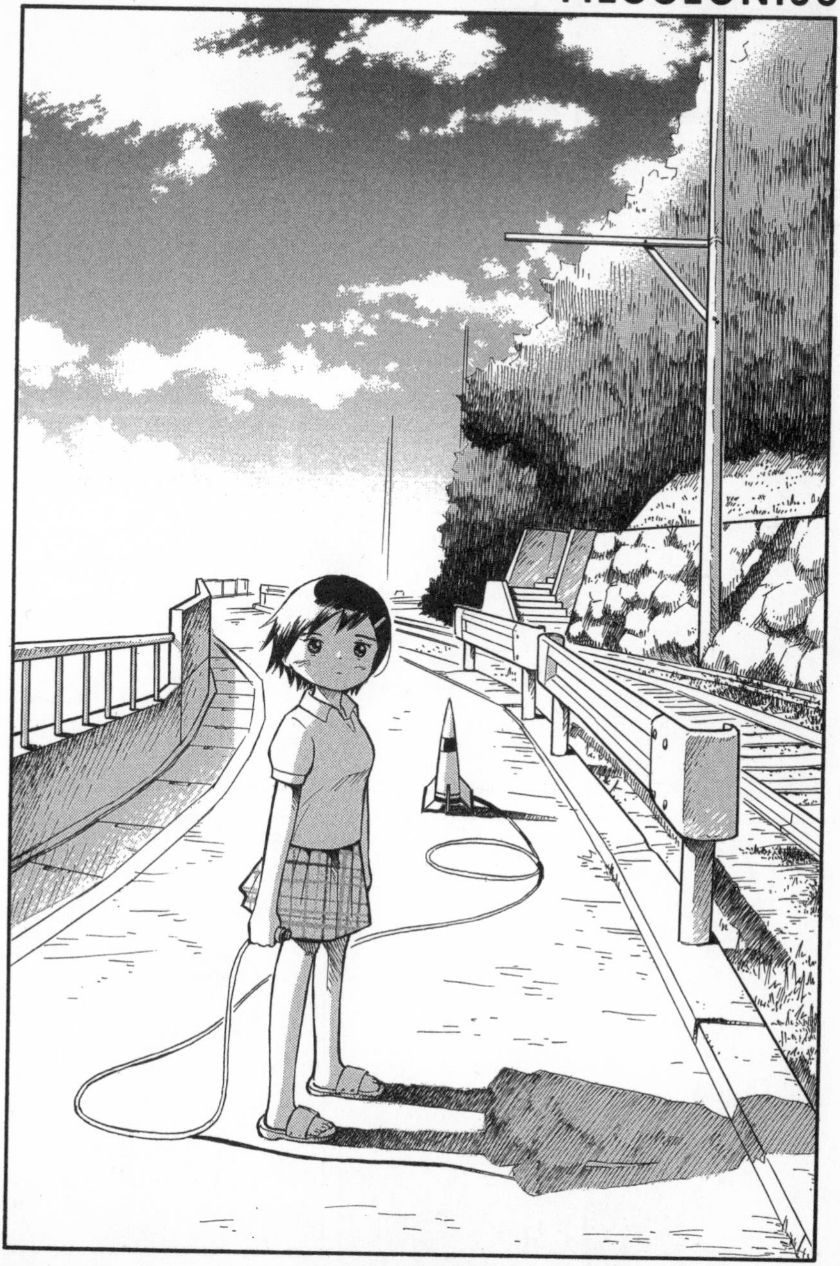

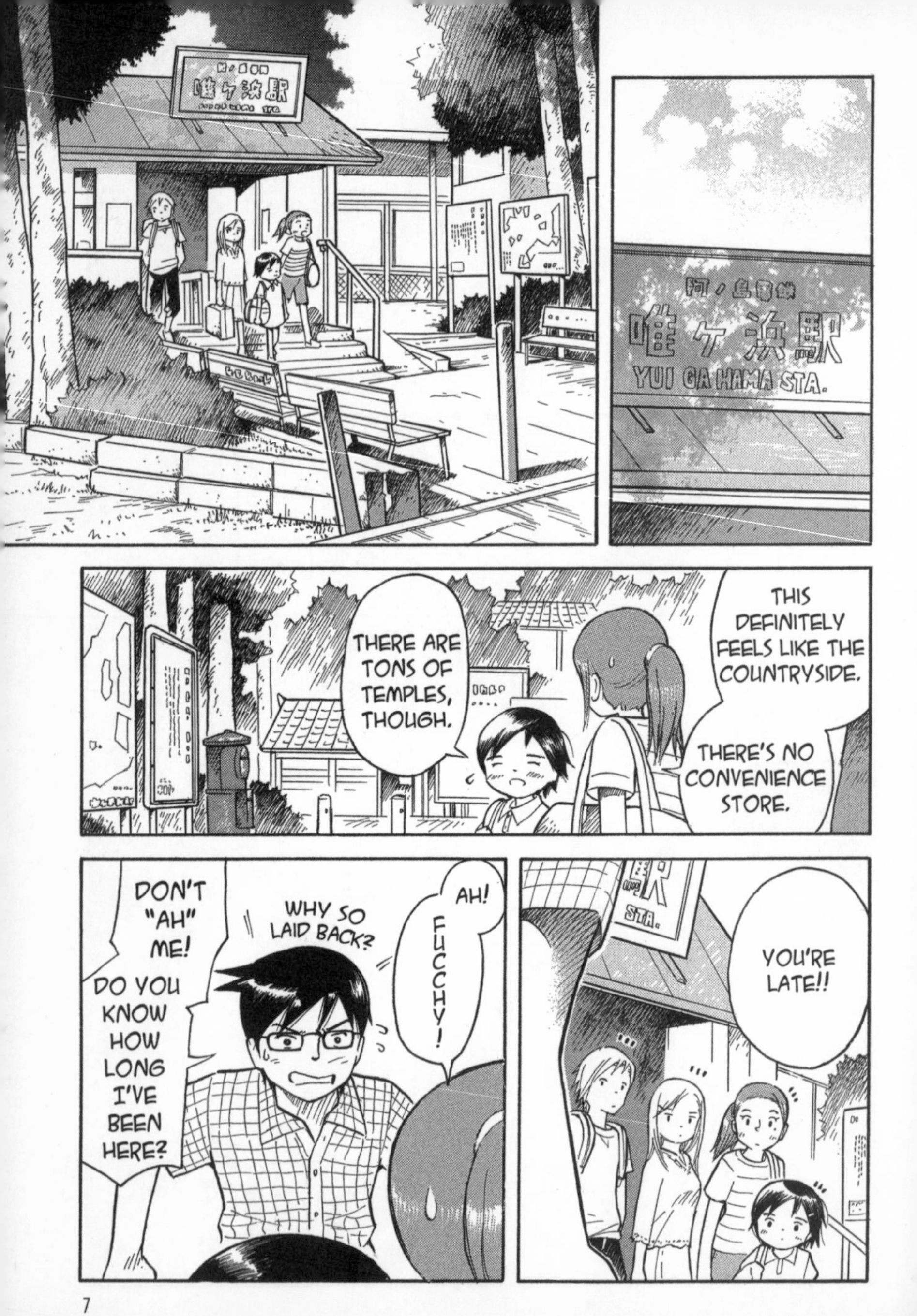
唯ヶ浜駅
YUI GA HAMA STA.
THIS DEFINITELY FEELS LIKE THE COUNTRYSIDE.
THERE'S NO CONVENIENCE STORE.
THERE ARE TONS OF TEMPLES, THOUGH.
YOU'RE LATE!!
STA.
AH! FUCCHY!
WHY SO LAID BACK?
DON'T "AH" ME!
DO YOU KNOW HOW LONG I'VE BEEN HERE?

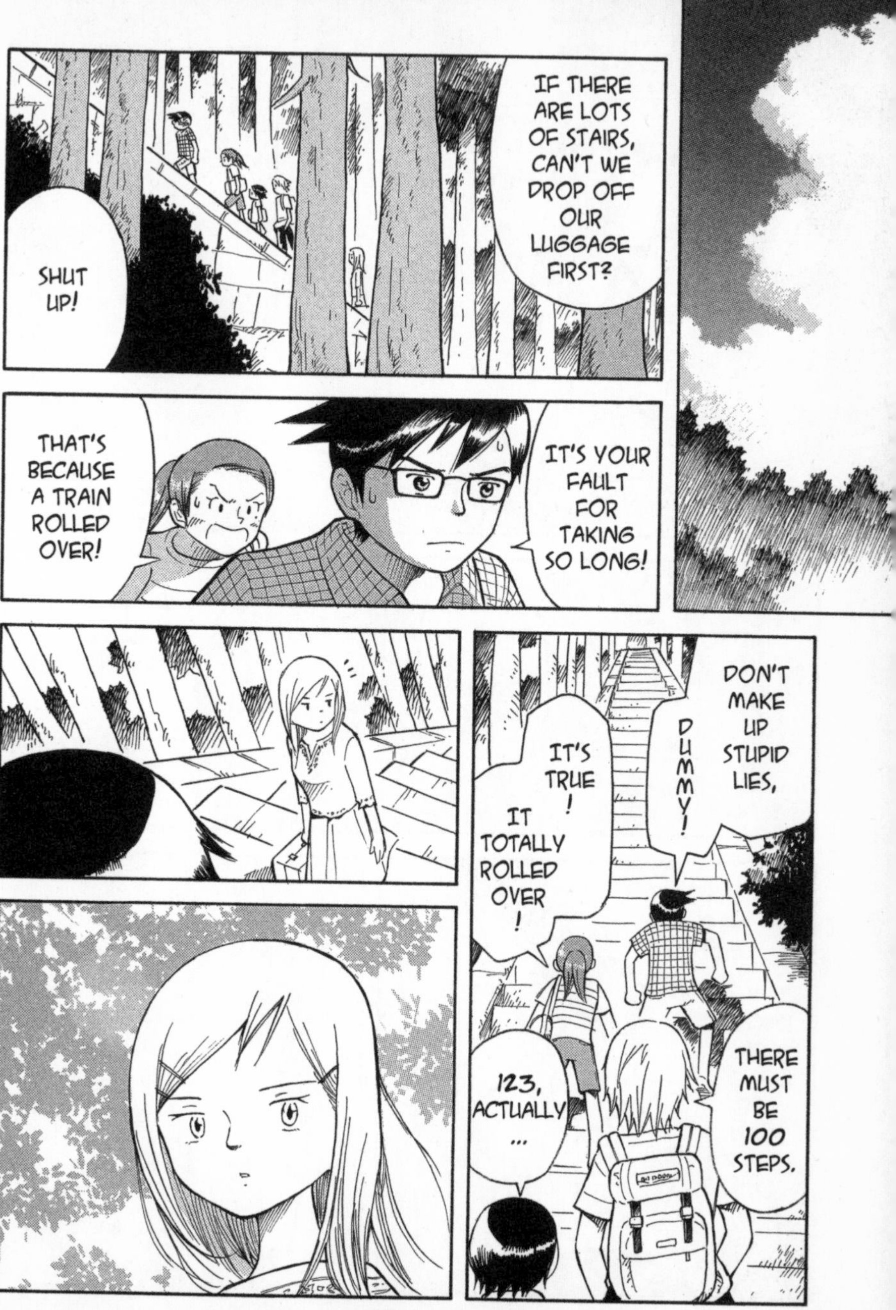
IF THERE ARE LOTS OF STAIRS, CAN'T WE DROP OFF OUR LUGGAGE FIRST?
SHUT UP!
IT'S YOUR FAULT FOR TAKING SO LONG!
THAT'S BECAUSE A TRAIN ROLLED OVER!
DON'T MAKE UP STUPID LIES,
DUMMY!
IT'S TRUE!
IT TOTALLY ROLLED OVER!
THERE MUST BE 100 STEPS.
123, ACTUALLY...

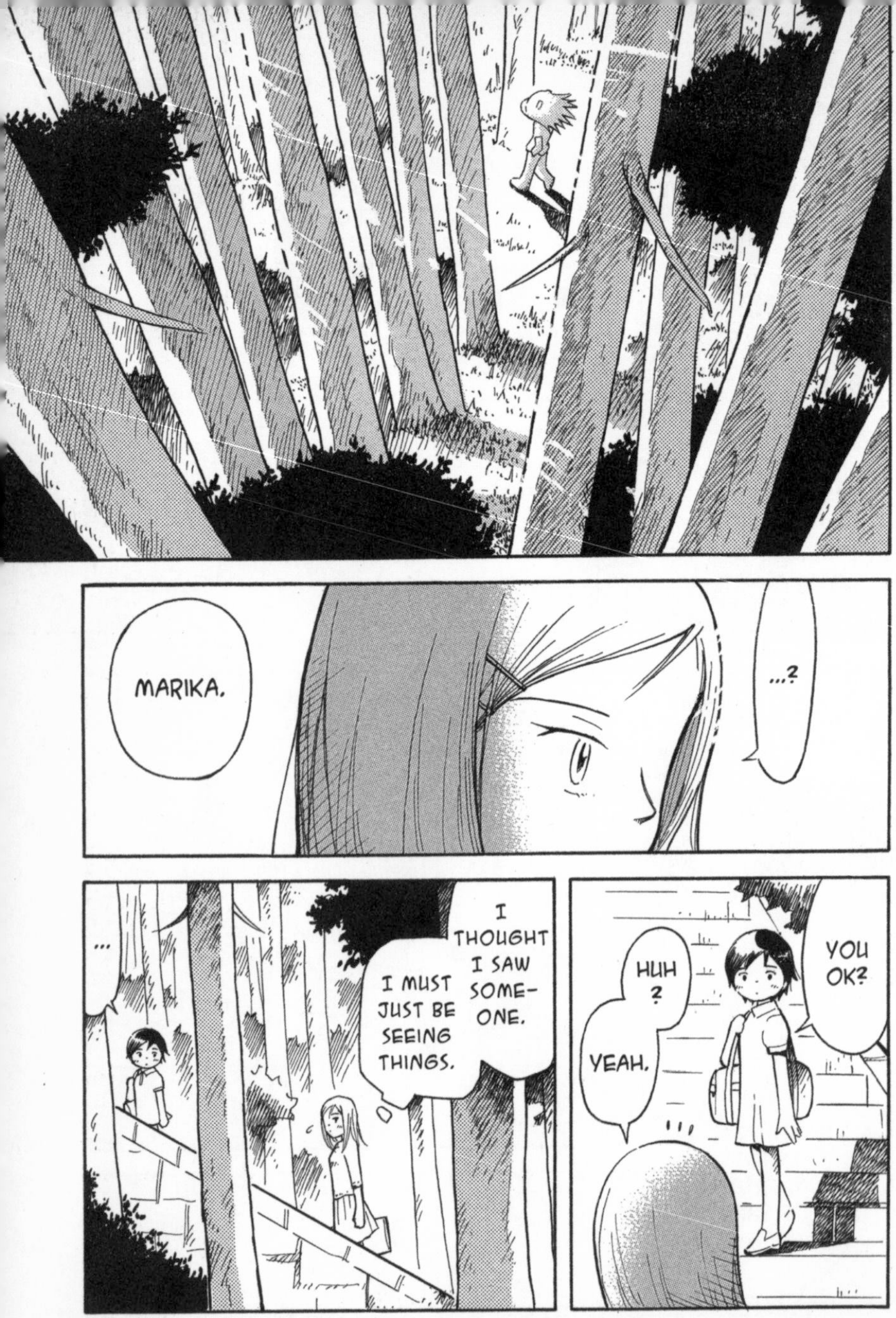
...?
MARIKA.
YOU OK?
HUH?
YEAH.
I THOUGHT I SAW SOME-ONE.
I MUST JUST BE SEEING THINGS.
...

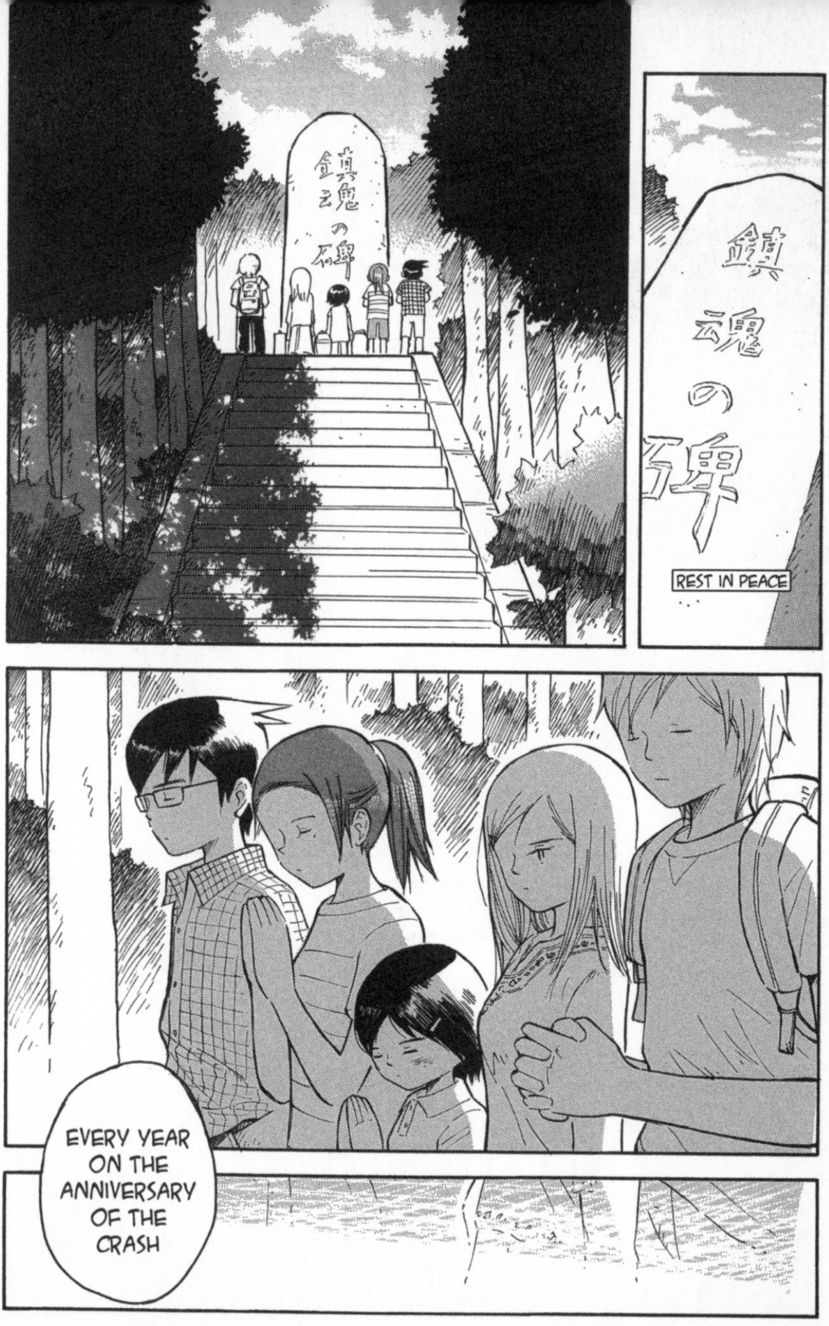
鎮魂の碑
REST IN PEACE
鎮魂の碑
EVERY YEAR ON THE ANNIVERSARY OF THE CRASH

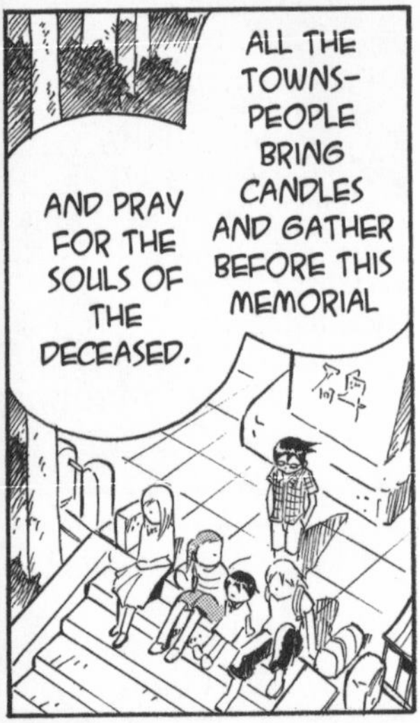
ALL THE TOWNSPEOPLE BRING CANDLES AND GATHER BEFORE THIS MEMORIAL
AND PRAY FOR THE SOULS OF THE DECEASED.

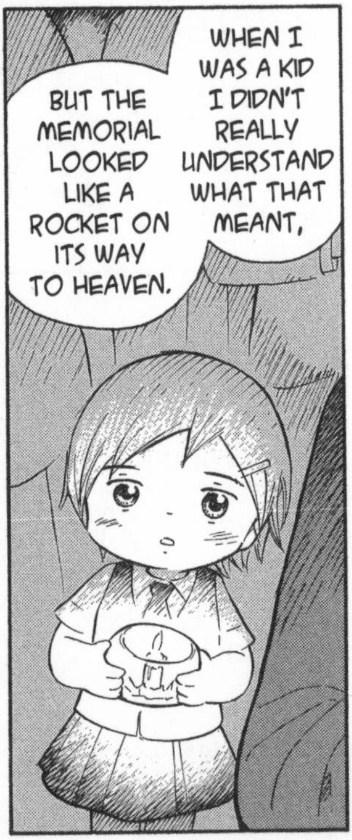
WHEN I WAS A KID I DIDN'T REALLY UNDERSTAND WHAT THAT MEANT,
BUT THE MEMORIAL LOOKED LIKE A ROCKET ON ITS WAY TO HEAVEN.

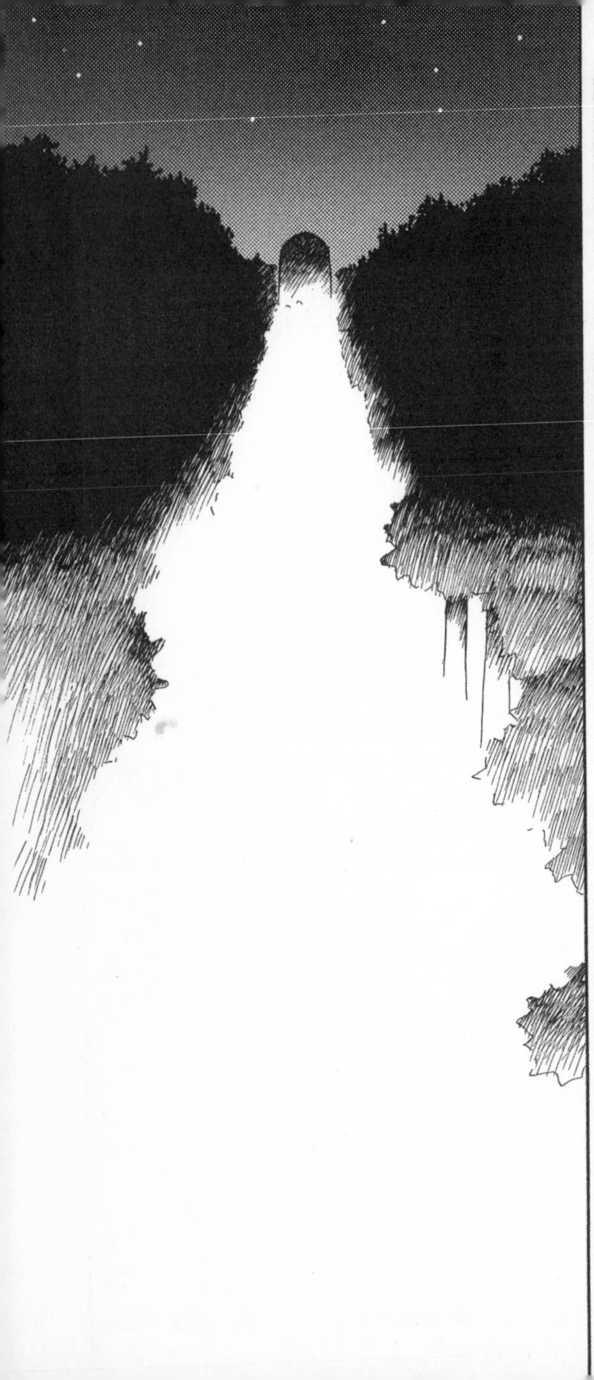

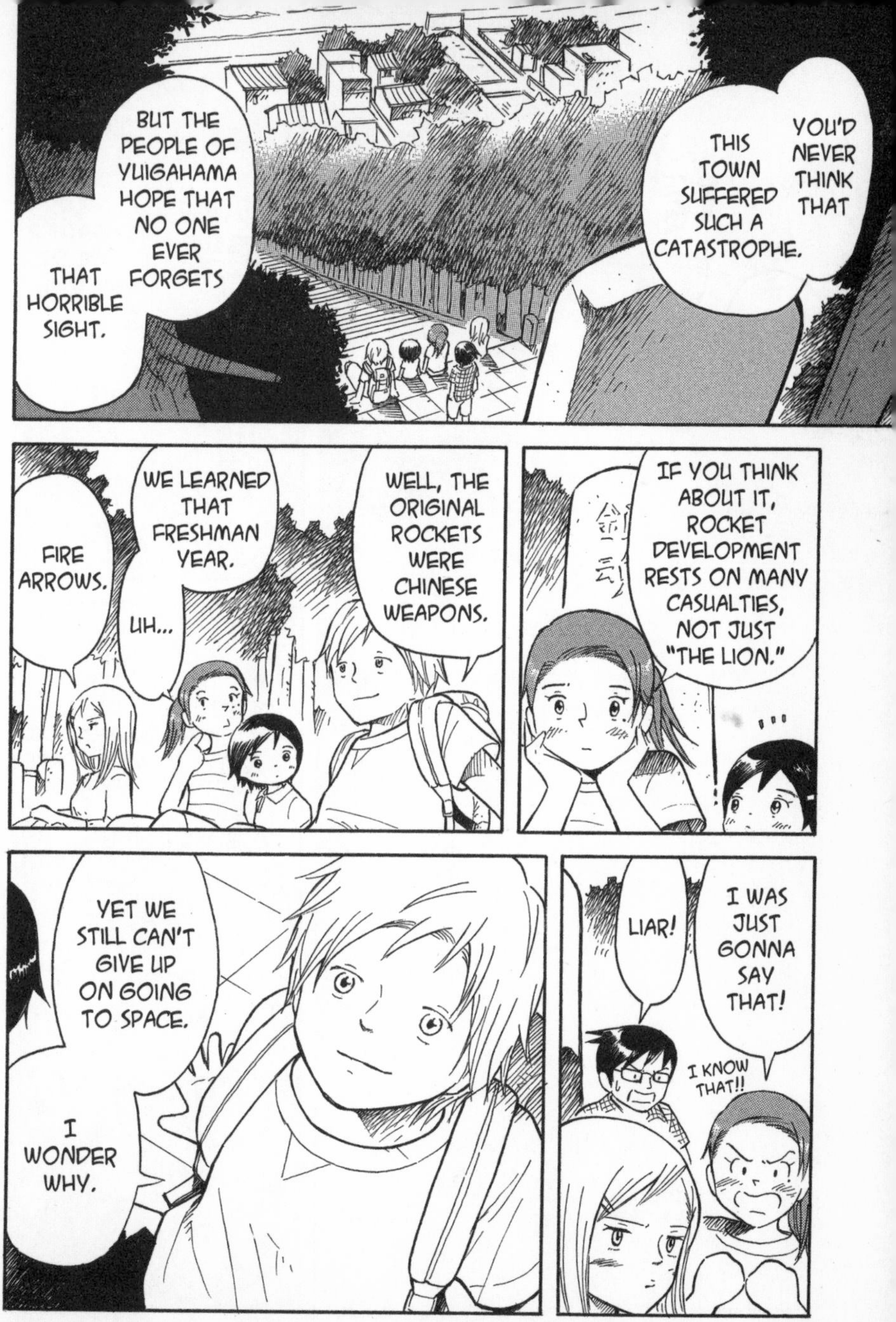
YOU'D NEVER THINK THAT
THIS TOWN SUFFERED SUCH A CATASTROPHE.
BUT THE PEOPLE OF YUIGAHAMA HOPE THAT NO ONE EVER FORGETS
THAT HORRIBLE SIGHT.
IF YOU THINK ABOUT IT, ROCKET DEVELOPMENT RESTS ON MANY CASUALTIES, NOT JUST "THE LION."
...
WELL, THE ORIGINAL ROCKETS WERE CHINESE WEAPONS.
WE LEARNED THAT FRESHMAN YEAR.
UH...
FIRE ARROWS.
I WAS JUST GONNA SAY THAT!
LIAR!
I KNOW THAT!!
YET WE STILL CAN'T GIVE UP ON GOING TO SPACE.
I WONDER WHY.

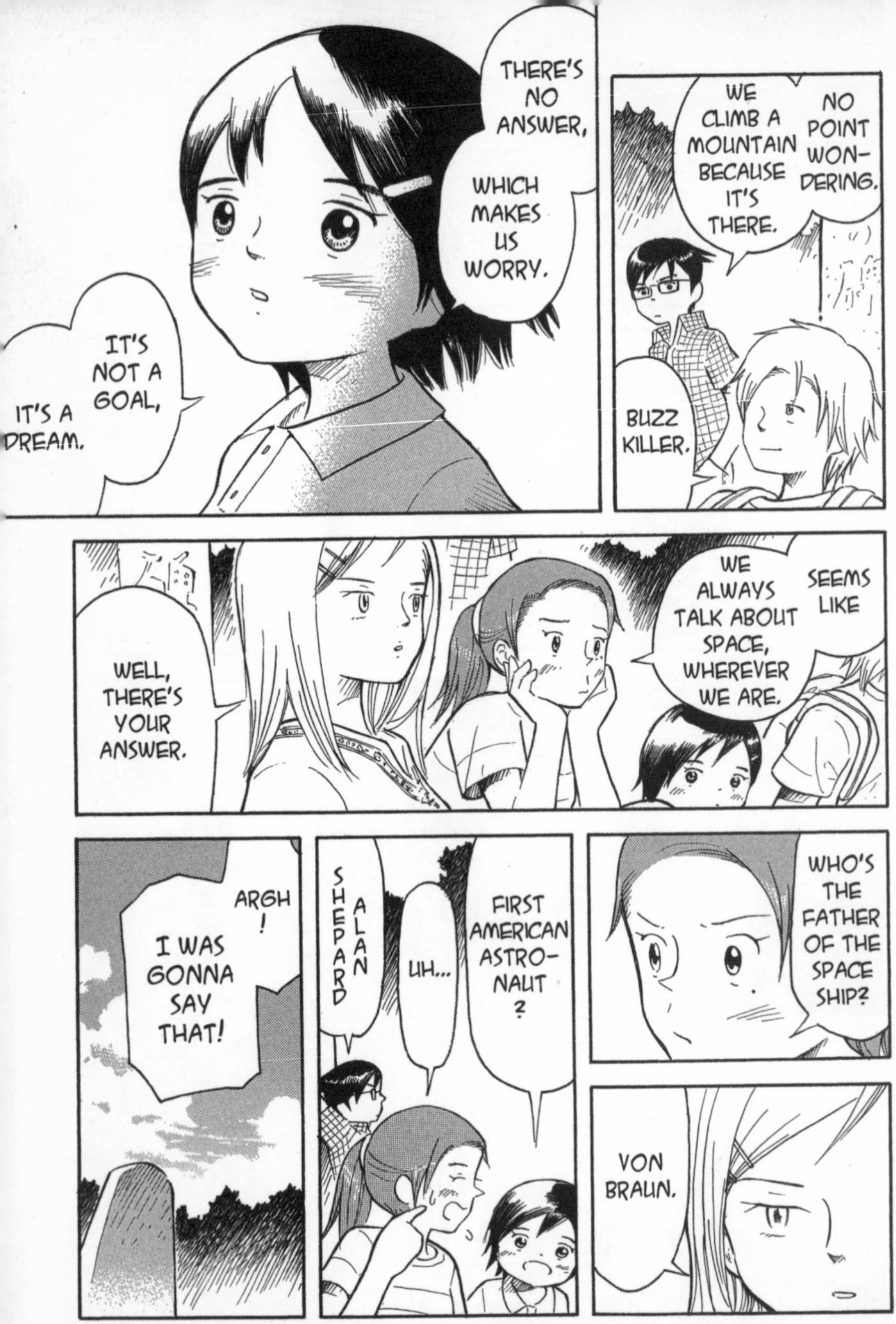
NO POINT WONDERING.
WE CLIMB A MOUNTAIN BECAUSE IT'S THERE.
BUZZ KILLER.
THERE'S NO ANSWER,
WHICH MAKES US WORRY.
IT'S NOT A GOAL,
IT'S A DREAM.
SEEMS LIKE
WE ALWAYS TALK ABOUT SPACE, WHEREVER WE ARE.
WELL, THERE'S YOUR ANSWER.
WHO'S THE FATHER OF THE SPACE SHIP?
VON BRAUN.
FIRST AMERICAN ASTRONAUT?
UH...
ALAN SHEPARD
ARGH!
I WAS GONNA SAY THAT!

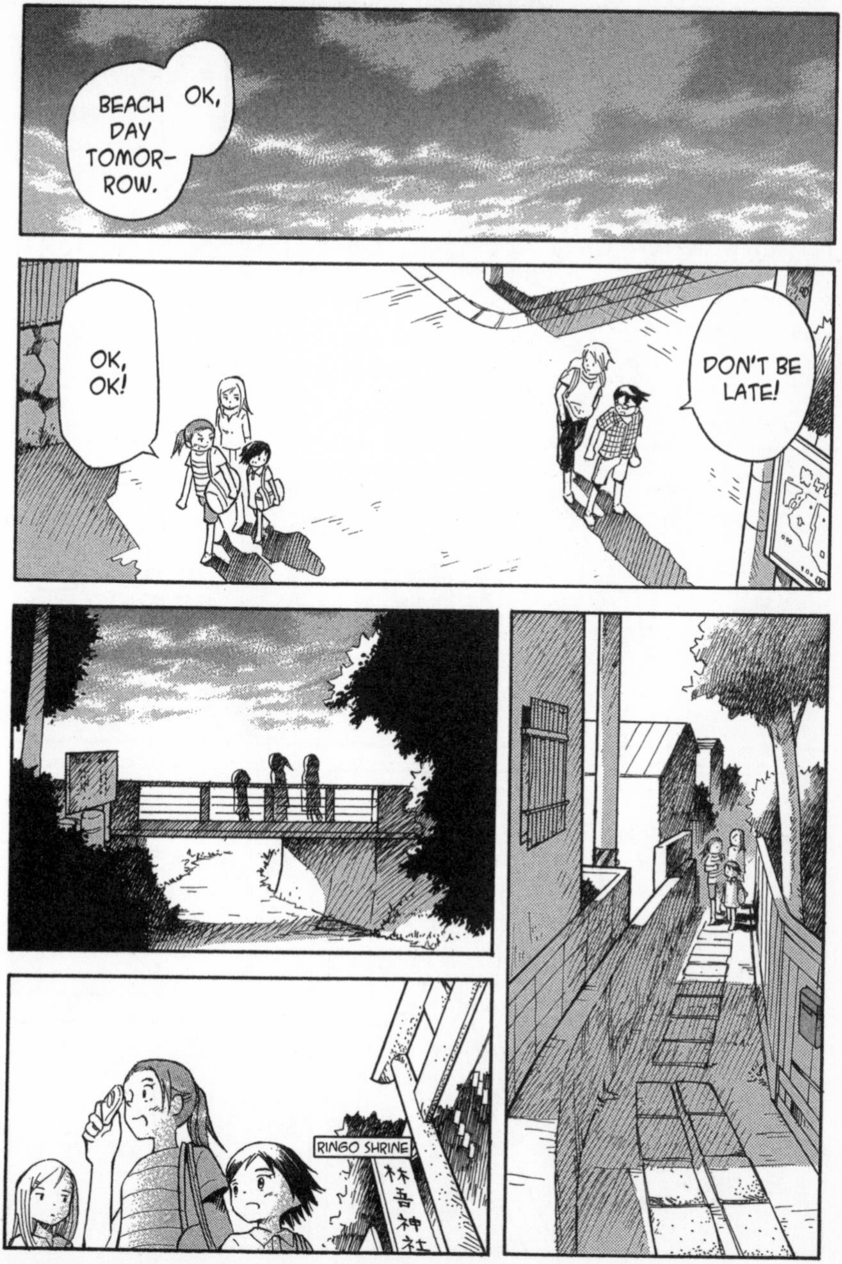
OK, BEACH DAY TOMORROW.
DON'T BE LATE!
OK, OK!
RINGO SHRINE
林吾神社

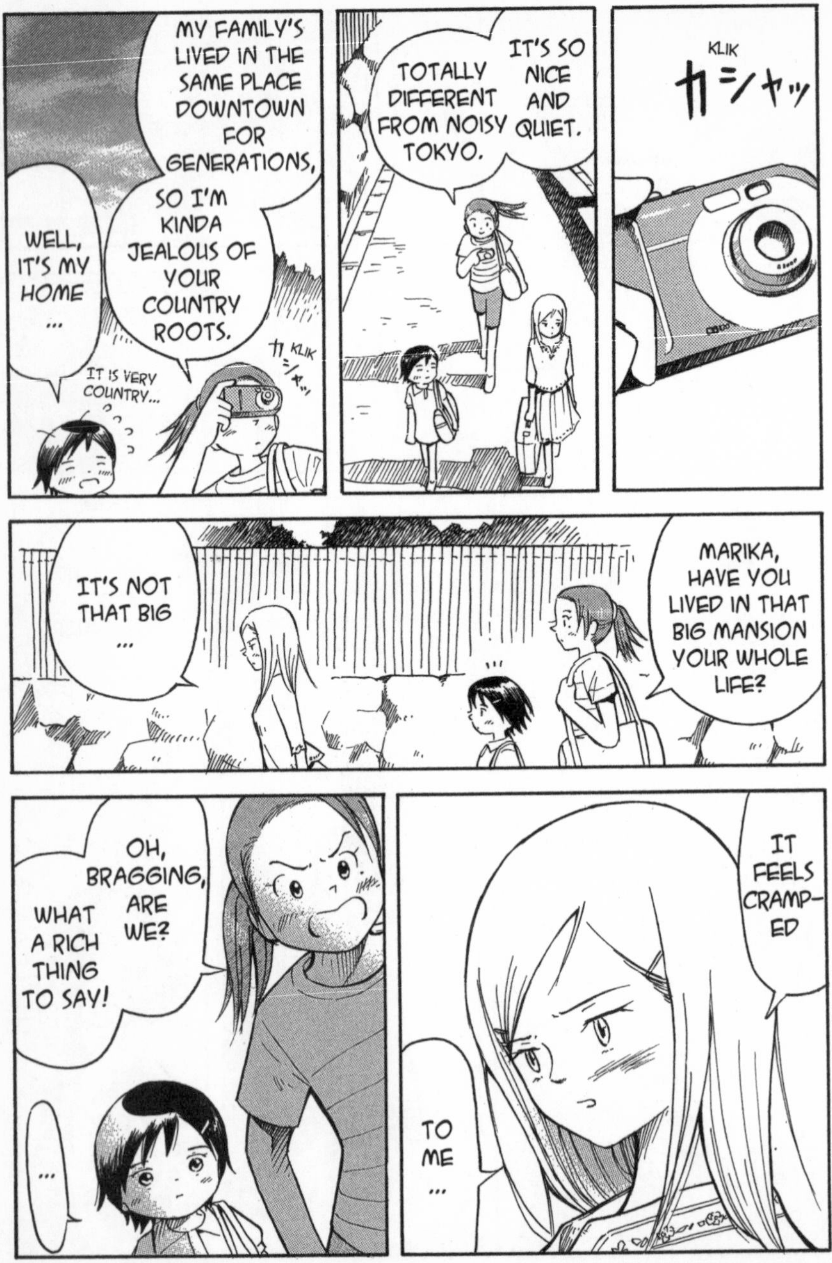
KLIK
カシャッ
IT'S SO NICE AND QUIET.
TOTALLY DIFFERENT FROM NOISY TOKYO.
MY FAMILY'S LIVED IN THE SAME PLACE DOWNTOWN FOR GENERATIONS,
SO I'M KINDA JEALOUS OF YOUR COUNTRY ROOTS.
KLIK
カシャッ
WELL, IT'S MY HOME ...
IT IS VERY COUNTRY...
MARIKA, HAVE YOU LIVED IN THAT BIG MANSION YOUR WHOLE LIFE?
IT'S NOT THAT BIG ...
IT FEELS CRAMP-ED
TO ME ...
OH, BRAGGING, ARE WE?
WHAT A RICH THING TO SAY!
...

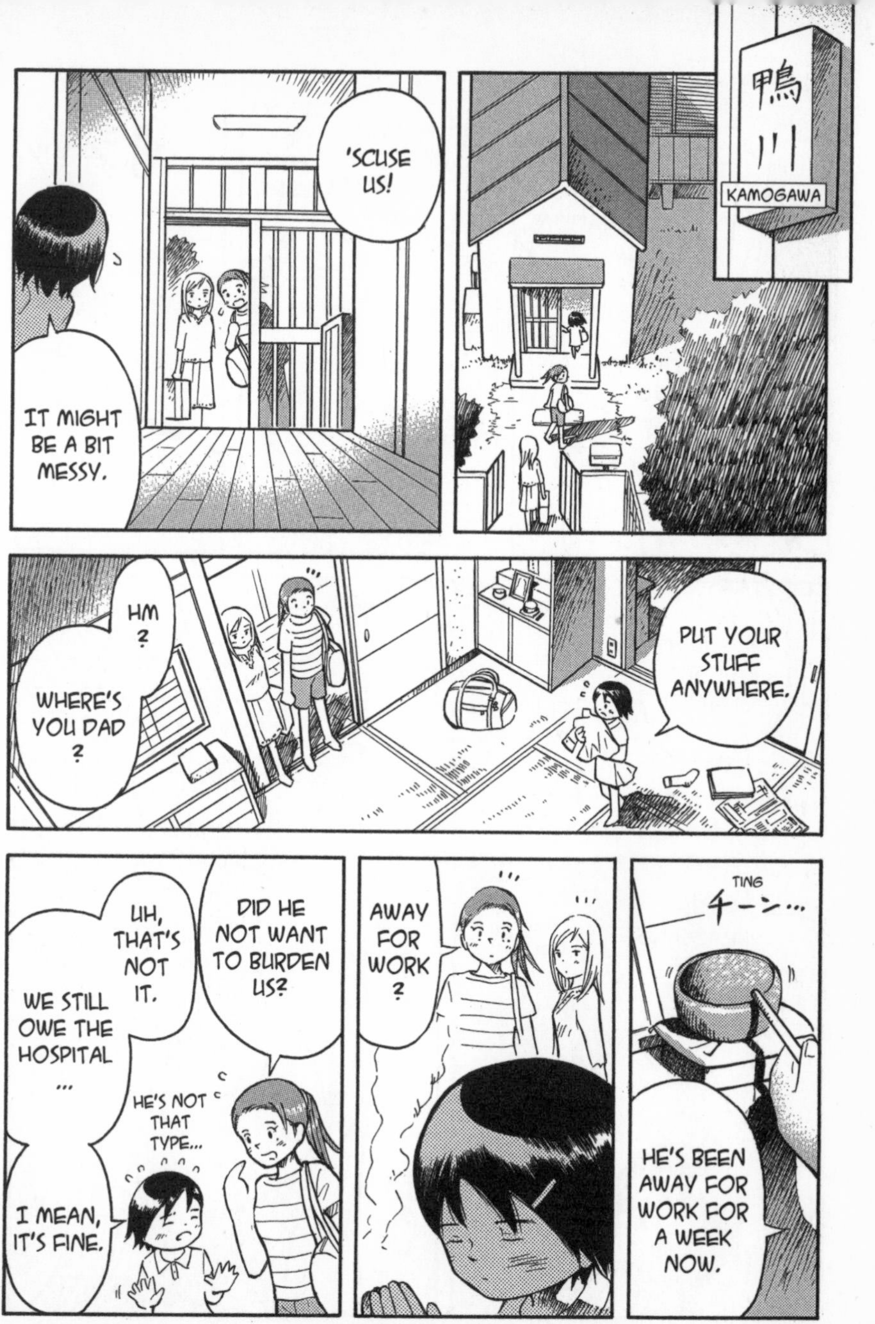

鴨川
KAMOGAWA
'SCUSE US!
IT MIGHT BE A BIT MESSY.
PUT YOUR STUFF ANYWHERE.
HM?
WHERE'S YOU DAD?
TING
チーン…
HE'S BEEN AWAY FOR WORK FOR A WEEK NOW.
AWAY FOR WORK?
DID HE NOT WANT TO BURDEN US?
UH, THAT'S NOT IT.
WE STILL OWE THE HOSPITAL ...
HE'S NOT THAT TYPE...
I MEAN, IT'S FINE.

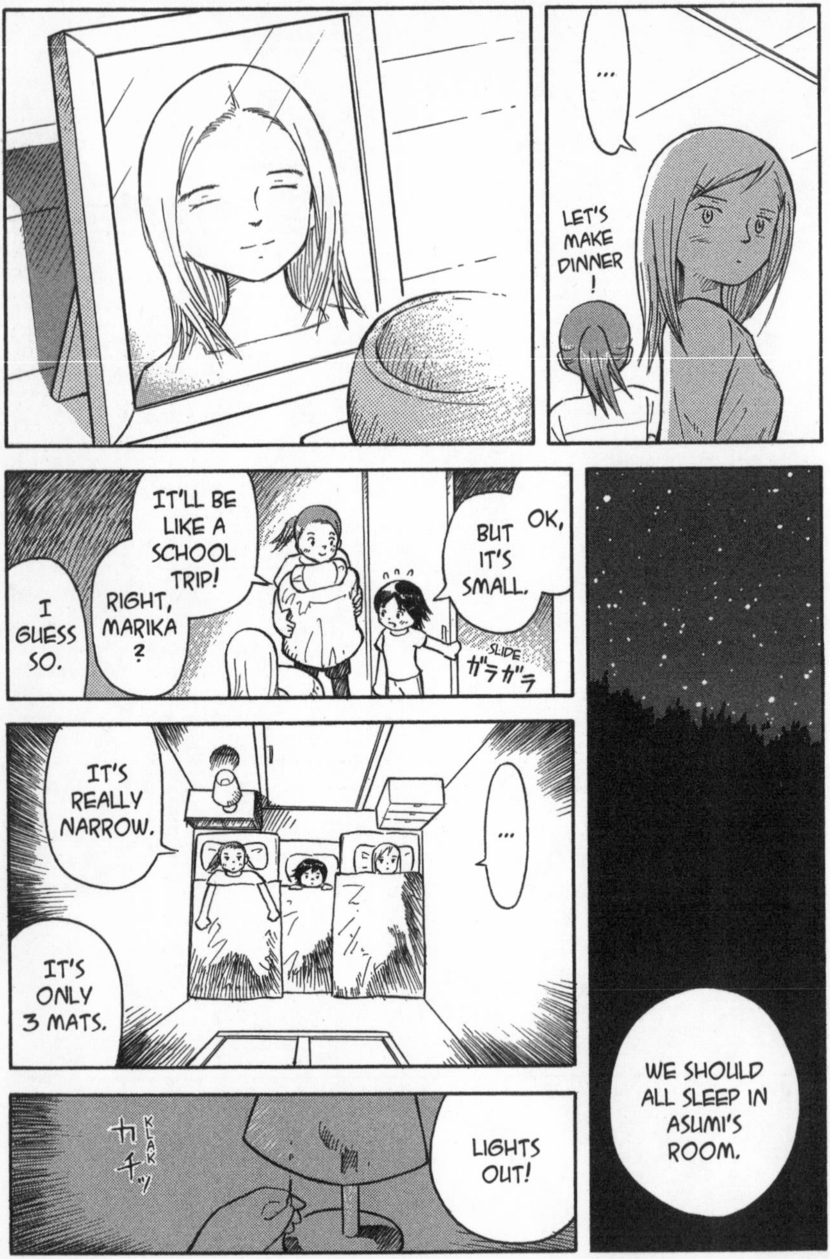
...
LET'S MAKE DINNER!
WE SHOULD ALL SLEEP IN ASUMI'S ROOM.
OK, BUT IT'S SMALL.
SLIDE
ガラガラ
IT'LL BE LIKE A SCHOOL TRIP!
RIGHT, MARIKA?
I GUESS SO.
...
IT'S REALLY NARROW.
IT'S ONLY 3 MATS.
LIGHTS OUT!
KLAK
カチッ

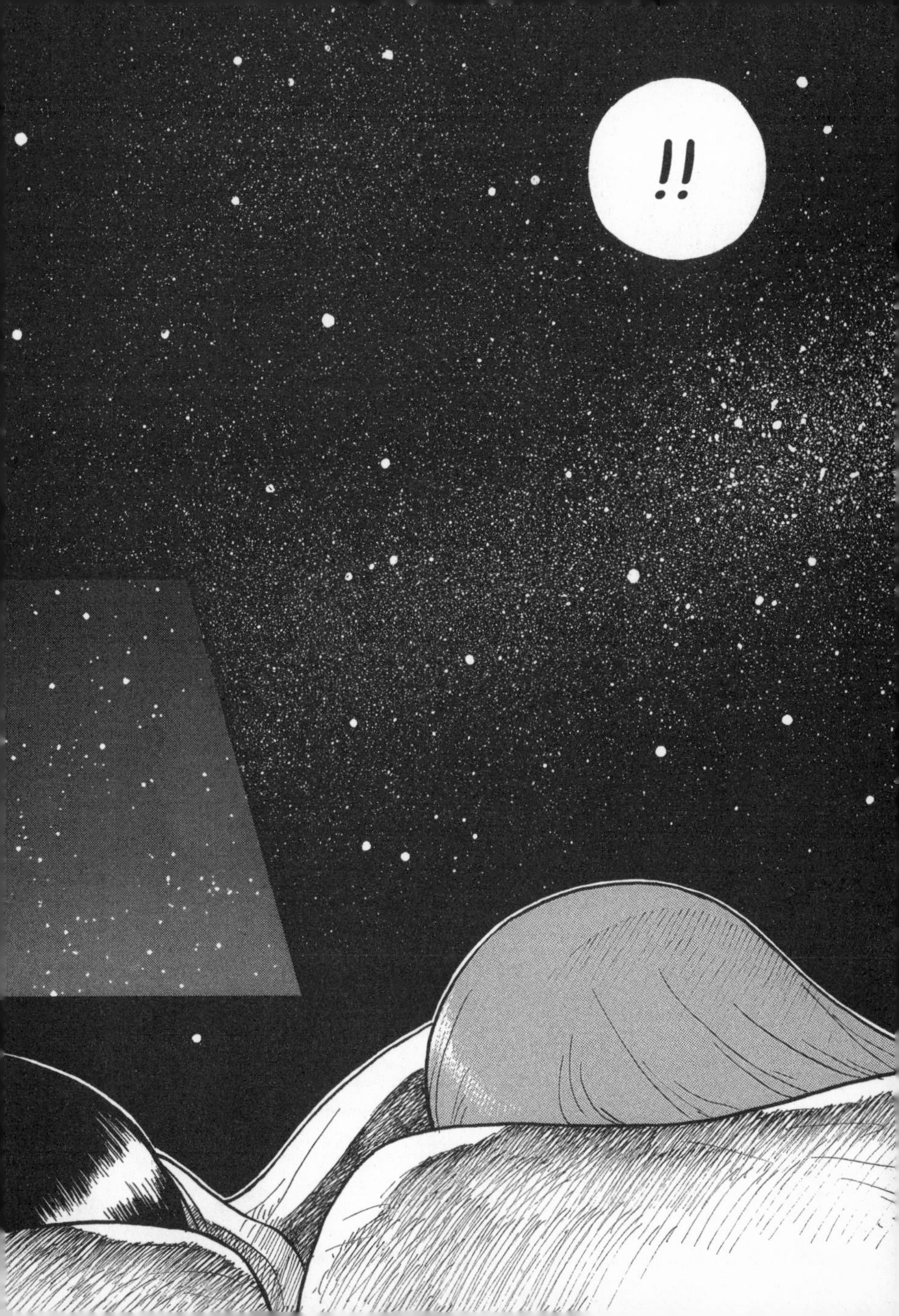
!!

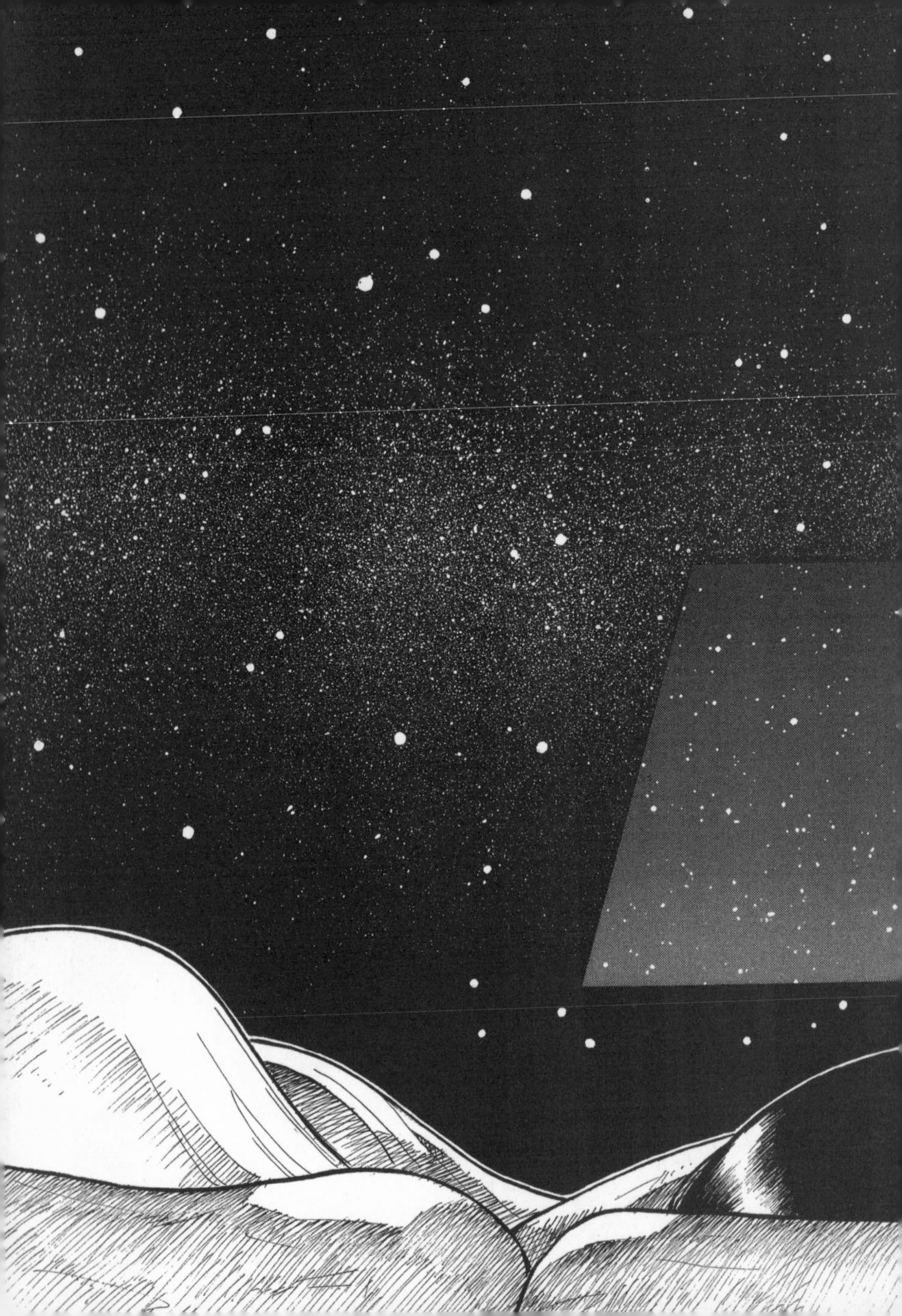

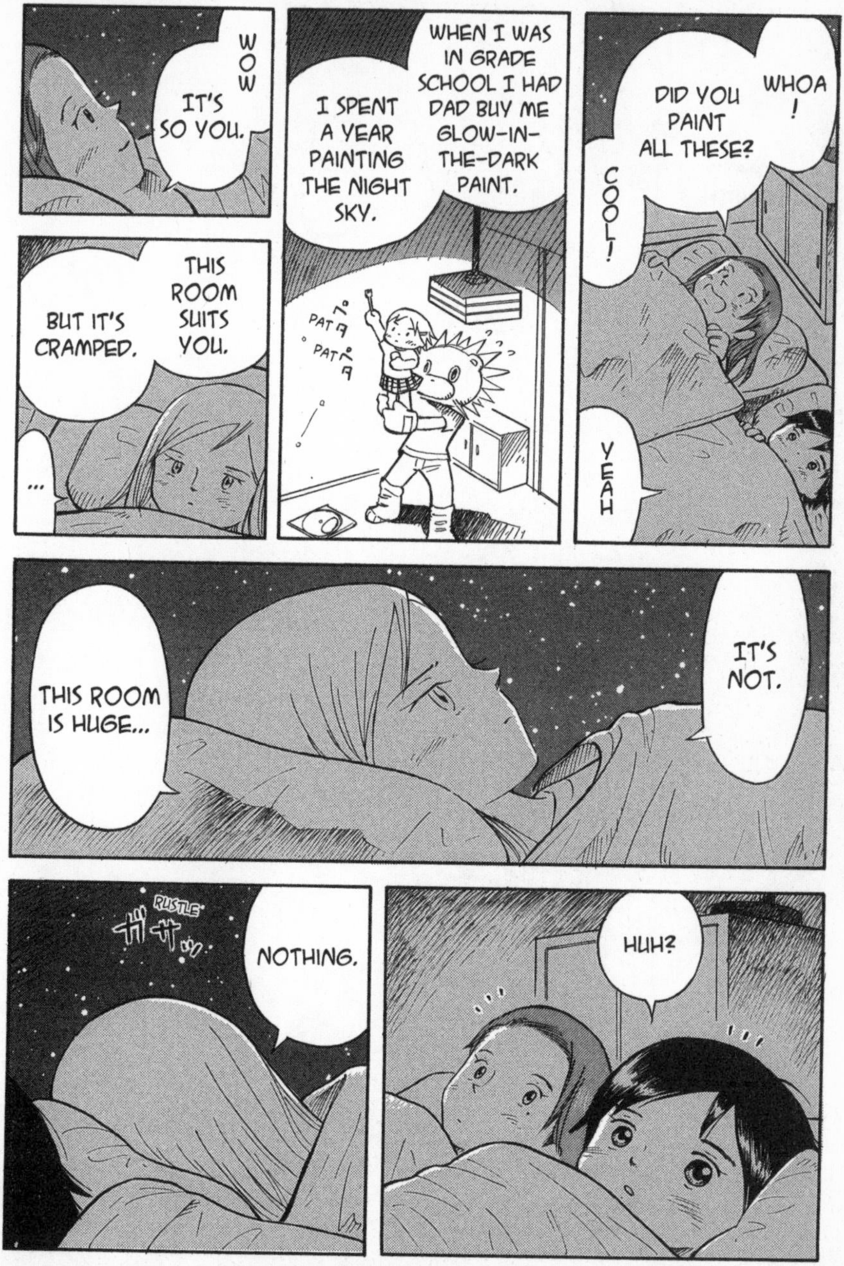
WHOA!
DID YOU PAINT ALL THESE?
COOL!
YEAH
WHEN I WAS IN GRADE SCHOOL I HAD DAD BUY ME GLOW-IN-THE-DARK PAINT.
I SPENT A YEAR PAINTING THE NIGHT SKY.
PAT
PAT
WOW
IT'S SO YOU.
THIS ROOM SUITS YOU.
BUT IT'S CRAMPED.
...
IT'S NOT.
THIS ROOM IS HUGE...
HUH?
NOTHING.
RUSTLE

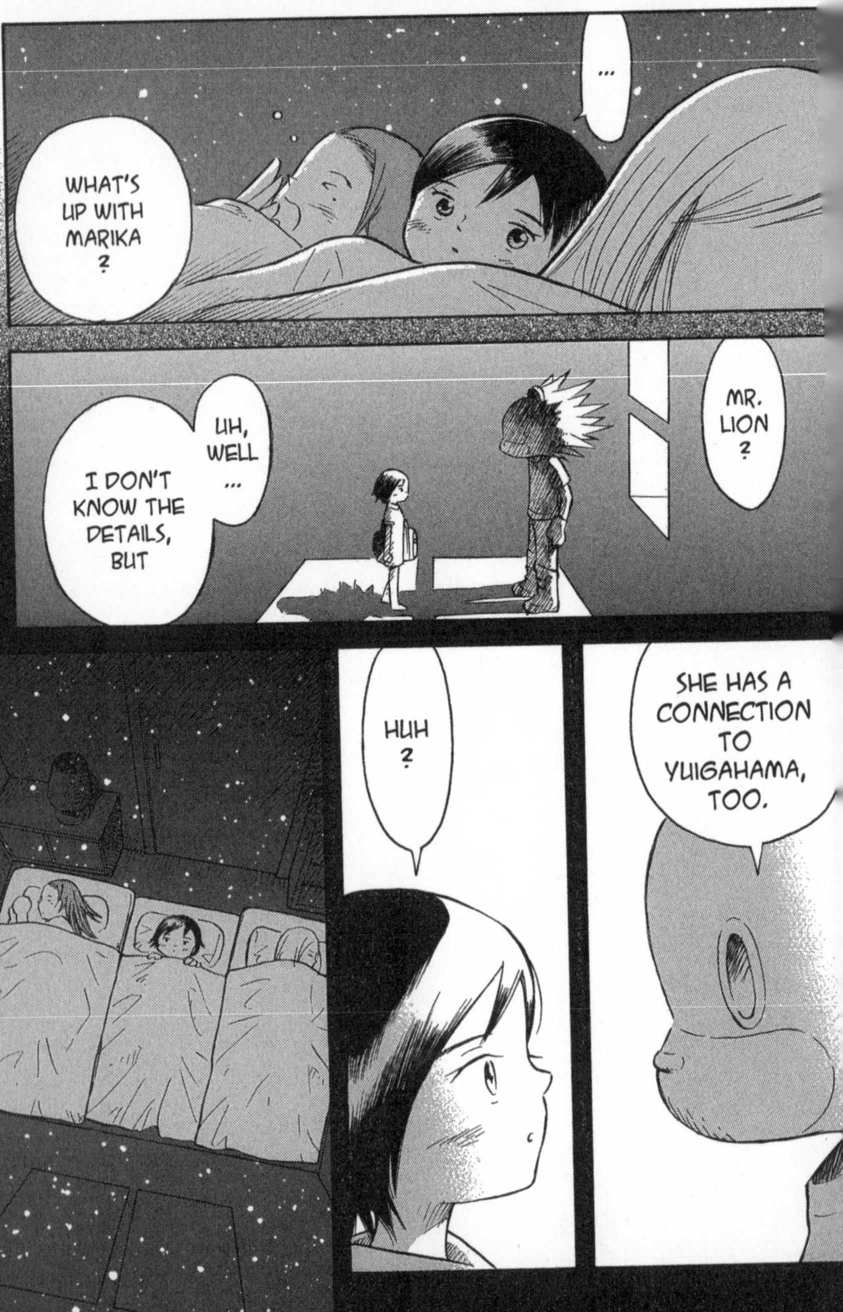
...
WHAT'S UP WITH MARIKA?
MR. LION?
UH, WELL...
I DON'T KNOW THE DETAILS, BUT
SHE HAS A CONNECTION TO YUIGAHAMA, TOO.
HUH?

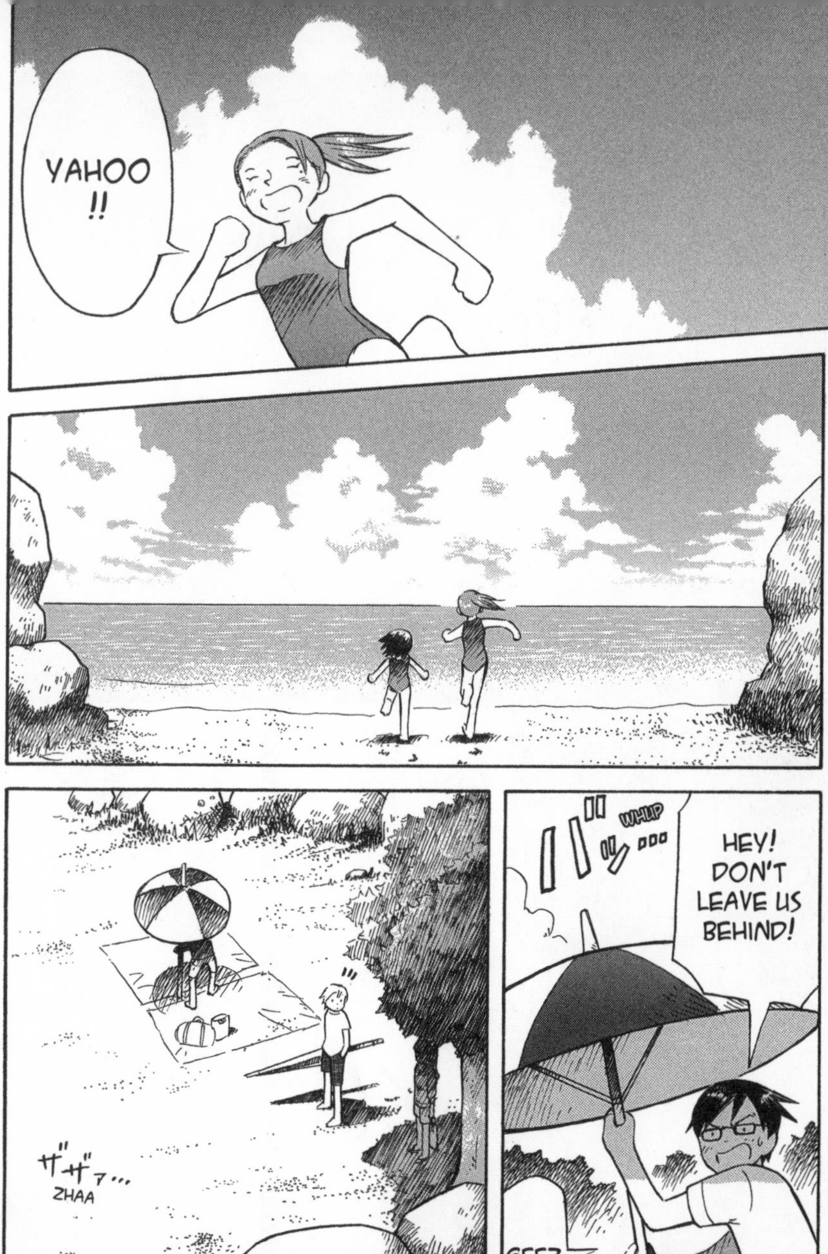
YAHOO !!
WHUP
HEY! DON'T LEAVE US BEHIND!
GEEZ.
ザザァ…
ZHAA

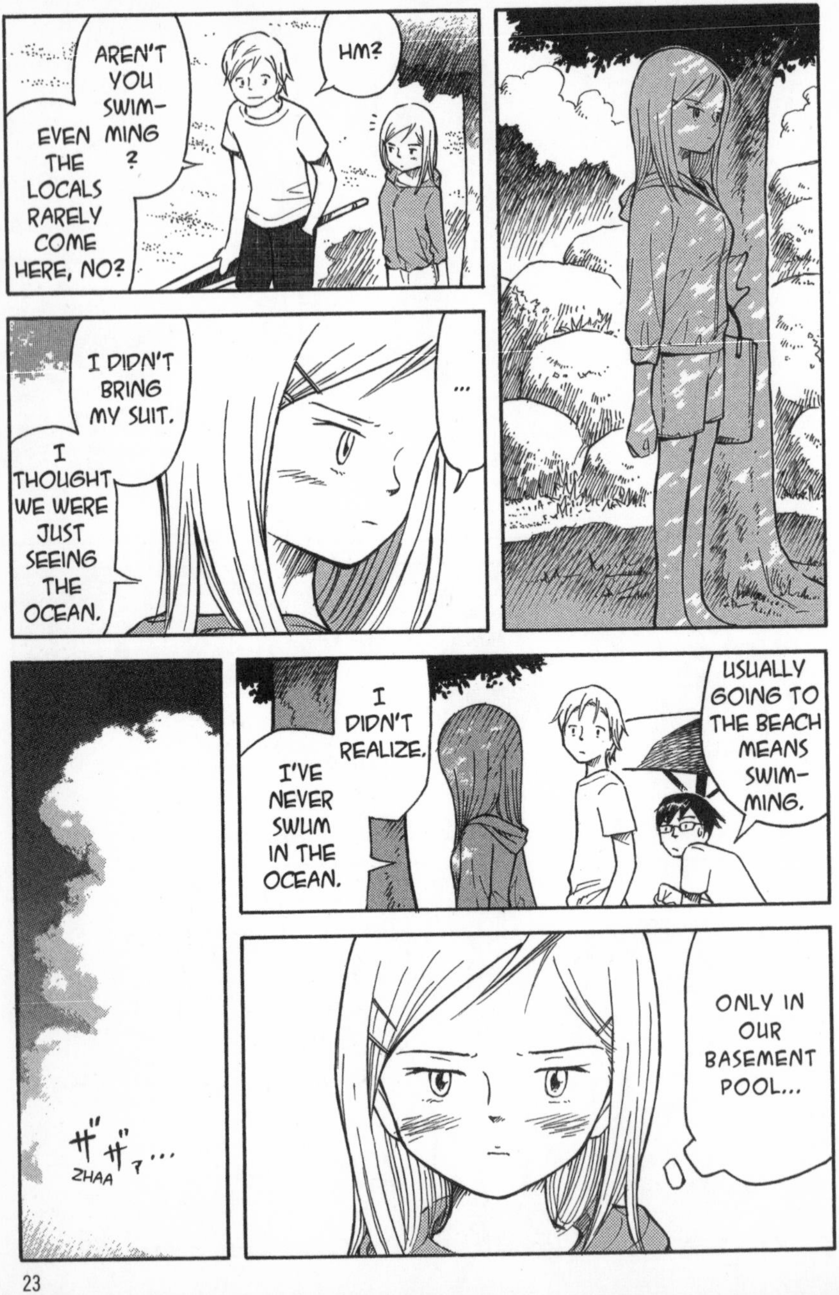
HM?
AREN'T YOU SWIMMING?
EVEN THE LOCALS RARELY COME HERE, NO?
...
I DIDN'T BRING MY SUIT.
I THOUGHT WE WERE JUST SEEING THE OCEAN.
USUALLY GOING TO THE BEACH MEANS SWIMMING.
I DIDN'T REALIZE.
I'VE NEVER SWUM IN THE OCEAN.
ONLY IN OUR BASEMENT POOL...
ザザァ...
ZHAA

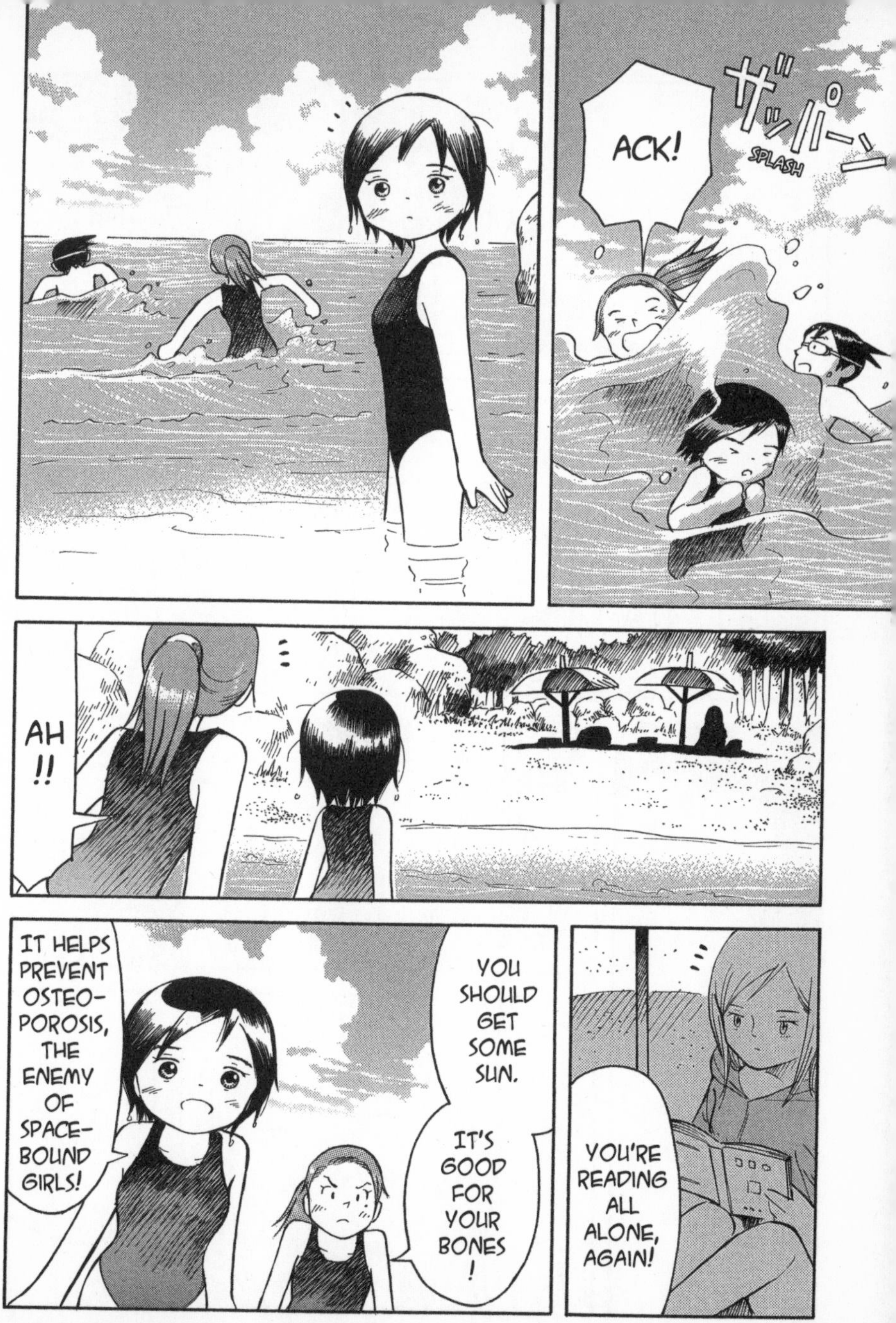
ACK!
ザッパーン
SPLASH
AH!!
YOU'RE READING ALL ALONE, AGAIN!
YOU SHOULD GET SOME SUN.
IT'S GOOD FOR YOUR BONES!
IT HELPS PREVENT OSTEO-POROSIS, THE ENEMY OF SPACE-BOUND GIRLS!

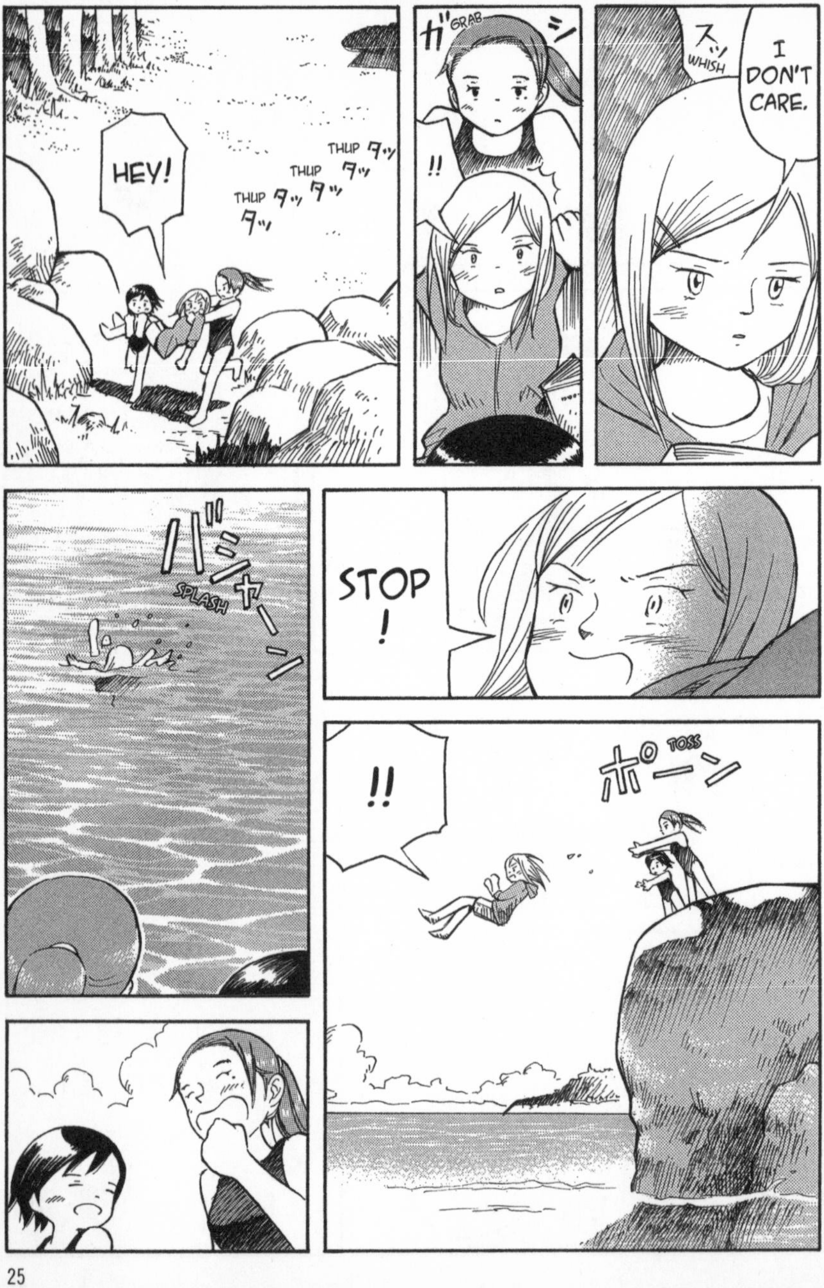

スッ WHISH
I DON'T CARE.
ガシ GRAB
!!
HEY!
THUP タッ
THUP タッ
THUP タッ
タッ
STOP!
!!
ポーン TOSS
バシャーン SPLASH

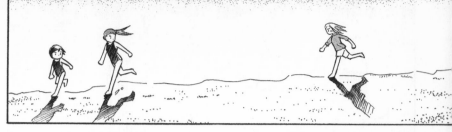

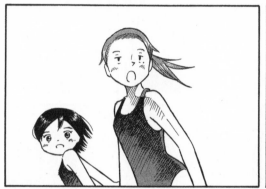

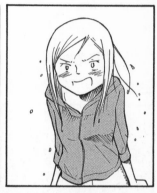

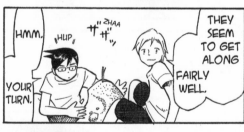

HMM.

HUP

ﾂﾞﾂﾞ ZHAA

YOUR TURN.

THEY SEEM TO GET ALONG FAIRLY WELL.

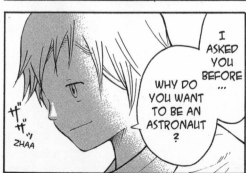

I ASKED YOU BEFORE...

WHY DO YOU WANT TO BE AN ASTRONAUT?

ﾂﾞ ﾂﾞ ﾂﾞ ZHAA

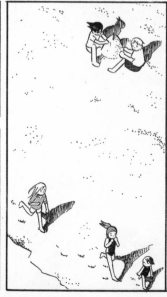

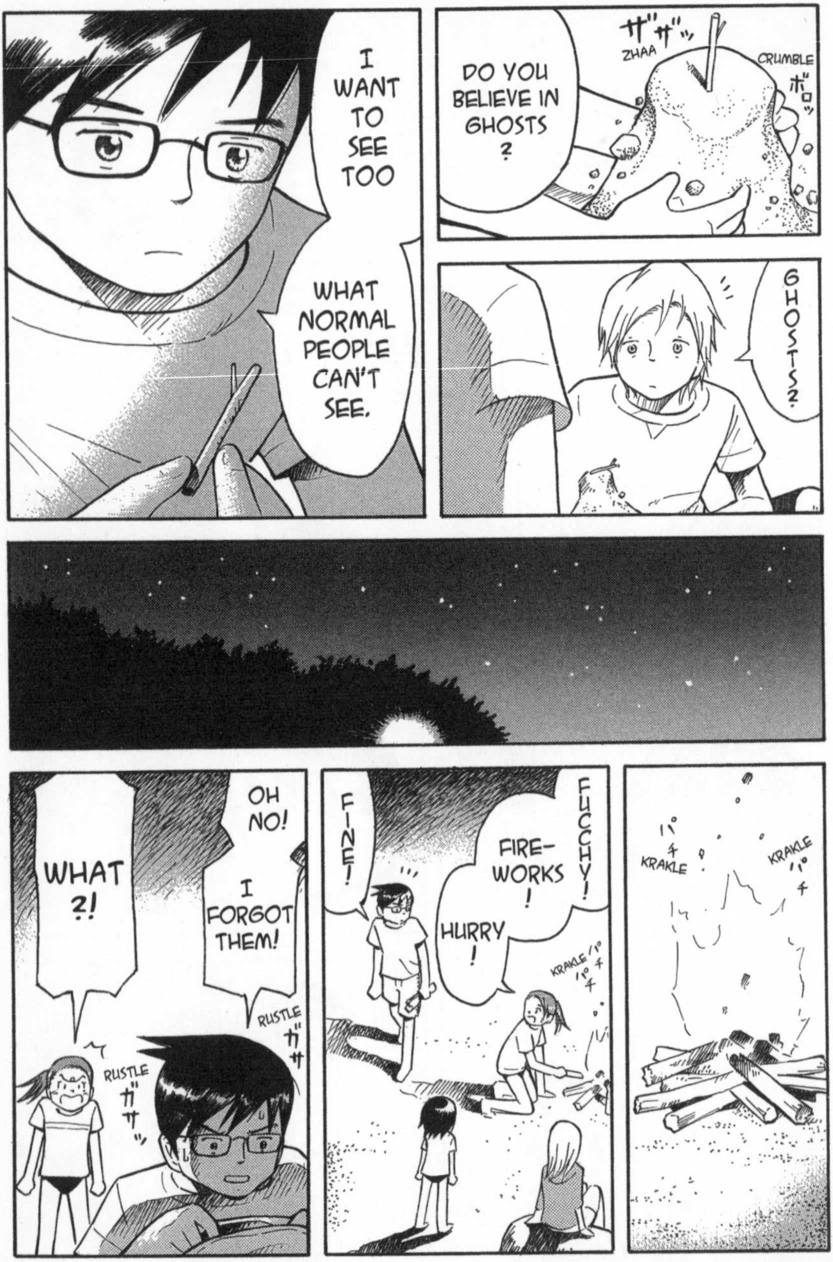
ザザッ
ZHAA
CRUMBLE
ボロッ
DO YOU BELIEVE IN GHOSTS?
GHOSTS?
I WANT TO SEE TOO
WHAT NORMAL PEOPLE CAN'T SEE.
パチ
KRAKLE
KRAKLE
パチ
FUCCHY!
FIRE-WORKS!
HURRY!
FINE!
KRAKLE パチ パチ
OH NO!
I FORGOT THEM!
RUSTLE
ガサ
WHAT?!
RUSTLE
ガサッ

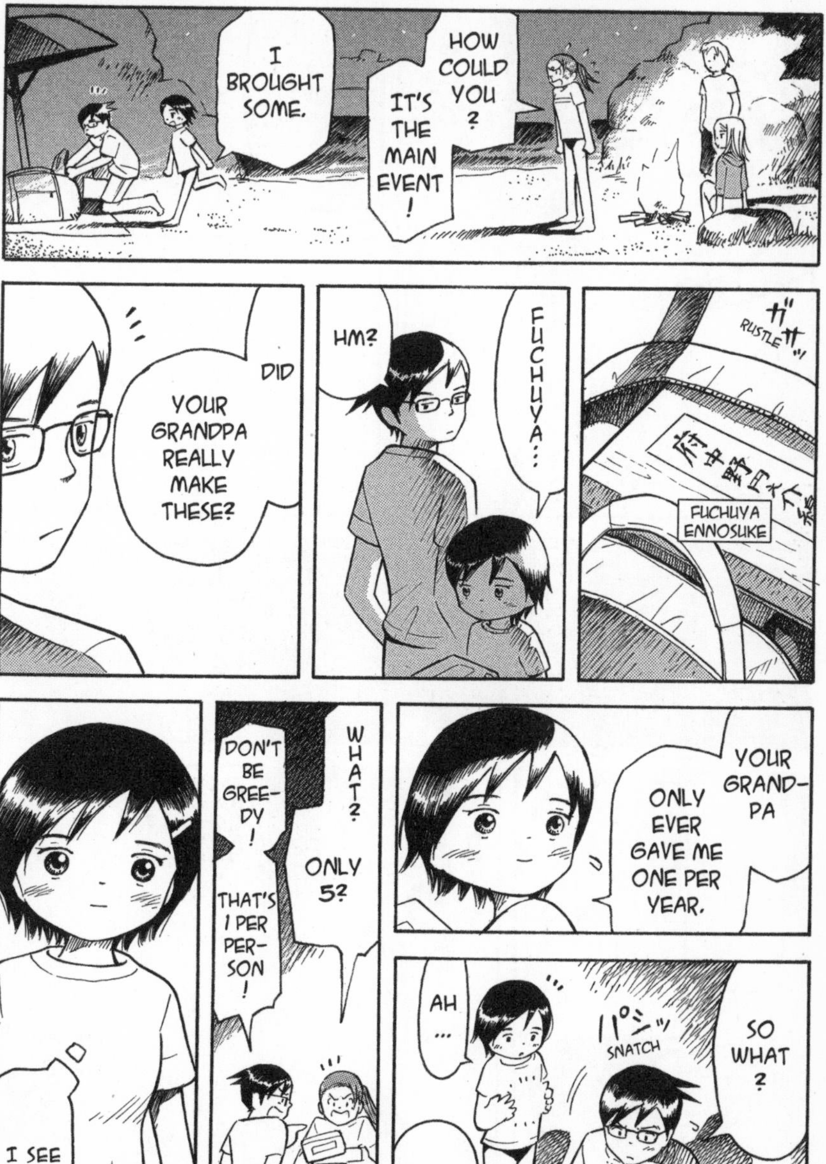
HOW COULD YOU?
IT'S THE MAIN EVENT!
I BROUGHT SOME.
ガサガサ
RUSTLE
FUCHUYA ENNOSUKE
FUCHUYA...
HM?
DID YOUR GRANDPA REALLY MAKE THESE?
YOUR GRANDPA ONLY EVER GAVE ME ONE PER YEAR.
SO WHAT?
パシッ
SNATCH
AH...
GEEZ.
WHAT?
DON'T BE GREEDY!
ONLY 5?
THAT'S 1 PER PERSON!
I SEE...

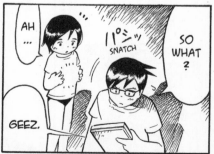

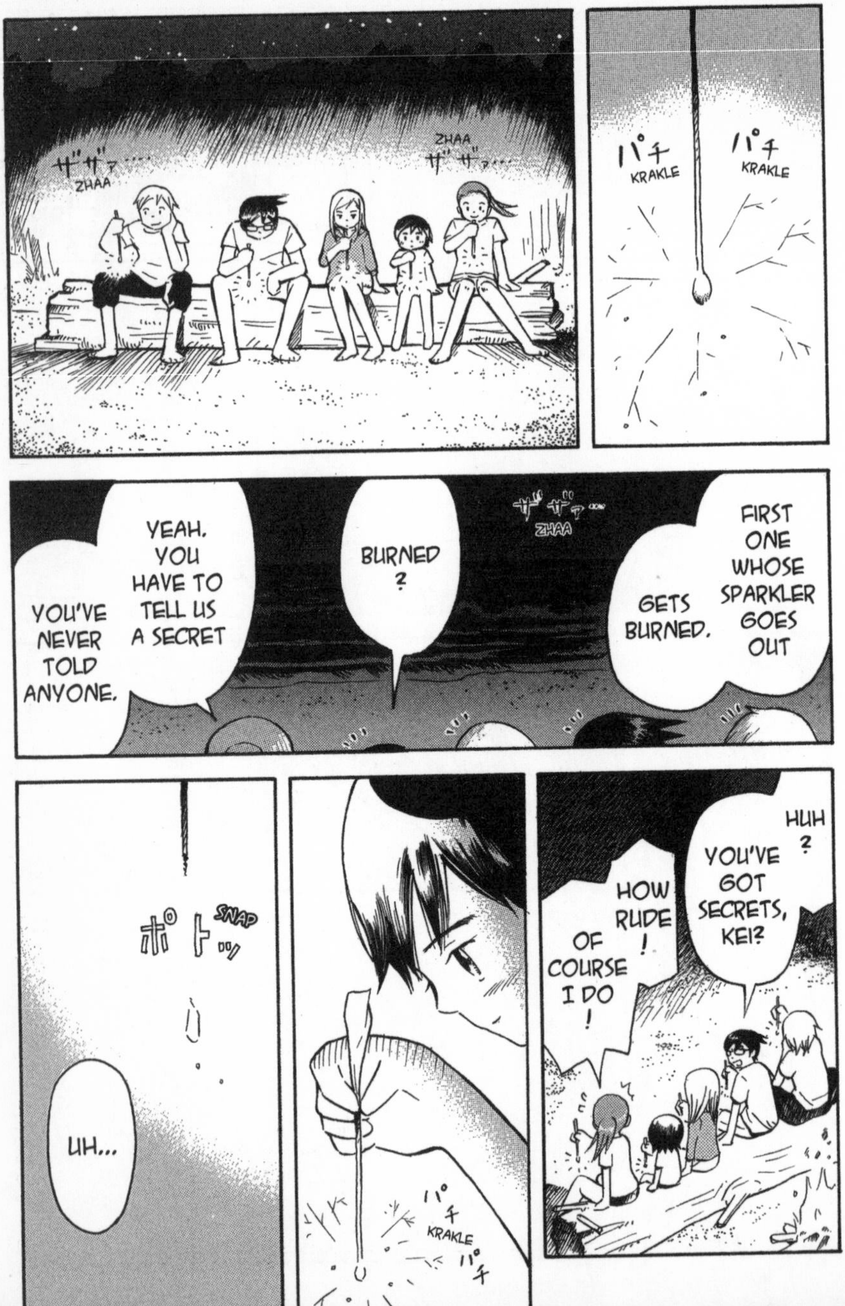
パチ
KRAKLE
パチ
KRAKLE
ZHAA
ザザァ……
ザザァ……
ZHAA
FIRST ONE WHOSE SPARKLER GOES OUT
GETS BURNED.
ザザァ…
ZHAA
BURNED?
YEAH. YOU HAVE TO TELL US A SECRET
YOU'VE NEVER TOLD ANYONE.
HUH?
YOU'VE GOT SECRETS, KEI?
HOW RUDE!
OF COURSE I DO!
パチ
KRAKLE
パチ
ポトッ
SNAP
UH...

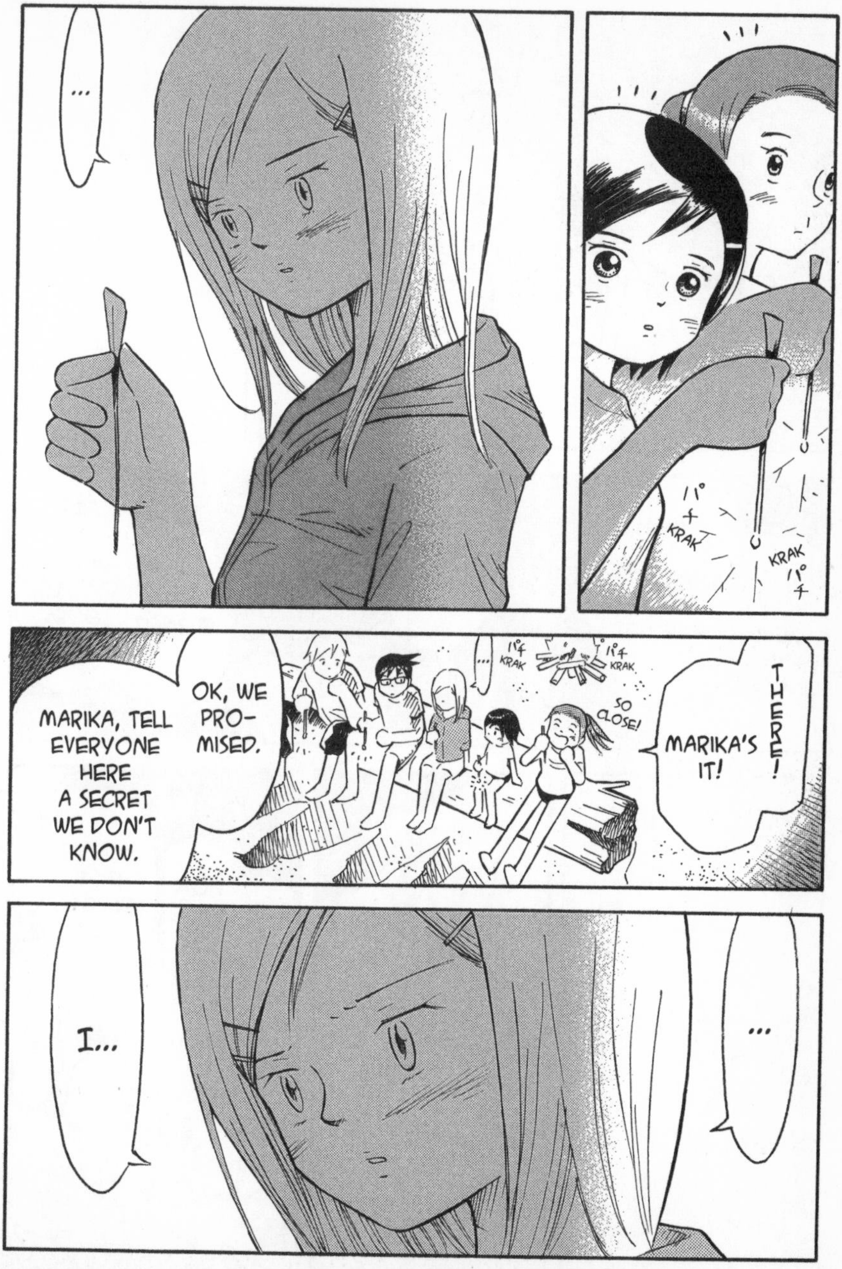
パチ KRAK
KRAK パチ
...
THERE!
MARIKA'S IT!
SO CLOSE!
パチ KRAK
パチ KRAK
...
OK, WE PRO-MISED.
MARIKA, TELL EVERYONE HERE A SECRET WE DON'T KNOW.
...
I...

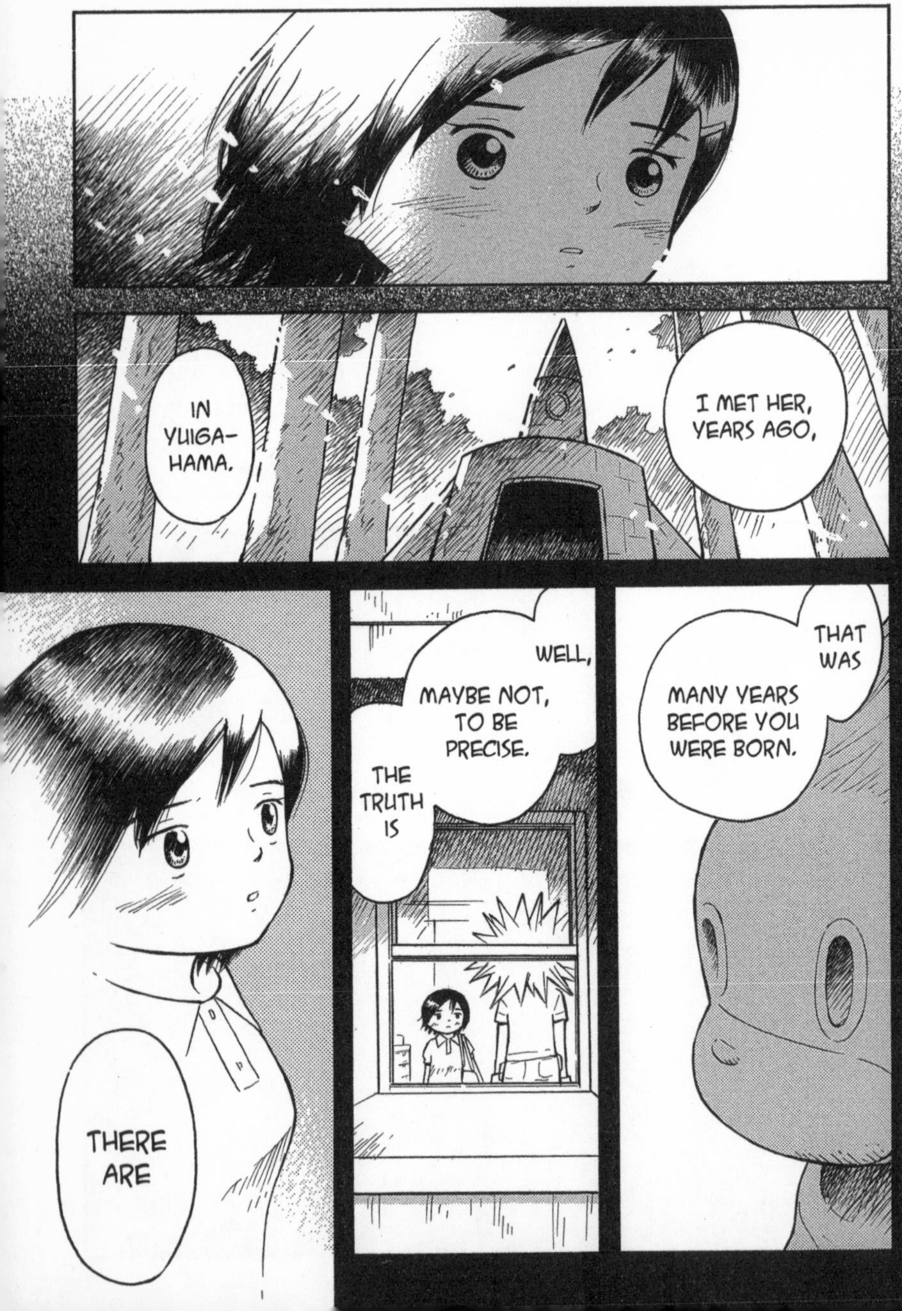
I MET HER, YEARS AGO,
IN YUIGA-HAMA.
THAT WAS MANY YEARS BEFORE YOU WERE BORN.
WELL, MAYBE NOT, TO BE PRECISE.
THE TRUTH IS
THERE ARE

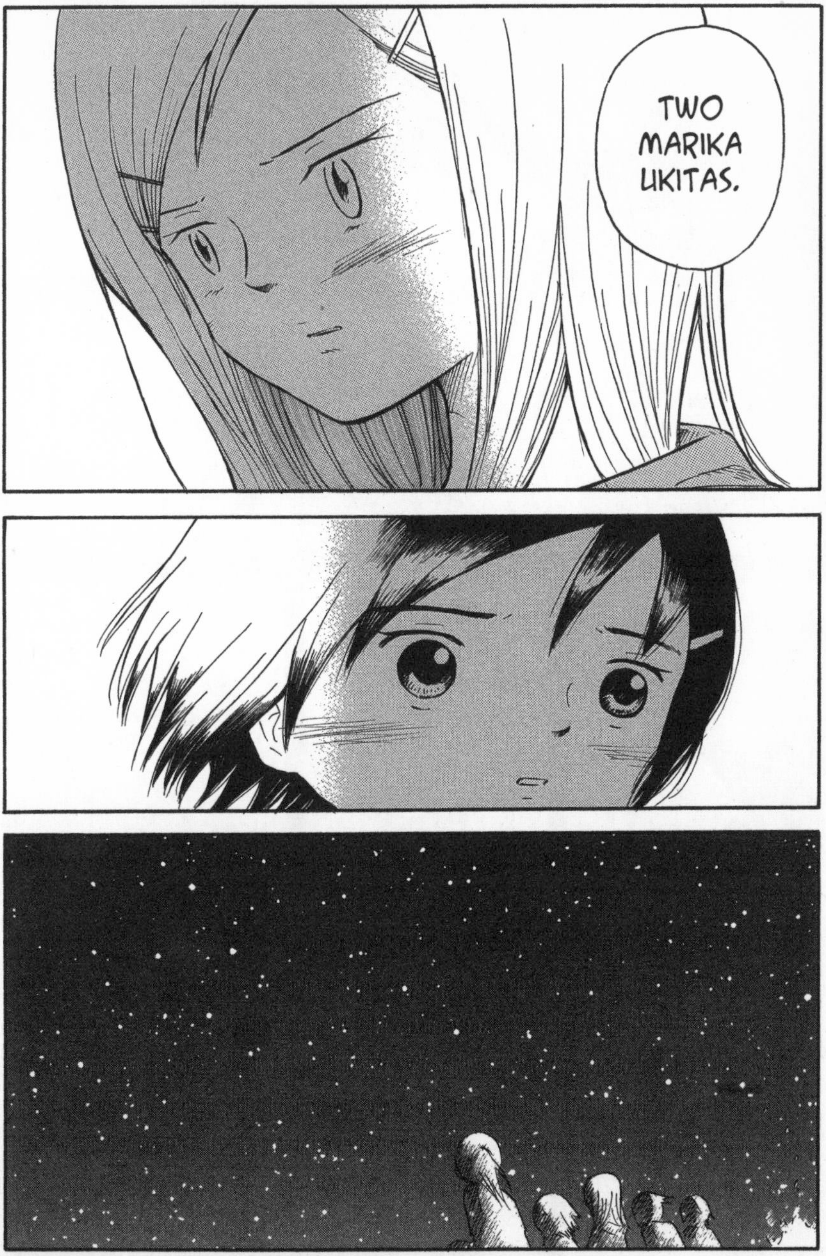
TWO MARIKA UKITAS.

MISSION:31

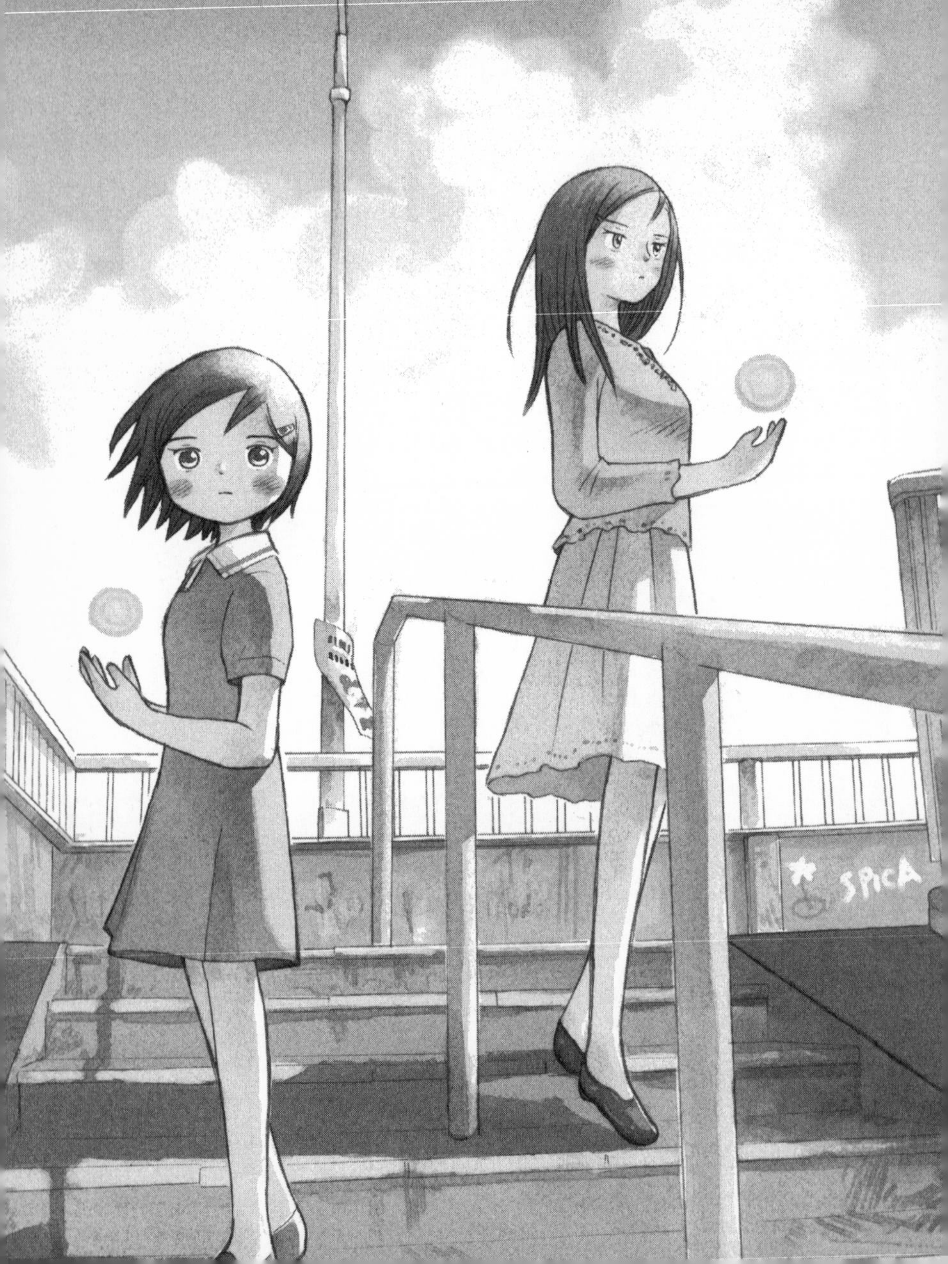
SPICA

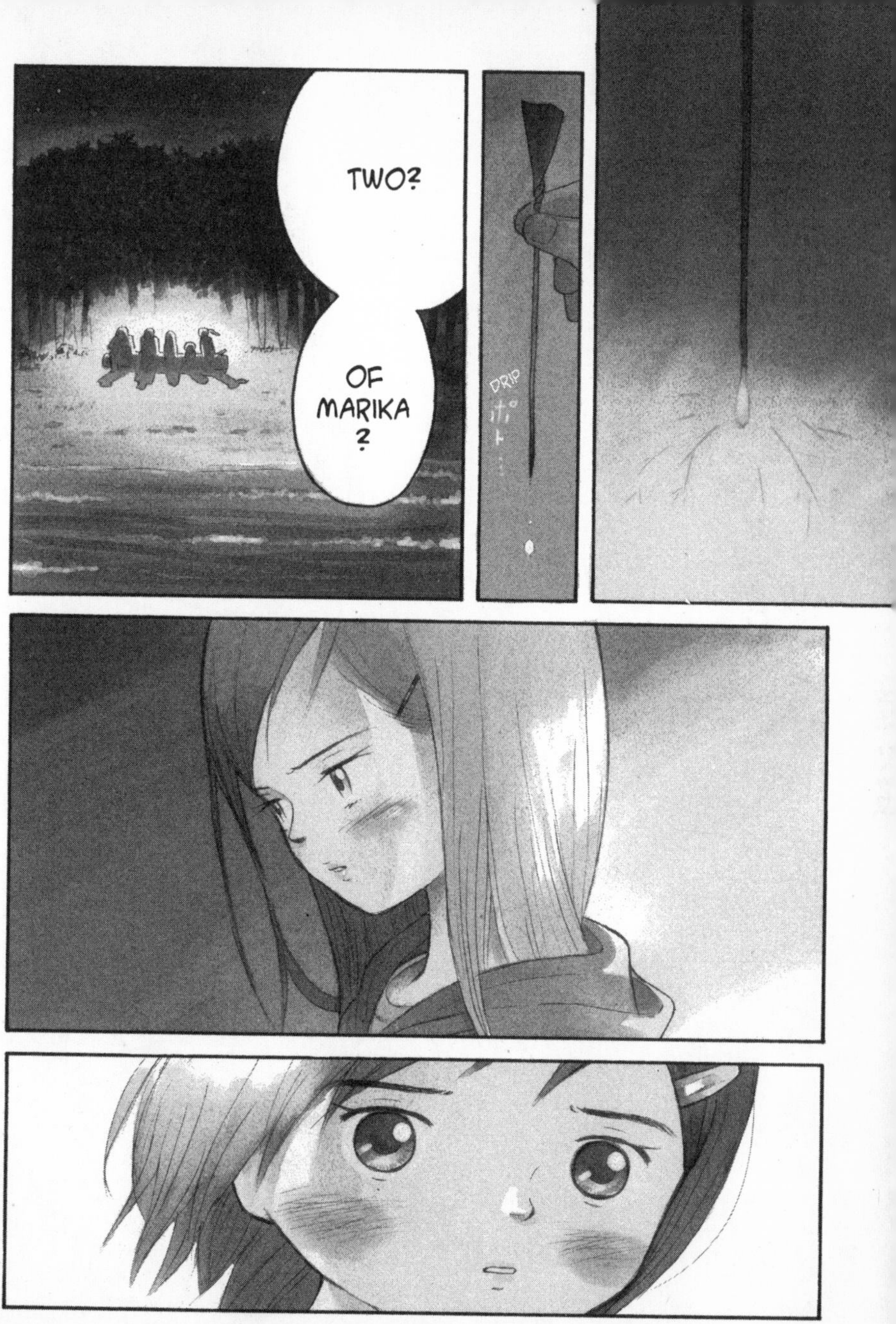
DRIP
ポト…
TWO?
OF MARIKA ?

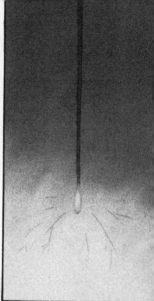

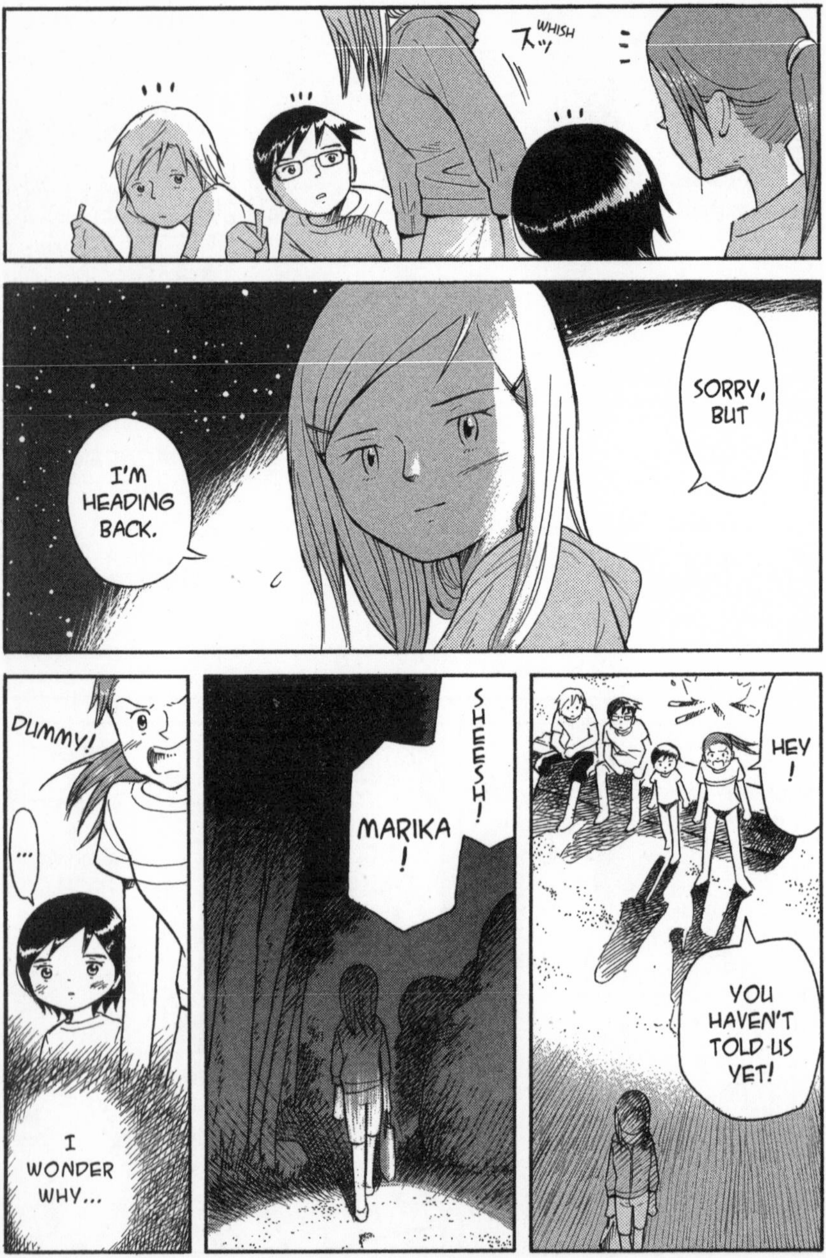
スッ
WHISH
SORRY, BUT
I'M HEADING BACK.
HEY!
YOU HAVEN'T TOLD US YET!
SHEESH!
MARIKA!
DUMMY!
...
I WONDER WHY...

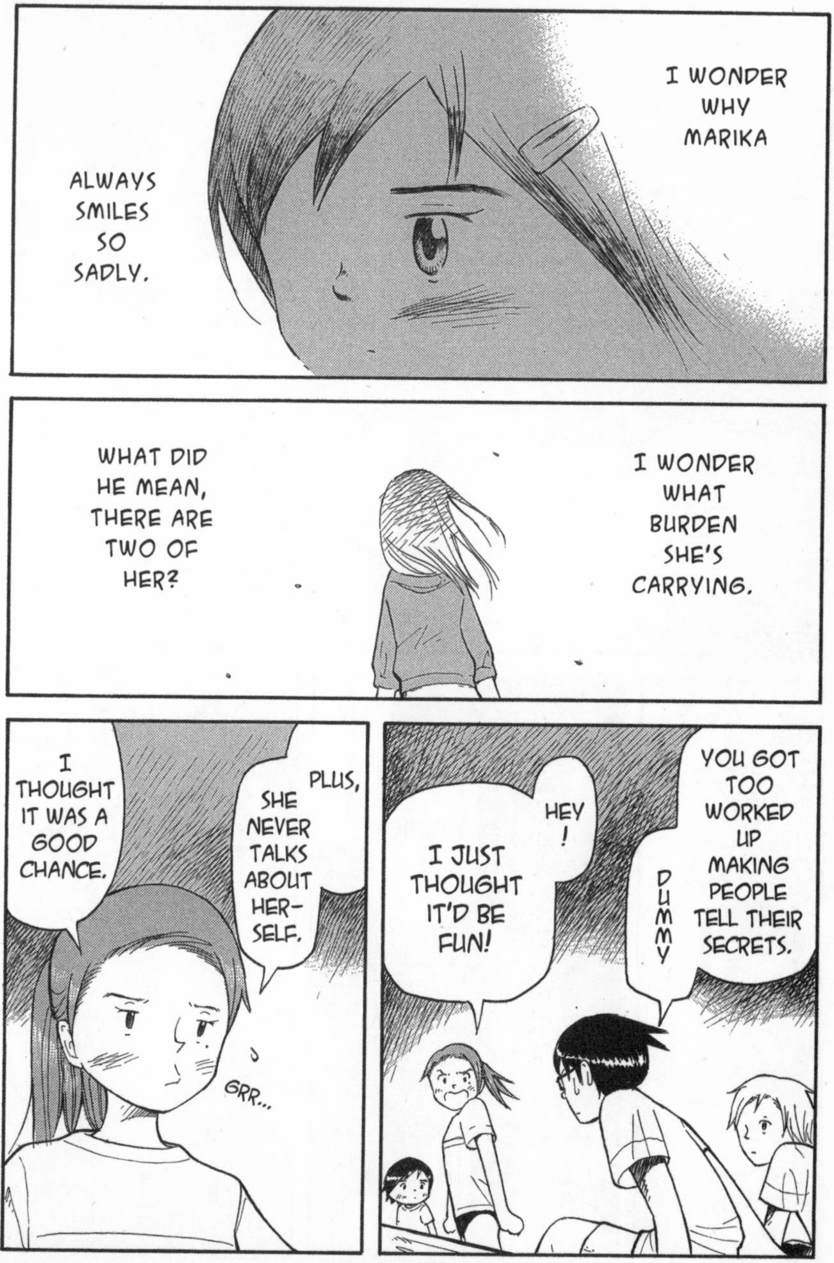
I WONDER WHY MARIKA
ALWAYS SMILES SO SADLY.
I WONDER WHAT BURDEN SHE'S CARRYING.
WHAT DID HE MEAN, THERE ARE TWO OF HER?
YOU GOT TOO WORKED UP MAKING PEOPLE TELL THEIR SECRETS.
DUMMY
HEY!
I JUST THOUGHT IT'D BE FUN!
PLUS, SHE NEVER TALKS ABOUT HER-SELF.
I THOUGHT IT WAS A GOOD CHANCE.
GRR...

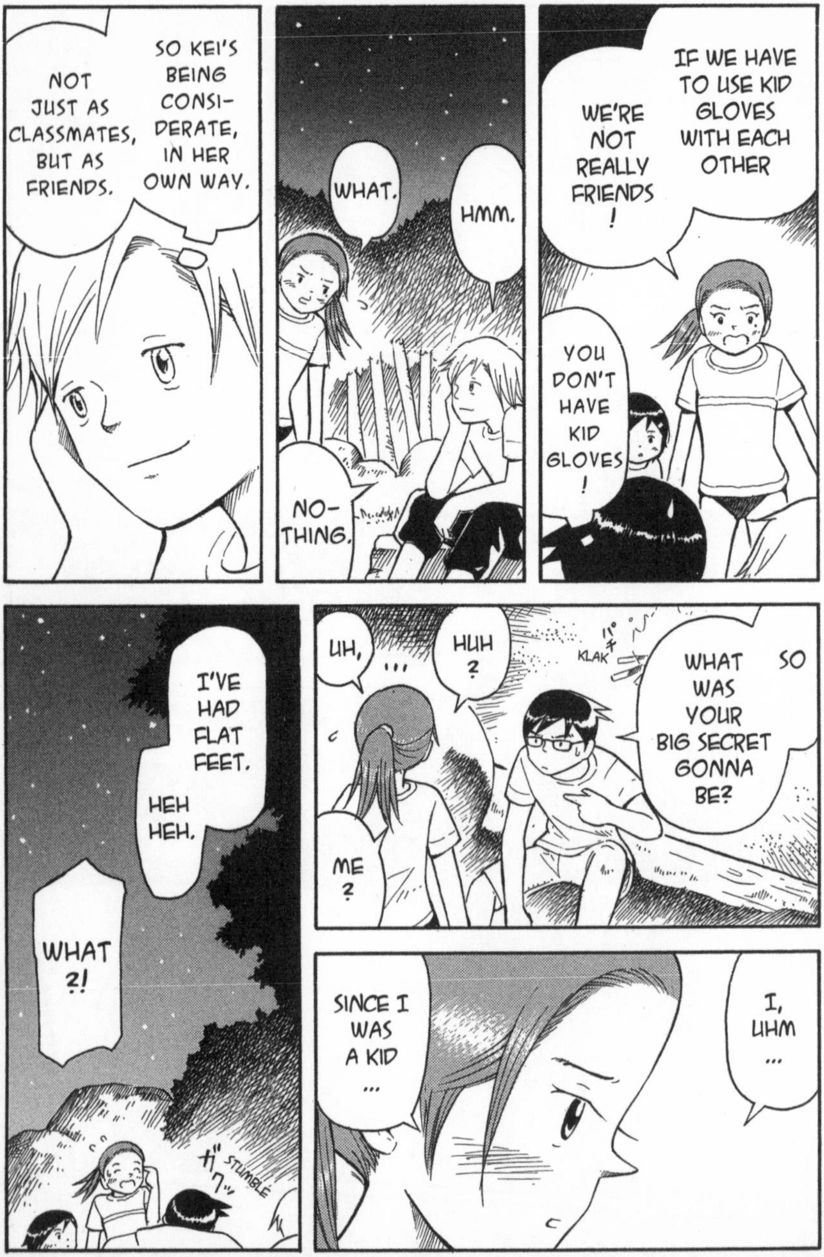
IF WE HAVE TO USE KID GLOVES WITH EACH OTHER
WE'RE NOT REALLY FRIENDS!
YOU DON'T HAVE KID GLOVES!
HMM.
WHAT.
NO-THING.
SO KEI'S BEING CONSI-DERATE, IN HER OWN WAY.
NOT JUST AS CLASSMATES, BUT AS FRIENDS.
SO
WHAT WAS YOUR BIG SECRET GONNA BE?
パチ
KLAK
HUH?
UH, ...
ME?
I, UHM ...
SINCE I WAS A KID ...
I'VE HAD FLAT FEET.
HEH HEH.
WHAT?!
ガク
STUMBLE

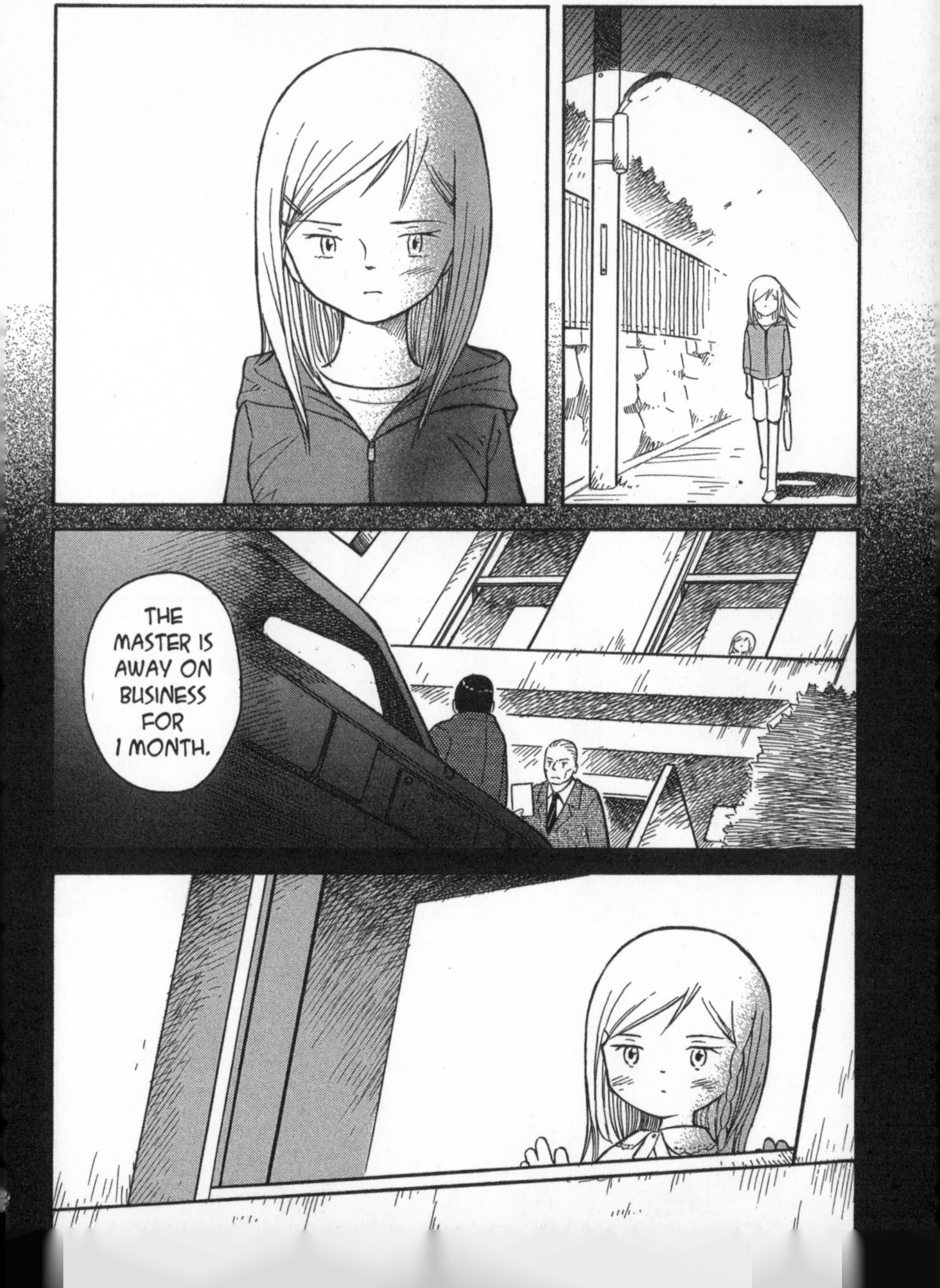
THE MASTER IS AWAY ON BUSINESS FOR 1 MONTH.

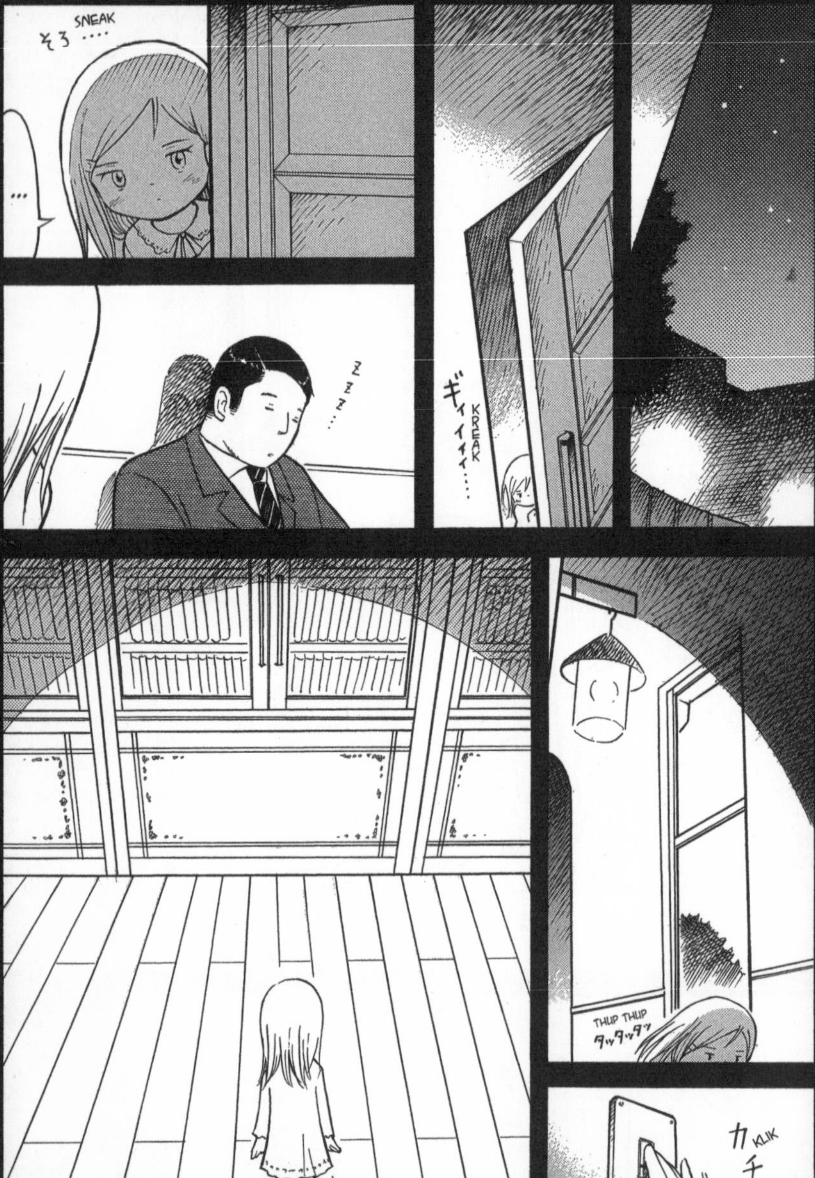
KREAK
ギィィィ……
SNEAK
そろ……
…
z z z…
THUP THUP
タッタッタッ
カチッ
KLIK

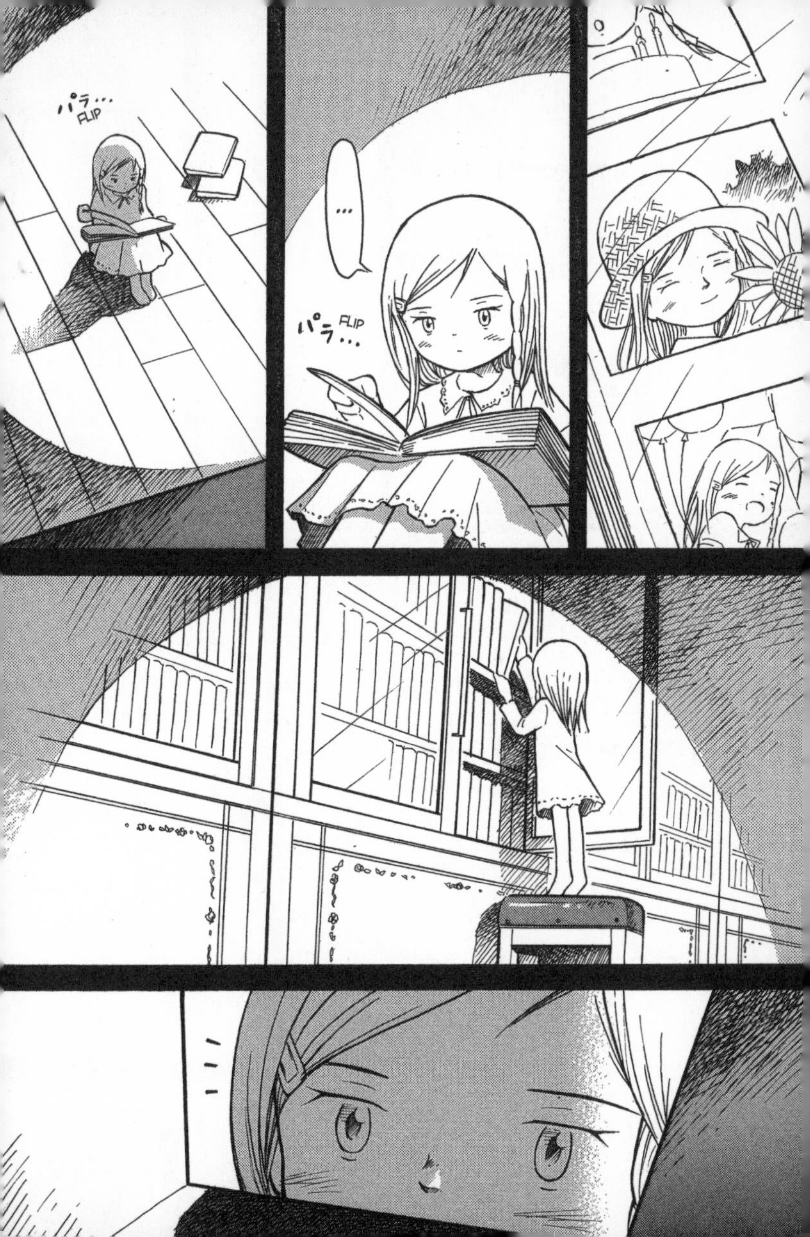
…
パラ… FLIP
パラ… FLIP

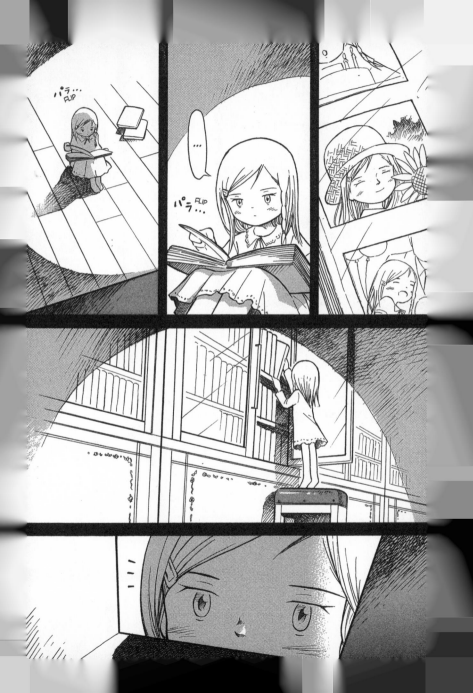

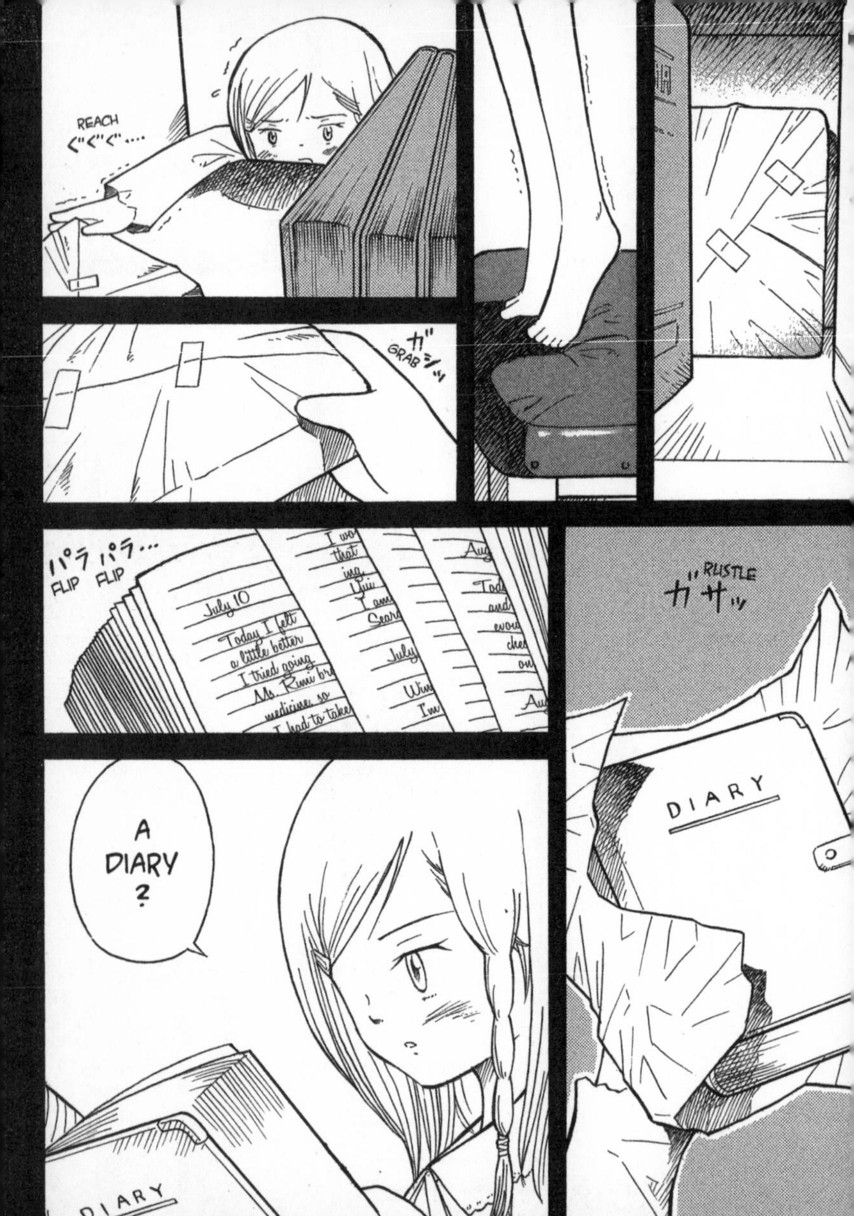
REACH
ぐぐぐ....
GRAB
ガシッ
RUSTLE
ガサッ
DIARY
パラ パラ...
FLIP FLIP
July 10
Today I felt
a little better
I tried going
medicines so
A DIARY?
DIARY

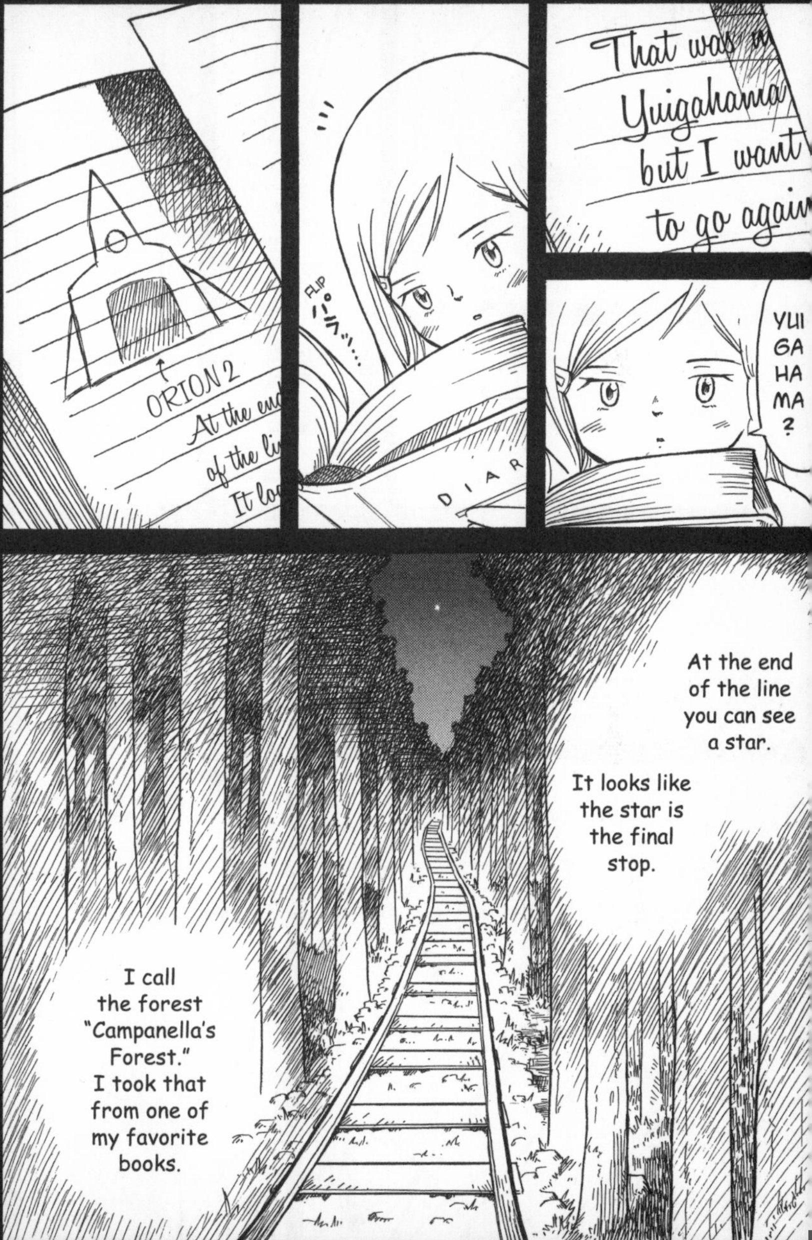
That was
Yuigahama
but I want
to go agai
YUI GA HA MA?
FLIP
ORION 2
At the end
of the li
It lo
DIAR
At the end of the line you can see a star.
It looks like the star is the final stop.
I call the forest "Campanella's Forest." I took that from one of my favorite books.

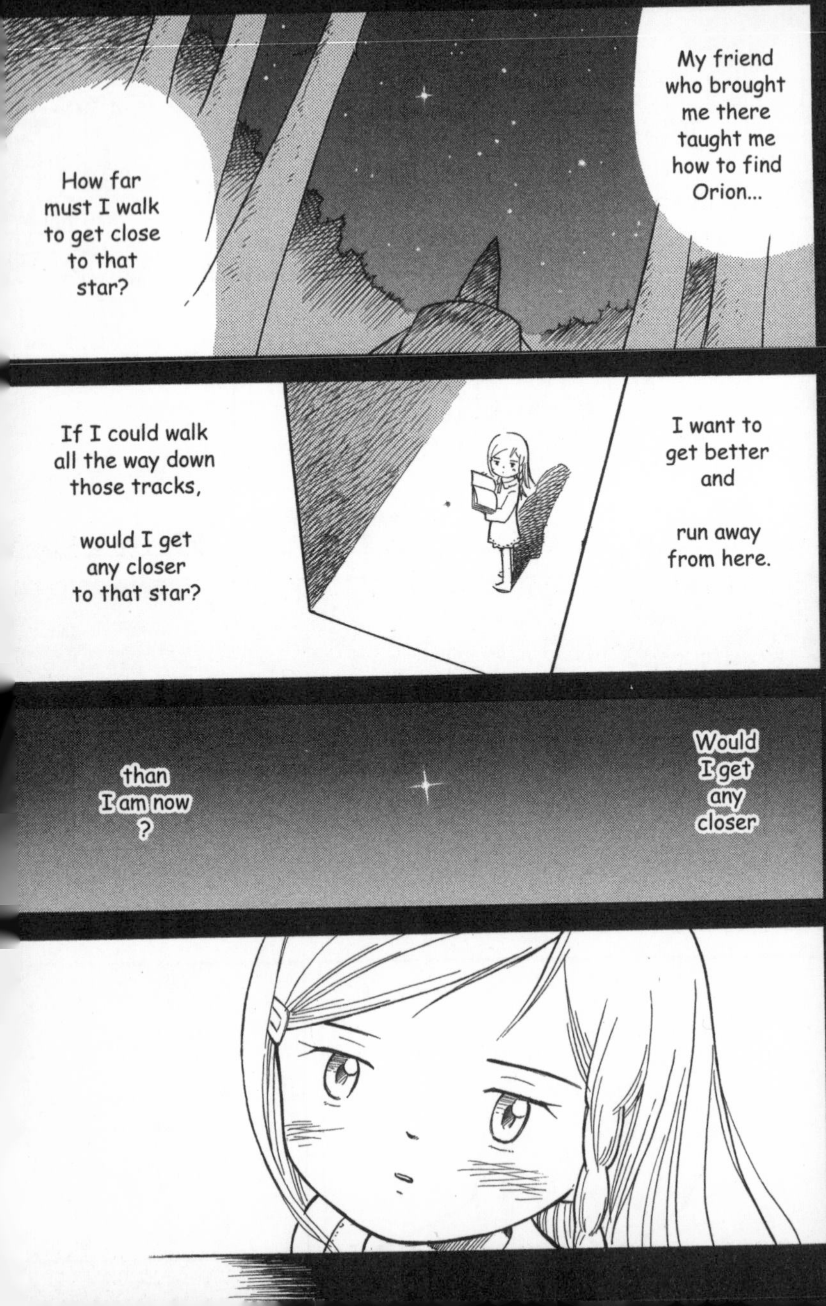
My friend who brought me there taught me how to find Orion...
How far must I walk to get close to that star?
I want to get better and
run away from here.
If I could walk all the way down those tracks,
would I get any closer to that star?
Would I get any closer
than I am now ?

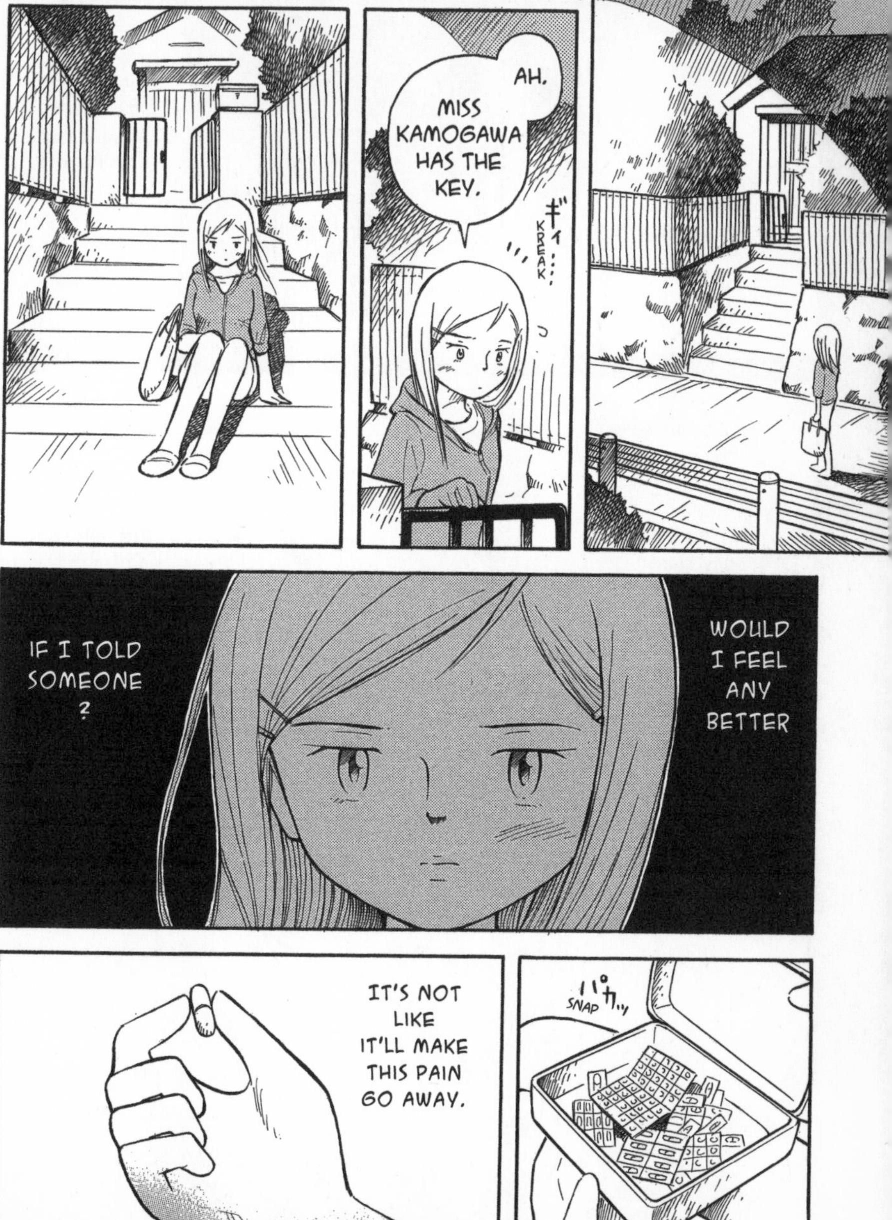
AH. MISS KAMOGAWA HAS THE KEY.
ギィ... KREAK
WOULD I FEEL ANY BETTER
IF I TOLD SOMEONE ?
パカッ SNAP
IT'S NOT LIKE IT'LL MAKE THIS PAIN GO AWAY.

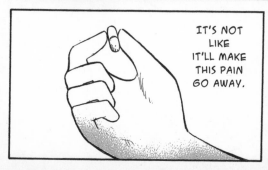

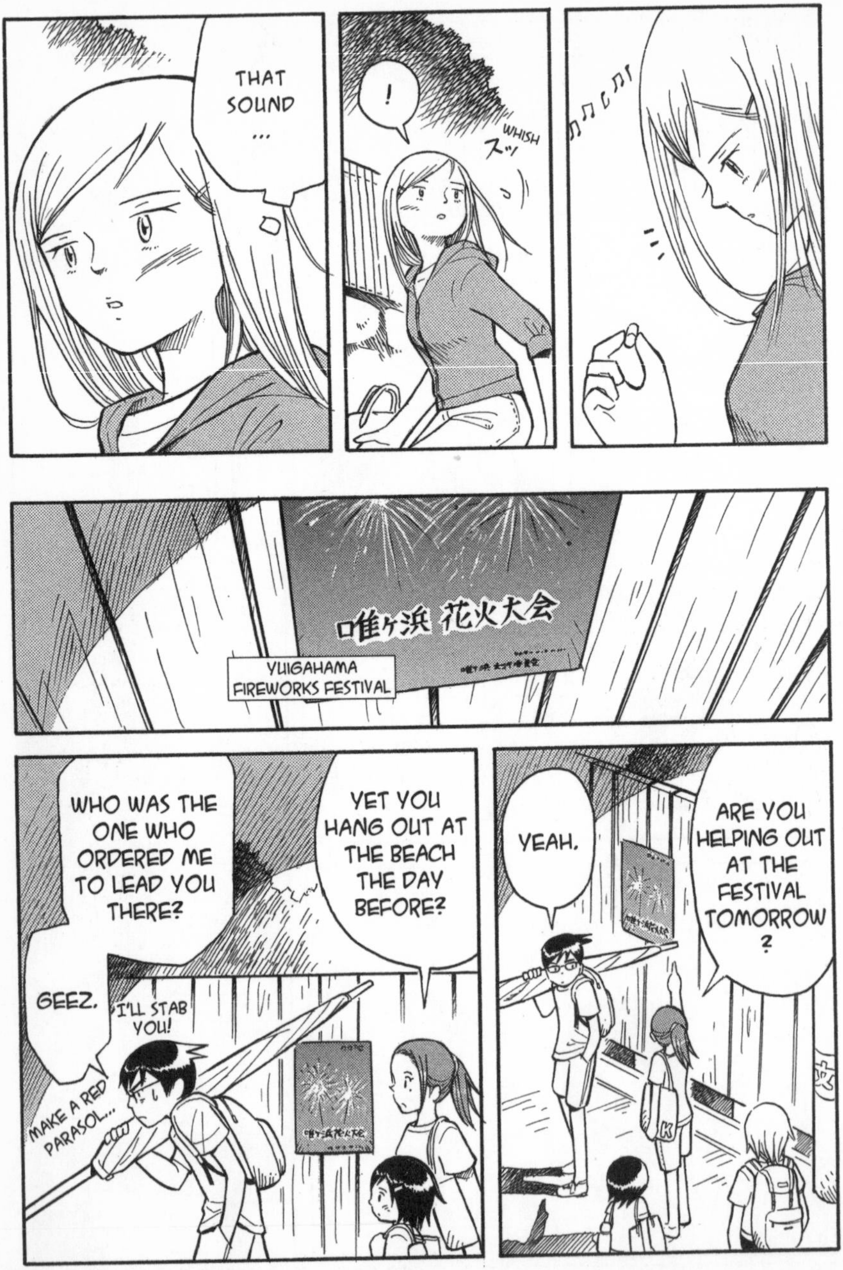
!
WHISH
ズッ
THAT SOUND ...
唯ヶ浜 花火大会
YUIGAHAMA FIREWORKS FESTIVAL
ARE YOU HELPING OUT AT THE FESTIVAL TOMORROW?
YEAH.
YET YOU HANG OUT AT THE BEACH THE DAY BEFORE?
WHO WAS THE ONE WHO ORDERED ME TO LEAD YOU THERE?
GEEZ.
I'LL STAB YOU!
MAKE A RED PARASOL...

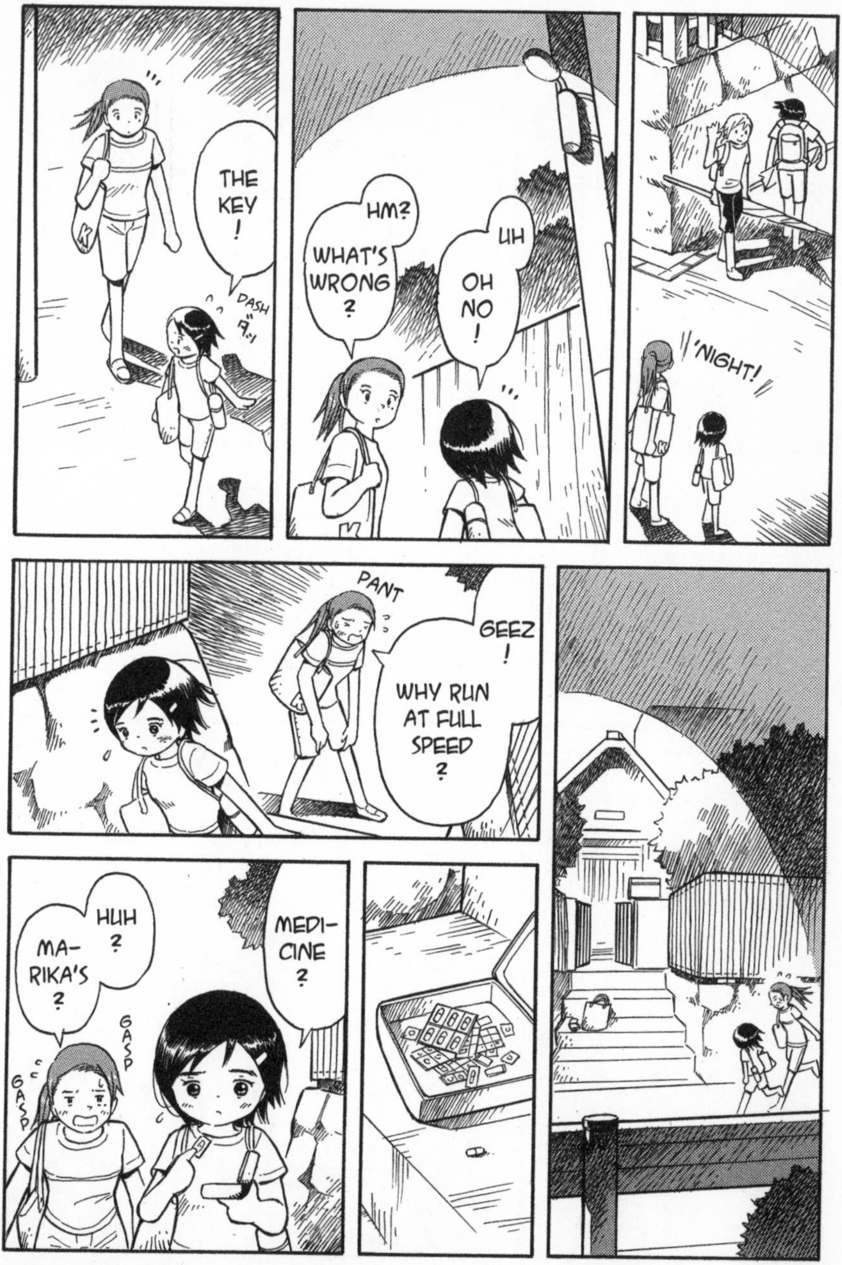
'NIGHT!
HM? WHAT'S WRONG?
UH OH NO!
THE KEY!
DASH ダッ
PANT
GEEZ! WHY RUN AT FULL SPEED?
MEDI-CINE?
HUH? MA-RIKA'S?
GASP GASP

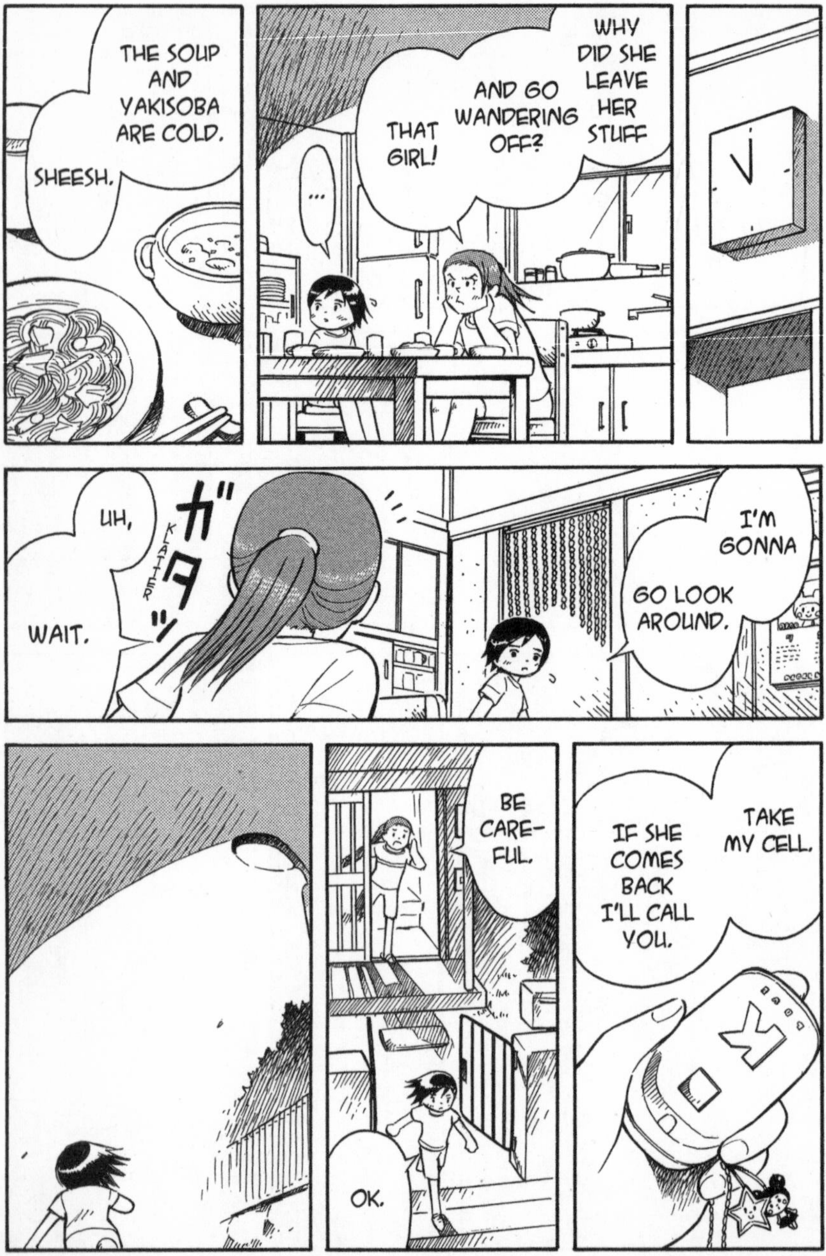
WHY DID SHE LEAVE HER STUFF
AND GO WANDERING OFF?
THAT GIRL!
...
THE SOUP AND YAKISOBA ARE COLD.
SHEESH.
I'M GONNA
GO LOOK AROUND.
ガタッ
KLATTER
UH,
WAIT.
TAKE MY CELL.
IF SHE COMES BACK I'LL CALL YOU.
BE CARE-FUL.
OK.

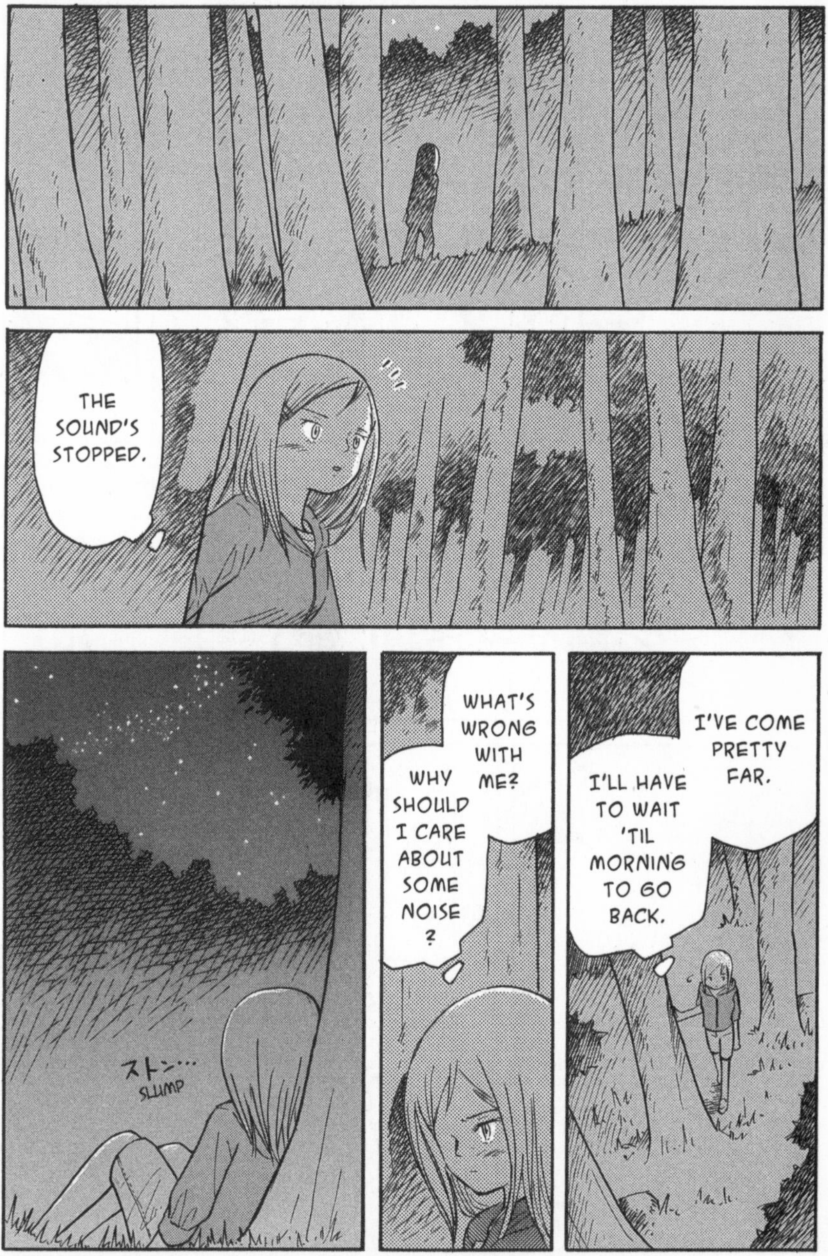
THE SOUND'S STOPPED.
I'VE COME PRETTY FAR.
I'LL HAVE TO WAIT 'TIL MORNING TO GO BACK.
WHAT'S WRONG WITH ME?
WHY SHOULD I CARE ABOUT SOME NOISE?
ストン…
SLUMP

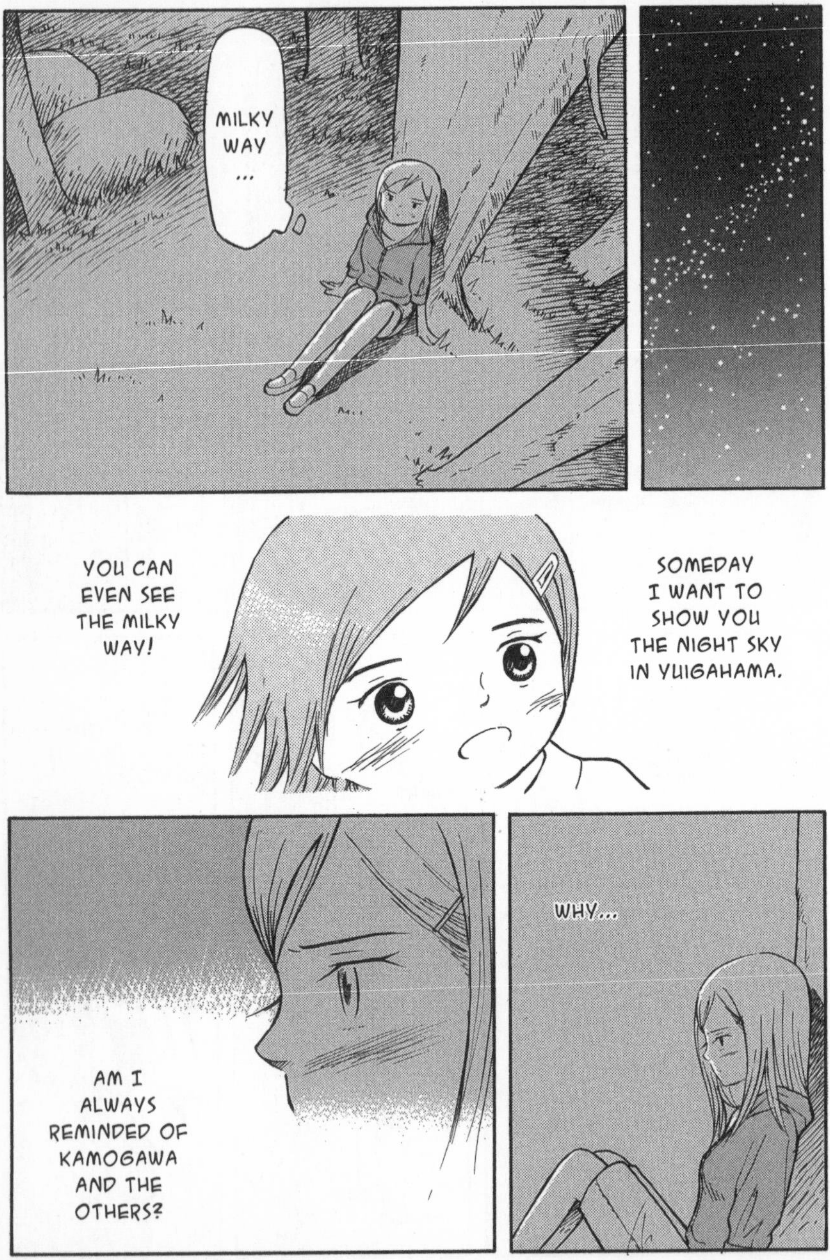
MILKY WAY ...
SOMEDAY I WANT TO SHOW YOU THE NIGHT SKY IN YUIGAHAMA.
YOU CAN EVEN SEE THE MILKY WAY!
WHY...
AM I ALWAYS REMINDED OF KAMOGAWA AND THE OTHERS?

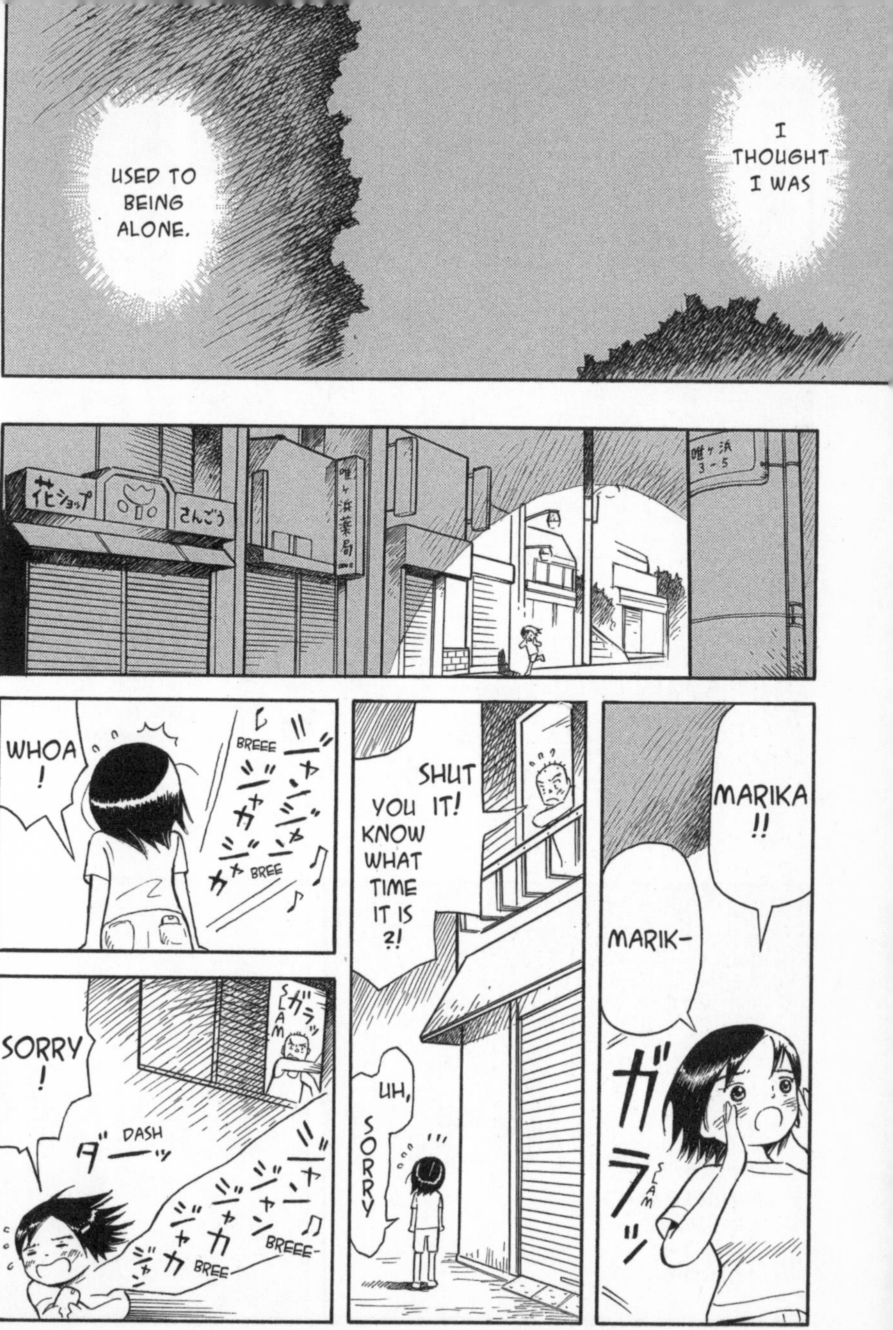
I THOUGHT I WAS
USED TO BEING ALONE.
唯ヶ浜 3-5
唯ヶ浜薬局
花ショップ さんごう
MARIKA!!
MARIK-
ガラッ
SLAM
SHUT IT!
YOU KNOW WHAT TIME IT IS?!
UH, SORRY
WHOA!
BREEE
BREE
SORRY!
ガラッ
SLAM
ダーッ
DASH
BREEE-
BREE

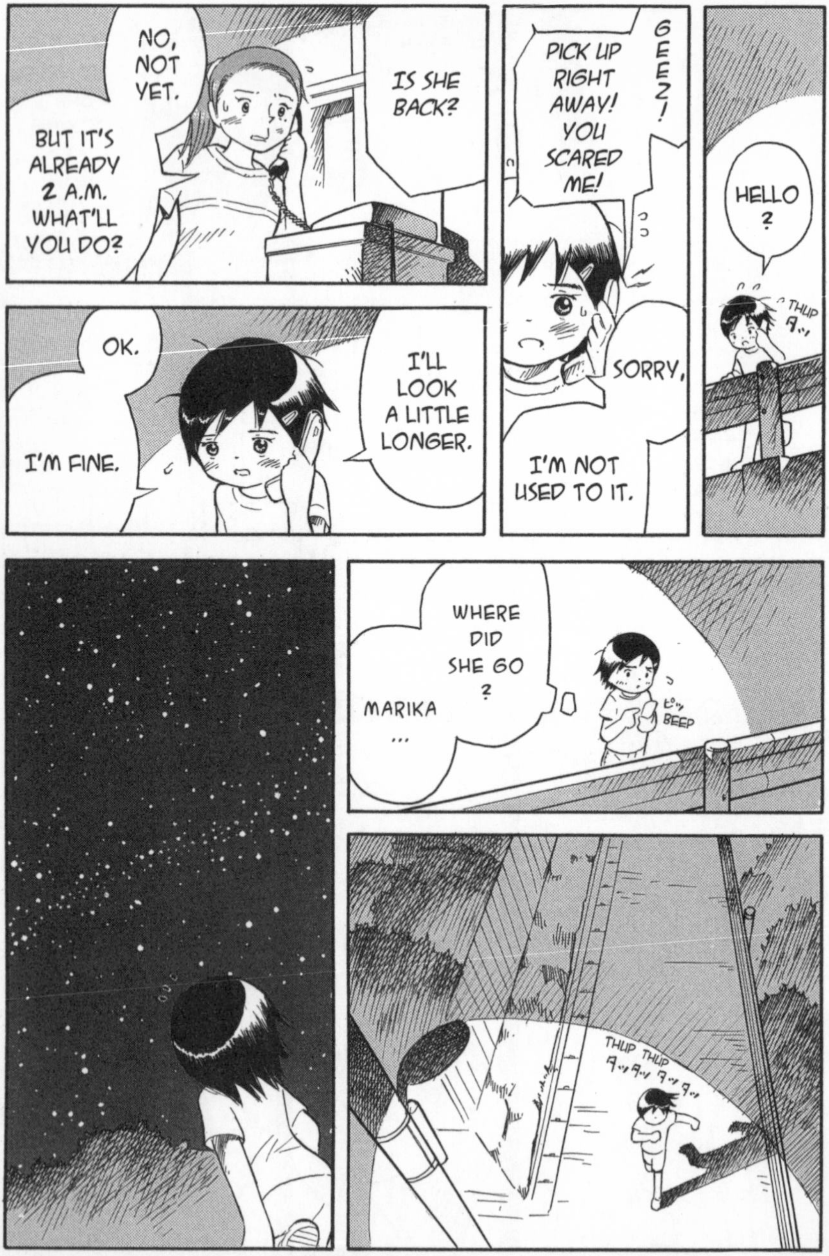
HELLO?
THUP
タッ
GEEZ!
PICK UP RIGHT AWAY! YOU SCARED ME!
SORRY,
I'M NOT USED TO IT.
IS SHE BACK?
NO, NOT YET.
BUT IT'S ALREADY 2 A.M. WHAT'LL YOU DO?
I'LL LOOK A LITTLE LONGER.
OK.
I'M FINE.
WHERE DID SHE GO?
MARIKA ...
ピッ
BEEP
THUP THUP
タッタッ タッタッ

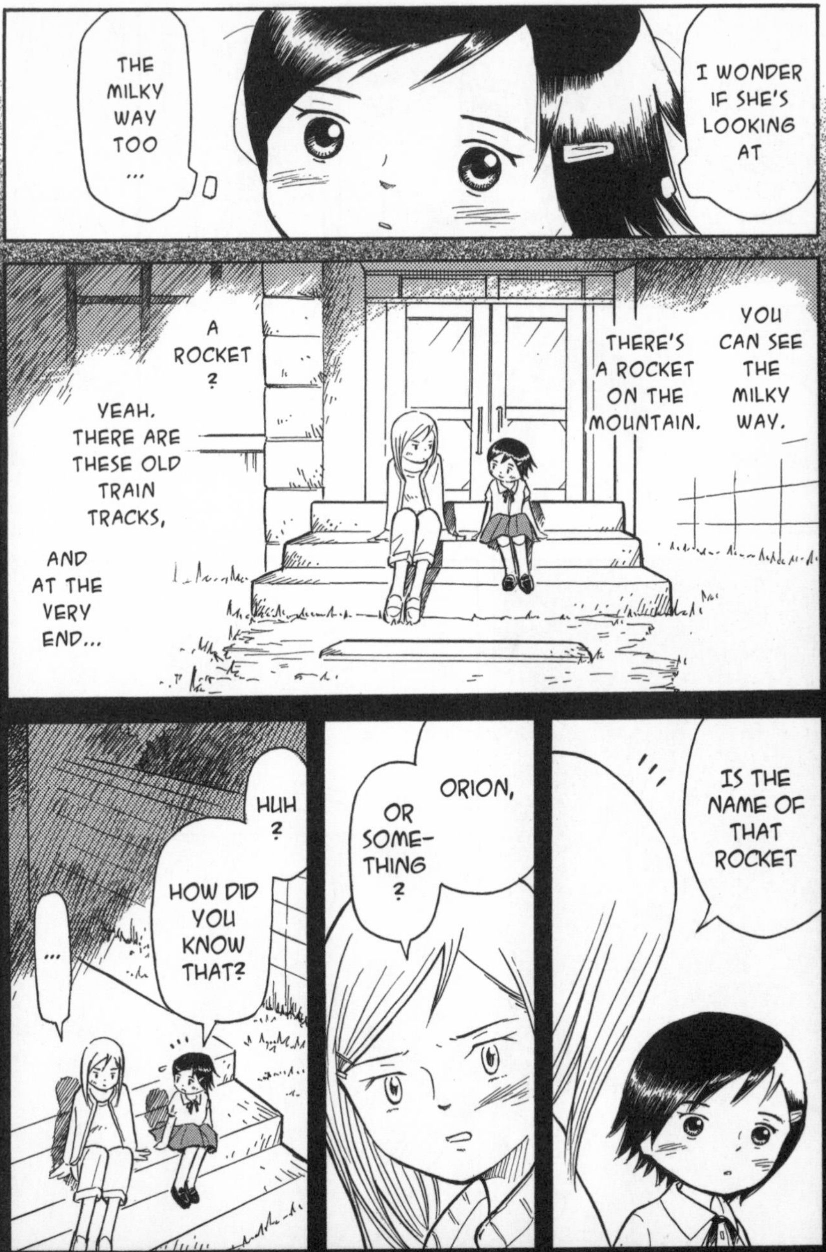
I WONDER IF SHE'S LOOKING AT
THE MILKY WAY TOO ...
YOU CAN SEE THE MILKY WAY.
THERE'S A ROCKET ON THE MOUNTAIN.
A ROCKET?
YEAH. THERE ARE THESE OLD TRAIN TRACKS,
AND AT THE VERY END...
IS THE NAME OF THAT ROCKET
ORION,
OR SOMETHING?
HUH?
HOW DID YOU KNOW THAT?
...

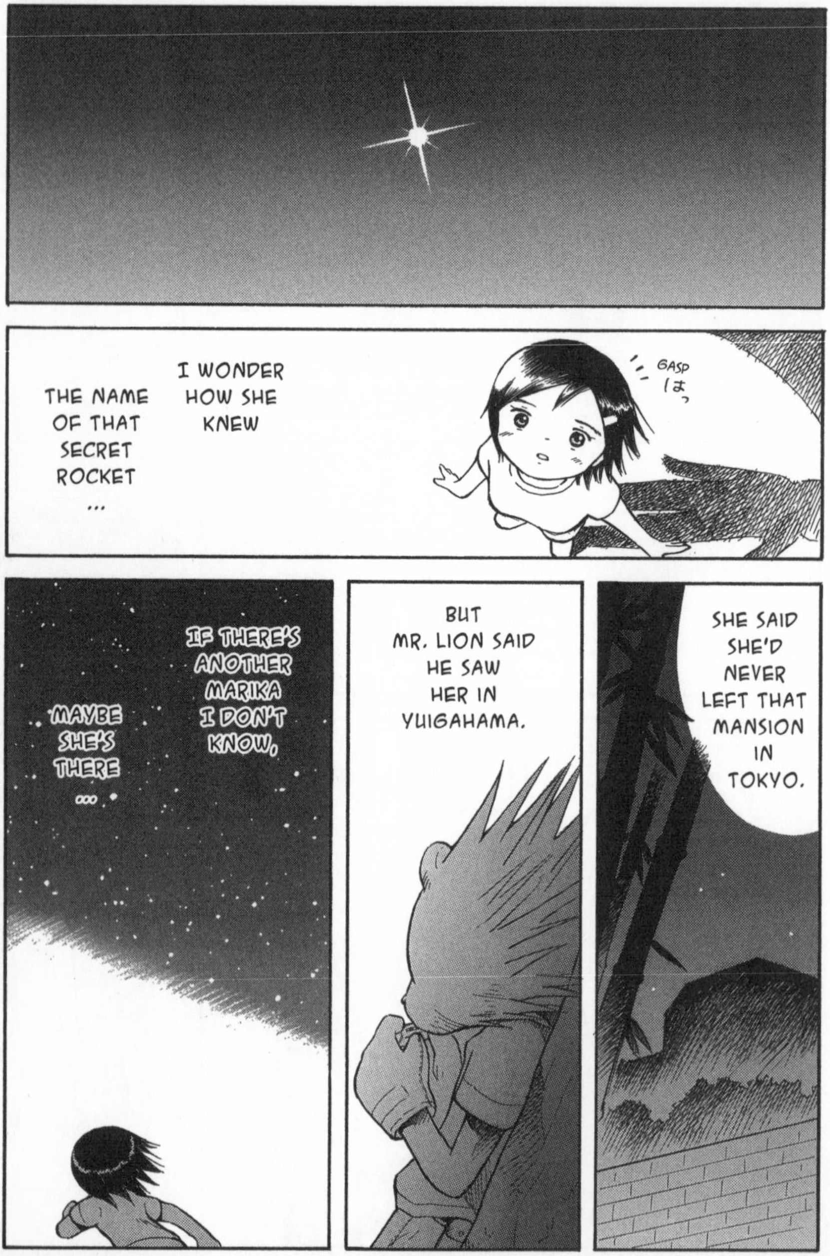
GASP はっ
I WONDER HOW SHE KNEW
THE NAME OF THAT SECRET ROCKET ...
SHE SAID SHE'D NEVER LEFT THAT MANSION IN TOKYO.
BUT MR. LION SAID HE SAW HER IN YUIGAHAMA.
IF THERE'S ANOTHER MARIKA I DON'T KNOW,
MAYBE SHE'S THERE ...

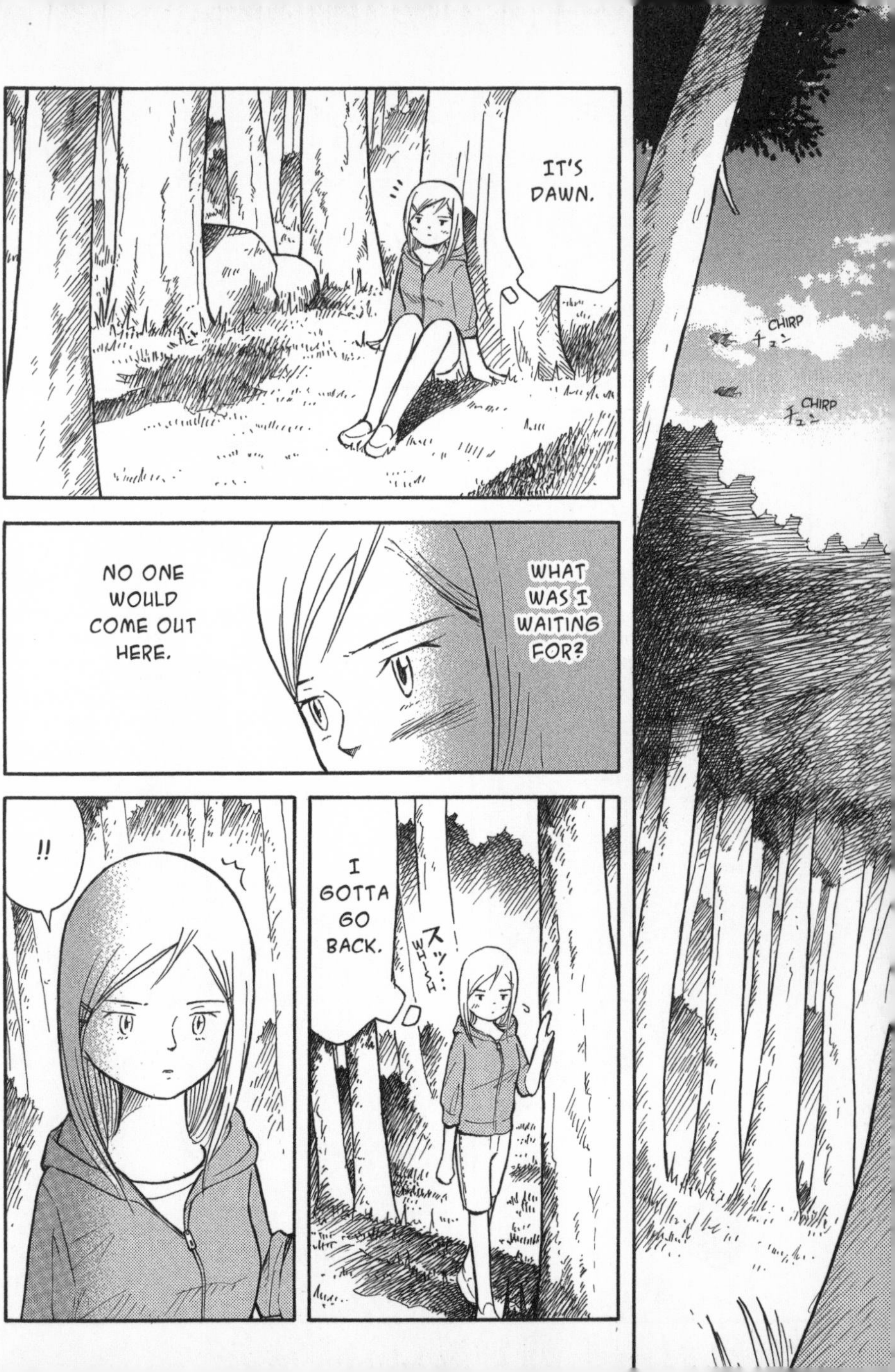
CHIRP チュン
CHIRP チュン
IT'S DAWN.
WHAT WAS I WAITING FOR?
NO ONE WOULD COME OUT HERE.
I GOTTA GO BACK.
スッ… WHISH
!!

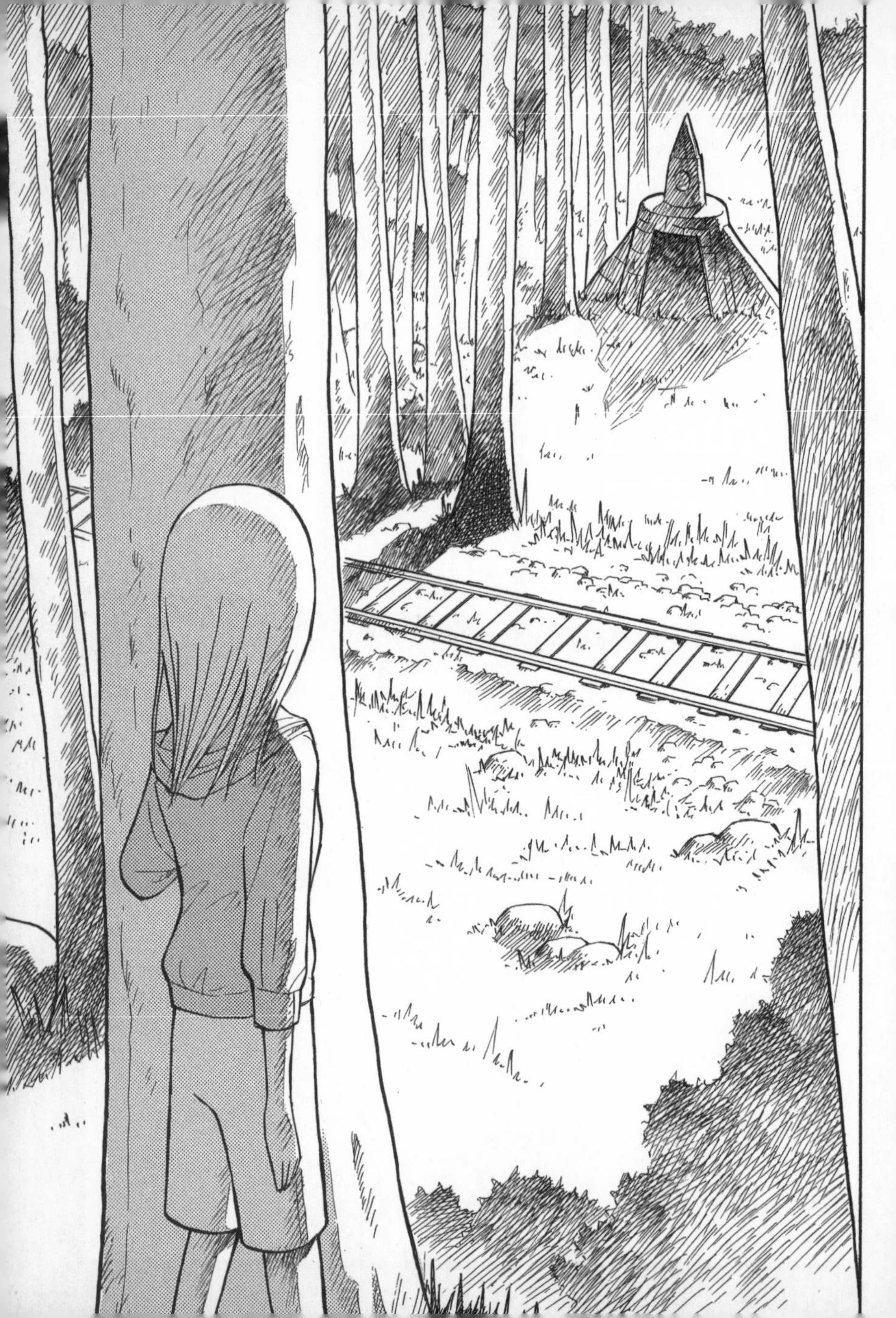

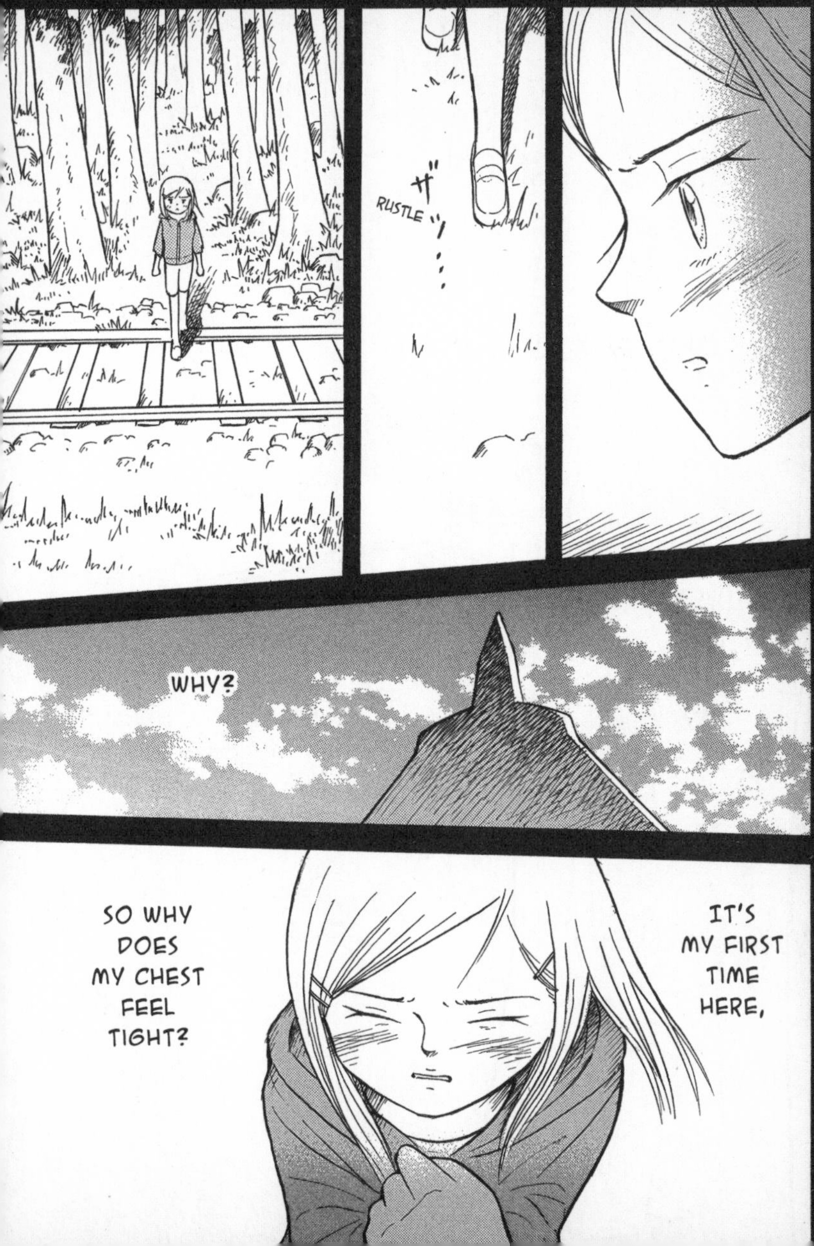
ザ
RUSTLE
WHY?
IT'S MY FIRST TIME HERE,
SO WHY DOES MY CHEST FEEL TIGHT?

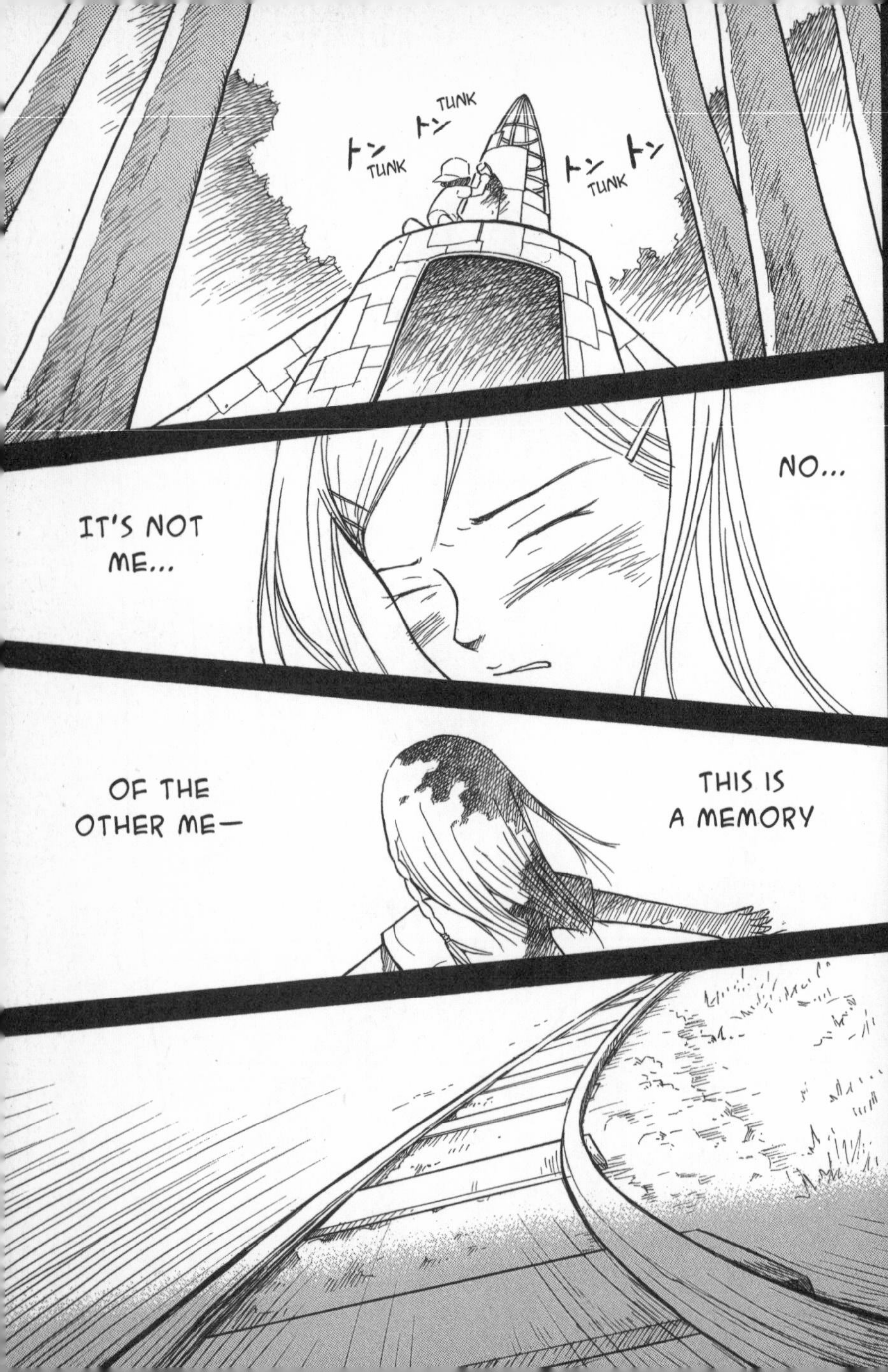
トン TUNK
トン TUNK
トン TUNK
トン TUNK
NO...
IT'S NOT ME...
THIS IS A MEMORY
OF THE OTHER ME—

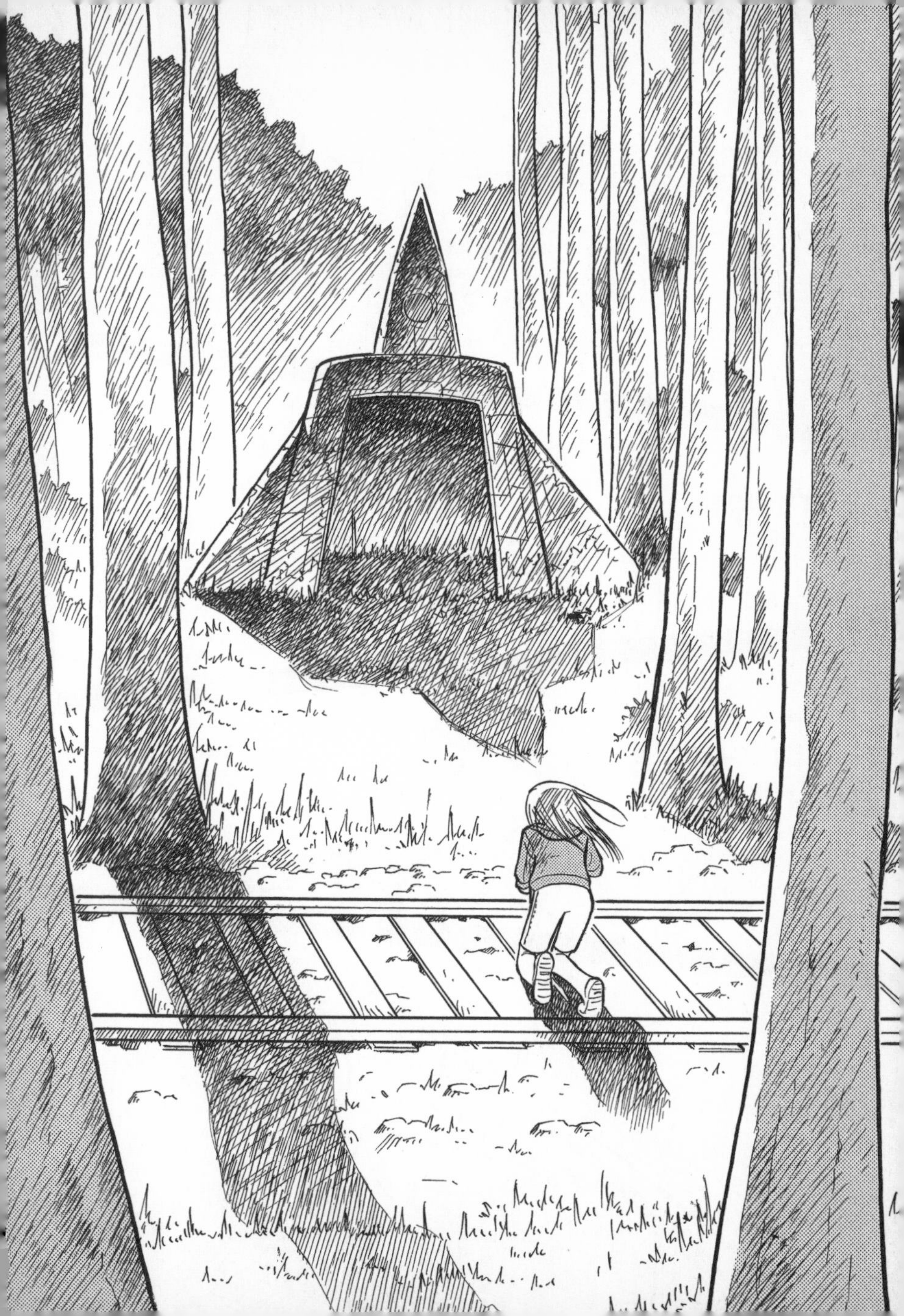

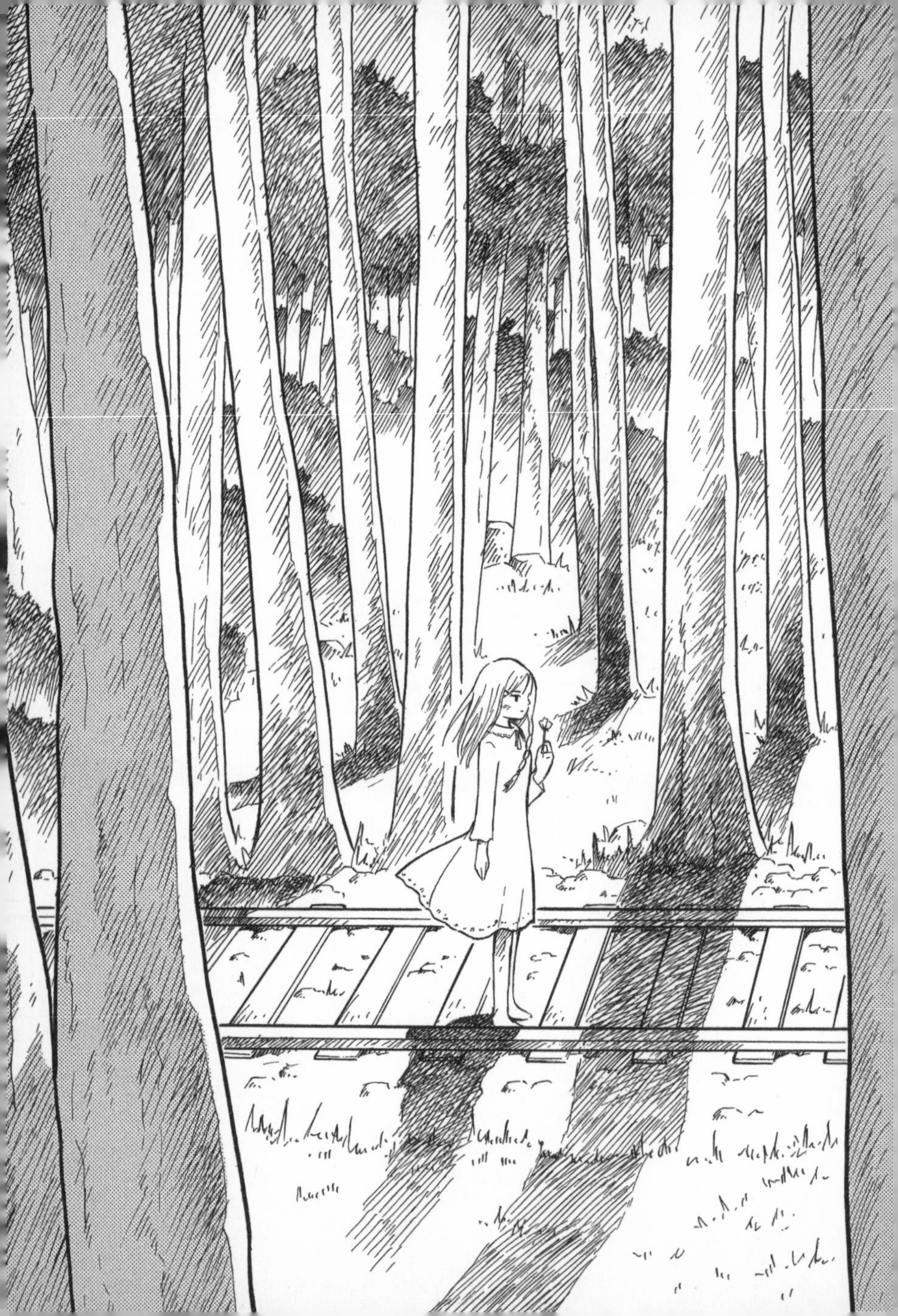

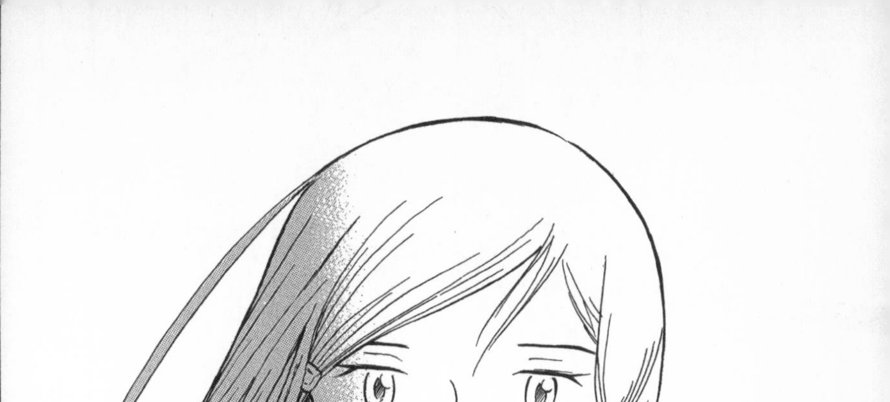
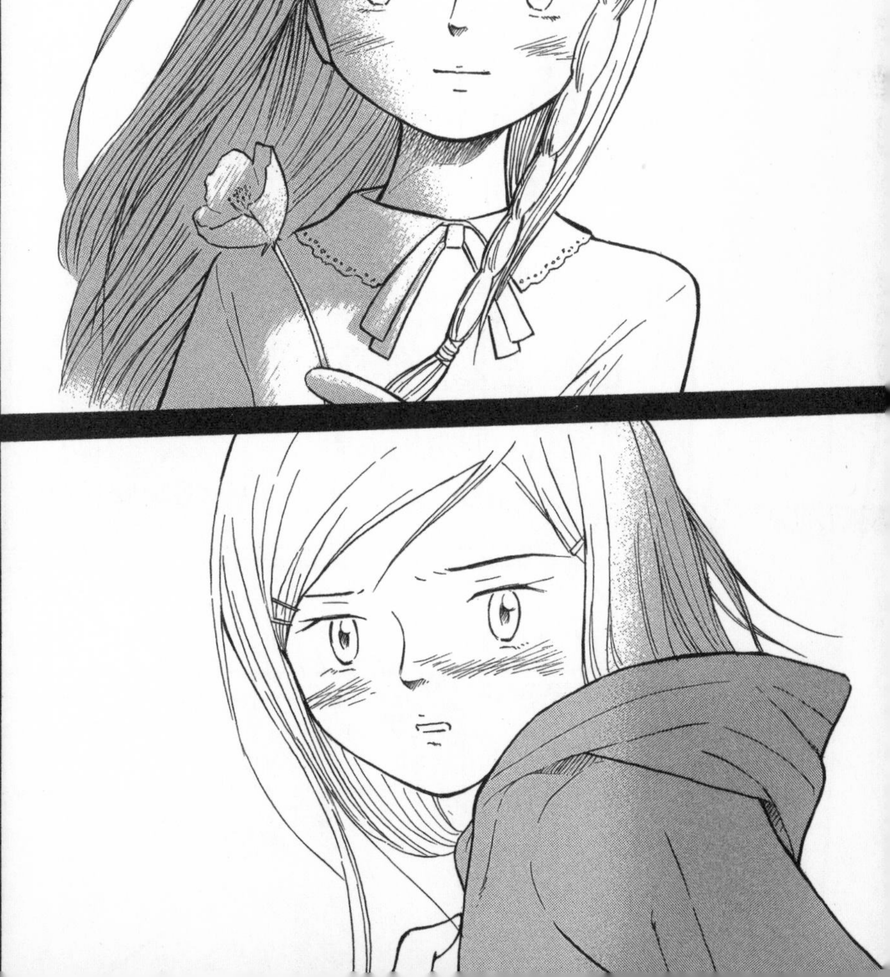

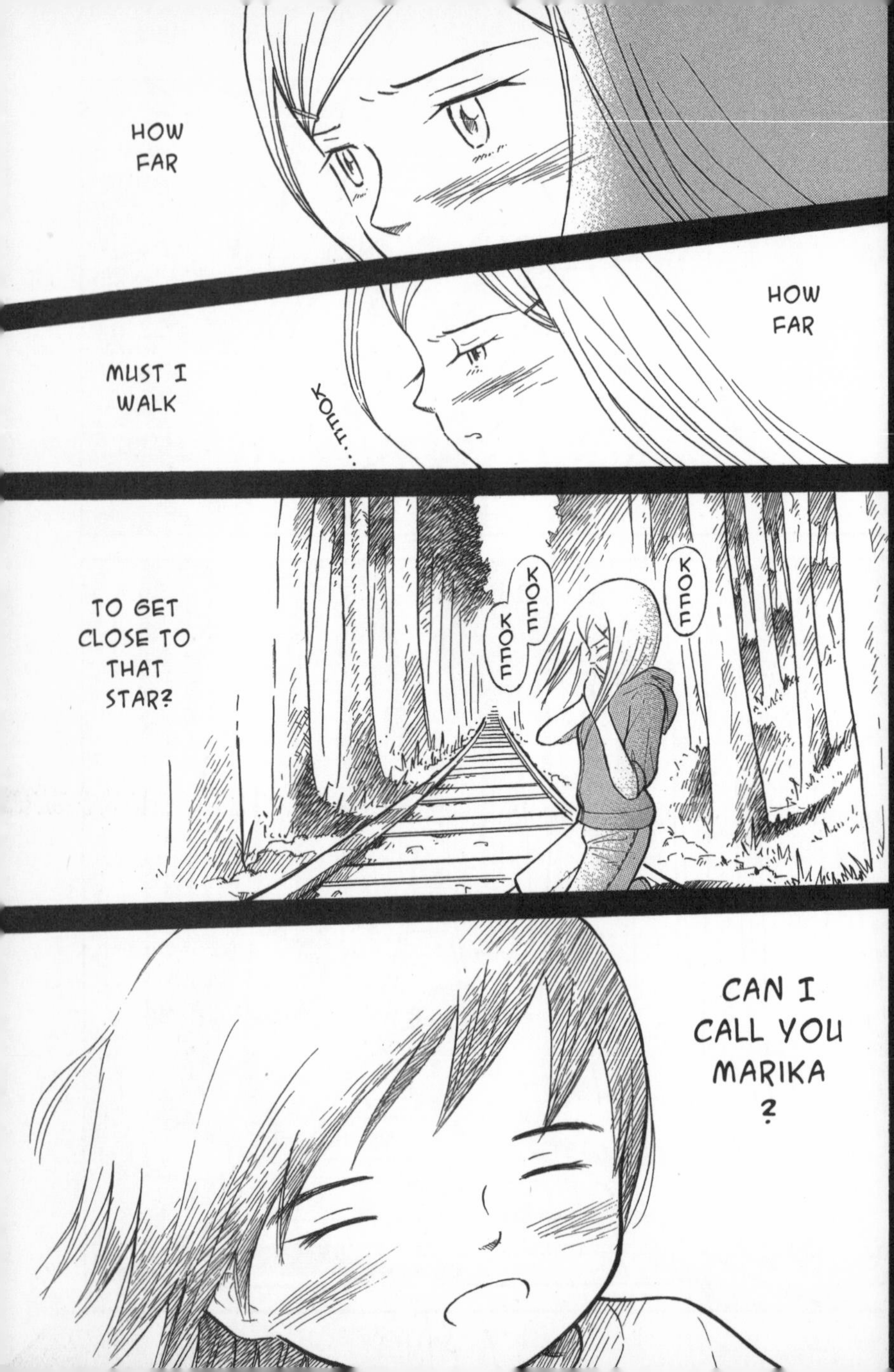
HOW FAR
HOW FAR
MUST I WALK
KOFF....
KOFF
KOFF KOFF
TO GET CLOSE TO THAT STAR?
CAN I CALL YOU MARIKA?

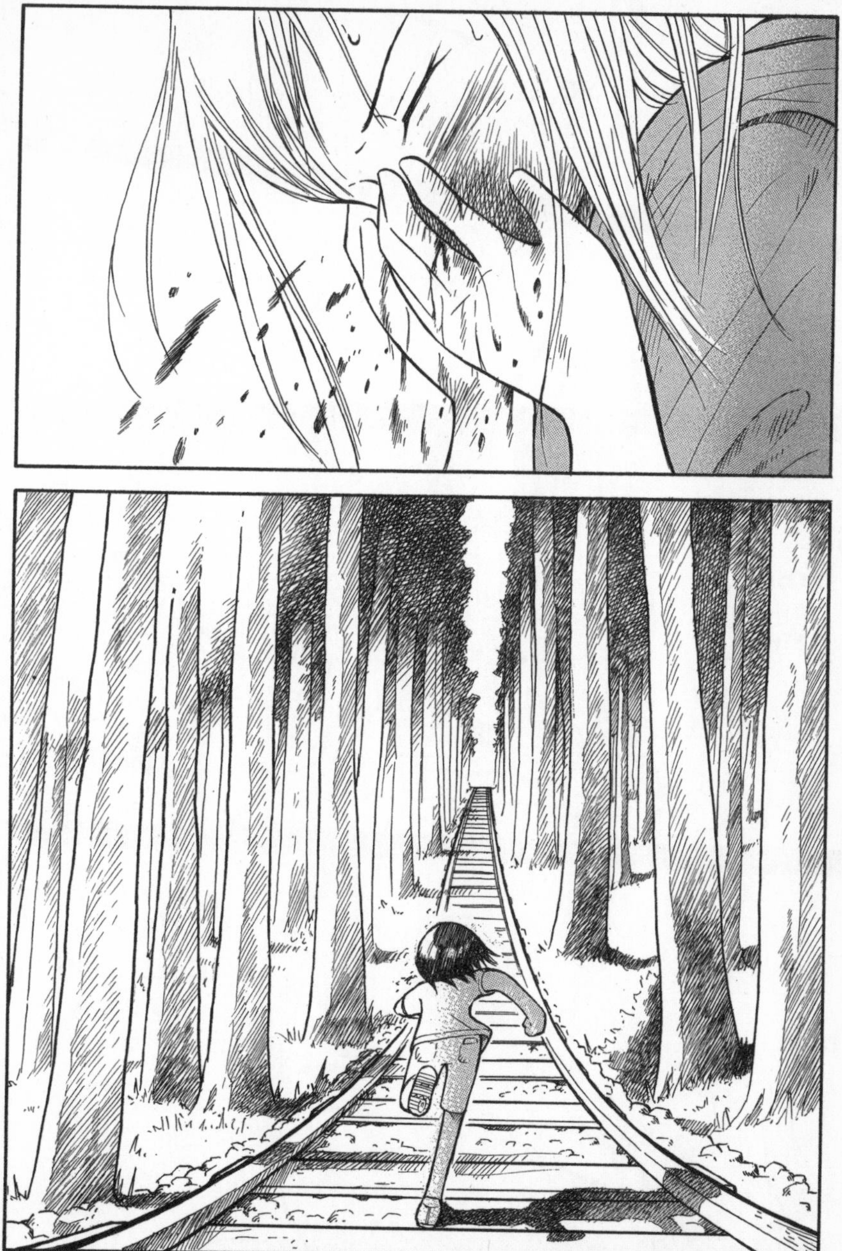

MISSION:32

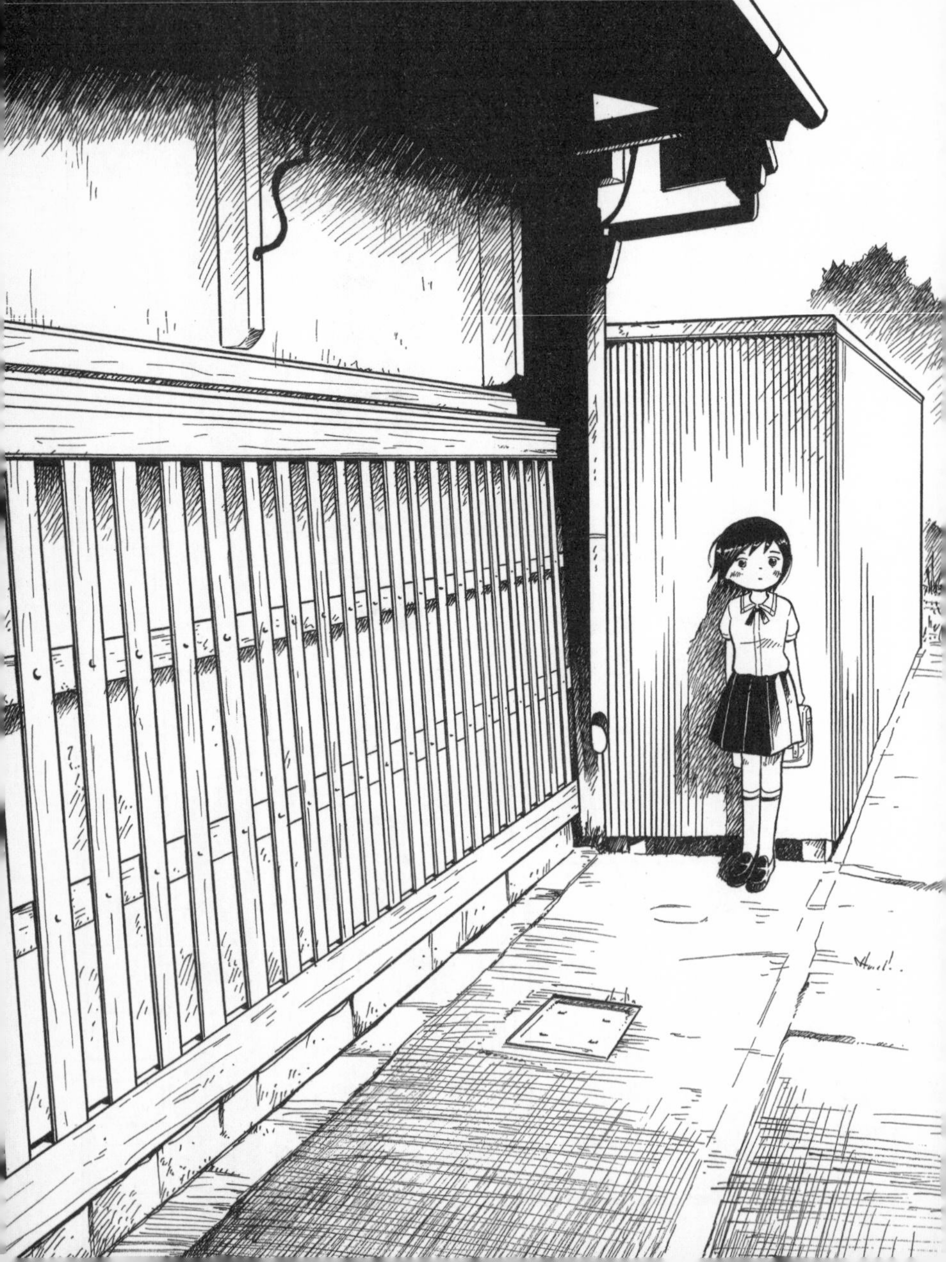

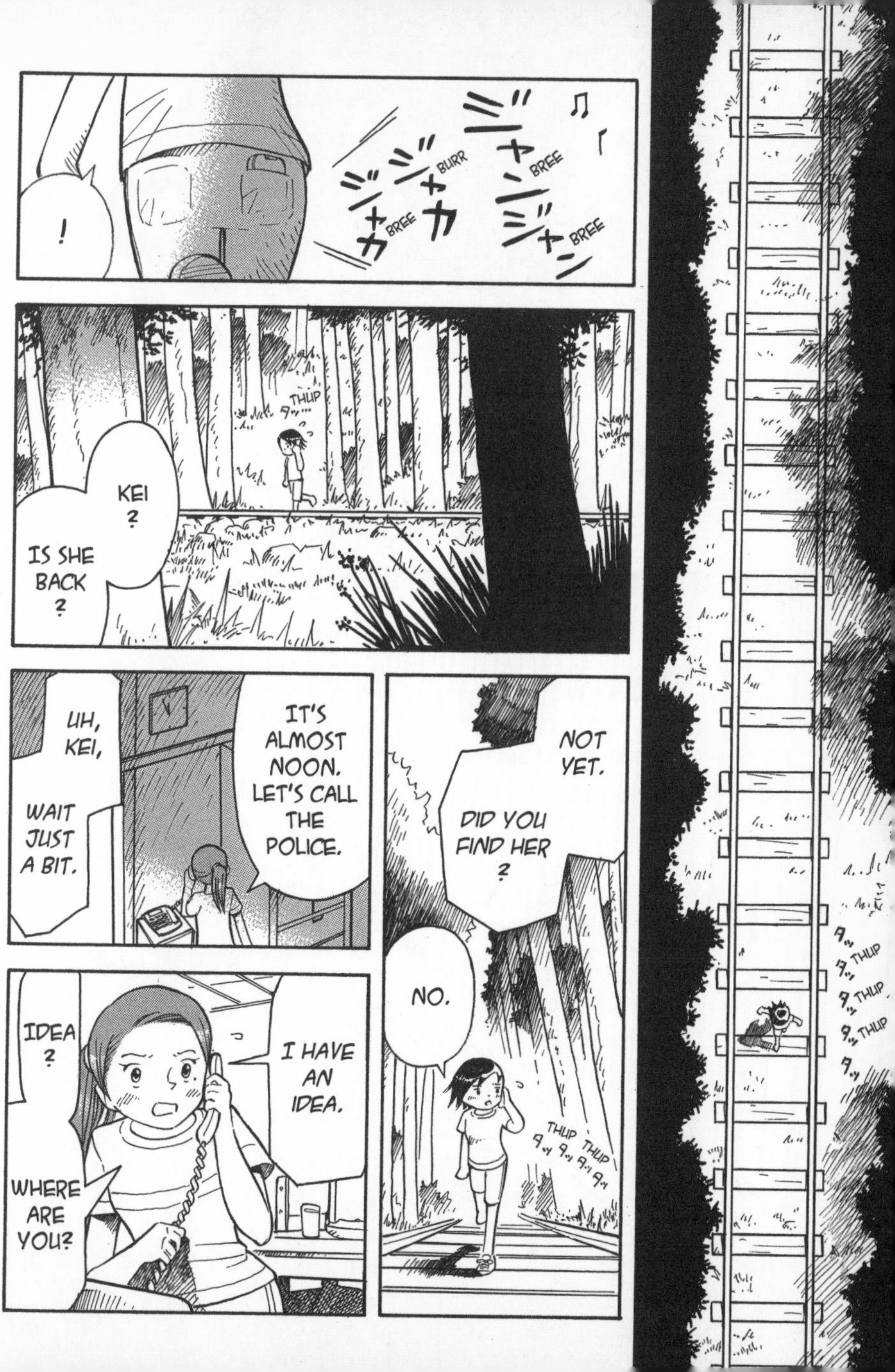

タッ THUP
タッ THUP
タッ THUP
タッ
ジャーンジャン BREE BREE
ジャカジャカ BURR BREE
!
タッ… THUP
KEI?
IS SHE BACK?
NOT YET.
DID YOU FIND HER?
IT'S ALMOST NOON. LET'S CALL THE POLICE.
UH, KEI,
WAIT JUST A BIT.
NO.
タッタッタッタッ THUP THUP
I HAVE AN IDEA.
IDEA?
WHERE ARE YOU?

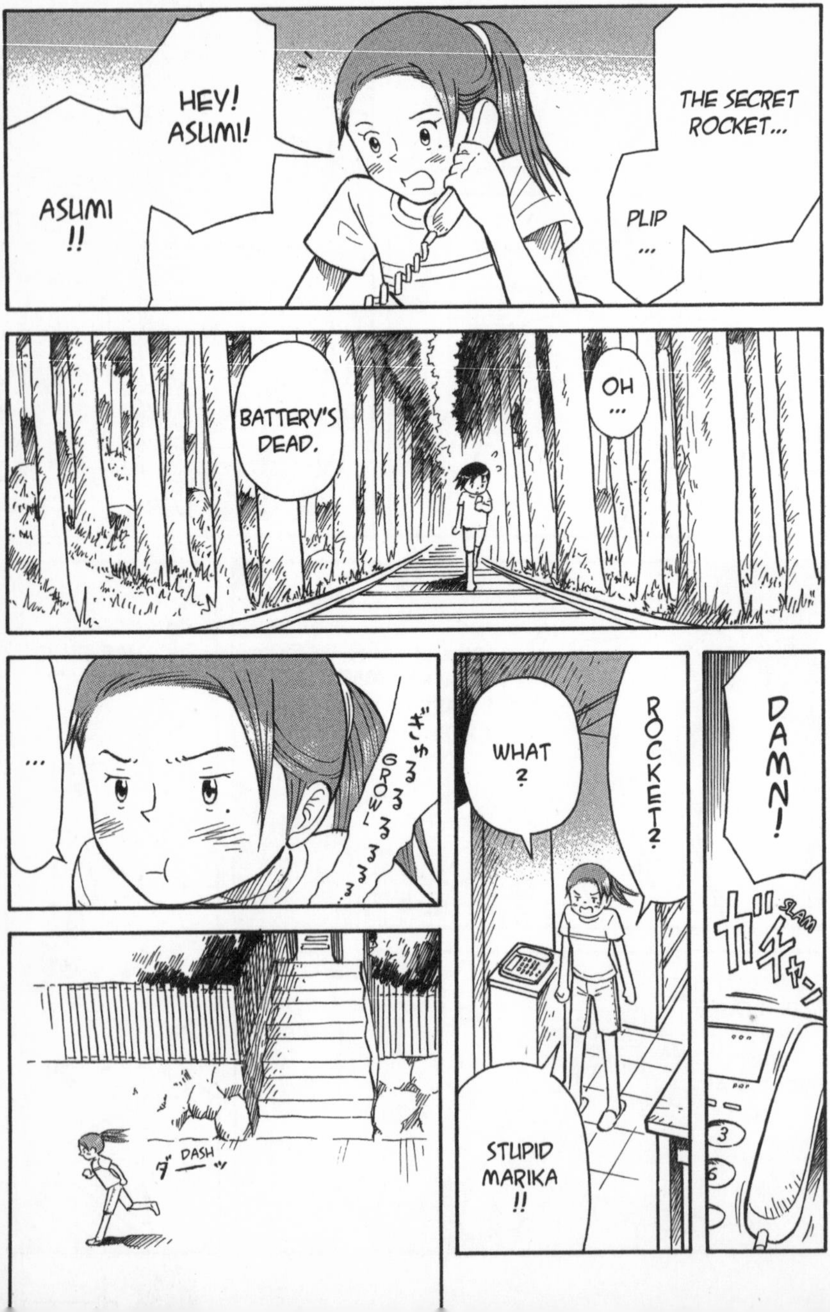
THE SECRET ROCKET...
PLIP ...
HEY! ASUMI!
ASUMI !!
OH ...
BATTERY'S DEAD.
DAMN!
ガチャーン
SLAM
ROCKET?
WHAT ?
STUPID MARIKA !!
...
ぎゅるるる
GROWL
るるるる...
ダーッ
DASH

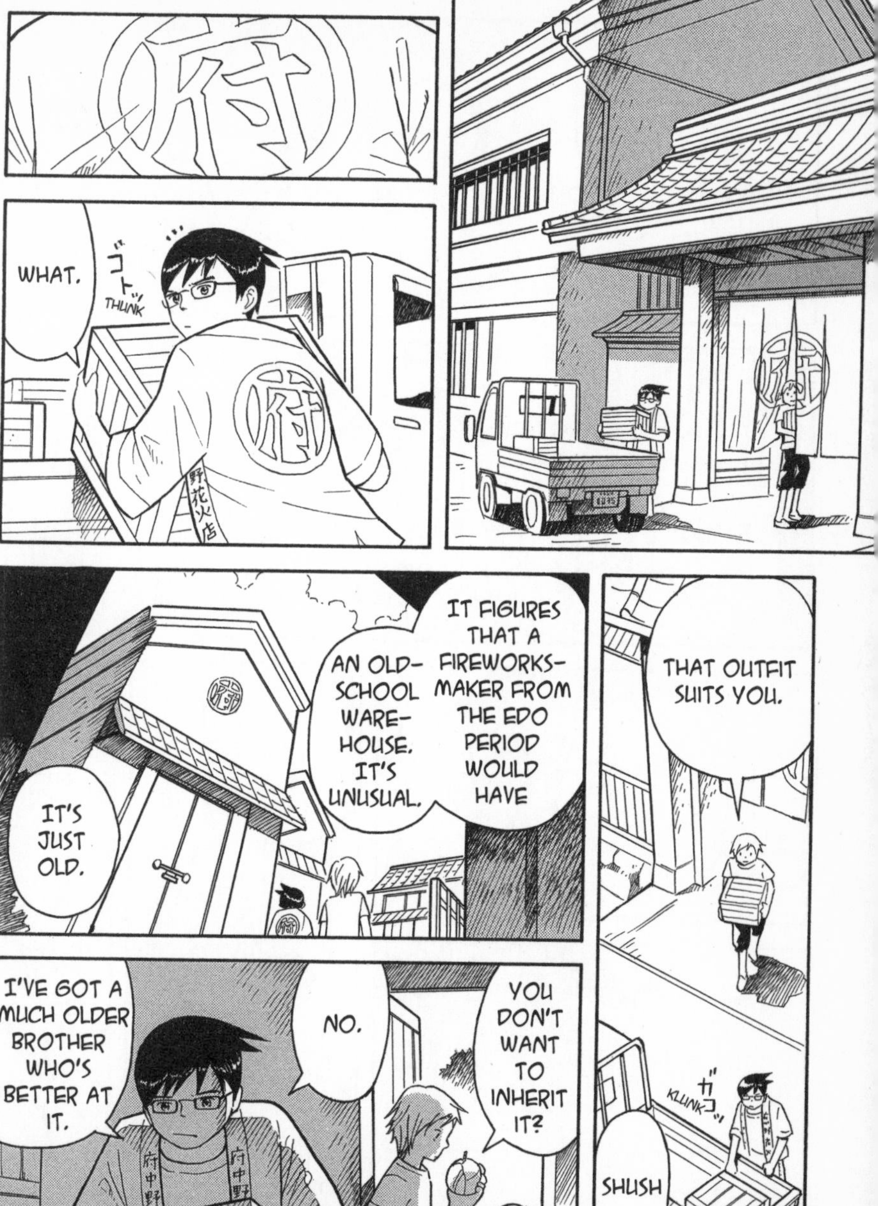
WHAT.
ゴトッ
THUNK
THAT OUTFIT SUITS YOU.
ガコッ
KLUNK
SHUSH
IT FIGURES THAT A FIREWORKS-MAKER FROM THE EDO PERIOD WOULD HAVE
AN OLD-SCHOOL WARE-HOUSE. IT'S UNUSUAL.
IT'S JUST OLD.
YOU DON'T WANT TO INHERIT IT?
NO.
I'VE GOT A MUCH OLDER BROTHER WHO'S BETTER AT IT.

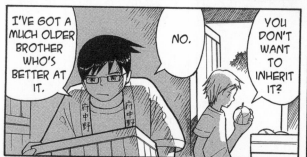

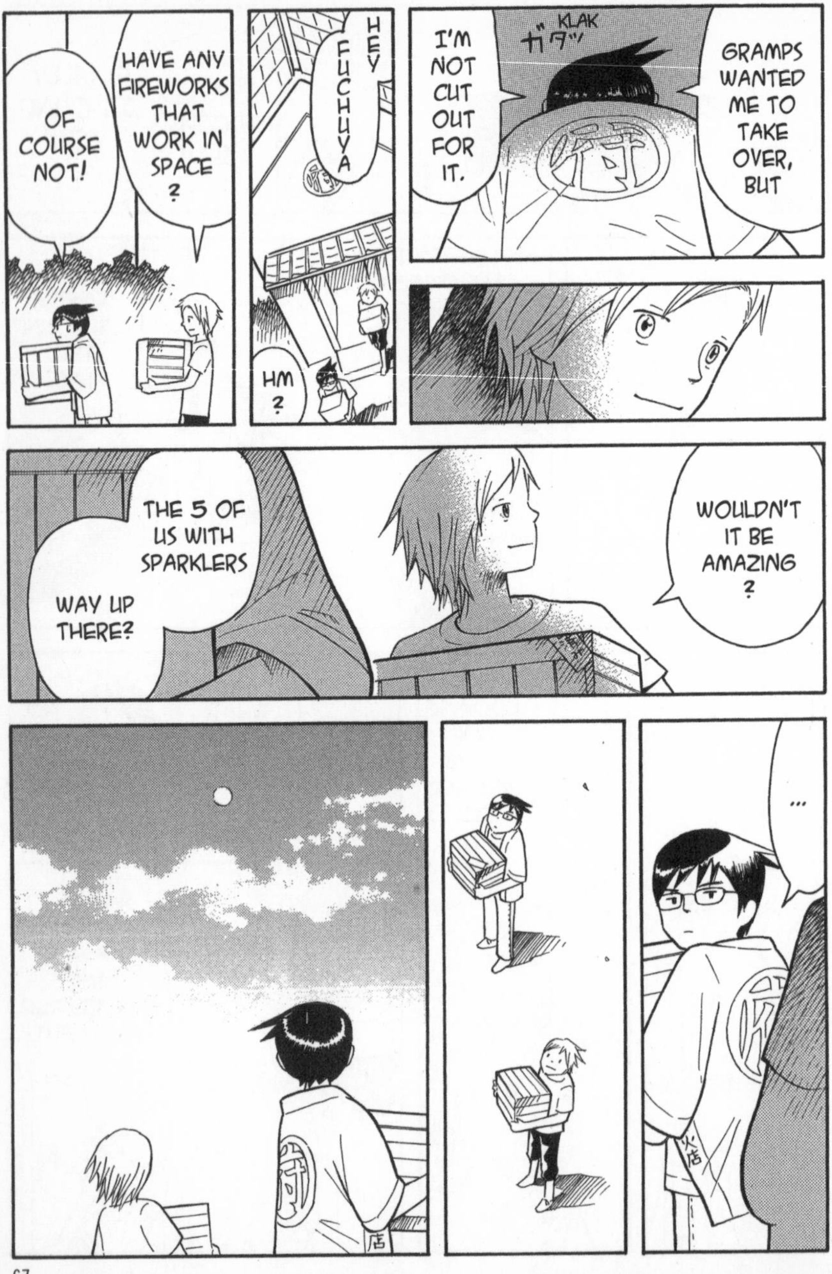
GRAMPS WANTED ME TO TAKE OVER, BUT
KLAK ガタッ
I'M NOT CUT OUT FOR IT.
HEY FUCHUYA
HM?
HAVE ANY FIREWORKS THAT WORK IN SPACE?
OF COURSE NOT!
WOULDN'T IT BE AMAZING?
THE 5 OF US WITH SPARKLERS
WAY UP THERE?
...

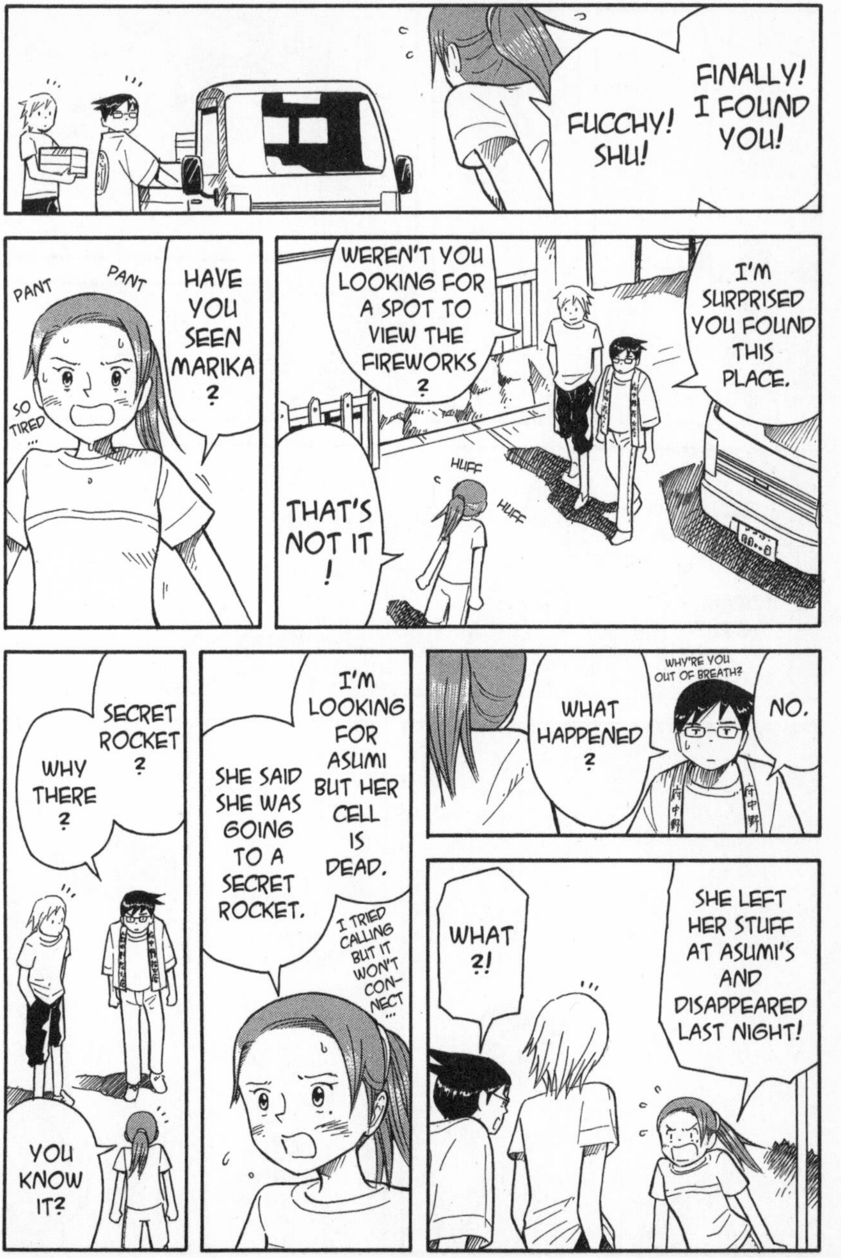
FINALLY! I FOUND YOU!
FUCCHY! SHU!
I'M SURPRISED YOU FOUND THIS PLACE.
WEREN'T YOU LOOKING FOR A SPOT TO VIEW THE FIREWORKS?
HUFF HUFF
THAT'S NOT IT!
HAVE YOU SEEN MARIKA?
PANT PANT
SO TIRED...
NO.
WHY'RE YOU OUT OF BREATH?
WHAT HAPPENED?
SHE LEFT HER STUFF AT ASUMI'S AND DISAPPEARED LAST NIGHT!
WHAT?!
I'M LOOKING FOR ASUMI BUT HER CELL IS DEAD.
SHE SAID SHE WAS GOING TO A SECRET ROCKET.
I TRIED CALLING BUT IT WON'T CONNECT...
SECRET ROCKET?
WHY THERE?
YOU KNOW IT?

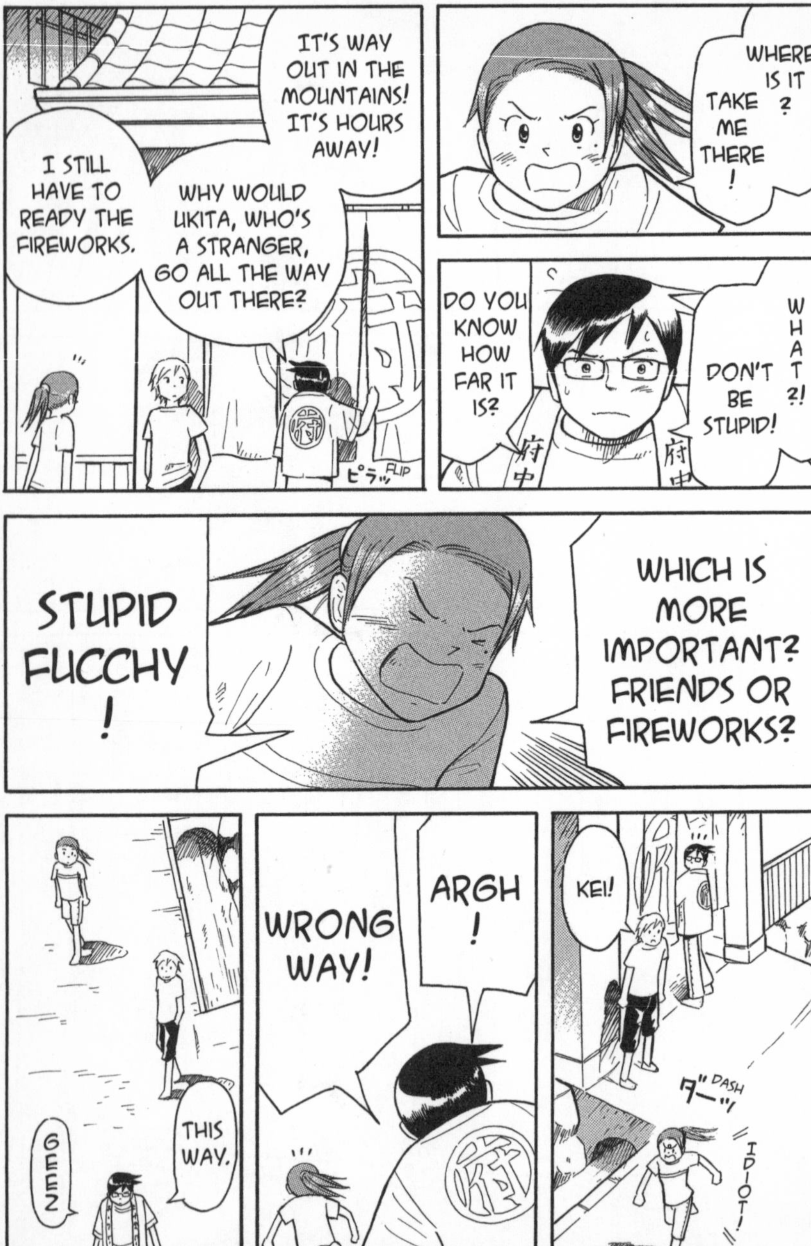
WHERE IS IT? TAKE ME THERE!
WHAT?!
DON'T BE STUPID!
DO YOU KNOW HOW FAR IT IS?
IT'S WAY OUT IN THE MOUNTAINS! IT'S HOURS AWAY!
I STILL HAVE TO READY THE FIREWORKS.
WHY WOULD UKITA, WHO'S A STRANGER, GO ALL THE WAY OUT THERE?
ピラッ FLIP
WHICH IS MORE IMPORTANT? FRIENDS OR FIREWORKS?
STUPID FUCCHY!
KEI!
ダーッ DASH
IDIOT!
ARGH!
WRONG WAY!
THIS WAY.
GEEZ

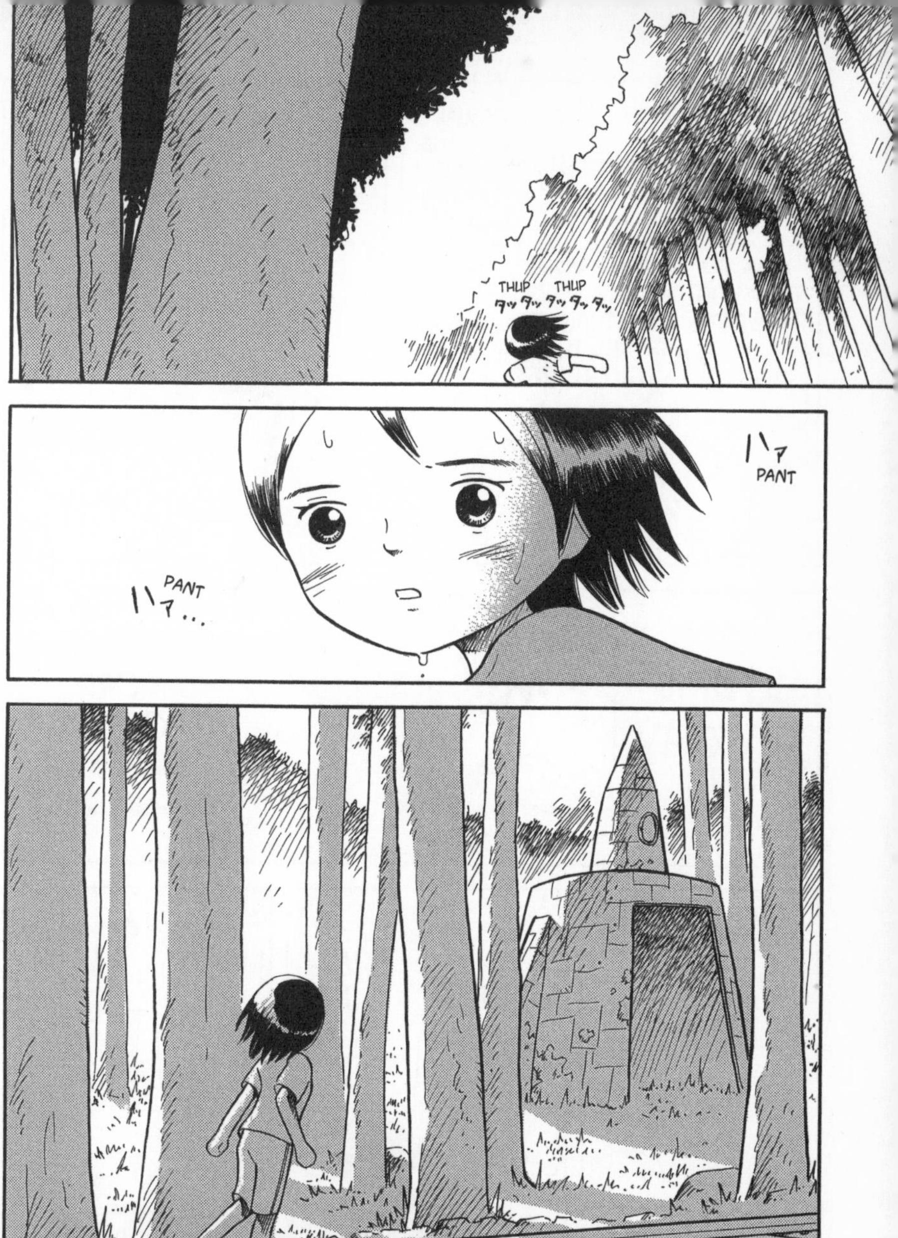
THUP THUP
タッタッタッタッタッ
ハァ
PANT
PANT
ハァ…

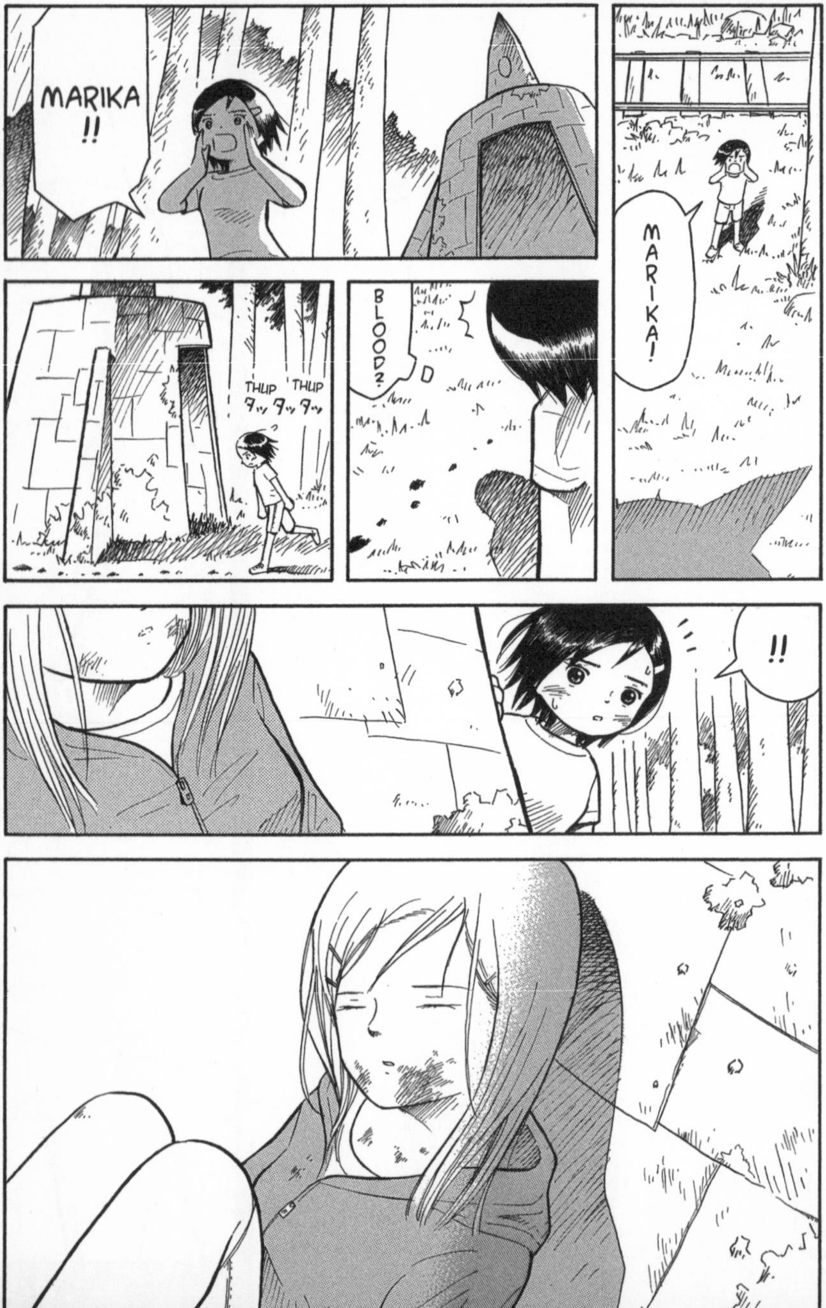
MARIKA!
MARIKA !!
BLOOD?
THUP THUP
タッタッタッ
!!

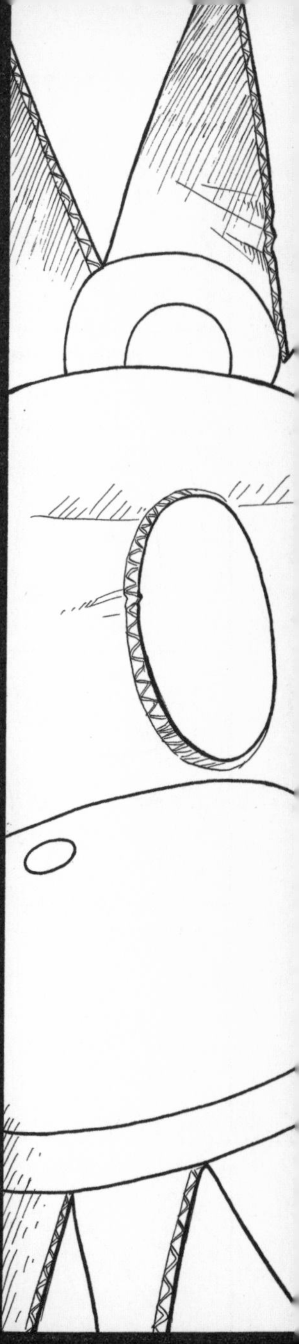
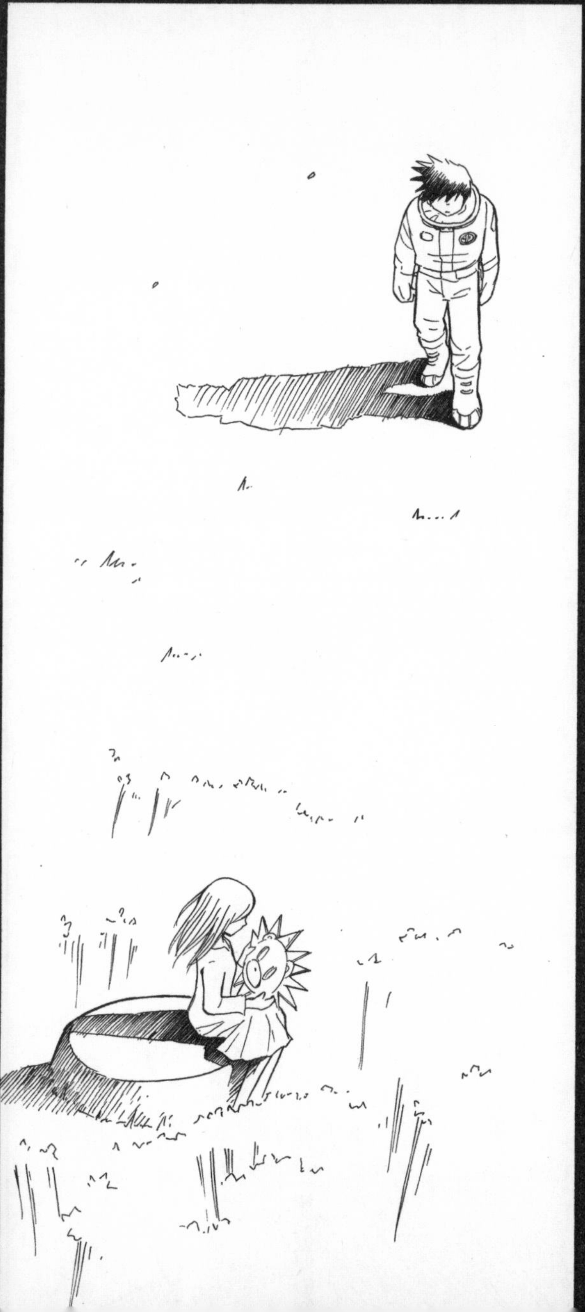

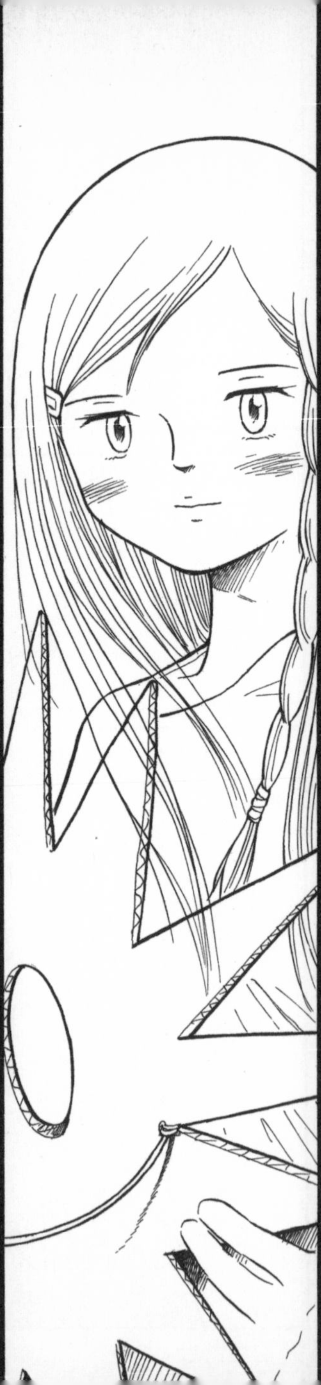
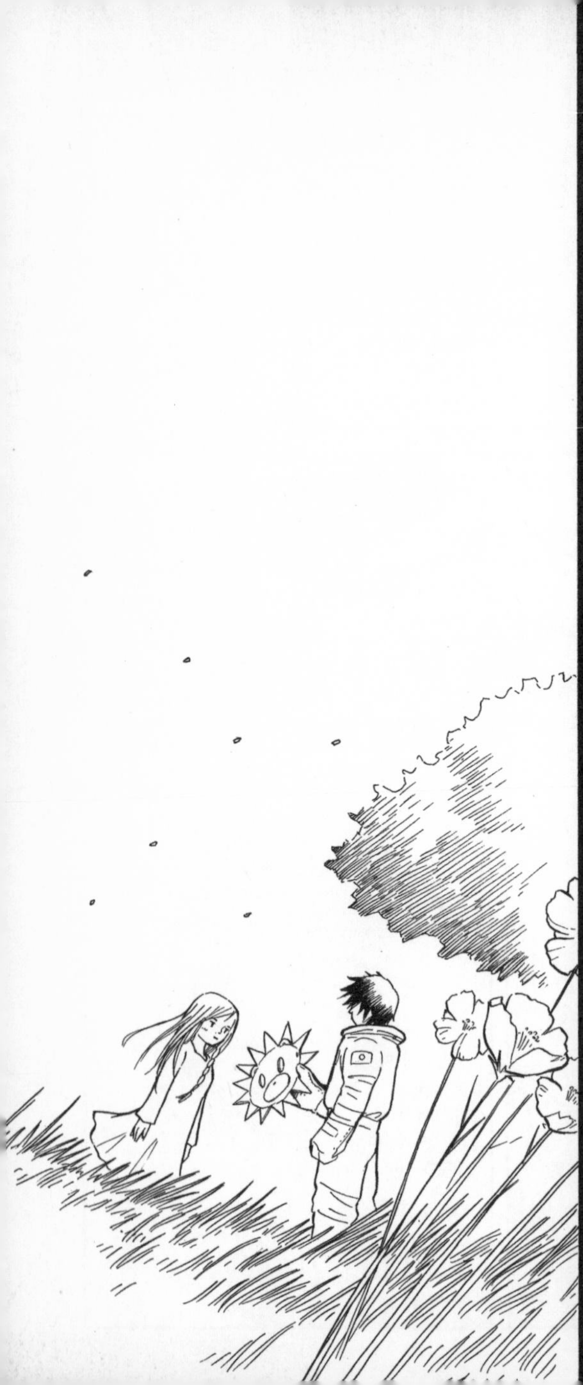

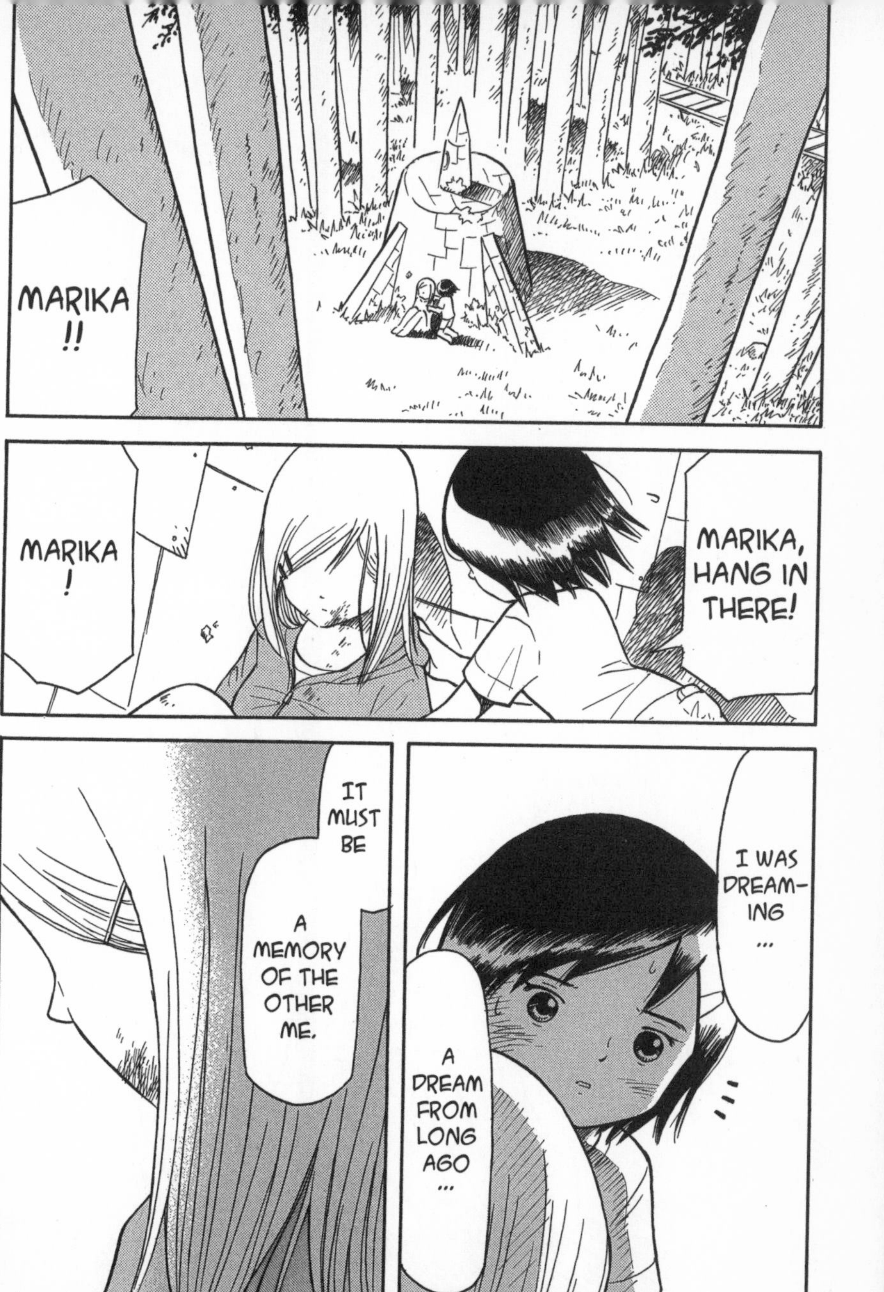
MARIKA !!
MARIKA, HANG IN THERE!
MARIKA !
I WAS DREAM-ING ...
A DREAM FROM LONG AGO ...
IT MUST BE
A MEMORY OF THE OTHER ME.

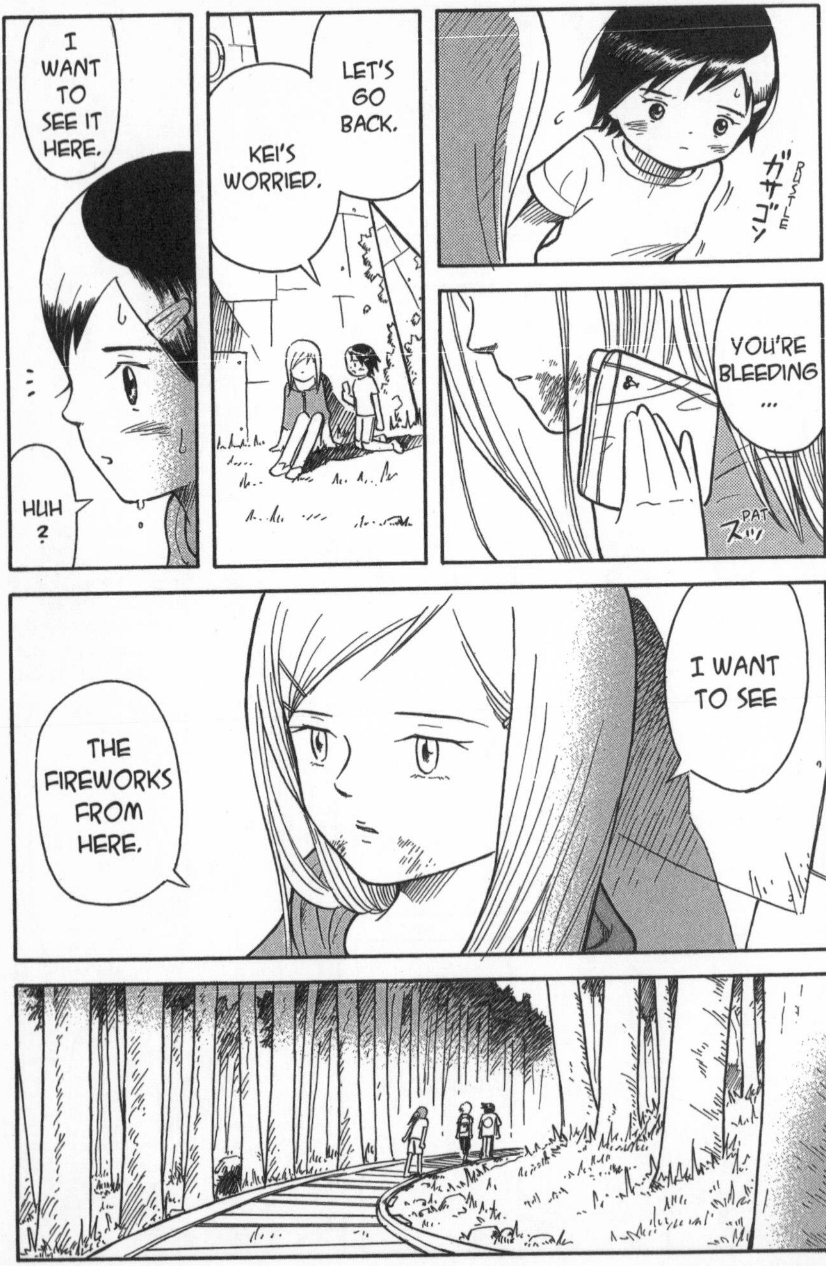
ガサゴソ
RUSTLE
YOU'RE BLEEDING ...
ズッ
PAT
LET'S GO BACK.
KEI'S WORRIED.
I WANT TO SEE IT HERE.
HUH?
I WANT TO SEE
THE FIREWORKS FROM HERE.

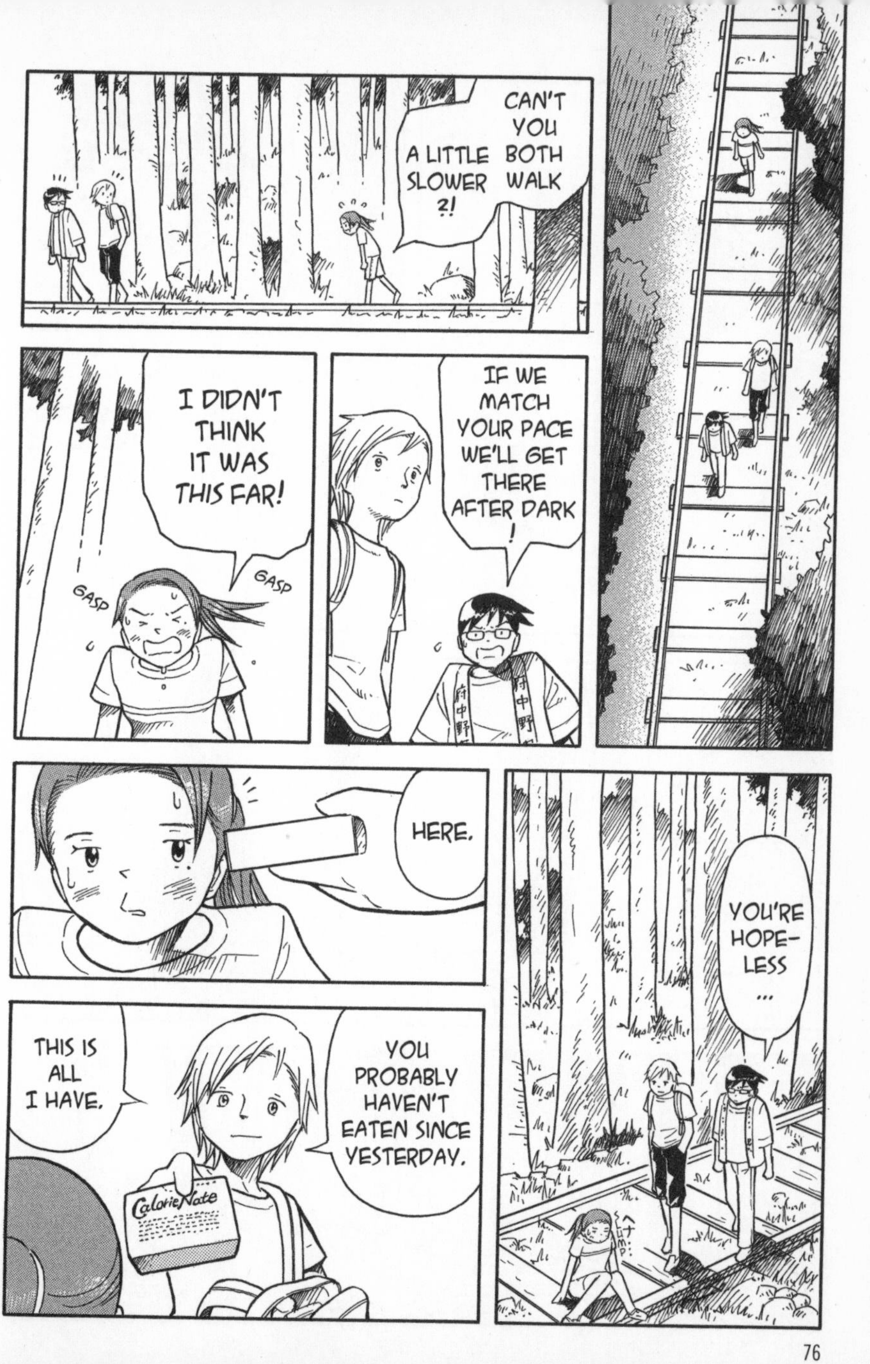
CAN'T YOU BOTH WALK A LITTLE SLOWER ?!
IF WE MATCH YOUR PACE WE'LL GET THERE AFTER DARK !
I DIDN'T THINK IT WAS THIS FAR!
GASP
GASP
YOU'RE HOPE-LESS ...
ヘナ
SLUMP
HERE.
YOU PROBABLY HAVEN'T EATEN SINCE YESTERDAY.
THIS IS ALL I HAVE.
CalorieNate

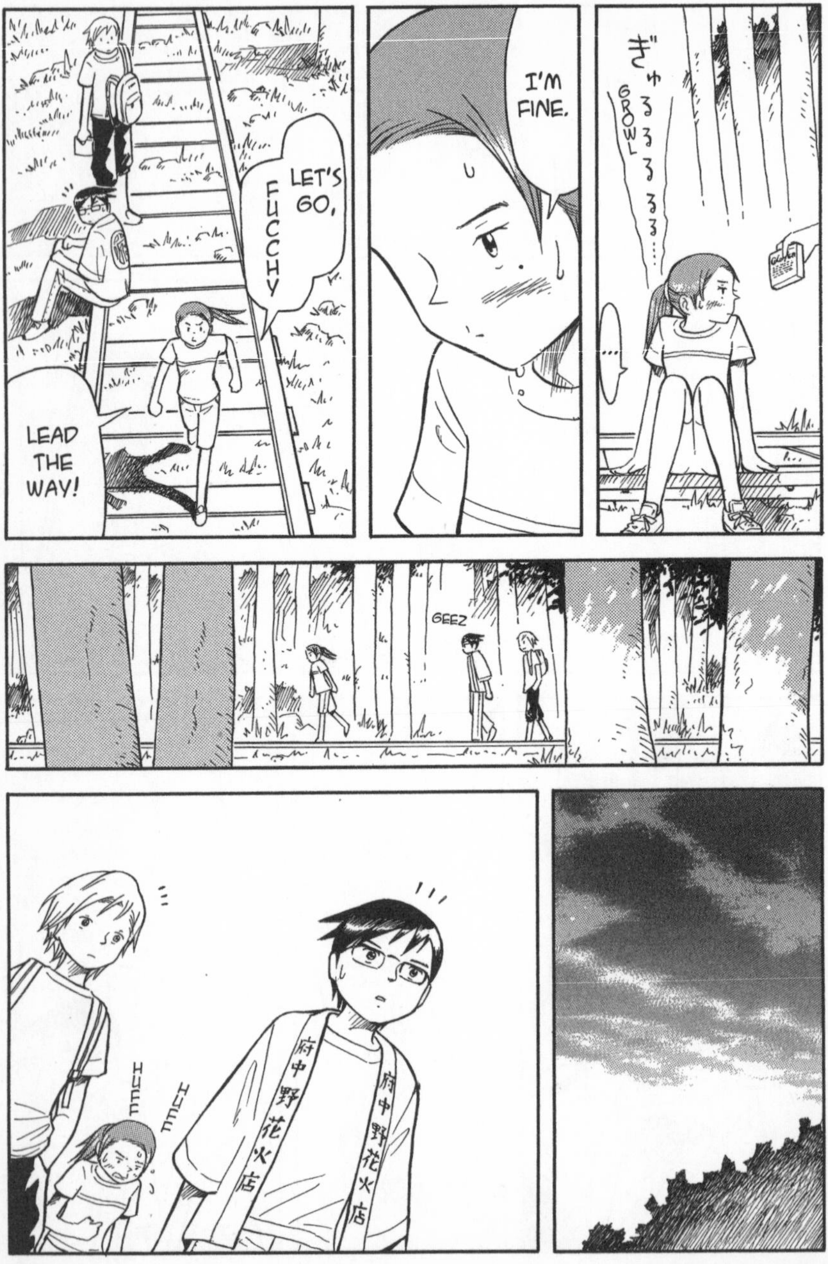
ぎゅるるるるる…
GROWL
…
I'M FINE.
LET'S GO, FUCCHY
LEAD THE WAY!
GEEZ
HUFF
HUFF
府中野花火店
府中野花火店

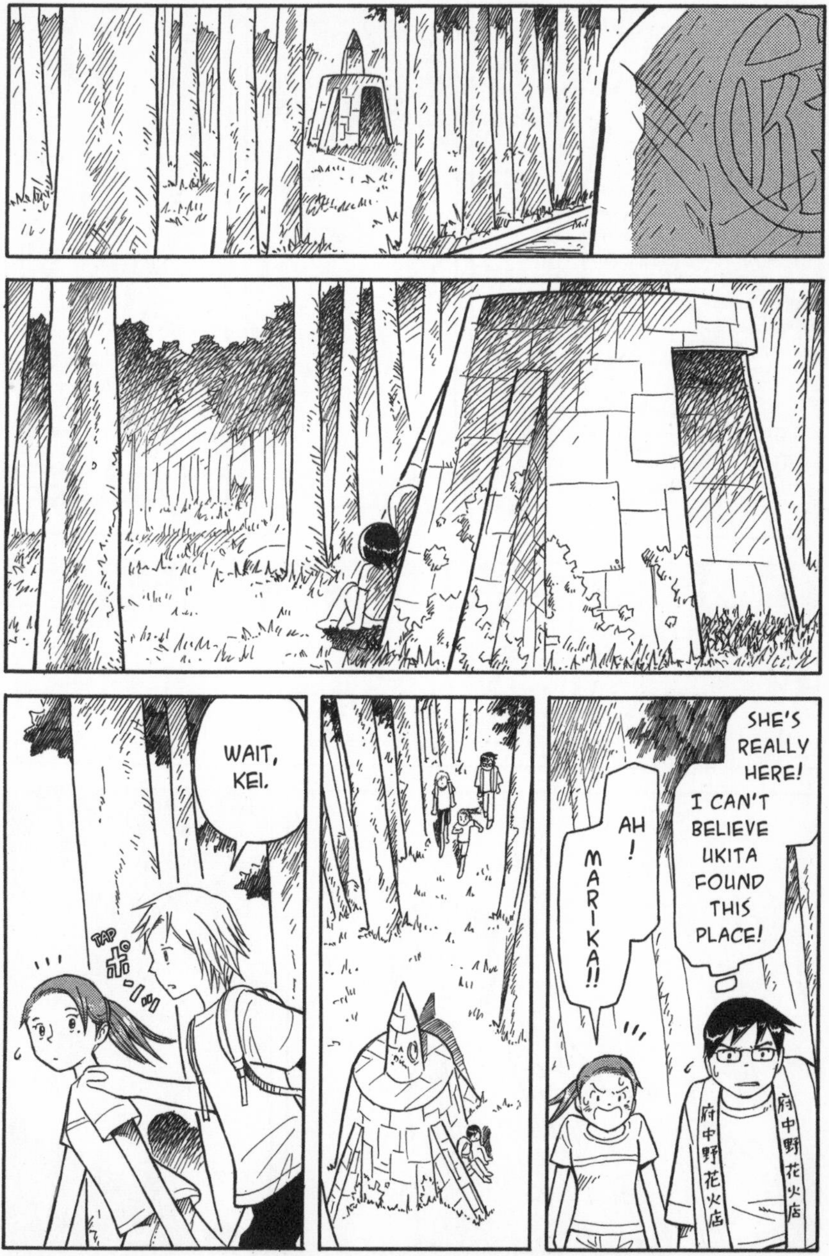
SHE'S REALLY HERE! I CAN'T BELIEVE UKITA FOUND THIS PLACE!
AH! MARIKA!!
府中野花火店
府中野花火店
WAIT, KEI.
TAP
ポンッ

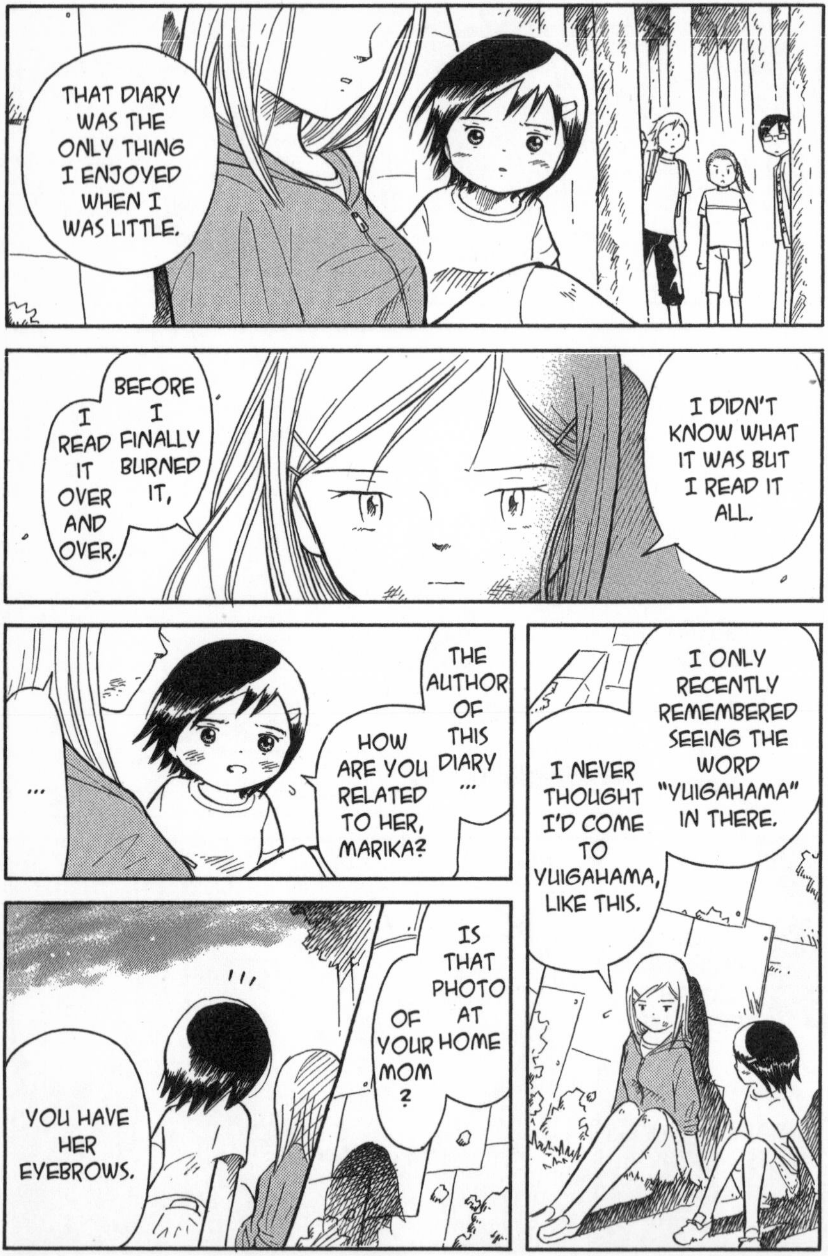
THAT DIARY WAS THE ONLY THING I ENJOYED WHEN I WAS LITTLE.
I DIDN'T KNOW WHAT IT WAS BUT I READ IT ALL.
BEFORE I FINALLY BURNED IT,
I READ IT OVER AND OVER.
I ONLY RECENTLY REMEMBERED SEEING THE WORD "YUIGAHAMA" IN THERE.
I NEVER THOUGHT I'D COME TO YUIGAHAMA, LIKE THIS.
THE AUTHOR OF THIS DIARY ...
HOW ARE YOU RELATED TO HER, MARIKA?
...
IS THAT PHOTO AT HOME
OF YOUR MOM ?
!!!
YOU HAVE HER EYEBROWS.

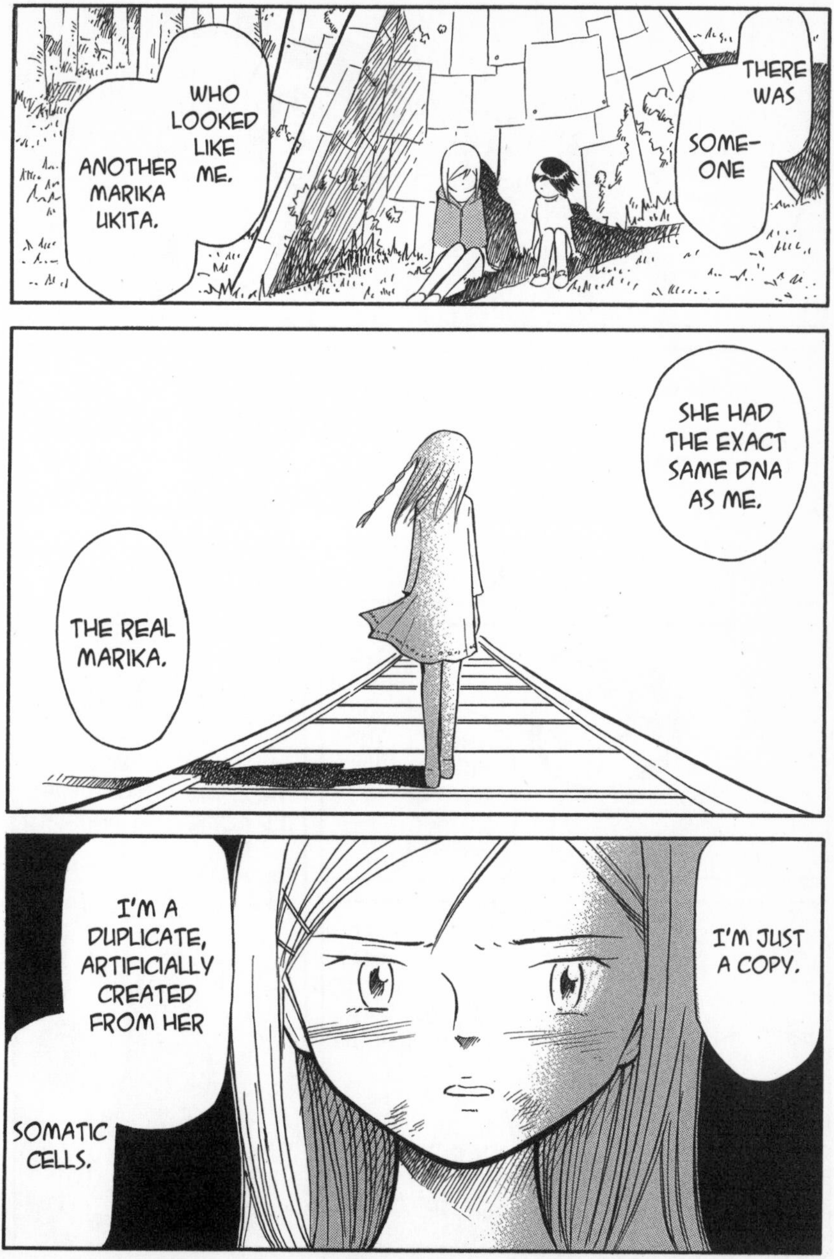
THERE WAS SOME-ONE
WHO LOOKED LIKE ME.
ANOTHER MARIKA UKITA.
SHE HAD THE EXACT SAME DNA AS ME.
THE REAL MARIKA.
I'M JUST A COPY.
I'M A DUPLICATE, ARTIFICIALLY CREATED FROM HER
SOMATIC CELLS.

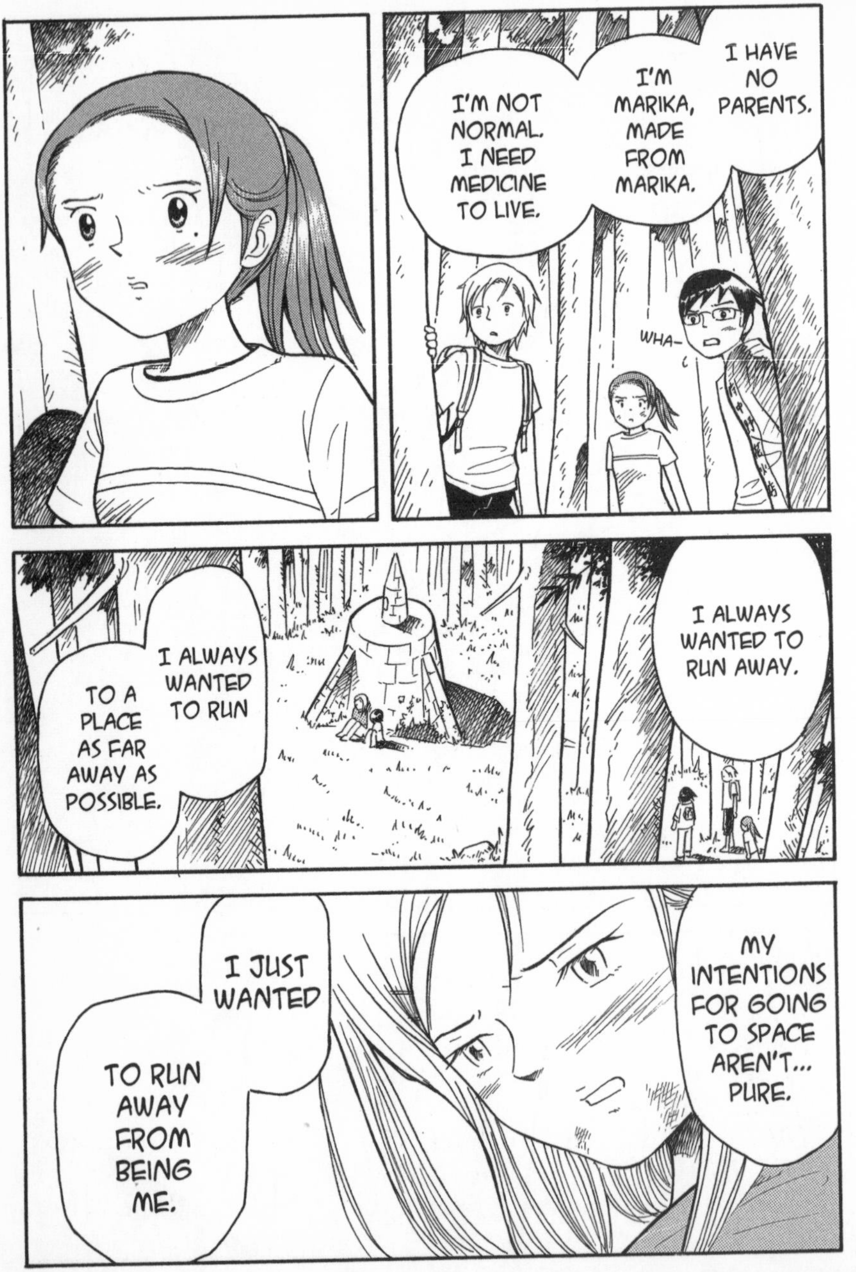
I HAVE NO PARENTS.
I'M MARIKA, MADE FROM MARIKA.
I'M NOT NORMAL. I NEED MEDICINE TO LIVE.
WHA-
I ALWAYS WANTED TO RUN AWAY.
I ALWAYS WANTED TO RUN
TO A PLACE AS FAR AWAY AS POSSIBLE.
MY INTENTIONS FOR GOING TO SPACE AREN'T... PURE.
I JUST WANTED
TO RUN AWAY FROM BEING ME.

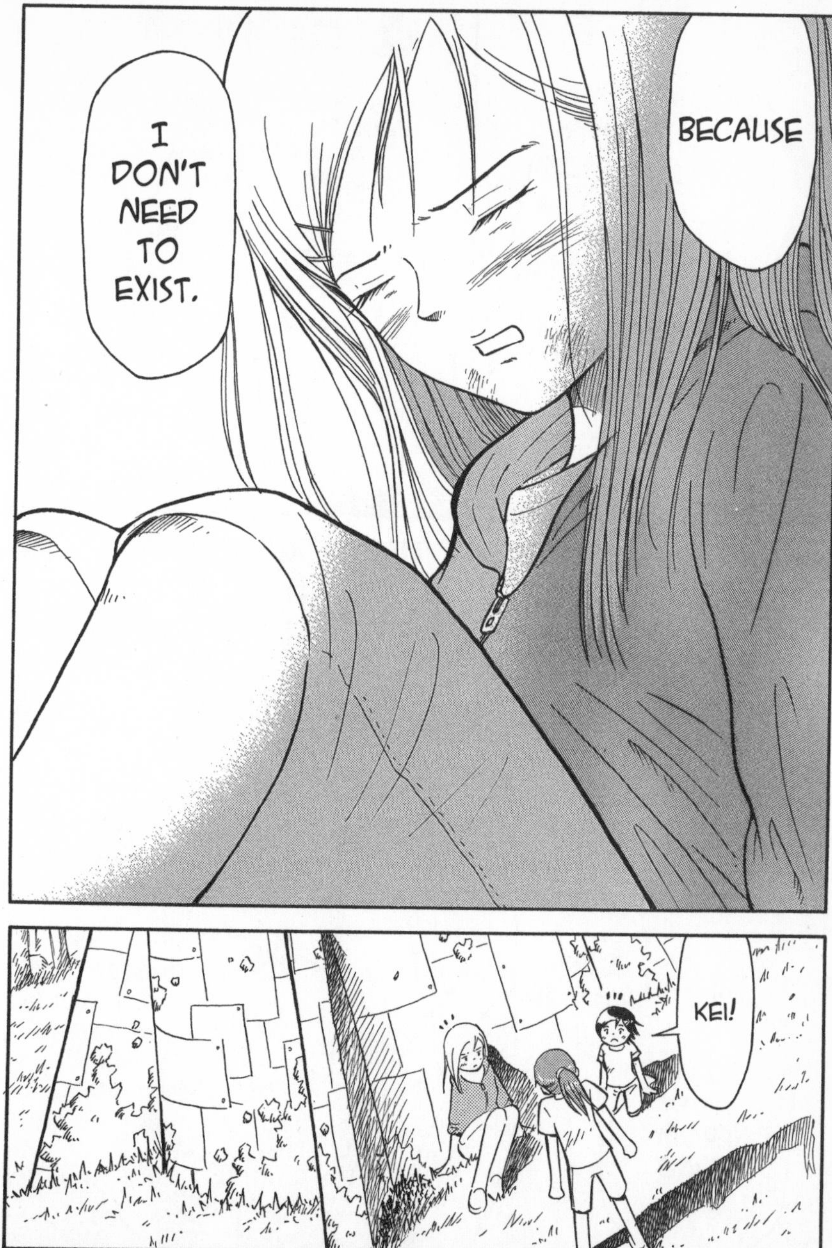
BECAUSE
I DON'T NEED TO EXIST.
KEI!

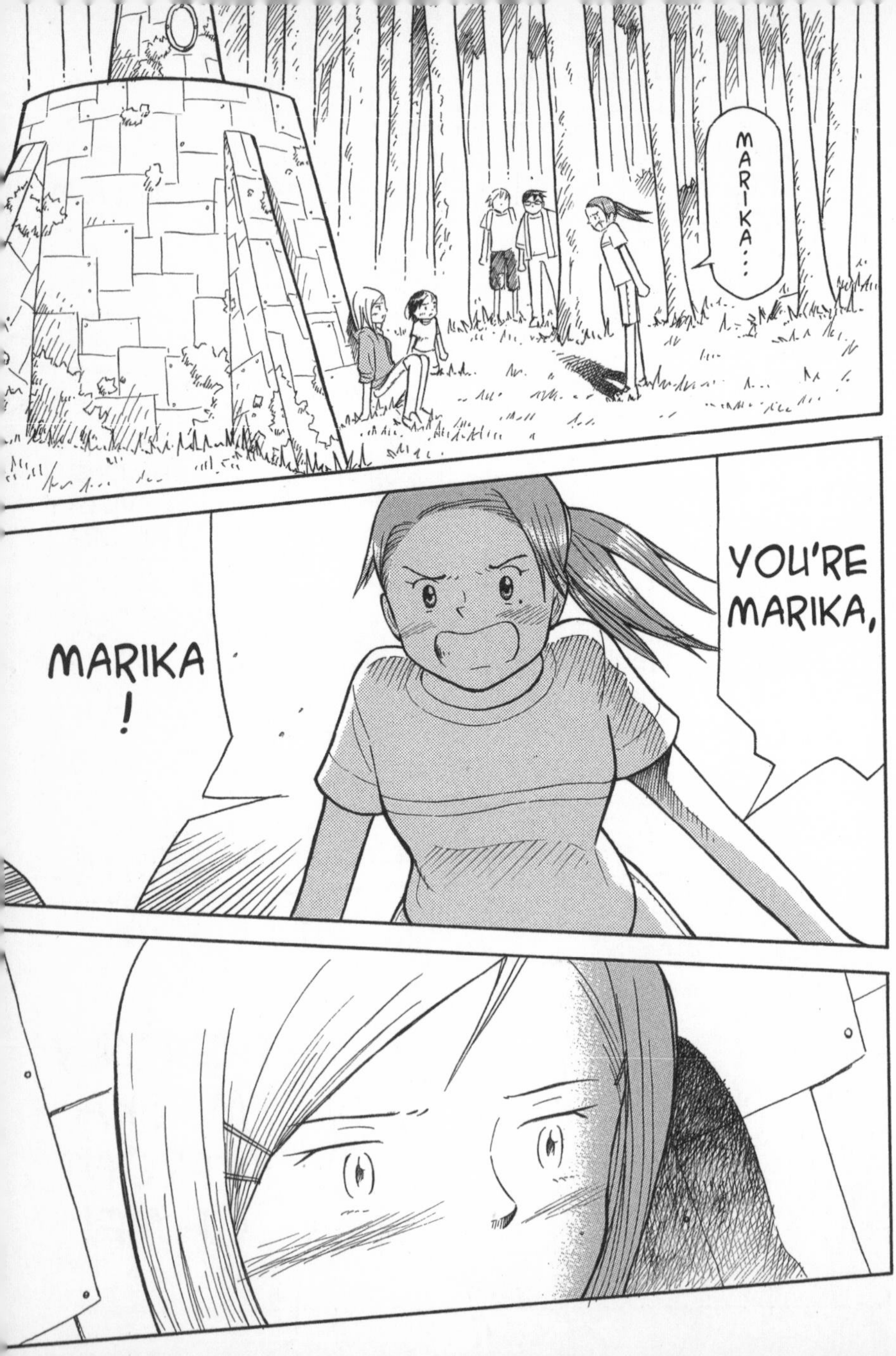
MARIKA...
YOU'RE MARIKA,
MARIKA!

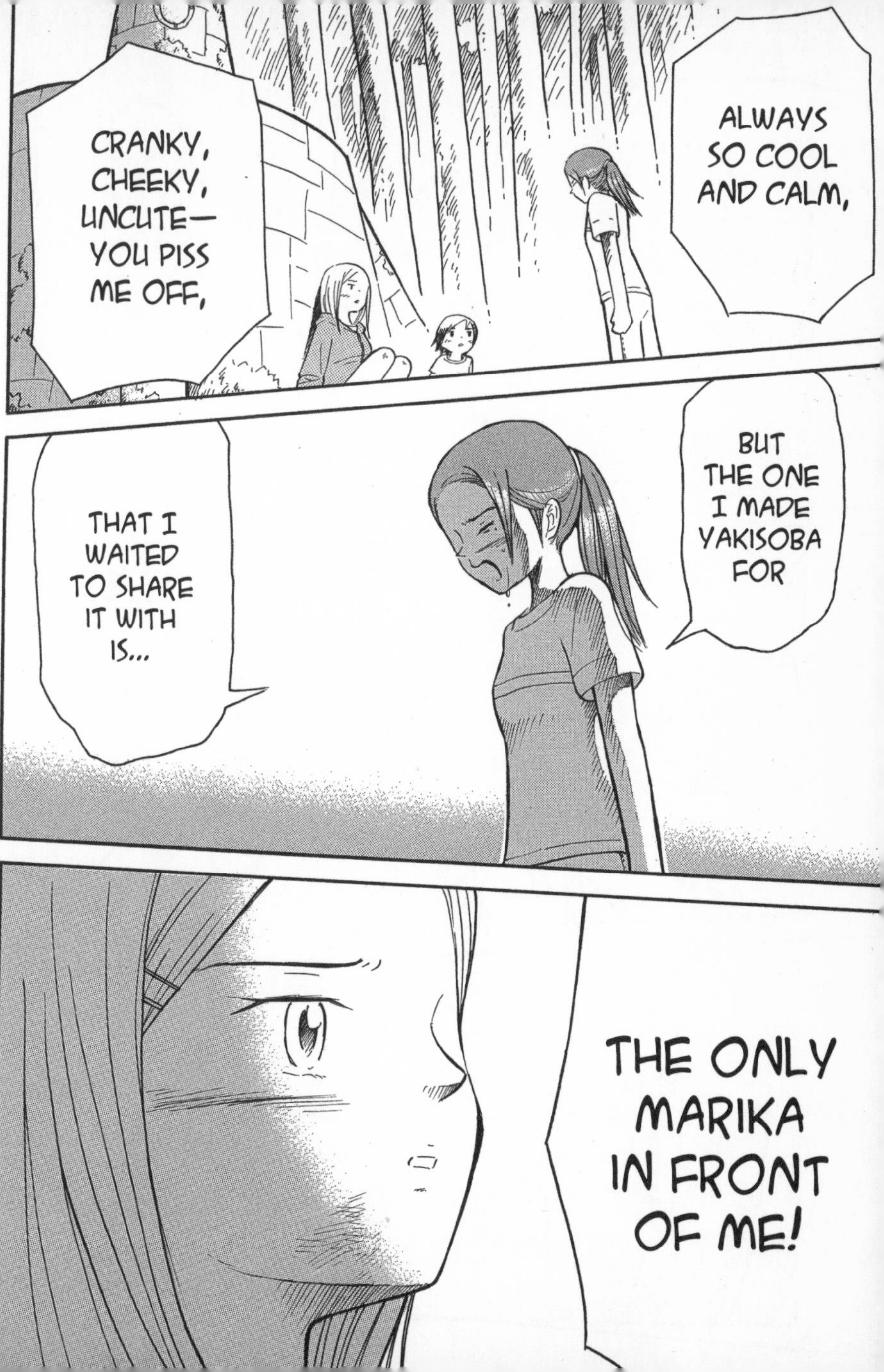
ALWAYS SO COOL AND CALM,
CRANKY, CHEEKY, UNCUTE— YOU PISS ME OFF,
BUT THE ONE I MADE YAKISOBA FOR
THAT I WAITED TO SHARE IT WITH IS...
THE ONLY MARIKA IN FRONT OF ME!

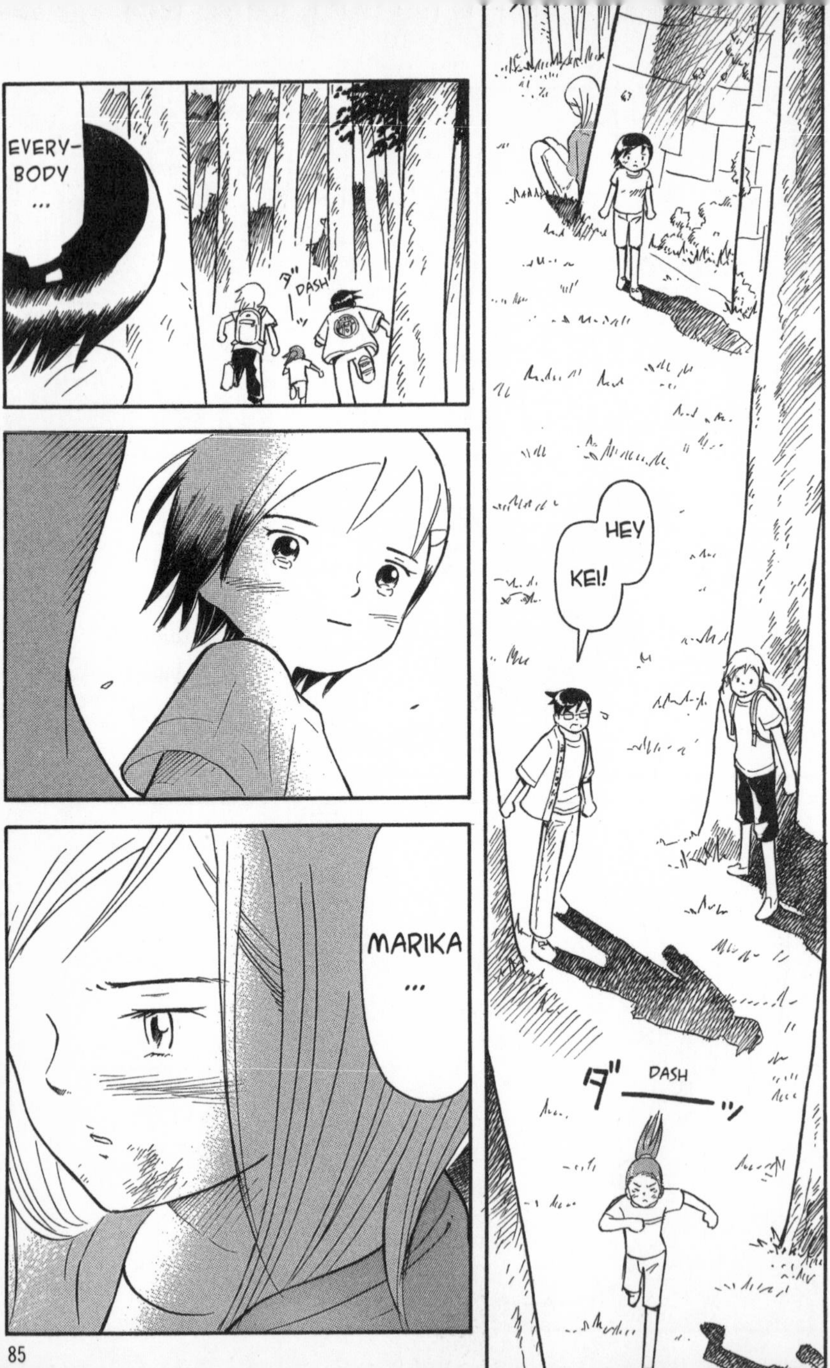
HEY KEI!
ダ— DASH ッ
EVERY-BODY ...
ダッ DASH
MARIKA ...

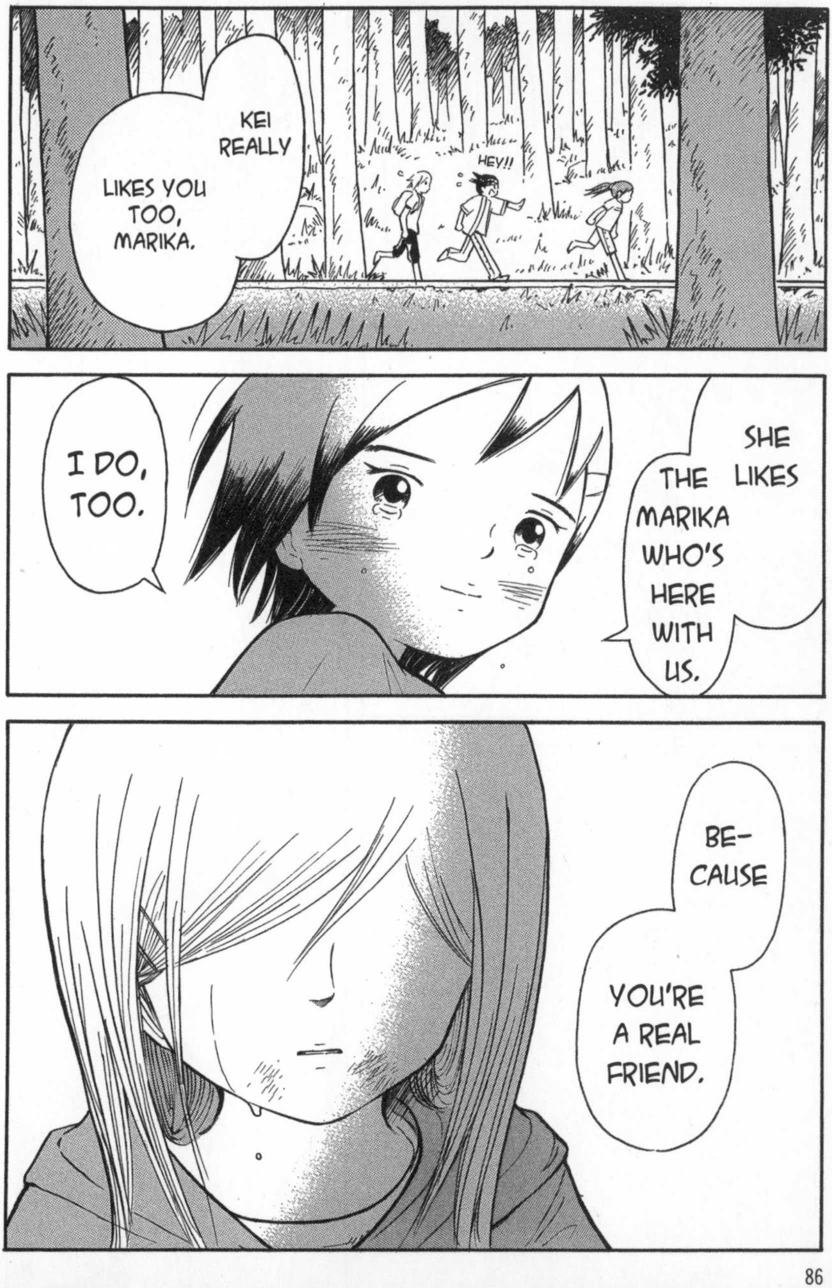
KEI REALLY LIKES YOU TOO, MARIKA.
HEY!!
SHE LIKES THE MARIKA WHO'S HERE WITH US.
I DO, TOO.
BE-CAUSE YOU'RE A REAL FRIEND.

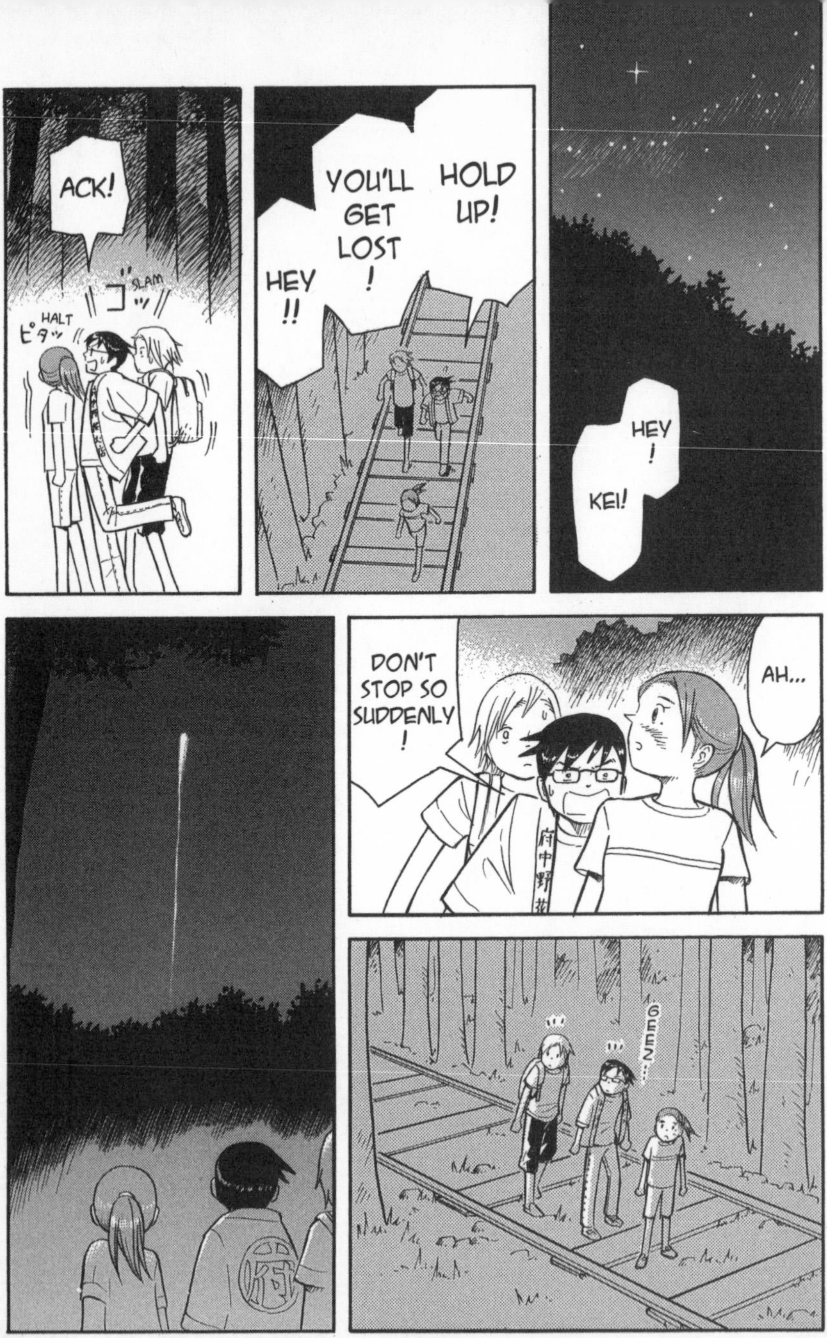
HEY! KEI!
HOLD UP!
YOU'LL GET LOST!
HEY!!
ACK!
ゴッ SLAM
ピタッ HALT
AH...
DON'T STOP SO SUDDENLY!
GEEZ...

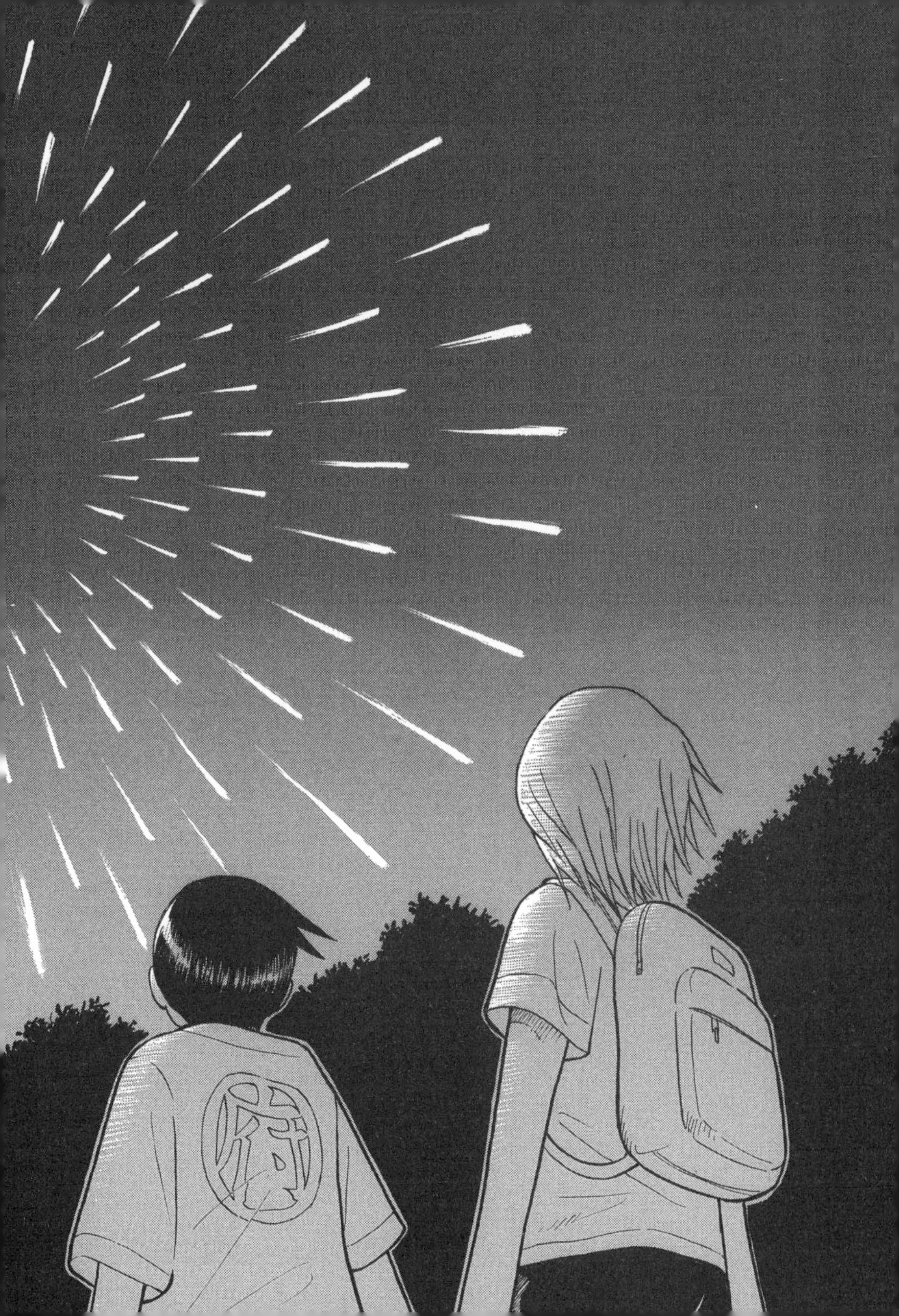

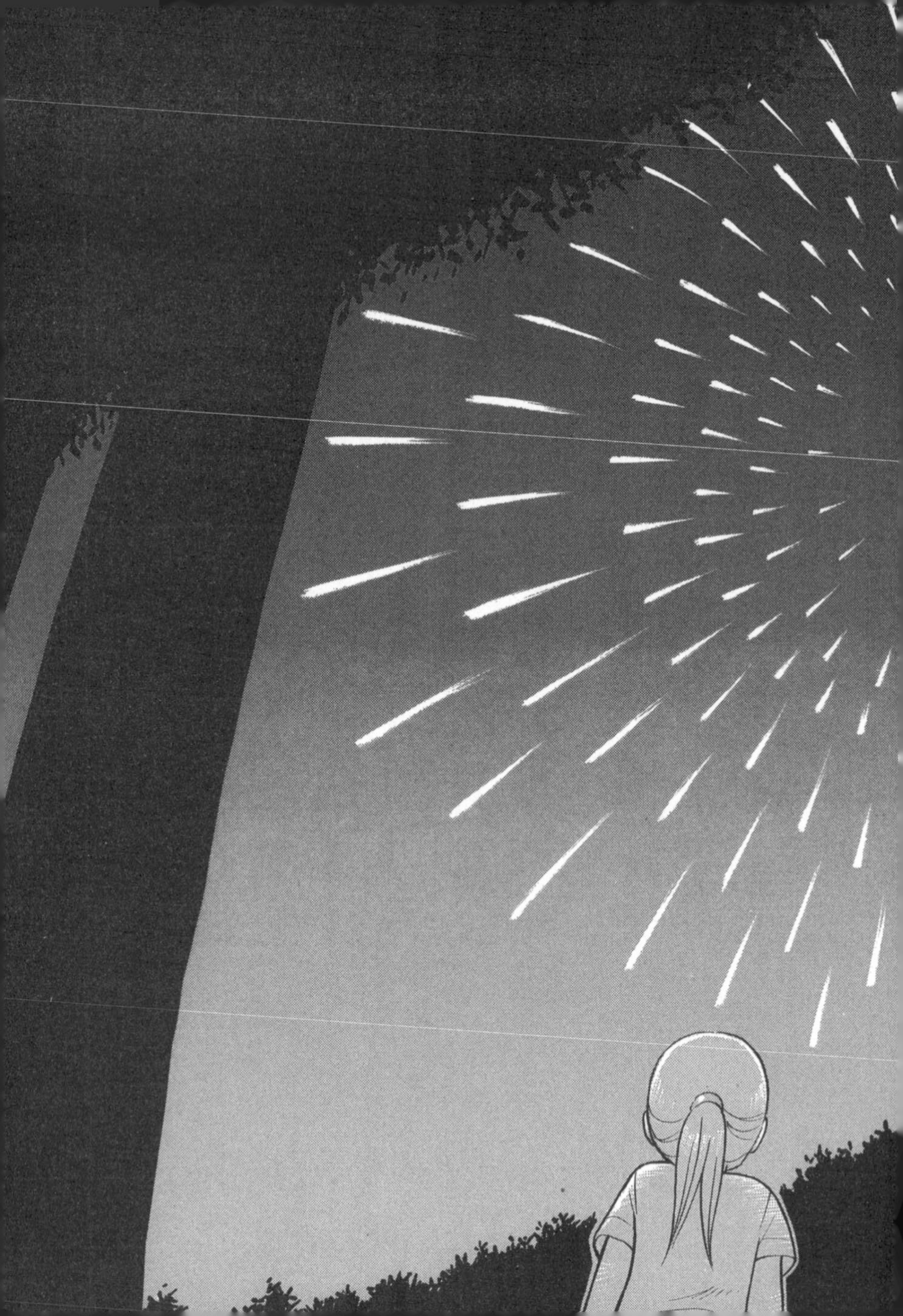

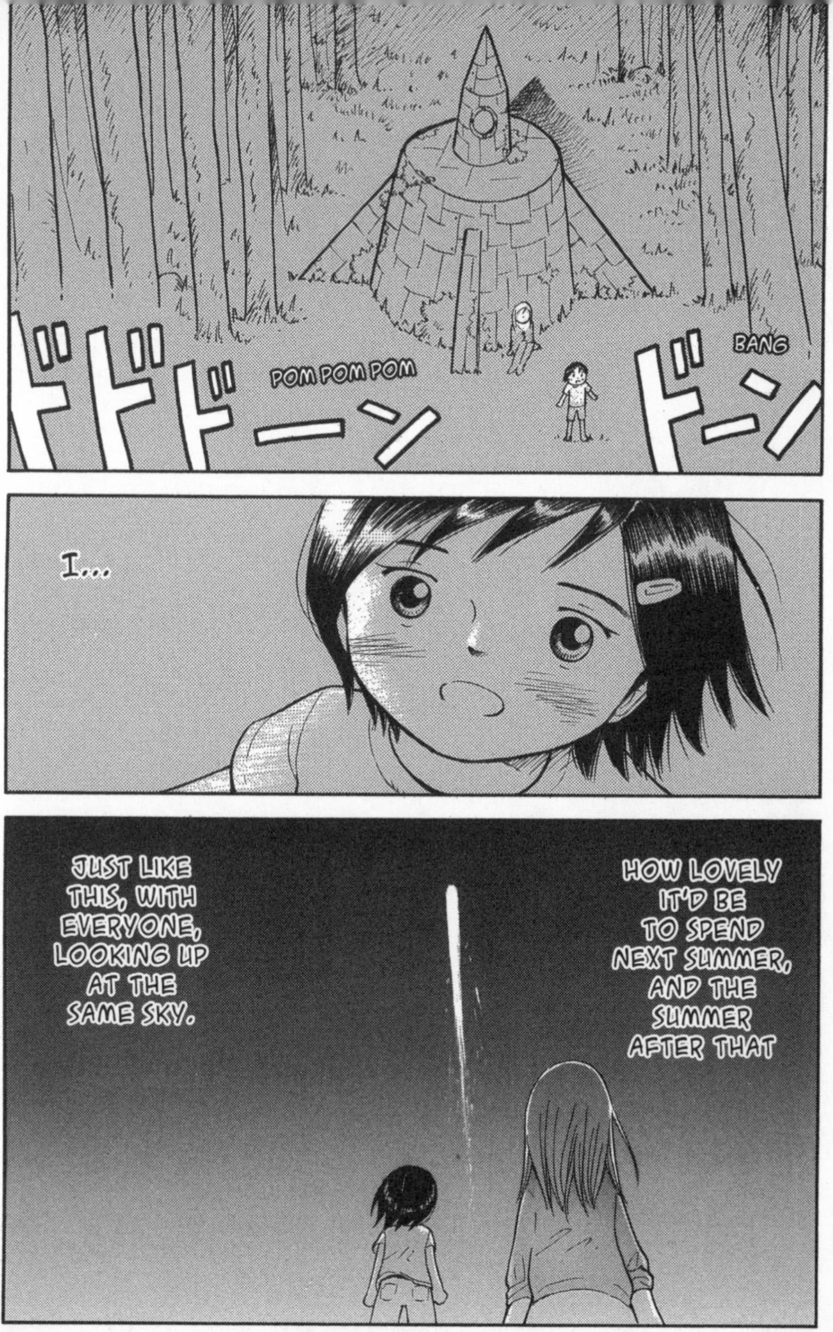
BANG
ドーン
POM POM POM
ドドドーン
I...
HOW LOVELY IT'D BE TO SPEND NEXT SUMMER, AND THE SUMMER AFTER THAT
JUST LIKE THIS, WITH EVERYONE, LOOKING UP AT THE SAME SKY.

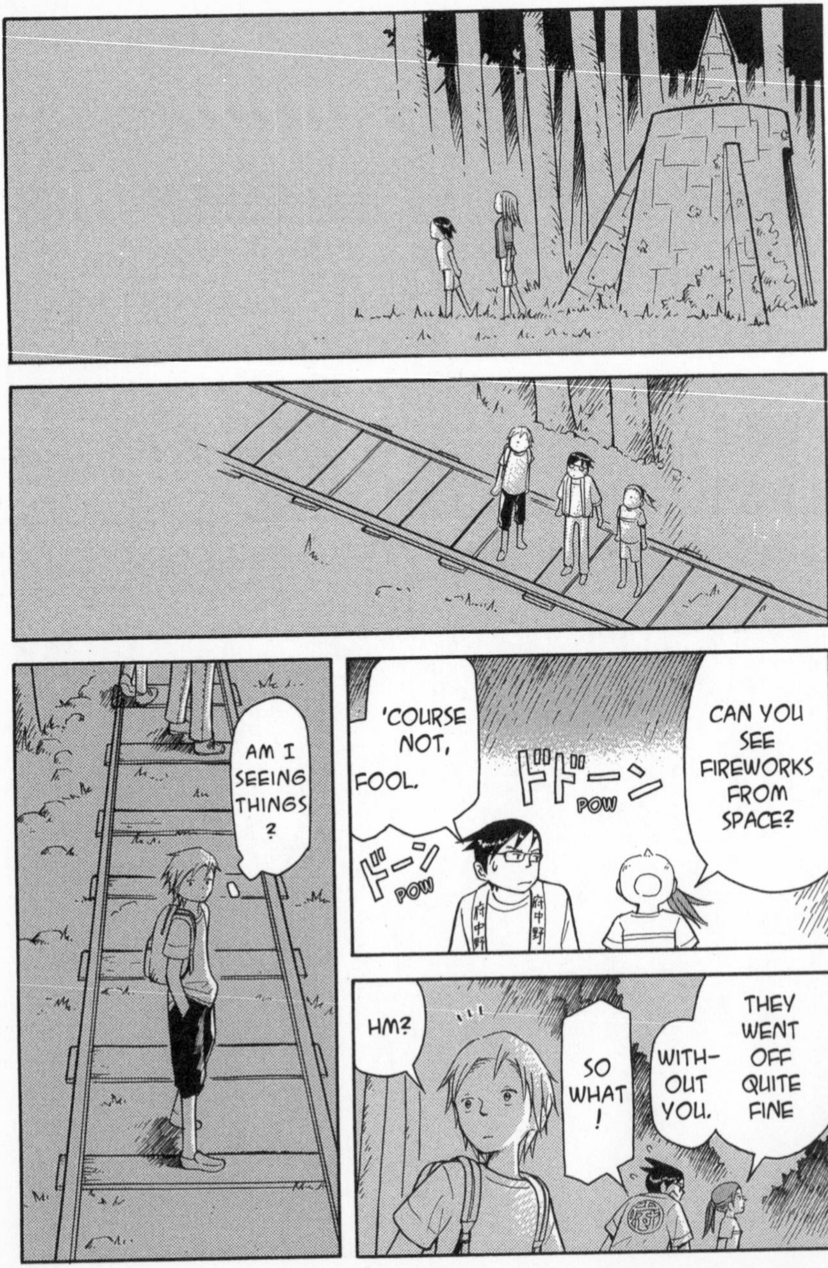
CAN YOU SEE FIREWORKS FROM SPACE?
ドドーン POW
'COURSE NOT, FOOL.
ドーン POW
THEY WENT OFF QUITE FINE WITHOUT YOU.
SO WHAT!
HM?
AM I SEEING THINGS?

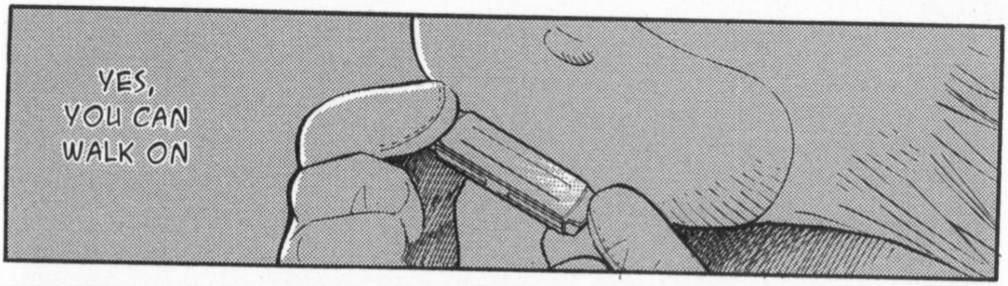
YES, YOU CAN WALK ON
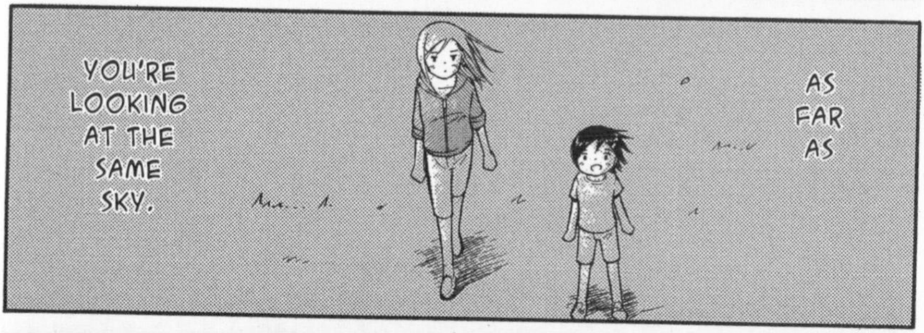
AS FAR AS
YOU'RE LOOKING AT THE SAME SKY.
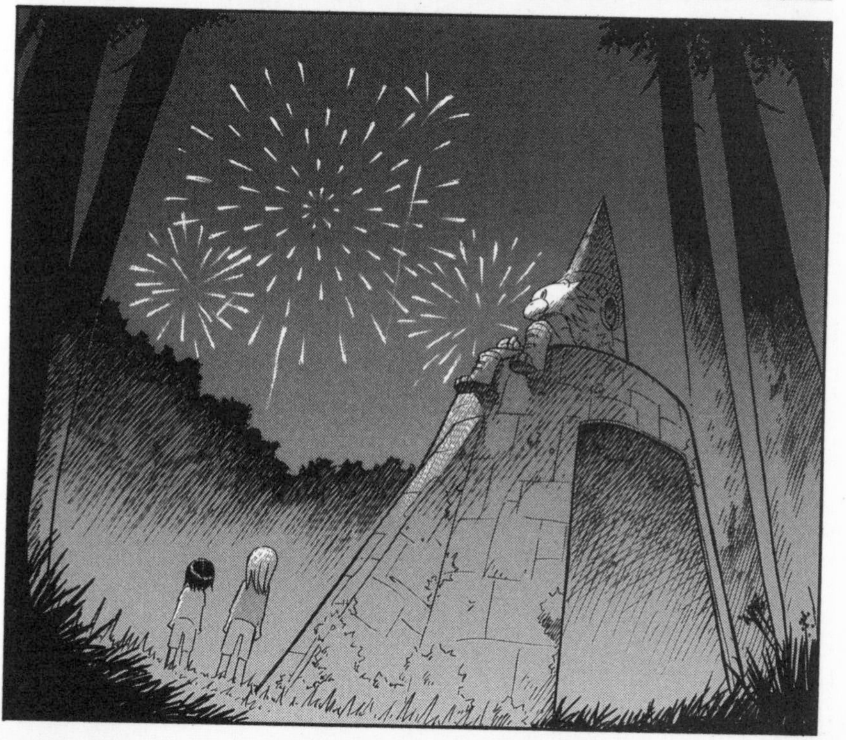

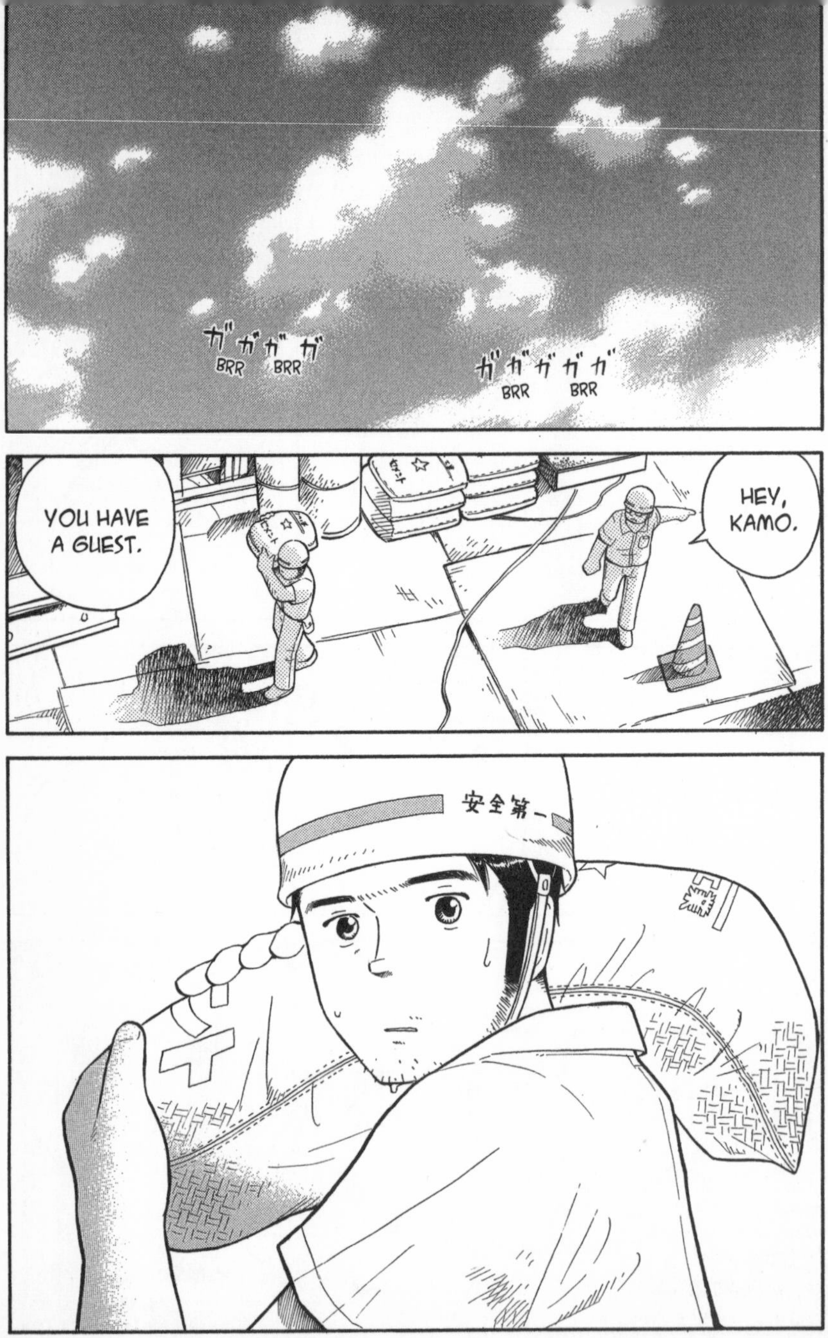
ガガガガガ
BRR BRR
ガガガガ
BRR BRR
HEY, KAMO.
YOU HAVE A GUEST.
安全第一

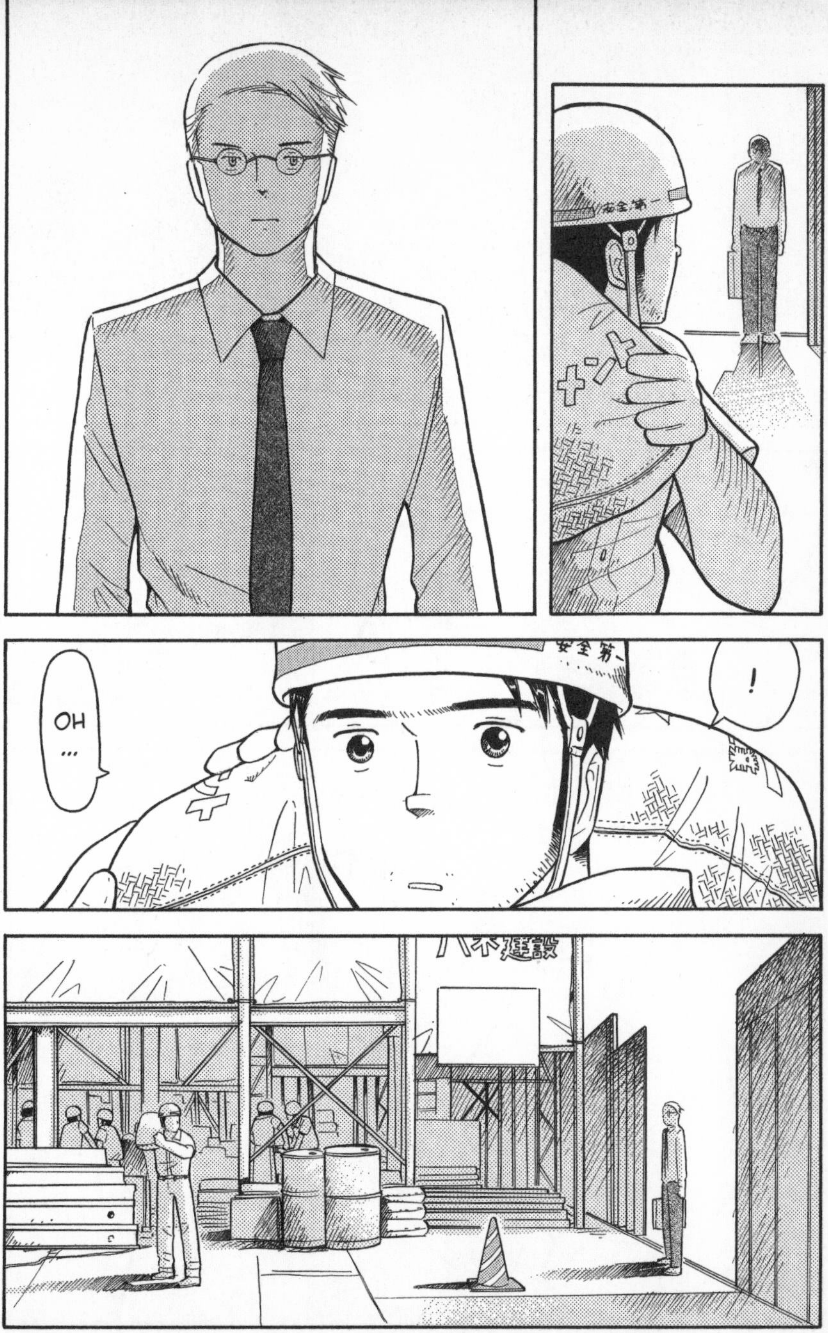
安全第一
安全第一
!
OH ...
八木建設

MISSION:33

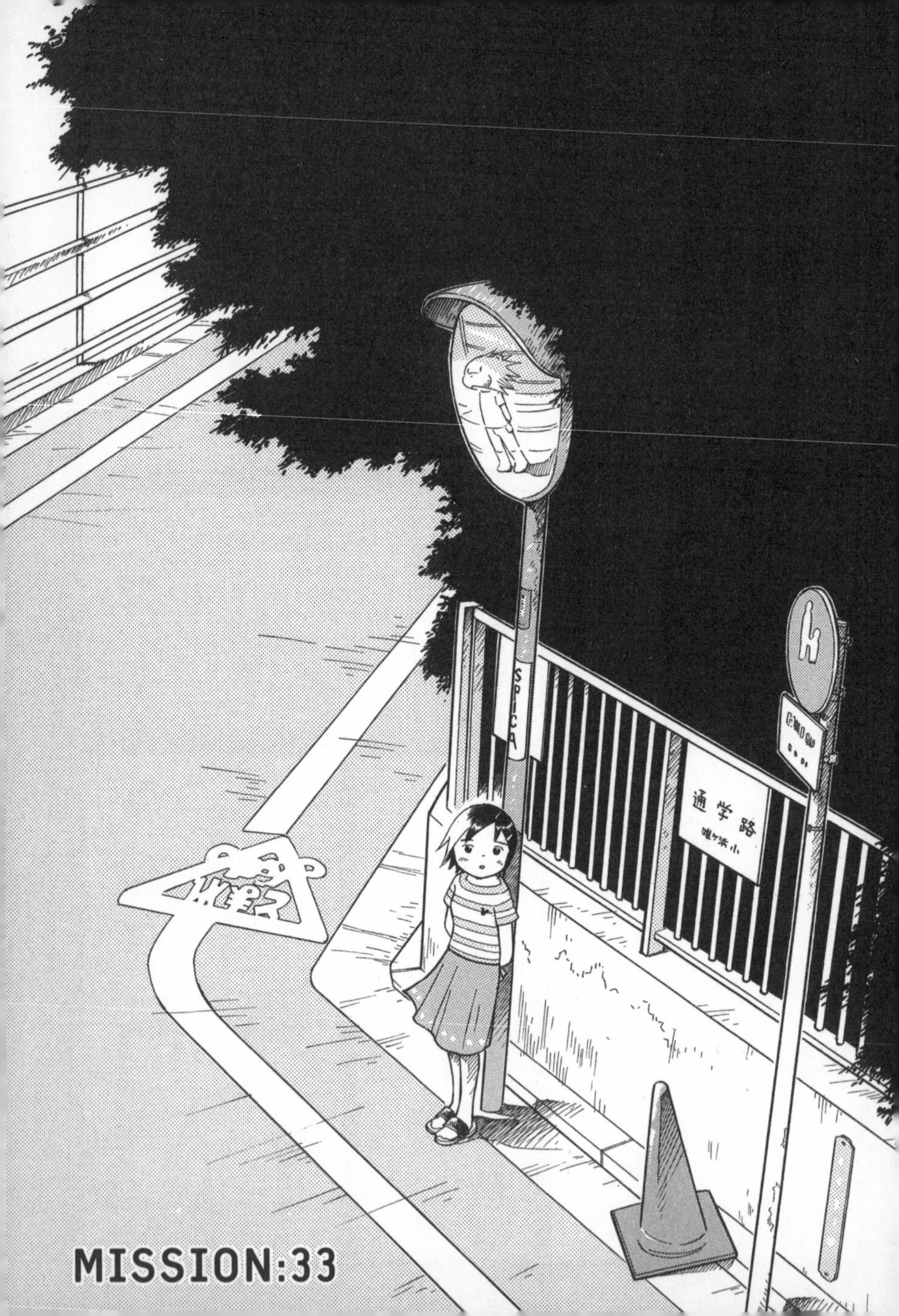
SPICA
通学路
唯ヶ浜小

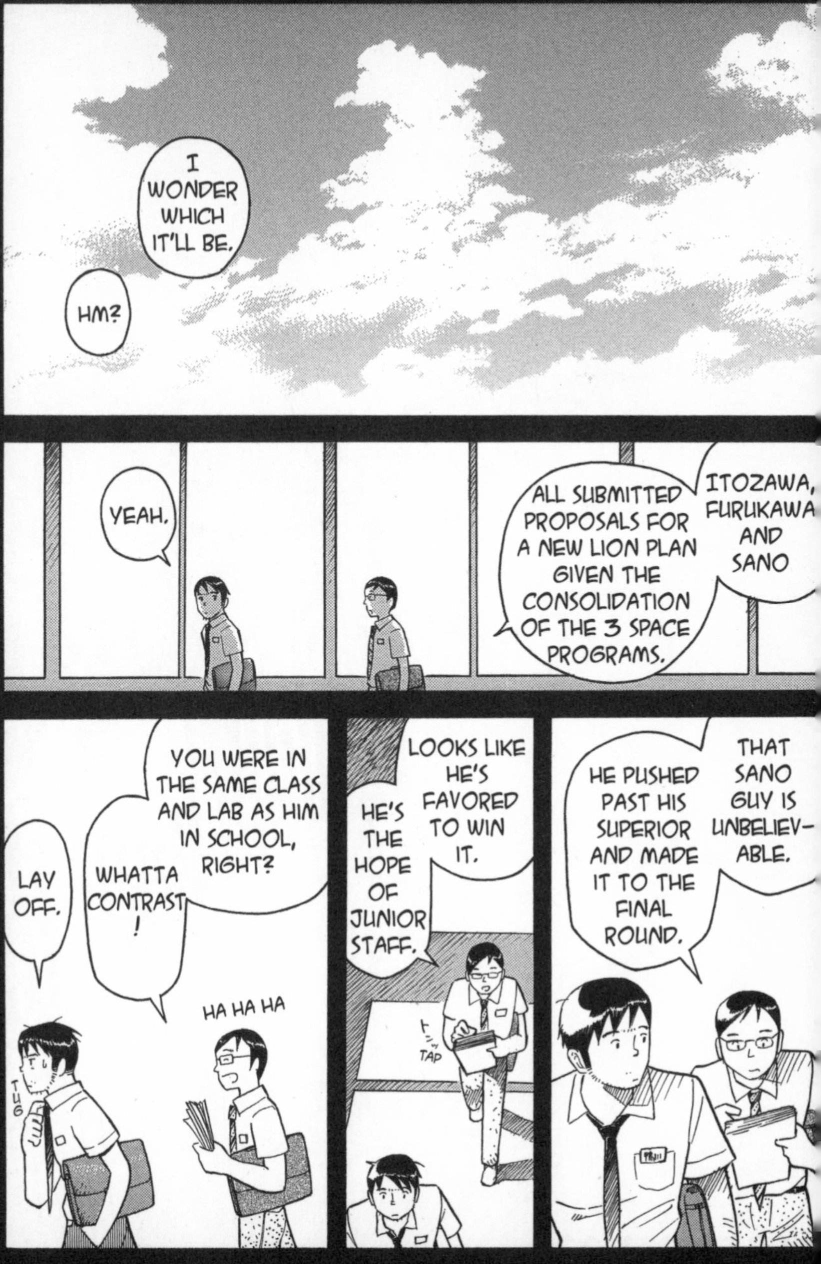
I WONDER WHICH IT'LL BE.
HM?
ITOZAWA, FURUKAWA AND SANO
ALL SUBMITTED PROPOSALS FOR A NEW LION PLAN GIVEN THE CONSOLIDATION OF THE 3 SPACE PROGRAMS.
YEAH.
THAT SANO GUY IS UNBELIEV-ABLE.
HE PUSHED PAST HIS SUPERIOR AND MADE IT TO THE FINAL ROUND.
LOOKS LIKE HE'S FAVORED TO WIN IT.
HE'S THE HOPE OF JUNIOR STAFF.
TAP
YOU WERE IN THE SAME CLASS AND LAB AS HIM IN SCHOOL, RIGHT?
WHATTA CONTRAST!
HA HA HA
LAY OFF.
TUG

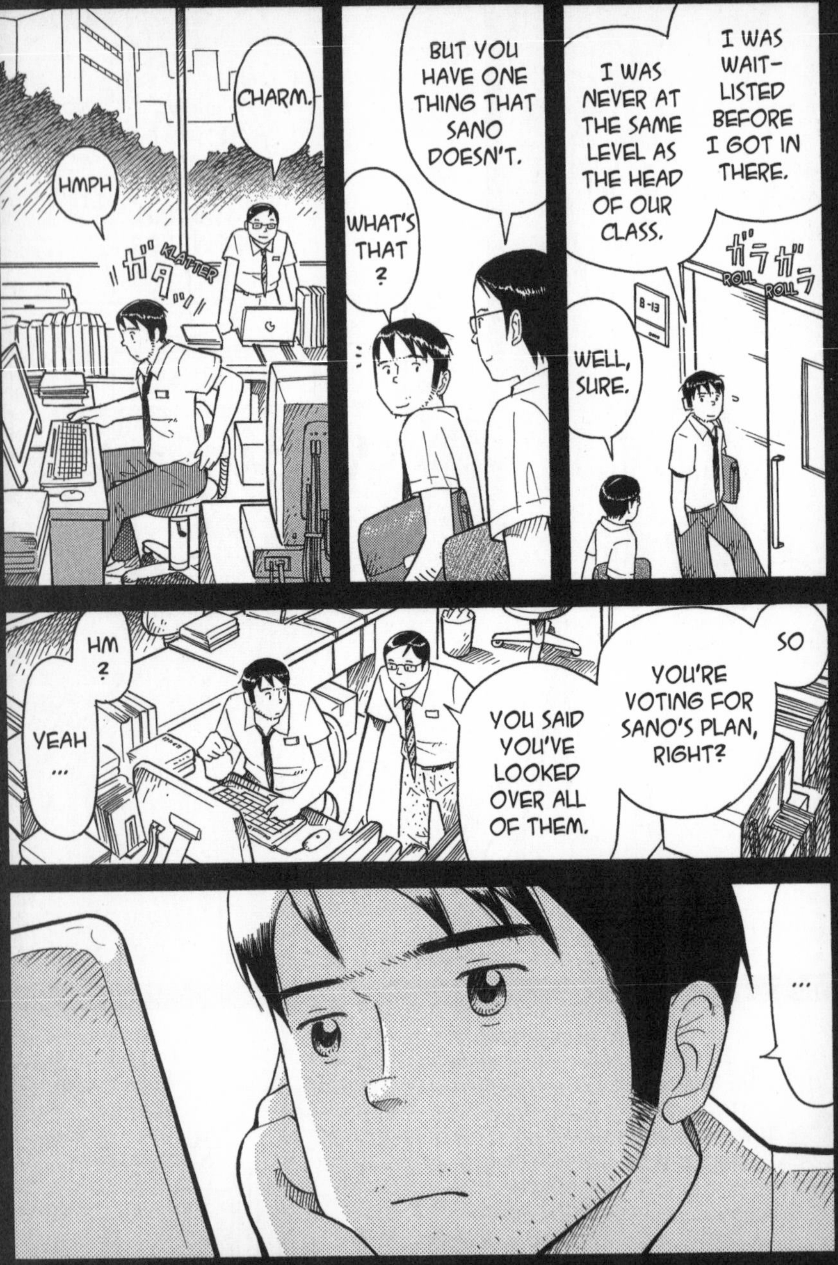
I WAS WAIT-LISTED BEFORE I GOT IN THERE.
I WAS NEVER AT THE SAME LEVEL AS THE HEAD OF OUR CLASS.
ガラガラ ROLL ROLL
WELL, SURE.
BUT YOU HAVE ONE THING THAT SANO DOESN'T.
WHAT'S THAT?
CHARM.
HMPH
ガタ KLATTER
SO YOU'RE VOTING FOR SANO'S PLAN, RIGHT?
YOU SAID YOU'VE LOOKED OVER ALL OF THEM.
HM?
YEAH ...
...

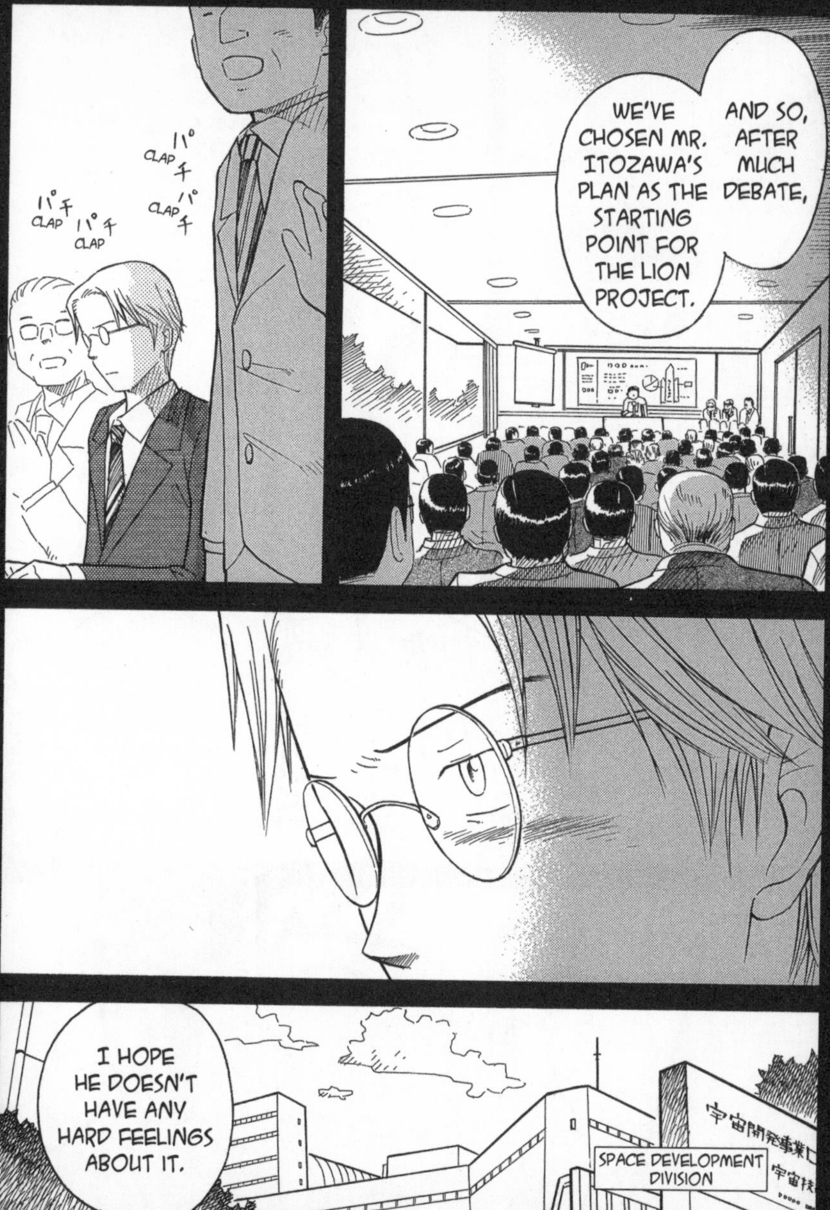
AND SO, AFTER MUCH DEBATE,
WE'VE CHOSEN MR. ITOZAWA'S PLAN AS THE STARTING POINT FOR THE LION PROJECT.
パチ CLAP
パチ CLAP
パチ CLAP
パチ CLAP
SPACE DEVELOPMENT DIVISION
I HOPE HE DOESN'T HAVE ANY HARD FEELINGS ABOUT IT.

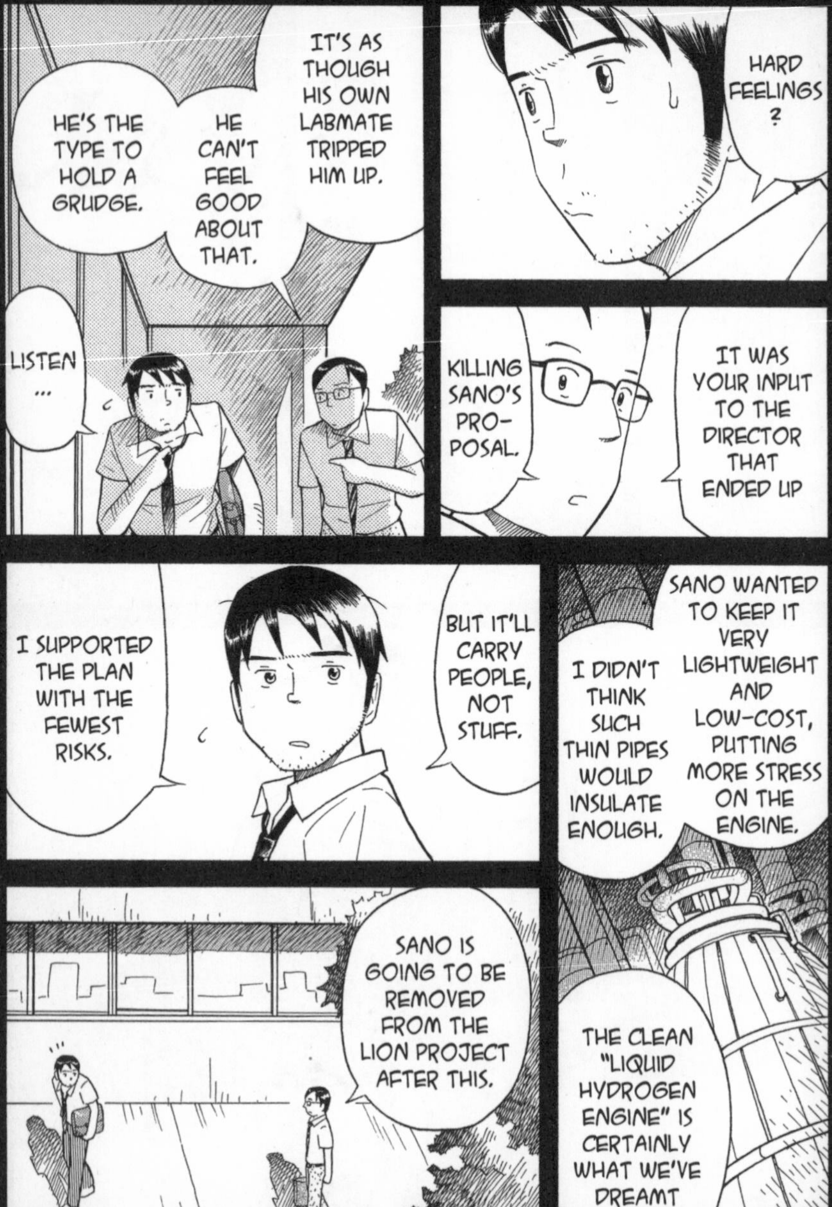
HARD FEELINGS?
IT WAS YOUR INPUT TO THE DIRECTOR THAT ENDED UP
KILLING SANO'S PRO-POSAL.
IT'S AS THOUGH HIS OWN LABMATE TRIPPED HIM UP.
HE CAN'T FEEL GOOD ABOUT THAT.
HE'S THE TYPE TO HOLD A GRUDGE.
LISTEN...
SANO WANTED TO KEEP IT VERY LIGHTWEIGHT AND LOW-COST, PUTTING MORE STRESS ON THE ENGINE.
I DIDN'T THINK SUCH THIN PIPES WOULD INSULATE ENOUGH.
THE CLEAN "LIQUID HYDROGEN ENGINE" IS CERTAINLY WHAT WE'VE DREAMT OF,
BUT IT'LL CARRY PEOPLE, NOT STUFF.
I SUPPORTED THE PLAN WITH THE FEWEST RISKS.
SANO IS GOING TO BE REMOVED FROM THE LION PROJECT AFTER THIS.

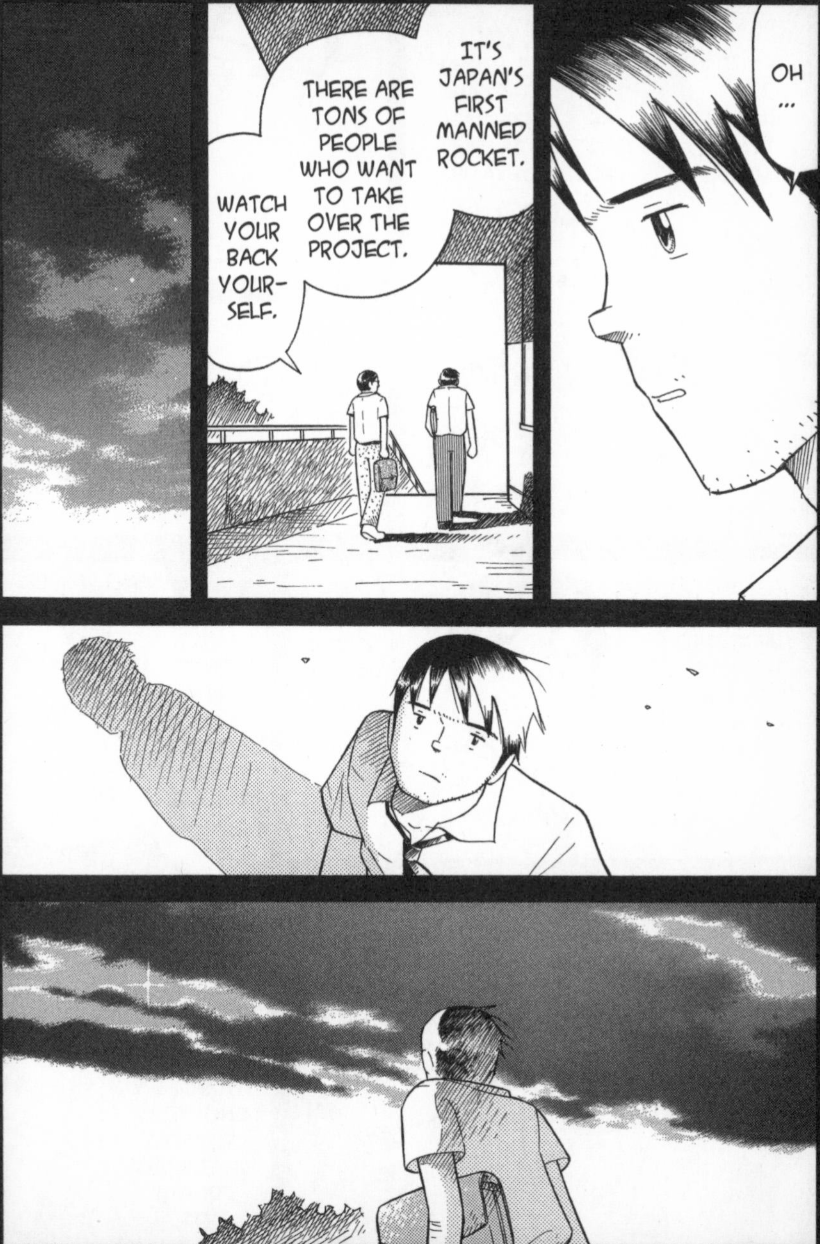
OH ...
IT'S JAPAN'S FIRST MANNED ROCKET.
THERE ARE TONS OF PEOPLE WHO WANT TO TAKE OVER THE PROJECT.
WATCH YOUR BACK YOURSELF.

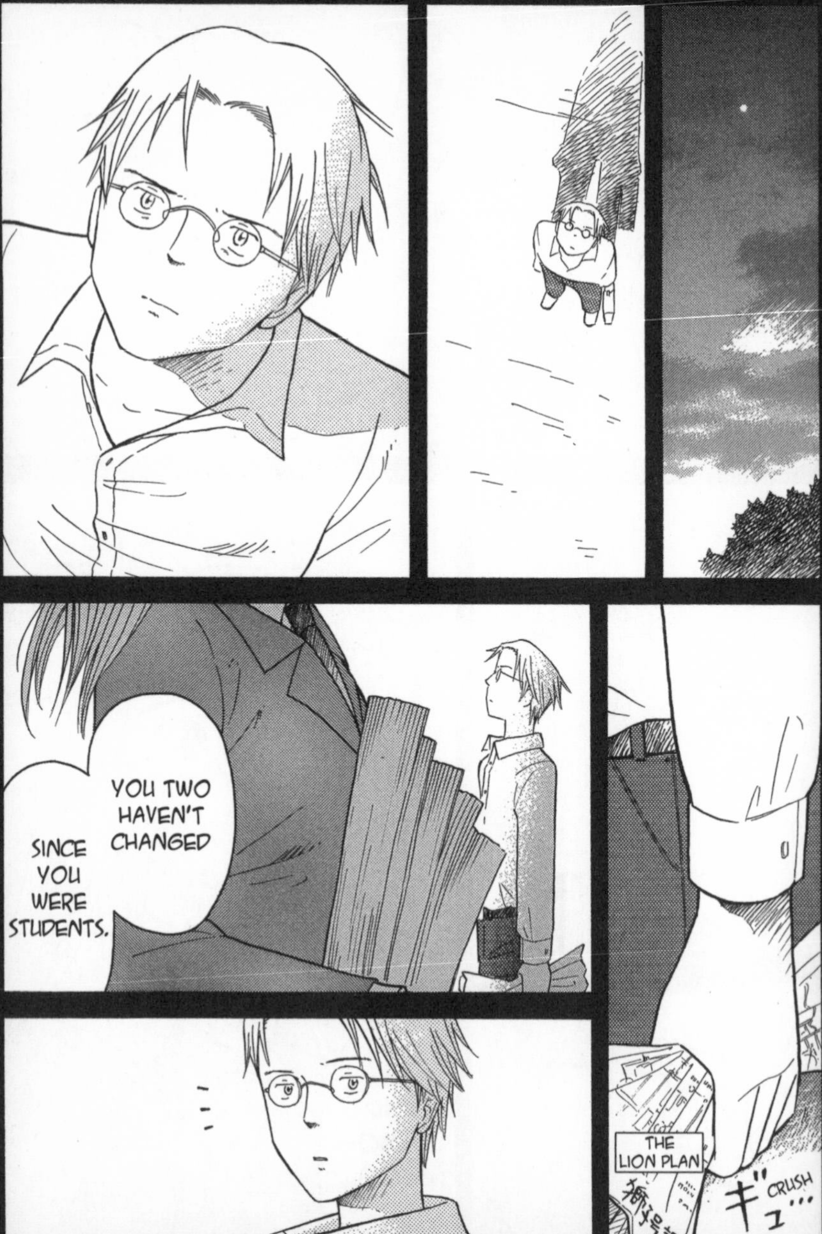
THE LION PLAN
ギュ…
CRUSH
YOU TWO HAVEN'T CHANGED SINCE YOU WERE STUDENTS.

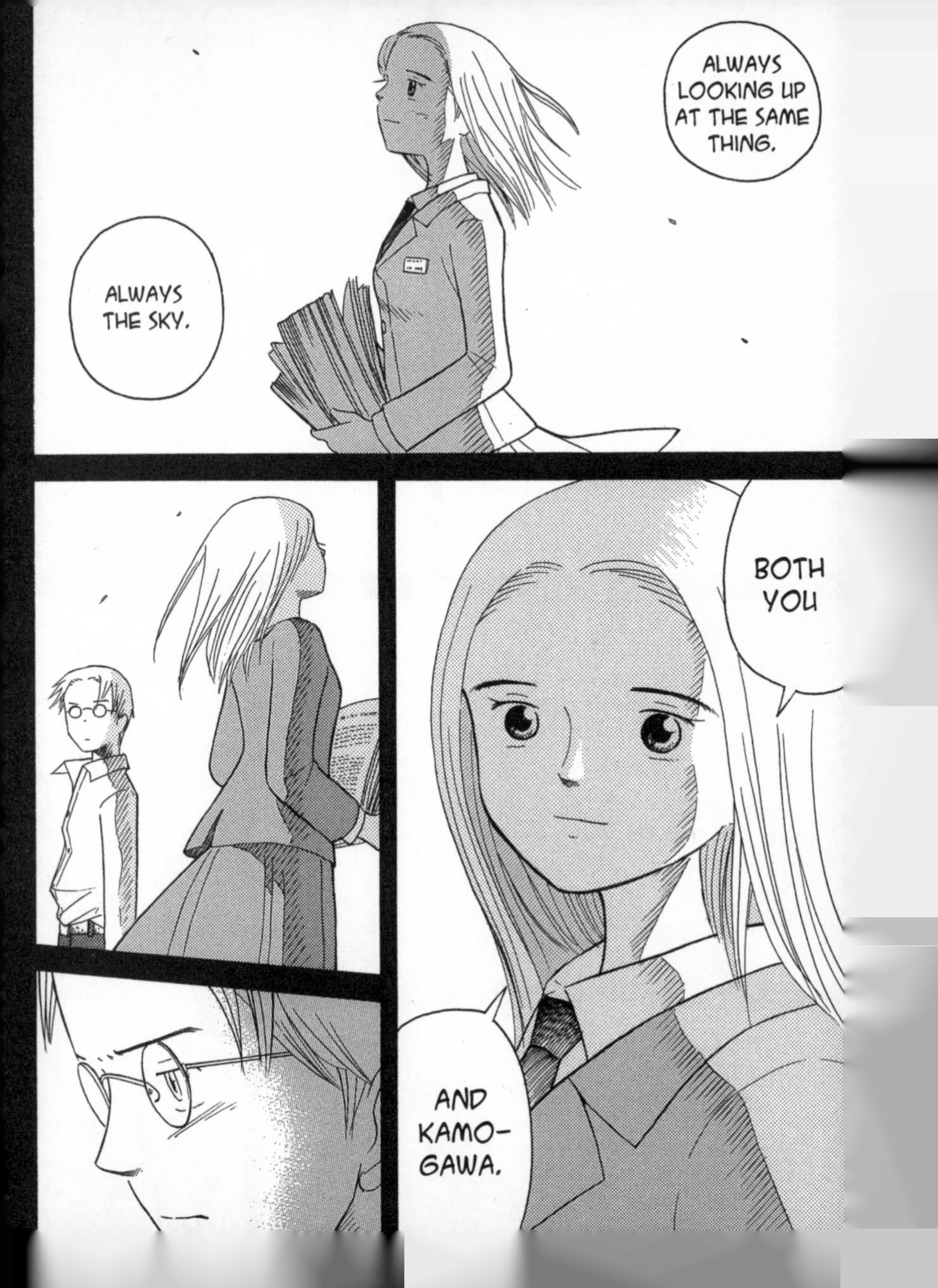
ALWAYS LOOKING UP AT THE SAME THING.
ALWAYS THE SKY.
BOTH YOU
AND KAMO-GAWA.

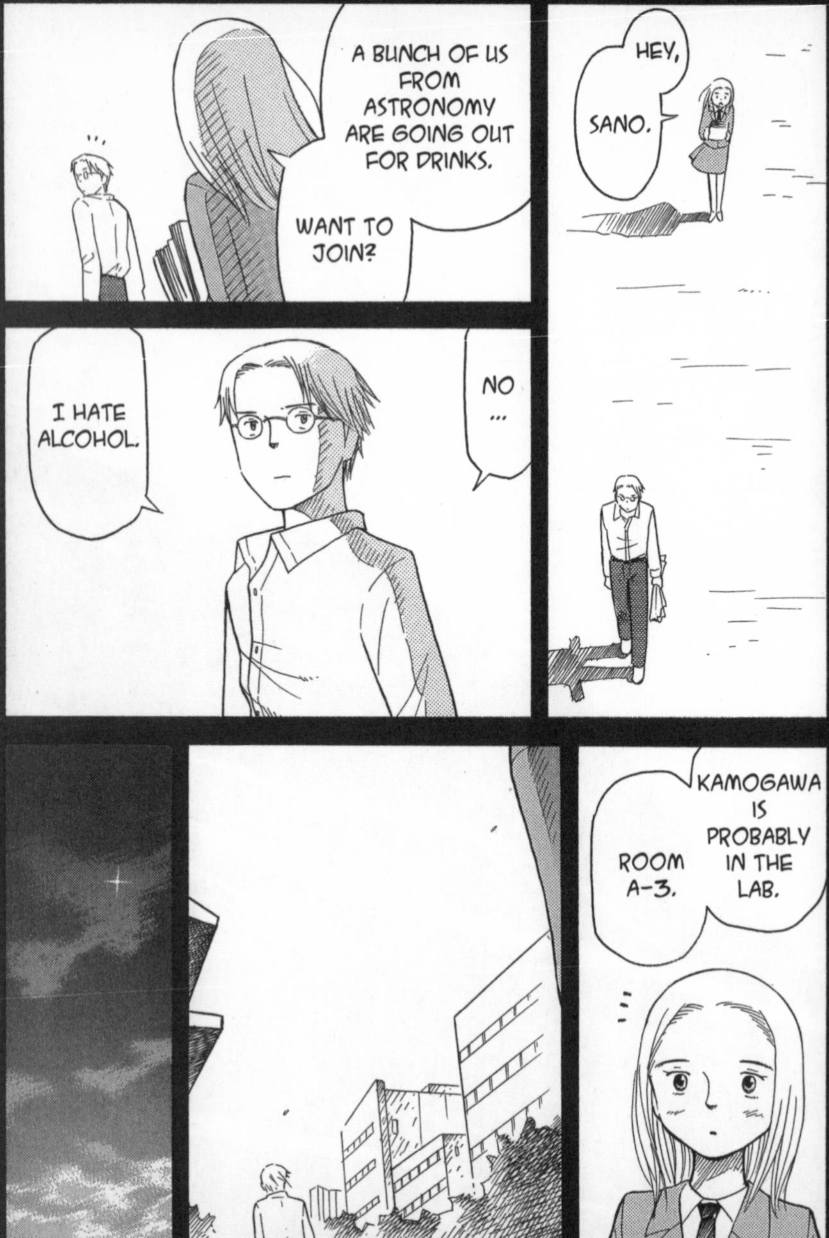
HEY,
SANO.
A BUNCH OF US FROM ASTRONOMY ARE GOING OUT FOR DRINKS.
WANT TO JOIN?
NO ...
I HATE ALCOHOL.
KAMOGAWA IS PROBABLY IN THE LAB.
ROOM A-3.

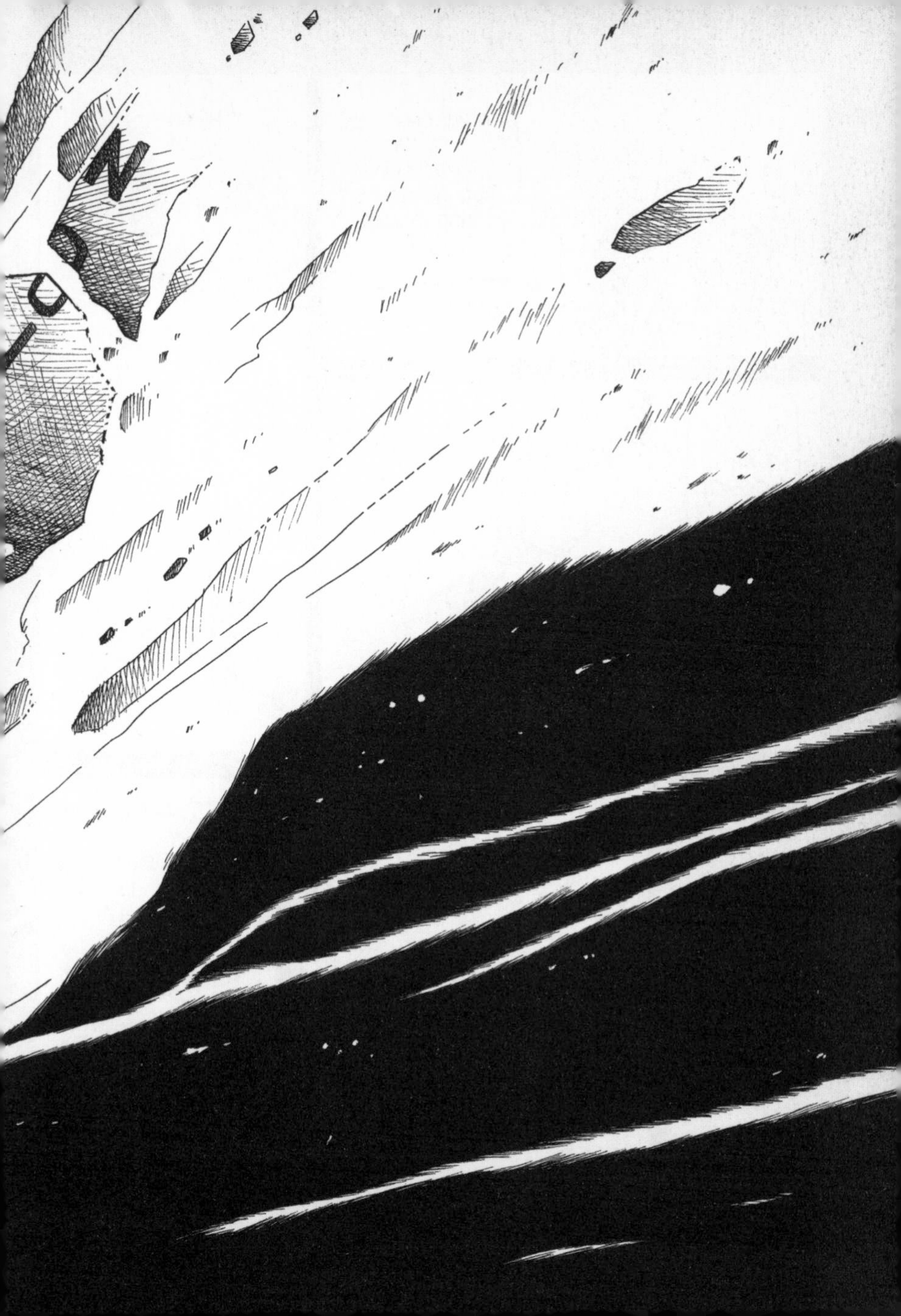

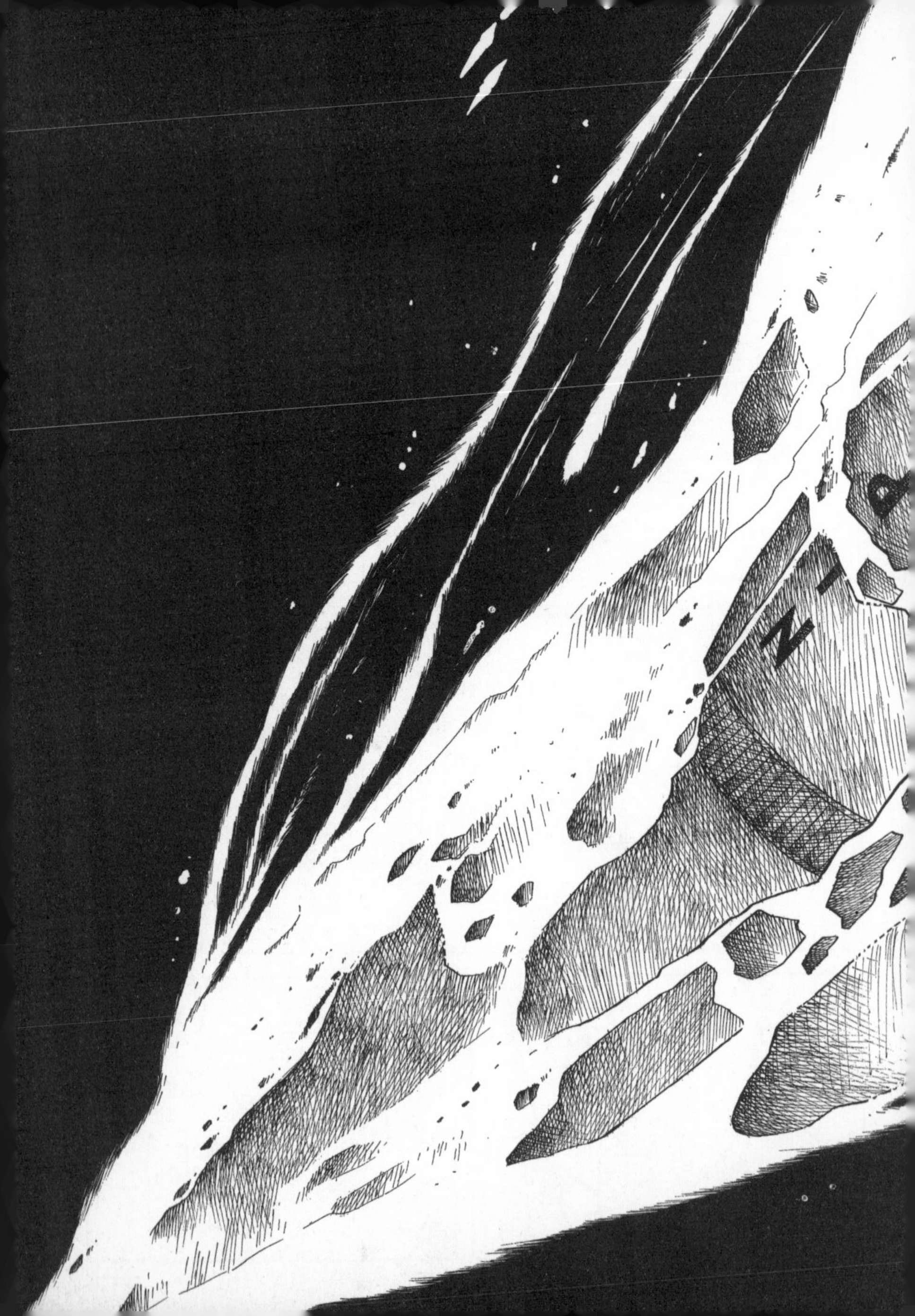

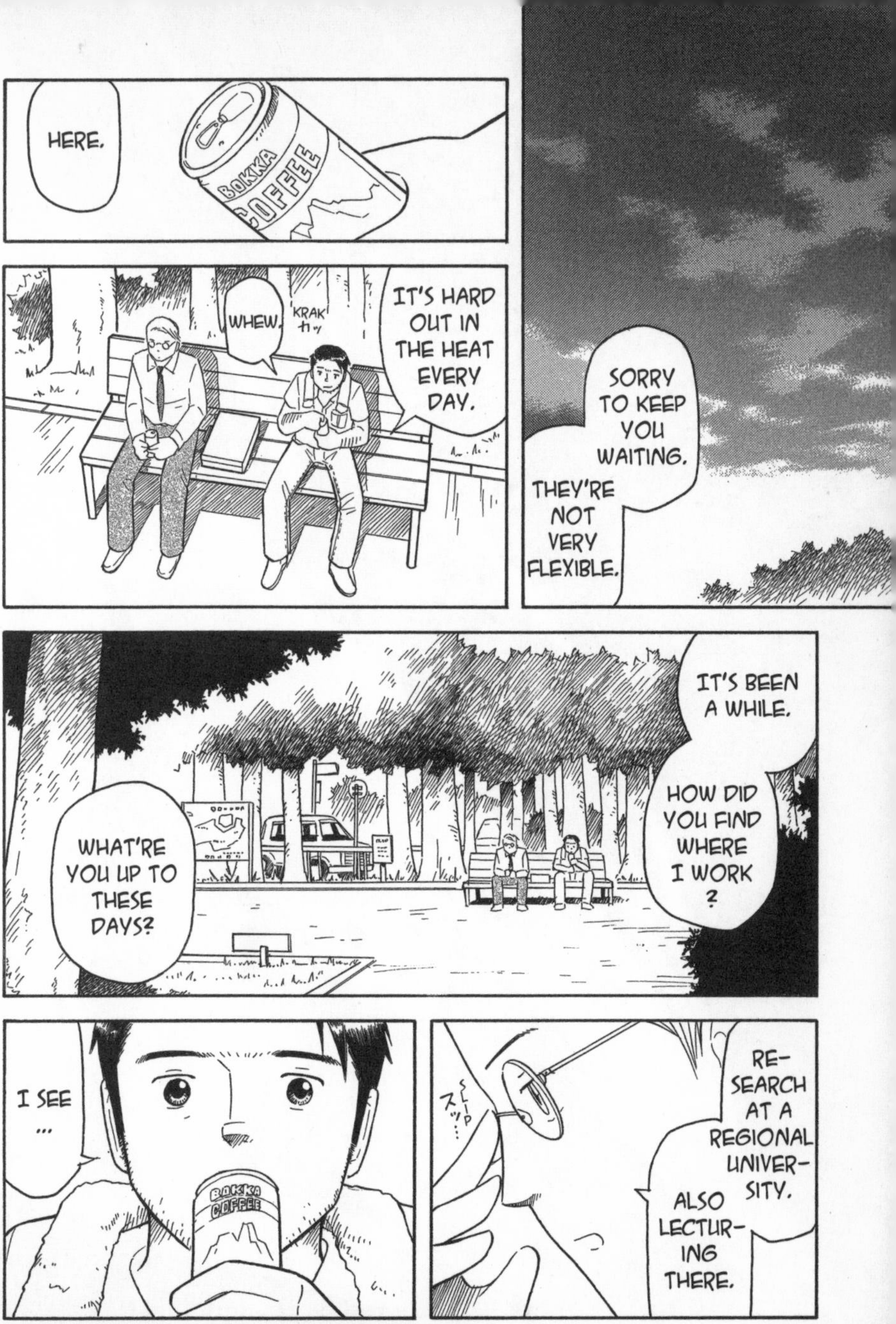
SORRY TO KEEP YOU WAITING.
THEY'RE NOT VERY FLEXIBLE.
HERE.
BOKKA COFFEE
IT'S HARD OUT IN THE HEAT EVERY DAY.
KRAK カッ
WHEW.
IT'S BEEN A WHILE.
HOW DID YOU FIND WHERE I WORK?
WHAT'RE YOU UP TO THESE DAYS?
RE-SEARCH AT A REGIONAL UNIVER-SITY.
ALSO LECTUR-ING THERE.
SLIP スッ…
I SEE…
BOKKA COFFEE

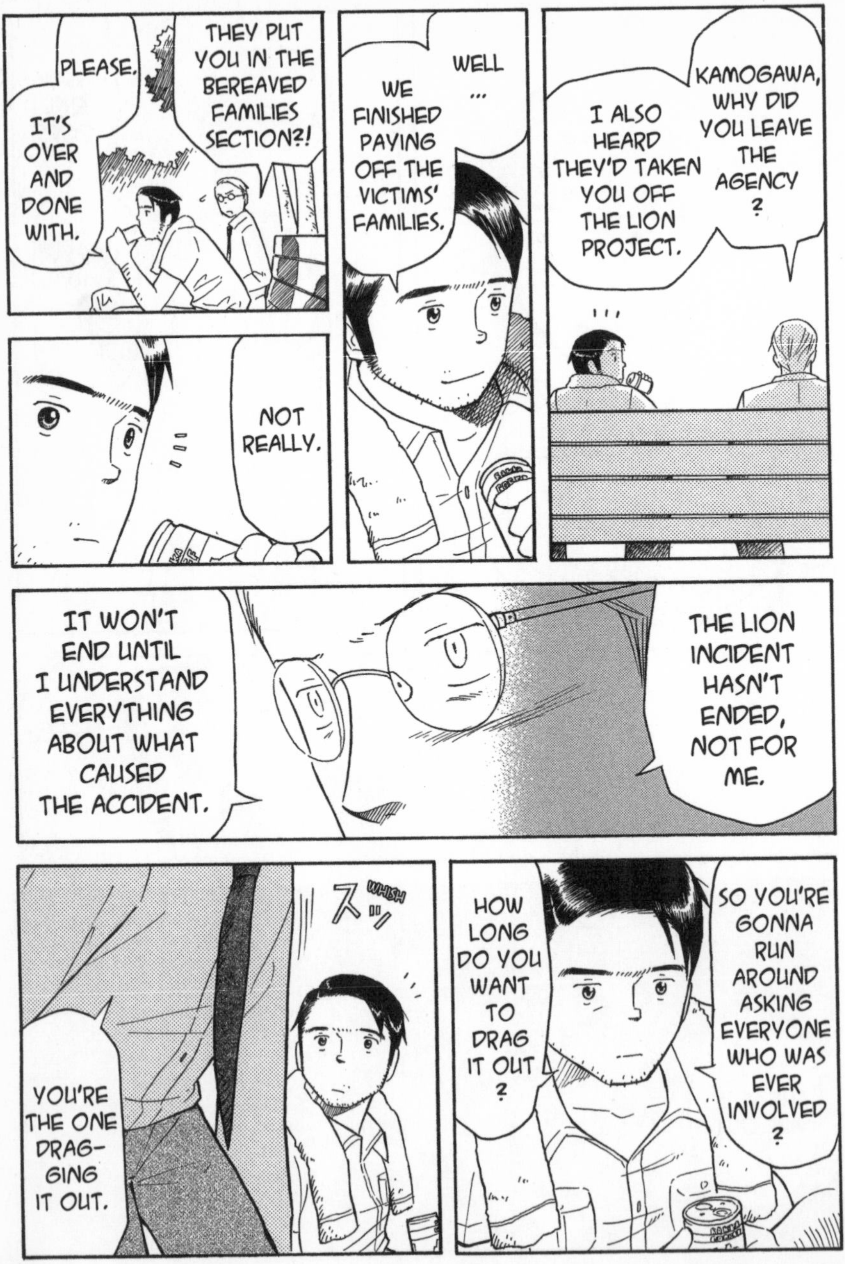
KAMOGAWA, WHY DID YOU LEAVE THE AGENCY?
I ALSO HEARD THEY'D TAKEN YOU OFF THE LION PROJECT.
WELL ...
WE FINISHED PAYING OFF THE VICTIMS' FAMILIES.
THEY PUT YOU IN THE BEREAVED FAMILIES SECTION?!
PLEASE.
IT'S OVER AND DONE WITH.
NOT REALLY.
THE LION INCIDENT HASN'T ENDED, NOT FOR ME.
IT WON'T END UNTIL I UNDERSTAND EVERYTHING ABOUT WHAT CAUSED THE ACCIDENT.
SO YOU'RE GONNA RUN AROUND ASKING EVERYONE WHO WAS EVER INVOLVED?
HOW LONG DO YOU WANT TO DRAG IT OUT?
WHISH
YOU'RE THE ONE DRAG-GING IT OUT.

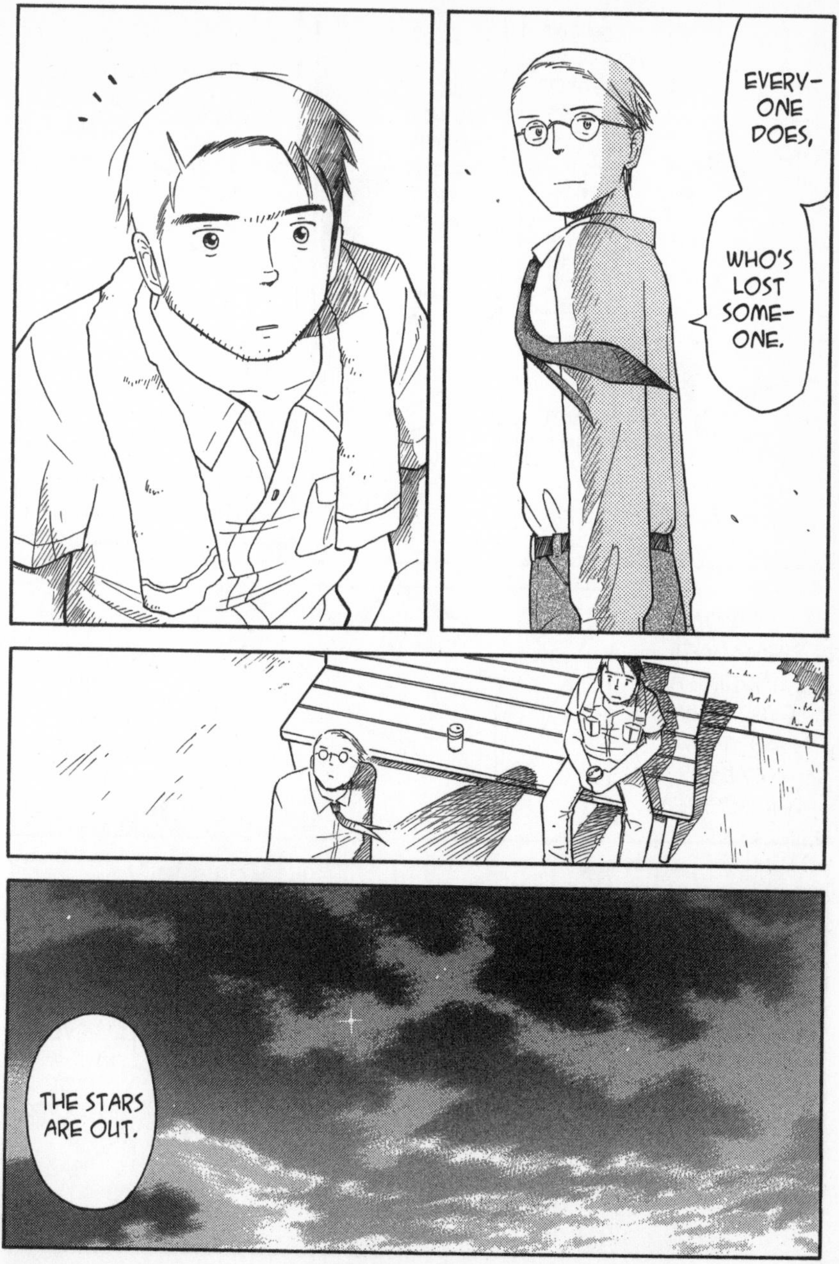
EVERY-ONE DOES,
WHO'S LOST SOME-ONE.
THE STARS ARE OUT.

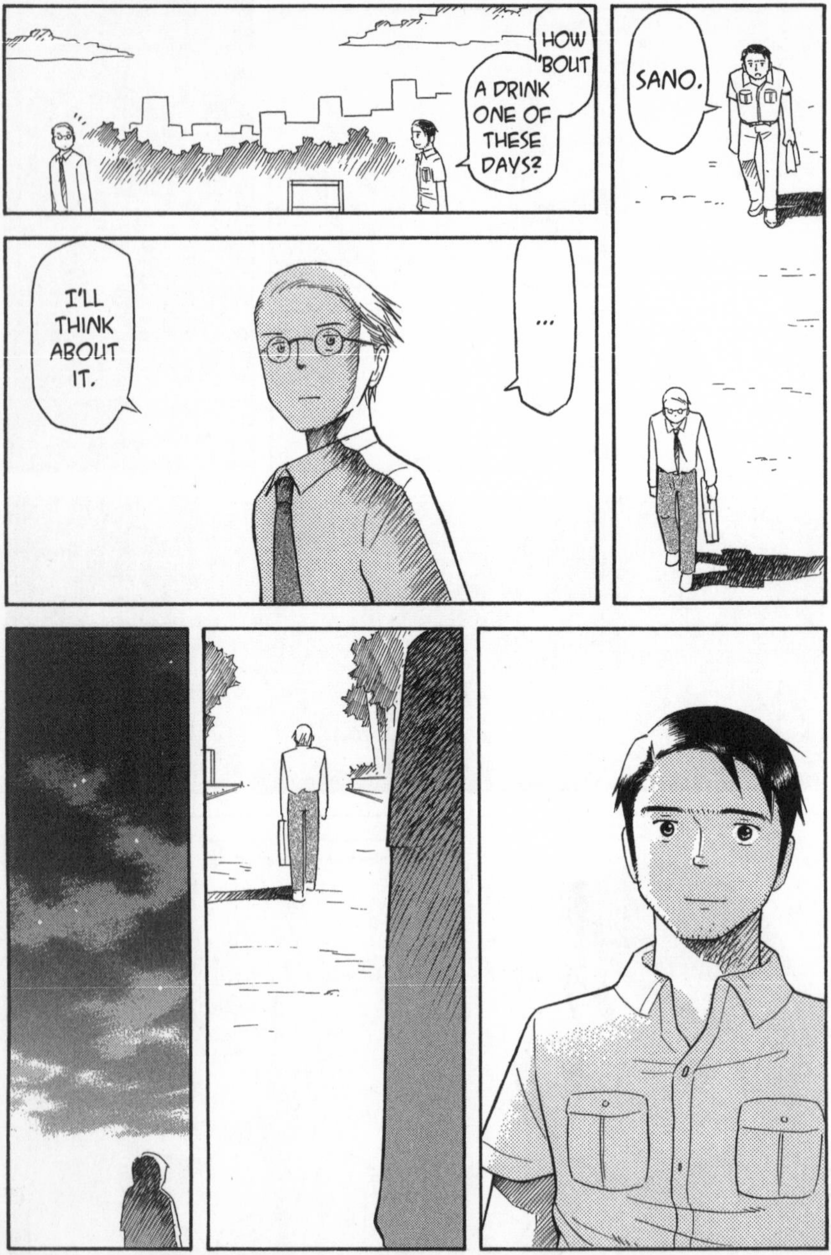
SANO.
HOW 'BOUT A DRINK ONE OF THESE DAYS?
...
I'LL THINK ABOUT IT.

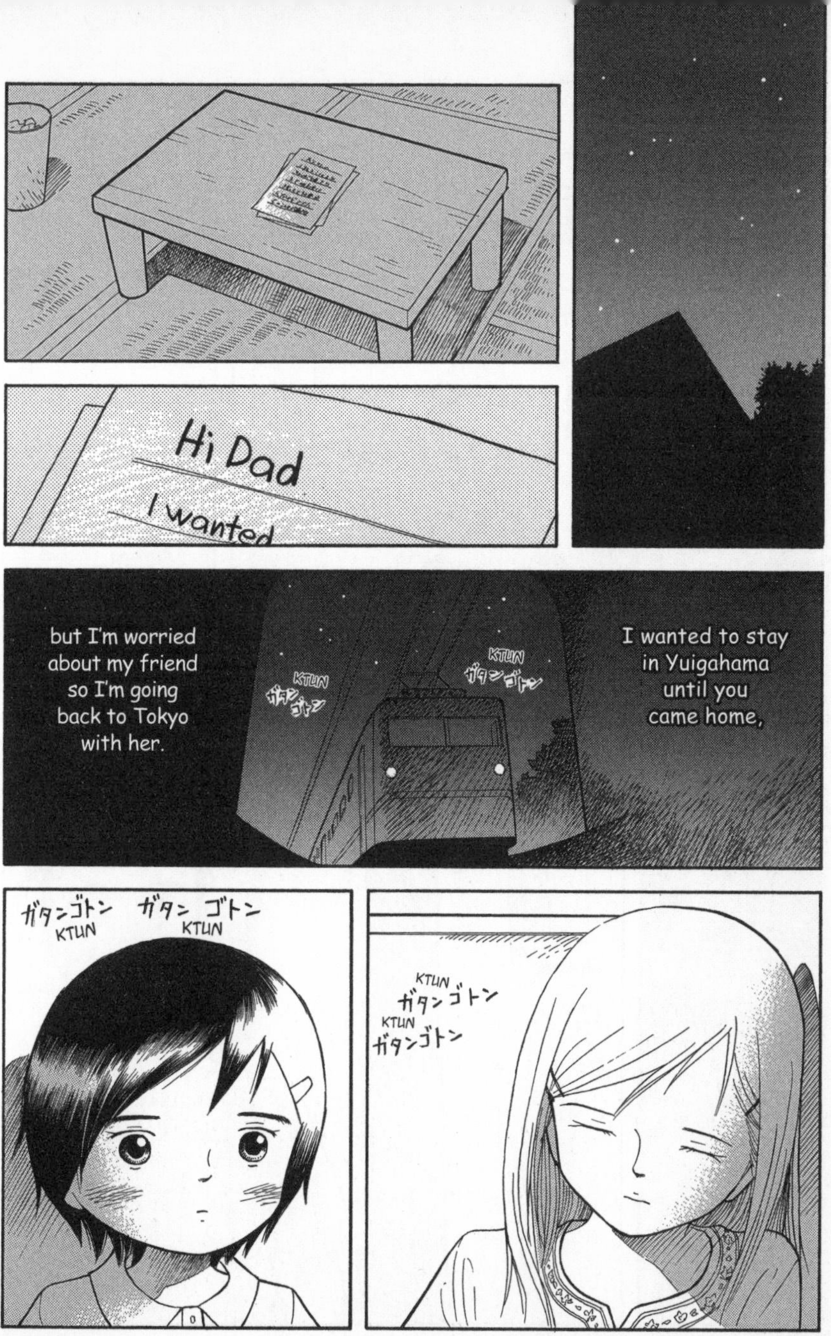
Hi Dad
I wanted
I wanted to stay in Yuigahama until you came home,
KTUN
ガタンゴトン
KTUN
ガタンゴトン
but I'm worried about my friend so I'm going back to Tokyo with her.
KTUN
ガタンゴトン
KTUN
ガタンゴトン
ガタン ゴトン
KTUN
ガタンゴトン
KTUN

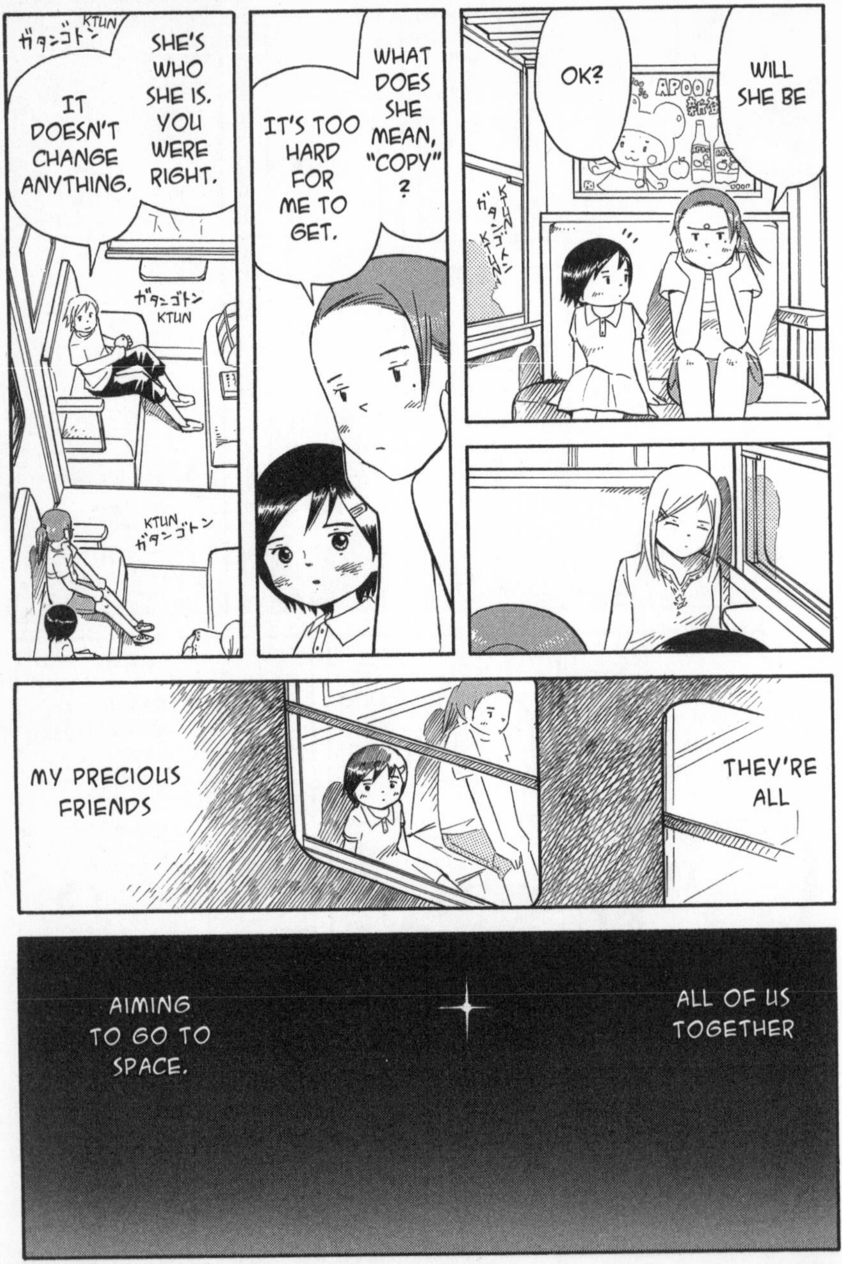
WILL SHE BE
OK?
KTUN ガタンゴトン KTUN
WHAT DOES SHE MEAN, "COPY"?
IT'S TOO HARD FOR ME TO GET.
ガタンゴトン KTUN
SHE'S WHO SHE IS. YOU WERE RIGHT.
IT DOESN'T CHANGE ANYTHING.
ガタンゴトン KTUN
KTUN ガタンゴトン
THEY'RE ALL
MY PRECIOUS FRIENDS
ALL OF US TOGETHER
AIMING TO GO TO SPACE.

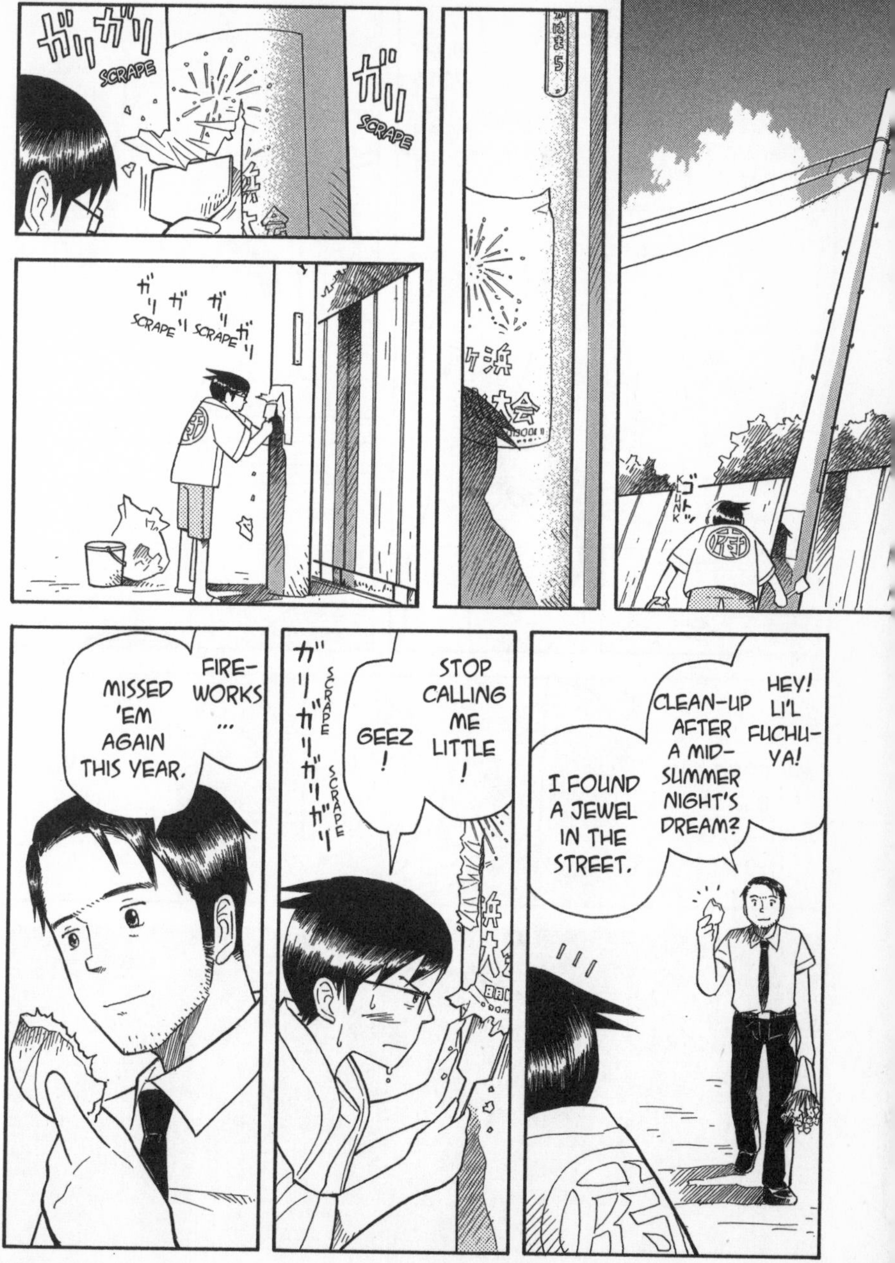
ガリ
SCRAPE
ガリガリ
SCRAPE
ガリガリガリ
SCRAPE SCRAPE
HEY! LI'L FUCHU-YA!
CLEAN-UP AFTER A MID-SUMMER NIGHT'S DREAM?
I FOUND A JEWEL IN THE STREET.
STOP CALLING ME LITTLE!
GEEZ!
ガリガリガリガリ
SCRAPE SCRAPE
FIRE-WORKS...
MISSED 'EM AGAIN THIS YEAR.

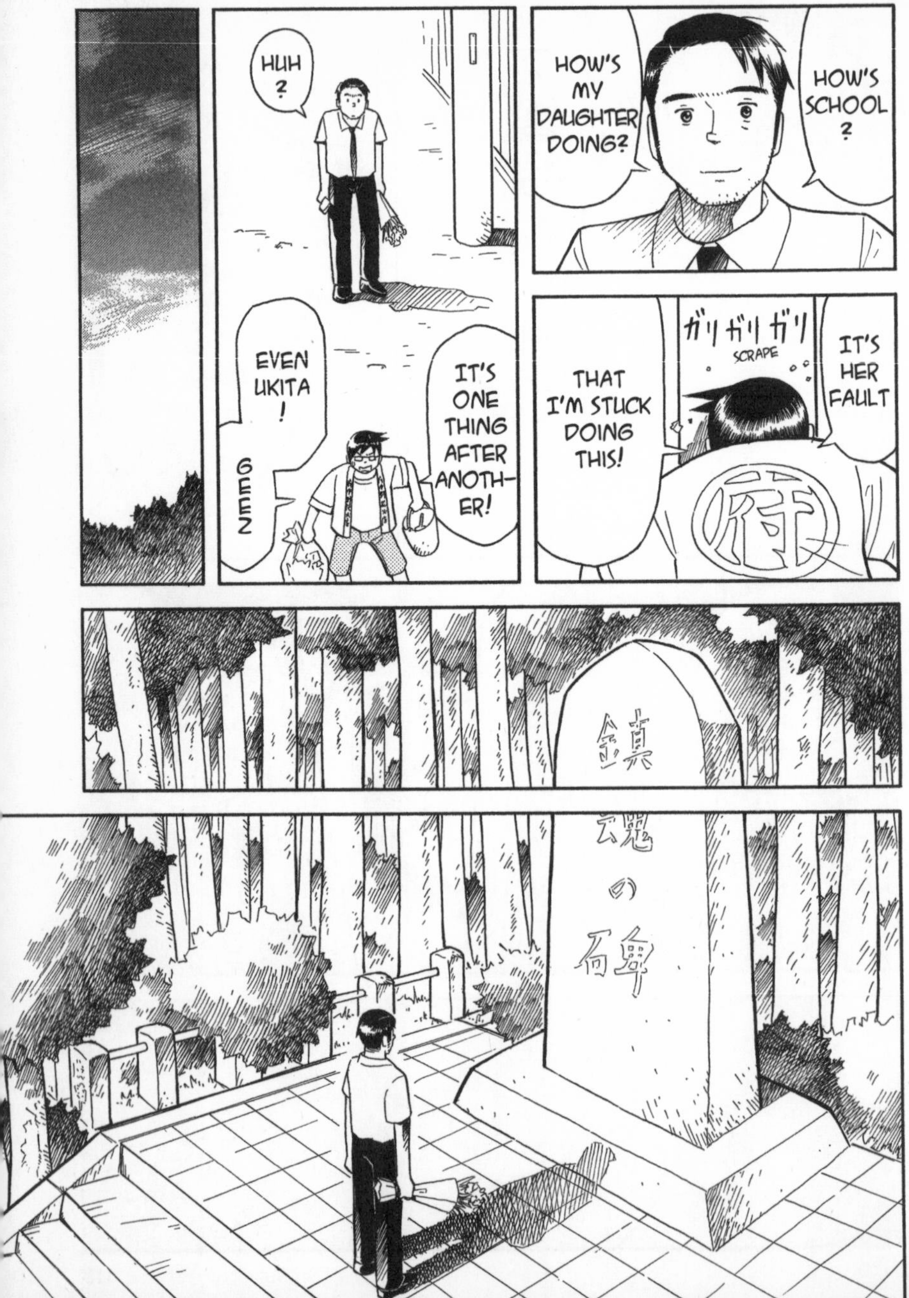
HOW'S SCHOOL?
HOW'S MY DAUGHTER DOING?
IT'S HER FAULT
ガリガリガリ SCRAPE
THAT I'M STUCK DOING THIS!
HUH?
IT'S ONE THING AFTER ANOTH-ER!
EVEN UKITA!
GEEZ
鎮魂の石碑

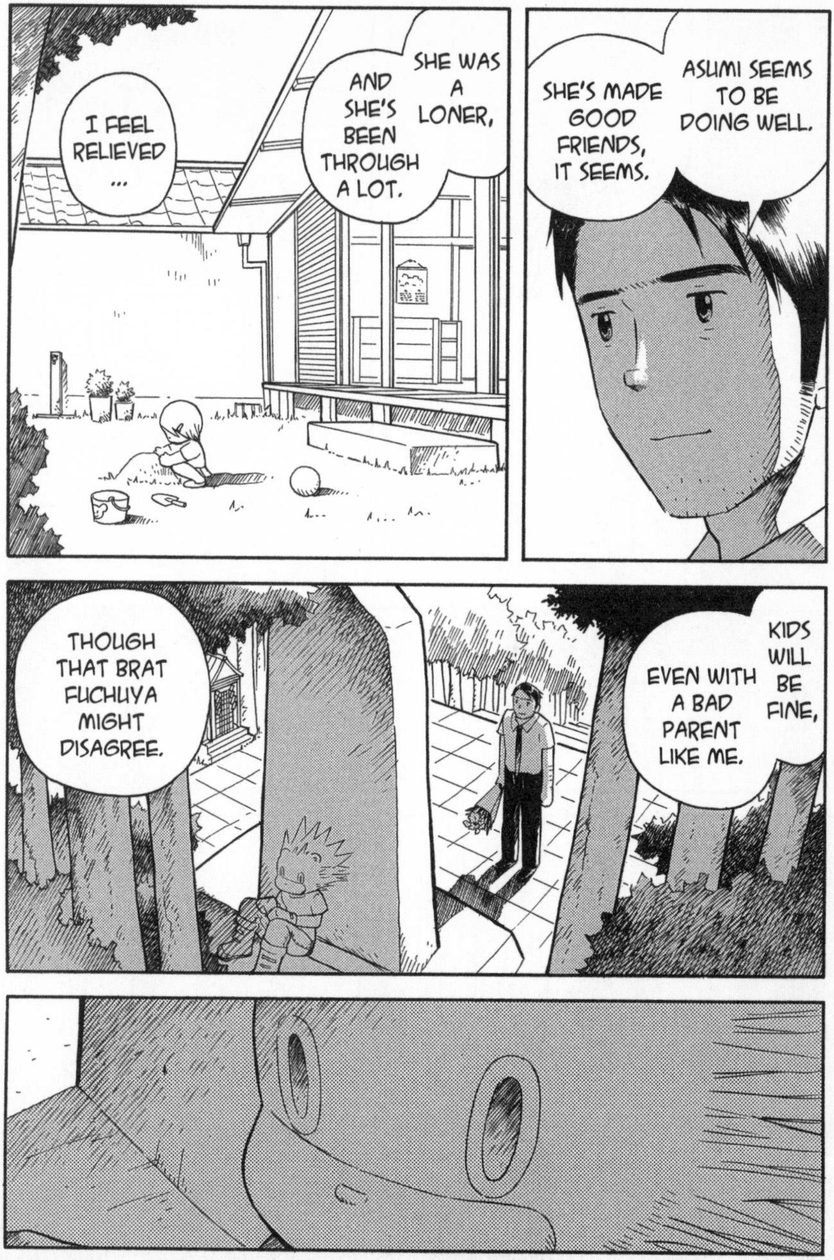
ASUMI SEEMS TO BE DOING WELL.
SHE'S MADE GOOD FRIENDS, IT SEEMS.
SHE WAS A LONER,
AND SHE'S BEEN THROUGH A LOT.
I FEEL RELIEVED ...
KIDS WILL BE FINE,
EVEN WITH A BAD PARENT LIKE ME.
THOUGH THAT BRAT FUCHUYA MIGHT DISAGREE.

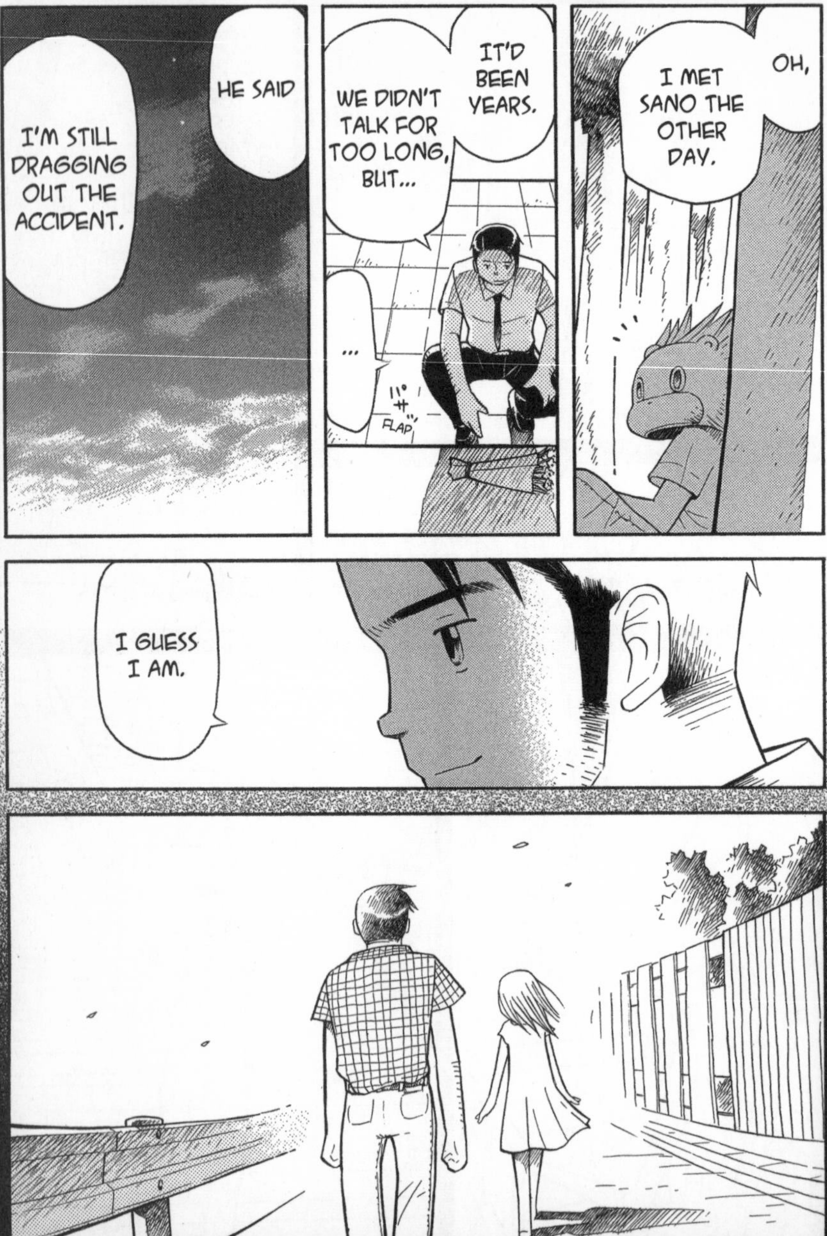
OH,
I MET SANO THE OTHER DAY.
IT'D BEEN YEARS.
WE DIDN'T TALK FOR TOO LONG, BUT...
...
FLAP
HE SAID
I'M STILL DRAGGING OUT THE ACCIDENT.
I GUESS I AM.

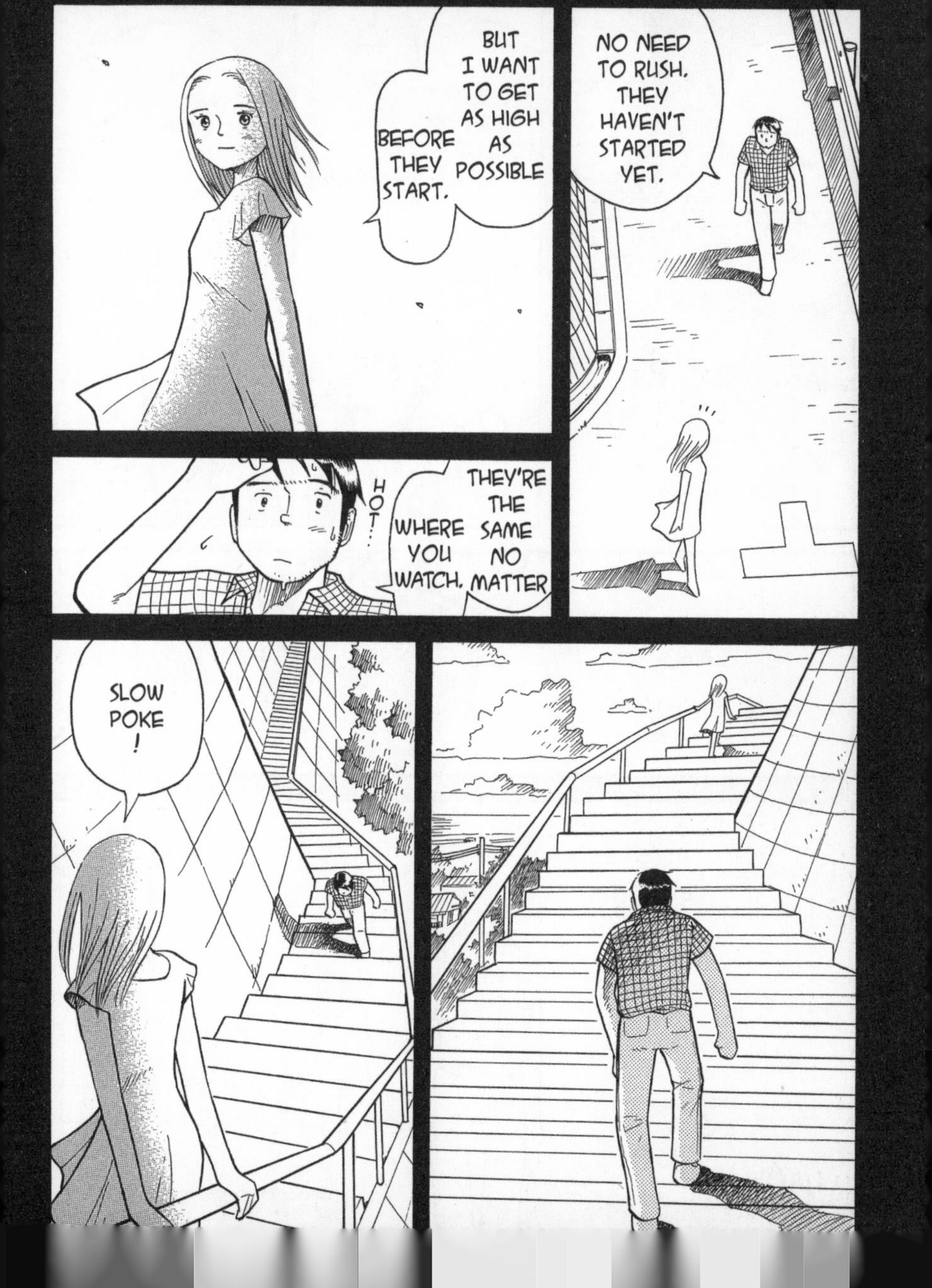
NO NEED TO RUSH. THEY HAVEN'T STARTED YET.
BUT I WANT TO GET AS HIGH AS POSSIBLE BEFORE THEY START.
THEY'RE THE SAME NO MATTER WHERE YOU WATCH.
HOT...
SLOW POKE!

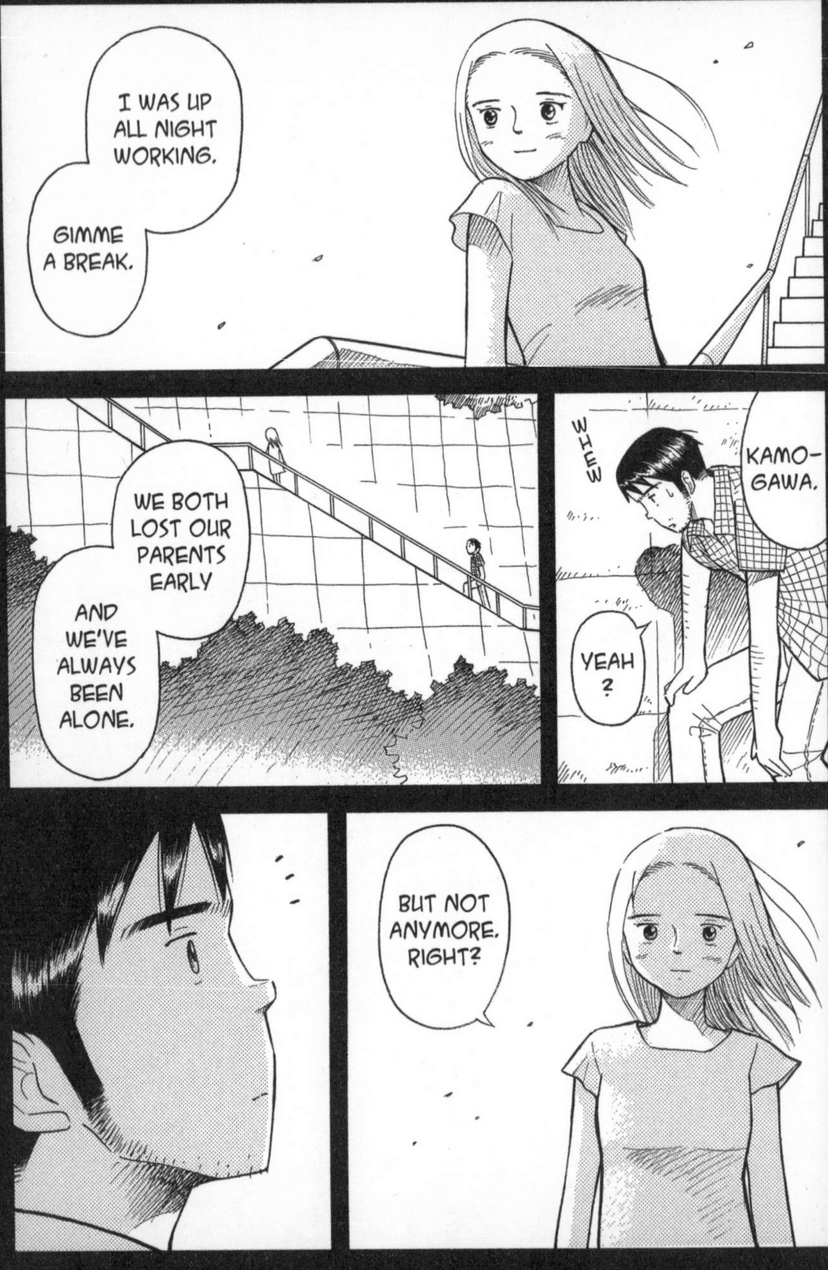
I WAS UP ALL NIGHT WORKING.
GIMME A BREAK.
KAMO-GAWA.
WHEW
YEAH?
WE BOTH LOST OUR PARENTS EARLY
AND WE'VE ALWAYS BEEN ALONE.
BUT NOT ANYMORE. RIGHT?

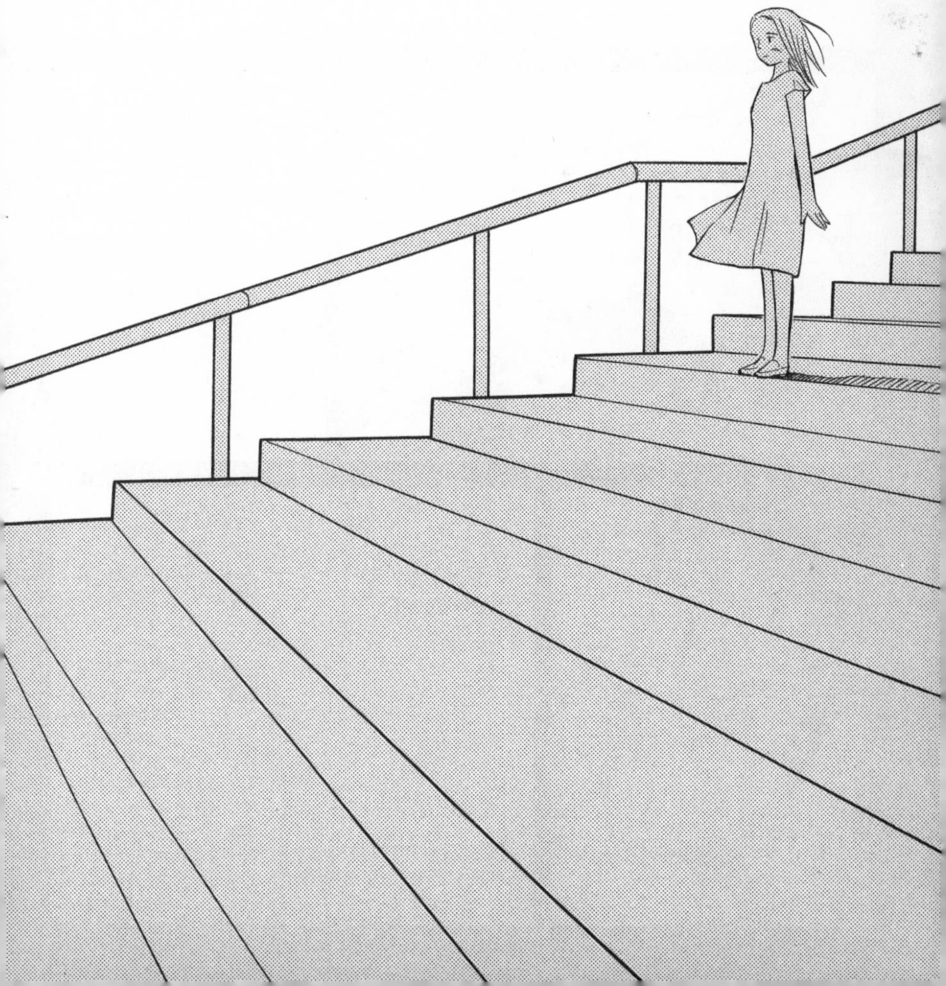

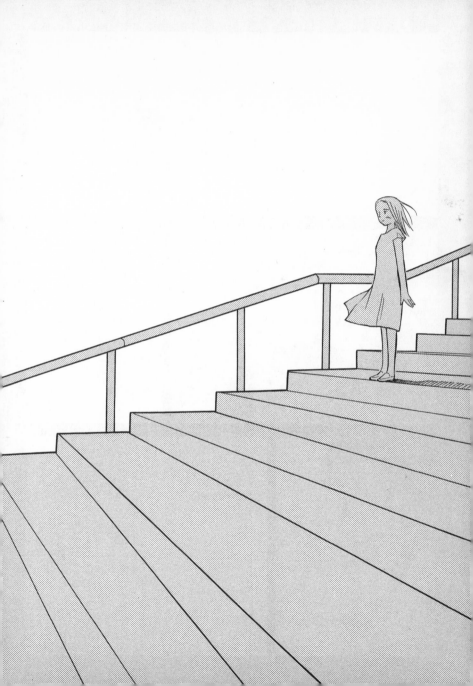

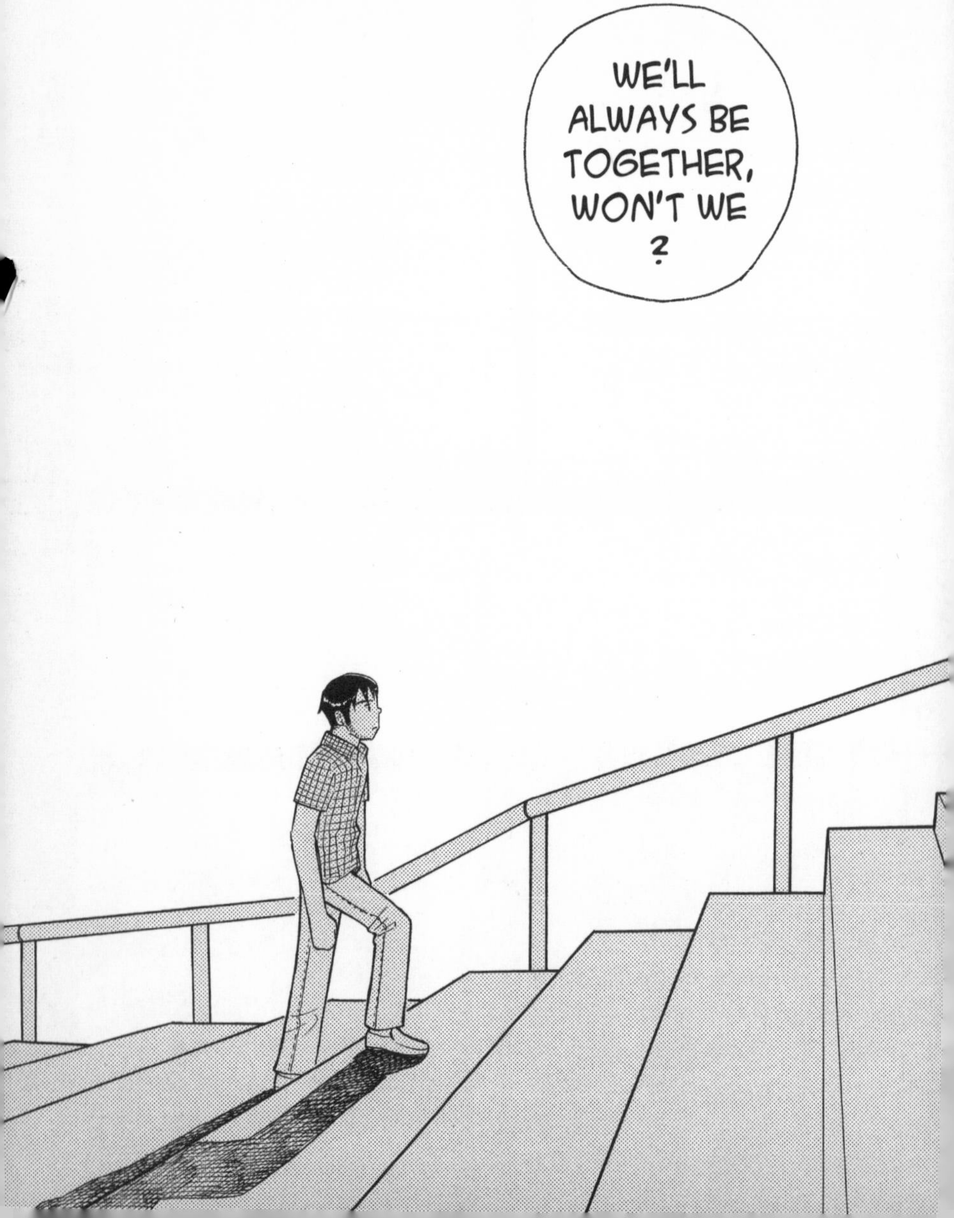
WE'LL ALWAYS BE TOGETHER, WON'T WE ?

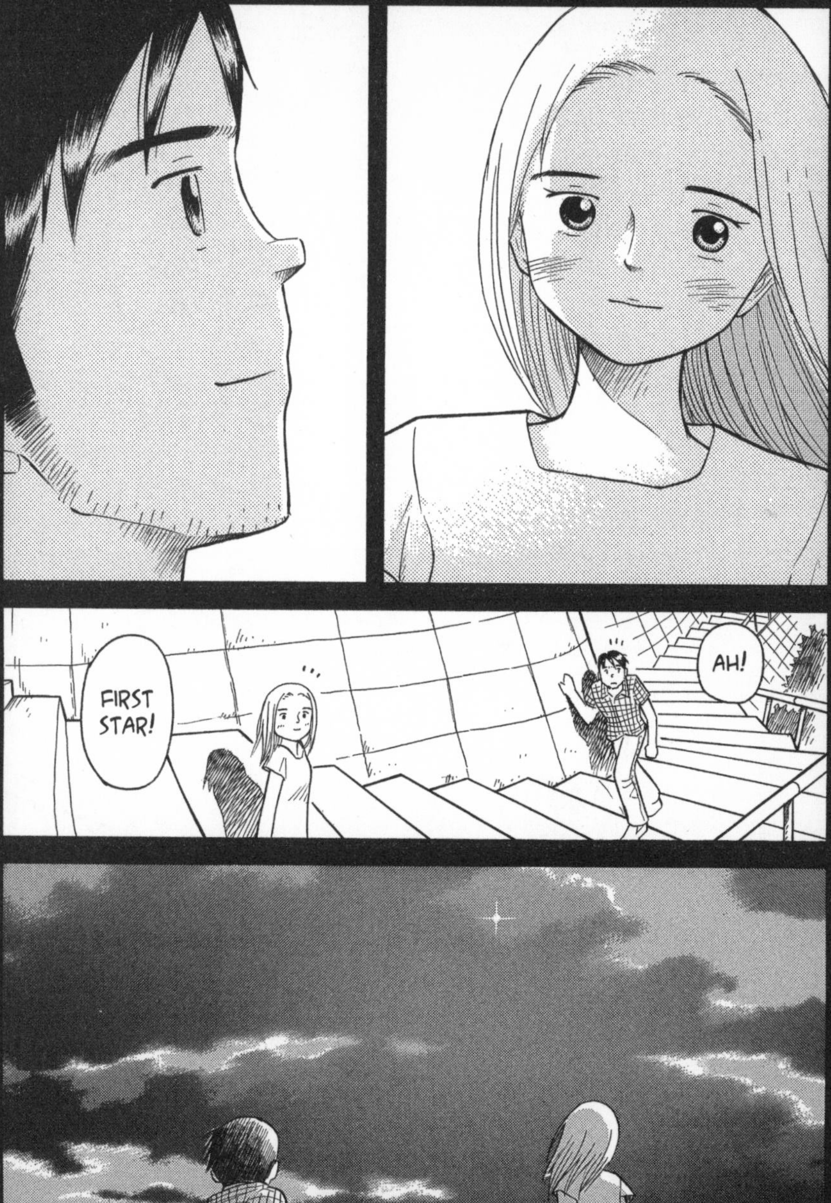
AH!
FIRST STAR!

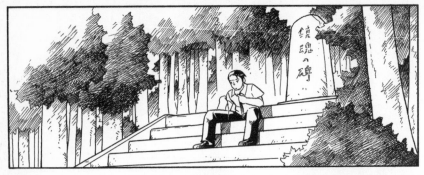

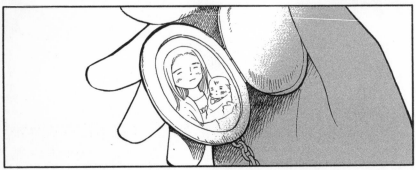

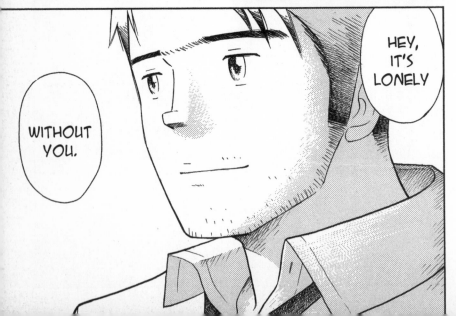

HEY, IT'S LONELY

WITHOUT YOU.

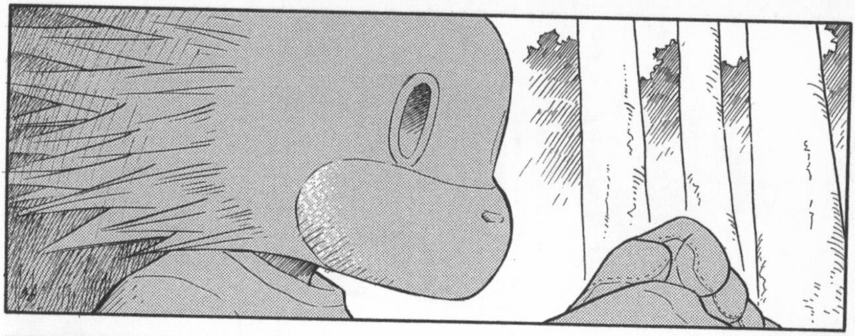

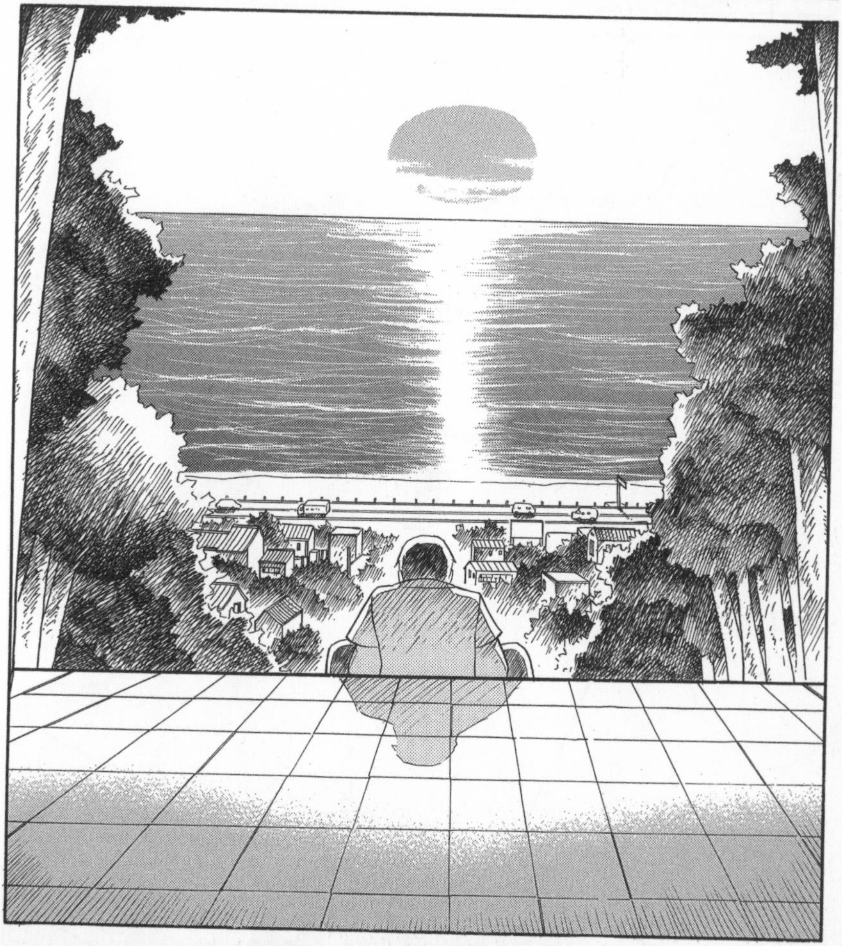

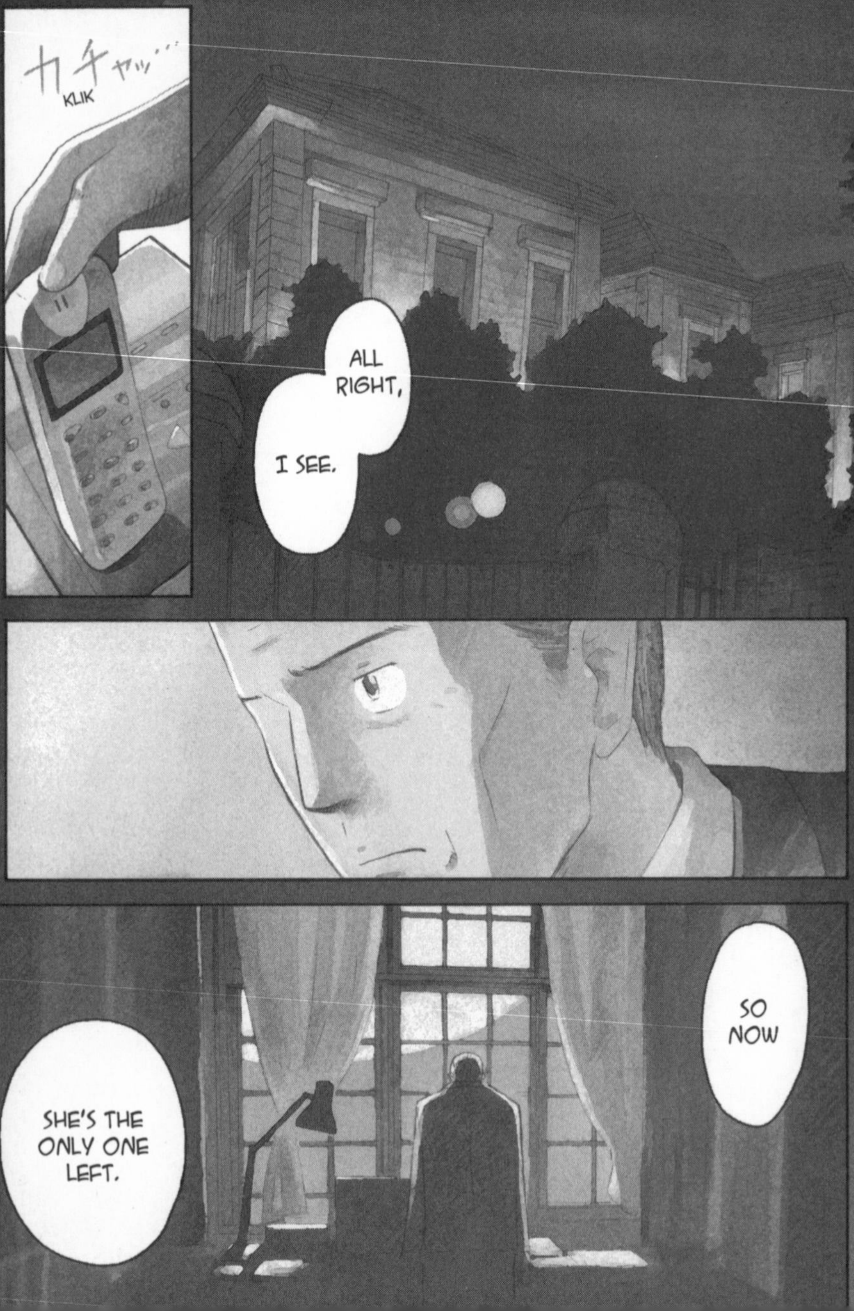
ALL RIGHT,
I SEE.
カチャッ…
KLIK
SO NOW
SHE'S THE ONLY ONE LEFT.

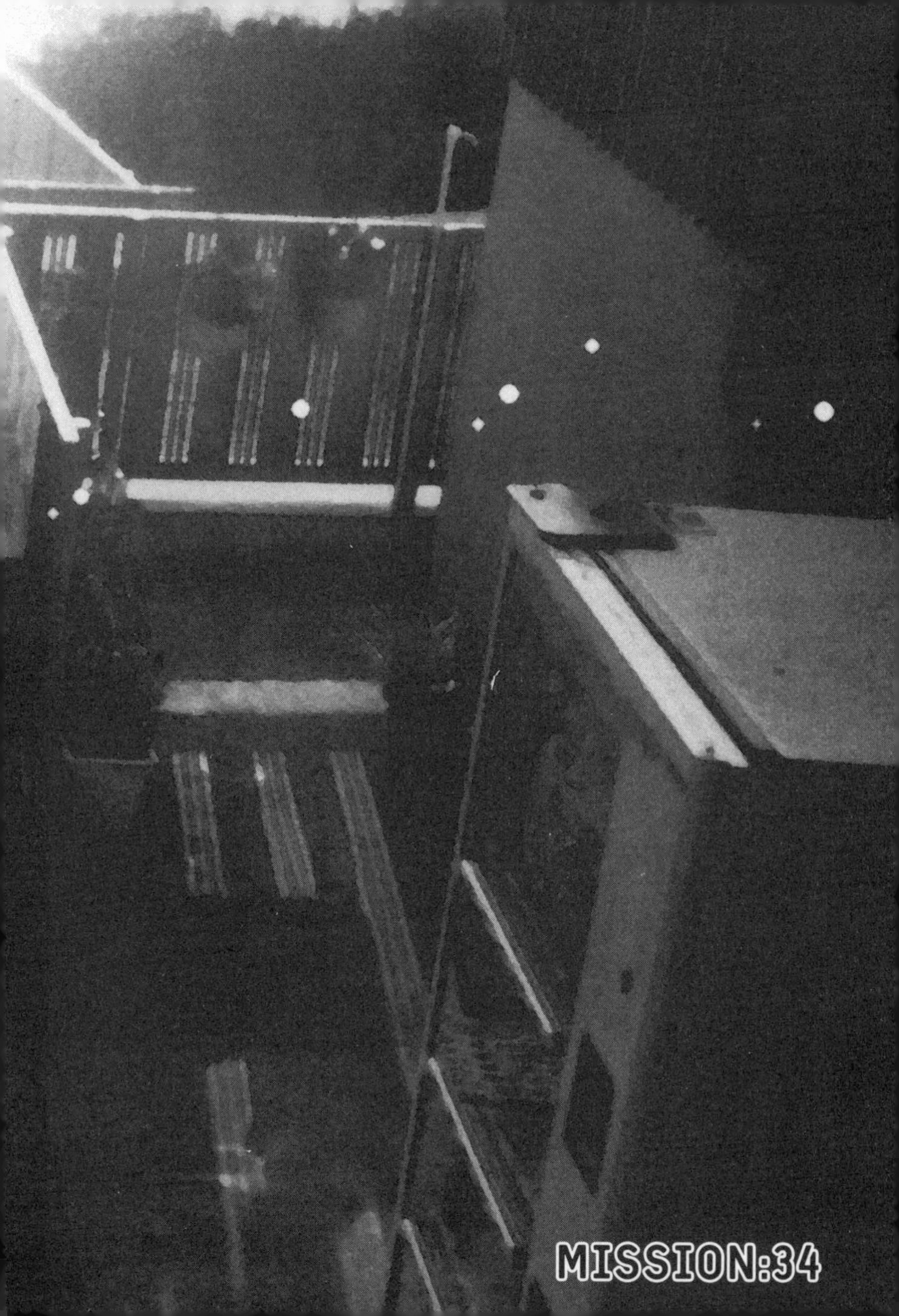

MISSION:34

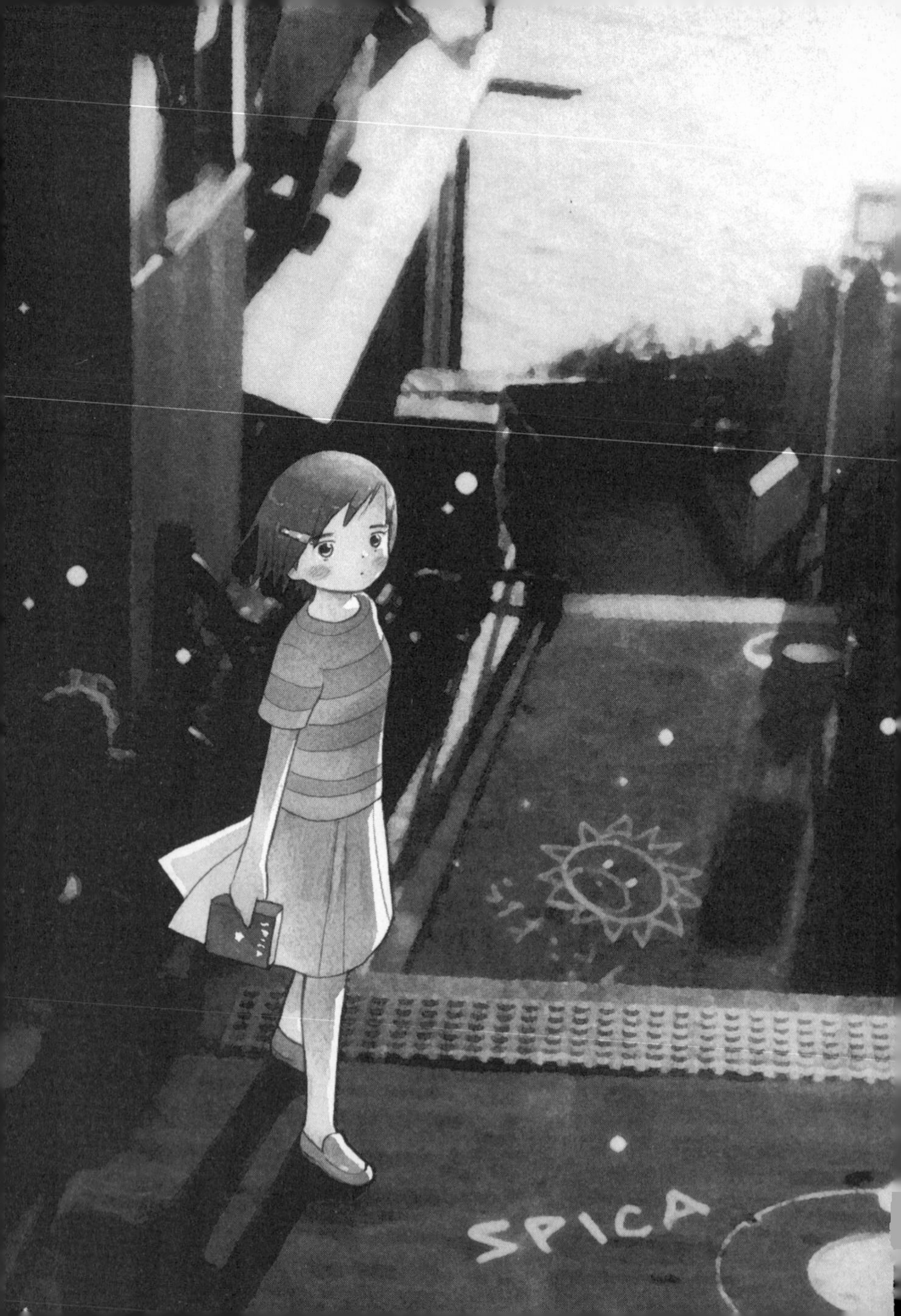
SPICA
SPICA

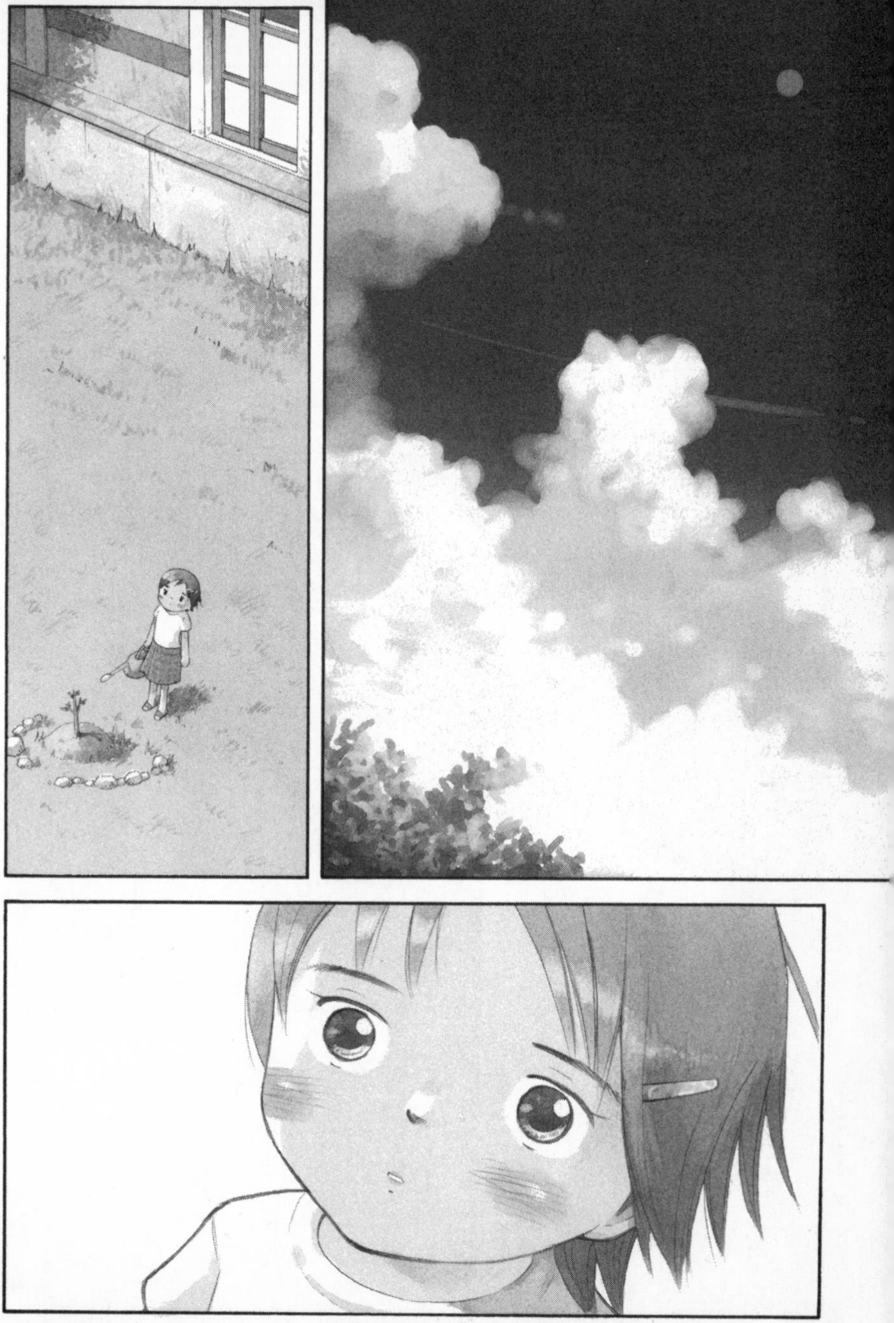

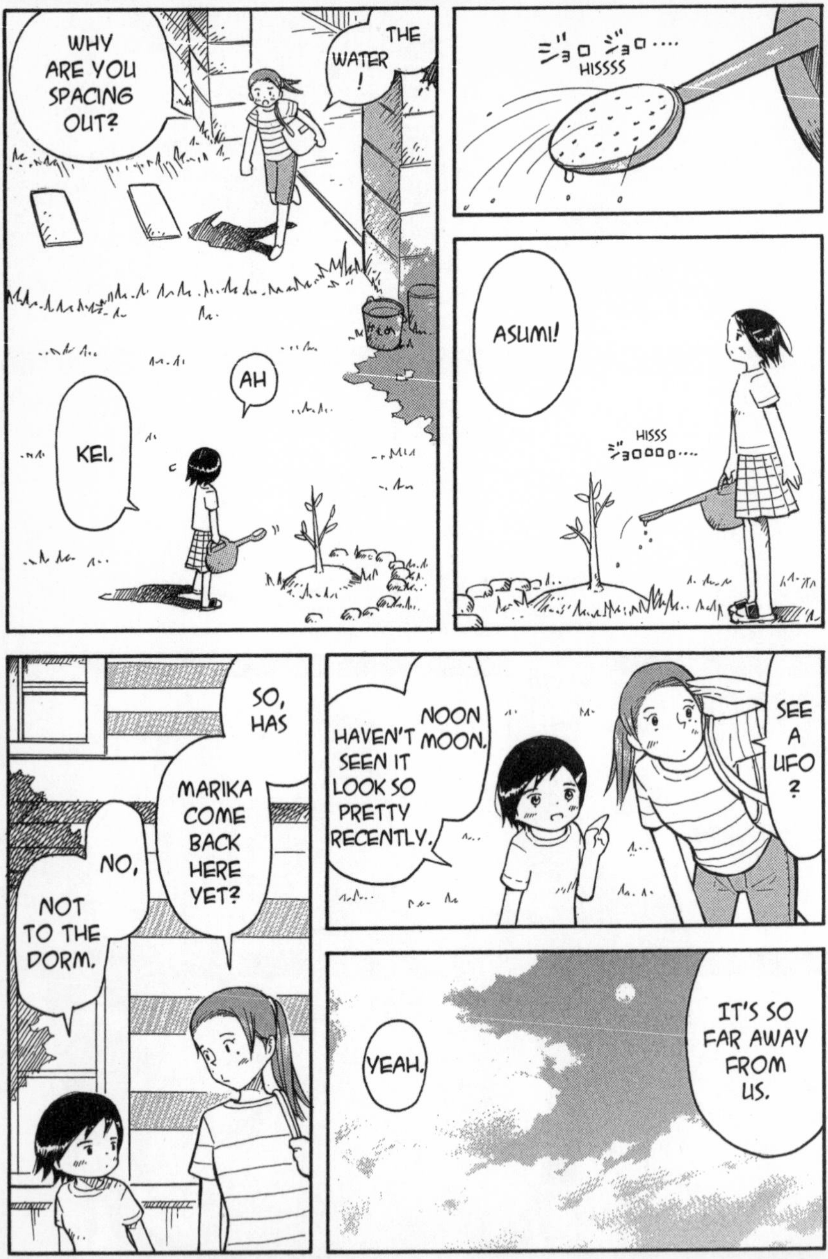
ジョロ ジョロ….
HISSSS
ASUMI!
HISSS
ジョロロロロ….
THE WATER!
WHY ARE YOU SPACING OUT?
AH
KEI.
SEE A UFO?
NOON MOON. HAVEN'T SEEN IT LOOK SO PRETTY RECENTLY.
IT'S SO FAR AWAY FROM US.
YEAH.
SO, HAS MARIKA COME BACK HERE YET?
NO, NOT TO THE DORM.

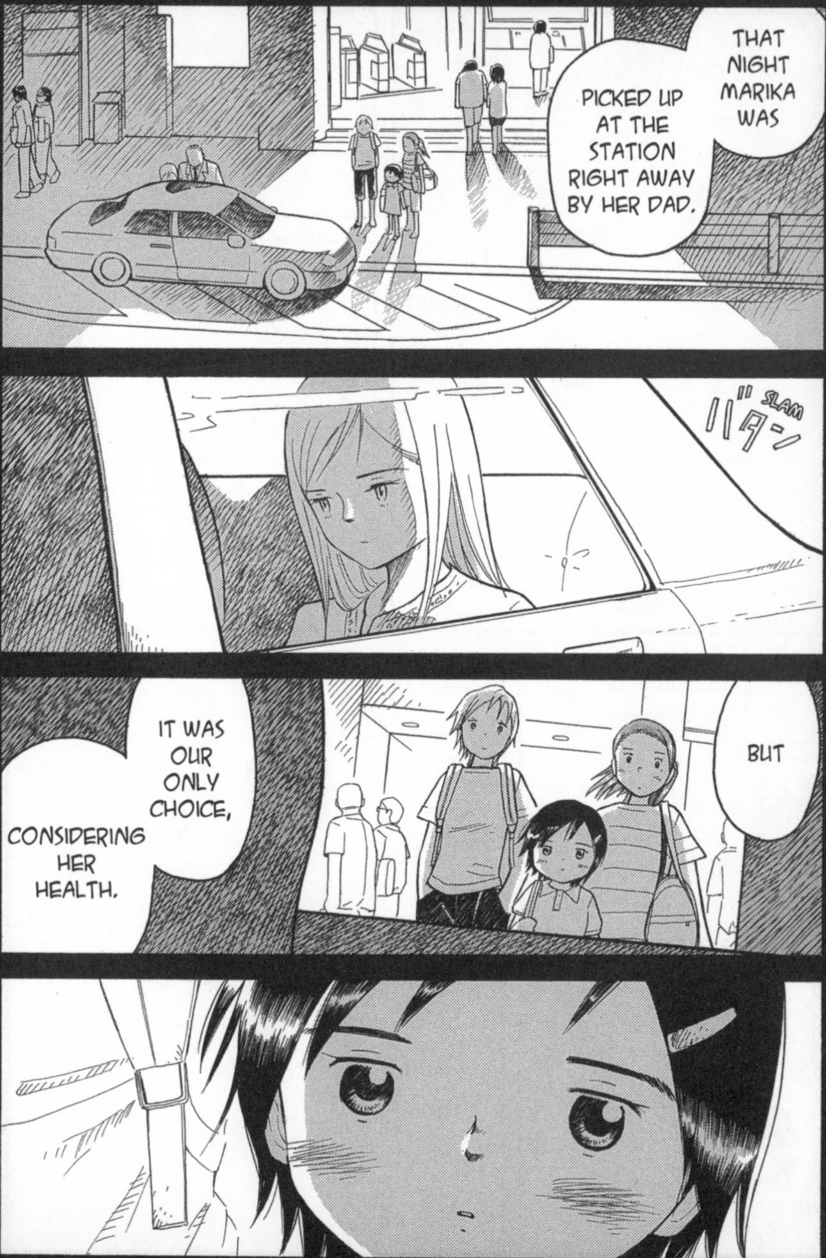
THAT NIGHT MARIKA WAS
PICKED UP AT THE STATION RIGHT AWAY BY HER DAD.
SLAM
バタン
BUT
IT WAS OUR ONLY CHOICE,
CONSIDERING HER HEALTH.

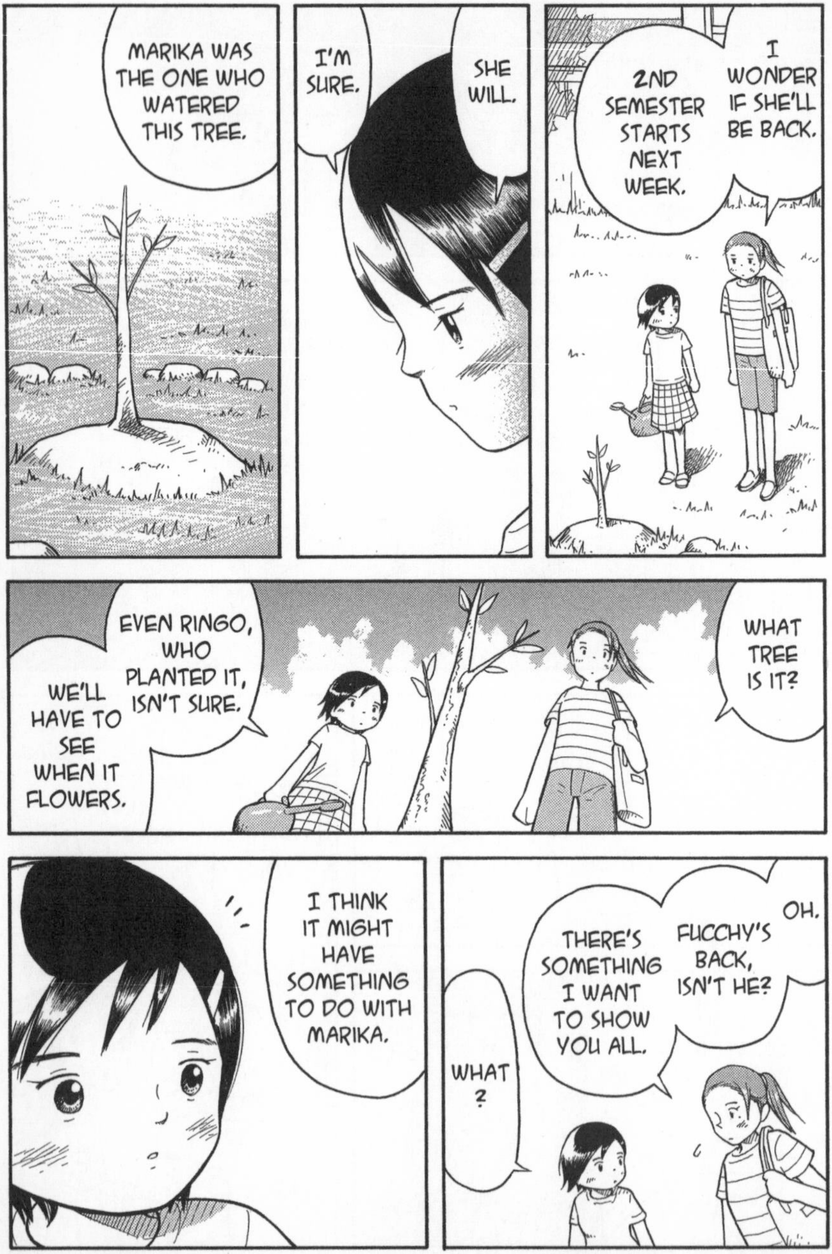
I WONDER IF SHE'LL BE BACK.
2ND SEMESTER STARTS NEXT WEEK.
SHE WILL.
I'M SURE.
MARIKA WAS THE ONE WHO WATERED THIS TREE.
WHAT TREE IS IT?
EVEN RINGO, WHO PLANTED IT, ISN'T SURE.
WE'LL HAVE TO SEE WHEN IT FLOWERS.
OH.
FUCCHY'S BACK, ISN'T HE?
THERE'S SOMETHING I WANT TO SHOW YOU ALL.
WHAT?
I THINK IT MIGHT HAVE SOMETHING TO DO WITH MARIKA.

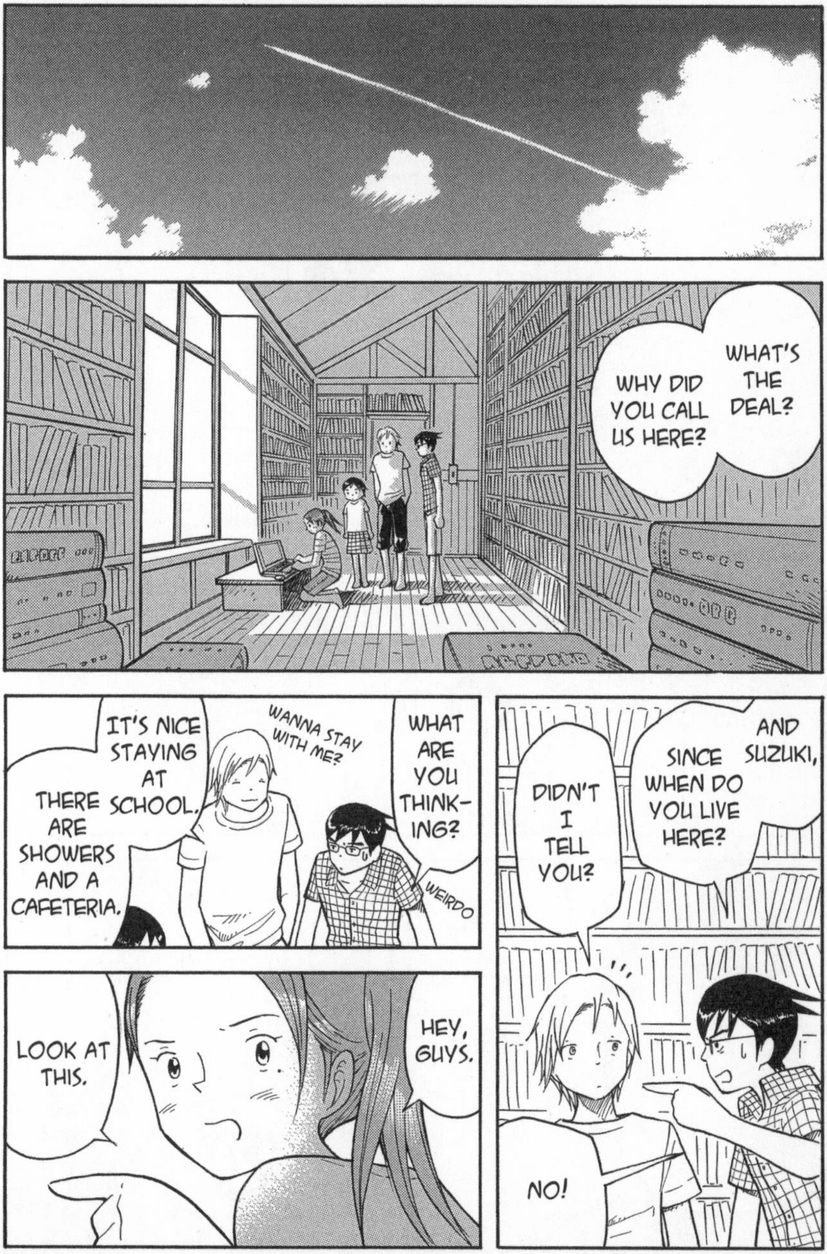
WHAT'S THE DEAL?
WHY DID YOU CALL US HERE?
AND SUZUKI, SINCE WHEN DO YOU LIVE HERE?
DIDN'T I TELL YOU?
NO!
WHAT ARE YOU THINKING?
WANNA STAY WITH ME?
IT'S NICE STAYING AT SCHOOL.
THERE ARE SHOWERS AND A CAFETERIA.
WEIRDO
HEY, GUYS.
LOOK AT THIS.

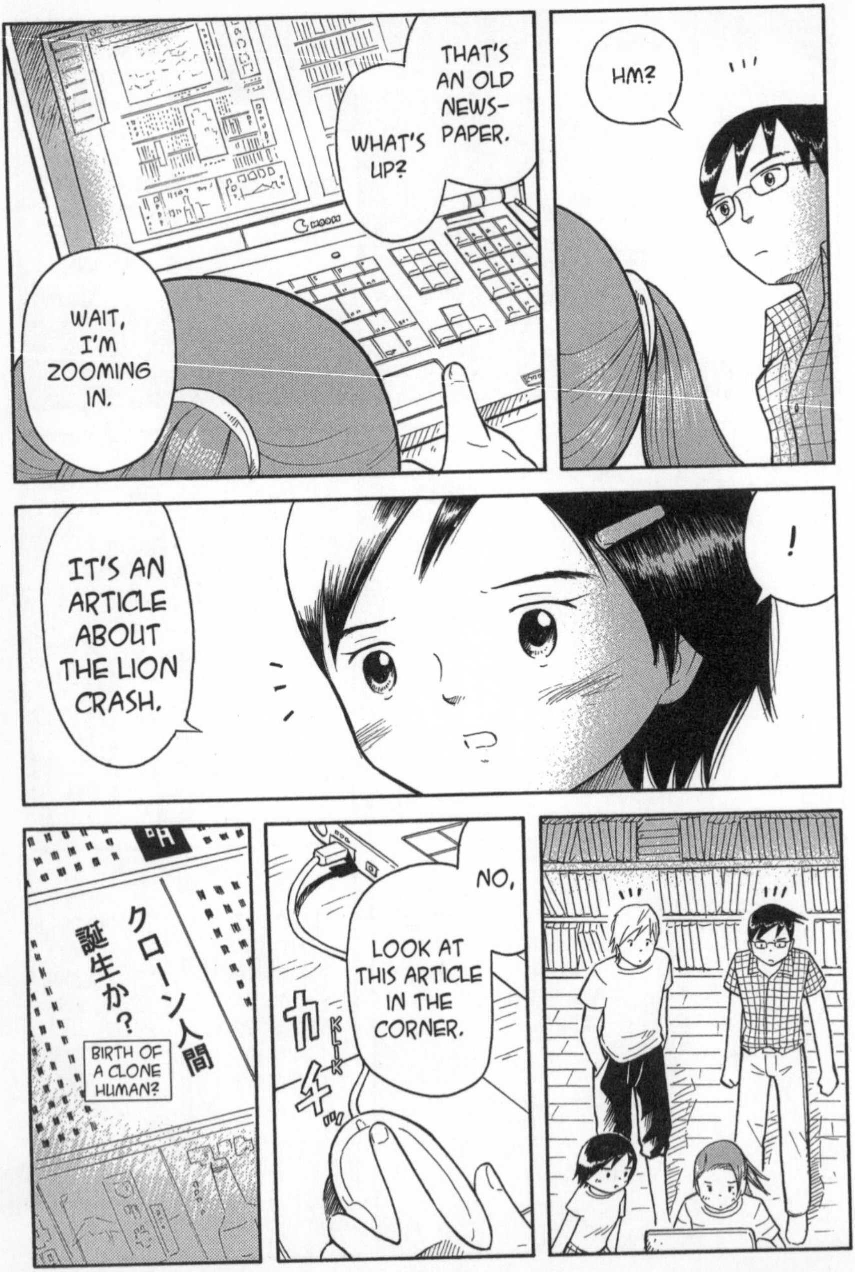
HM?
THAT'S AN OLD NEWS-PAPER.
WHAT'S UP?
WAIT, I'M ZOOMING IN.
!
IT'S AN ARTICLE ABOUT THE LION CRASH.
NO,
LOOK AT THIS ARTICLE IN THE CORNER.
カチッ
KLIK
クローン人間誕生か？
BIRTH OF A CLONE HUMAN?

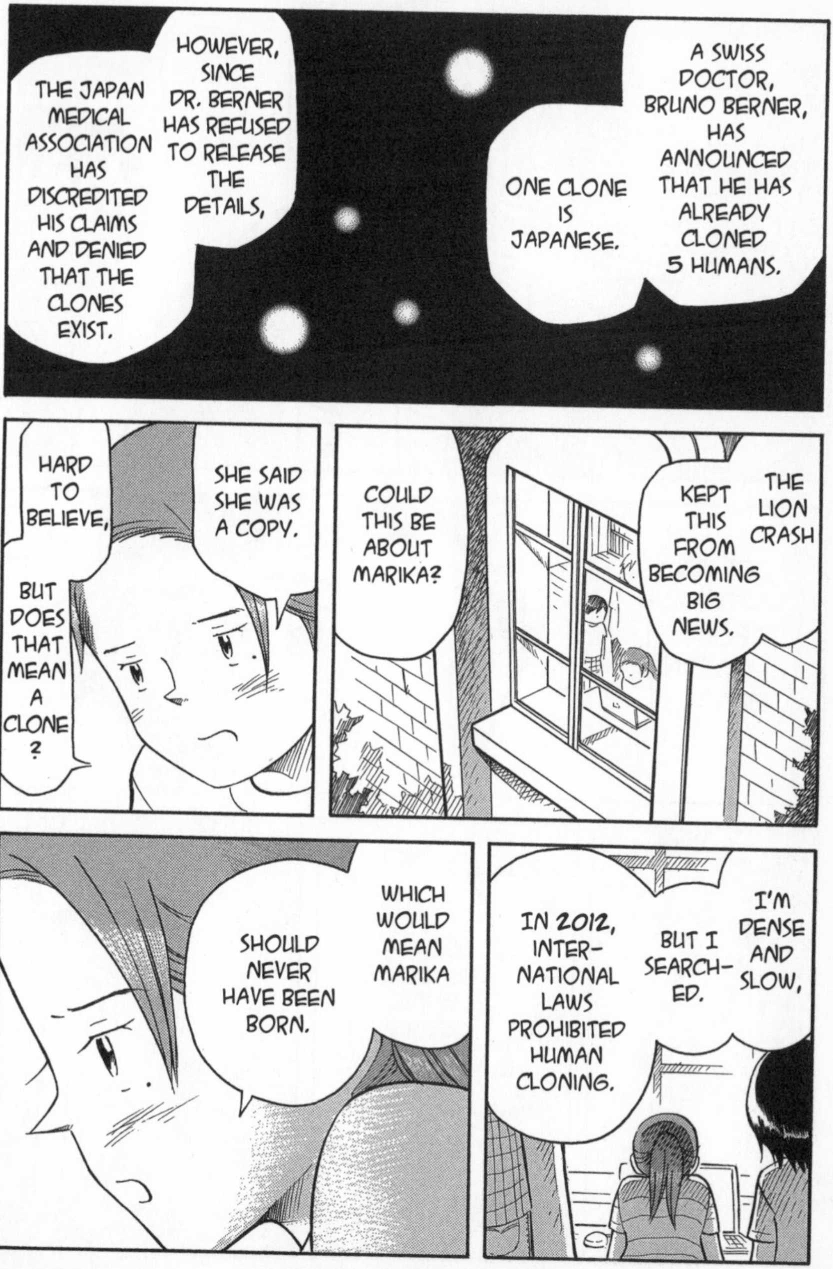
A SWISS DOCTOR, BRUNO BERNER, HAS ANNOUNCED THAT HE HAS ALREADY CLONED 5 HUMANS.
ONE CLONE IS JAPANESE.
HOWEVER, SINCE DR. BERNER HAS REFUSED TO RELEASE THE DETAILS,
THE JAPAN MEDICAL ASSOCIATION HAS DISCREDITED HIS CLAIMS AND DENIED THAT THE CLONES EXIST.
THE LION CRASH
KEPT THIS FROM BECOMING BIG NEWS.
COULD THIS BE ABOUT MARIKA?
SHE SAID SHE WAS A COPY.
HARD TO BELIEVE,
BUT DOES THAT MEAN A CLONE?
I'M DENSE AND SLOW,
BUT I SEARCH-ED.
IN 2012, INTER-NATIONAL LAWS PROHIBITED HUMAN CLONING.
WHICH WOULD MEAN MARIKA
SHOULD NEVER HAVE BEEN BORN.

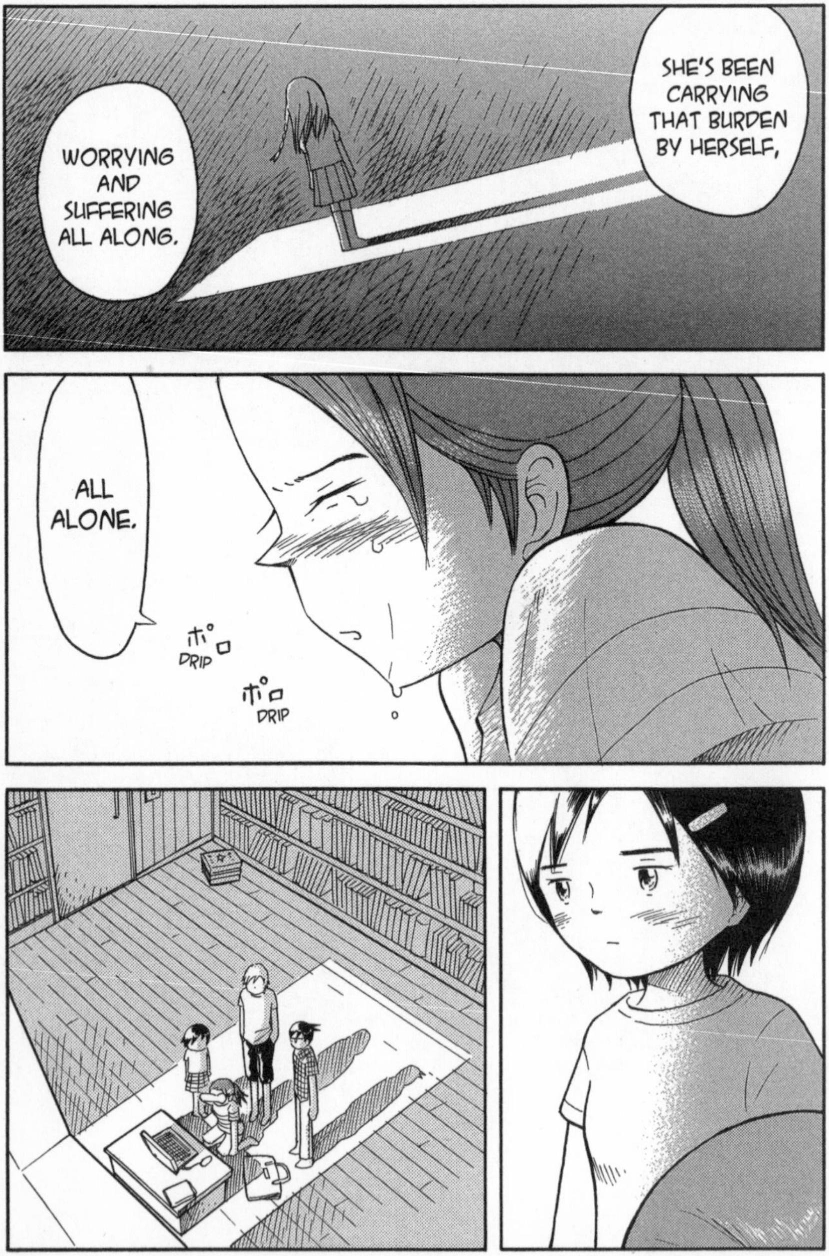
SHE'S BEEN CARRYING THAT BURDEN BY HERSELF,
WORRYING AND SUFFERING ALL ALONG.
ALL ALONE.
ポロ
DRIP
ポロ
DRIP

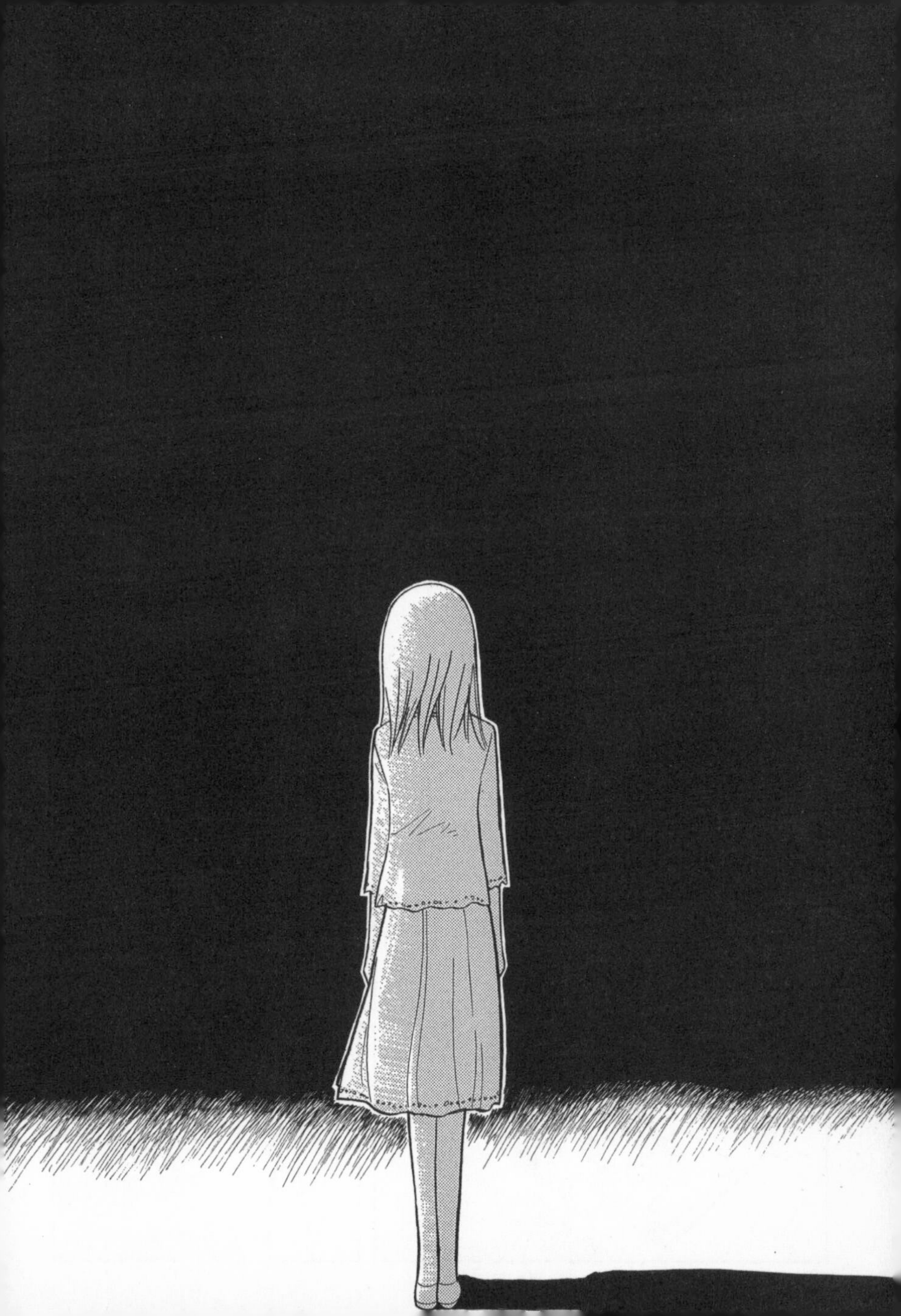

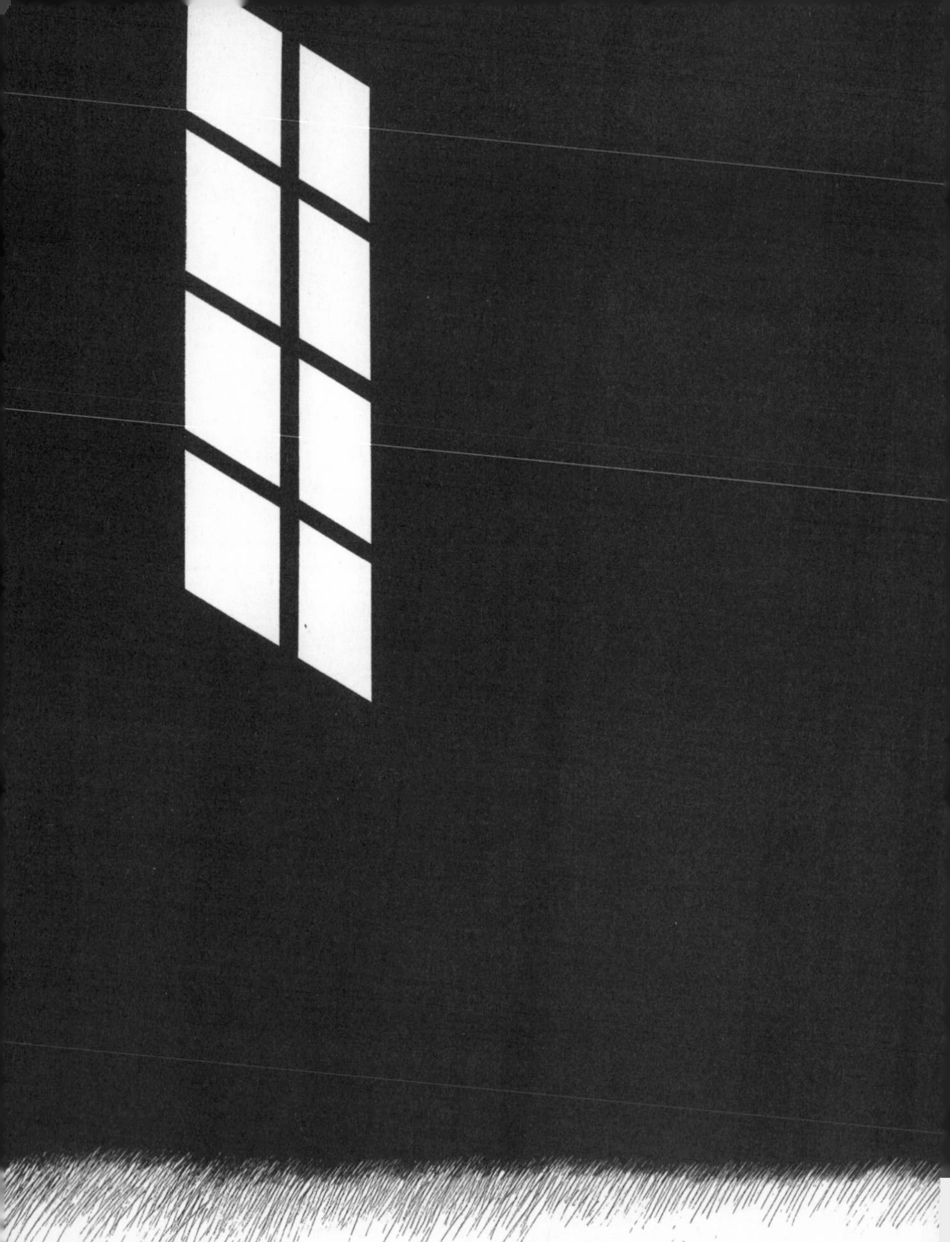

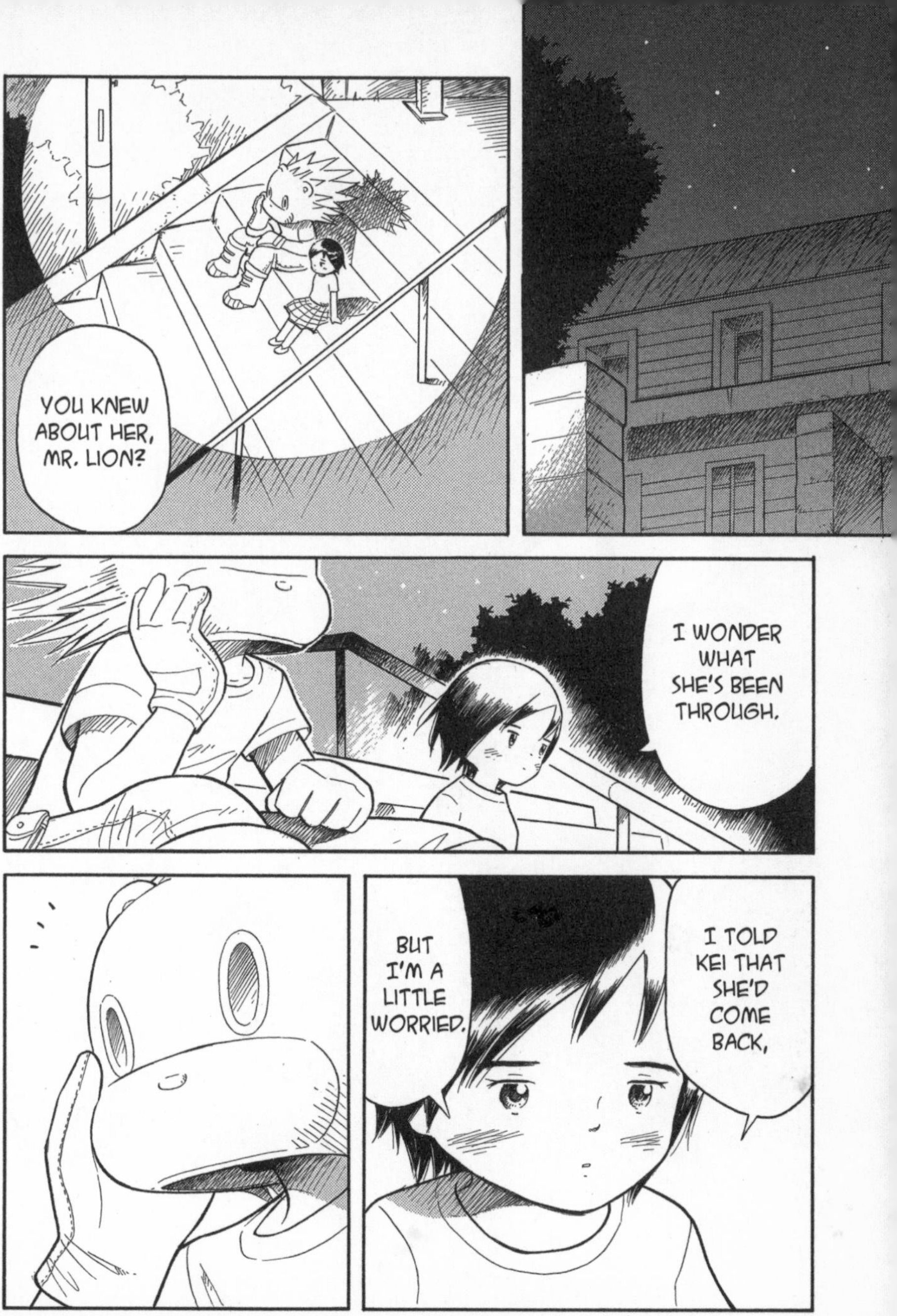
YOU KNEW ABOUT HER, MR. LION?
I WONDER WHAT SHE'S BEEN THROUGH.
I TOLD KEI THAT SHE'D COME BACK,
BUT I'M A LITTLE WORRIED.

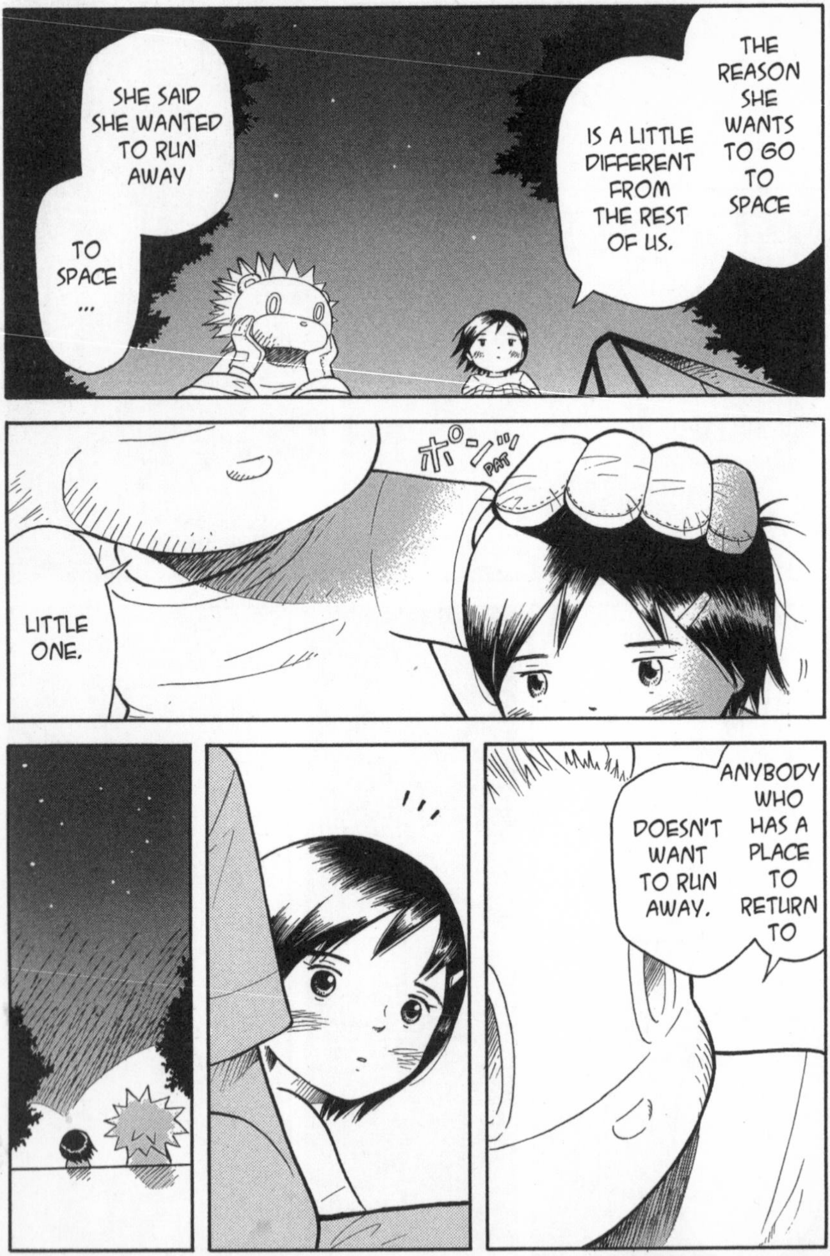
THE REASON SHE WANTS TO GO TO SPACE
IS A LITTLE DIFFERENT FROM THE REST OF US.
SHE SAID SHE WANTED TO RUN AWAY
TO SPACE ...
ポーンッ
PAT
LITTLE ONE.
ANYBODY WHO HAS A PLACE TO RETURN TO
DOESN'T WANT TO RUN AWAY.

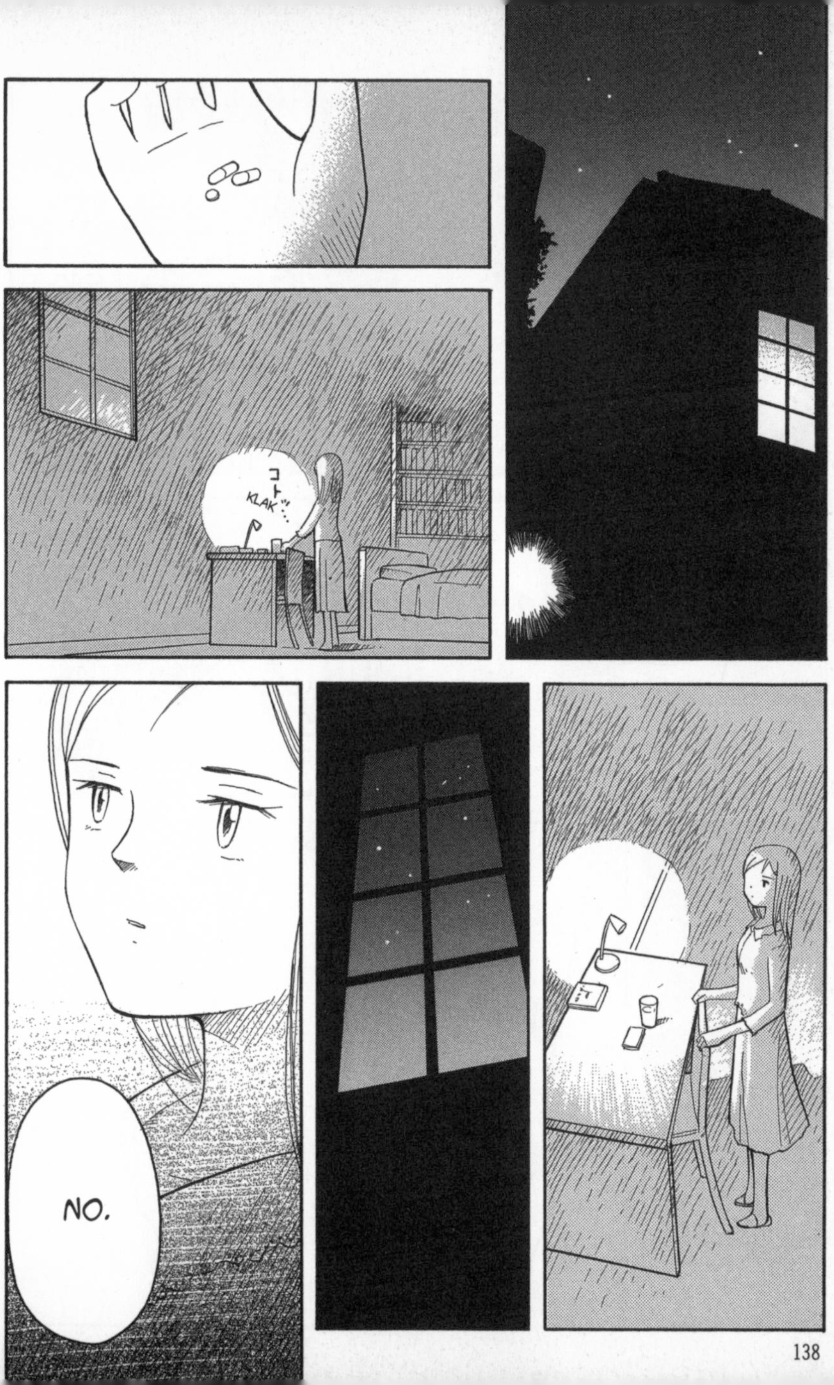
コトッ…
KLAK
NO.

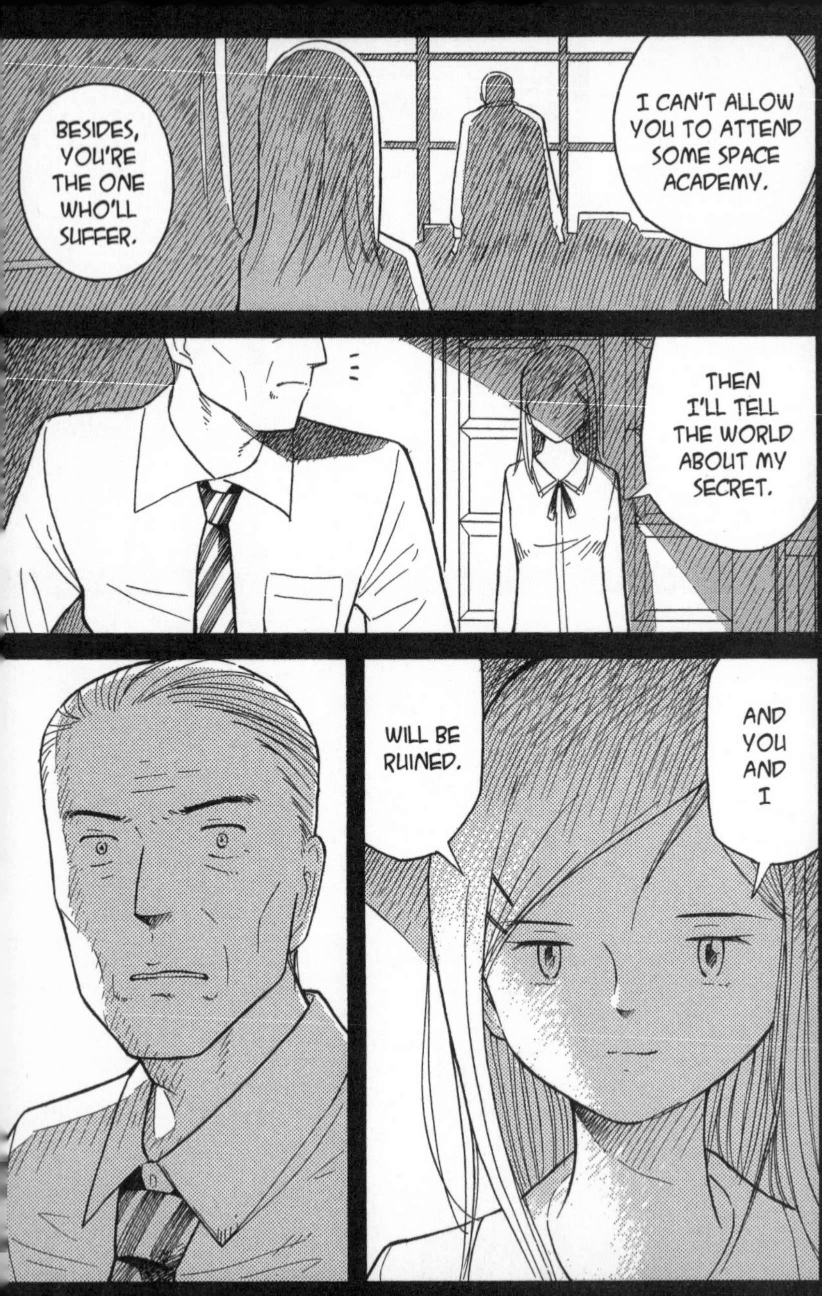
I CAN'T ALLOW YOU TO ATTEND SOME SPACE ACADEMY.
BESIDES, YOU'RE THE ONE WHO'LL SUFFER.
THEN I'LL TELL THE WORLD ABOUT MY SECRET.
AND YOU AND I
WILL BE RUINED.

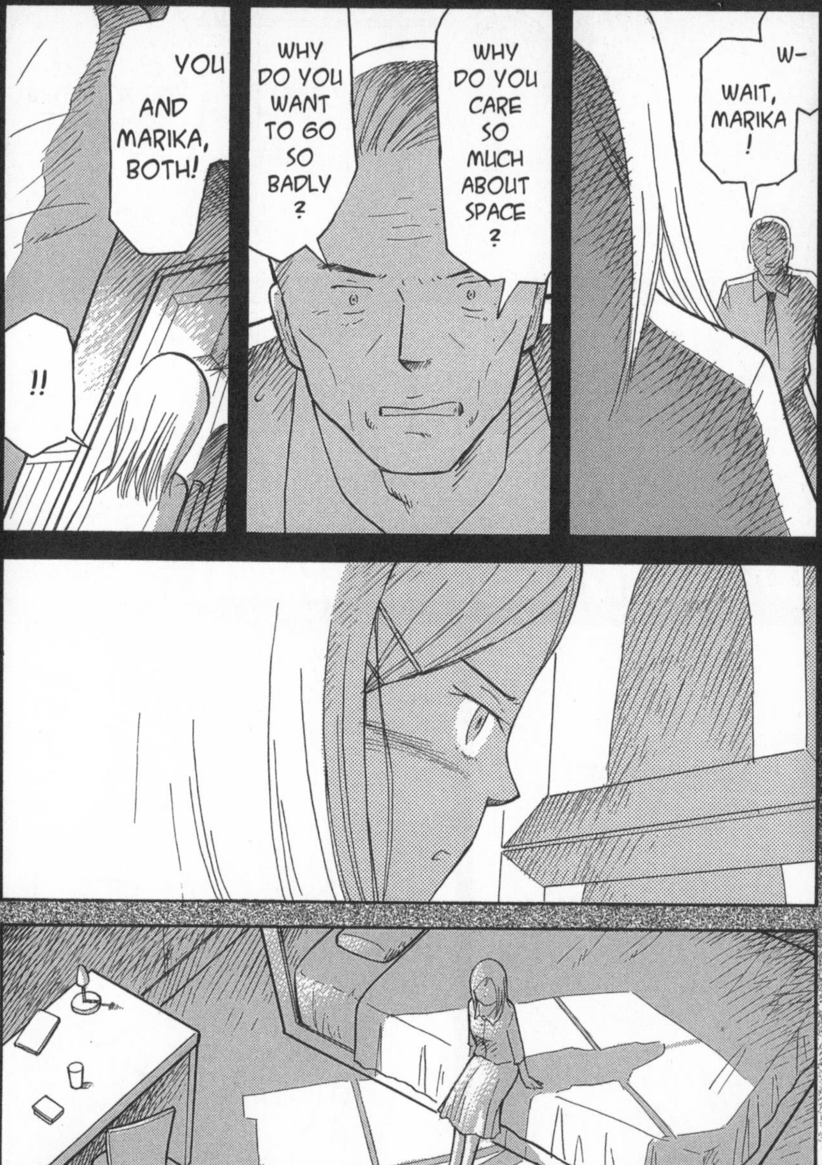
W- WAIT, MARIKA!
WHY DO YOU CARE SO MUCH ABOUT SPACE?
WHY DO YOU WANT TO GO SO BADLY?
YOU AND MARIKA, BOTH!
!!

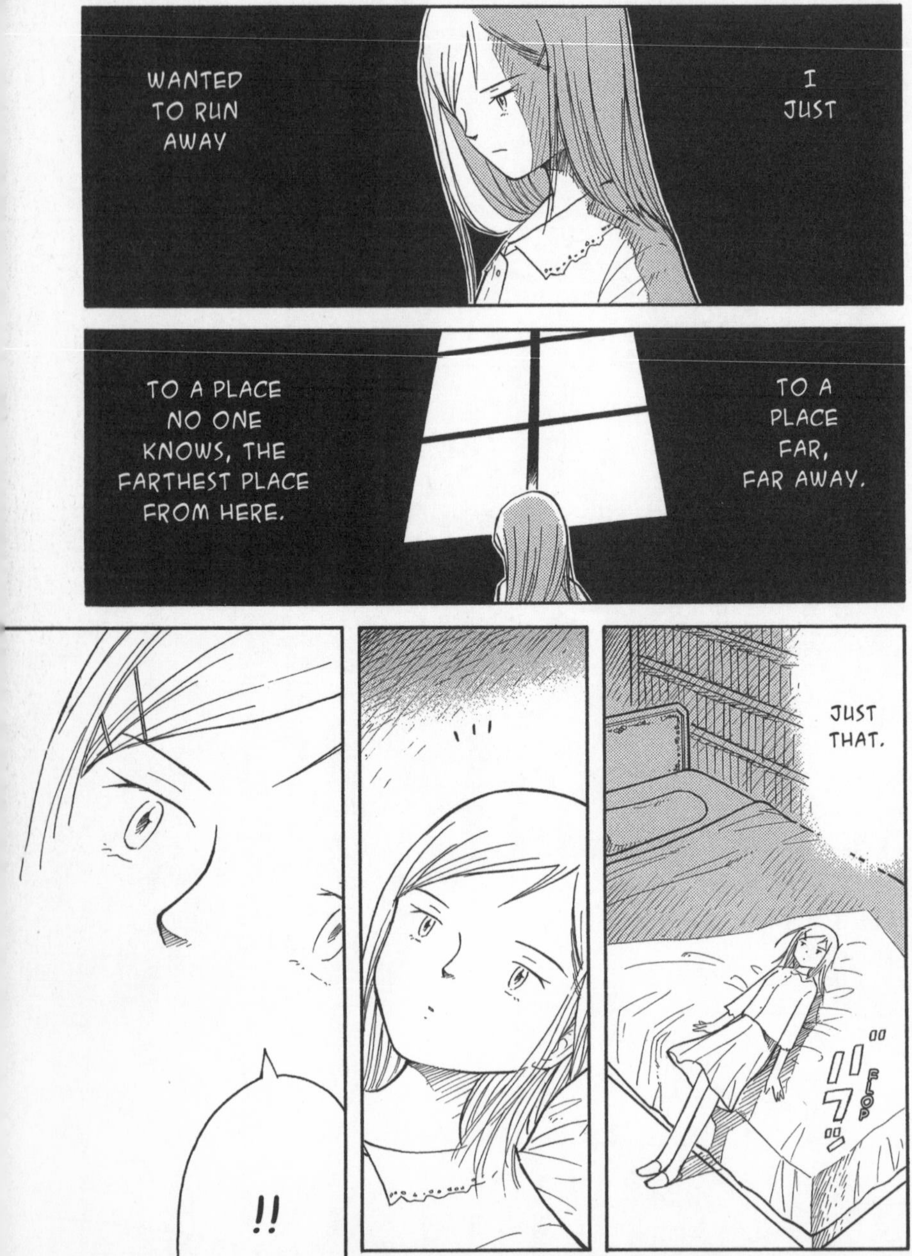

I JUST
WANTED TO RUN AWAY
TO A PLACE FAR, FAR AWAY.
TO A PLACE NO ONE KNOWS, THE FARTHEST PLACE FROM HERE.
JUST THAT.
FLOP
!!

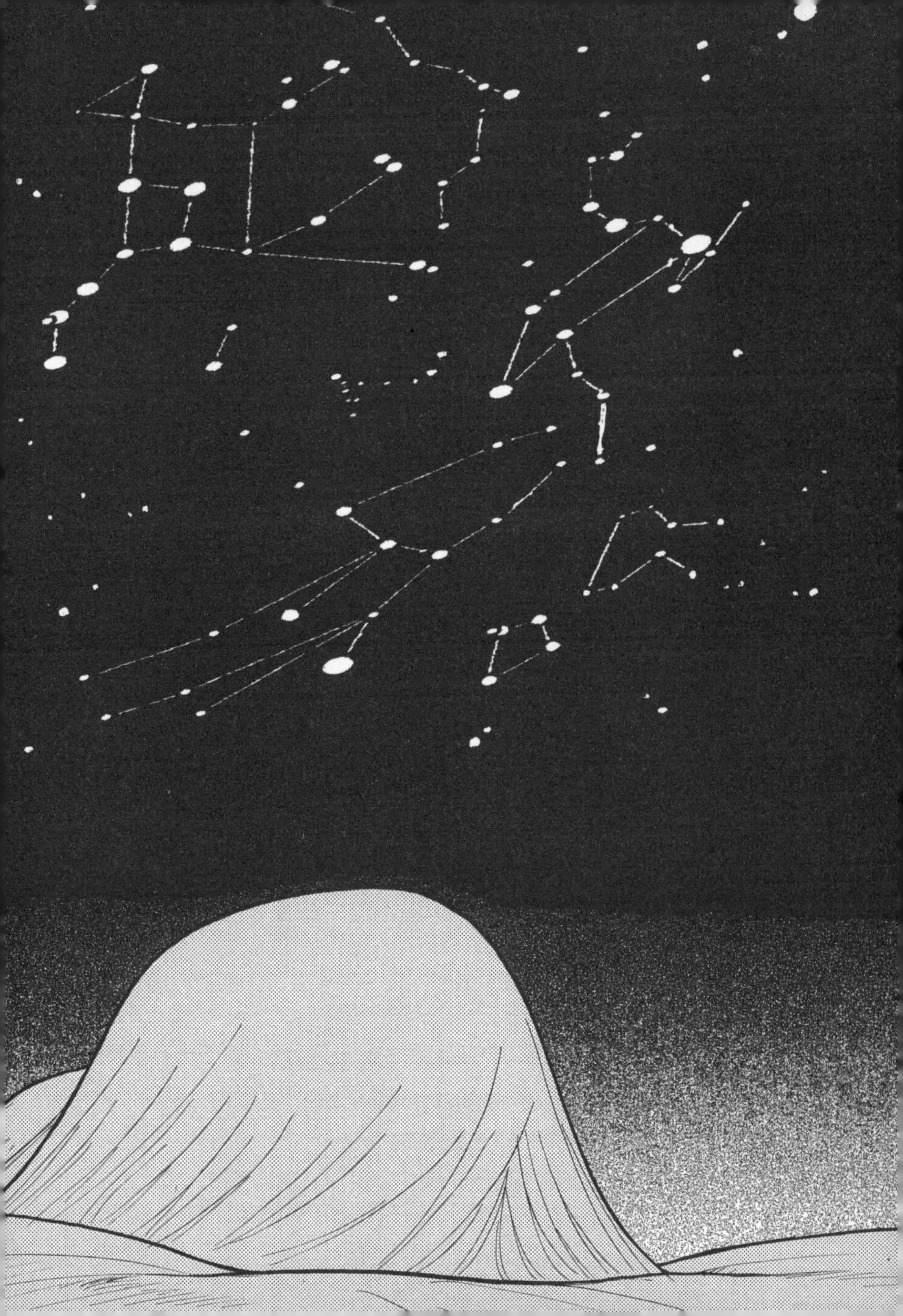

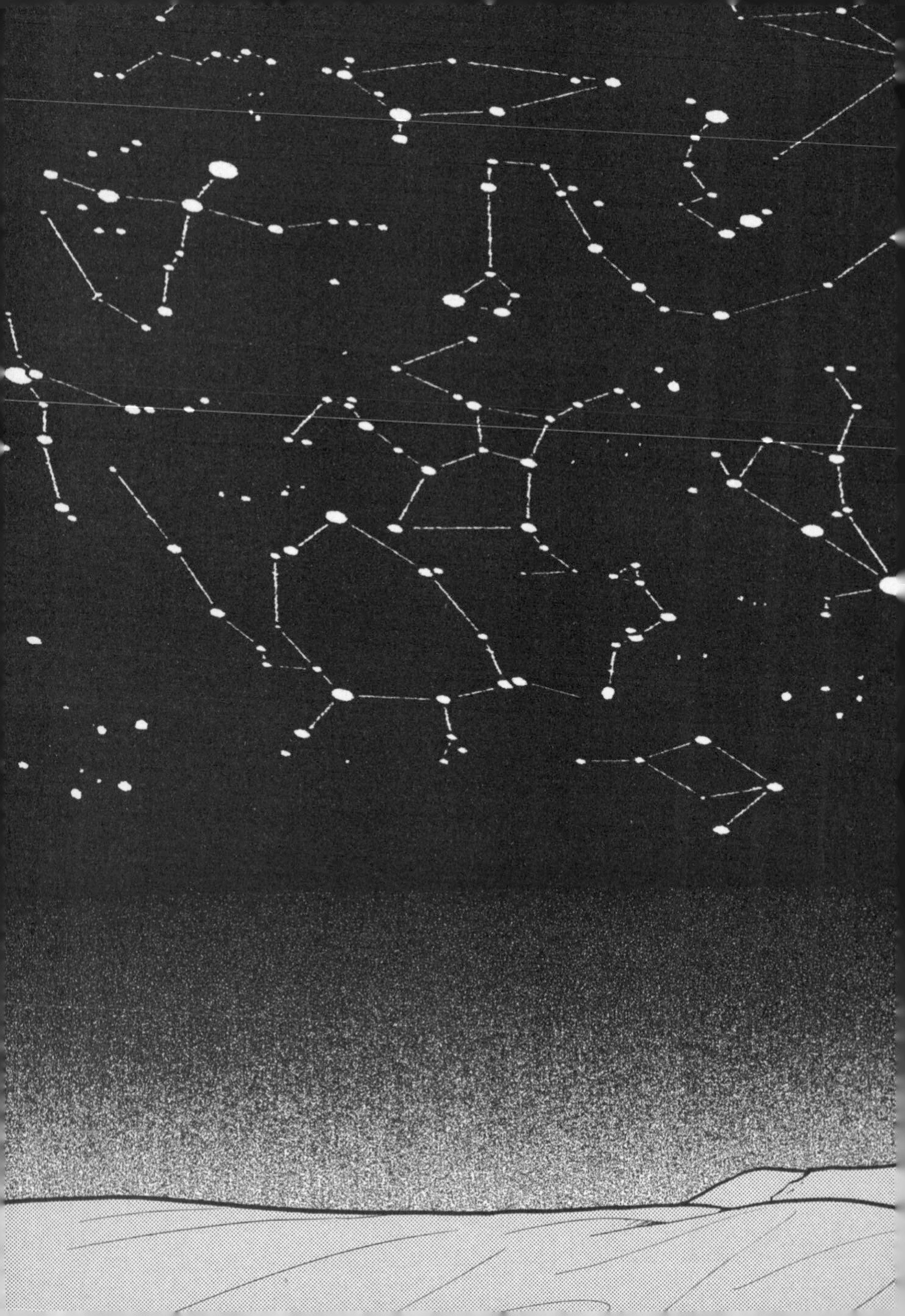

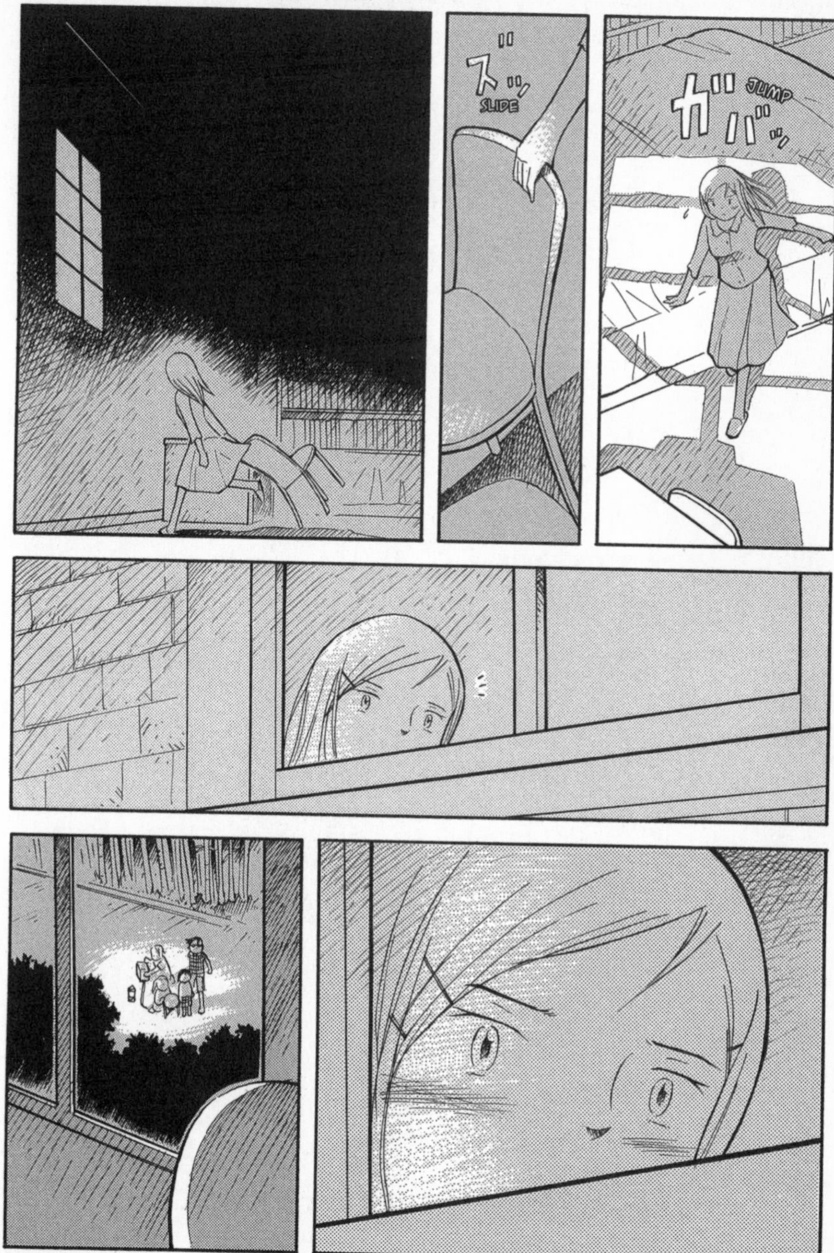
ガバッ
JUMP
ズッ
SLIDE

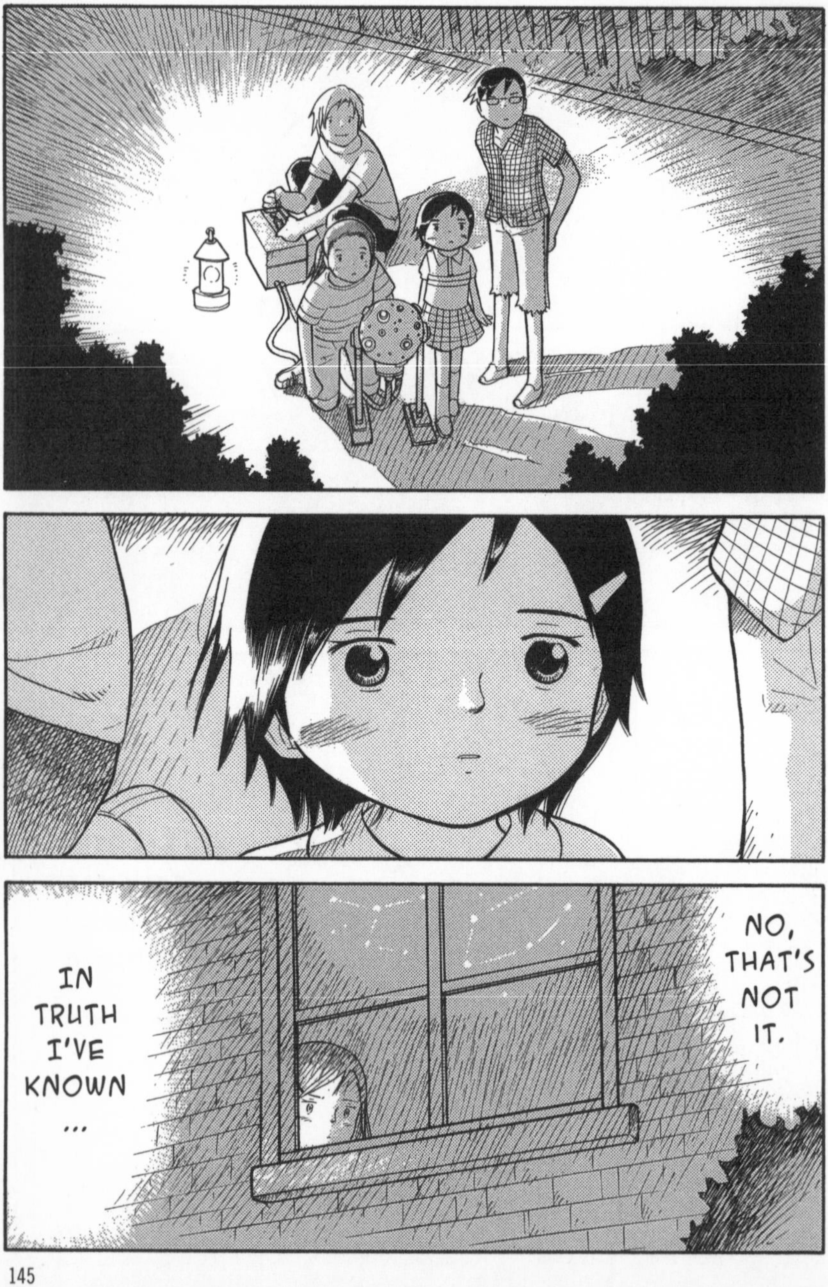
NO, THAT'S NOT IT.
IN TRUTH I'VE KNOWN ...

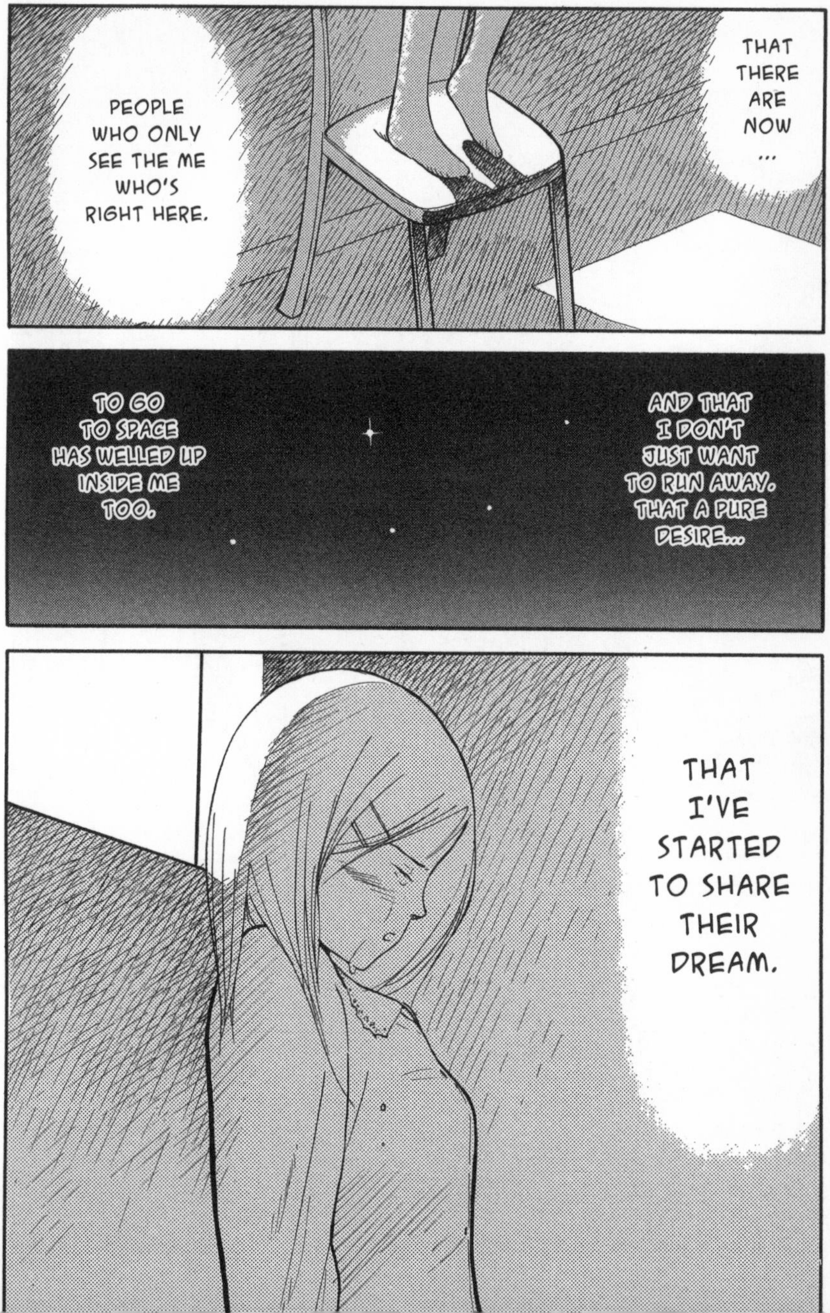
THAT THERE ARE NOW ...
PEOPLE WHO ONLY SEE THE ME WHO'S RIGHT HERE.
AND THAT I DON'T JUST WANT TO RUN AWAY. THAT A PURE DESIRE...
TO GO TO SPACE HAS WELLED UP INSIDE ME TOO.
THAT I'VE STARTED TO SHARE THEIR DREAM.

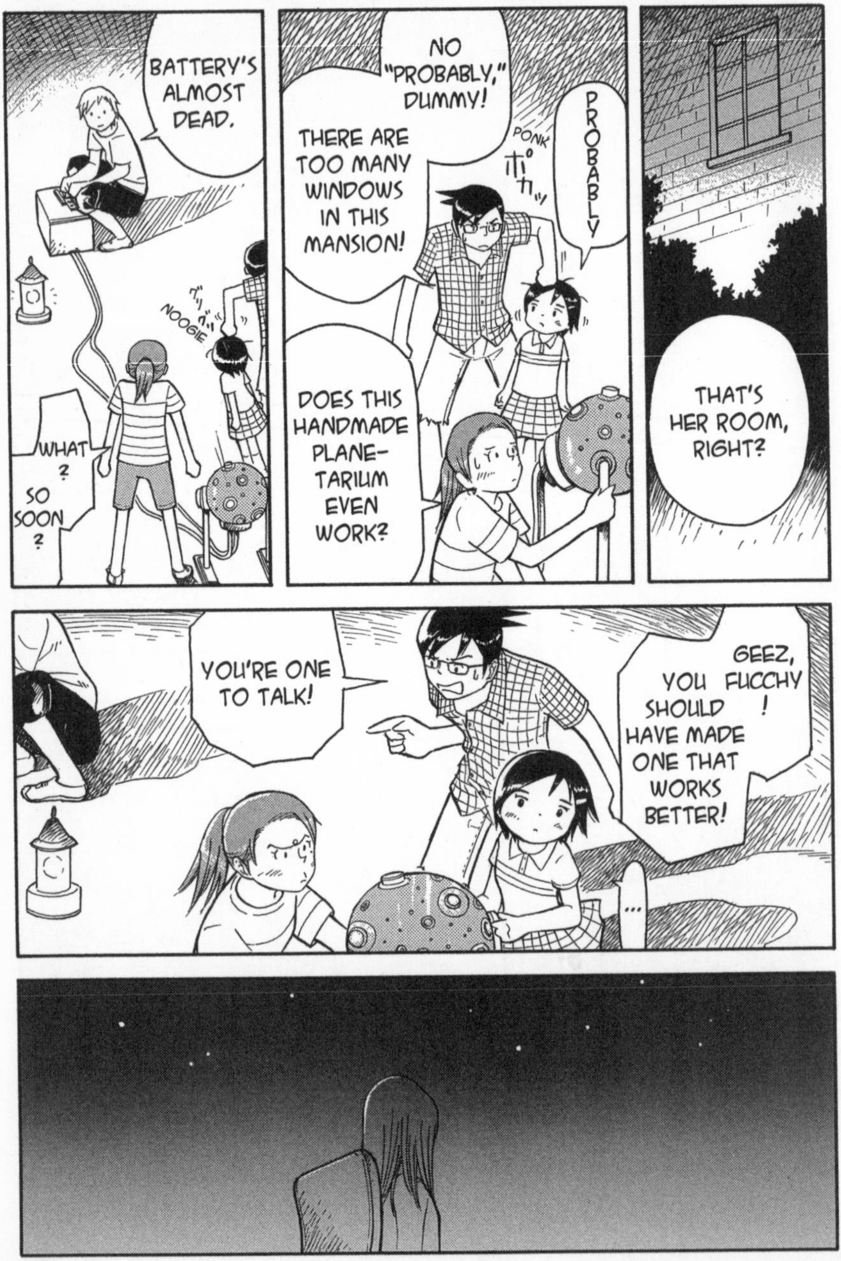
THAT'S HER ROOM, RIGHT?
PROBABLY
PONK
NO "PROBABLY," DUMMY!
THERE ARE TOO MANY WINDOWS IN THIS MANSION!
DOES THIS HANDMADE PLANETARIUM EVEN WORK?
BATTERY'S ALMOST DEAD.
NOOGIE
WHAT? SO SOON?
GEEZ, FUCCHY! YOU SHOULD HAVE MADE ONE THAT WORKS BETTER!
YOU'RE ONE TO TALK!
...

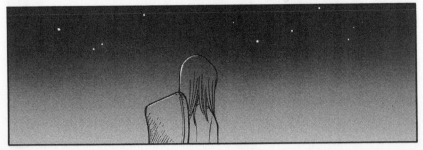

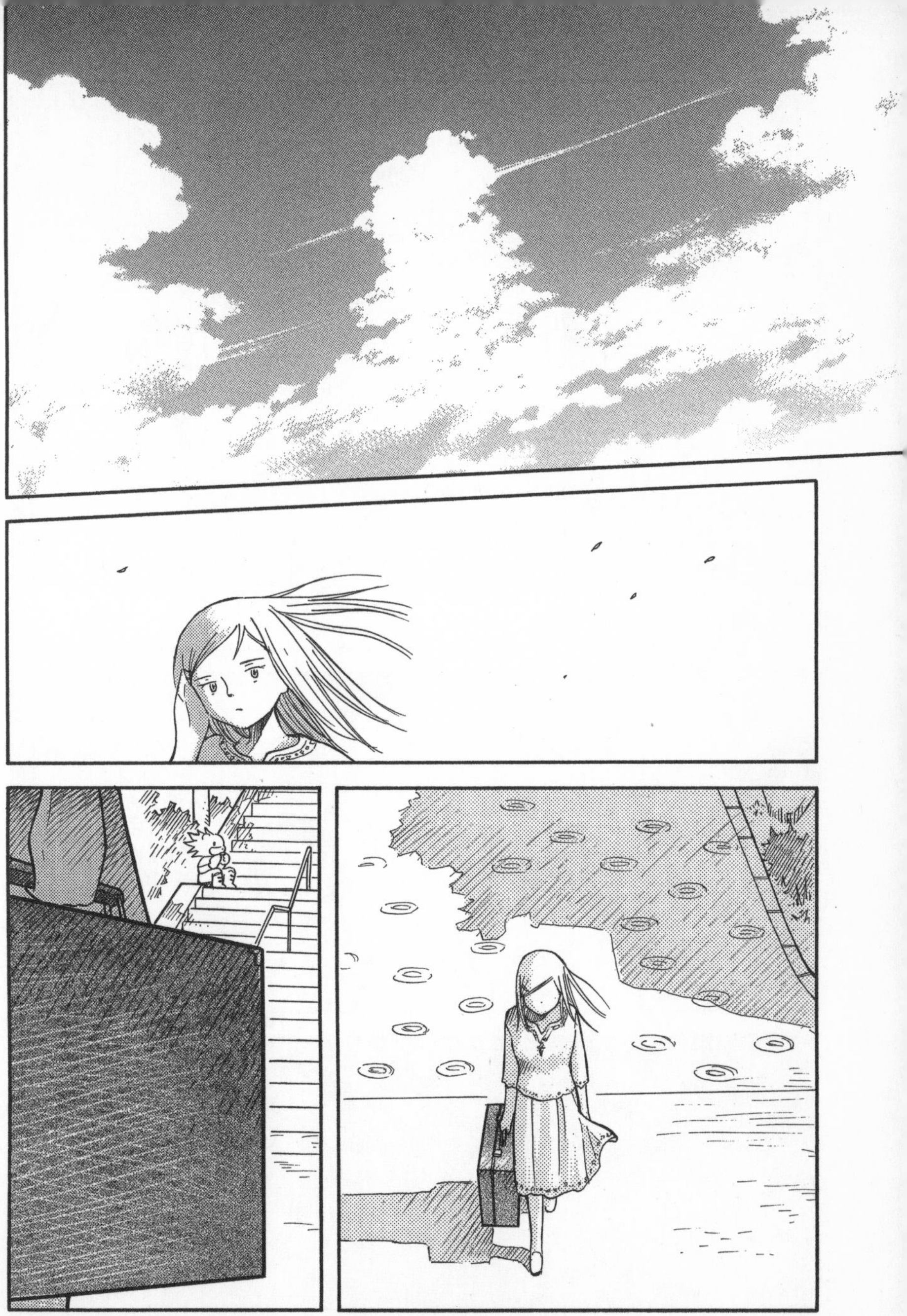

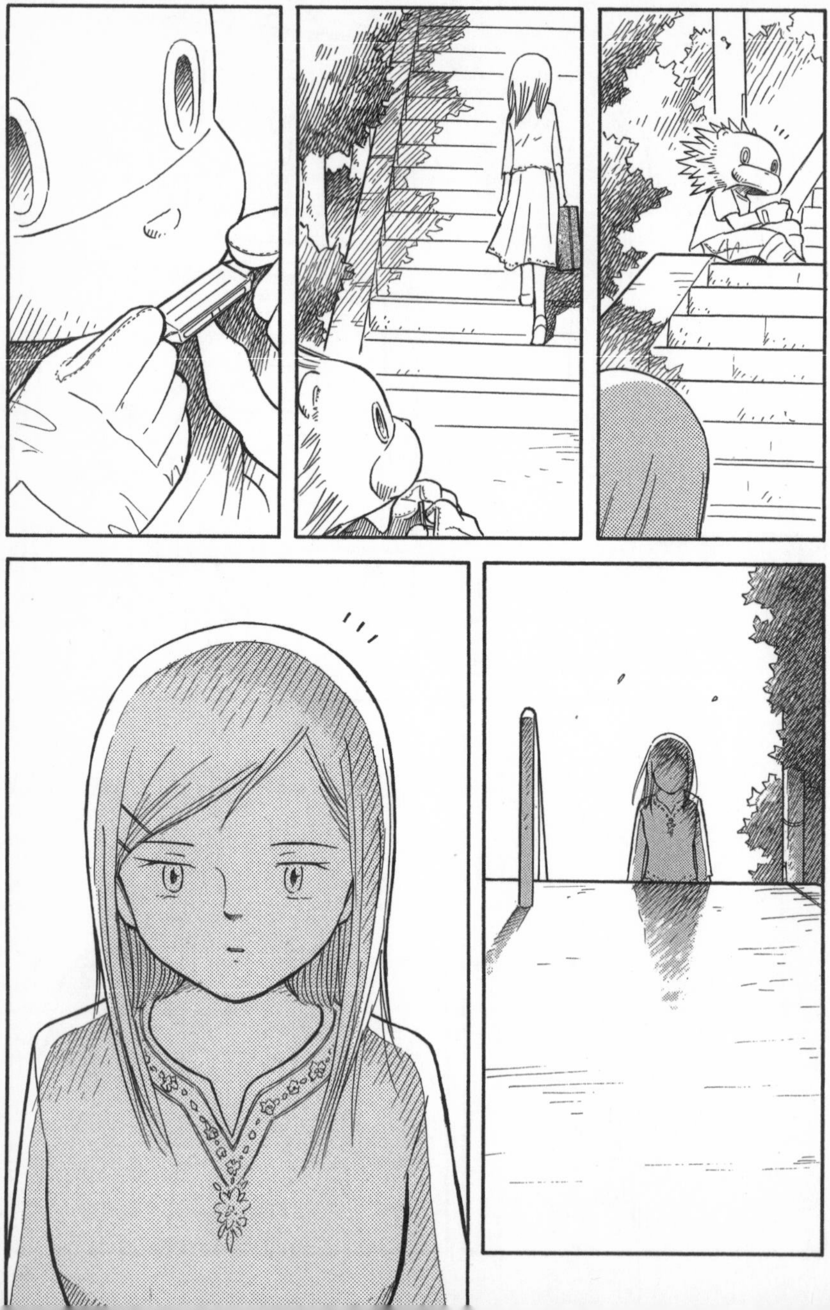

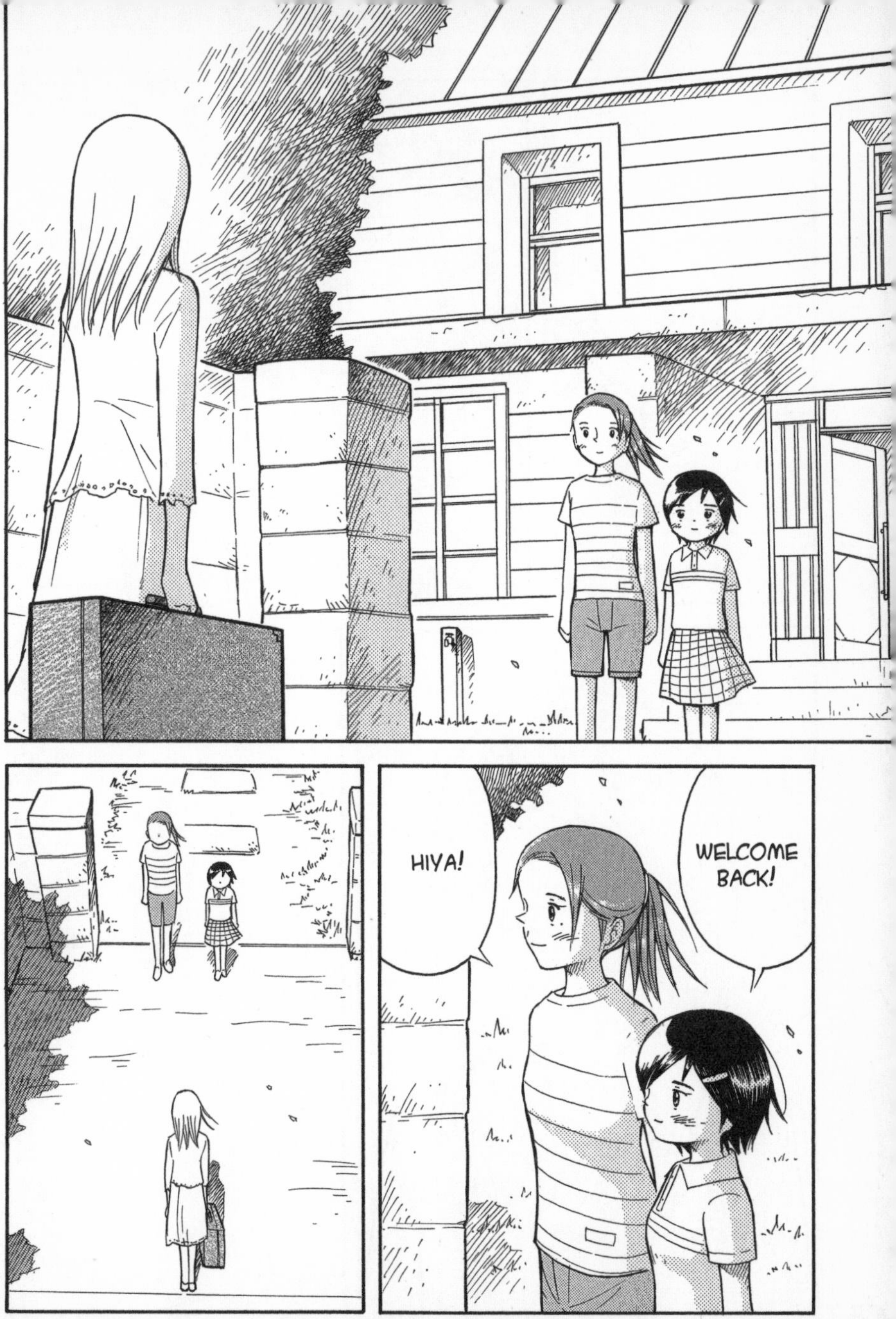
WELCOME BACK!
HIYA!

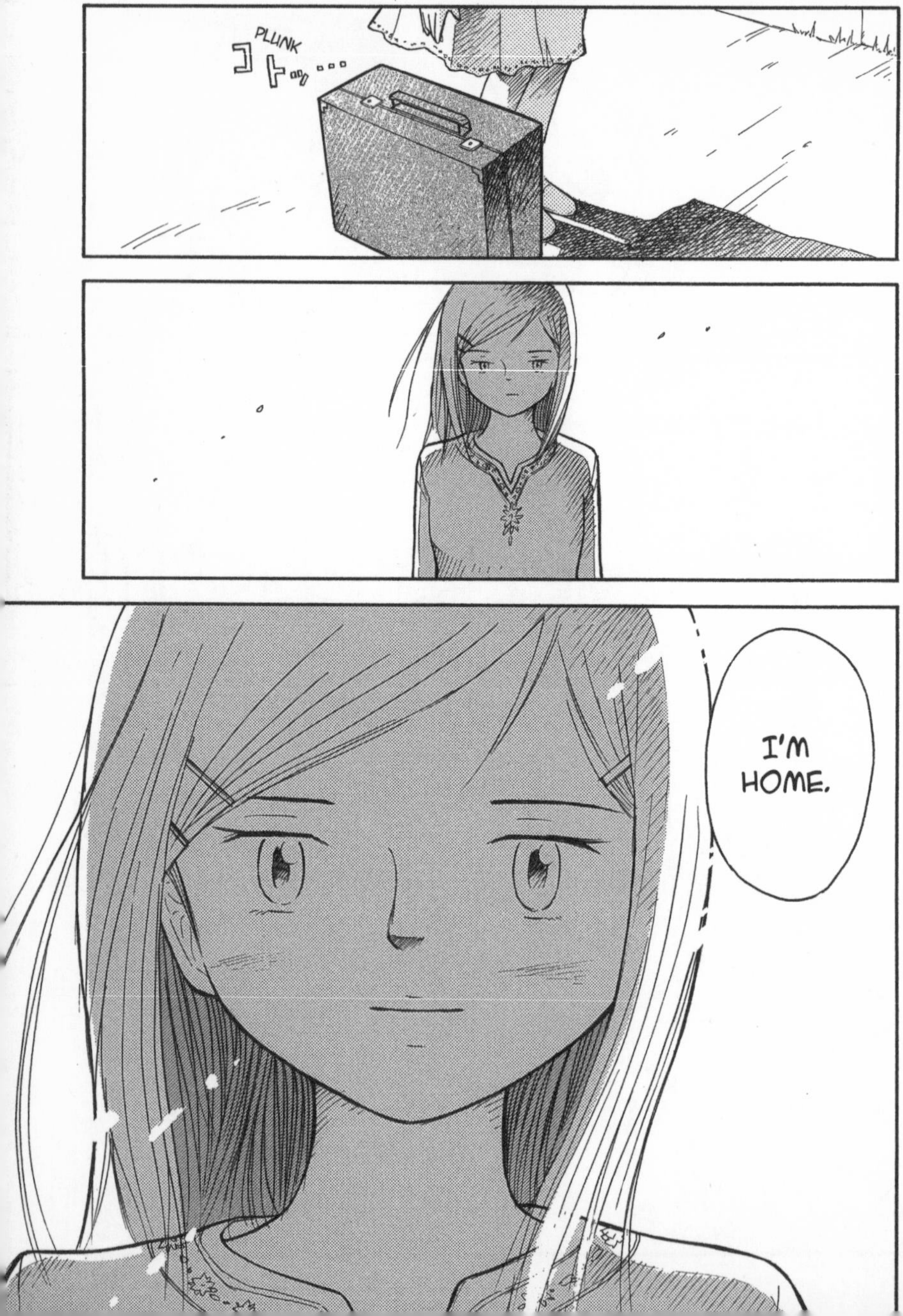
PLUNK
コトッ...
I'M HOME.

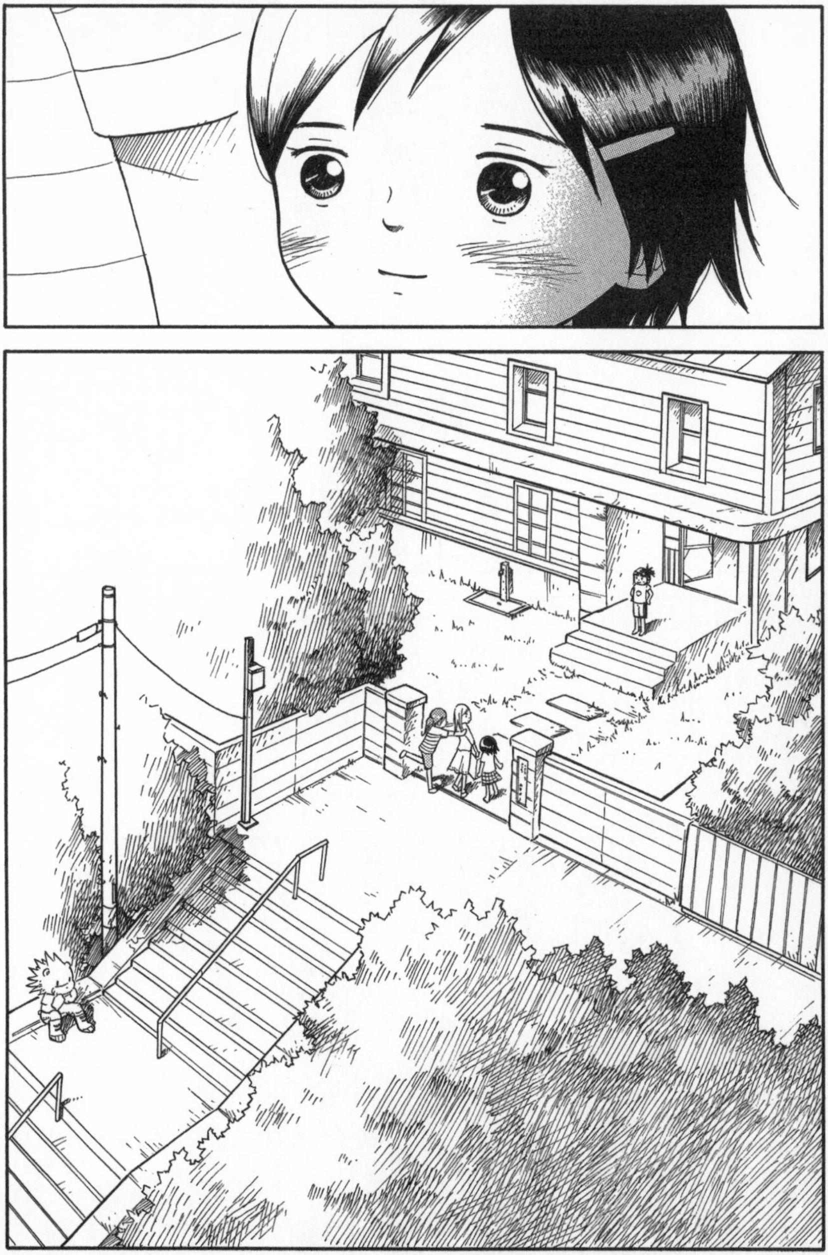

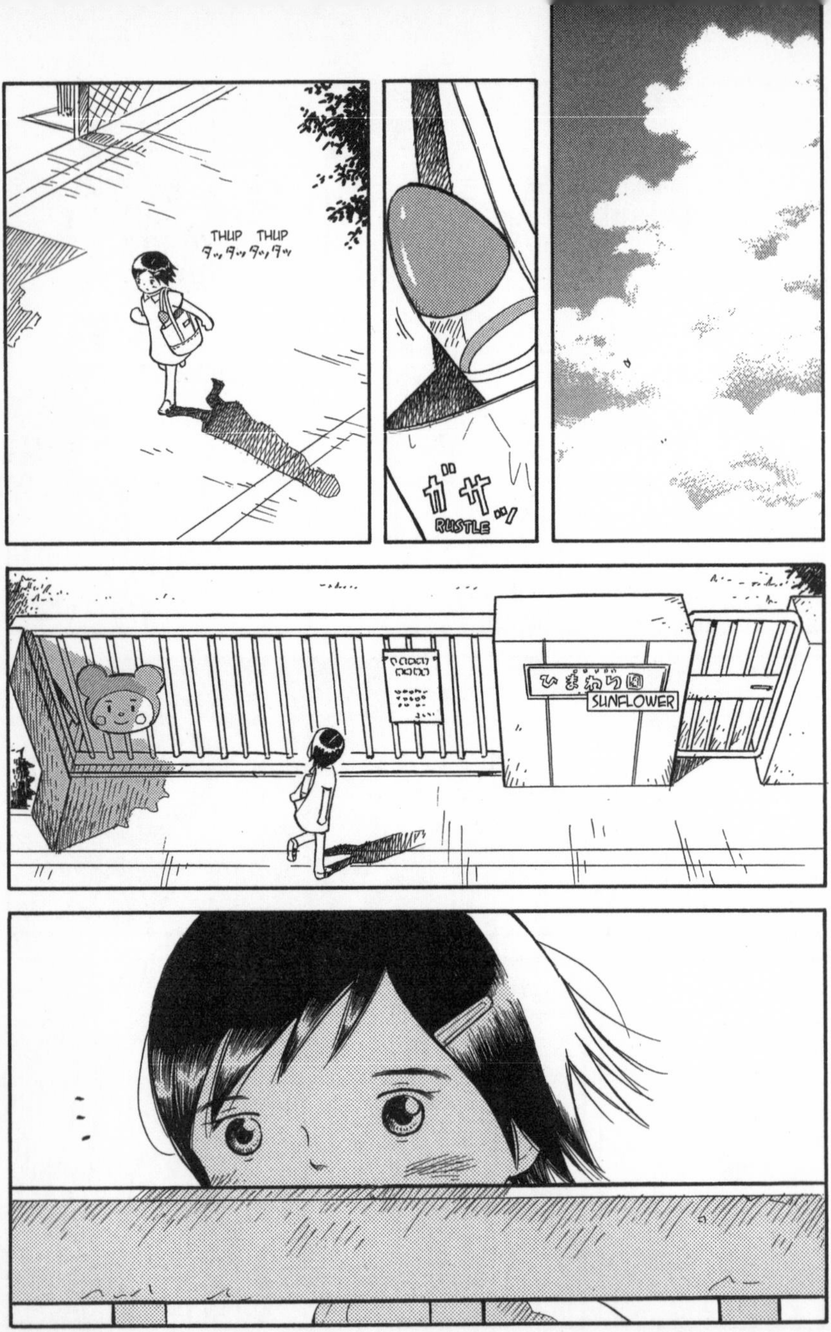
ガサッ
RUSTLE
THUP THUP
タッタッタッタッ
ひまわり園
SUNFLOWER

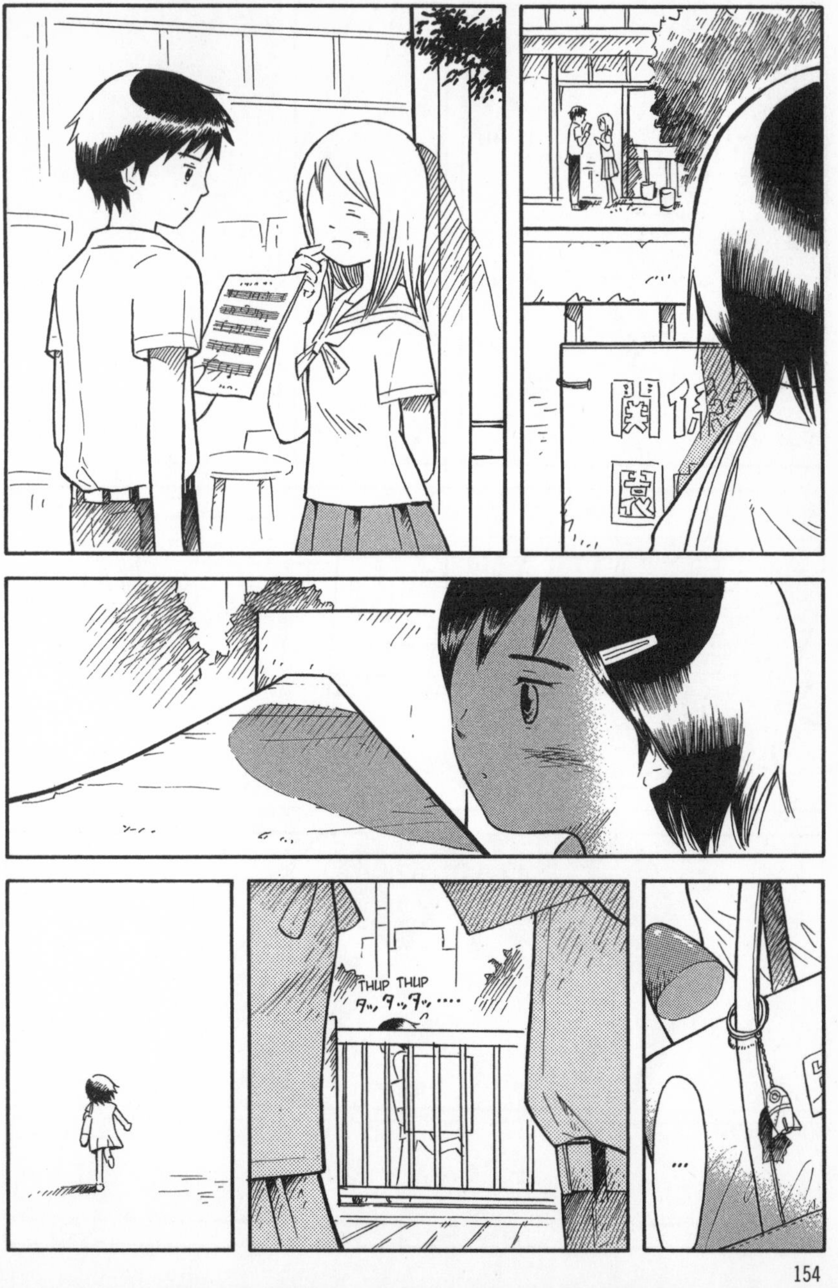
関係
…
THUP THUP
タッ、タッタッ、…

MISSION:35

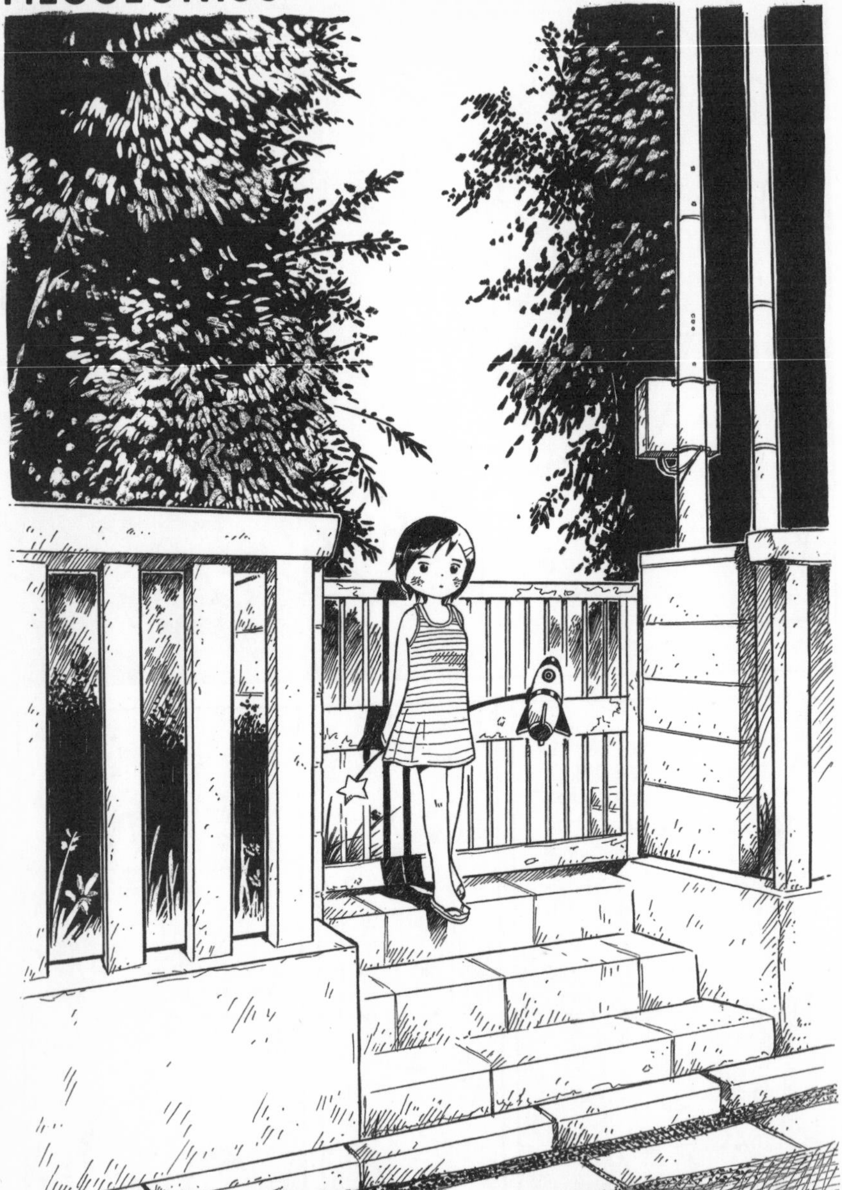

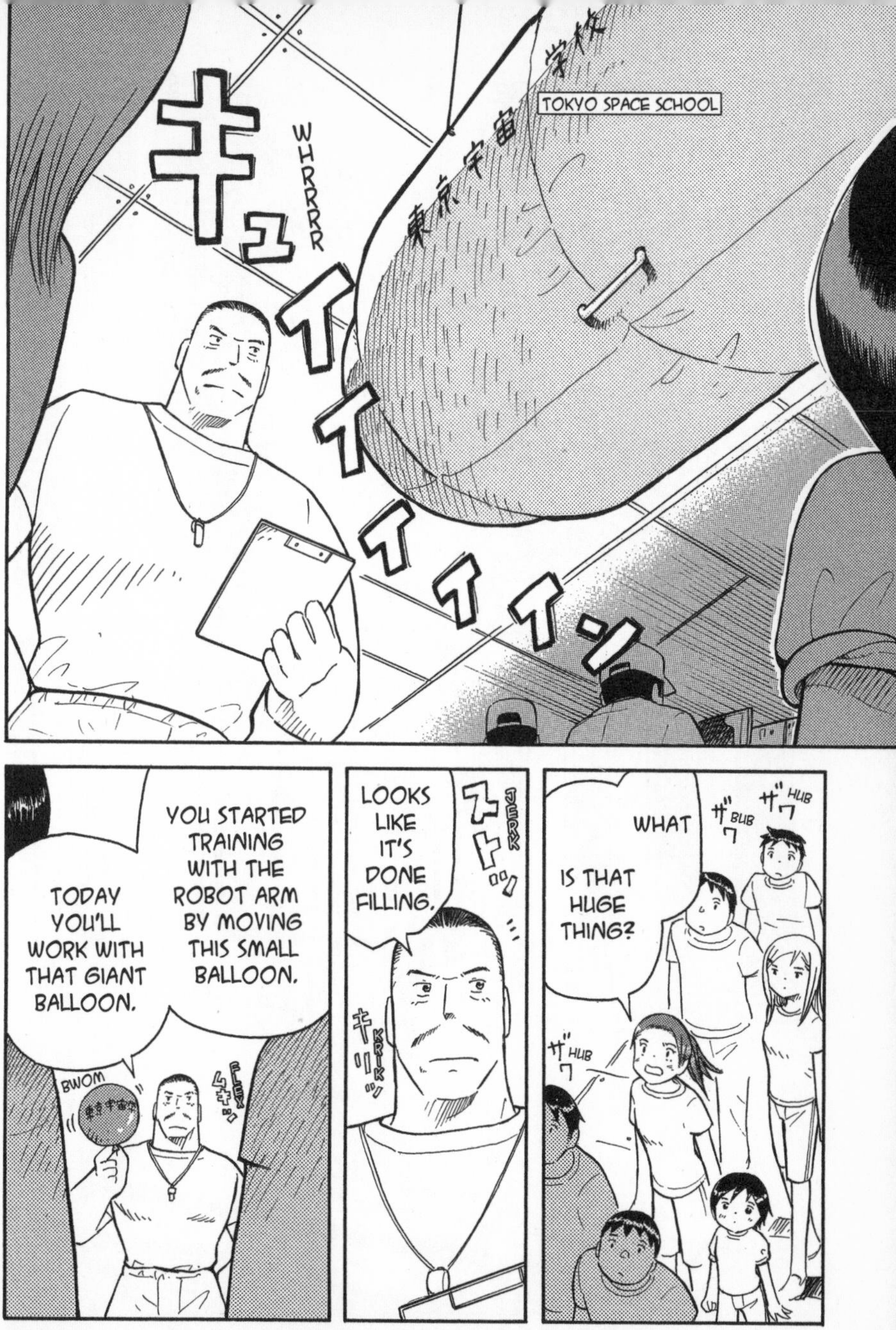
東京宇宙学校
TOKYO SPACE SCHOOL
キュイイイイーン
WHRRRR
WHAT IS THAT HUGE THING?
ザワ HUB
ザワ BUB
ザワ HUB
LOOKS LIKE IT'S DONE FILLING.
JERK
KRIK
YOU STARTED TRAINING WITH THE ROBOT ARM BY MOVING THIS SMALL BALLOON.
TODAY YOU'LL WORK WITH THAT GIANT BALLOON.
BWOM
FLEX

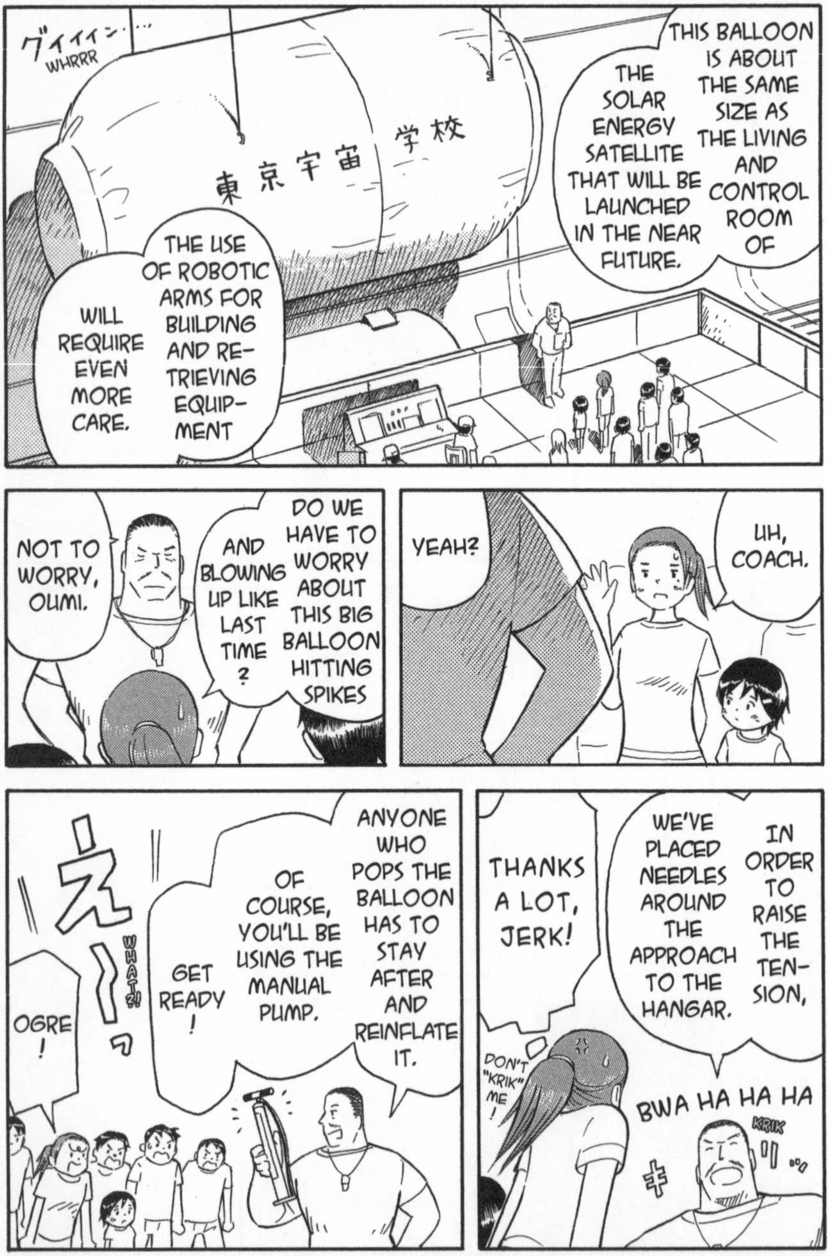
グイイイン…
WHRRR
THIS BALLOON IS ABOUT THE SAME SIZE AS THE LIVING AND CONTROL ROOM OF
THE SOLAR ENERGY SATELLITE THAT WILL BE LAUNCHED IN THE NEAR FUTURE.
東京宇宙学校
THE USE OF ROBOTIC ARMS FOR BUILDING AND RE-TRIEVING EQUIP-MENT
WILL REQUIRE EVEN MORE CARE.
UH, COACH.
YEAH?
DO WE HAVE TO WORRY ABOUT THIS BIG BALLOON HITTING SPIKES
AND BLOWING UP LIKE LAST TIME?
NOT TO WORRY, OUMI.
IN ORDER TO RAISE THE TEN-SION,
WE'VE PLACED NEEDLES AROUND THE APPROACH TO THE HANGAR.
THANKS A LOT, JERK!
BWA HA HA HA
KRIK
DON'T "KRIK" ME!
ANYONE WHO POPS THE BALLOON HAS TO STAY AFTER AND REINFLATE IT.
OF COURSE, YOU'LL BE USING THE MANUAL PUMP.
GET READY!
えーっ
WHAT?!
OGRE!

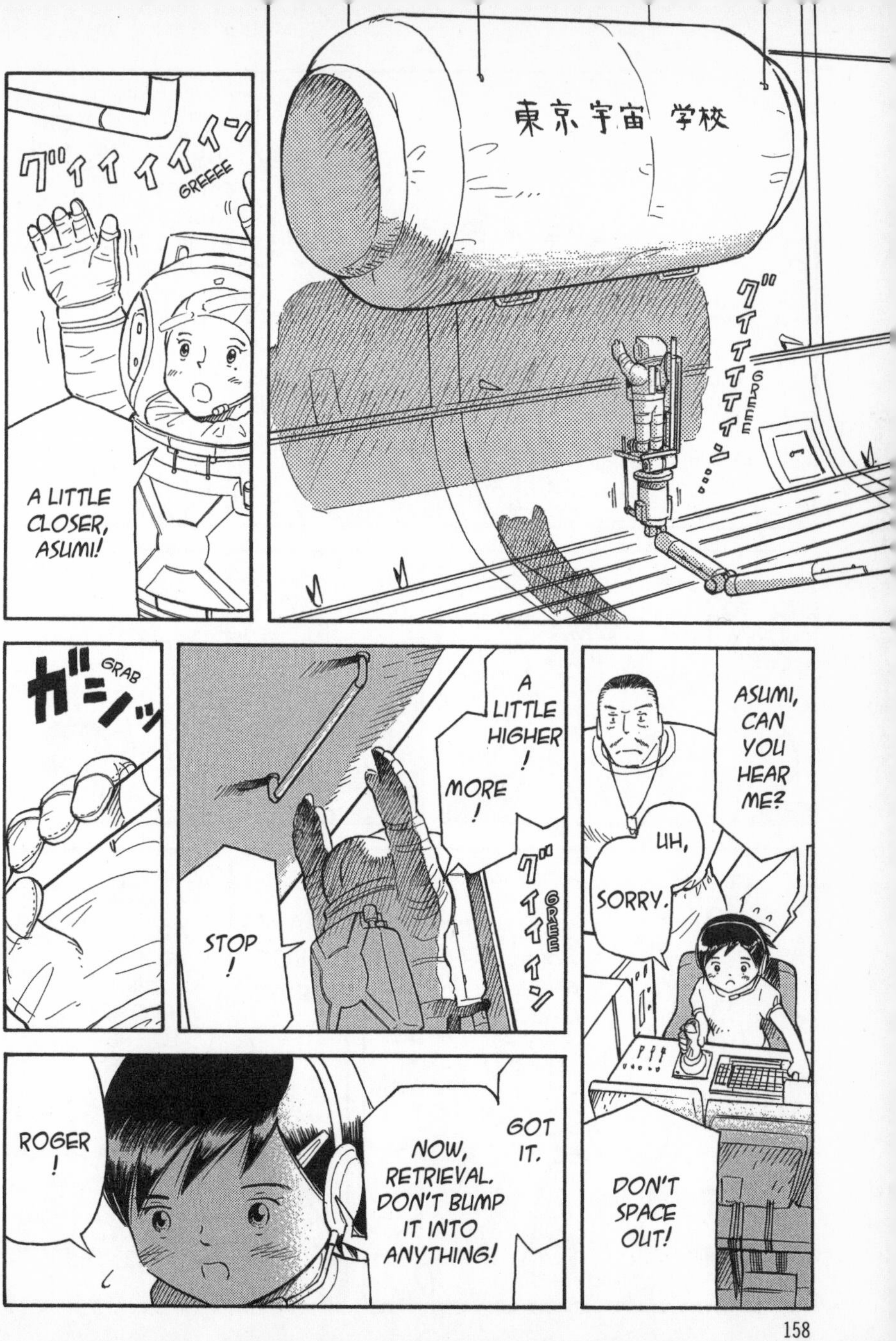
東京宇宙 学校
グィィィィン…
GREEE
グィィィィン
GREEEE
A LITTLE CLOSER, ASUMI!
ASUMI, CAN YOU HEAR ME?
UH, SORRY.
DON'T SPACE OUT!
A LITTLE HIGHER!
MORE!
グィィン
GREE
STOP!
ガシッ
GRAB
GOT IT.
NOW, RETRIEVAL. DON'T BUMP IT INTO ANYTHING!
ROGER!

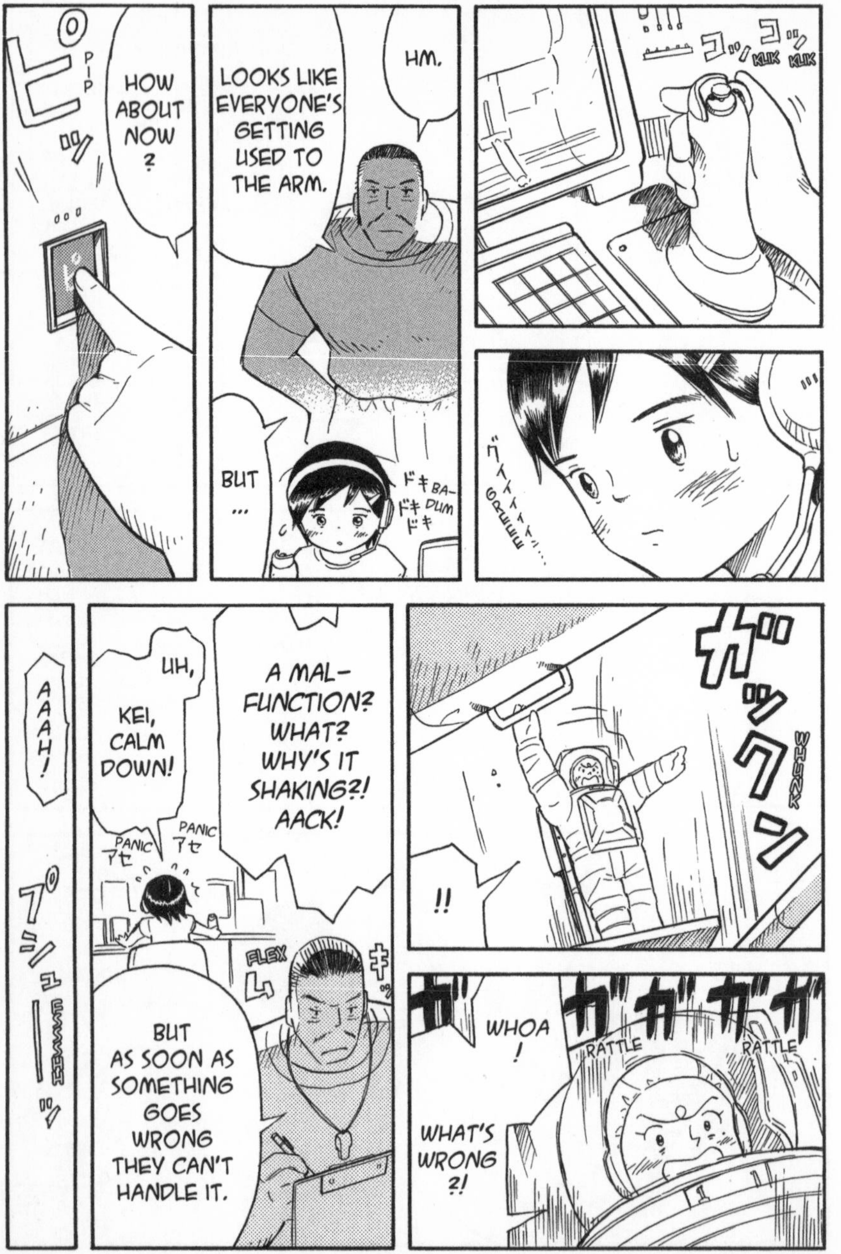

コッ コッ
KLIK KLIK
グィィィィ…
GRWEEE…
HM.
LOOKS LIKE EVERYONE'S GETTING USED TO THE ARM.
BUT …
ドキドキドキ
BA-DUM
ピッ
PIP
HOW ABOUT NOW?
ガックン
WHUNK
!!
ガガガガ
RATTLE RATTLE
WHOA!
WHAT'S WRONG?!
A MAL-FUNCTION? WHAT? WHY'S IT SHAKING?! AACK!
UH,
KEI, CALM DOWN!
アセ アセ
PANIC PANIC
キッ
ム
FLEX
BUT AS SOON AS SOMETHING GOES WRONG THEY CAN'T HANDLE IT.
AAAAH!
プシュー
FSSSSH

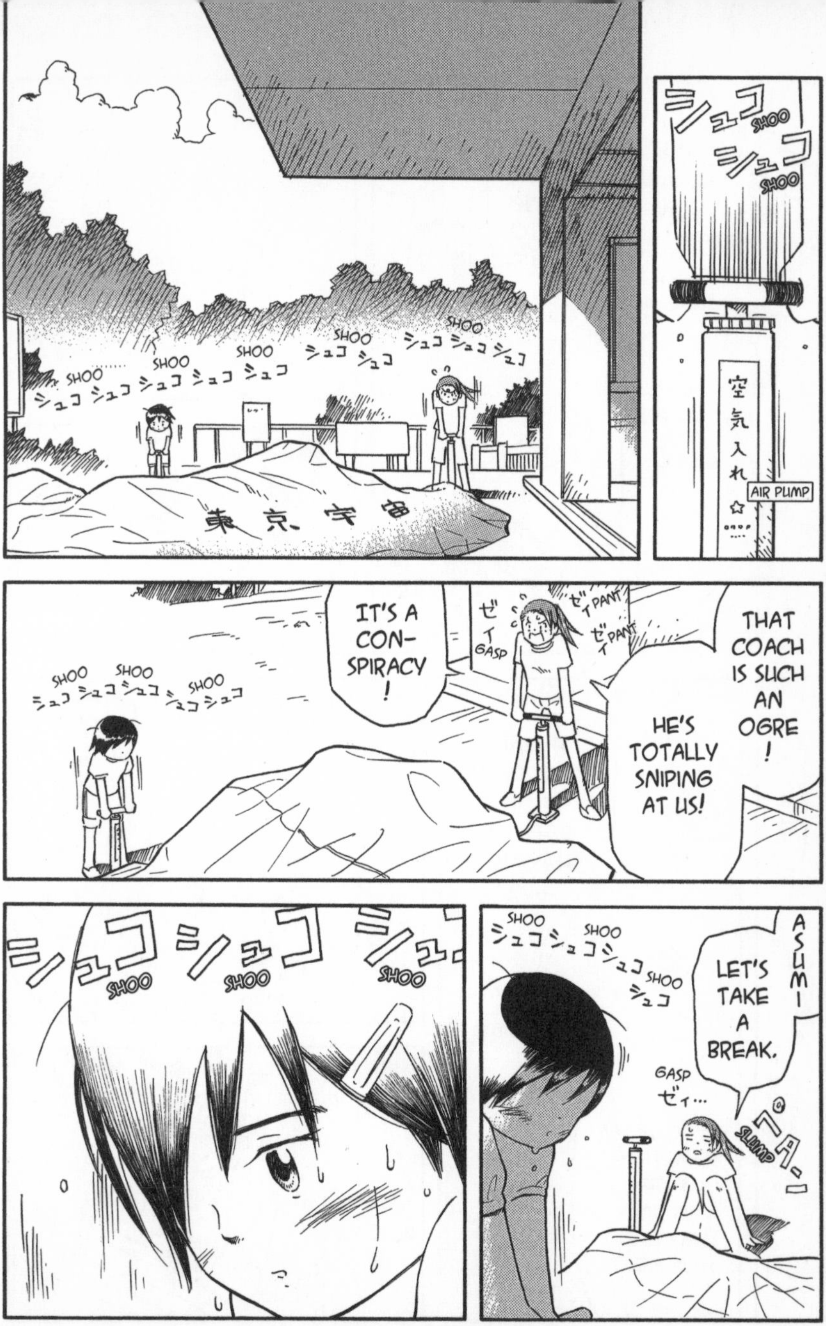
シュコ SHOO
シュコ SHOO
空気入れ☆
AIR PUMP
シュコ SHOO シュコ シュコ SHOO シュコ シュコ SHOO シュコ シュコ SHOO シュコ シュコ……
東京宇宙
THAT COACH IS SUCH AN OGRE!
HE'S TOTALLY SNIPING AT US!
ゼイ PANT
ゼイ PANT
ゼイ GASP
IT'S A CON-SPIRACY!
シュコ SHOO シュコ SHOO シュコ シュコ SHOO シュコ
ASUMI
LET'S TAKE A BREAK.
GASP ゼィ…
ペタ- SLUMP
シュコ SHOO シュコ SHOO シュコ シュコ SHOO
シュコ SHOO シュコ SHOO シュコ SHOO

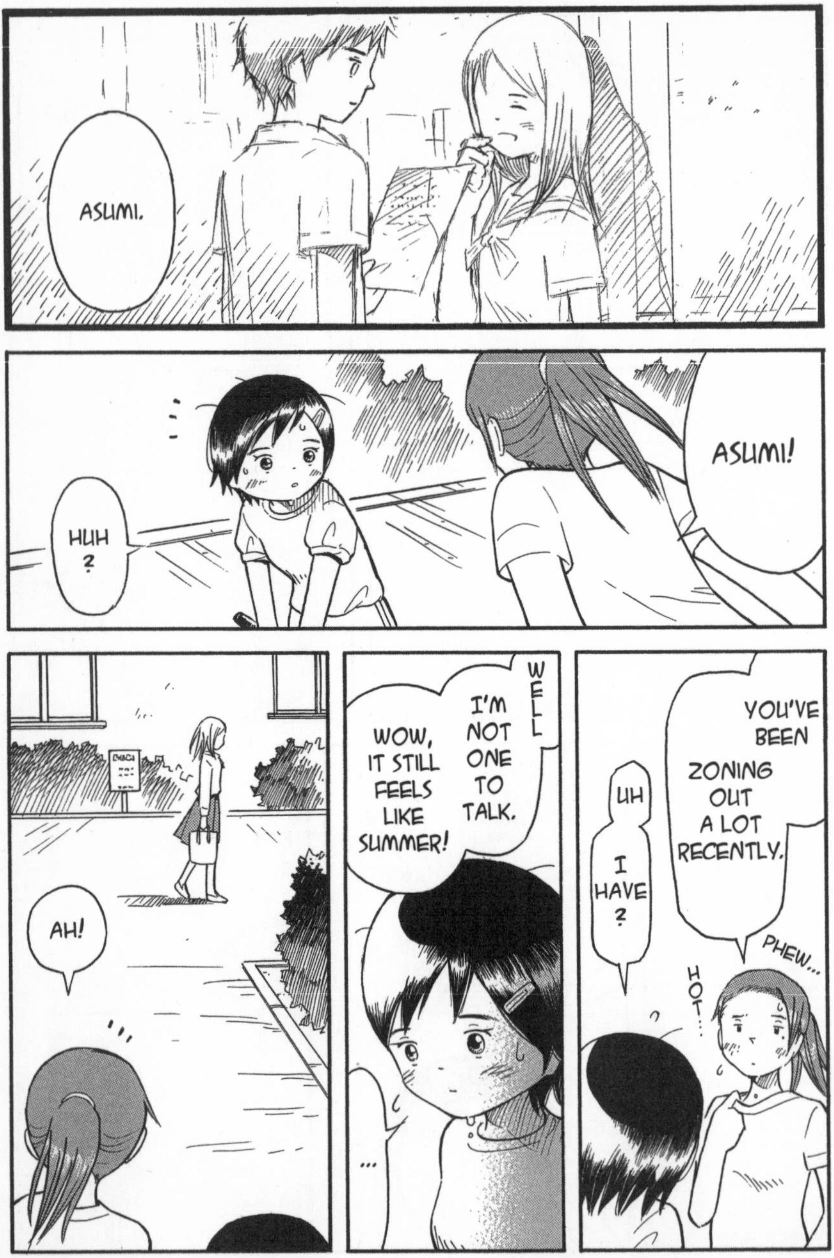
ASUMI.
ASUMI!
HUH ?
YOU'VE BEEN ZONING OUT A LOT RECENTLY.
PHEW...
HOT...
UH I HAVE ?
WELL I'M NOT ONE TO TALK.
WOW, IT STILL FEELS LIKE SUMMER!
...
AH!

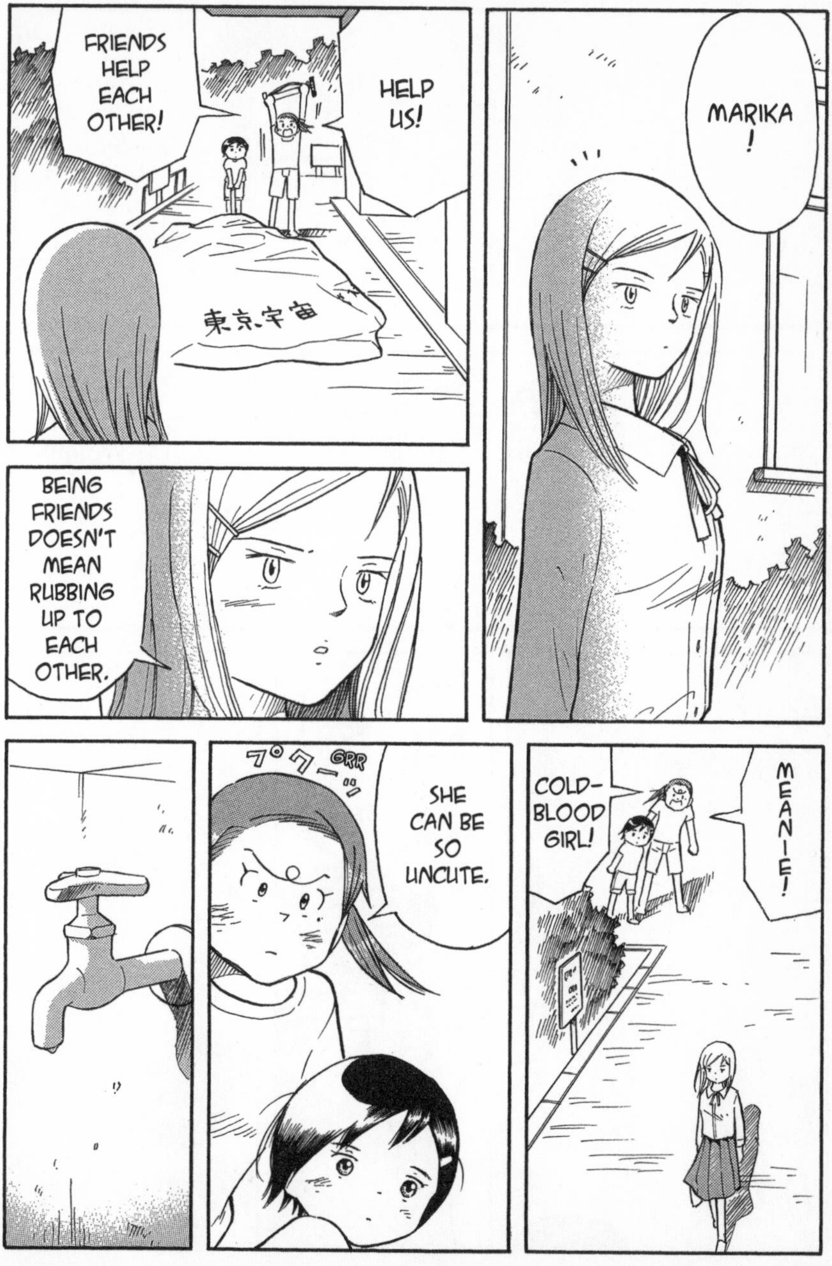
MARIKA!
HELP US!
FRIENDS HELP EACH OTHER!
東京宇宙
BEING FRIENDS DOESN'T MEAN RUBBING UP TO EACH OTHER.
MEANIE!
COLD-BLOOD GIRL!
プクーッ
GRR
SHE CAN BE SO UNCUTE.

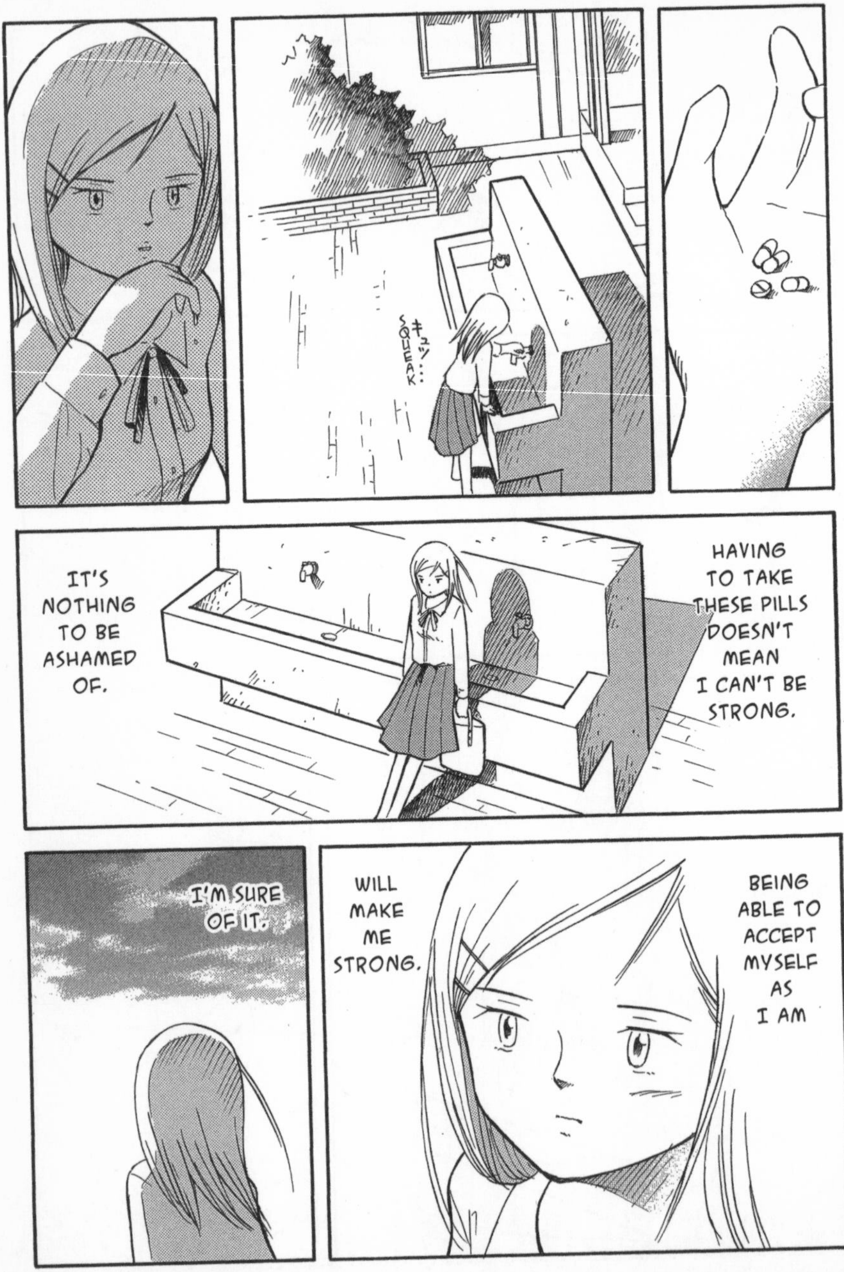
キュッ…
SQUEAK
HAVING TO TAKE THESE PILLS DOESN'T MEAN I CAN'T BE STRONG.
IT'S NOTHING TO BE ASHAMED OF.
BEING ABLE TO ACCEPT MYSELF AS I AM
WILL MAKE ME STRONG.
I'M SURE OF IT.

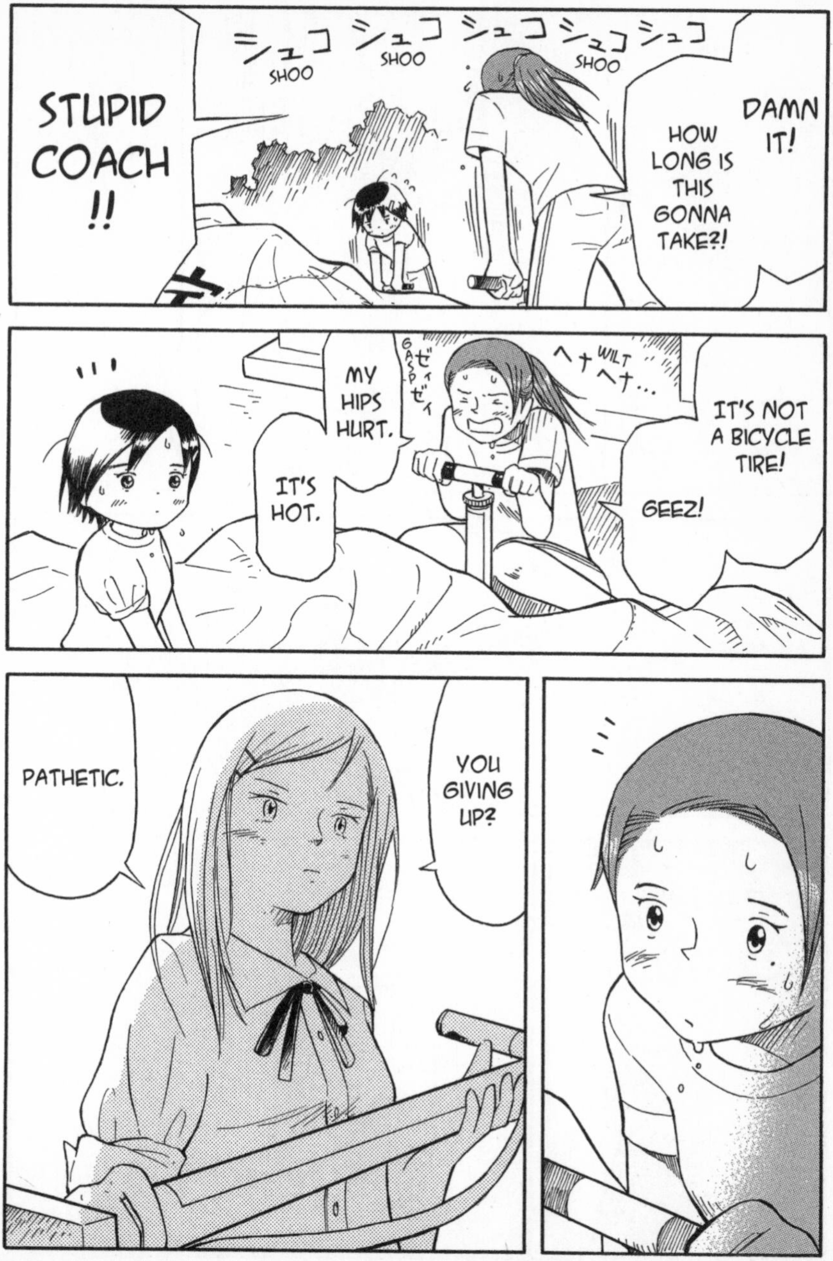
DAMN IT!
HOW LONG IS THIS GONNA TAKE?!
シュコ シュコ シュコ シュコ シュコ
SHOO SHOO SHOO
STUPID COACH!!
IT'S NOT A BICYCLE TIRE!
GEEZ!
ヘナヘナ…
WILT
ゼィゼィ
GASP
MY HIPS HURT.
IT'S HOT.
YOU GIVING UP?
PATHETIC.

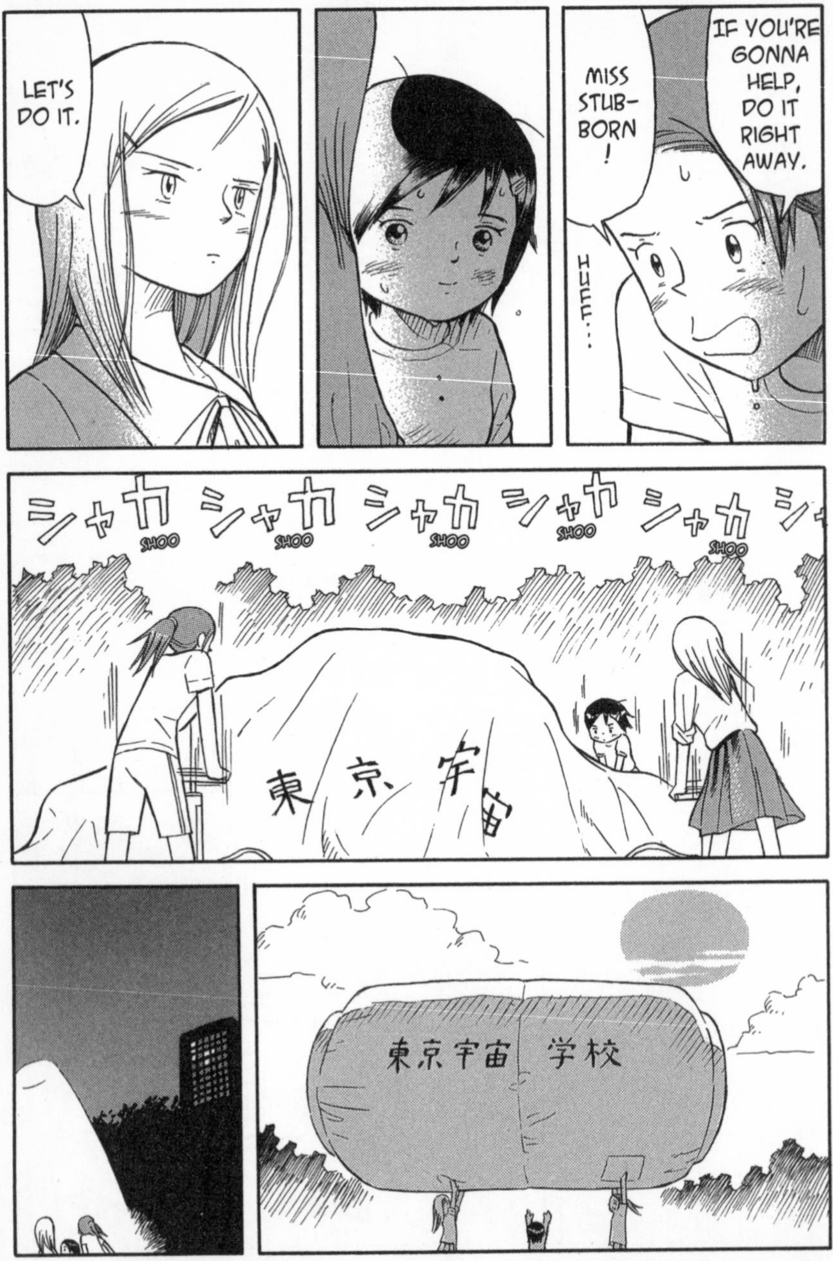

IF YOU'RE GONNA HELP, DO IT RIGHT AWAY.
MISS STUB-BORN!
HUFF...
LET'S DO IT.
シャカ シャカ シャカ シャカ シャカ シャ
SHOO SHOO SHOO SHOO SHOO
東京宇宙
東京宇宙 学校

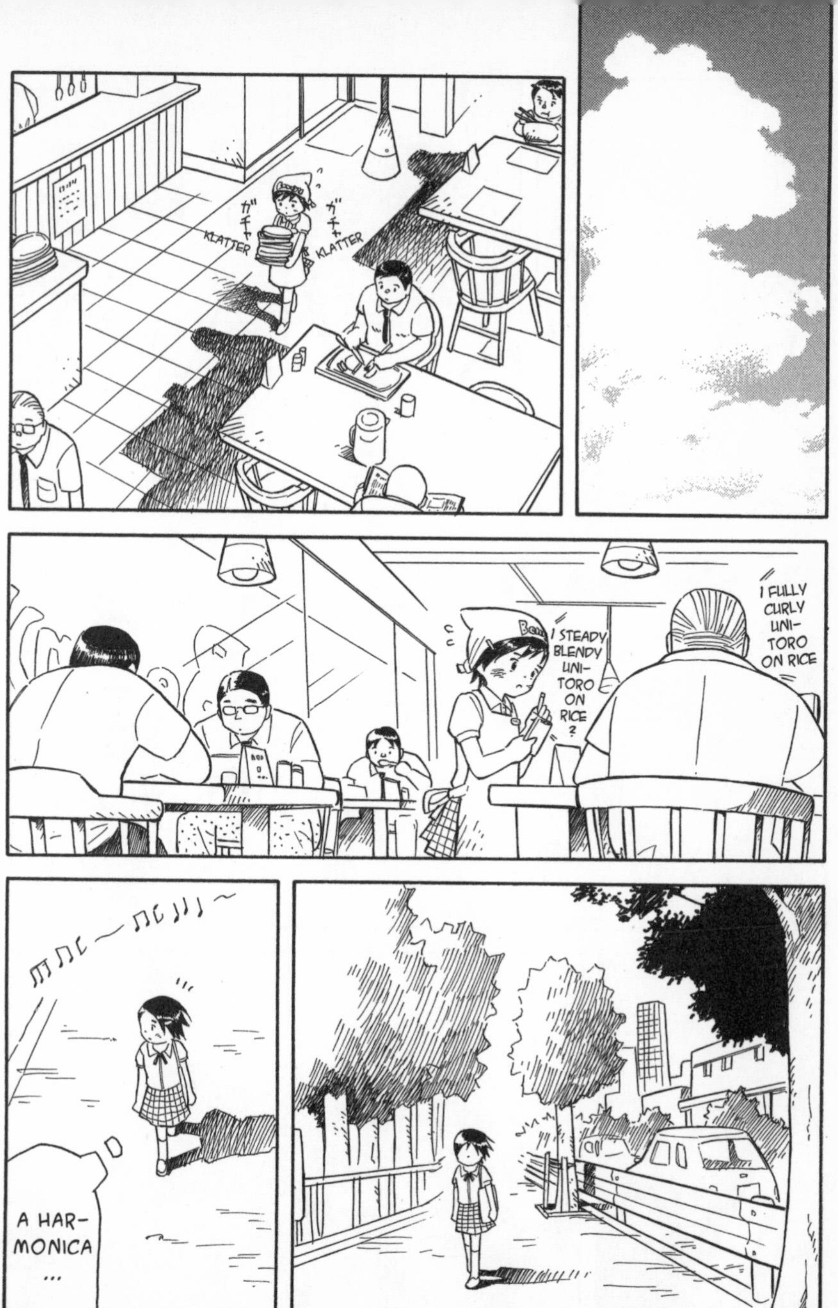
ガチャ
KLATTER
ガチャ
KLATTER
I FULLY CURLY UNI-TORO ON RICE
I STEADY BLENDY UNI-TORO ON RICE ?
A HAR-MONICA ...

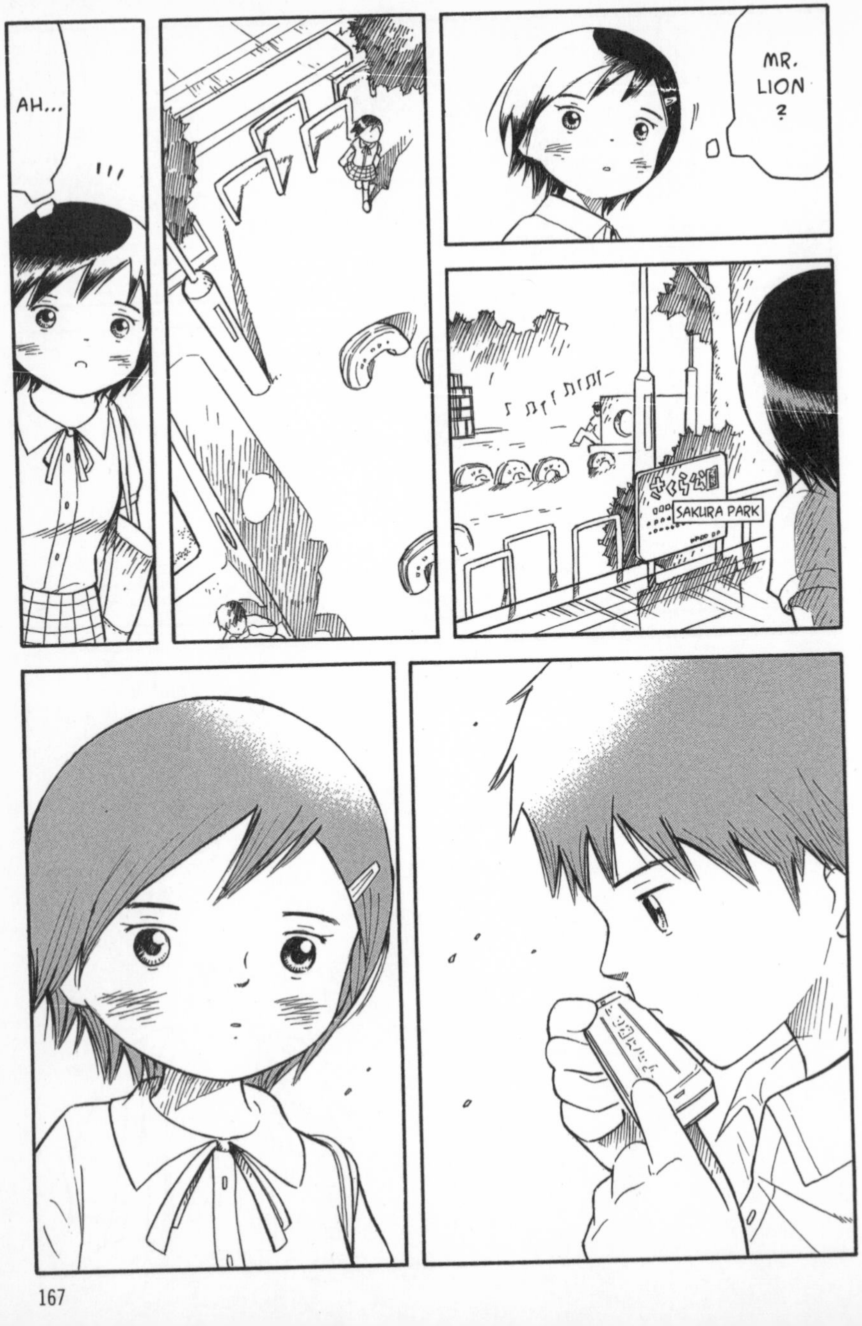
MR. LION?
さくら公園
SAKURA PARK
AH...
!!!

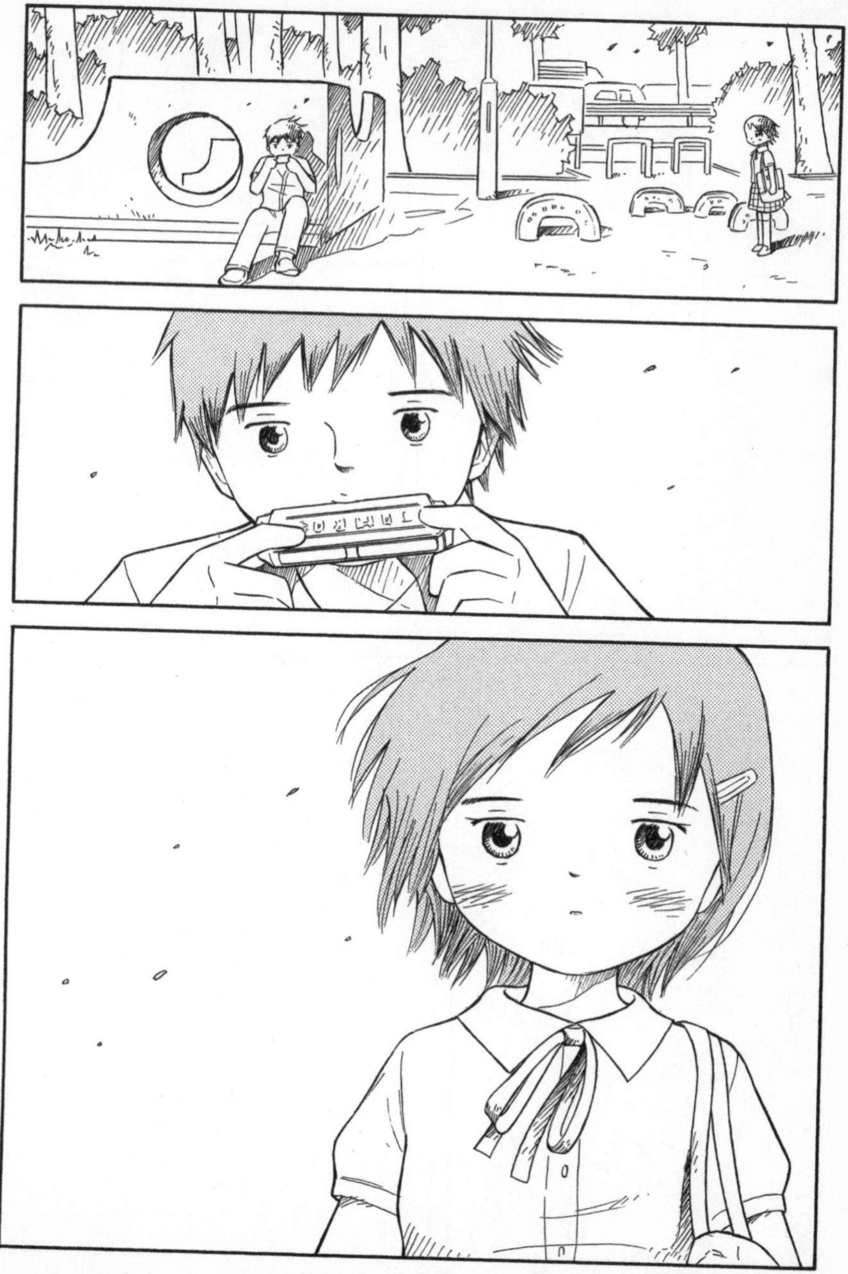

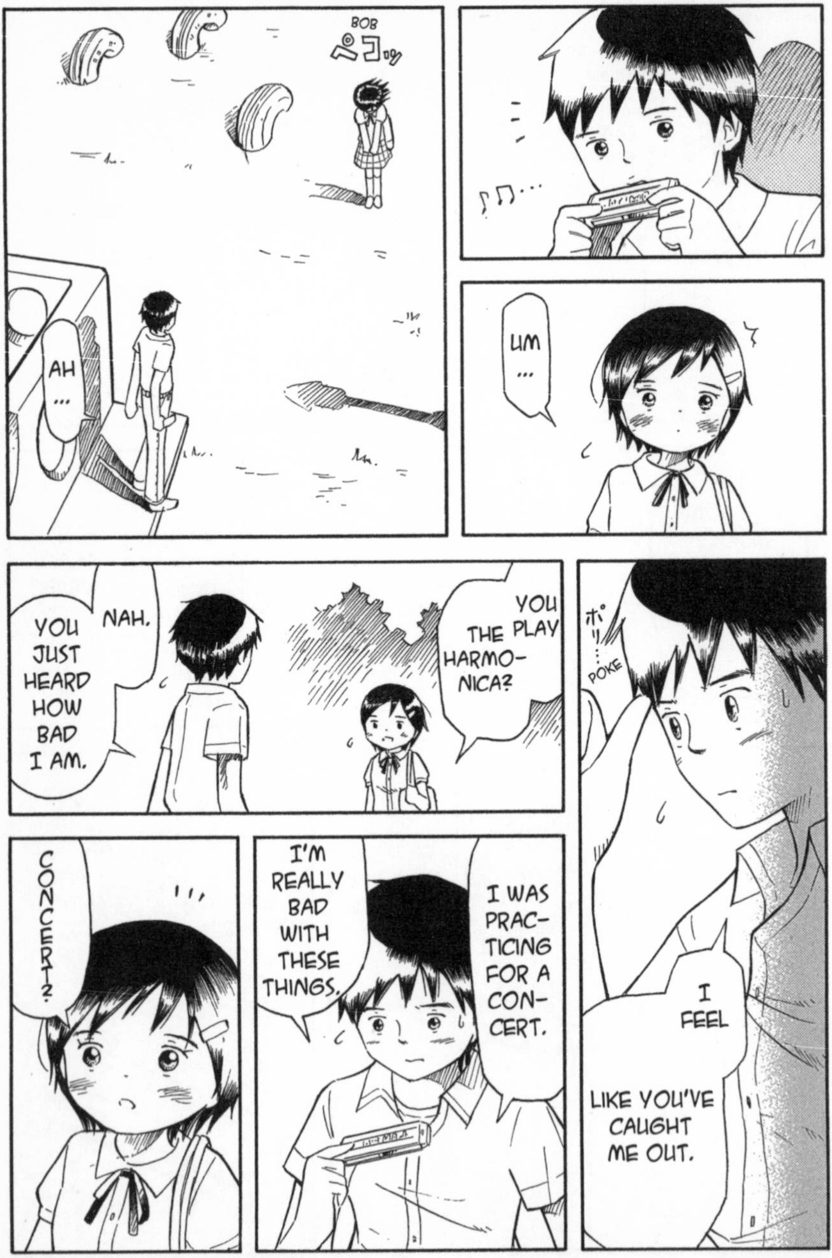

UM ...
ペコッ
BOB
AH ...
ポリ…
POKE
I FEEL
LIKE YOU'VE CAUGHT ME OUT.
YOU PLAY THE HARMONICA?
NAH.
YOU JUST HEARD HOW BAD I AM.
I WAS PRACTICING FOR A CONCERT.
I'M REALLY BAD WITH THESE THINGS.
CONCERT?

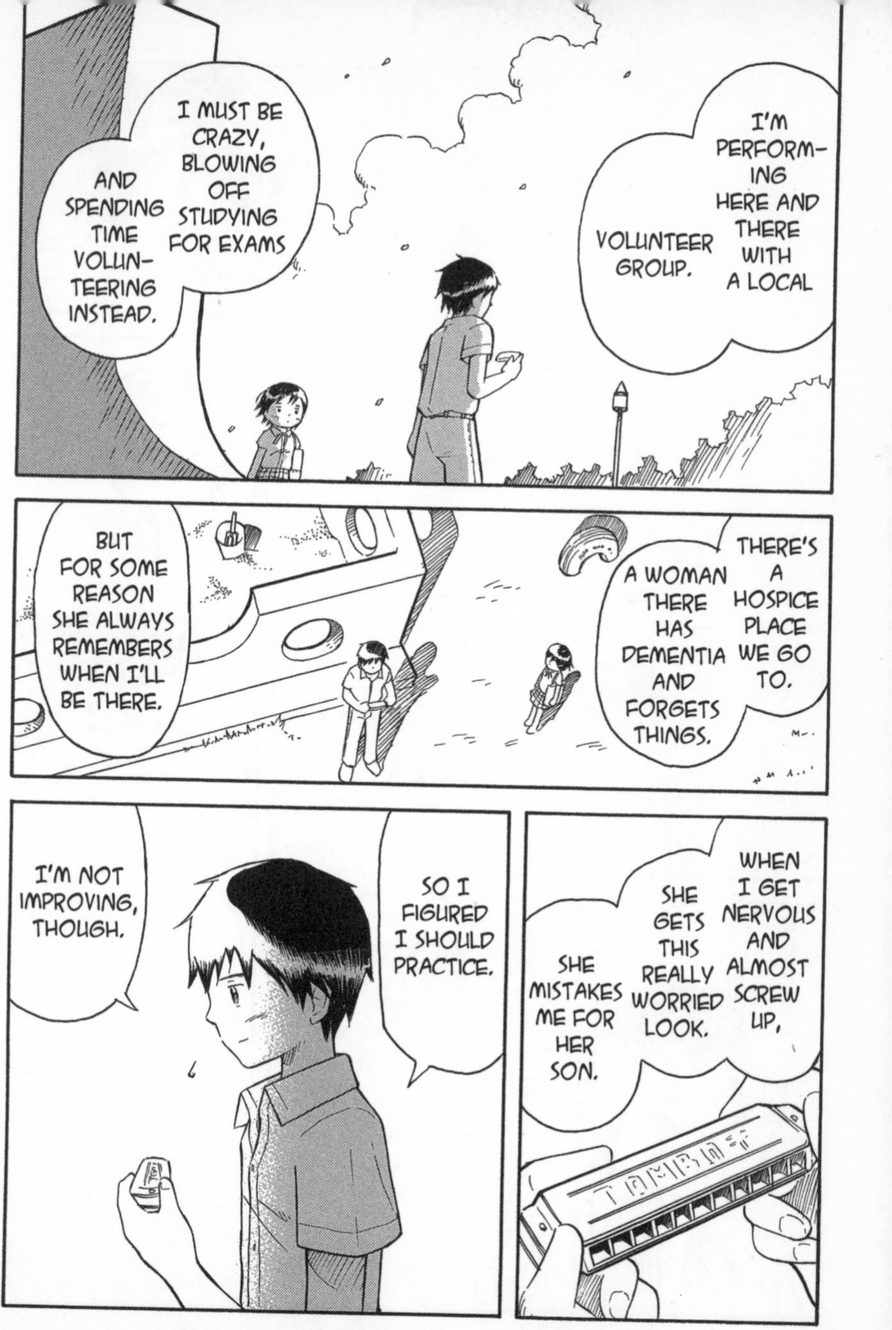
I'M PERFORMING HERE AND THERE WITH A LOCAL
VOLUNTEER GROUP.
I MUST BE CRAZY, BLOWING OFF STUDYING FOR EXAMS
AND SPENDING TIME VOLUNTEERING INSTEAD.
THERE'S A HOSPICE PLACE WE GO TO.
A WOMAN THERE HAS DEMENTIA AND FORGETS THINGS.
BUT FOR SOME REASON SHE ALWAYS REMEMBERS WHEN I'LL BE THERE.
WHEN I GET NERVOUS AND ALMOST SCREW UP,
SHE GETS THIS REALLY WORRIED LOOK.
SHE MISTAKES ME FOR HER SON.
SO I FIGURED I SHOULD PRACTICE.
I'M NOT IMPROVING, THOUGH.

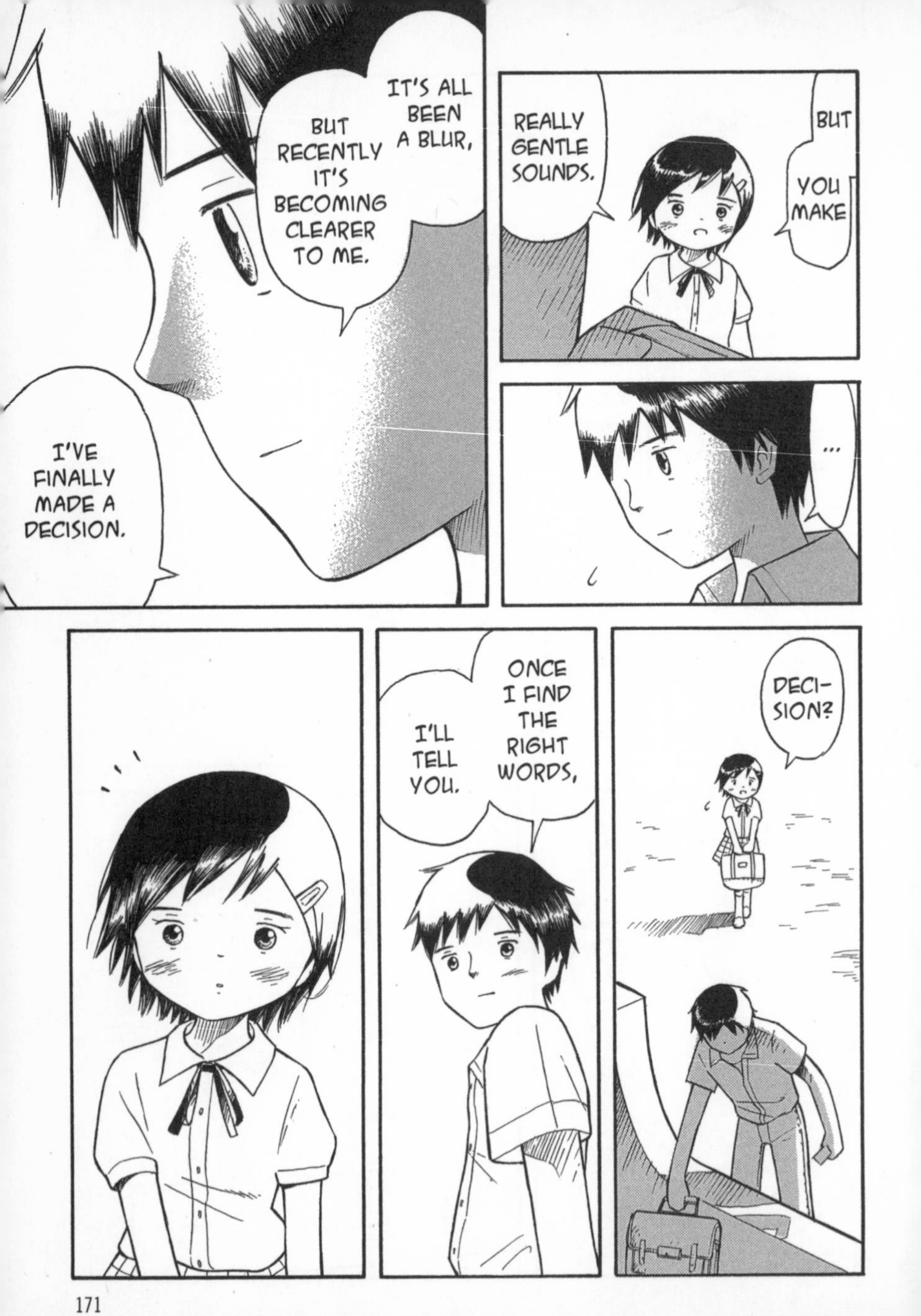
BUT YOU MAKE
REALLY GENTLE SOUNDS.
...
IT'S ALL BEEN A BLUR,
BUT RECENTLY IT'S BECOMING CLEARER TO ME.
I'VE FINALLY MADE A DECISION.
DECI-SION?
ONCE I FIND THE RIGHT WORDS,
I'LL TELL YOU.

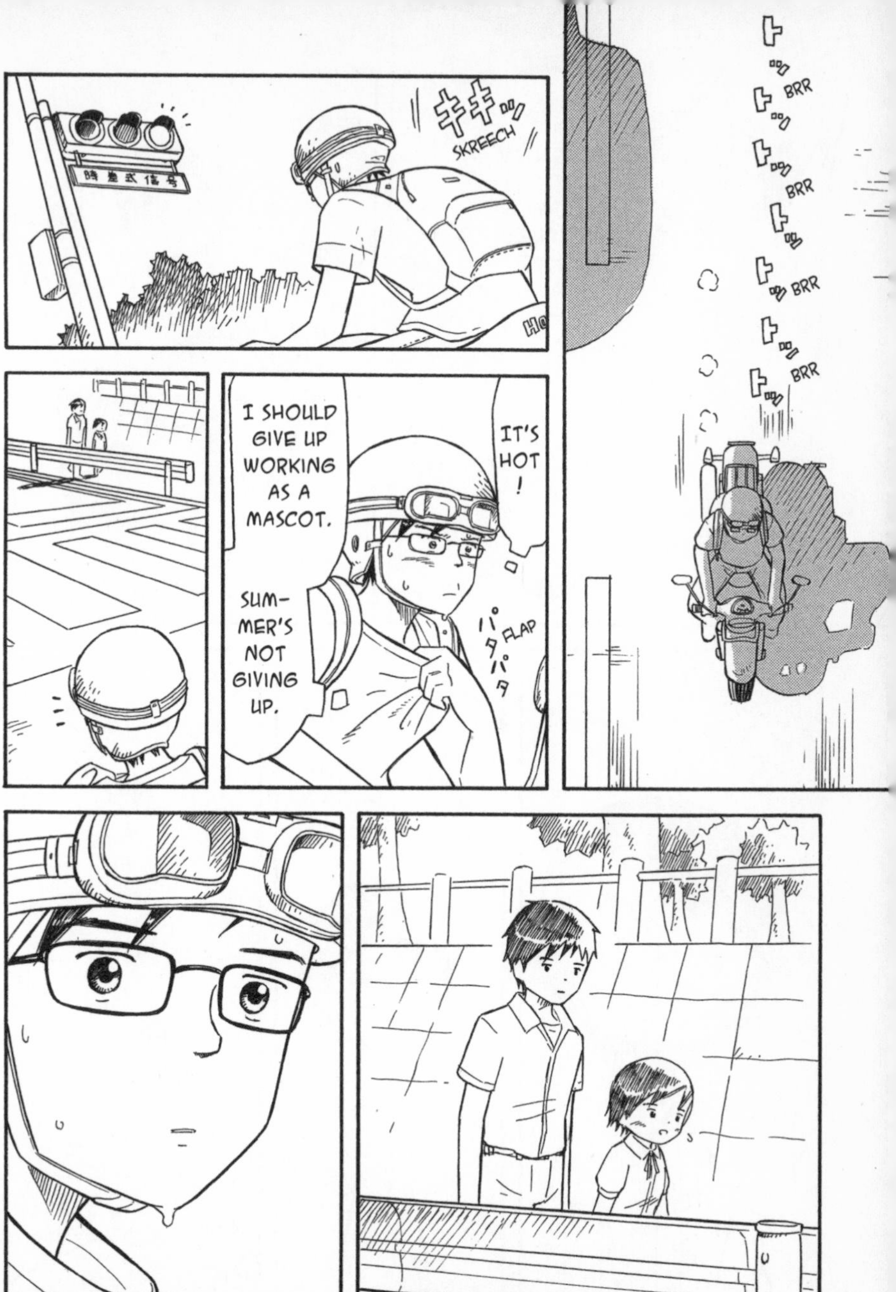

トッ
BRR
トッ
トッ
BRR
トッ
トッ
BRR
トッ
BRR
トッ
キキッ
SKREECH
時差式信号
IT'S HOT!
I SHOULD GIVE UP WORKING AS A MASCOT.
SUMMER'S NOT GIVING UP.
パタパタ
FLAP

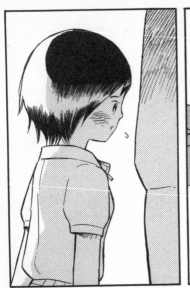

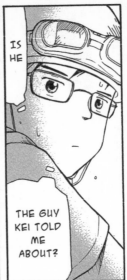

IS HE

THE GUY KEI TOLD ME ABOUT?

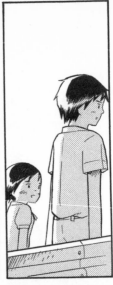

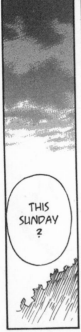

THIS SUNDAY?

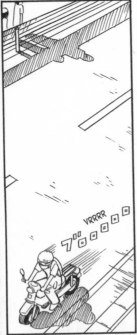

VRRRR

ブ°ㅇㅇㅇㅇ

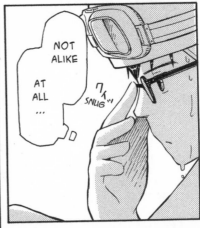

NOT ALIKE

AT ALL...

クヘ" SNUG

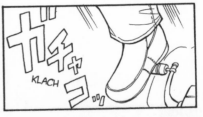

ガチャコ"

KLACH

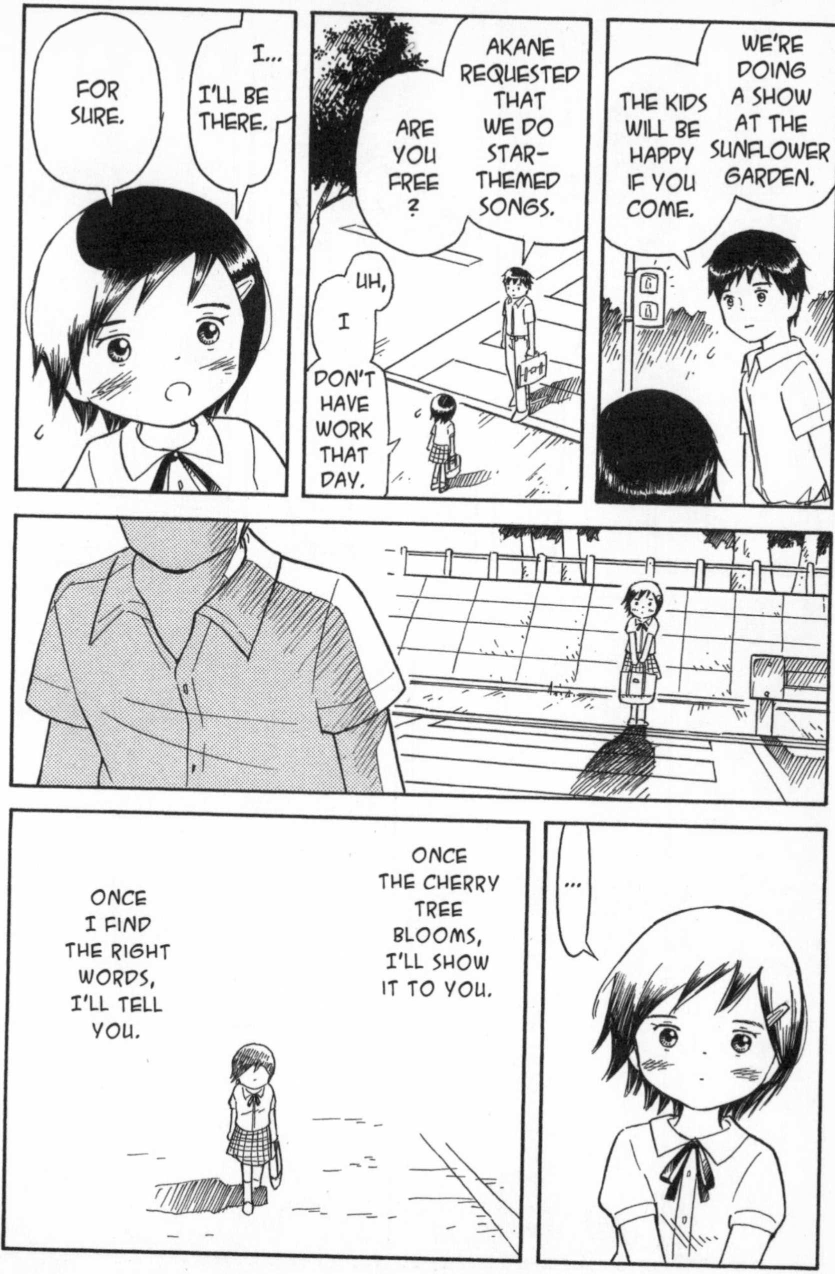
WE'RE DOING A SHOW AT THE SUNFLOWER GARDEN.
THE KIDS WILL BE HAPPY IF YOU COME.
AKANE REQUESTED THAT WE DO STAR-THEMED SONGS.
ARE YOU FREE?
UH, I DON'T HAVE WORK THAT DAY.
I... I'LL BE THERE.
FOR SURE.
...
ONCE THE CHERRY TREE BLOOMS, I'LL SHOW IT TO YOU.
ONCE I FIND THE RIGHT WORDS, I'LL TELL YOU.

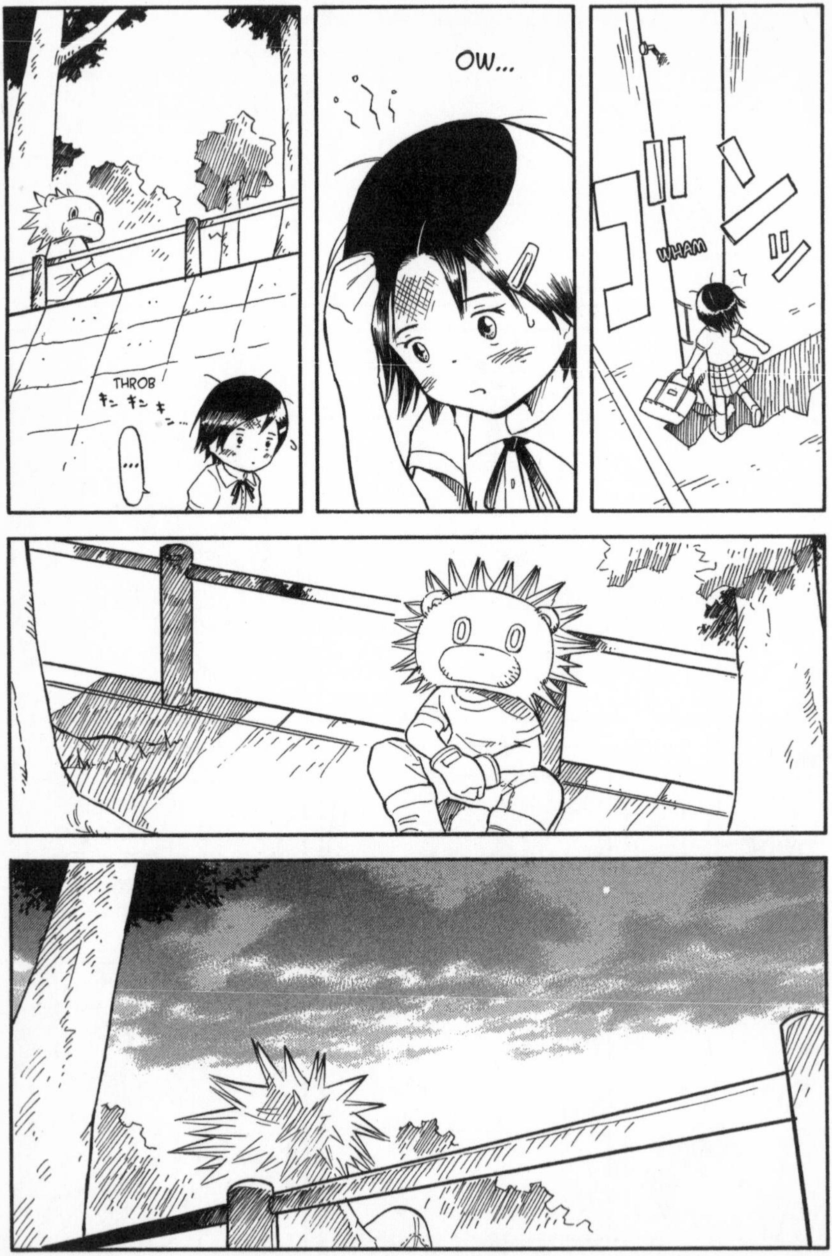
ゴンッ
WHAM
OW...
THROB
キン キン キン...
...

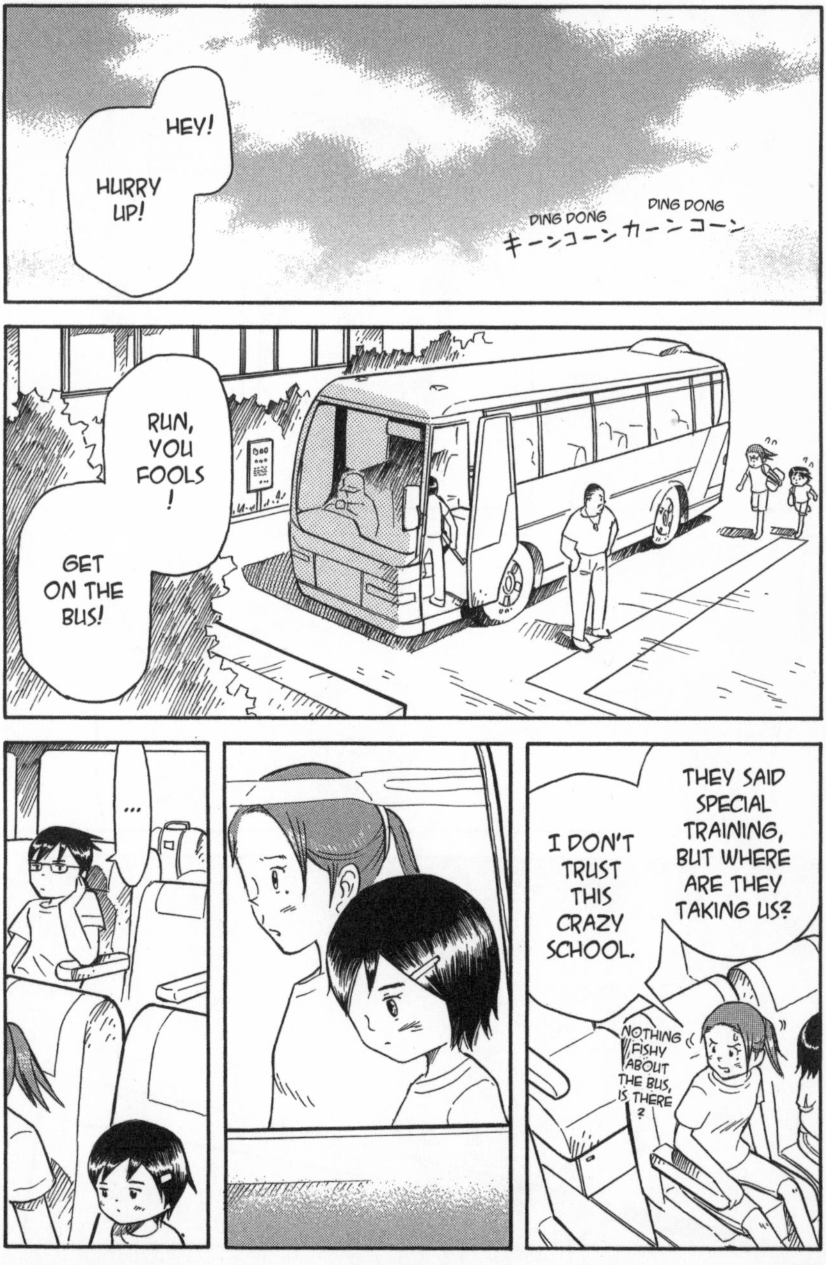
HEY! HURRY UP!
DING DONG キーンコーン DING DONG カーンコーン
RUN, YOU FOOLS!
GET ON THE BUS!
THEY SAID SPECIAL TRAINING, BUT WHERE ARE THEY TAKING US?
I DON'T TRUST THIS CRAZY SCHOOL.
NOTHING FISHY ABOUT THE BUS, IS THERE?
...

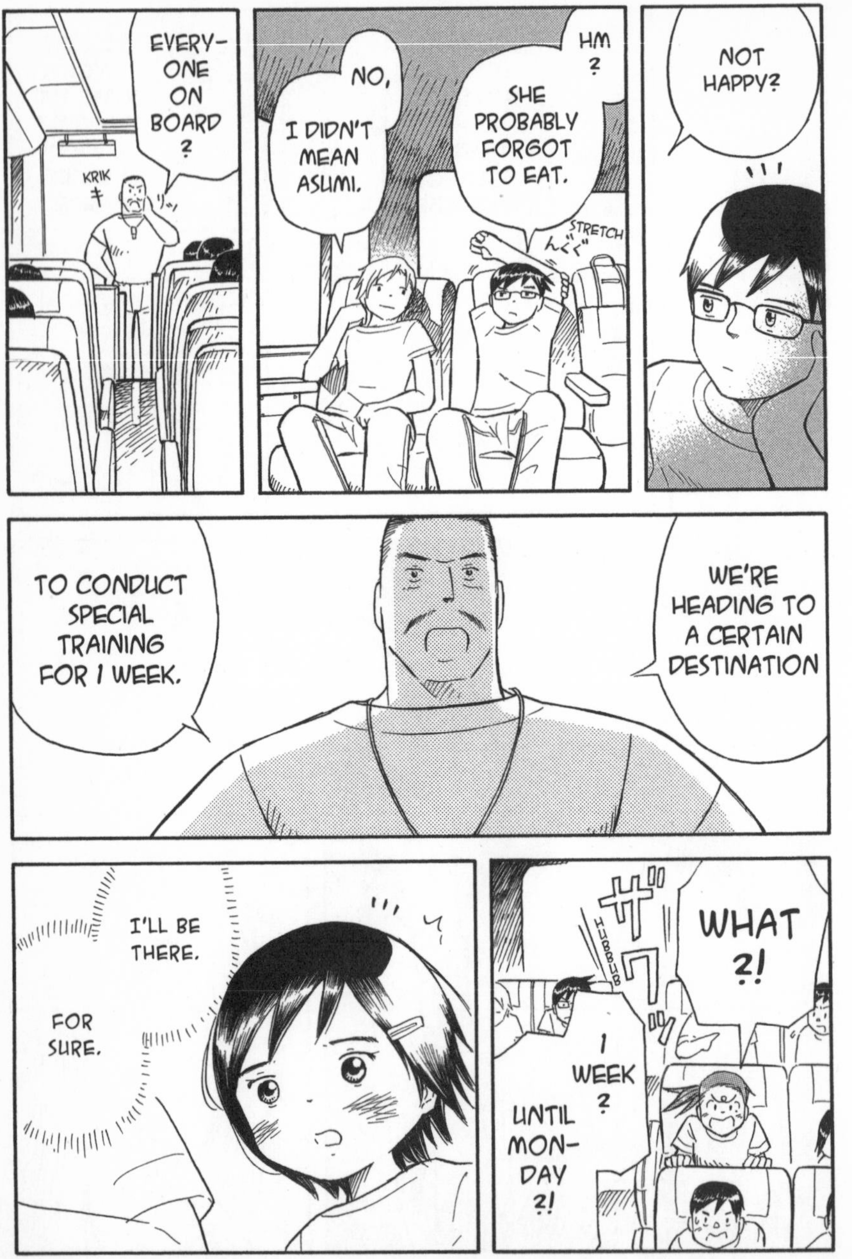
NOT HAPPY?
HM?
SHE PROBABLY FORGOT TO EAT.
STRETCH
NO,
I DIDN'T MEAN ASUMI.
EVERY-ONE ON BOARD?
KRIK
WE'RE HEADING TO A CERTAIN DESTINATION
TO CONDUCT SPECIAL TRAINING FOR 1 WEEK.
WHAT?!
HUBBUB
1 WEEK?
UNTIL MON-DAY?!
I'LL BE THERE.
FOR SURE.

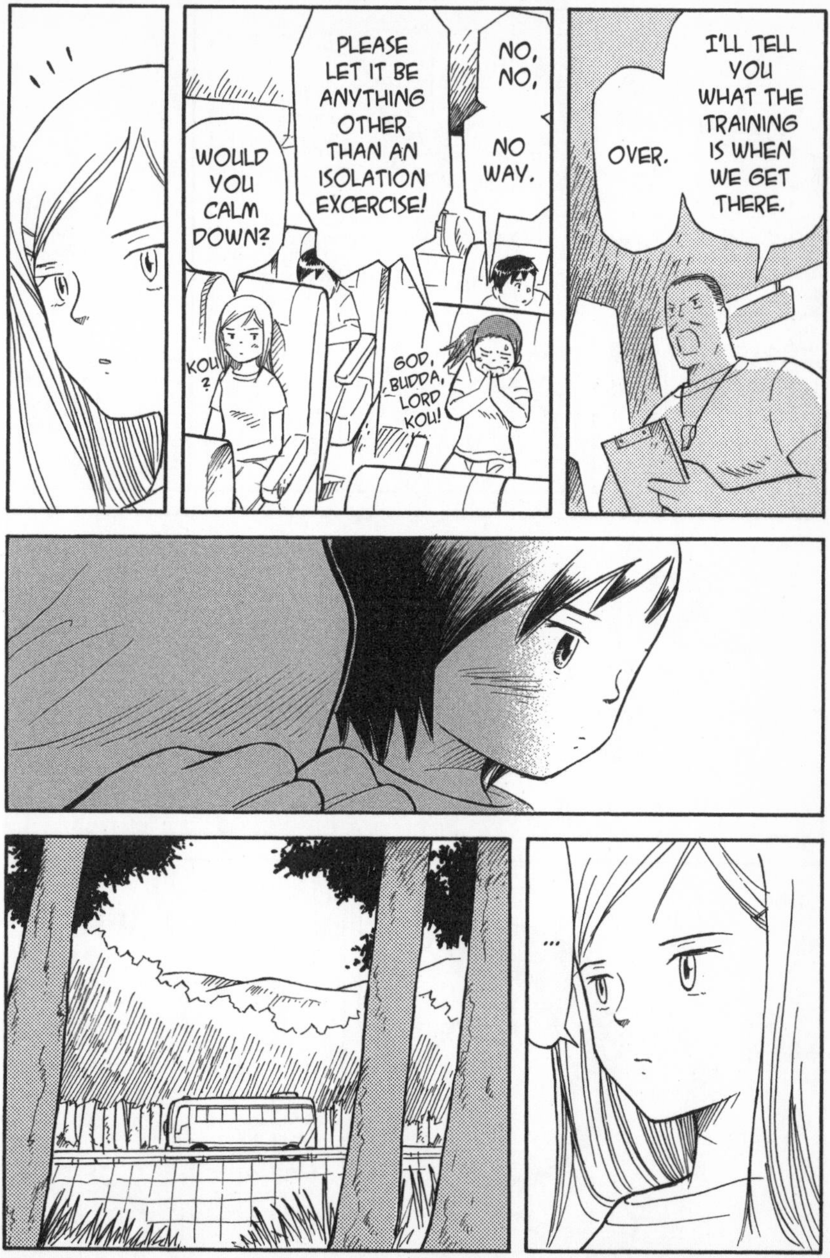
I'LL TELL YOU WHAT THE TRAINING IS WHEN WE GET THERE.
OVER.
NO, NO,
NO WAY.
PLEASE LET IT BE ANYTHING OTHER THAN AN ISOLATION EXCERCISE!
WOULD YOU CALM DOWN?
GOD, BUDDA, LORD KOU!
KOU?
...

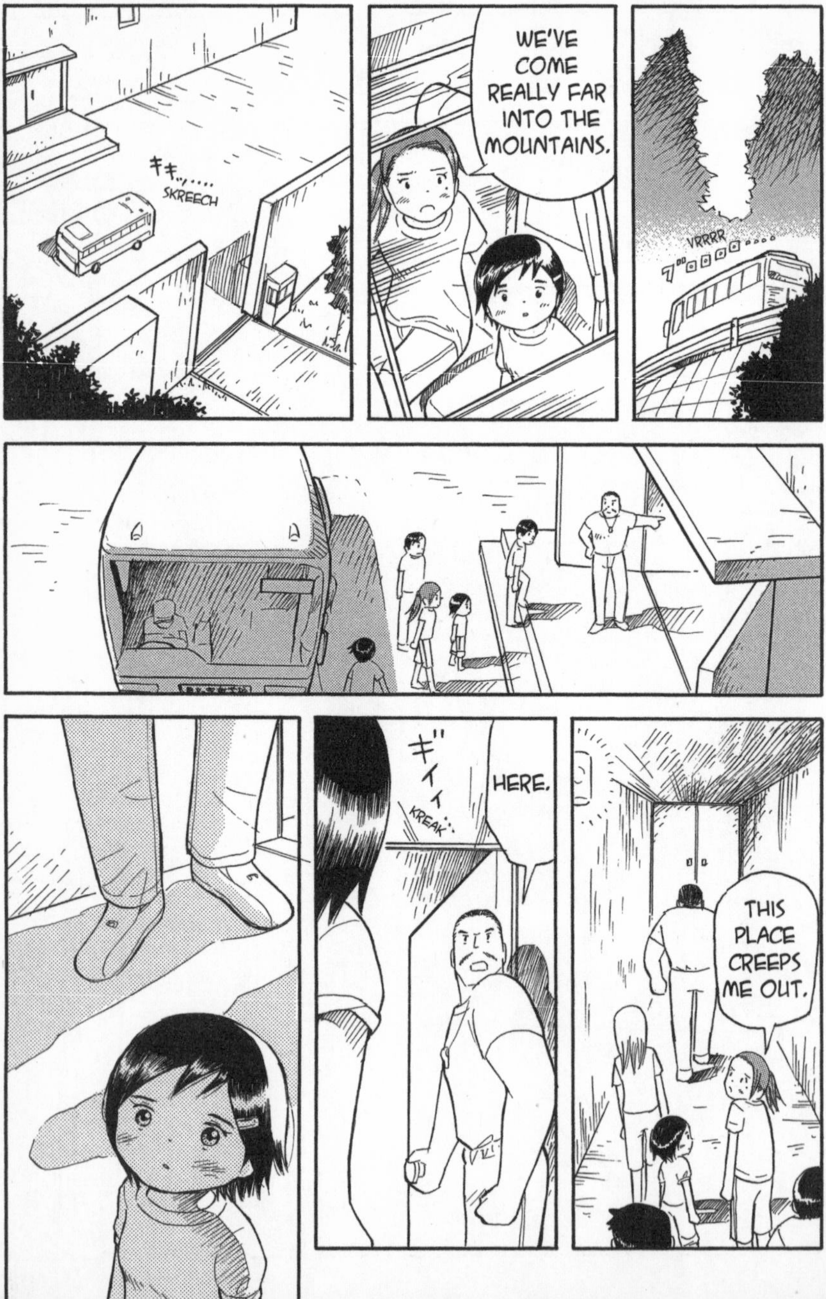
VRRRR
WE'VE COME REALLY FAR INTO THE MOUNTAINS.
SKREECH
THIS PLACE CREEPS ME OUT.
HERE.
ギイィ
KREAK

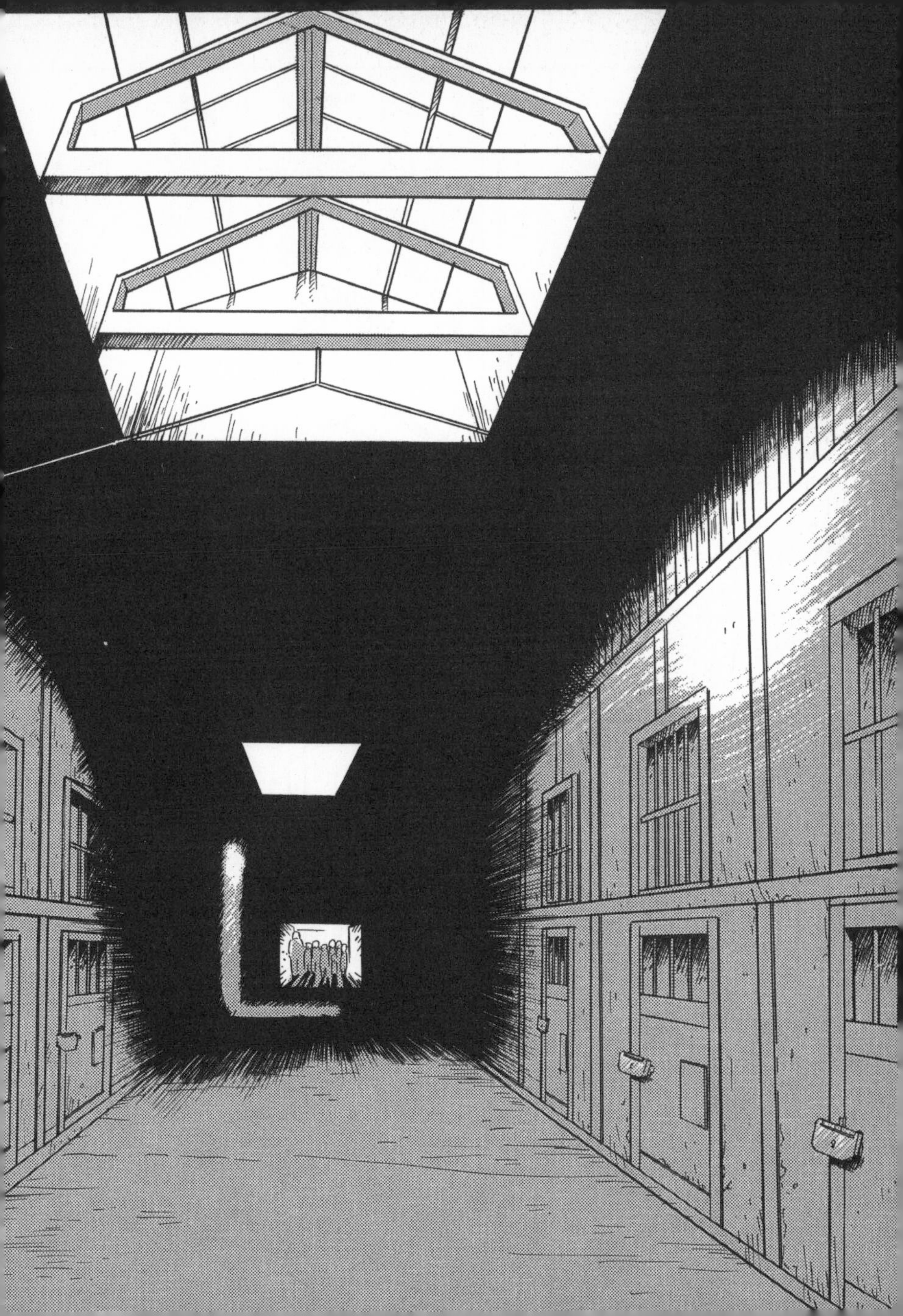

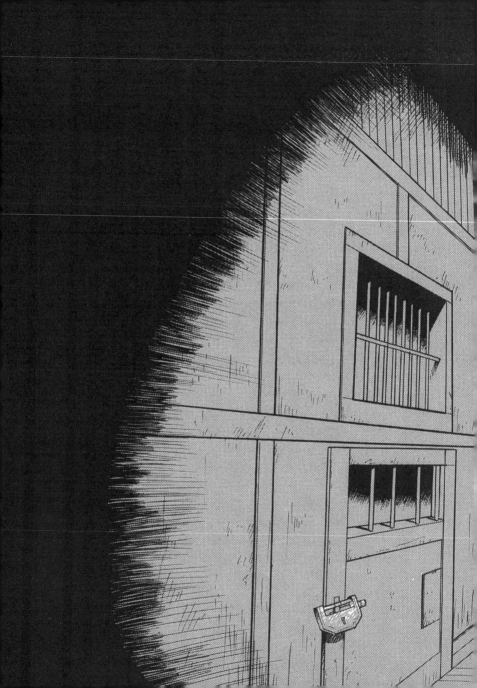

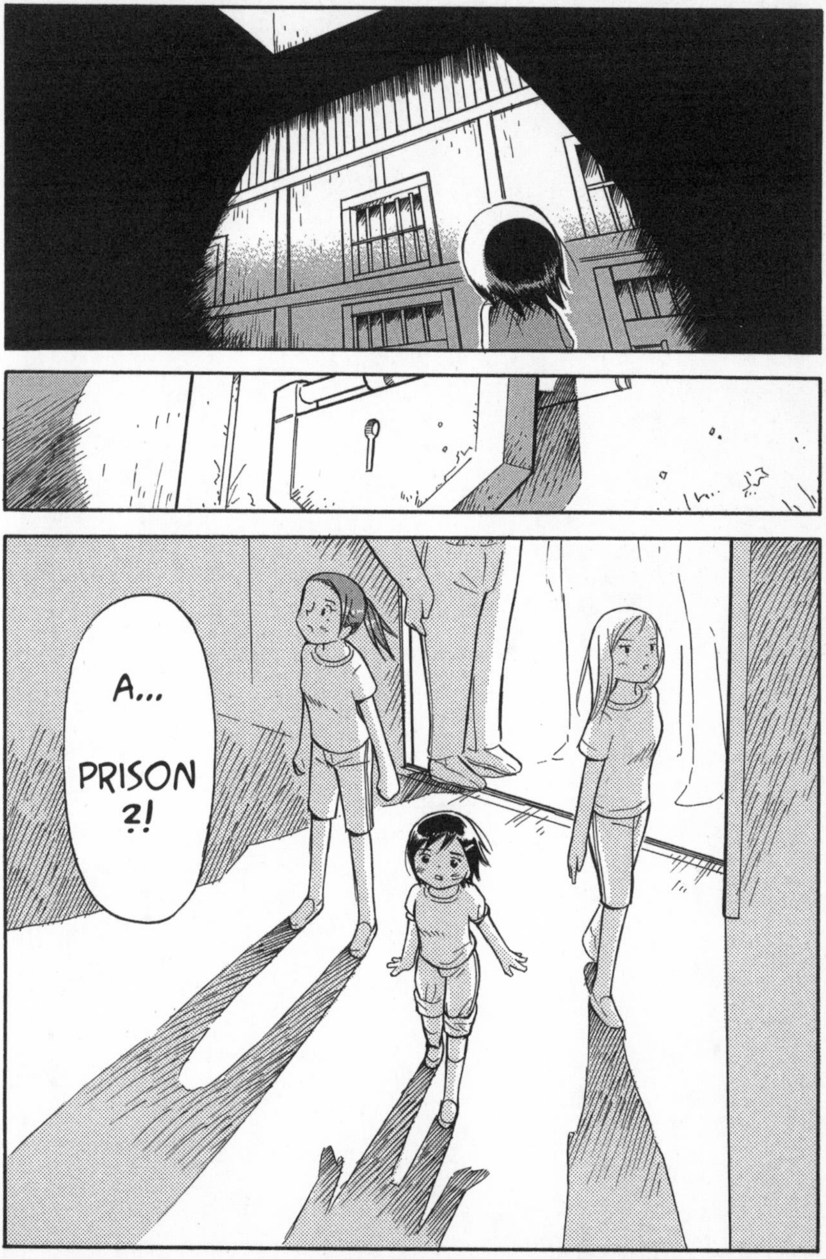
A... PRISON ?!

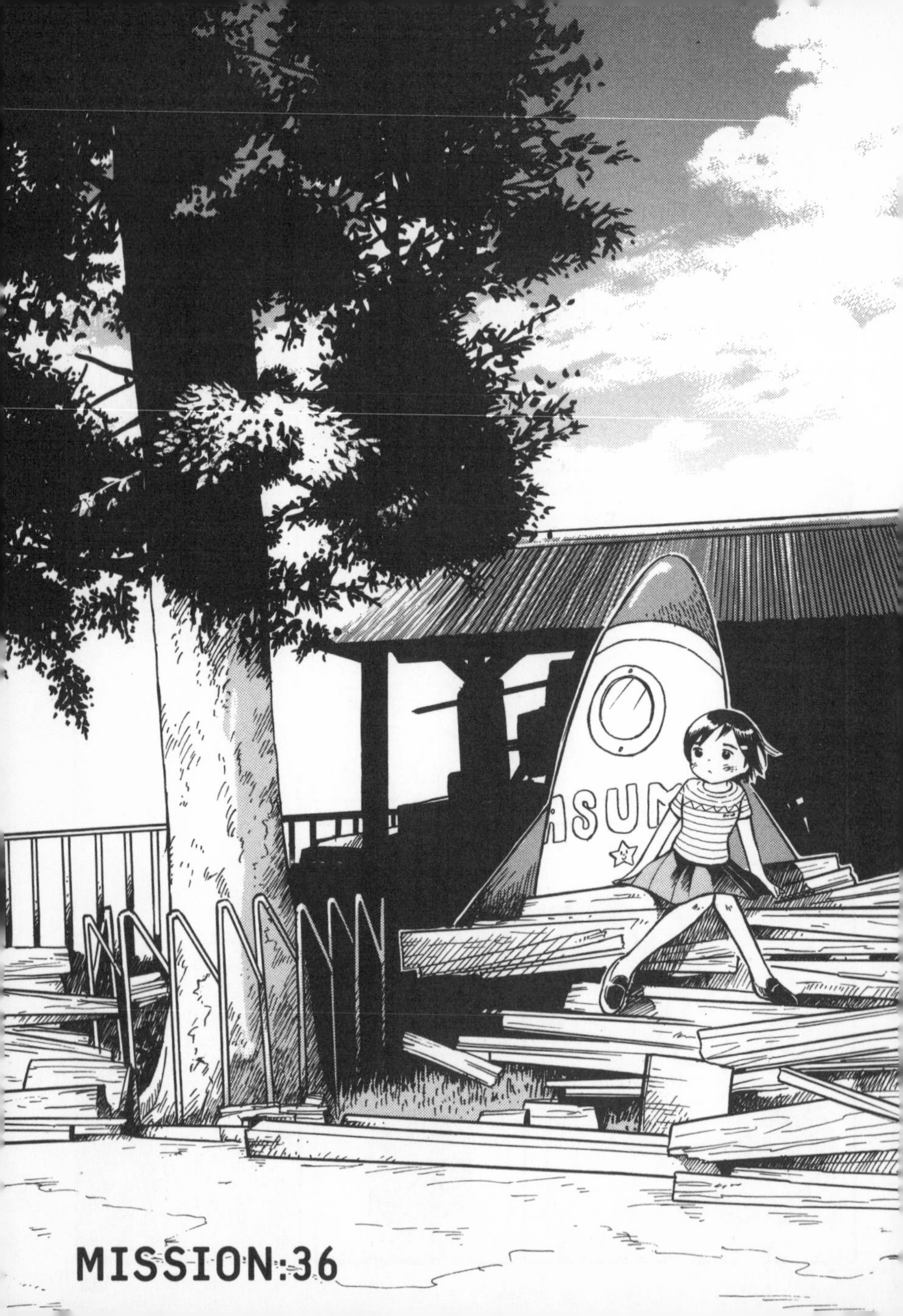
ASUM

MISSION:36

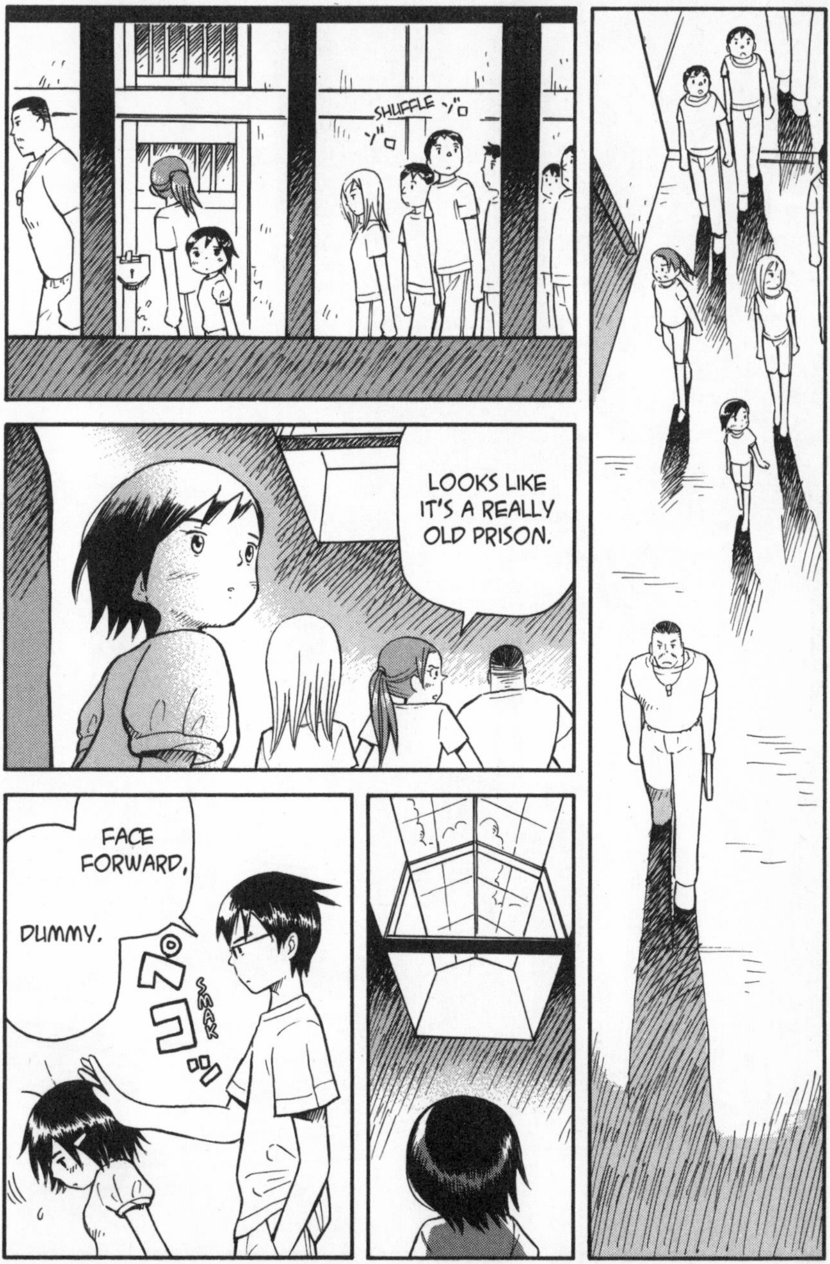
SHUFFLE ゾロ
ゾロ
LOOKS LIKE IT'S A REALLY OLD PRISON.
FACE FORWARD,
DUMMY.
SMAK

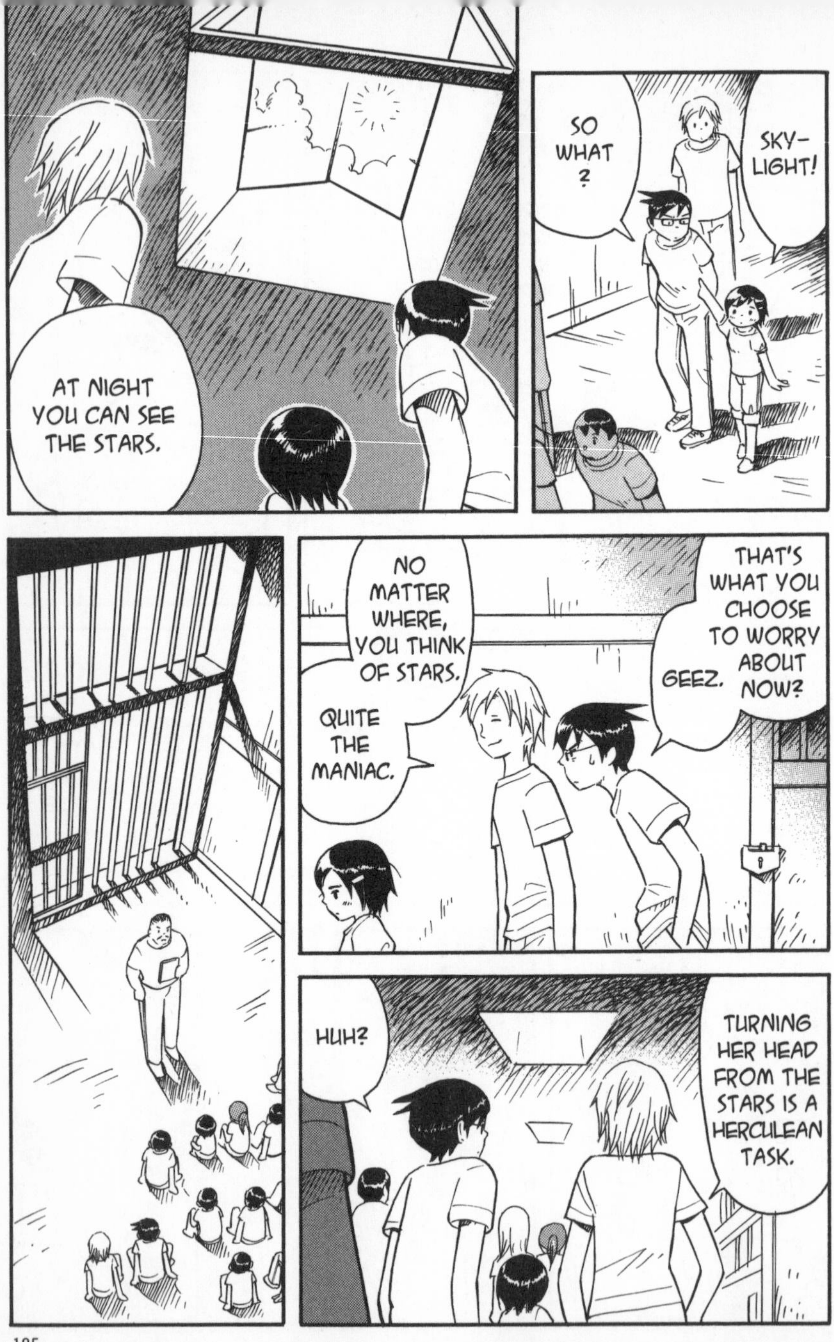
SKY-LIGHT!
SO WHAT?
AT NIGHT YOU CAN SEE THE STARS.
THAT'S WHAT YOU CHOOSE TO WORRY ABOUT NOW?
GEEZ.
NO MATTER WHERE, YOU THINK OF STARS.
QUITE THE MANIAC.
TURNING HER HEAD FROM THE STARS IS A HERCULEAN TASK.
HUH?

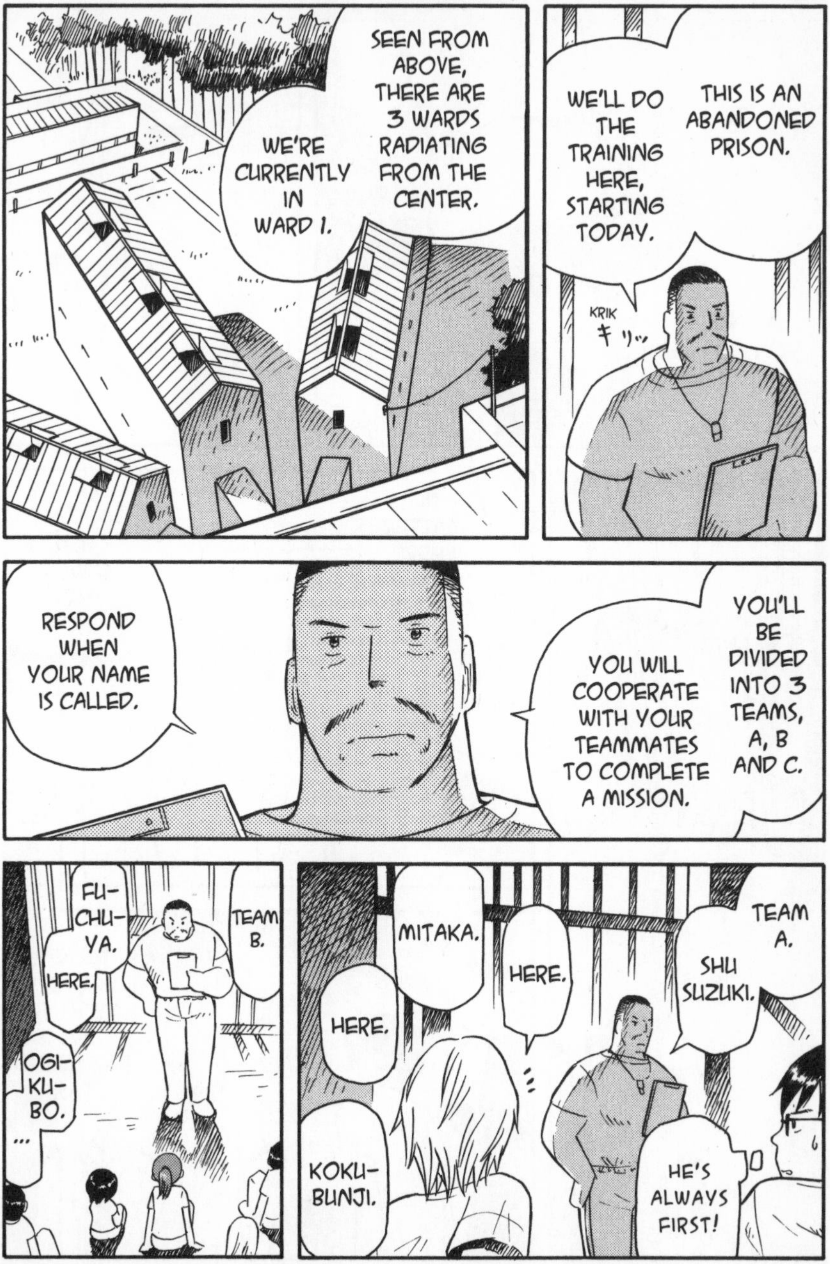
THIS IS AN ABANDONED PRISON.
WE'LL DO THE TRAINING HERE, STARTING TODAY.
KRIK
キリッ
SEEN FROM ABOVE, THERE ARE 3 WARDS RADIATING FROM THE CENTER.
WE'RE CURRENTLY IN WARD 1.
YOU'LL BE DIVIDED INTO 3 TEAMS, A, B AND C.
YOU WILL COOPERATE WITH YOUR TEAMMATES TO COMPLETE A MISSION.
RESPOND WHEN YOUR NAME IS CALLED.
TEAM A.
SHU SUZUKI.
HERE.
MITAKA.
HERE.
...
KOKUBUNJI.
HE'S ALWAYS FIRST!
TEAM B.
FU-CHU-YA.
HERE.
OGI-KU-BO.
...

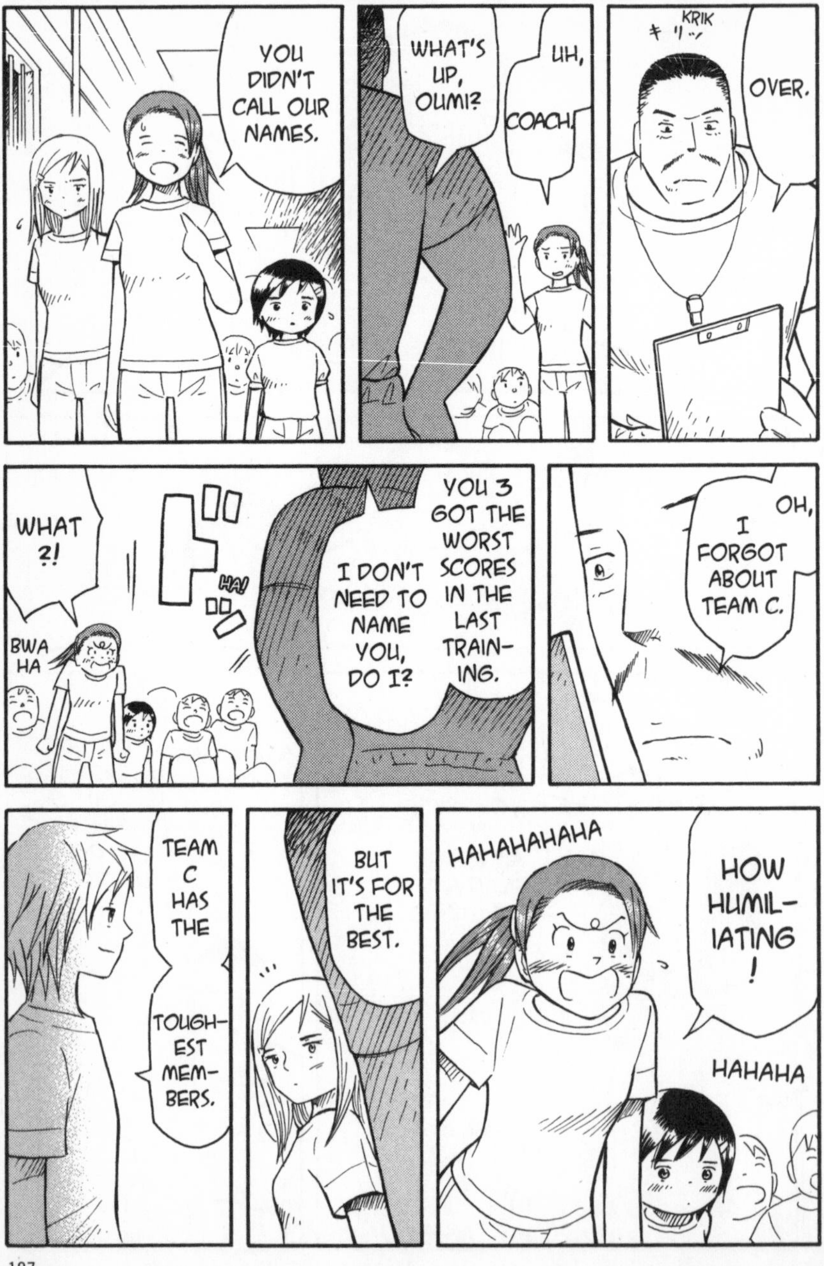
KRIK
キリッ
OVER.
UH, COACH.
WHAT'S UP, OUMI?
YOU DIDN'T CALL OUR NAMES.
OH, I FORGOT ABOUT TEAM C.
YOU 3 GOT THE WORST SCORES IN THE LAST TRAINING.
I DON'T NEED TO NAME YOU, DO I?
HA!
WHAT ?!
BWA HA
HOW HUMILIATING!
HAHAHAHAHA
HAHAHA
BUT IT'S FOR THE BEST.
TEAM C HAS THE TOUGHEST MEMBERS.

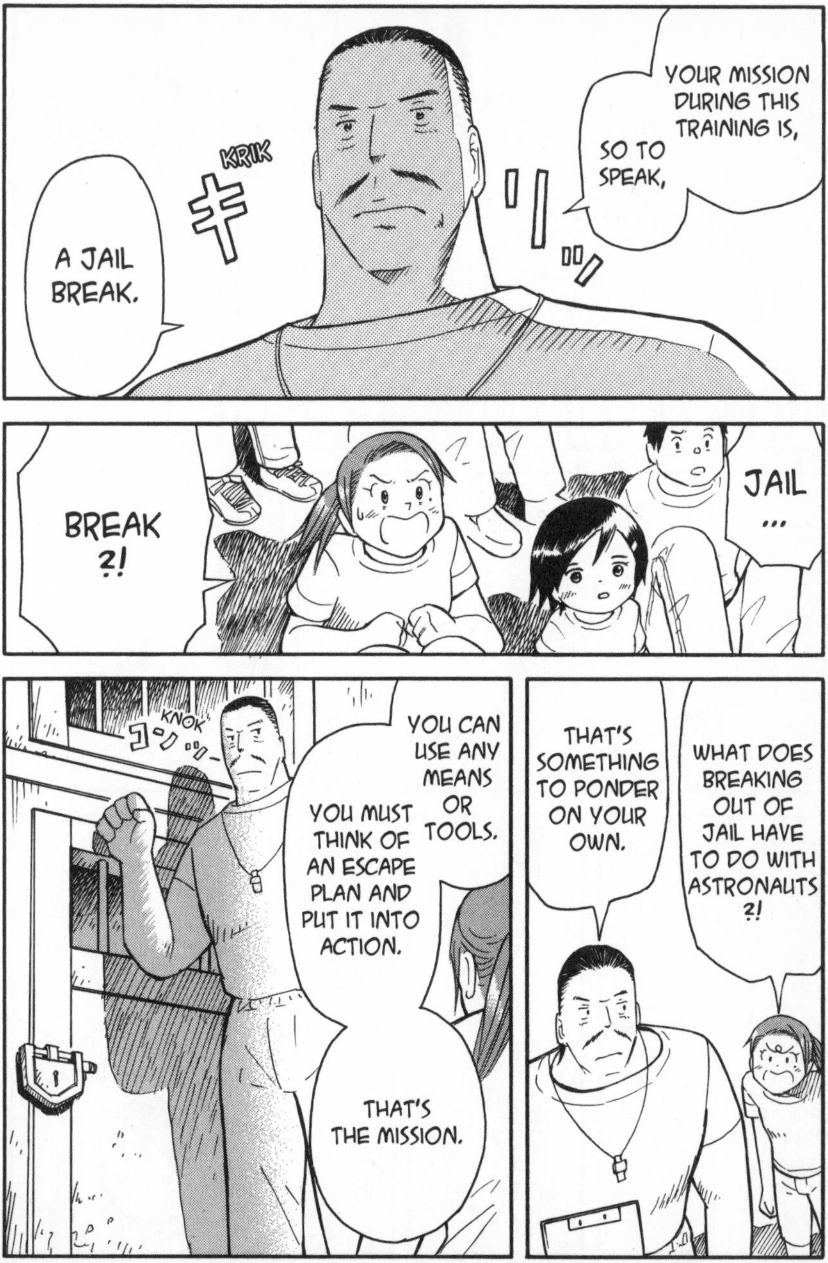
YOUR MISSION DURING THIS TRAINING IS,
SO TO SPEAK,
KRIK
A JAIL BREAK.
JAIL ...
BREAK ?!
WHAT DOES BREAKING OUT OF JAIL HAVE TO DO WITH ASTRONAUTS ?!
THAT'S SOMETHING TO PONDER ON YOUR OWN.
YOU CAN USE ANY MEANS OR TOOLS.
YOU MUST THINK OF AN ESCAPE PLAN AND PUT IT INTO ACTION.
KNOK
THAT'S THE MISSION.

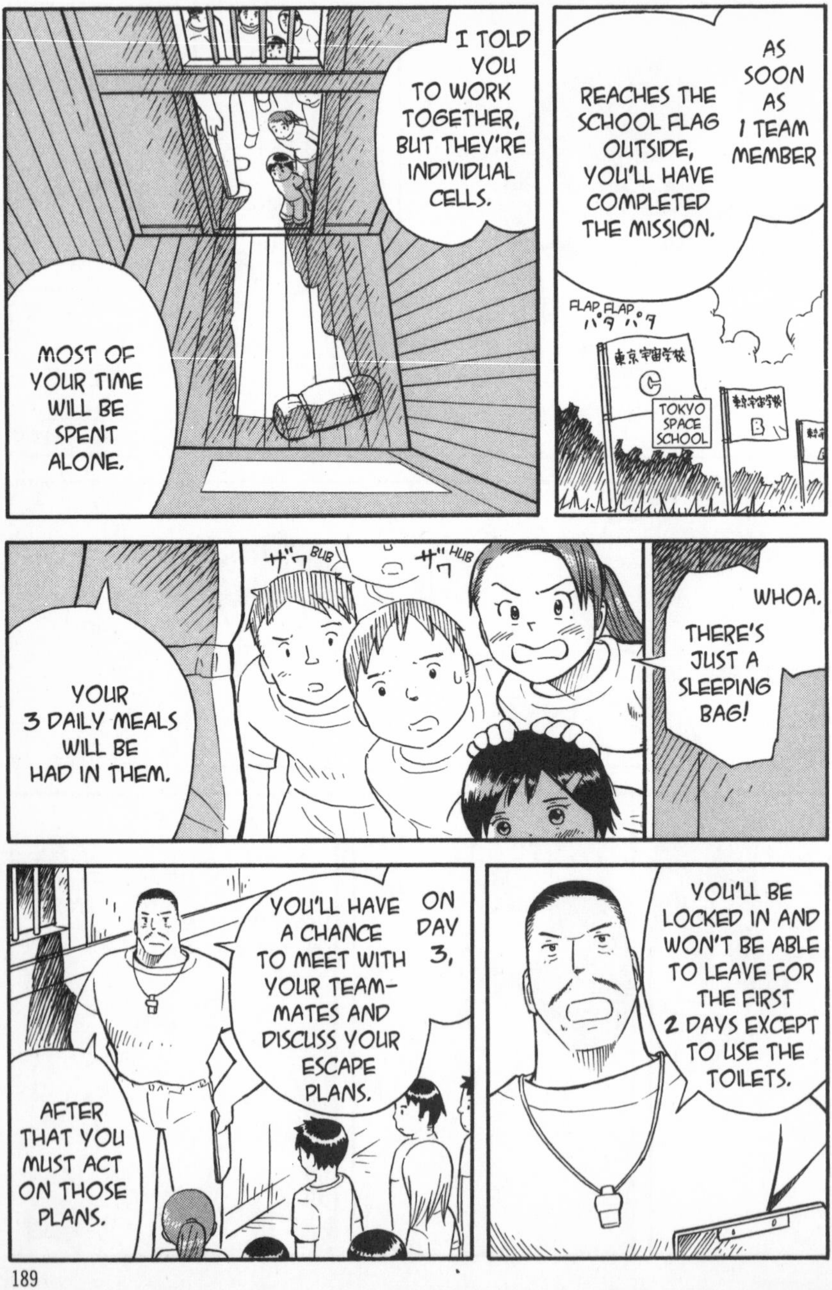
AS SOON AS 1 TEAM MEMBER
REACHES THE SCHOOL FLAG OUTSIDE, YOU'LL HAVE COMPLETED THE MISSION.
FLAP FLAP
パタパタ
東京宇宙学校
C
TOKYO SPACE SCHOOL
B
I TOLD YOU TO WORK TOGETHER, BUT THEY'RE INDIVIDUAL CELLS.
MOST OF YOUR TIME WILL BE SPENT ALONE.
WHOA.
THERE'S JUST A SLEEPING BAG!
ザワ BUB
ザワ HUB
YOUR 3 DAILY MEALS WILL BE HAD IN THEM.
YOU'LL BE LOCKED IN AND WON'T BE ABLE TO LEAVE FOR THE FIRST 2 DAYS EXCEPT TO USE THE TOILETS.
ON DAY 3,
YOU'LL HAVE A CHANCE TO MEET WITH YOUR TEAM-MATES AND DISCUSS YOUR ESCAPE PLANS.
AFTER THAT YOU MUST ACT ON THOSE PLANS.

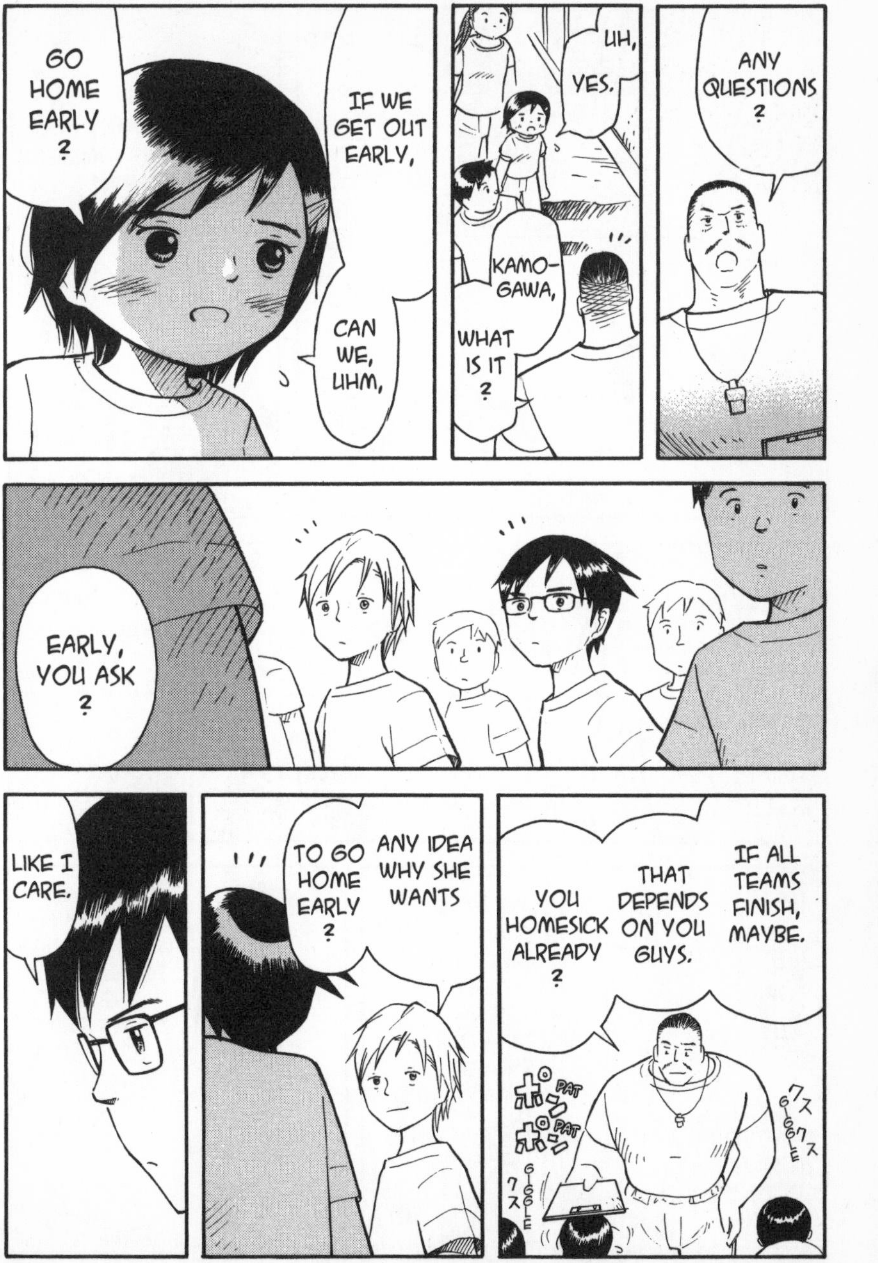
ANY QUESTIONS?
UH, YES.
KAMO-GAWA, WHAT IS IT?
IF WE GET OUT EARLY,
CAN WE, UHM,
GO HOME EARLY?
EARLY, YOU ASK?
IF ALL TEAMS FINISH, MAYBE.
THAT DEPENDS ON YOU GUYS.
YOU HOMESICK ALREADY?
GIGGLE
PAT
PAT
GIGGLE
ANY IDEA WHY SHE WANTS TO GO HOME EARLY?
LIKE I CARE.

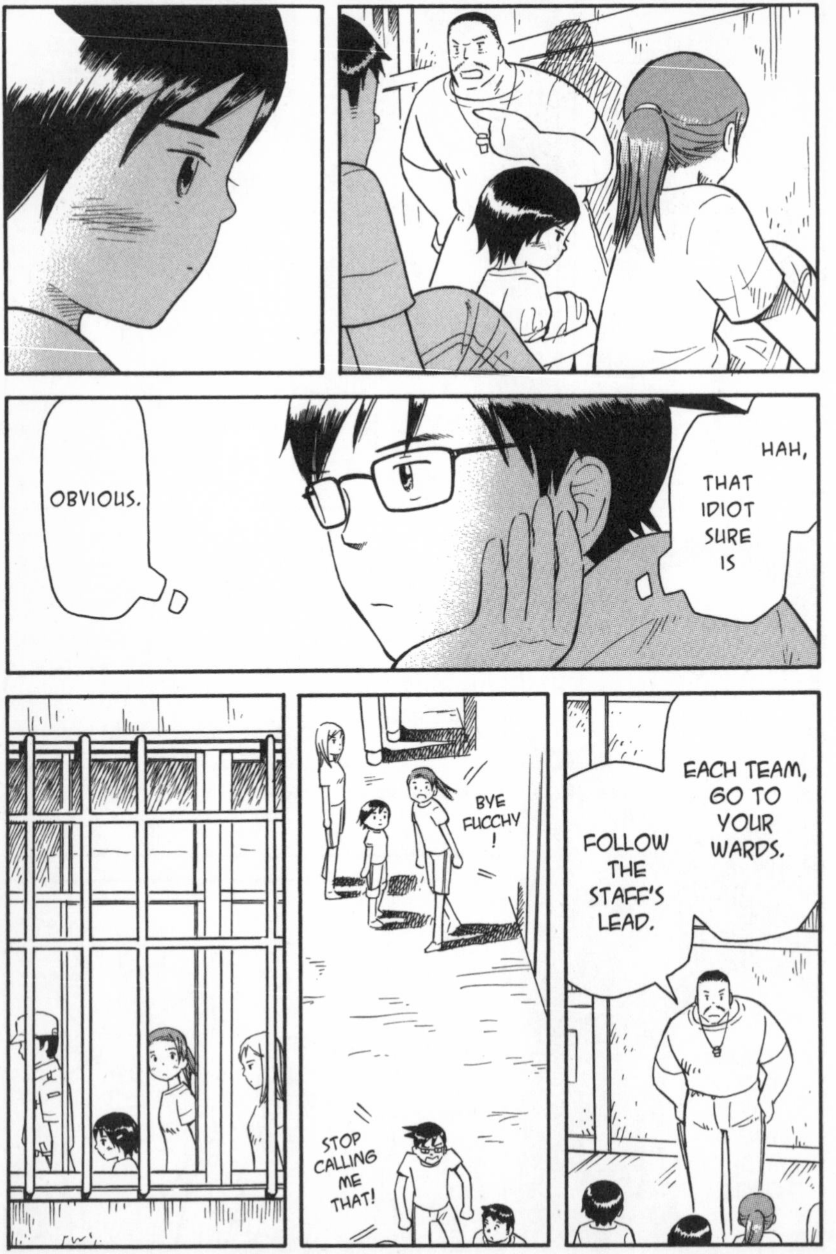
HAH, THAT IDIOT SURE IS
OBVIOUS.
EACH TEAM, GO TO YOUR WARDS.
FOLLOW THE STAFF'S LEAD.
BYE FUCCHY!
STOP CALLING ME THAT!

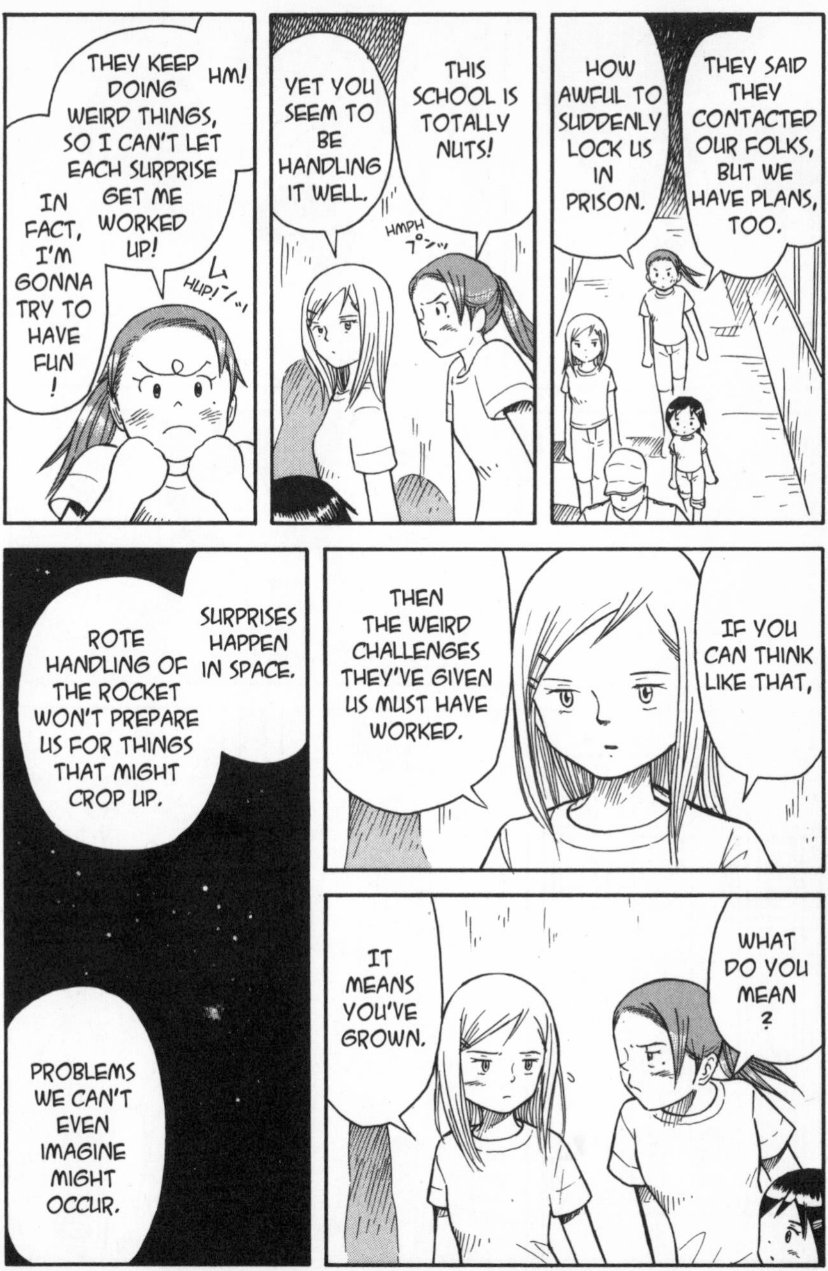
THEY SAID THEY CONTACTED OUR FOLKS, BUT WE HAVE PLANS, TOO.
HOW AWFUL TO SUDDENLY LOCK US IN PRISON.
THIS SCHOOL IS TOTALLY NUTS!
HMPH
YET YOU SEEM TO BE HANDLING IT WELL.
THEY KEEP DOING WEIRD THINGS, SO I CAN'T LET EACH SURPRISE GET ME WORKED UP!
HM!
HUP!
IN FACT, I'M GONNA TRY TO HAVE FUN!
IF YOU CAN THINK LIKE THAT,
THEN THE WEIRD CHALLENGES THEY'VE GIVEN US MUST HAVE WORKED.
WHAT DO YOU MEAN?
IT MEANS YOU'VE GROWN.
SURPRISES HAPPEN IN SPACE.
ROTE HANDLING OF THE ROCKET WON'T PREPARE US FOR THINGS THAT MIGHT CROP UP.
PROBLEMS WE CAN'T EVEN IMAGINE MIGHT OCCUR.

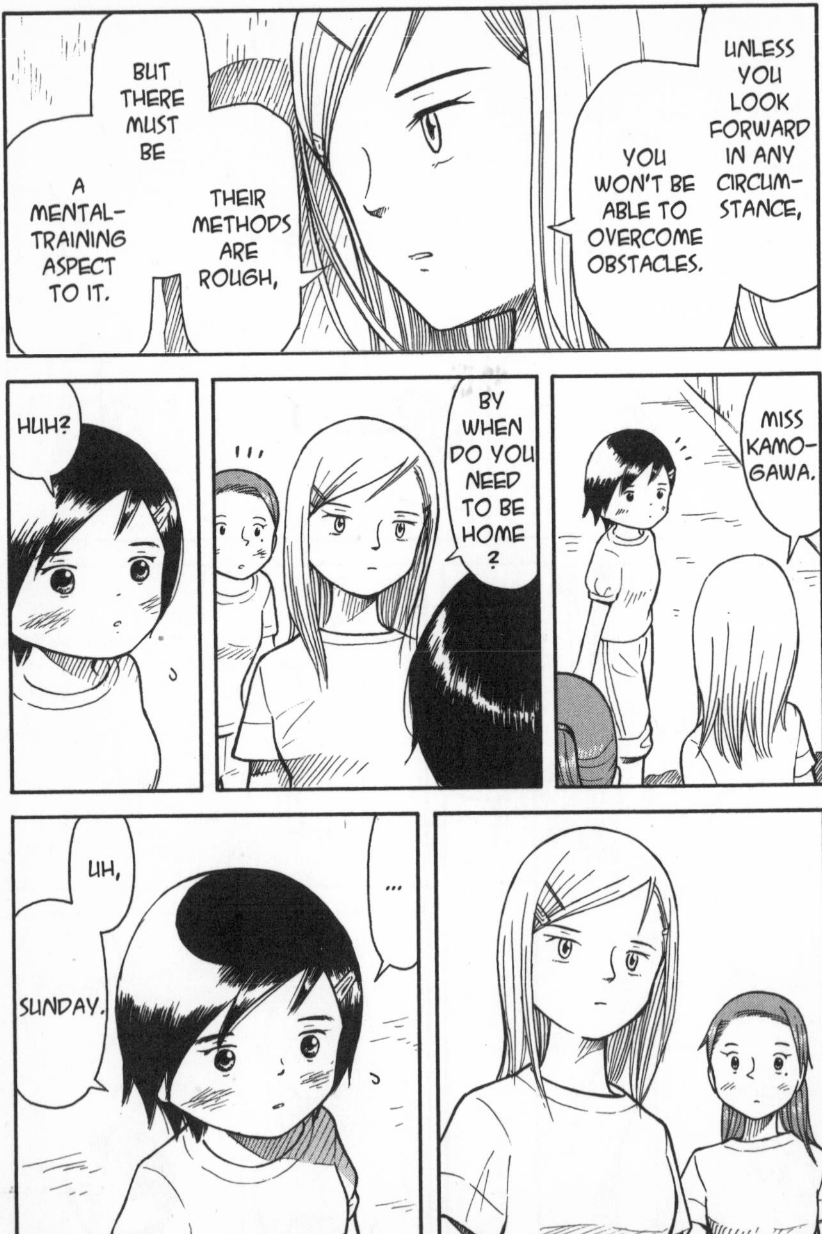
UNLESS YOU LOOK FORWARD IN ANY CIRCUM-STANCE,
YOU WON'T BE ABLE TO OVERCOME OBSTACLES.
THEIR METHODS ARE ROUGH,
BUT THERE MUST BE
A MENTAL-TRAINING ASPECT TO IT.
MISS KAMO-GAWA.
BY WHEN DO YOU NEED TO BE HOME?
HUH?
...
UH,
SUNDAY.

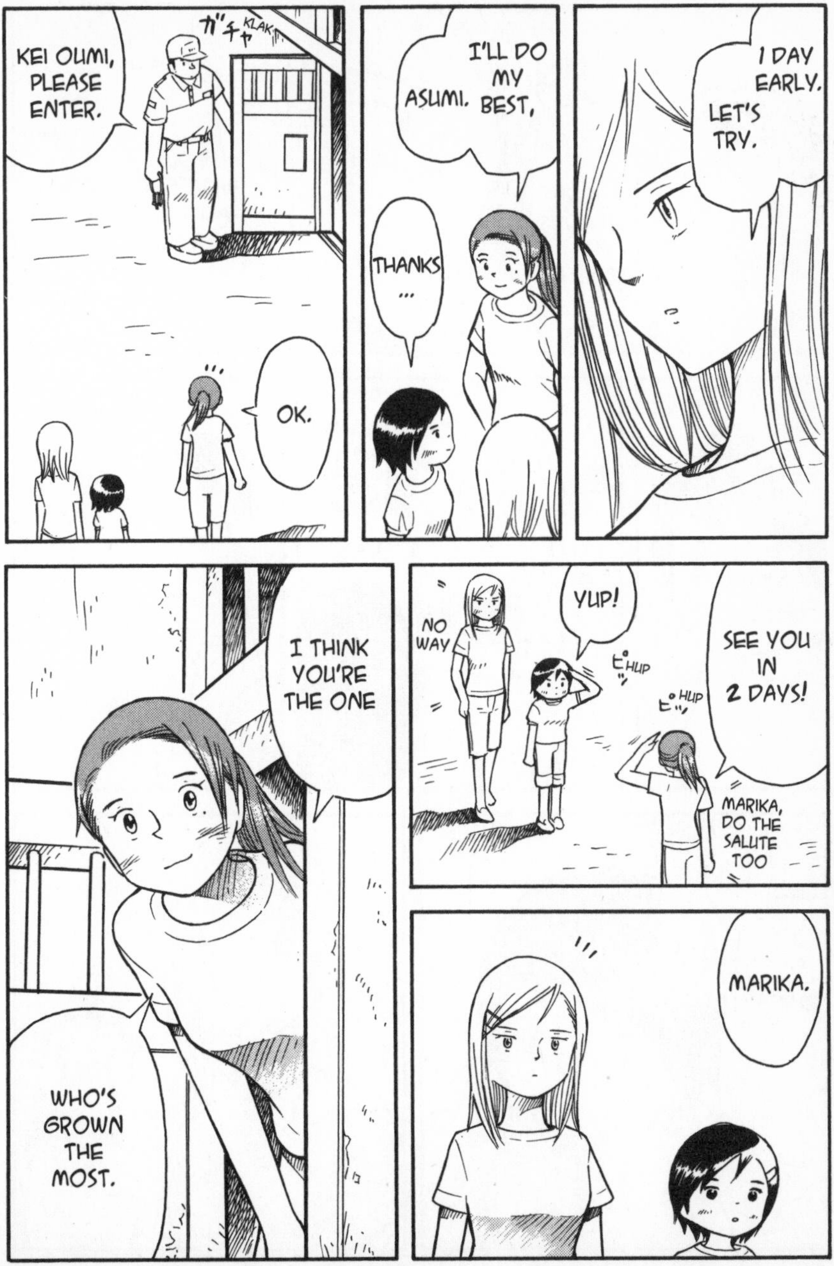
1 DAY EARLY.
LET'S TRY.
I'LL DO MY BEST,
ASUMI.
THANKS ...
ガチャ KLAK
KEI OUMI, PLEASE ENTER.
OK.
SEE YOU IN 2 DAYS!
YUP!
ピッ HUP
ピッ HUP
NO WAY
MARIKA, DO THE SALUTE TOO
MARIKA.
I THINK YOU'RE THE ONE
WHO'S GROWN THE MOST.

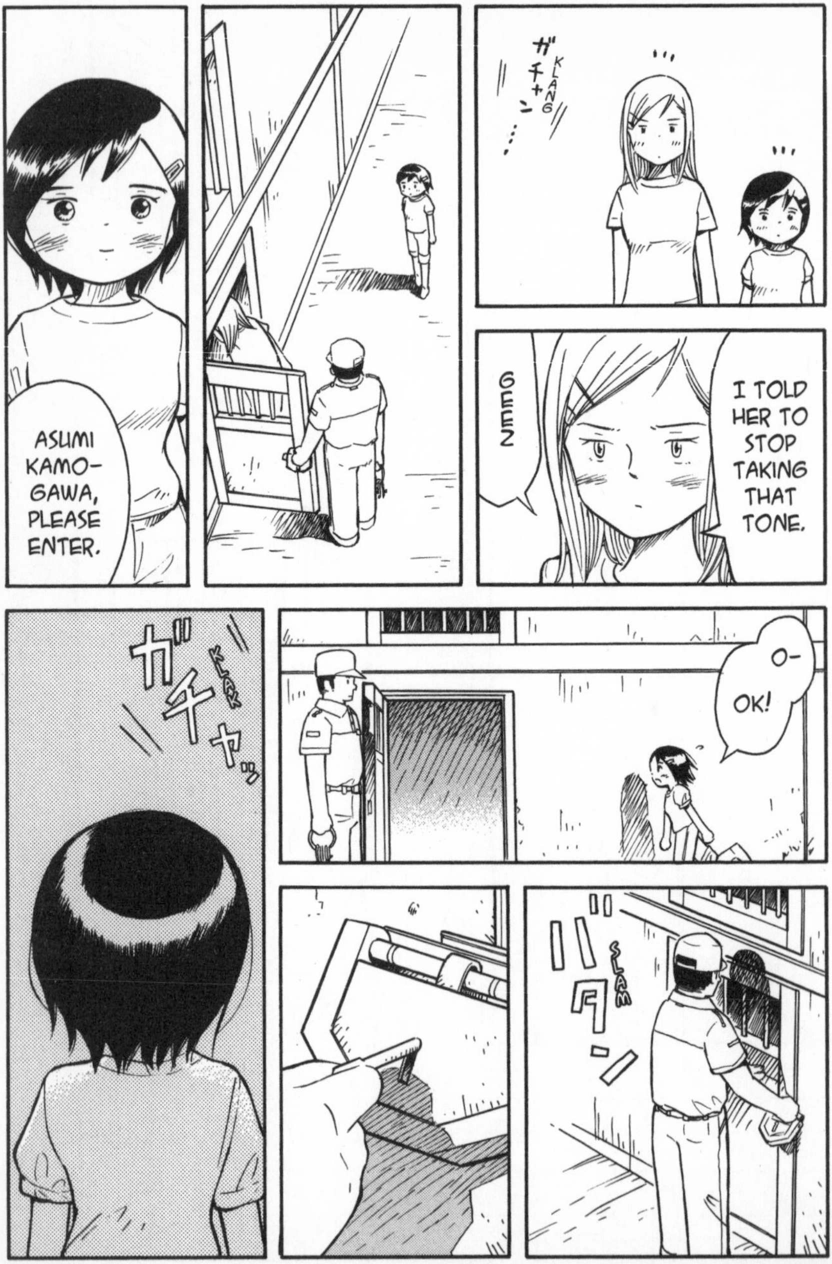

ガチャン…
KLANG
I TOLD HER TO STOP TAKING THAT TONE.
GEEZ
ASUMI KAMOGAWA, PLEASE ENTER.
O- OK!
バタン
SLAM
ガチャッ
KLAK

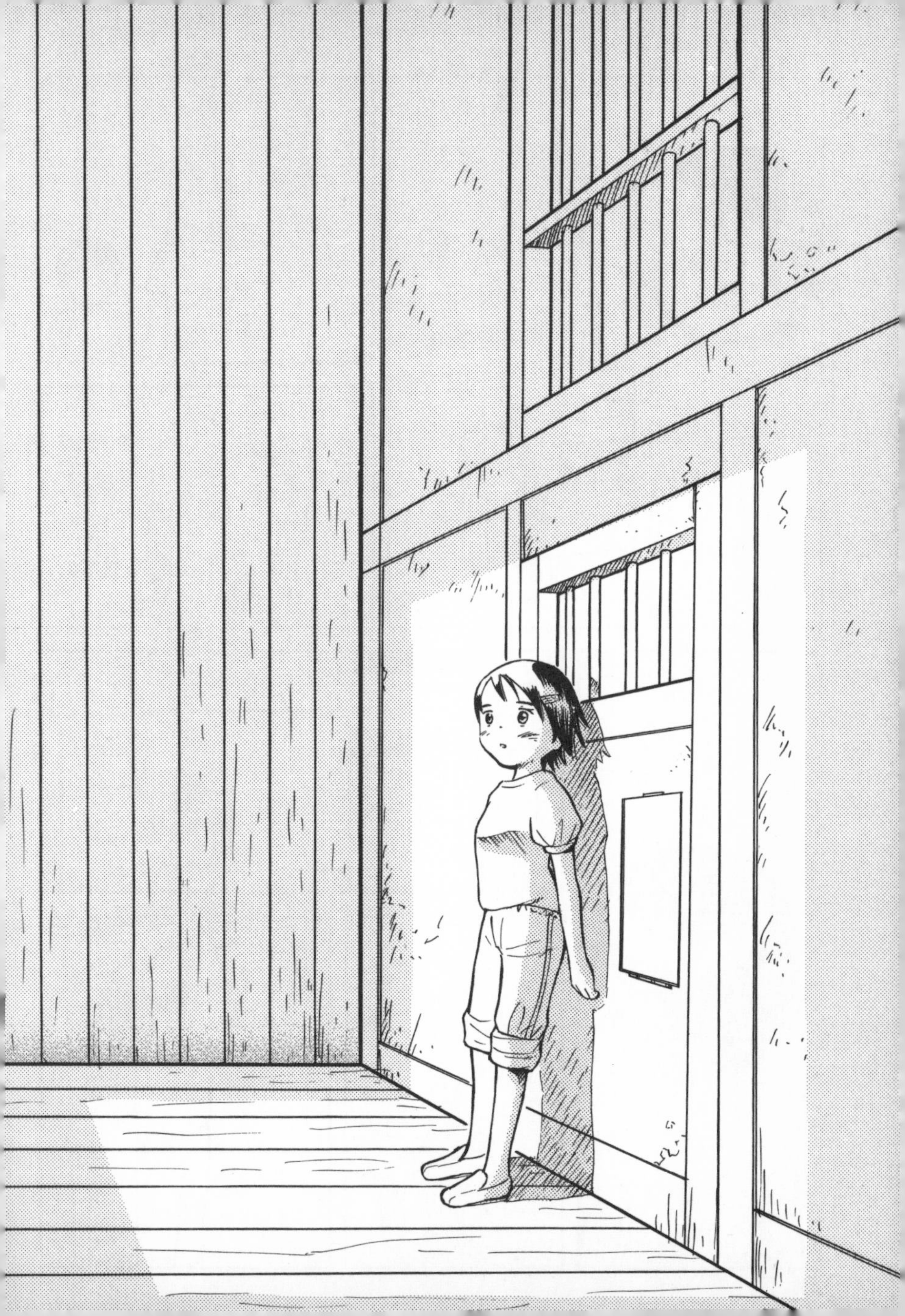

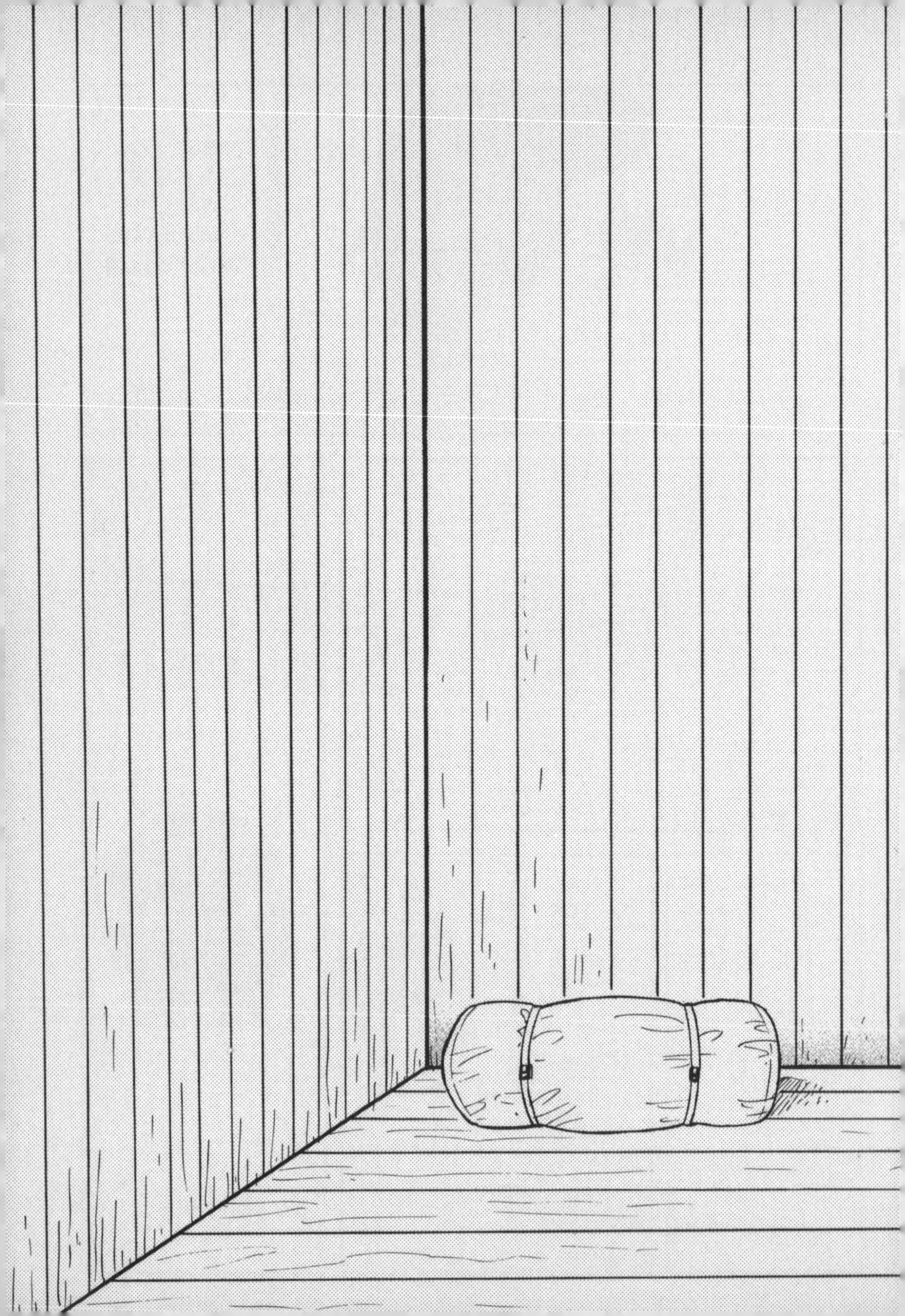

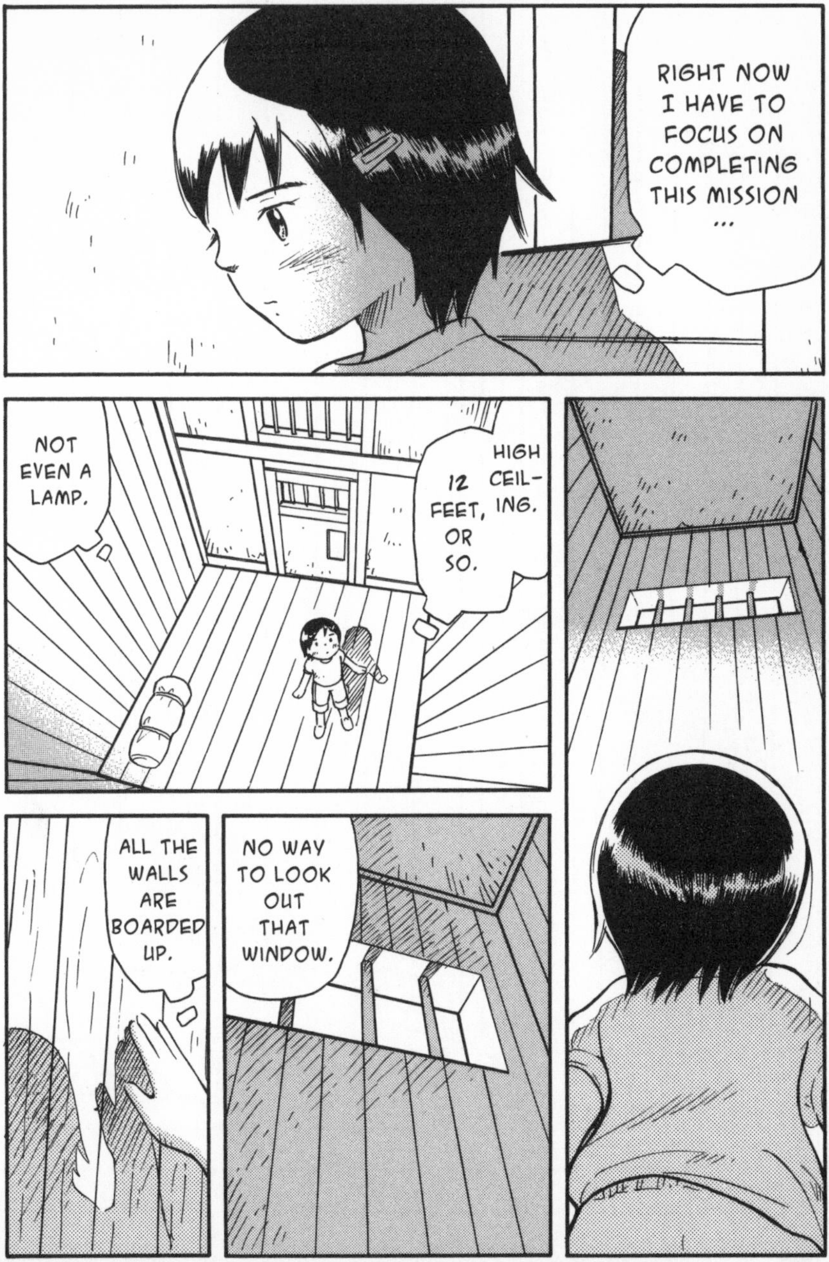
RIGHT NOW I HAVE TO FOCUS ON COMPLETING THIS MISSION ...
HIGH CEILING. 12 FEET, OR SO.
NOT EVEN A LAMP.
NO WAY TO LOOK OUT THAT WINDOW.
ALL THE WALLS ARE BOARDED UP.

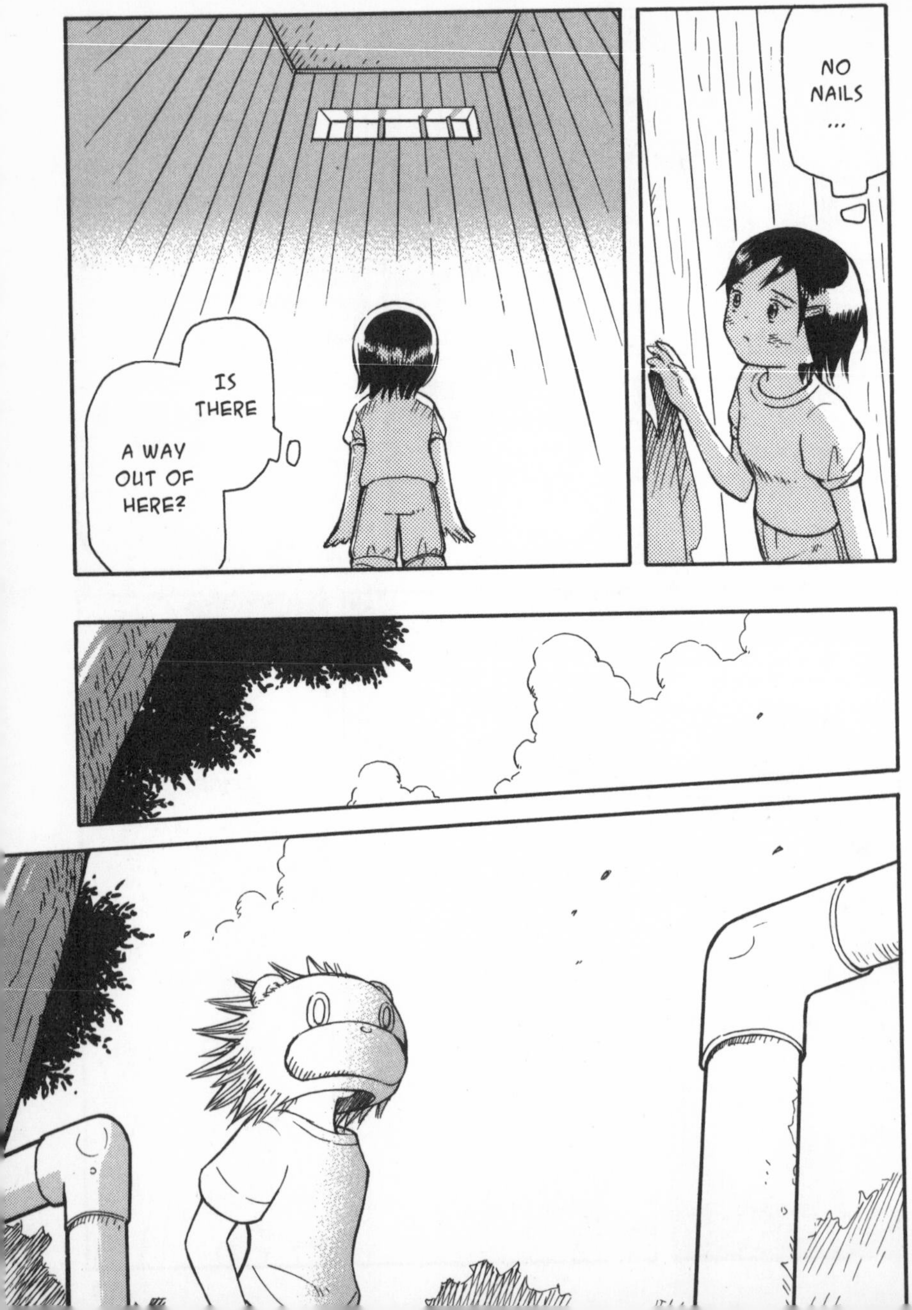
NO NAILS ...
IS THERE A WAY OUT OF HERE?

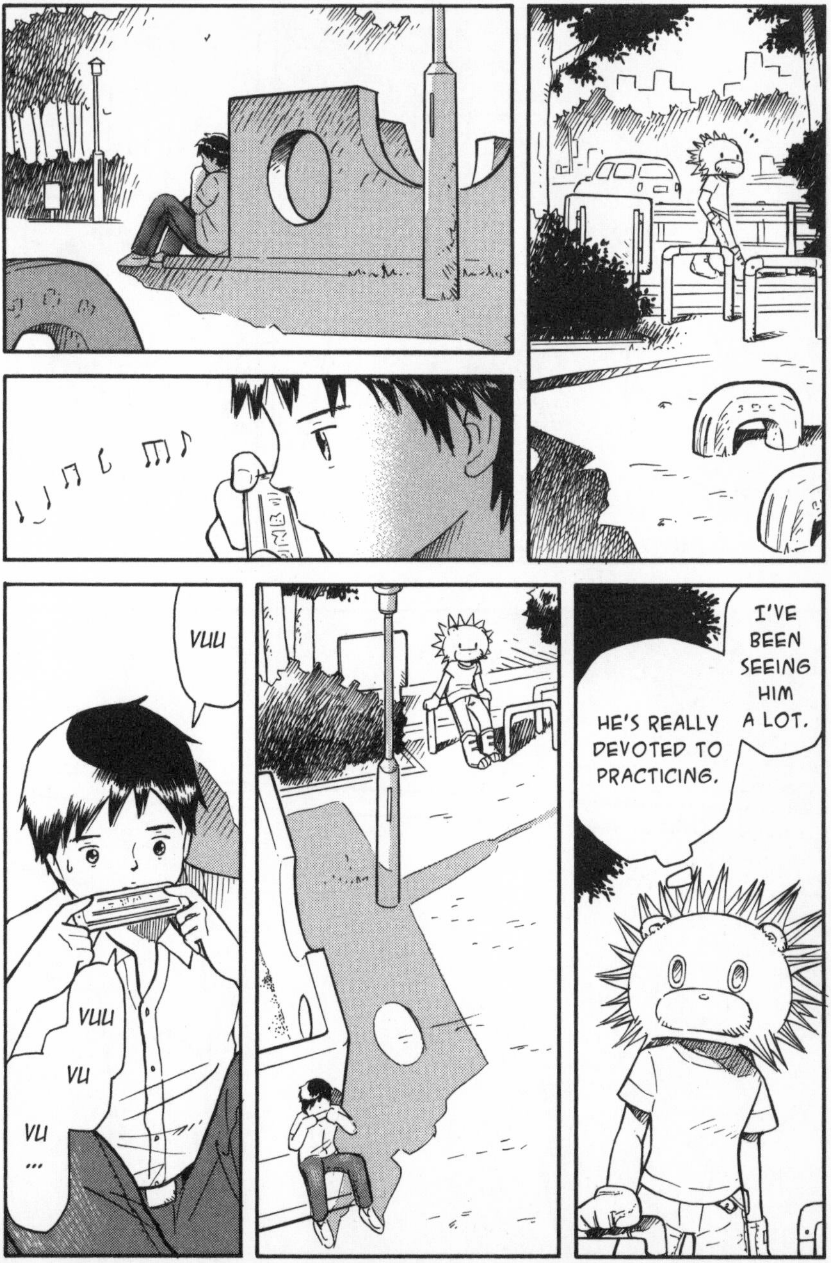
I'VE BEEN SEEING HIM A LOT.
HE'S REALLY DEVOTED TO PRACTICING.
VUU
VUU
VU
VU ...

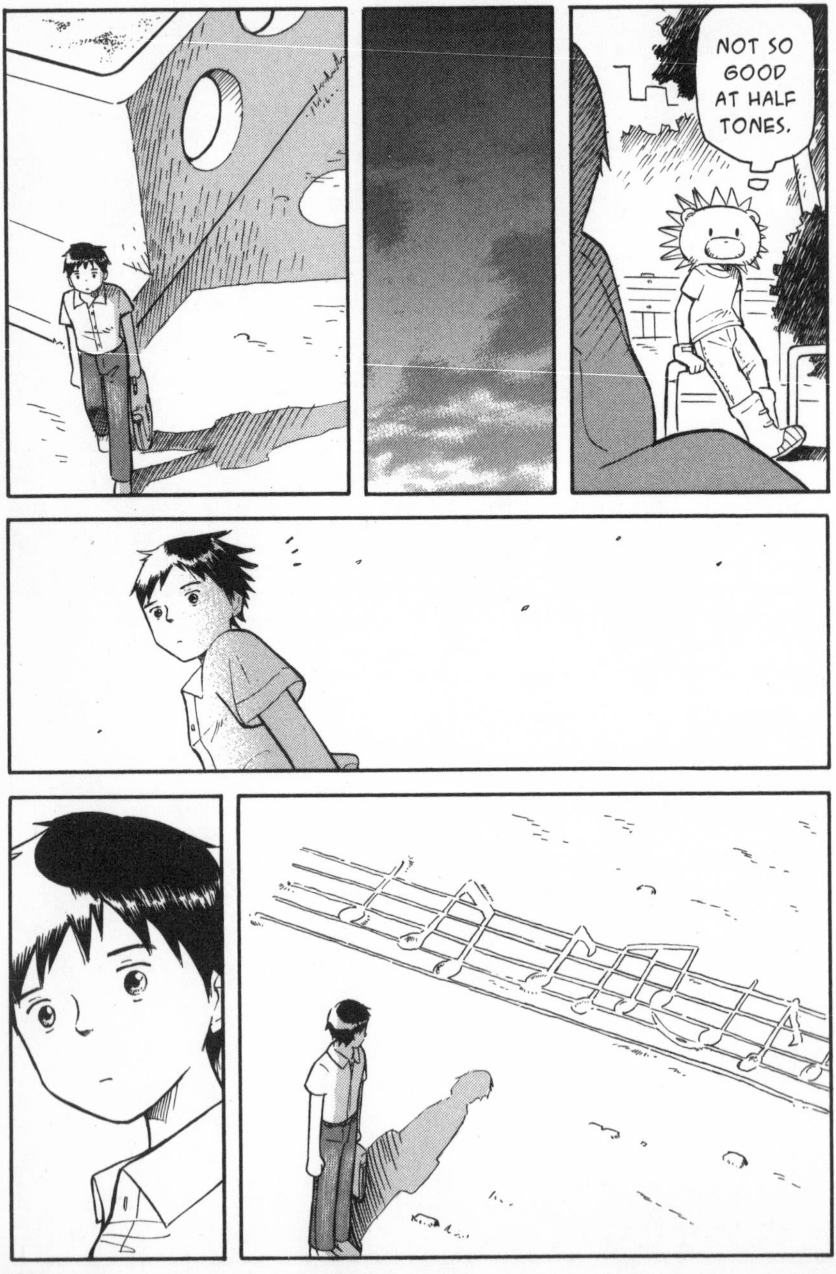
NOT SO GOOD AT HALF TONES.

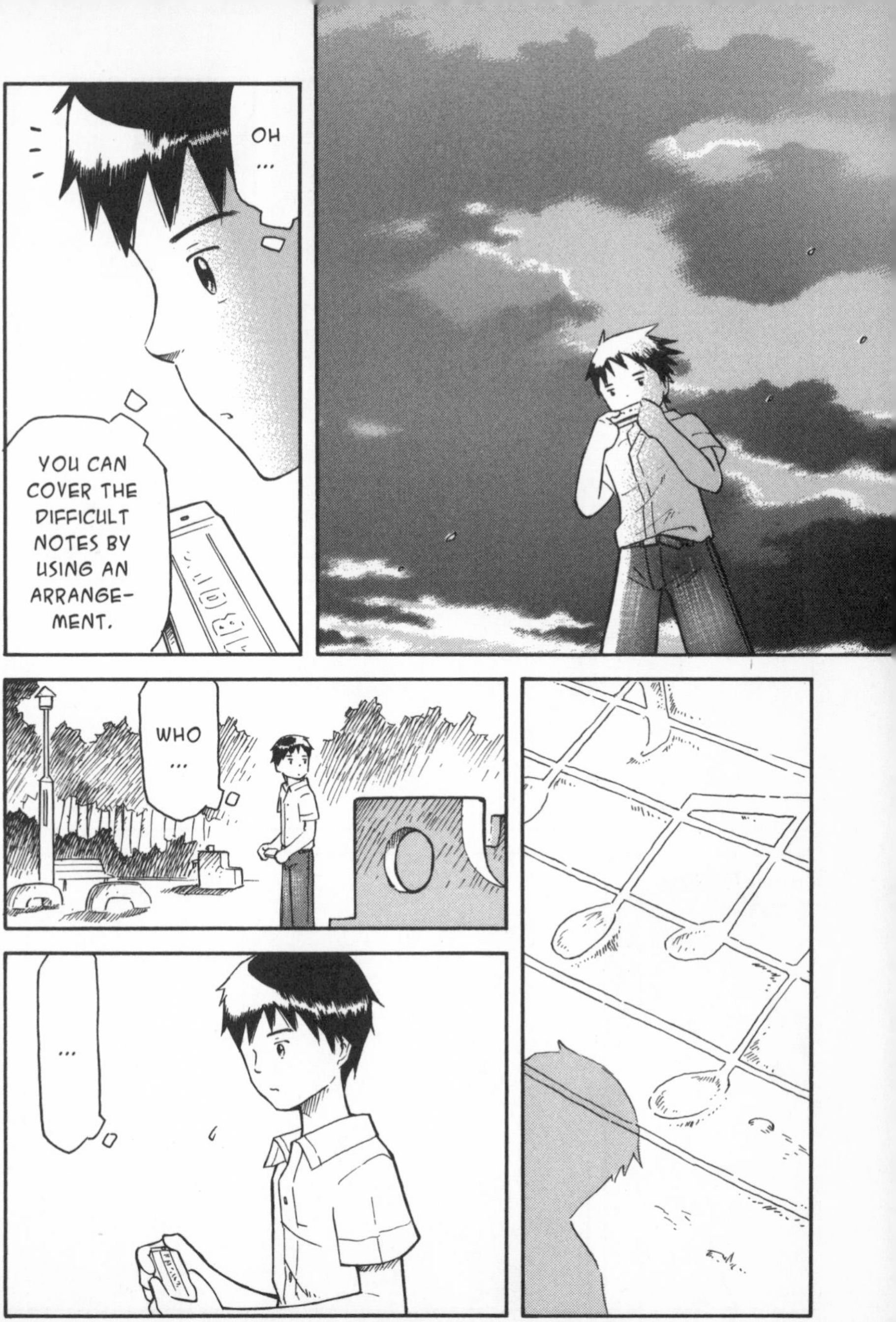
OH ...
YOU CAN COVER THE DIFFICULT NOTES BY USING AN ARRANGE-MENT.
WHO ...
...

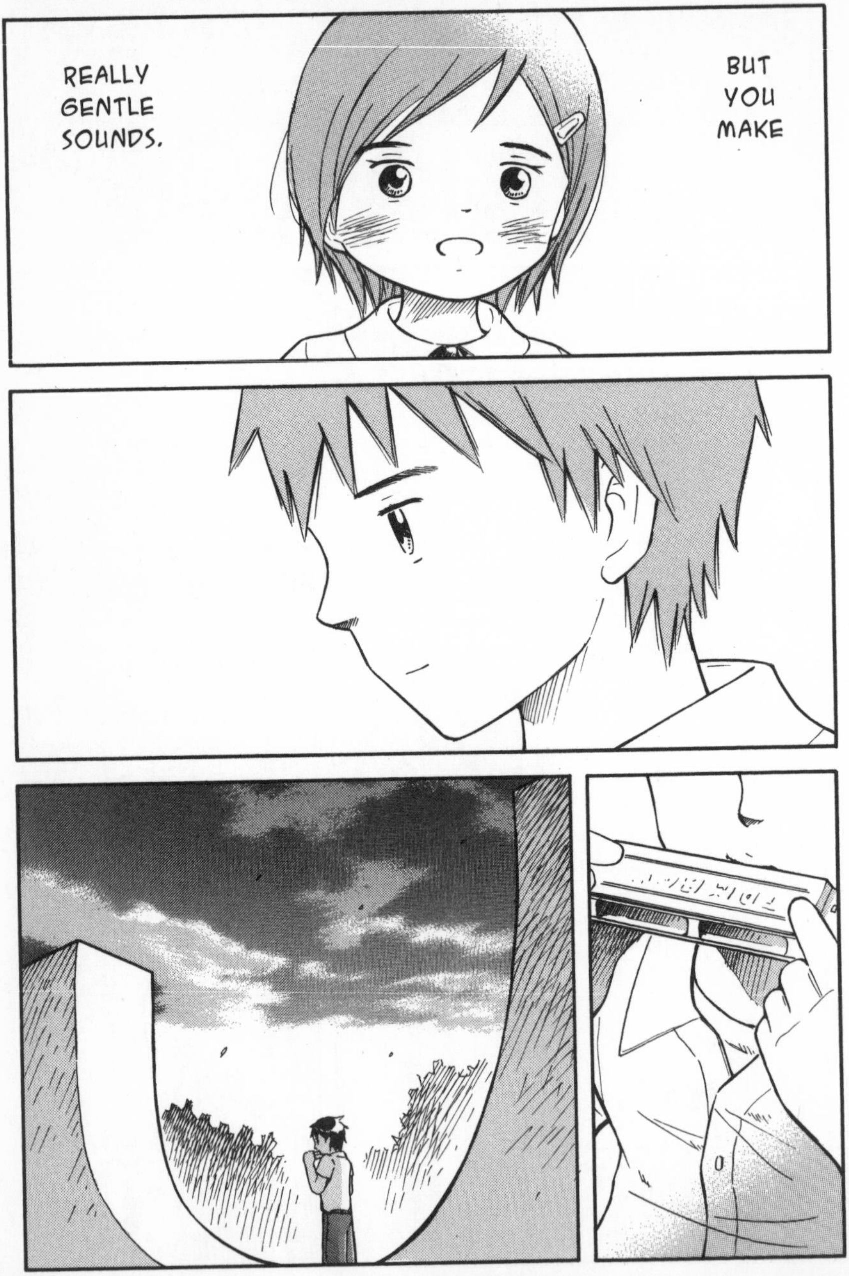
BUT YOU MAKE
REALLY GENTLE SOUNDS.

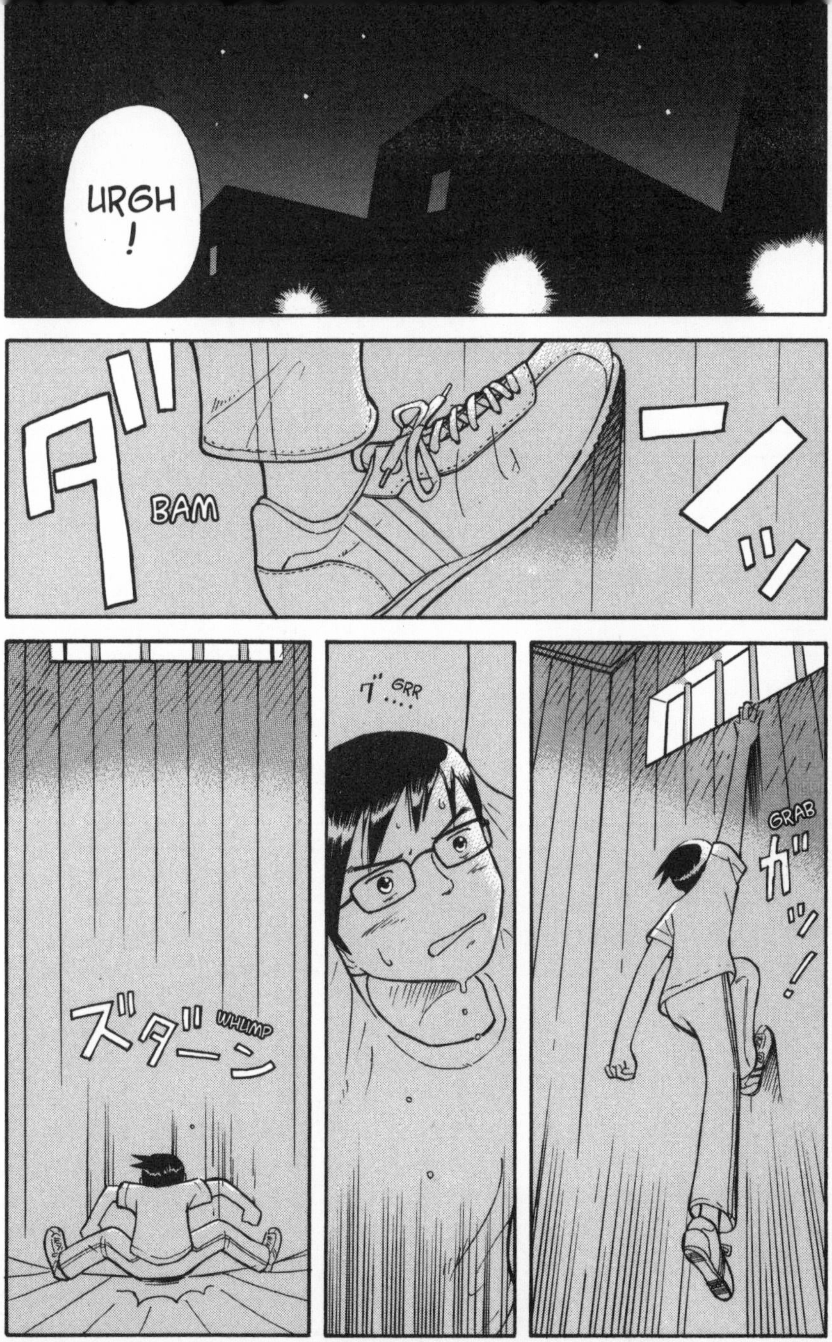
URGH!
ダーンッ
BAM
ガッ!
GRAB
ヴ…
GRR
ズダーン
WHUMP

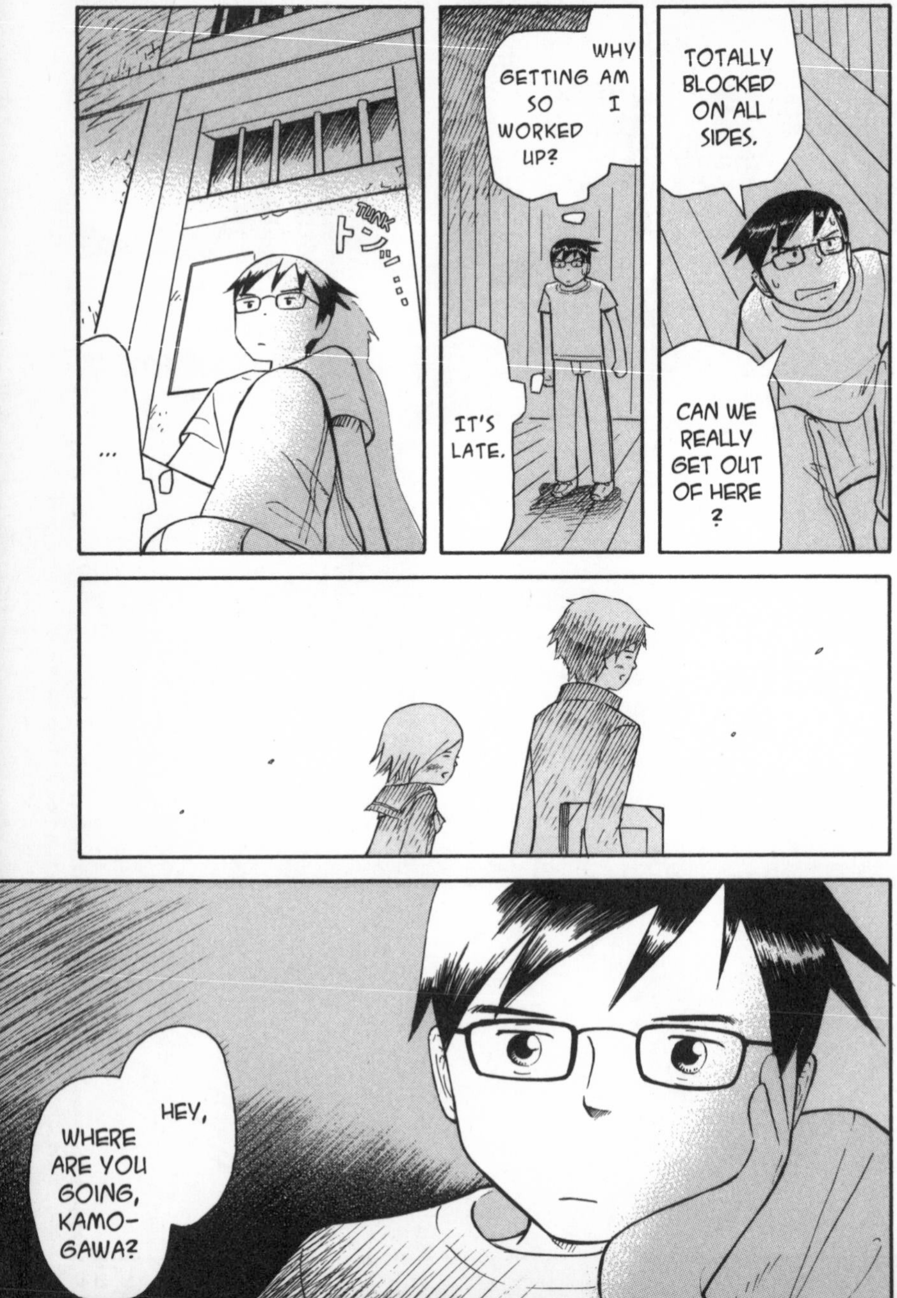
TOTALLY BLOCKED ON ALL SIDES.
CAN WE REALLY GET OUT OF HERE?
WHY AM I GETTING SO WORKED UP?
IT'S LATE.
TUNK
トンッ
...
HEY, WHERE ARE YOU GOING, KAMOGAWA?

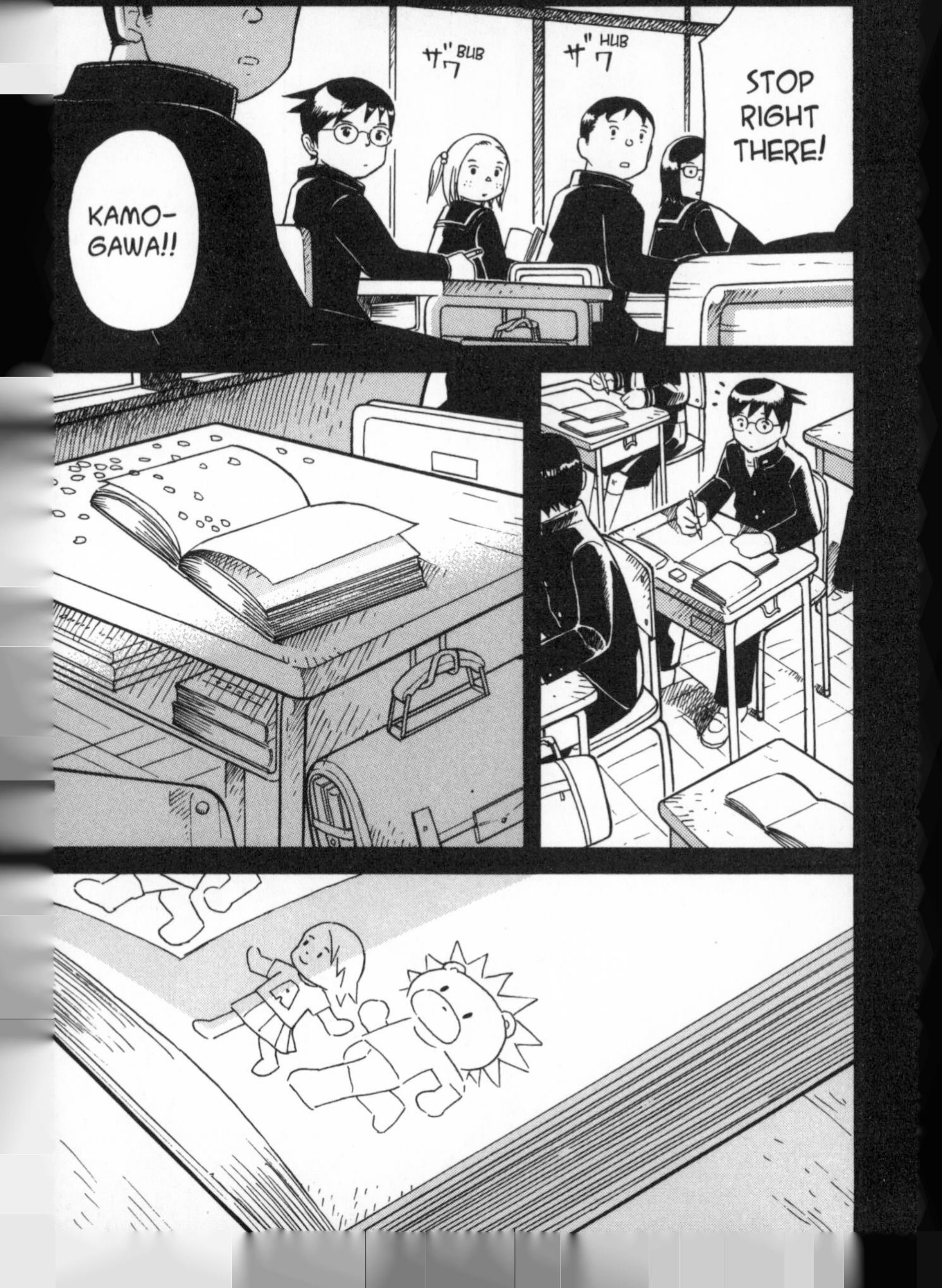
STOP RIGHT THERE!
ザワ HUB
ザワ BUB
KAMO-GAWA!!

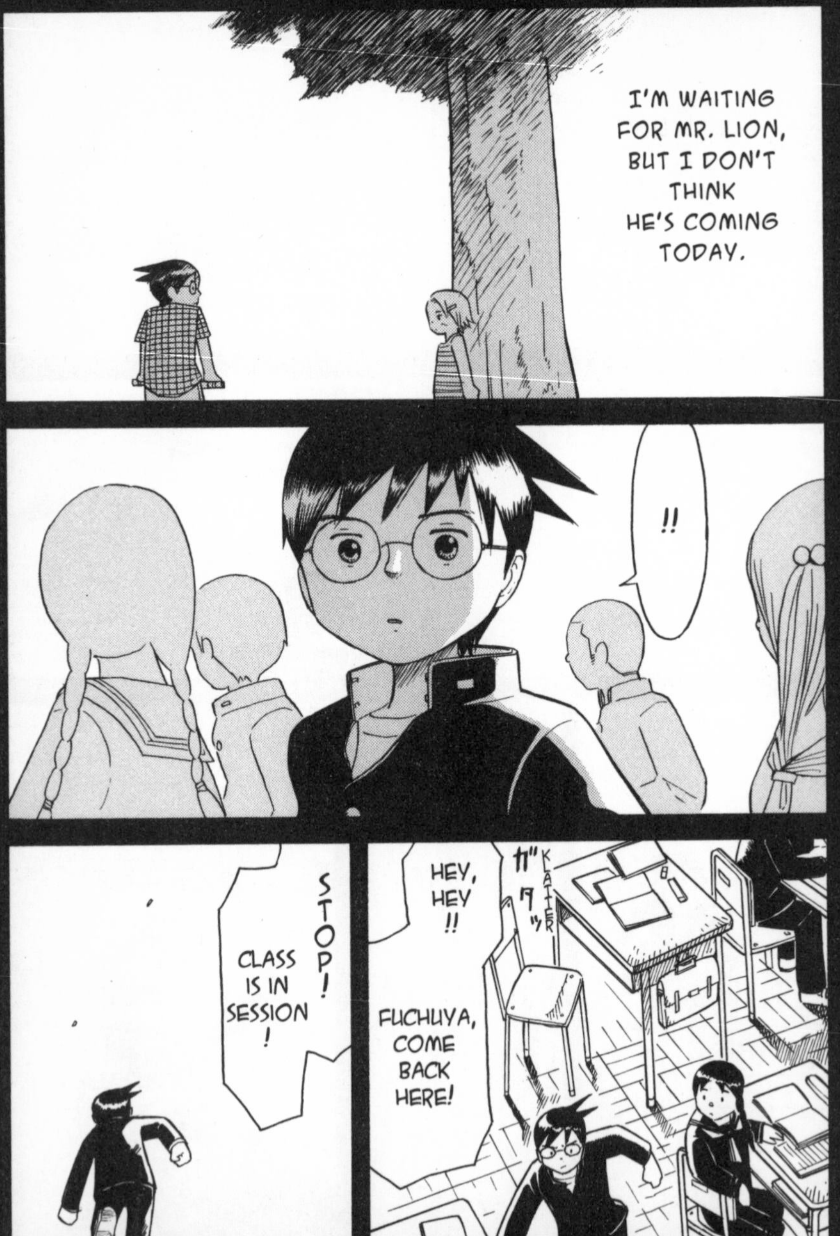
I'M WAITING FOR MR. LION, BUT I DON'T THINK HE'S COMING TODAY.
!!
ガタッ
KLATTER
HEY, HEY!!
FUCHUYA, COME BACK HERE!
STOP!
CLASS IS IN SESSION!

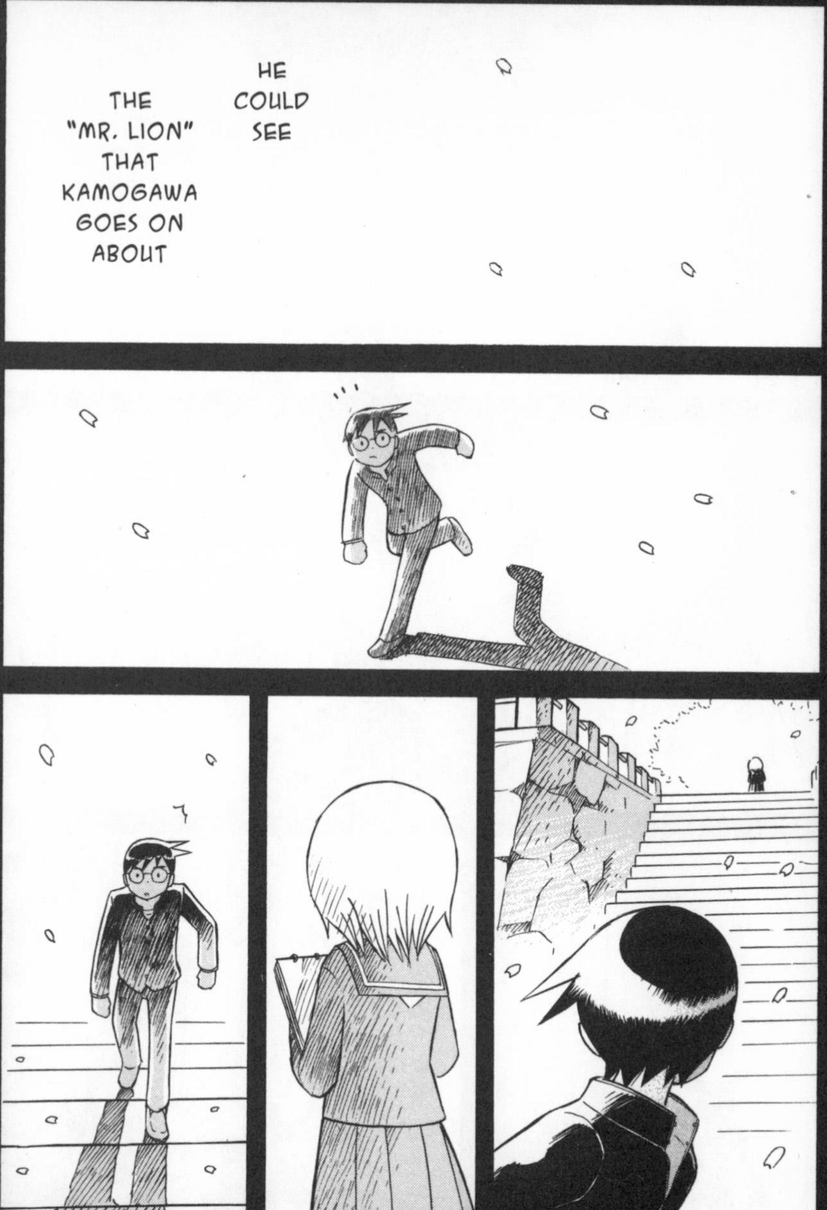
HE COULD SEE
THE "MR. LION" THAT KAMOGAWA GOES ON ABOUT

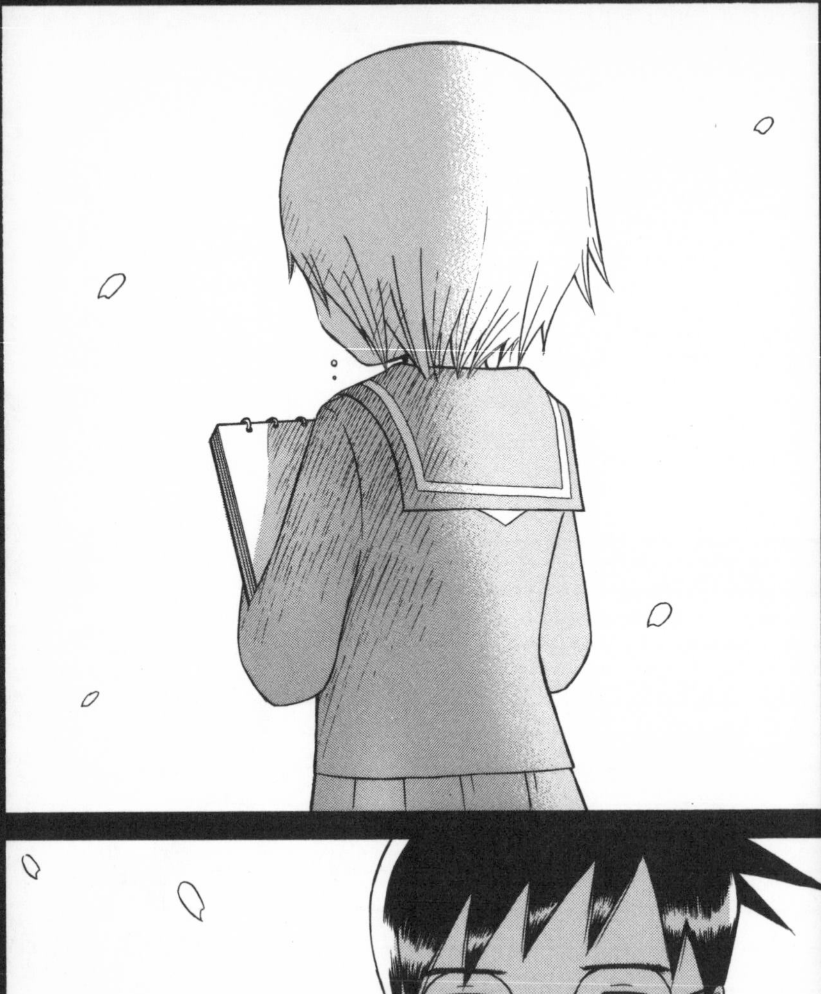
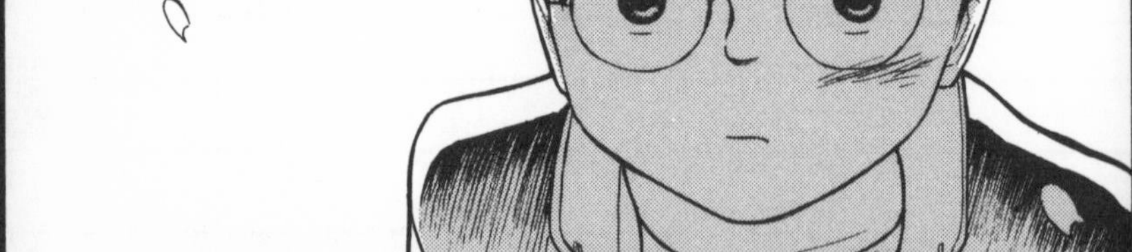

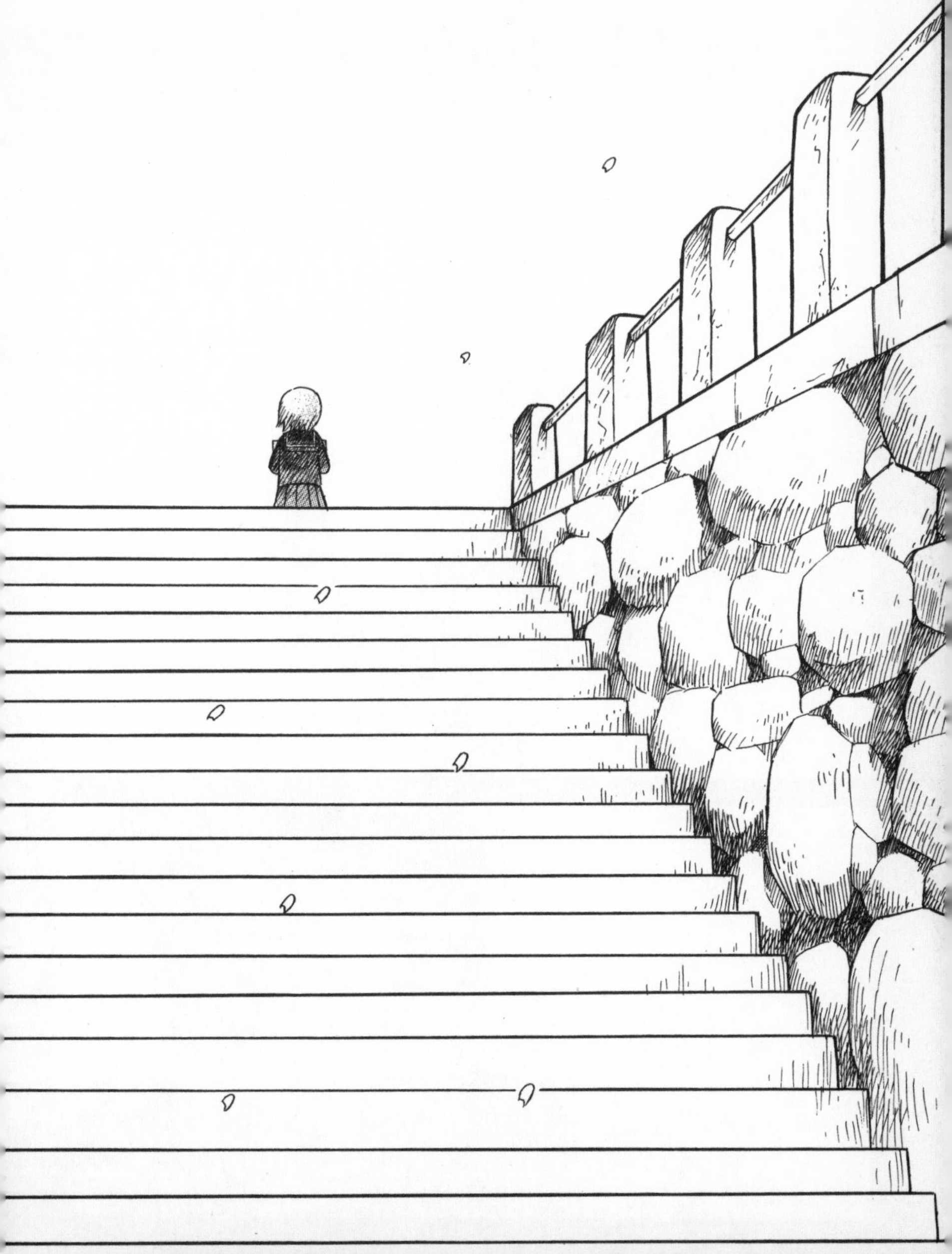

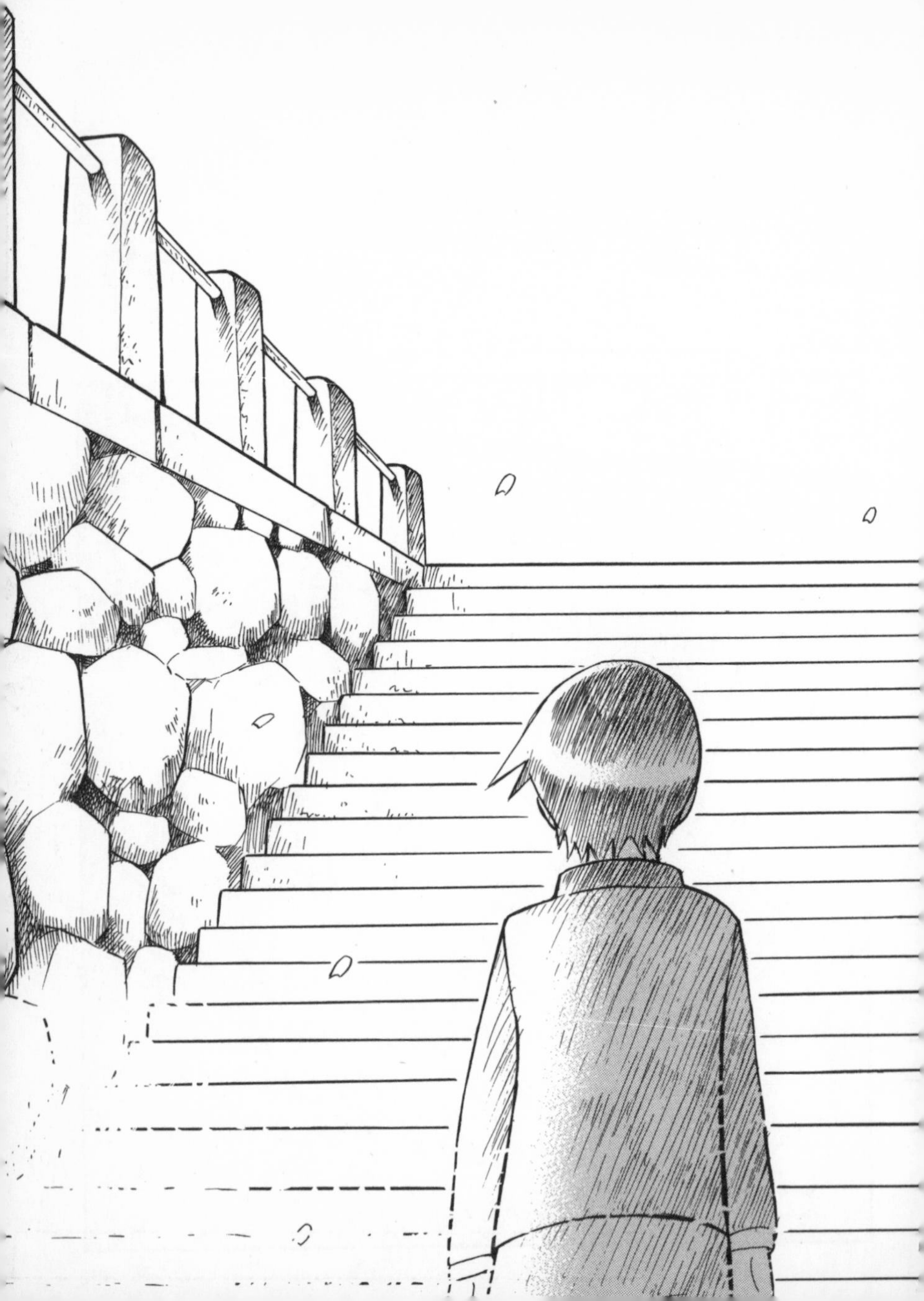

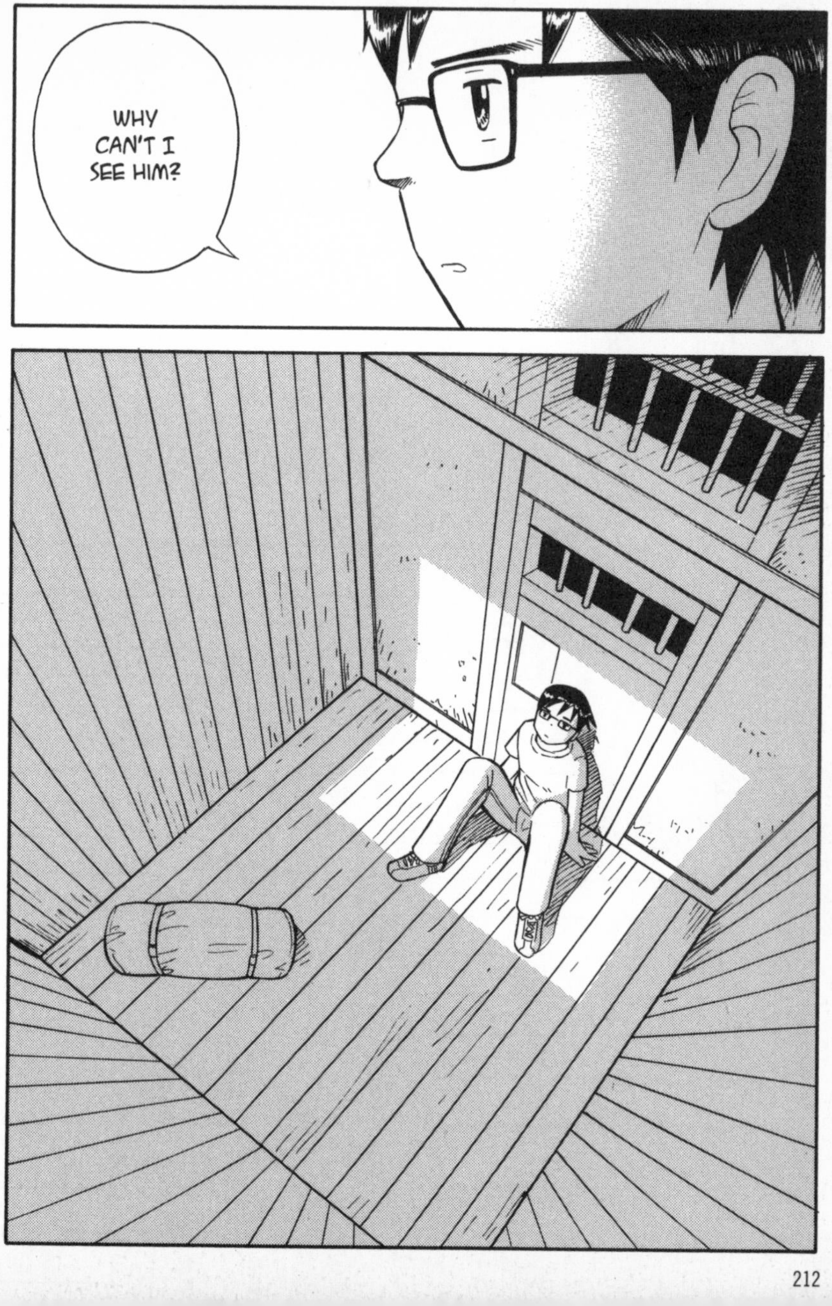
WHY CAN'T I SEE HIM?

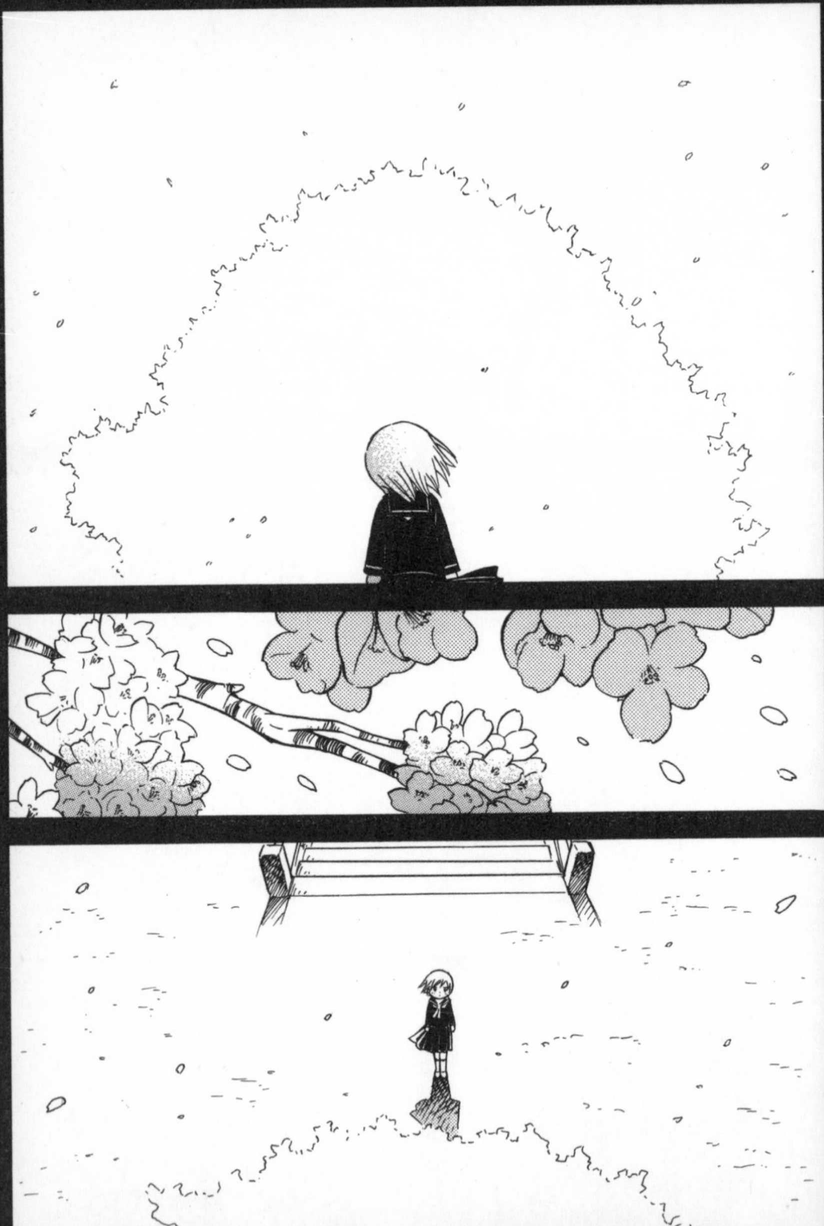

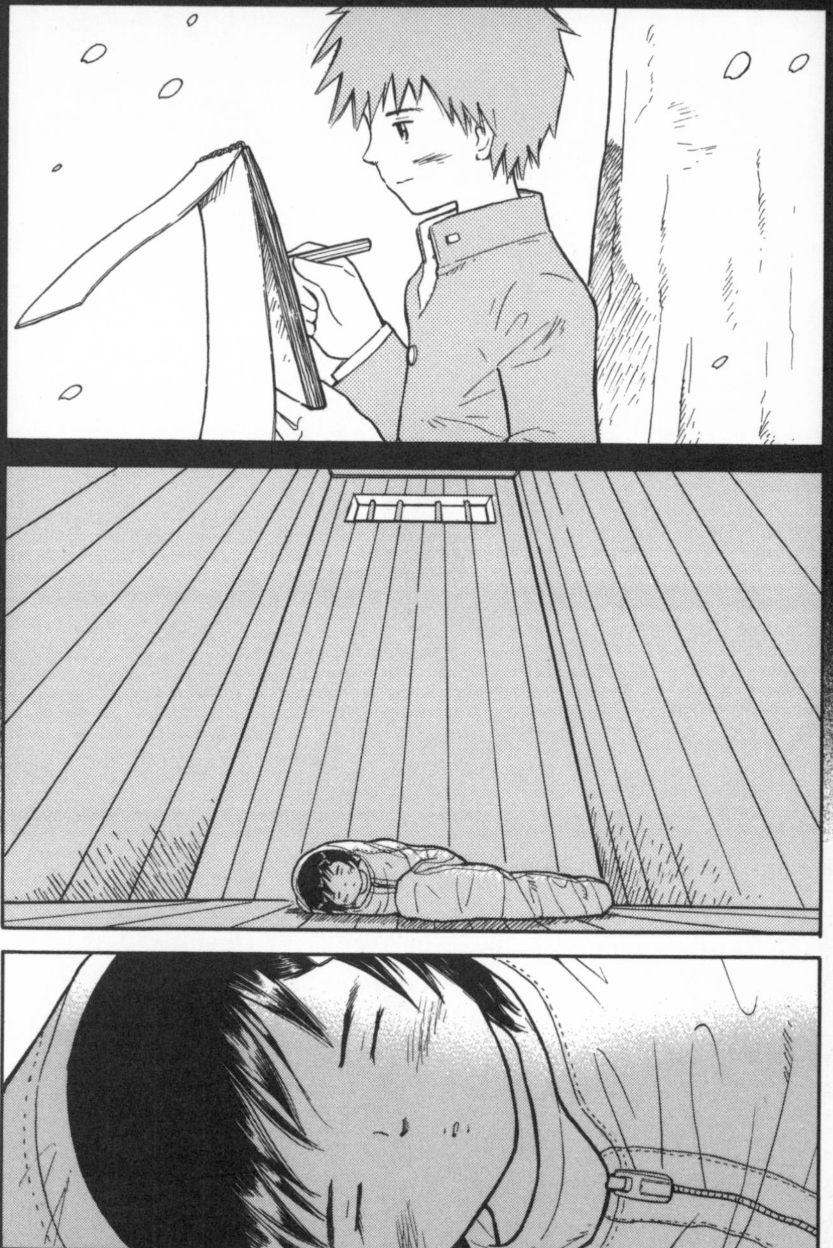

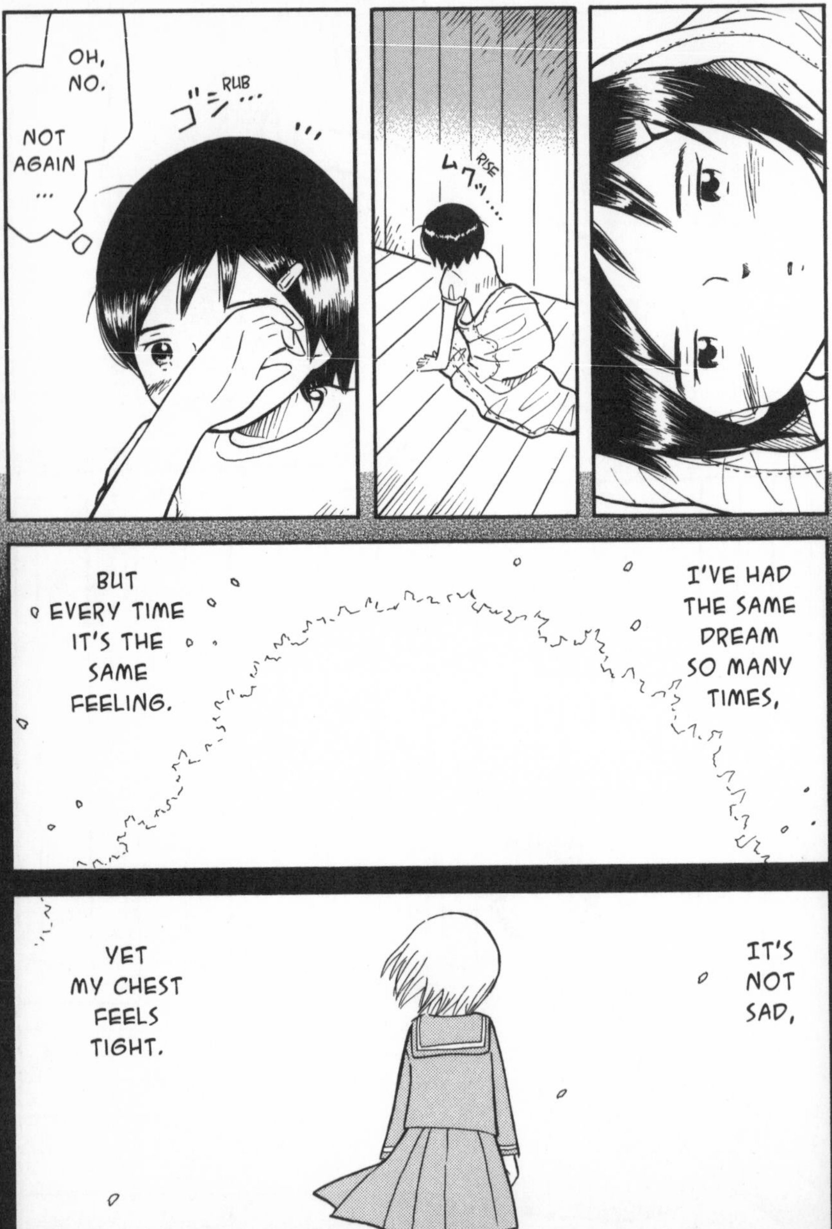
ムクッ…
RISE
OH, NO.
NOT AGAIN …
ゴシ
RUB…
I'VE HAD THE SAME DREAM SO MANY TIMES,
BUT EVERY TIME IT'S THE SAME FEELING.
IT'S NOT SAD,
YET MY CHEST FEELS TIGHT.

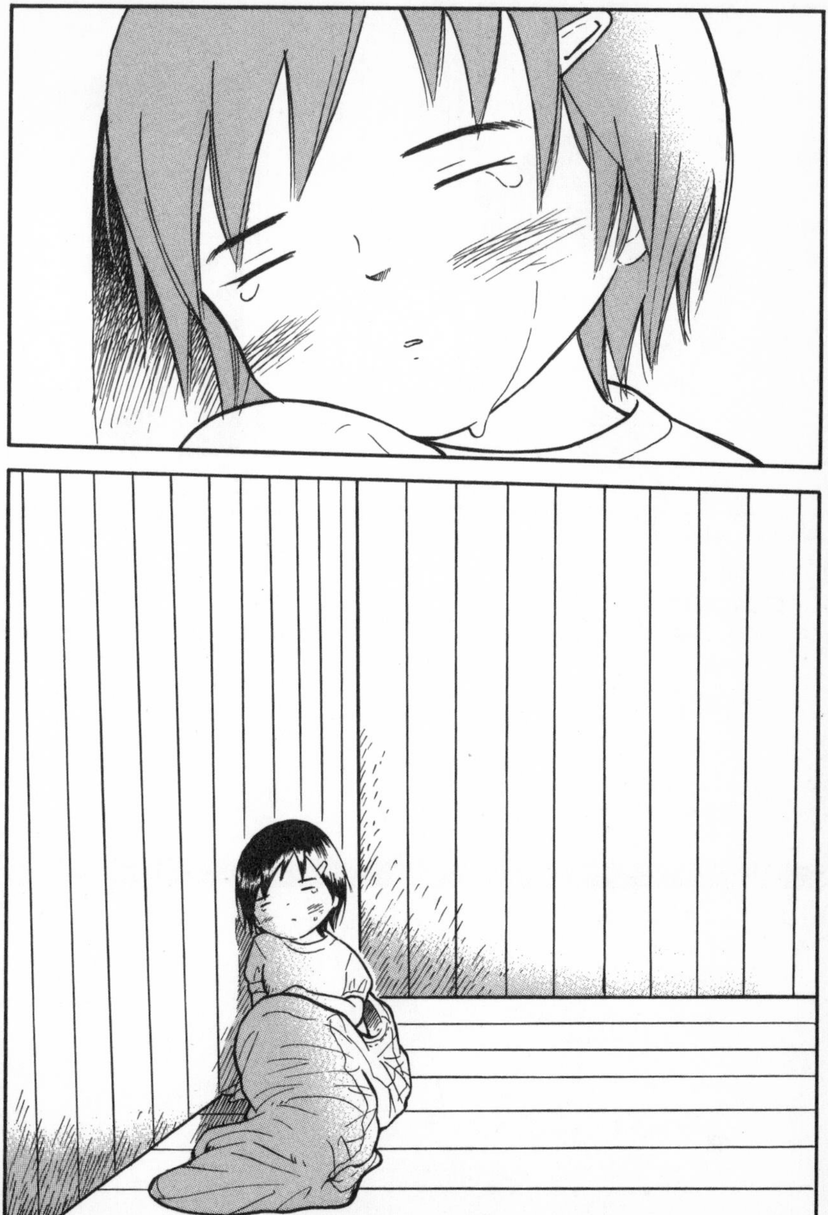

MISSION:37

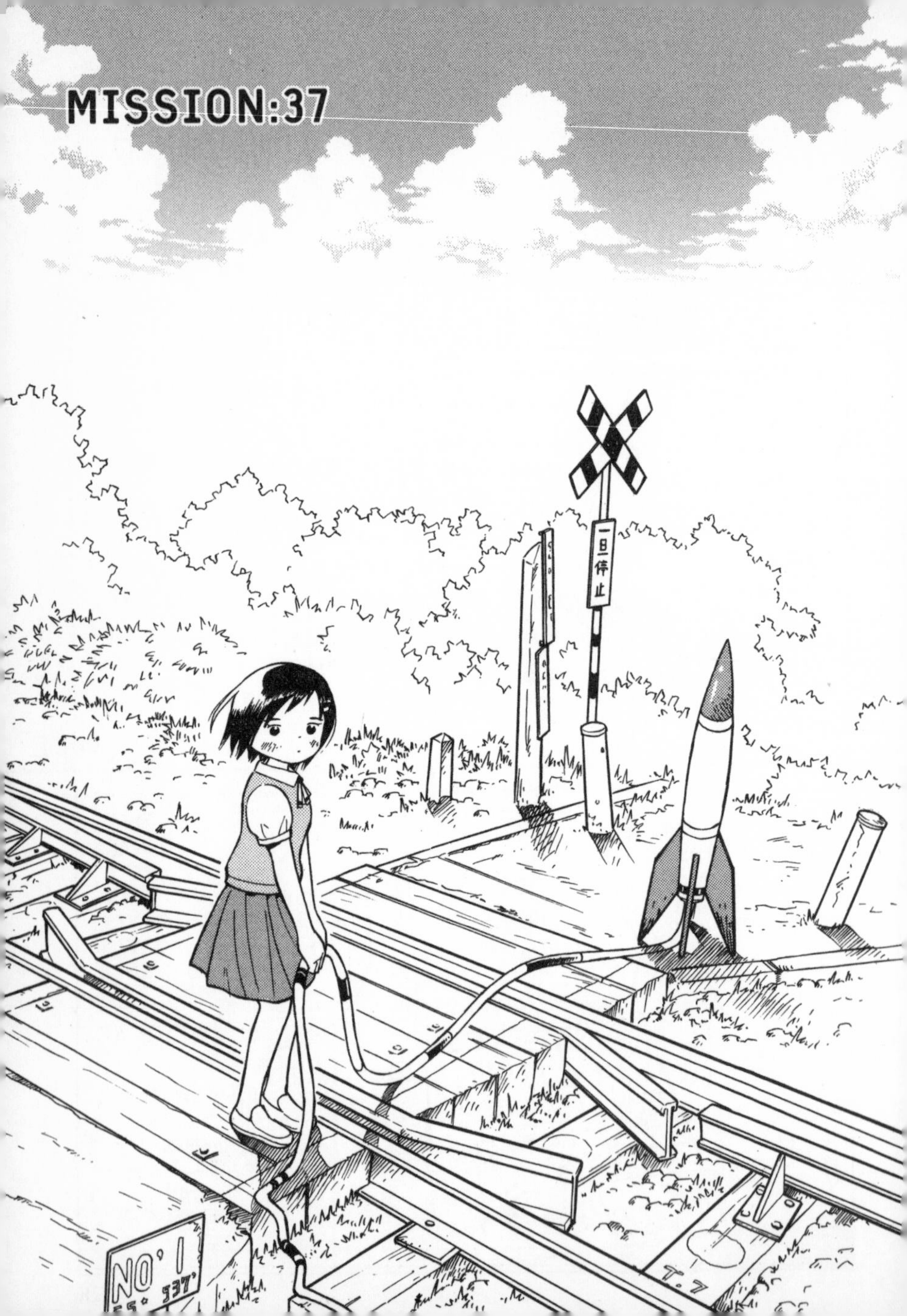
一旦停止

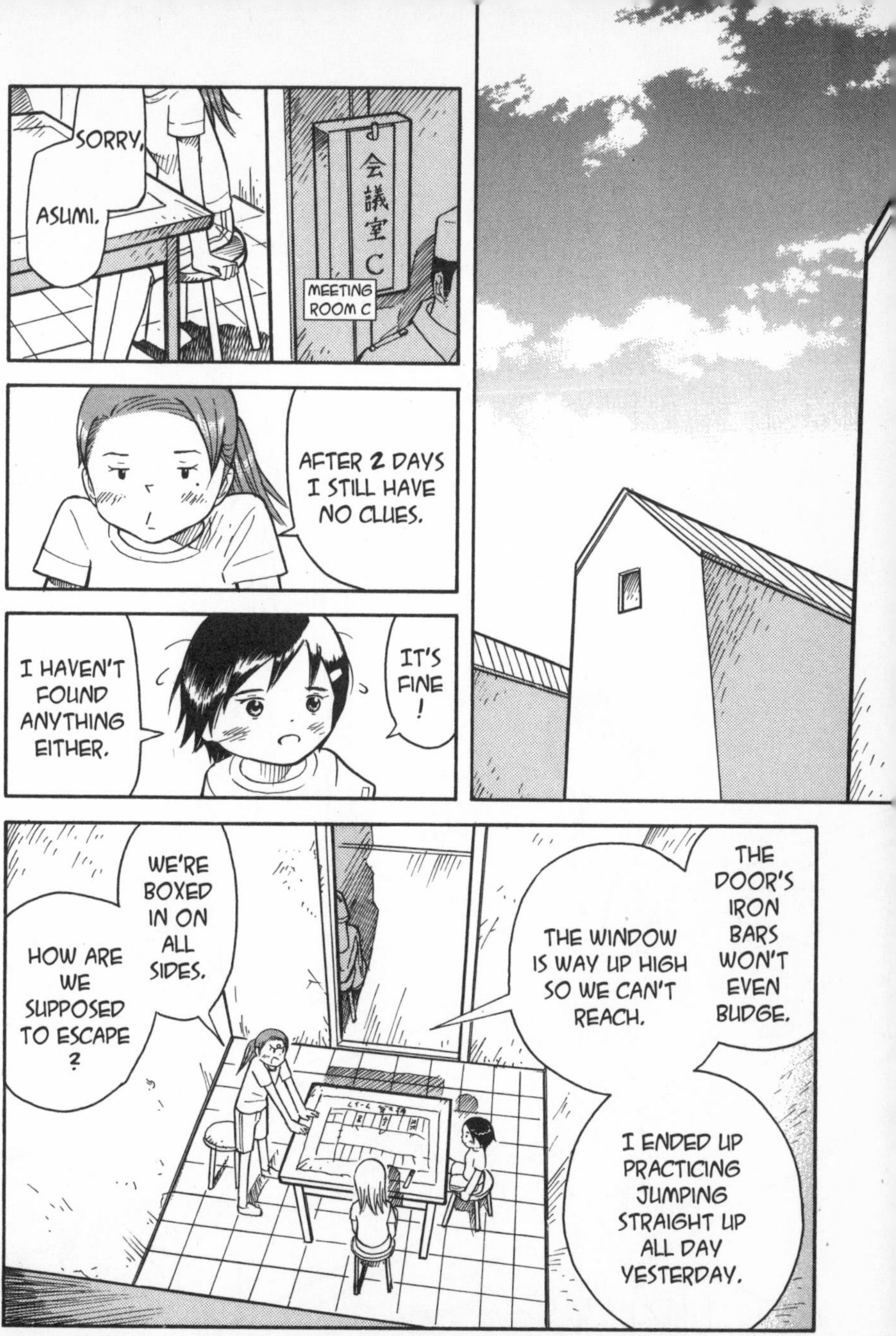
会議室C
MEETING ROOM C
SORRY, ASUMI.
AFTER 2 DAYS I STILL HAVE NO CLUES.
IT'S FINE!
I HAVEN'T FOUND ANYTHING EITHER.
THE DOOR'S IRON BARS WON'T EVEN BUDGE.
THE WINDOW IS WAY UP HIGH SO WE CAN'T REACH.
I ENDED UP PRACTICING JUMPING STRAIGHT UP ALL DAY YESTERDAY.
WE'RE BOXED IN ON ALL SIDES.
HOW ARE WE SUPPOSED TO ESCAPE?

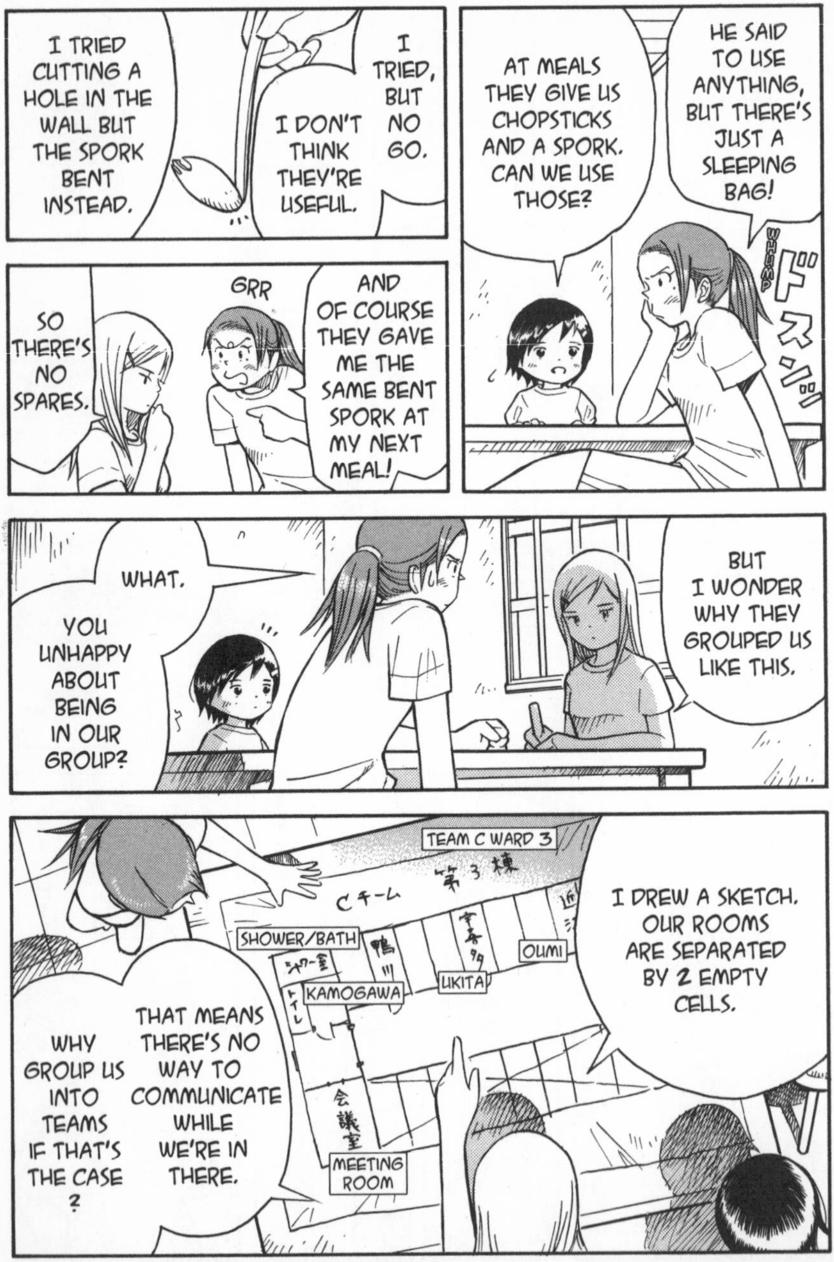
HE SAID TO USE ANYTHING, BUT THERE'S JUST A SLEEPING BAG!
WHUMP
ドスン
AT MEALS THEY GIVE US CHOPSTICKS AND A SPORK. CAN WE USE THOSE?
I TRIED, BUT NO GO.
I DON'T THINK THEY'RE USEFUL.
I TRIED CUTTING A HOLE IN THE WALL BUT THE SPORK BENT INSTEAD.
AND OF COURSE THEY GAVE ME THE SAME BENT SPORK AT MY NEXT MEAL!
GRR
SO THERE'S NO SPARES.
BUT I WONDER WHY THEY GROUPED US LIKE THIS.
WHAT.
YOU UNHAPPY ABOUT BEING IN OUR GROUP?
I DREW A SKETCH. OUR ROOMS ARE SEPARATED BY 2 EMPTY CELLS.
TEAM C WARD 3
第3棟
Cチーム
OUMI
宇喜多
UKITA
鴨川
KAMOGAWA
シャワー室
SHOWER/BATH
トイレ
会議室
MEETING ROOM
THAT MEANS THERE'S NO WAY TO COMMUNICATE WHILE WE'RE IN THERE.
WHY GROUP US INTO TEAMS IF THAT'S THE CASE?

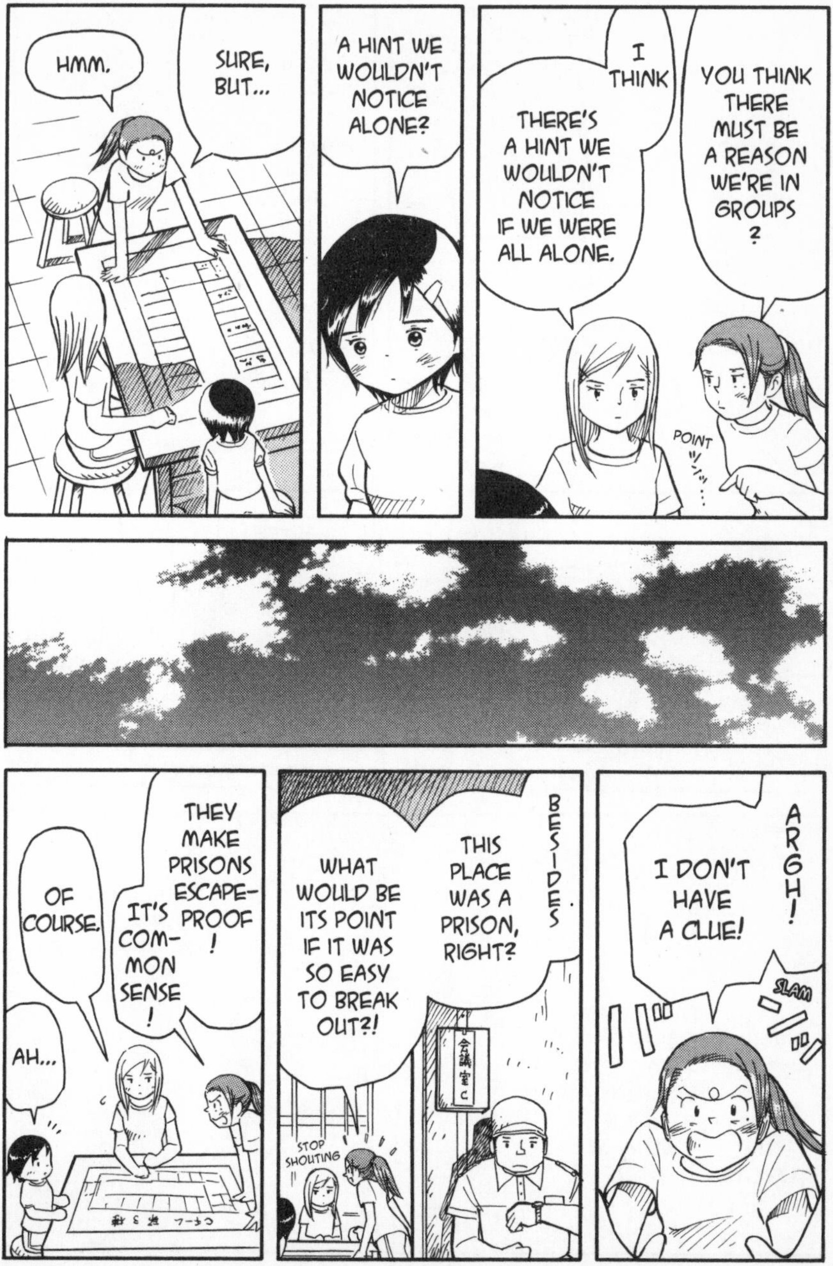
YOU THINK THERE MUST BE A REASON WE'RE IN GROUPS?
I THINK
THERE'S A HINT WE WOULDN'T NOTICE IF WE WERE ALL ALONE.
POINT
A HINT WE WOULDN'T NOTICE ALONE?
SURE, BUT...
HMM.
ARGH!
I DON'T HAVE A CLUE!
SLAM
BESIDES.
THIS PLACE WAS A PRISON, RIGHT?
WHAT WOULD BE ITS POINT IF IT WAS SO EASY TO BREAK OUT?!
STOP SHOUTING
THEY MAKE PRISONS ESCAPE-PROOF!
IT'S COM-MON SENSE!
OF COURSE.
AH...

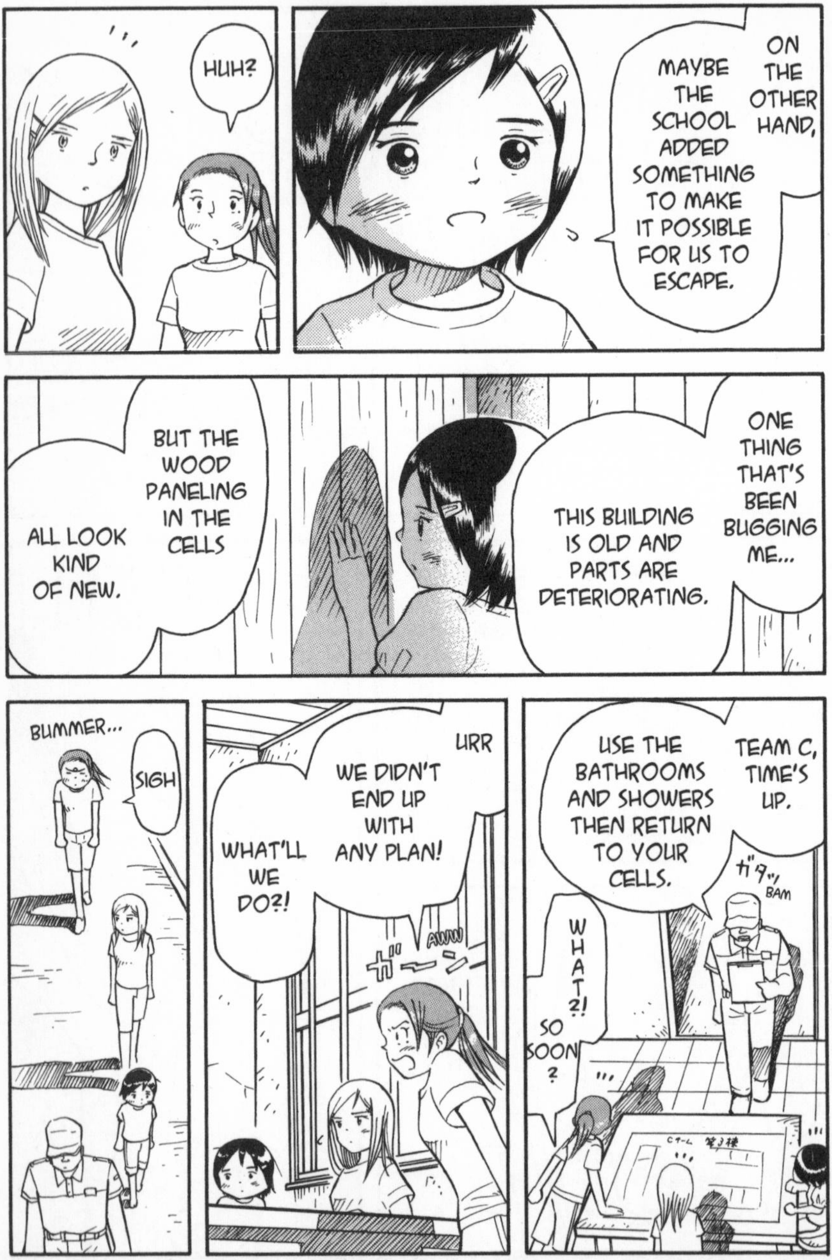
ON THE OTHER HAND,
MAYBE THE SCHOOL ADDED SOMETHING TO MAKE IT POSSIBLE FOR US TO ESCAPE.
HUH?
ONE THING THAT'S BEEN BUGGING ME...
THIS BUILDING IS OLD AND PARTS ARE DETERIORATING.
BUT THE WOOD PANELING IN THE CELLS
ALL LOOK KIND OF NEW.
TEAM C, TIME'S UP.
USE THE BATHROOMS AND SHOWERS THEN RETURN TO YOUR CELLS.
ガタッ
BAM
WHAT?!
SO SOON?
URR
WE DIDN'T END UP WITH ANY PLAN!
WHAT'LL WE DO?!
AWW
ガーン
BUMMER...
SIGH

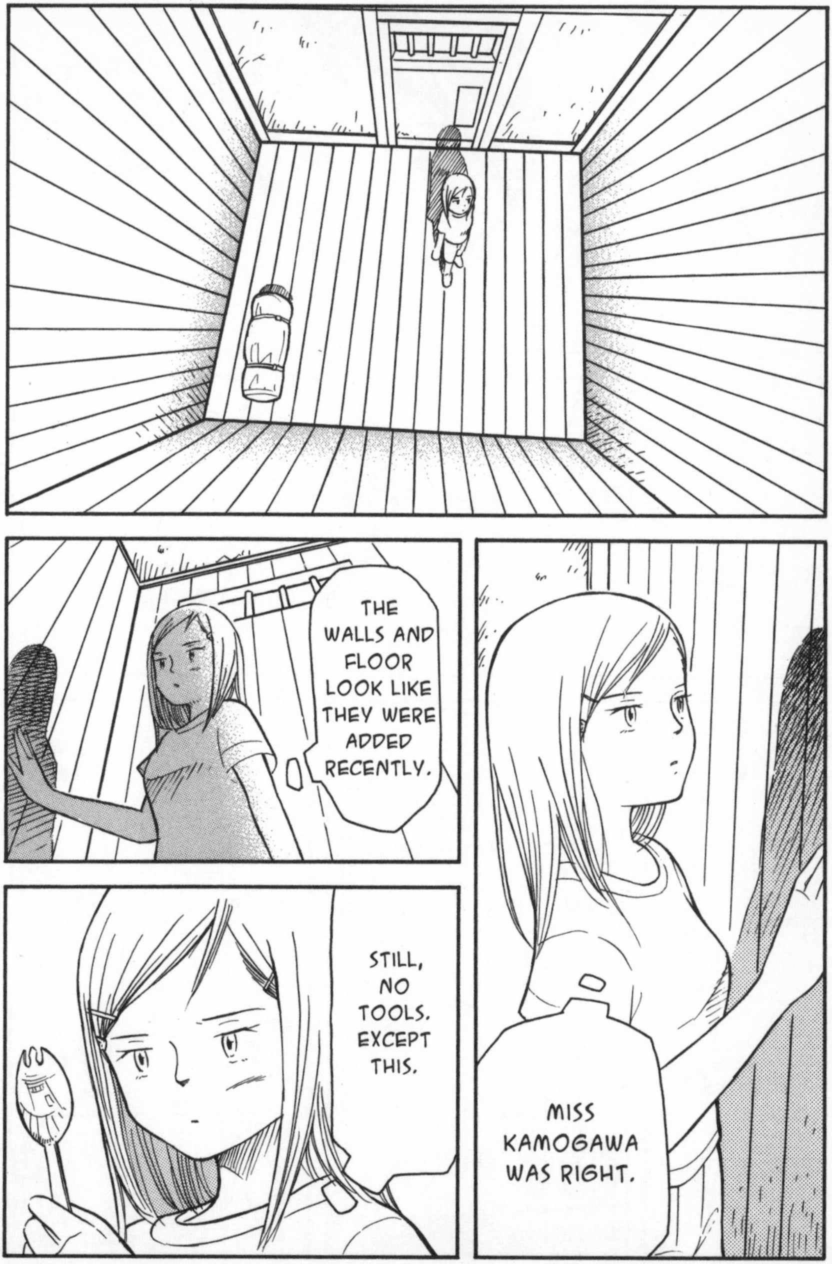
MISS KAMOGAWA WAS RIGHT.
THE WALLS AND FLOOR LOOK LIKE THEY WERE ADDED RECENTLY.
STILL, NO TOOLS. EXCEPT THIS.

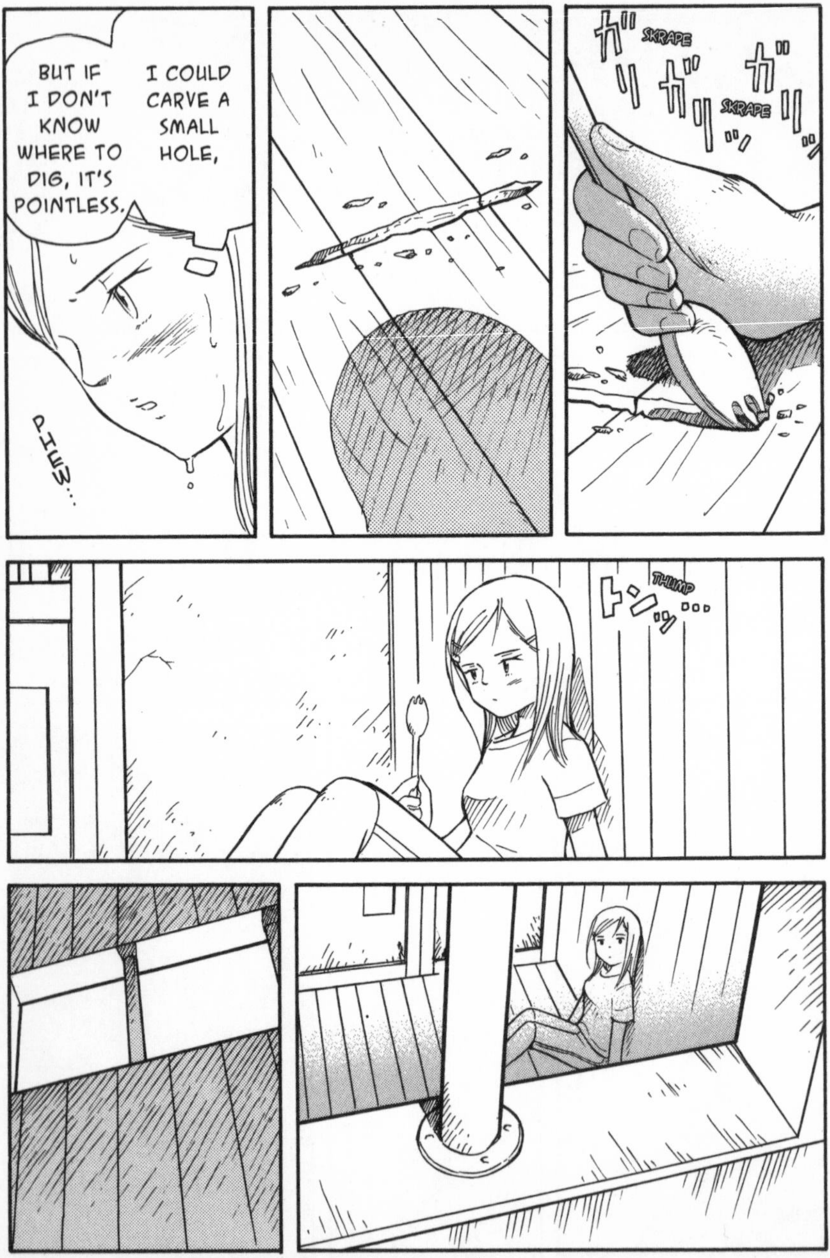
ガリッ
SKRAPE
ガリッ
SKRAPE
ガリッ
I COULD CARVE A SMALL HOLE,
BUT IF I DON'T KNOW WHERE TO DIG, IT'S POINTLESS.
PHEW...
トンッ
THUMP

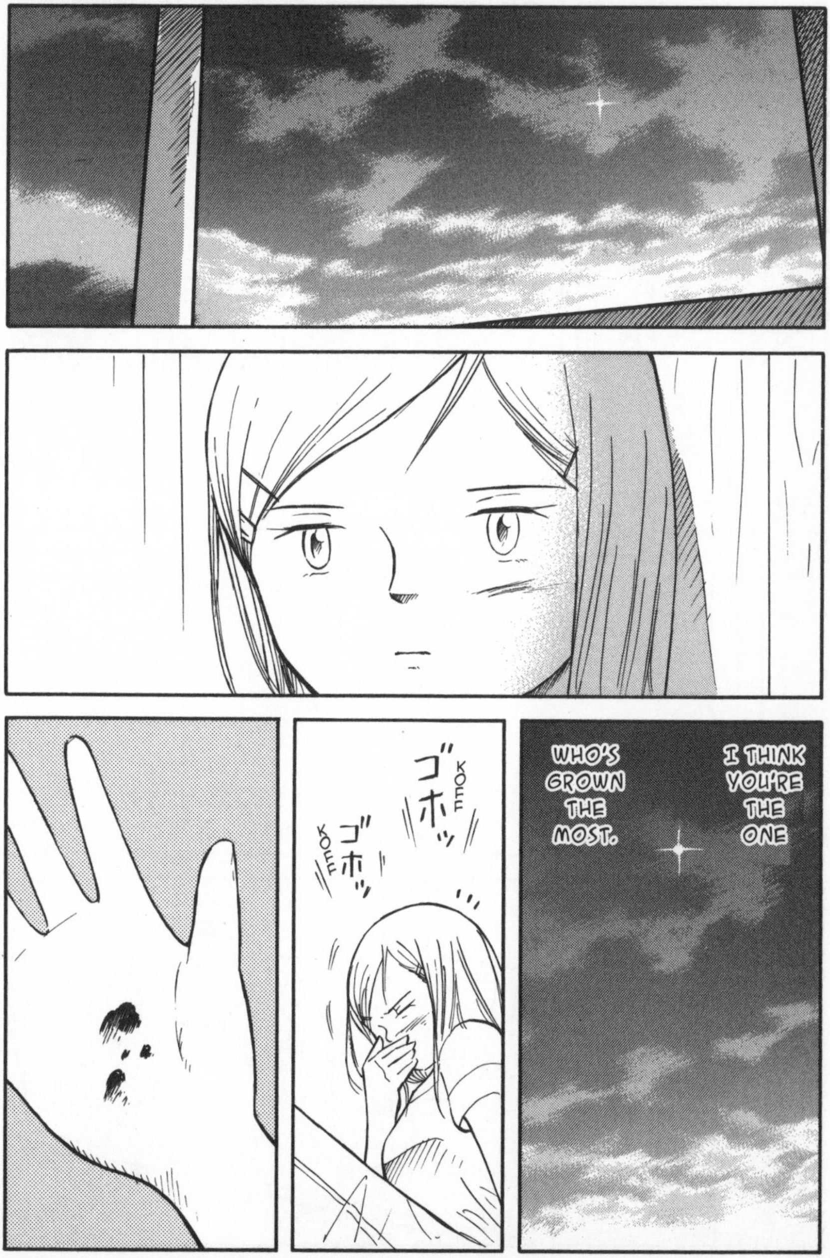
I THINK YOU'RE THE ONE
WHO'S GROWN THE MOST.
ゴホッ
KOFF
ゴホッ
KOFF

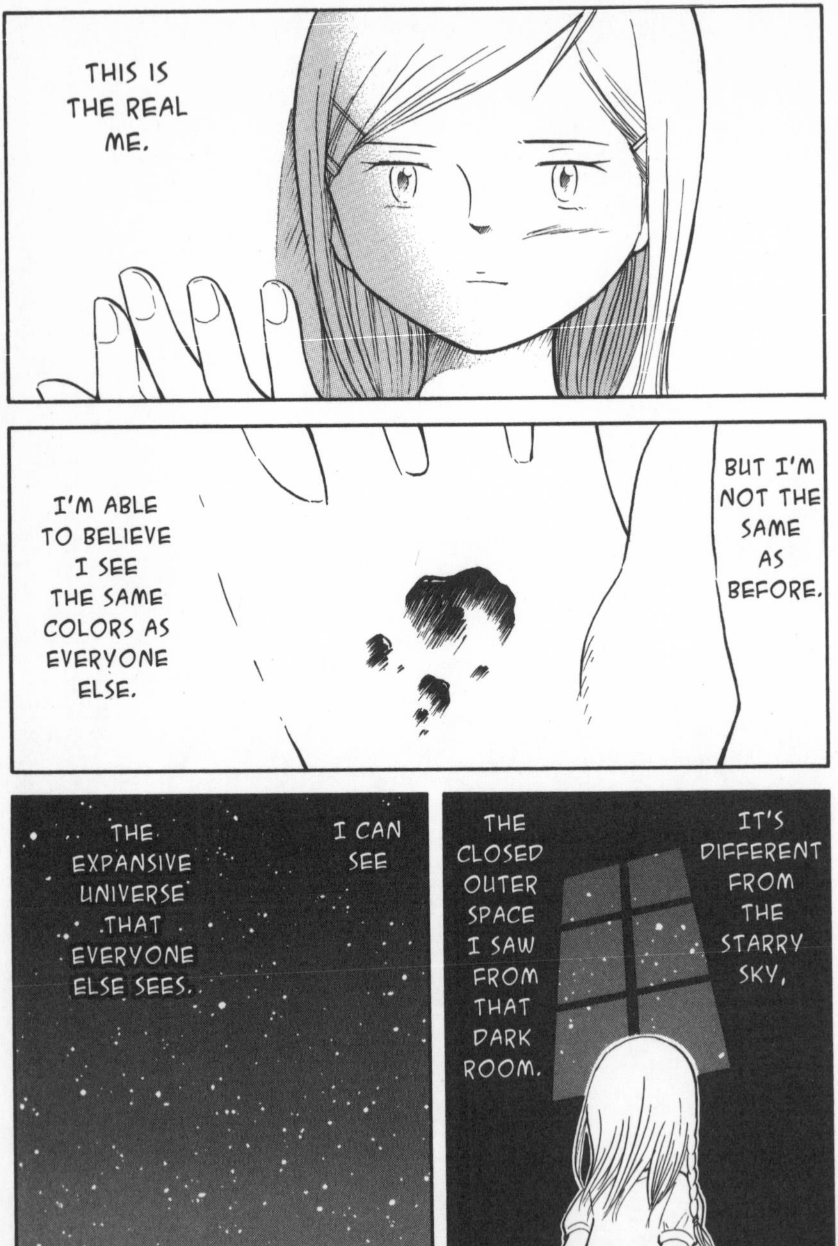
THIS IS THE REAL ME.
BUT I'M NOT THE SAME AS BEFORE.
I'M ABLE TO BELIEVE I SEE THE SAME COLORS AS EVERYONE ELSE.
IT'S DIFFERENT FROM THE STARRY SKY,
THE CLOSED OUTER SPACE I SAW FROM THAT DARK ROOM.
I CAN SEE
THE EXPANSIVE UNIVERSE THAT EVERYONE ELSE SEES.

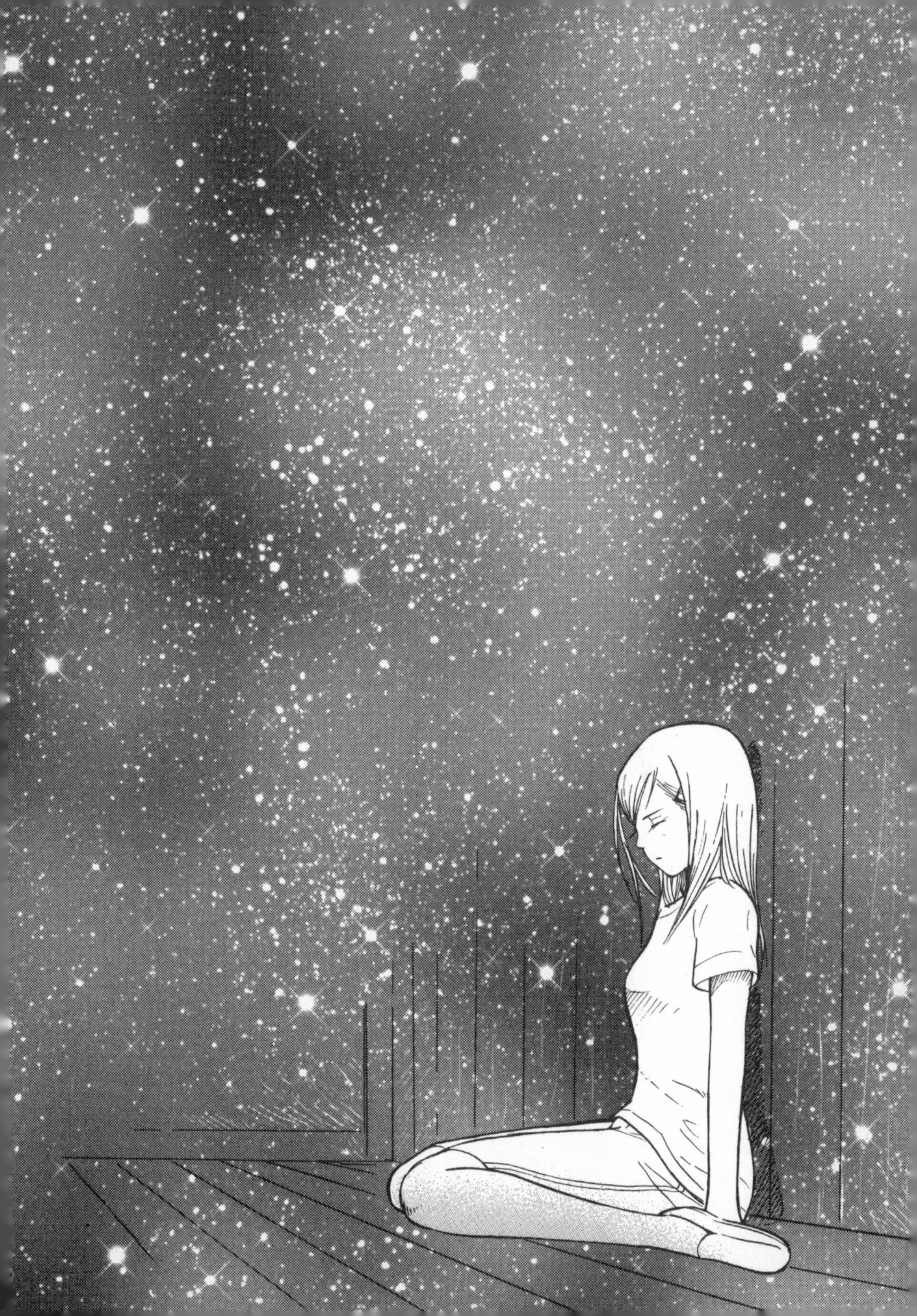

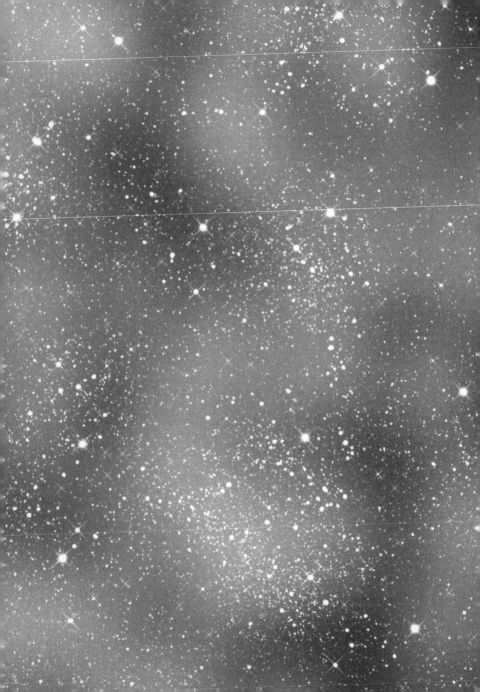

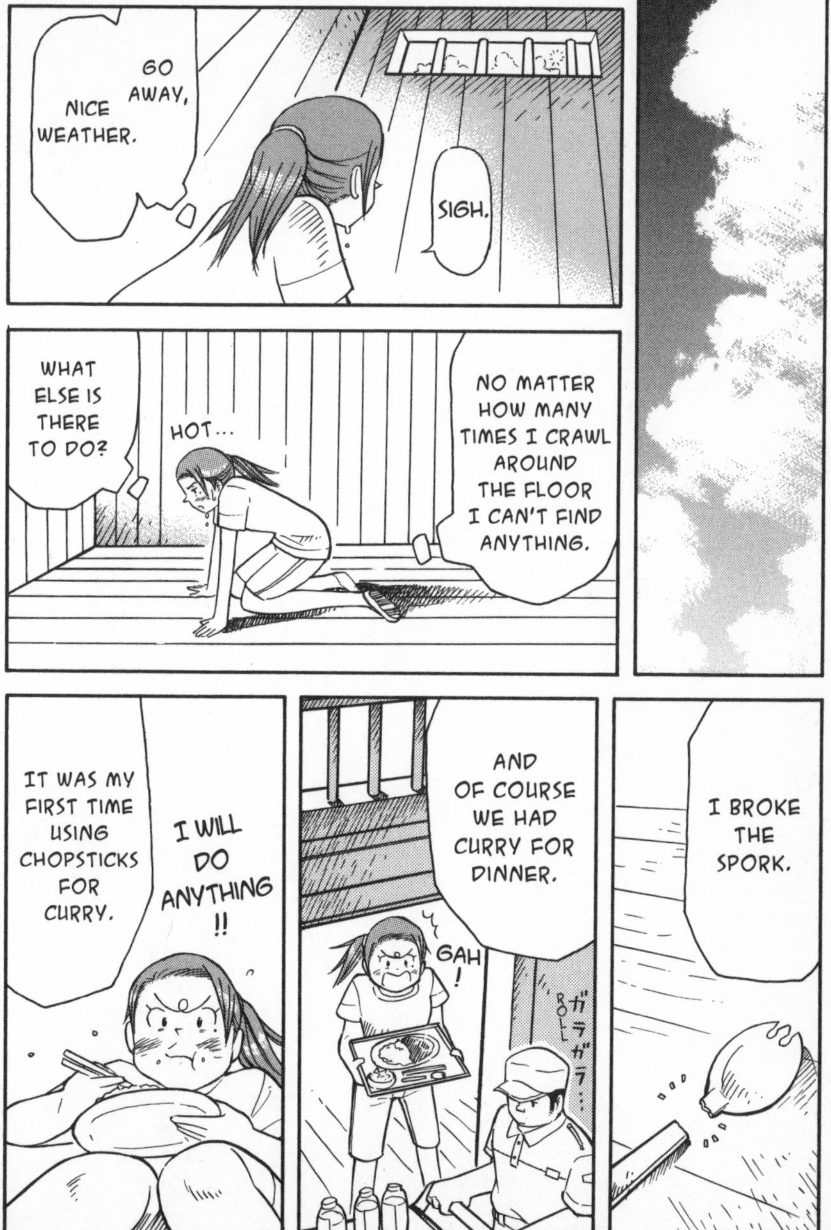
SIGH.
GO AWAY, NICE WEATHER.
NO MATTER HOW MANY TIMES I CRAWL AROUND THE FLOOR I CAN'T FIND ANYTHING.
HOT...
WHAT ELSE IS THERE TO DO?
I BROKE THE SPORK.
AND OF COURSE WE HAD CURRY FOR DINNER.
GAH!
ROLL
ガラガラ…
I WILL DO ANYTHING!!
IT WAS MY FIRST TIME USING CHOPSTICKS FOR CURRY.

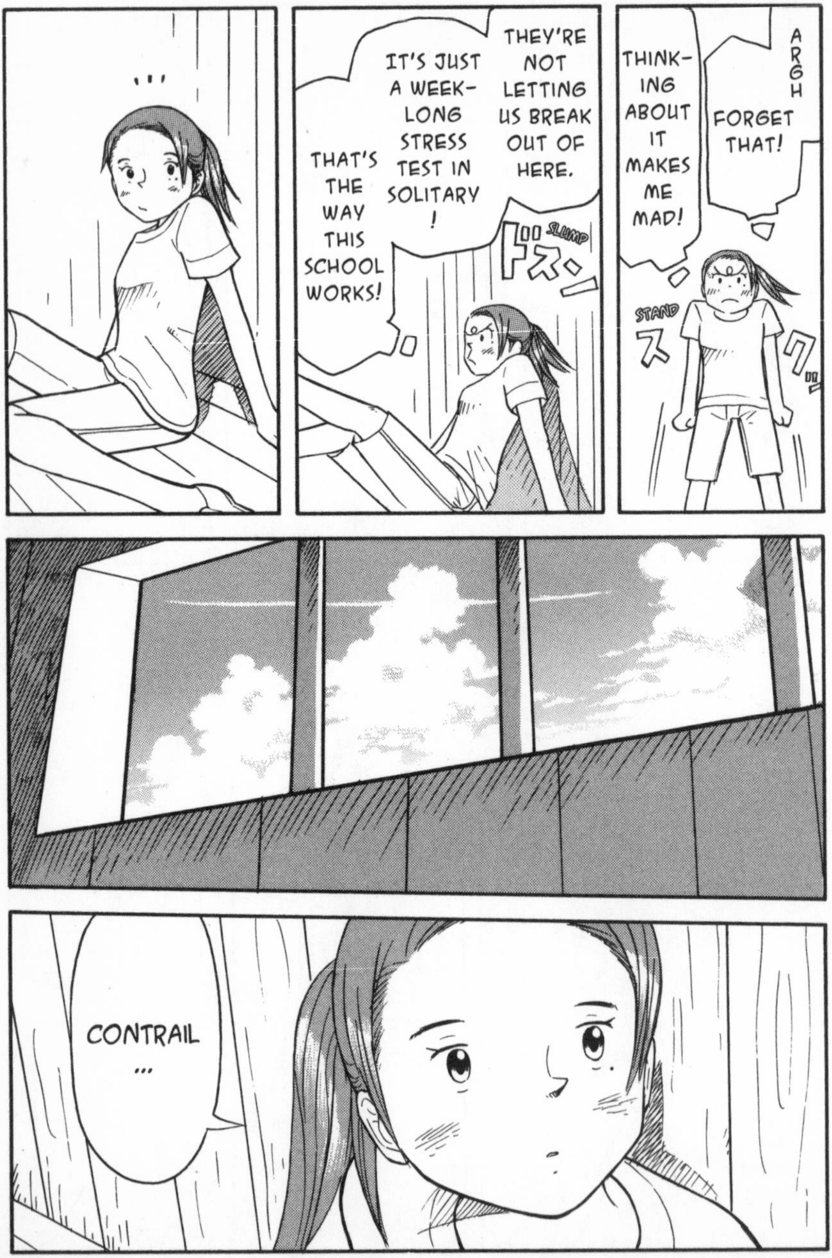
ARGH
FORGET THAT!
THINKING ABOUT IT MAKES ME MAD!
STAND
THEY'RE NOT LETTING US BREAK OUT OF HERE.
IT'S JUST A WEEK-LONG STRESS TEST IN SOLITARY!
THAT'S THE WAY THIS SCHOOL WORKS!
SLUMP
...
CONTRAIL ...

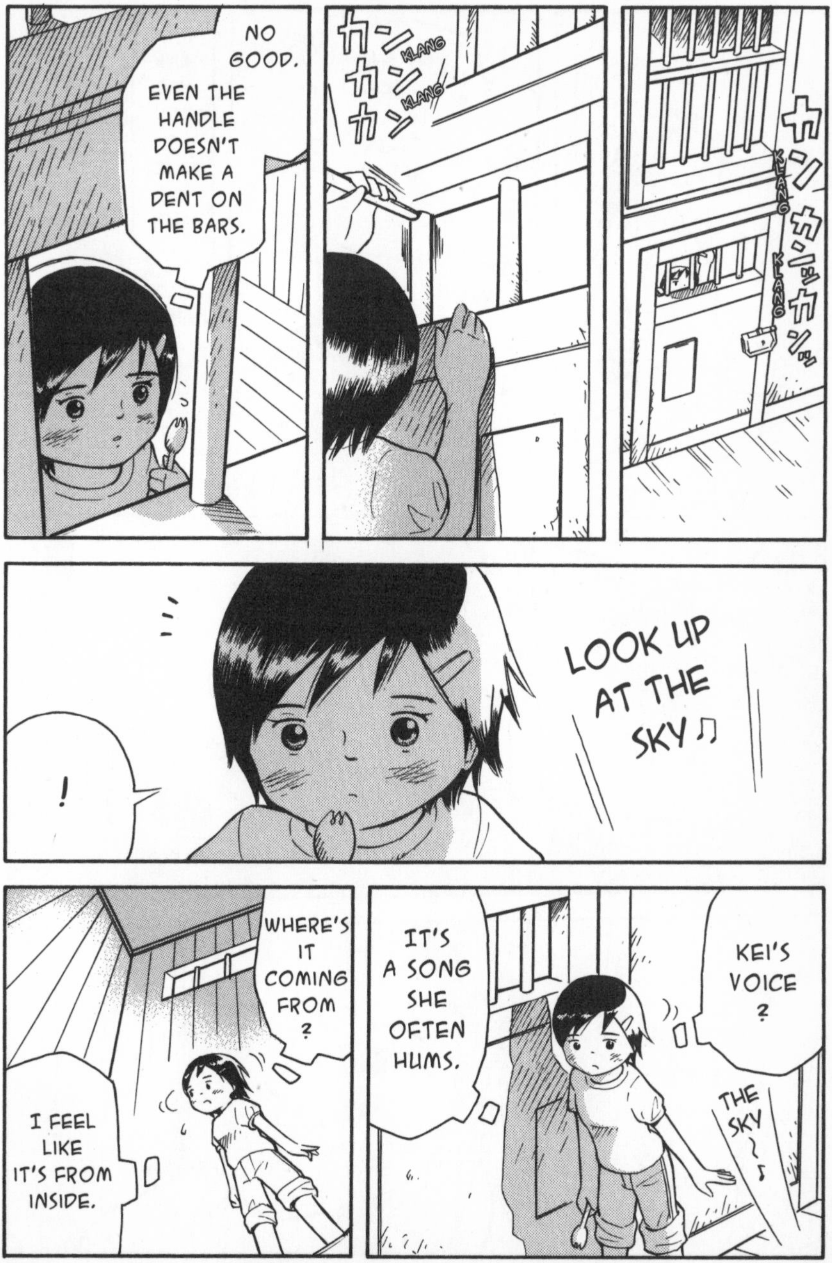
KLANG KLANG
KLANG KLANG
NO GOOD.
EVEN THE HANDLE DOESN'T MAKE A DENT ON THE BARS.
LOOK UP AT THE SKY♫
!
KEI'S VOICE?
THE SKY~♪
IT'S A SONG SHE OFTEN HUMS.
WHERE'S IT COMING FROM?
I FEEL LIKE IT'S FROM INSIDE.

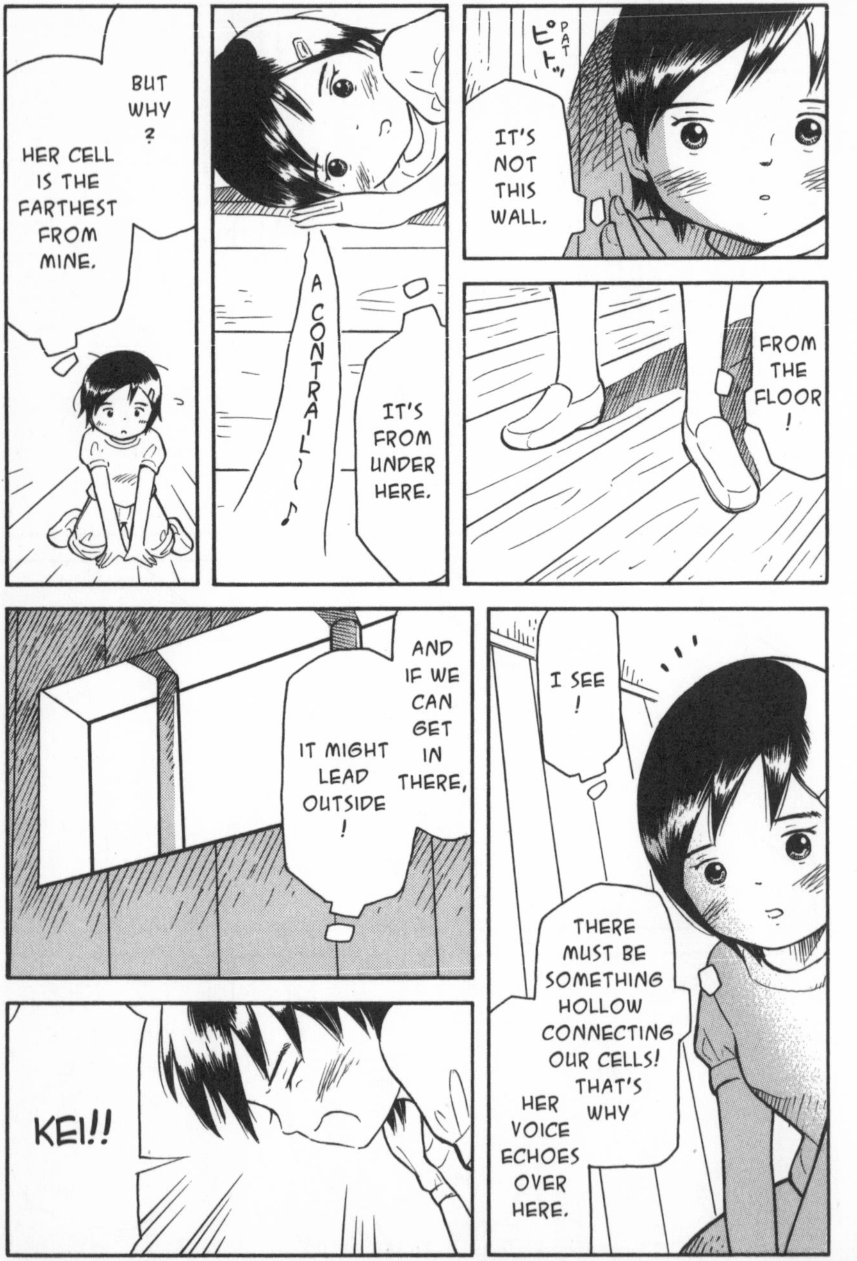
ピトッ PAT
IT'S NOT THIS WALL.
FROM THE FLOOR!
A CONTRAIL~♪
IT'S FROM UNDER HERE.
BUT WHY?
HER CELL IS THE FARTHEST FROM MINE.
I SEE!
THERE MUST BE SOMETHING HOLLOW CONNECTING OUR CELLS! THAT'S WHY HER VOICE ECHOES OVER HERE.
AND IF WE CAN GET IN THERE,
IT MIGHT LEAD OUTSIDE!
KEI!!

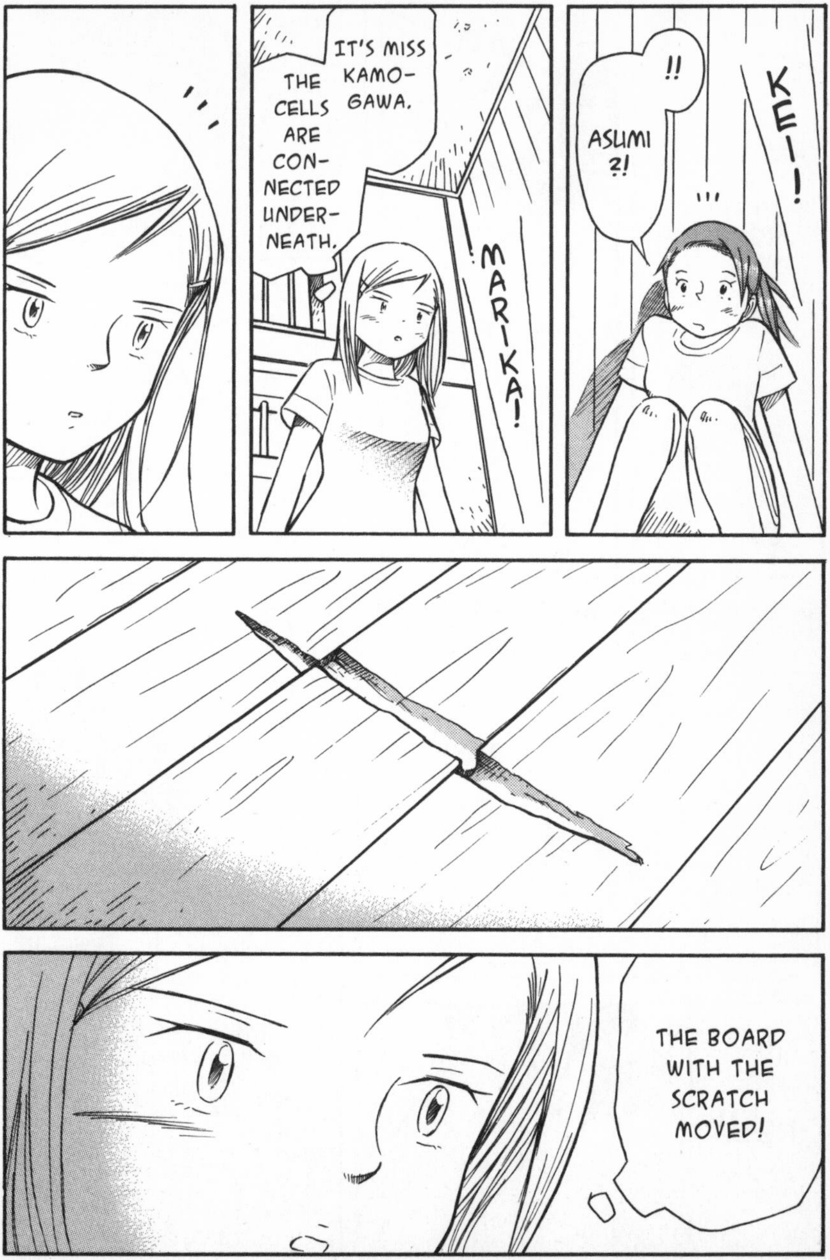
KEI!
!!
ASUMI?!
IT'S MISS KAMO-GAWA.
THE CELLS ARE CON-NECTED UNDER-NEATH.
MARIKA!
THE BOARD WITH THE SCRATCH MOVED!

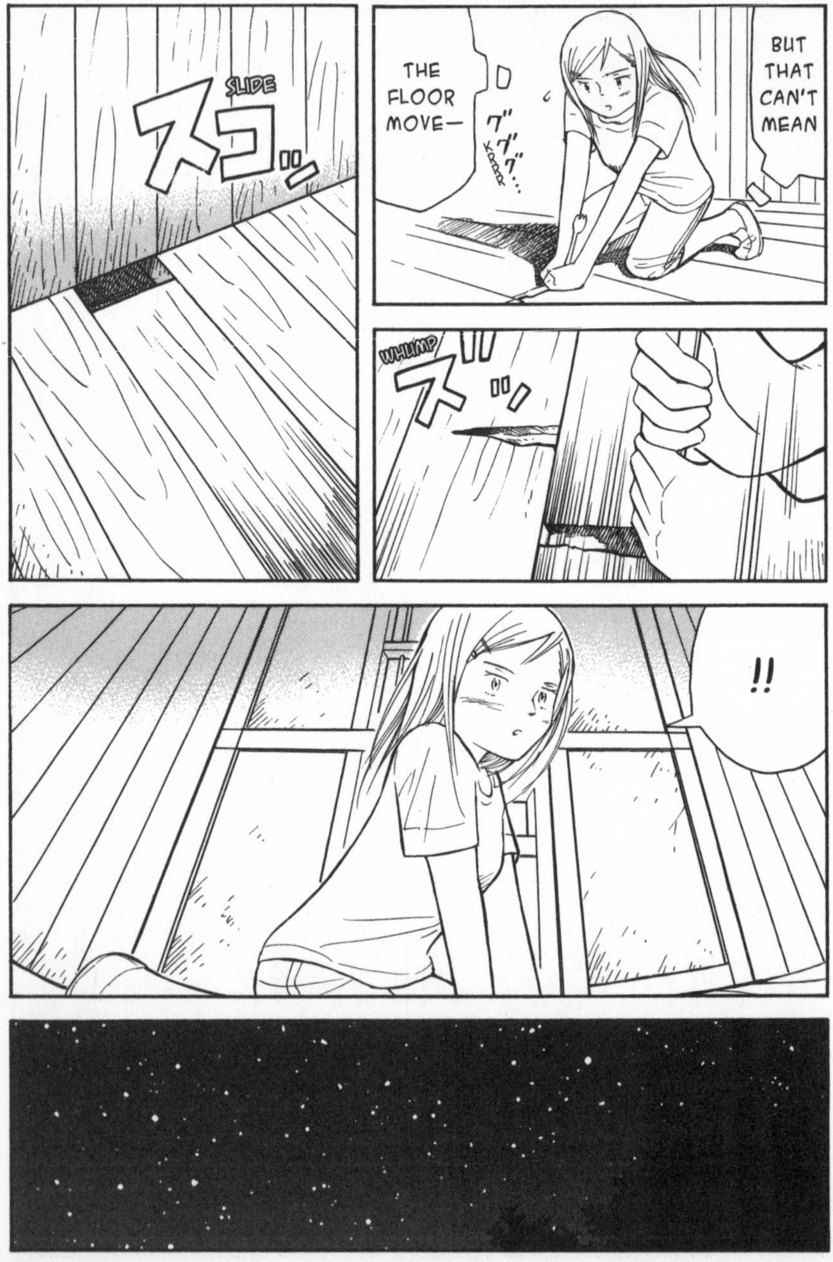
BUT THAT CAN'T MEAN
THE FLOOR MOVE—
KRRRR
WHUMP
ズッ
SLIDE
スコッ
!!

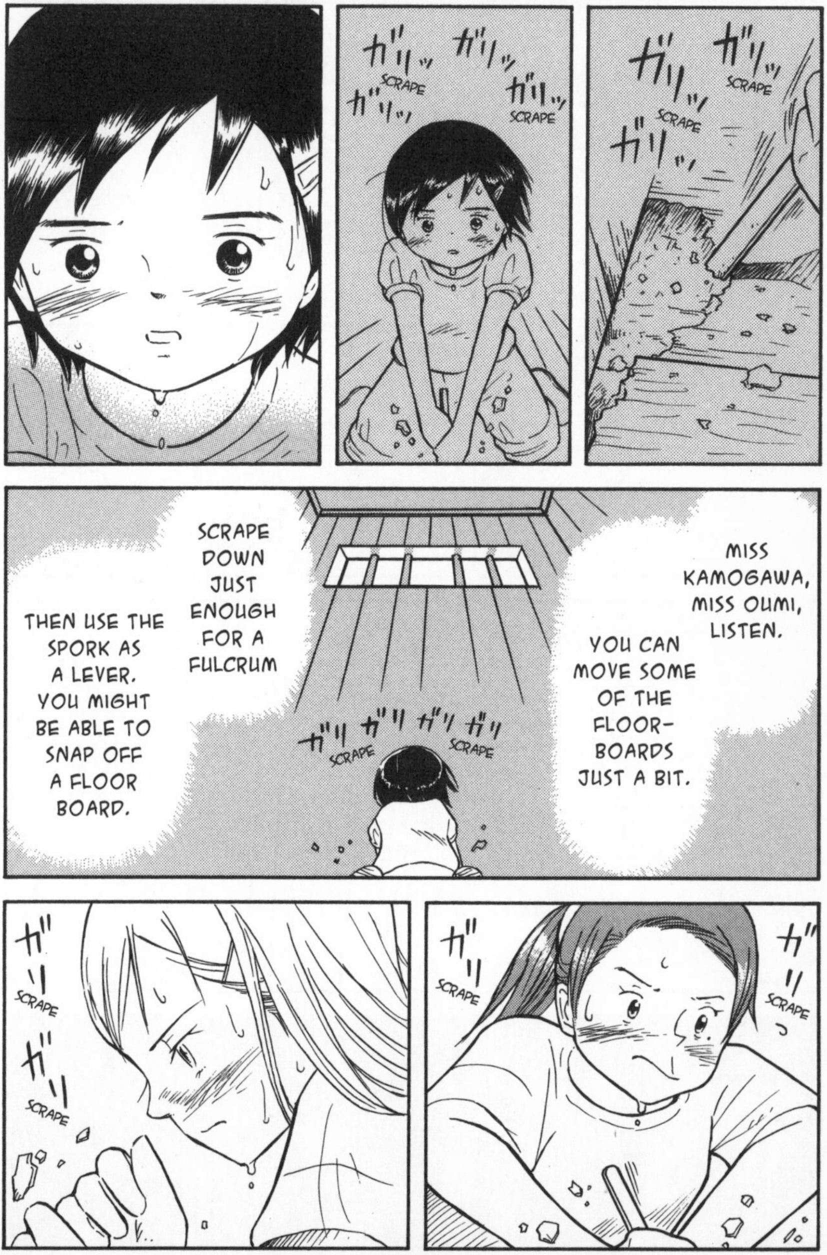
ガリッ
SCRAPE
ガリッ
ガリッ
SCRAPE
ガリッ
ガリッ
ガリッ
SCRAPE
ガリッ
SCRAPE
ガリッ
MISS KAMOGAWA, MISS OUMI, LISTEN.
YOU CAN MOVE SOME OF THE FLOOR-BOARDS JUST A BIT.
ガリ ガリ ガリ ガリ
SCRAPE
SCRAPE
SCRAPE DOWN JUST ENOUGH FOR A FULCRUM
THEN USE THE SPORK AS A LEVER. YOU MIGHT BE ABLE TO SNAP OFF A FLOOR BOARD.
ガリ
SCRAPE
ガリ
SCRAPE
ガリ
SCRAPE
ガリ
SCRAPE

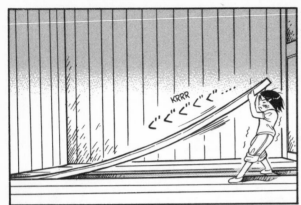

KRRR
く"く"く"く"く"....

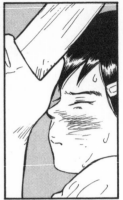

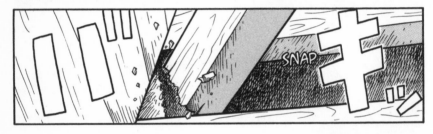

SNAP
キ
"

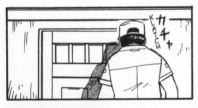

KLATCH
カ
チ
ャ

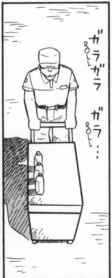

ガ"ラ
ROLL
ガ"ラ
ROLL

ガ"ラ
ROLL
..

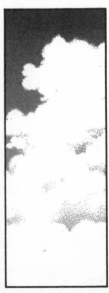

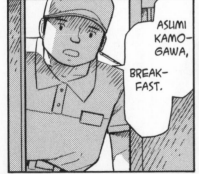

ASUMI
KAMO-
GAWA,

BREAK-
FAST.

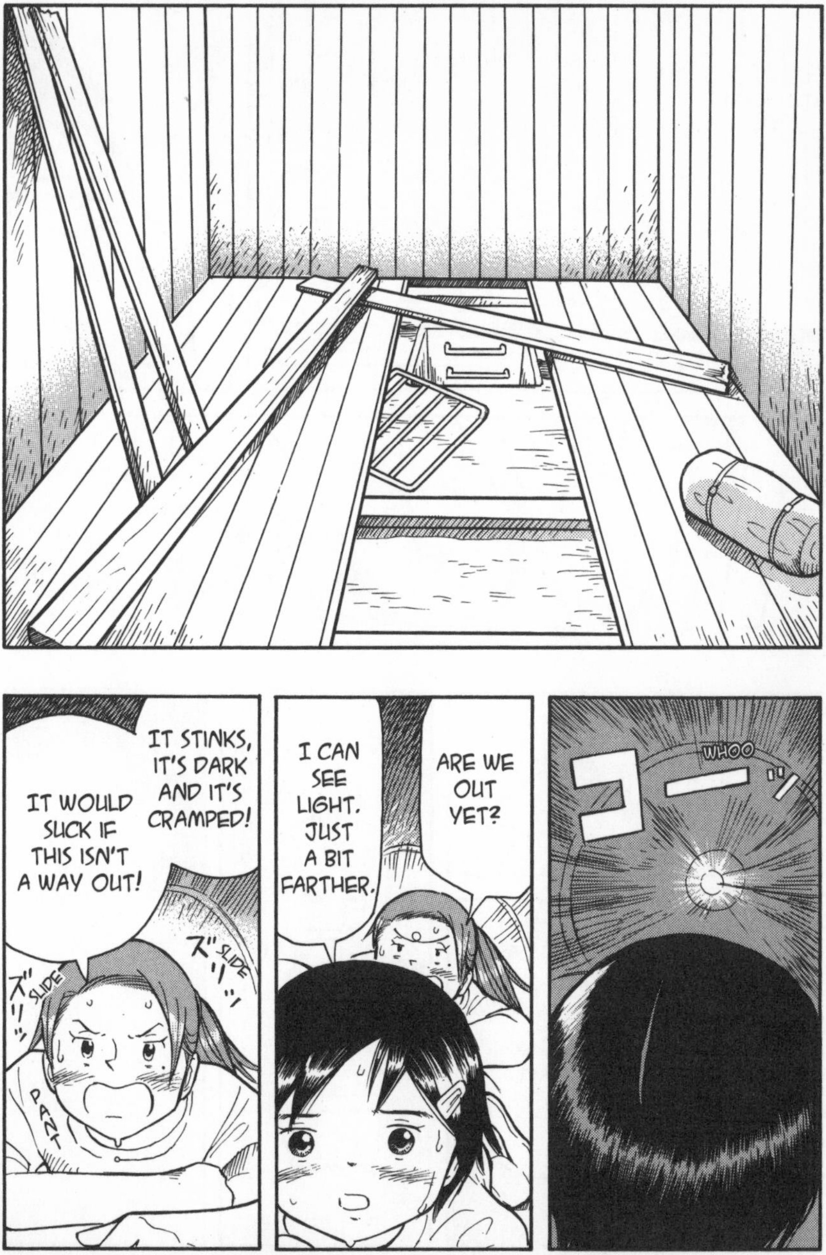
コー
WHOO
ARE WE OUT YET?
I CAN SEE LIGHT. JUST A BIT FARTHER.
IT STINKS, IT'S DARK AND IT'S CRAMPED!
IT WOULD SUCK IF THIS ISN'T A WAY OUT!
ズリッ
SLIDE
ズリッ
SLIDE
PANT

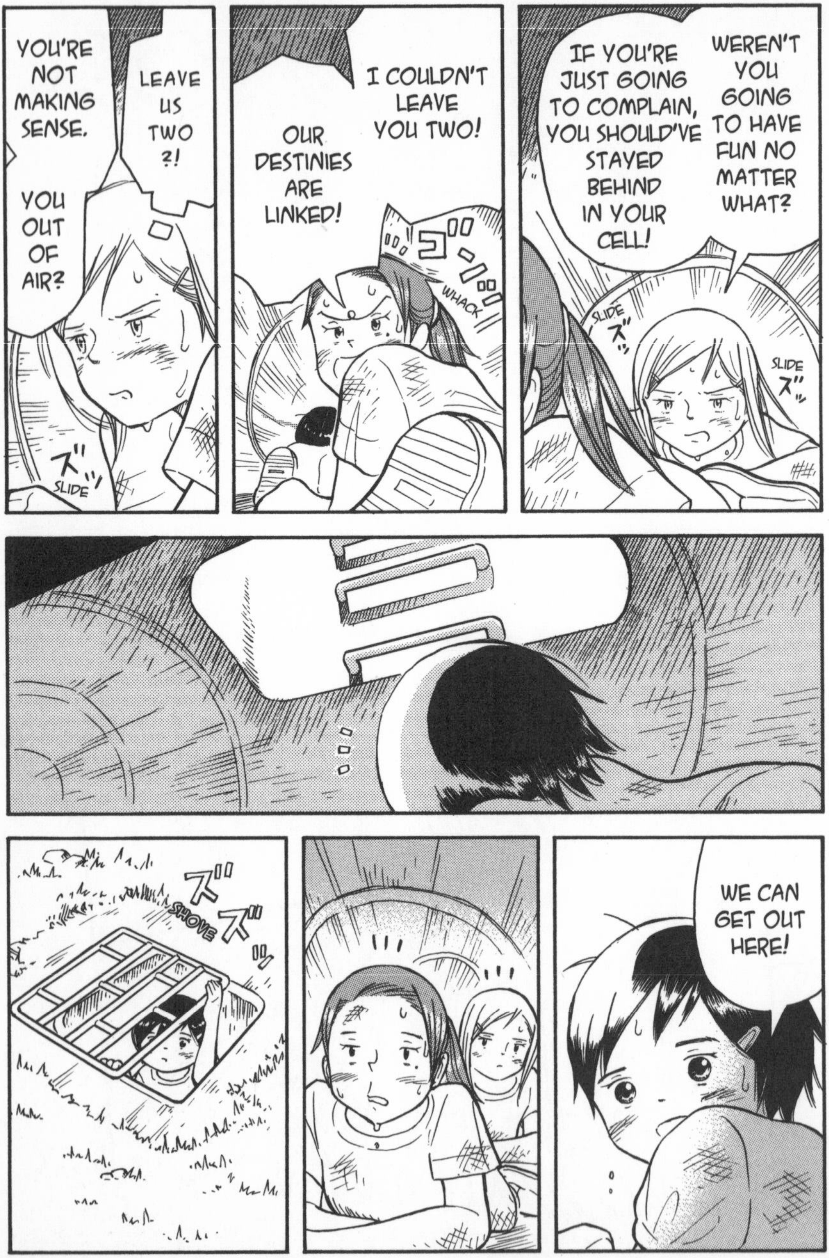
WEREN'T YOU GOING TO HAVE FUN NO MATTER WHAT?
IF YOU'RE JUST GOING TO COMPLAIN, YOU SHOULD'VE STAYED BEHIND IN YOUR CELL!
SLIDE
SLIDE
I COULDN'T LEAVE YOU TWO!
OUR DESTINIES ARE LINKED!
WHACK
LEAVE US TWO ?!
YOU'RE NOT MAKING SENSE.
YOU OUT OF AIR?
SLIDE
WE CAN GET OUT HERE!
SHOVE

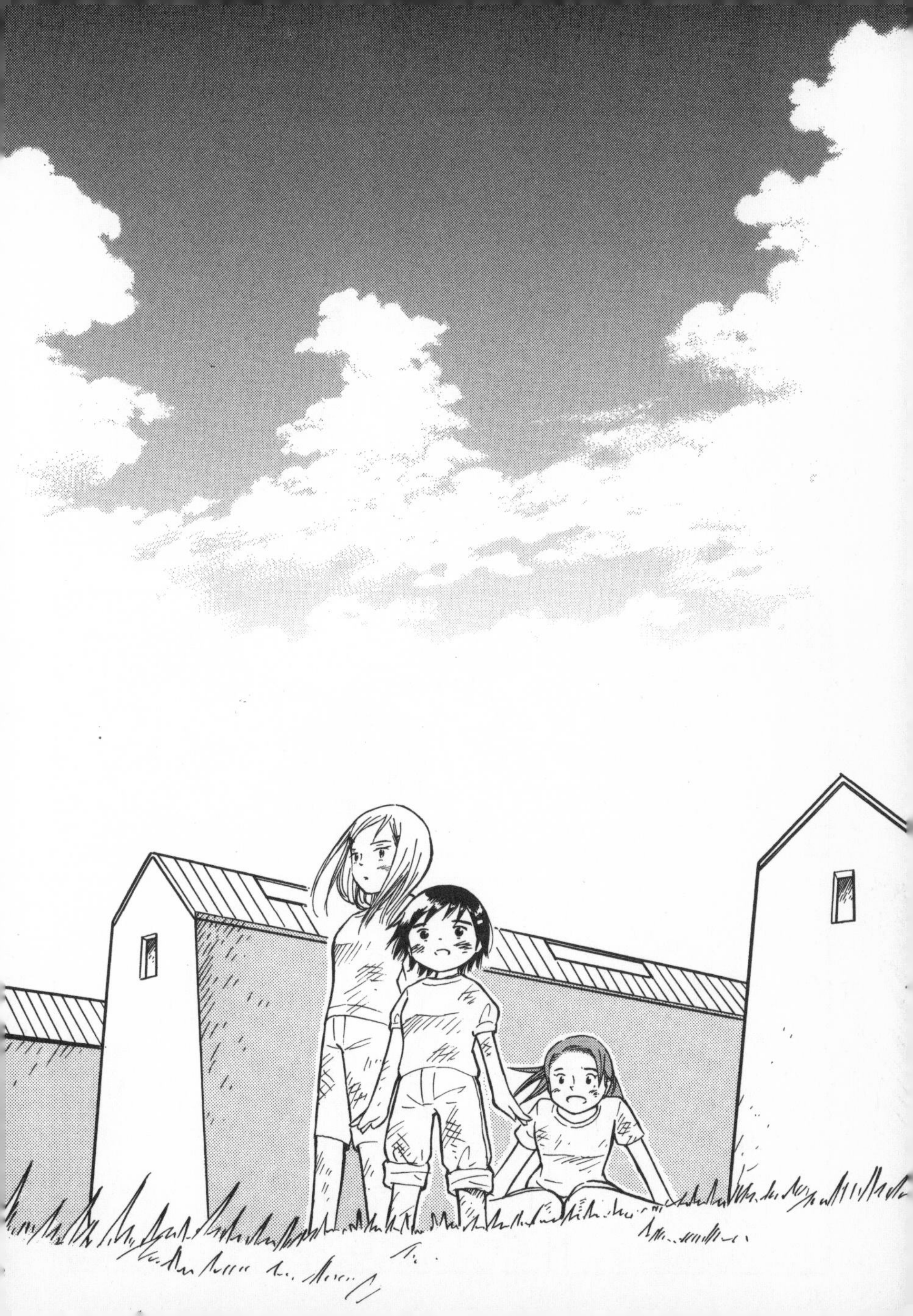

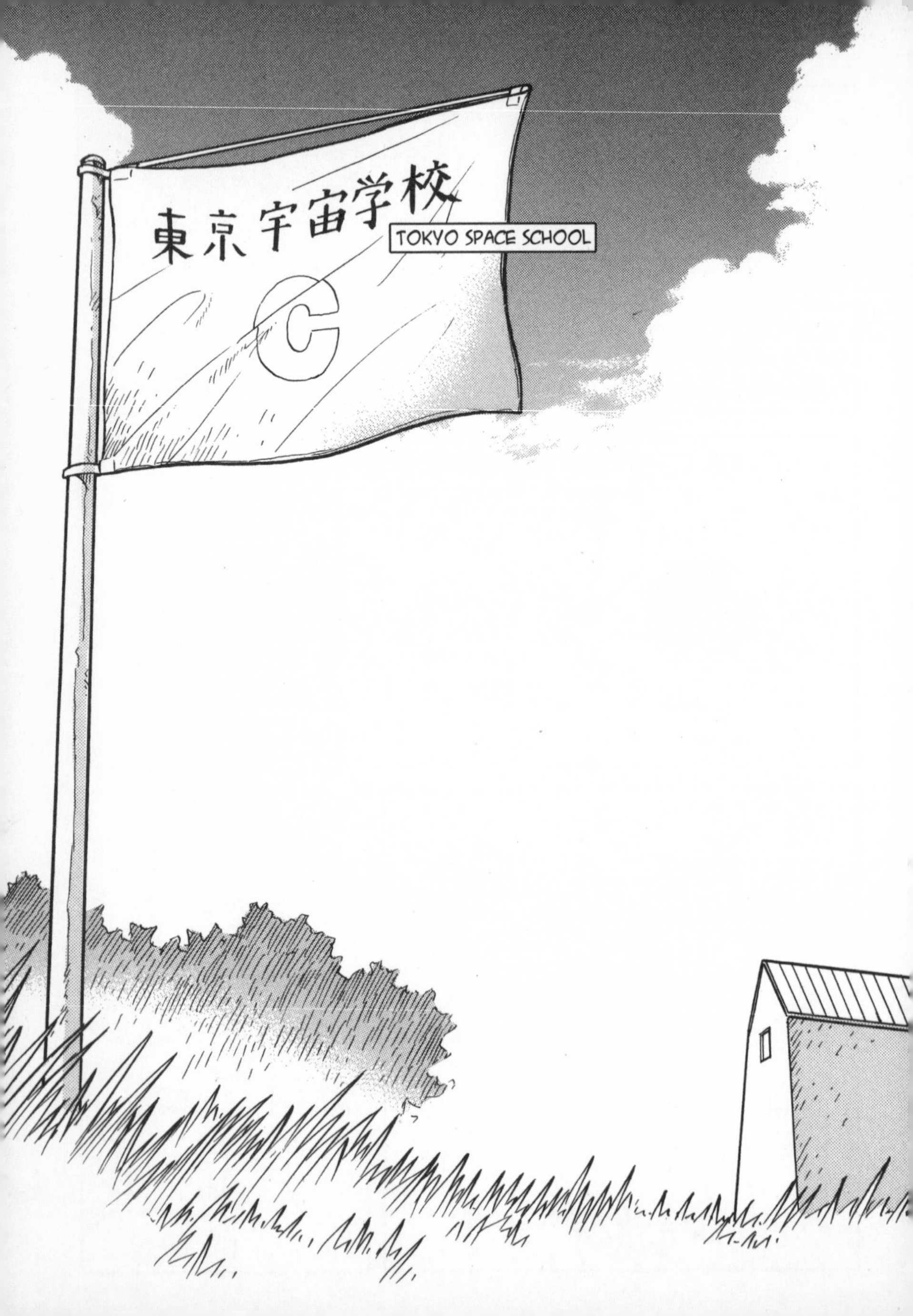
東京宇宙学校
TOKYO SPACE SCHOOL
C

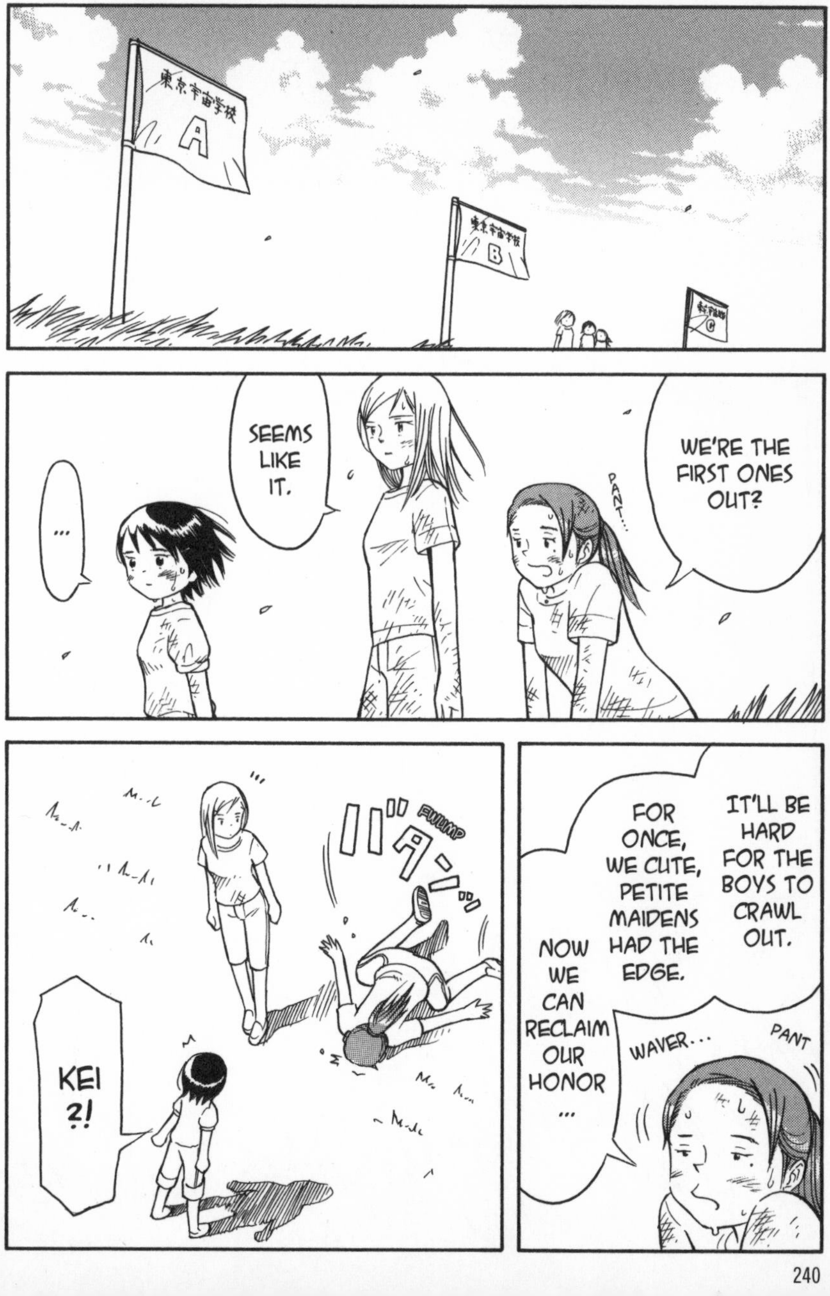
東京宇宙学校
A
東京宇宙学校
B
WE'RE THE FIRST ONES OUT?
PANT...
SEEMS LIKE IT.
...
IT'LL BE HARD FOR THE BOYS TO CRAWL OUT.
FOR ONCE, WE CUTE, PETITE MAIDENS HAD THE EDGE.
NOW WE CAN RECLAIM OUR HONOR...
PANT
WAVER...
バタン
FWUMP
KEI?!

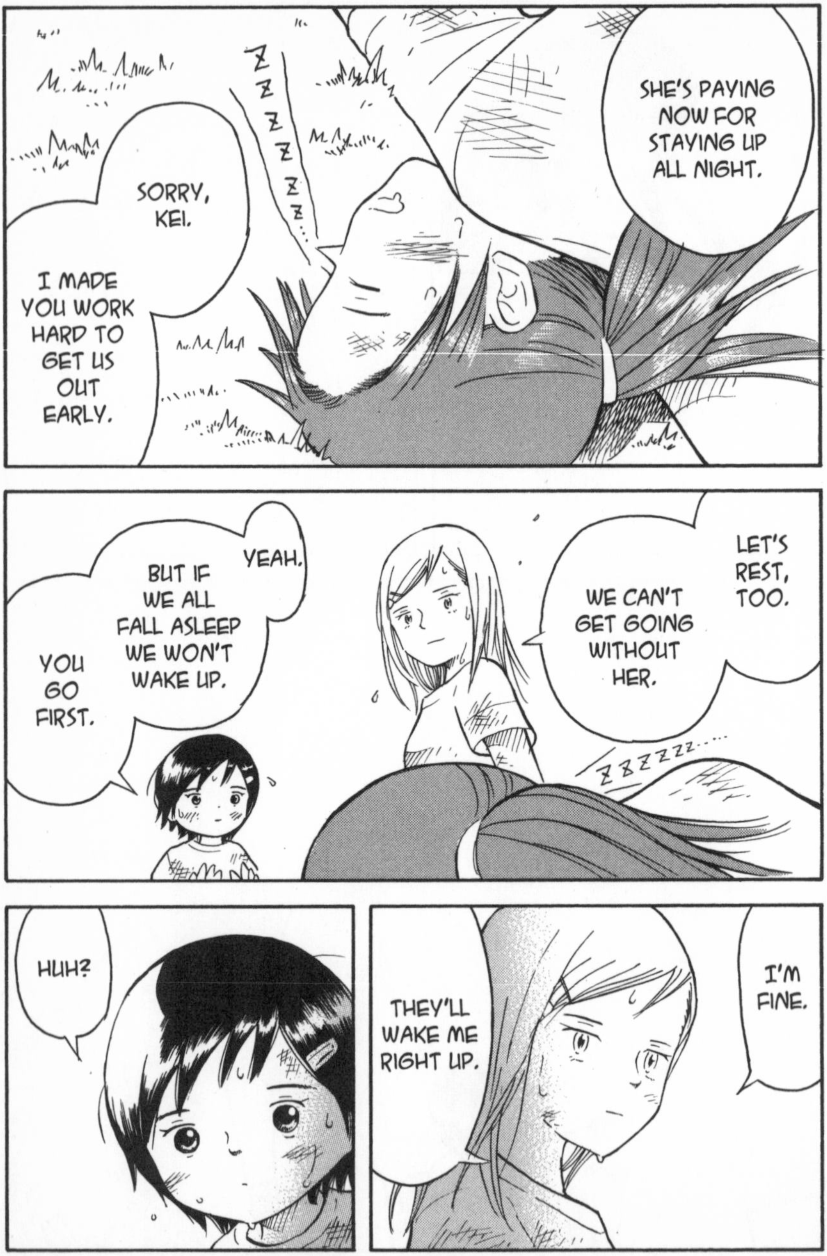
SHE'S PAYING NOW FOR STAYING UP ALL NIGHT.
ZZZZZZ...
SORRY, KEI.
I MADE YOU WORK HARD TO GET US OUT EARLY.
LET'S REST, TOO.
WE CAN'T GET GOING WITHOUT HER.
ZZZZZZ....
YEAH.
BUT IF WE ALL FALL ASLEEP WE WON'T WAKE UP.
YOU GO FIRST.
I'M FINE.
THEY'LL WAKE ME RIGHT UP.
HUH?

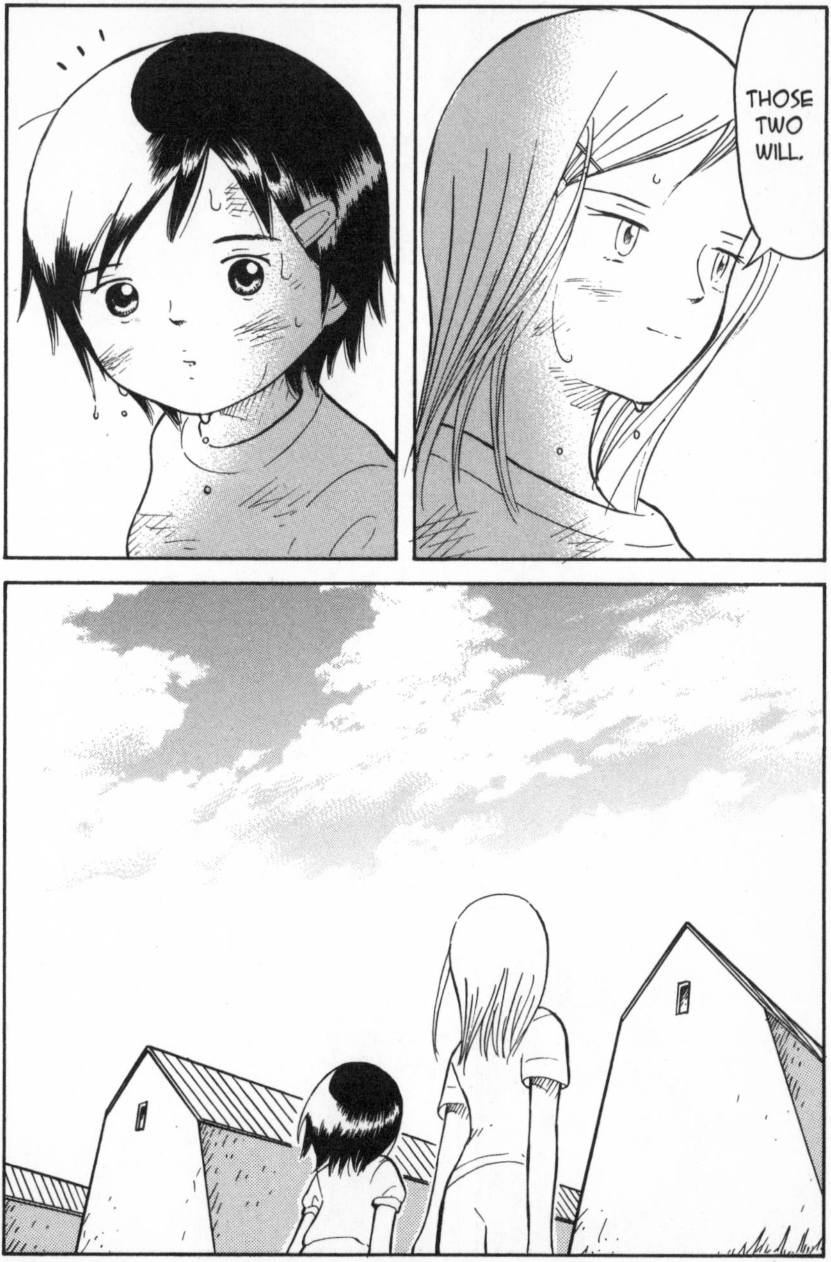
THOSE TWO WILL.

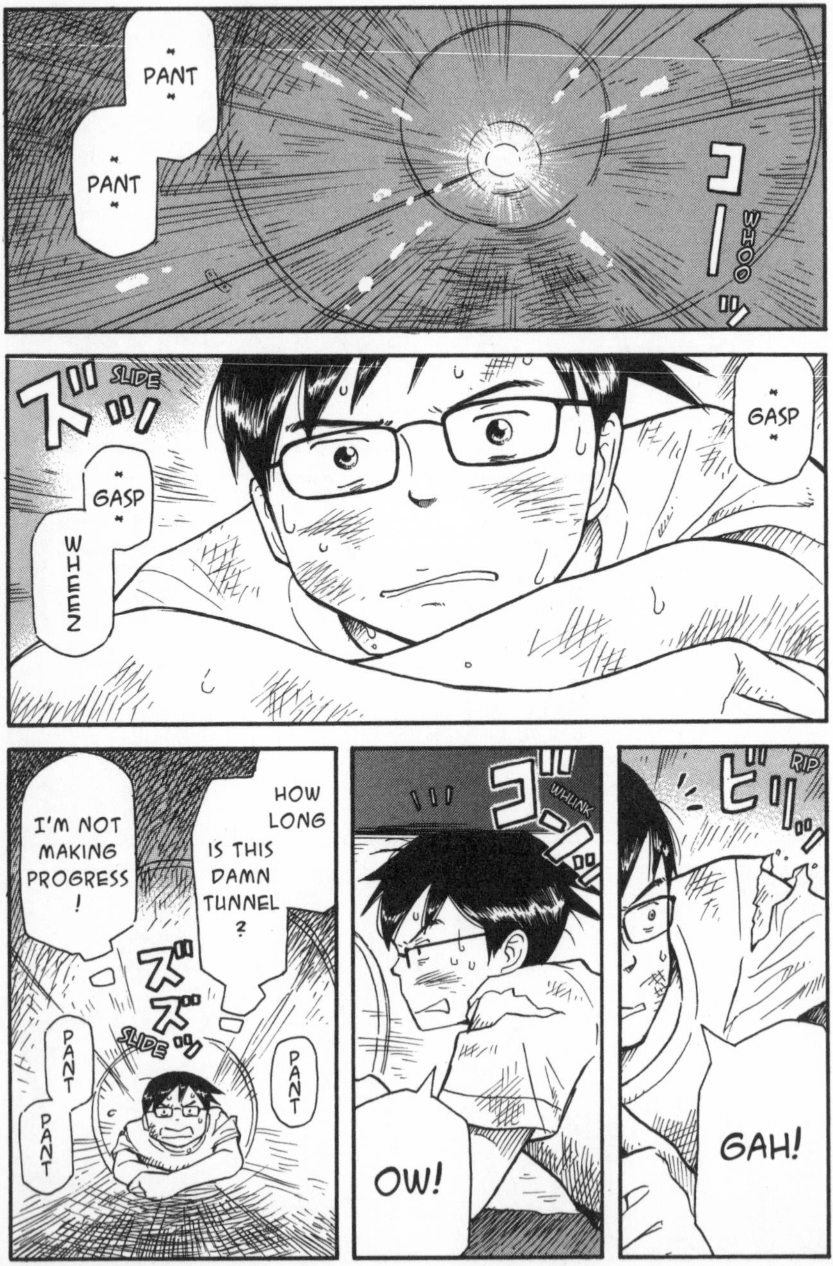
WHOO
PANT
PANT
GASP
SLIDE
GASP
WHEEZ
RIP
GAH!
WHUNK
OW!
HOW LONG IS THIS DAMN TUNNEL?
I'M NOT MAKING PROGRESS!
SLIDE
PANT
PANT PANT

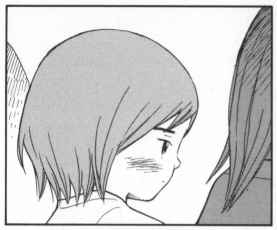

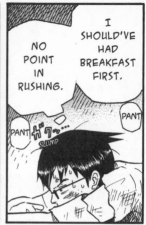

I SHOULD'VE HAD BREAKFAST FIRST.

NO POINT IN RUSHING.

PANT

PANT

ガクッ...
SLUMP

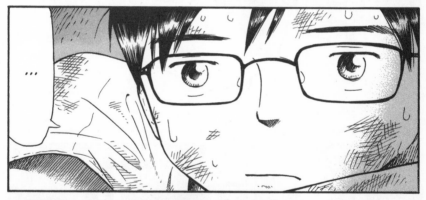

...

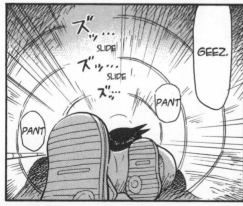

ズッ....
SLIDE

ズッ....
SLIDE

ズッ...

GEEZ.

PANT

PANT

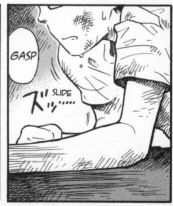

GASP

ズッ...
SLIDE

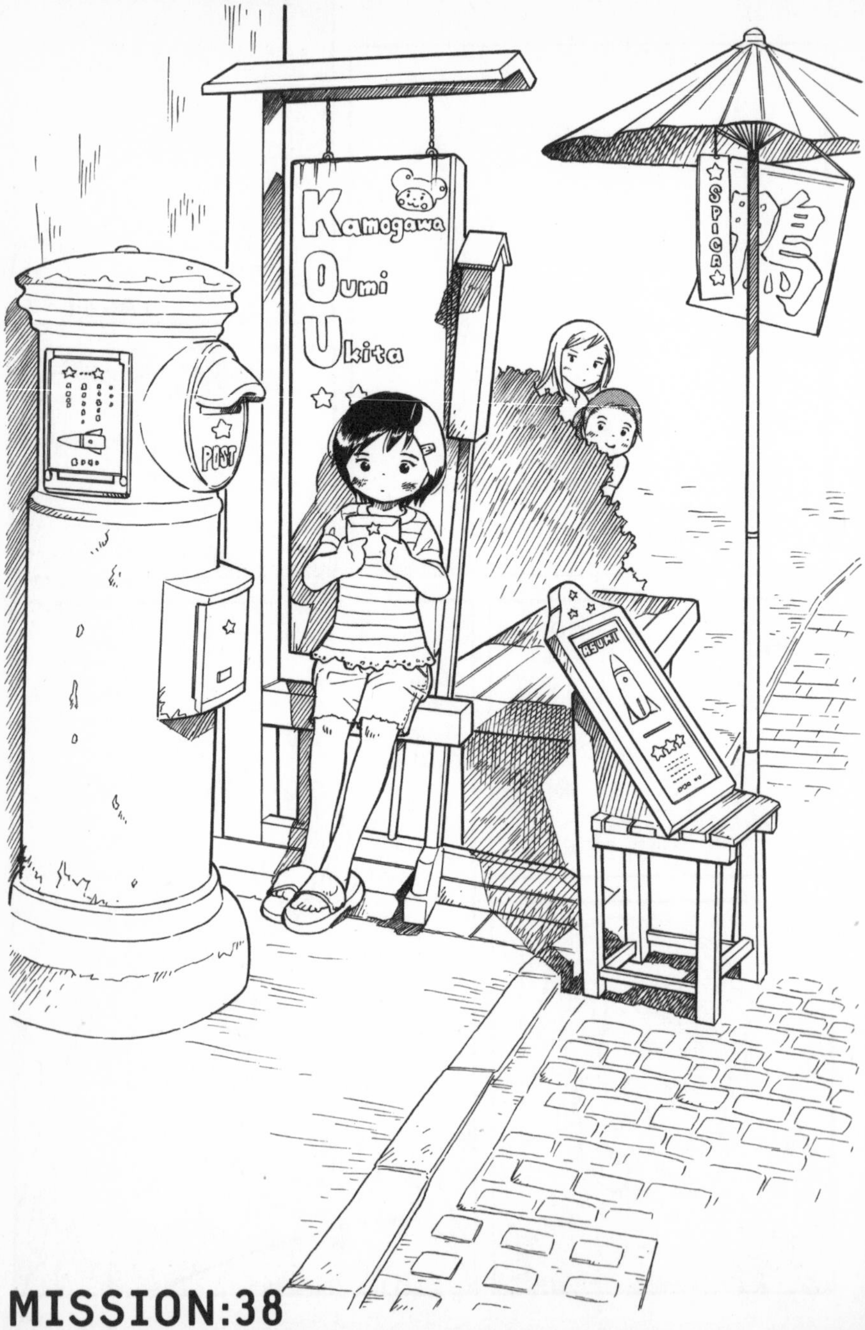
Kamogawa
Oumi
Ukita
POST
SPICA
ASUMI

MISSION:38

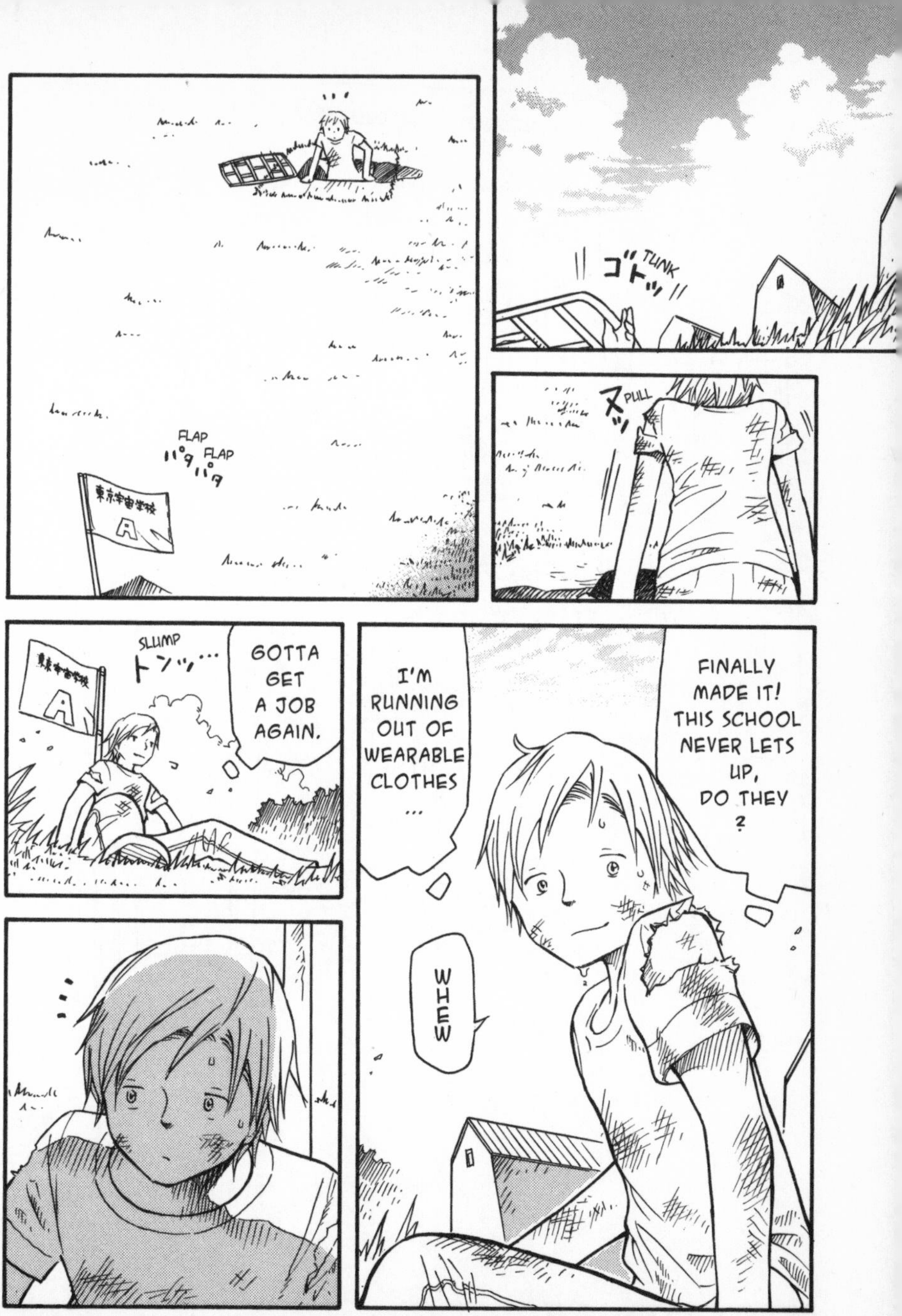
ゴトッ
TUNK
ヌッ
PULL
パタパタ
FLAP FLAP
東京宇宙学校
A
FINALLY MADE IT! THIS SCHOOL NEVER LETS UP, DO THEY?
I'M RUNNING OUT OF WEARABLE CLOTHES...
WHEW
トンッ…
SLUMP
GOTTA GET A JOB AGAIN.
東京宇宙学校
A

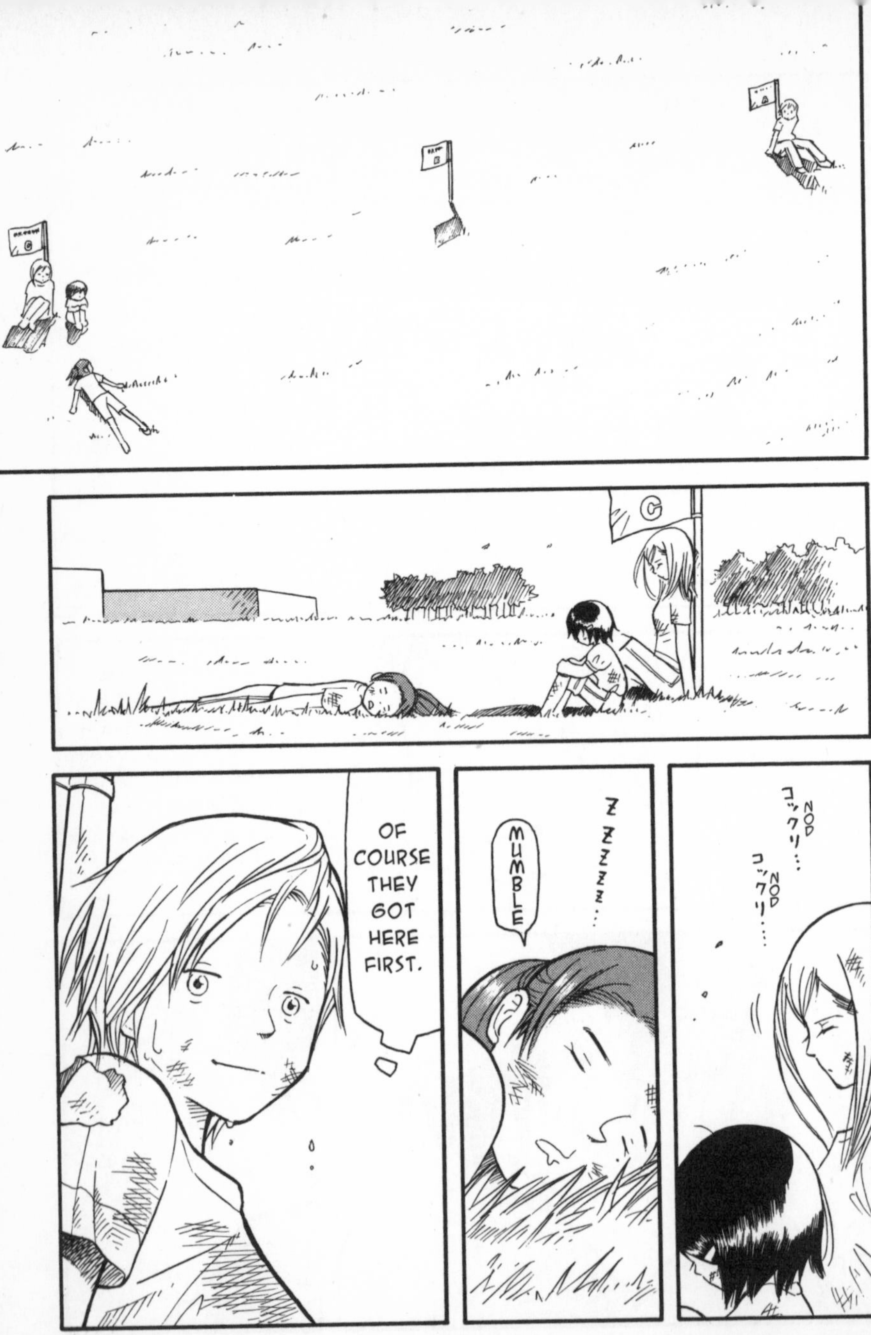
NOD
コックリ…
NOD
コックリ…
Z Z ZZZZ…
MUMBLE
OF COURSE THEY GOT HERE FIRST.

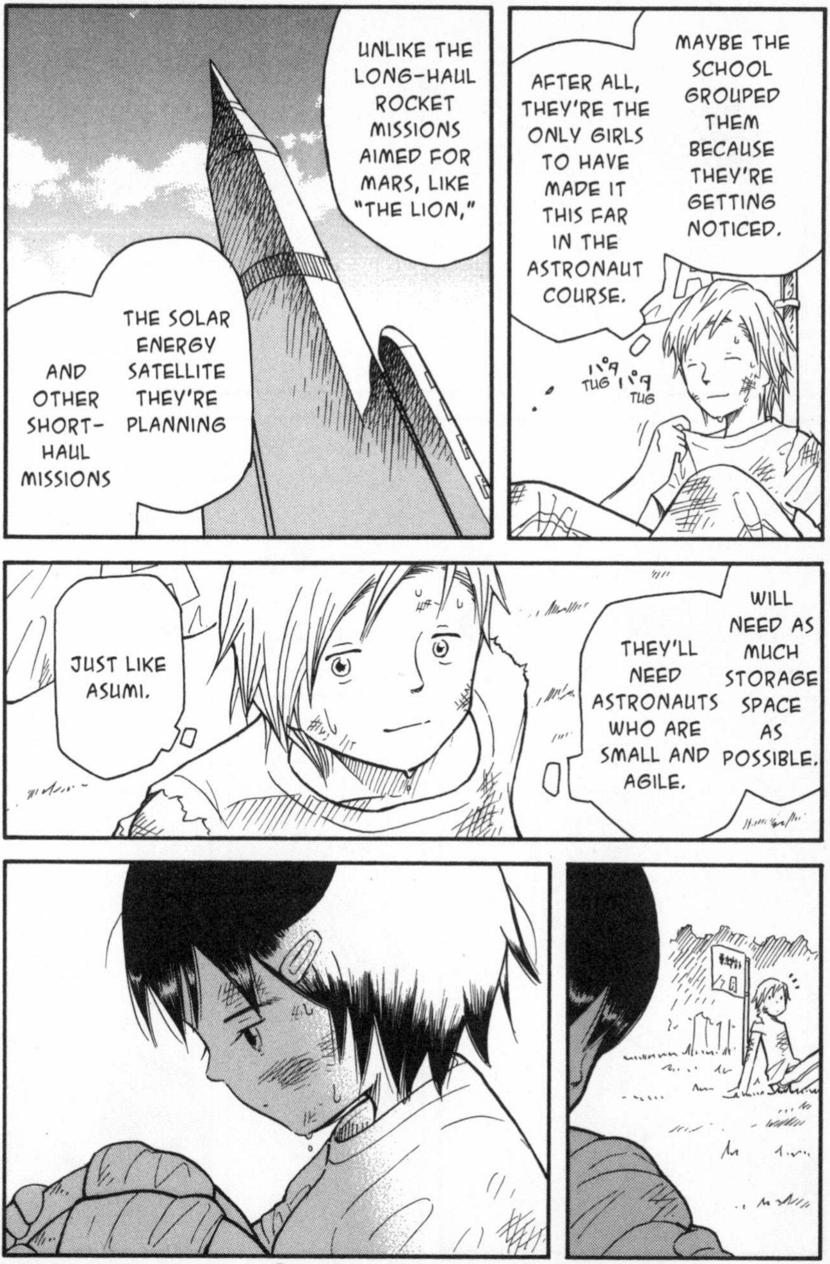
MAYBE THE SCHOOL GROUPED THEM BECAUSE THEY'RE GETTING NOTICED.
AFTER ALL, THEY'RE THE ONLY GIRLS TO HAVE MADE IT THIS FAR IN THE ASTRONAUT COURSE.
パタ TUG パタ TUG
UNLIKE THE LONG-HAUL ROCKET MISSIONS AIMED FOR MARS, LIKE "THE LION,"
THE SOLAR ENERGY SATELLITE THEY'RE PLANNING
AND OTHER SHORT-HAUL MISSIONS
WILL NEED AS MUCH STORAGE SPACE AS POSSIBLE.
THEY'LL NEED ASTRONAUTS WHO ARE SMALL AND AGILE.
JUST LIKE ASUMI.

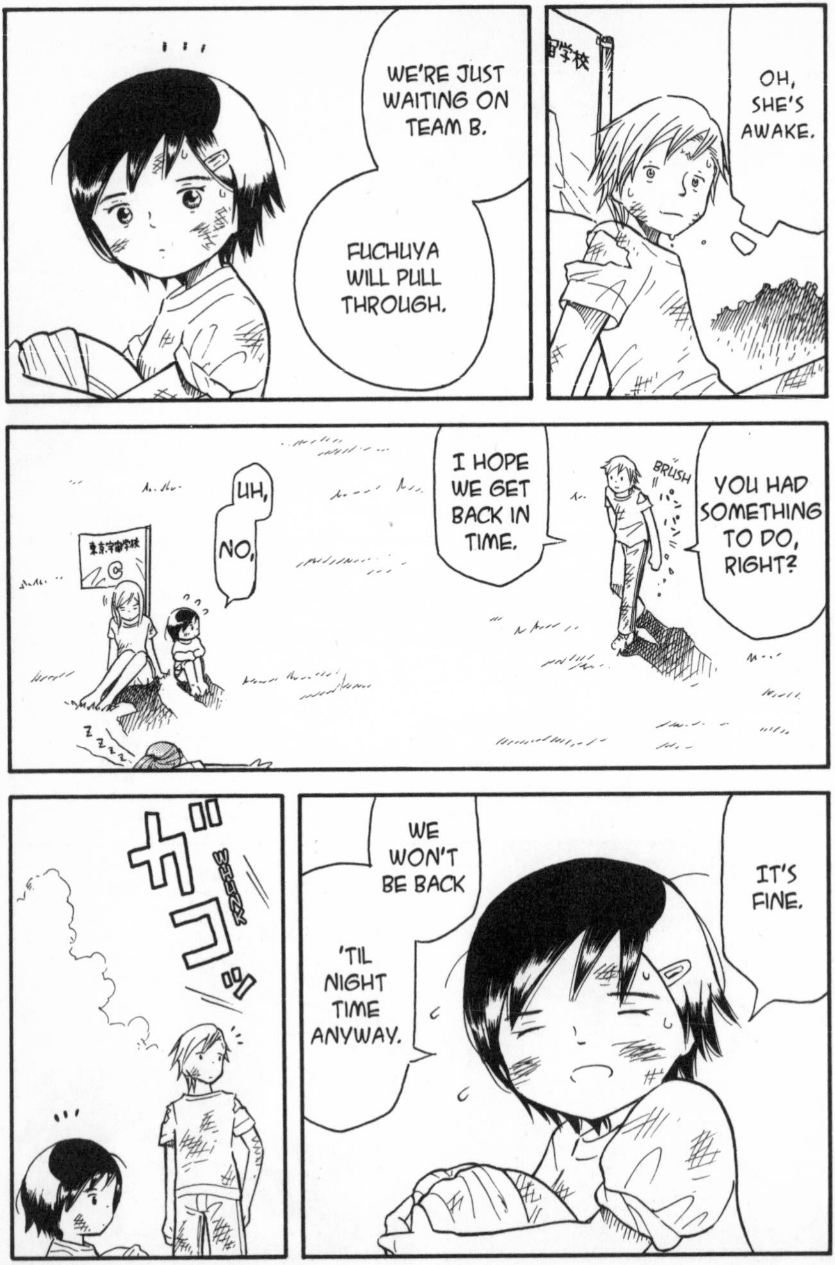
OH, SHE'S AWAKE.
WE'RE JUST WAITING ON TEAM B.
FUCHUYA WILL PULL THROUGH.
YOU HAD SOMETHING TO DO, RIGHT?
BRUSH
I HOPE WE GET BACK IN TIME.
UH,
NO,
東京宇宙学校
IT'S FINE.
WE WON'T BE BACK
'TIL NIGHT TIME ANYWAY.
ガコッ
WHUNK

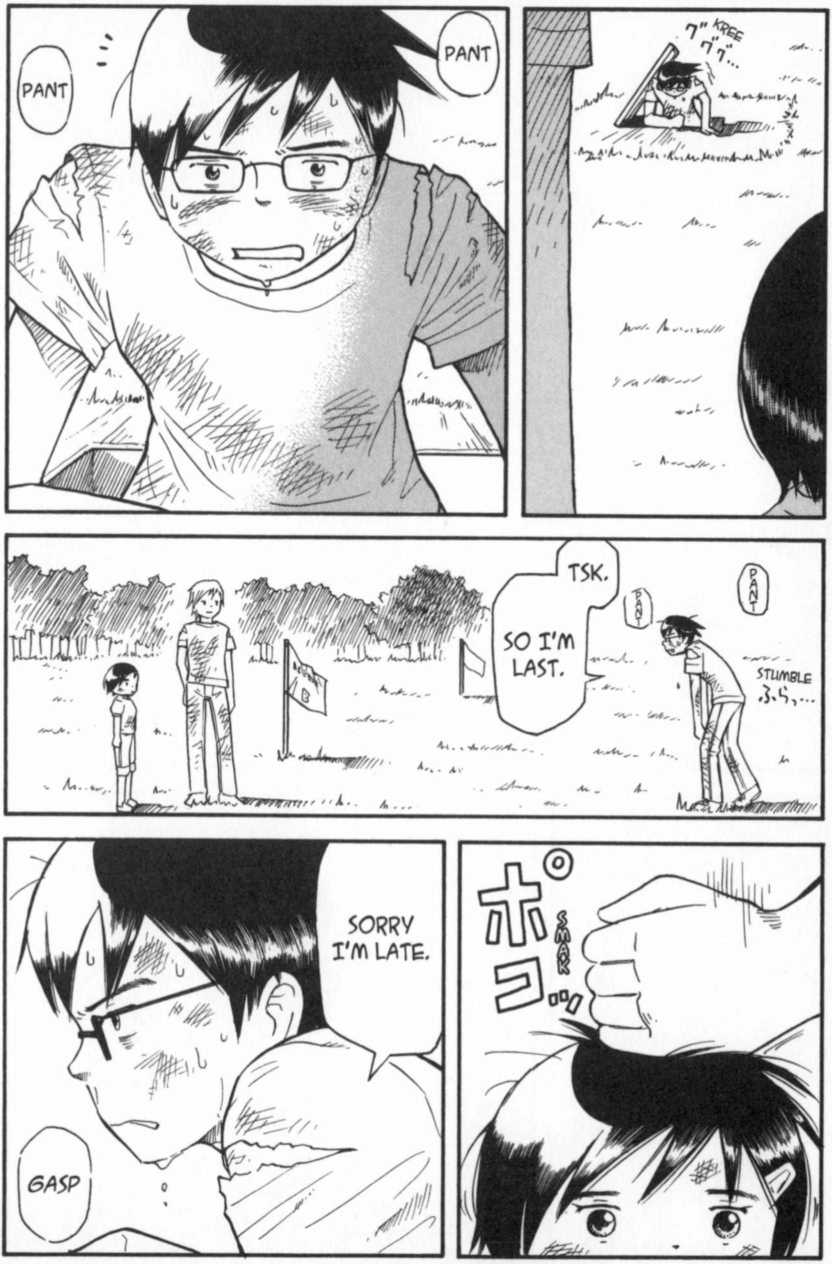
グ
KREE
ググ...
PANT
PANT
PANT
PANT
TSK.
SO I'M LAST.
STUMBLE
ふらっ...
ポコッ
SMAK
SORRY I'M LATE.
GASP

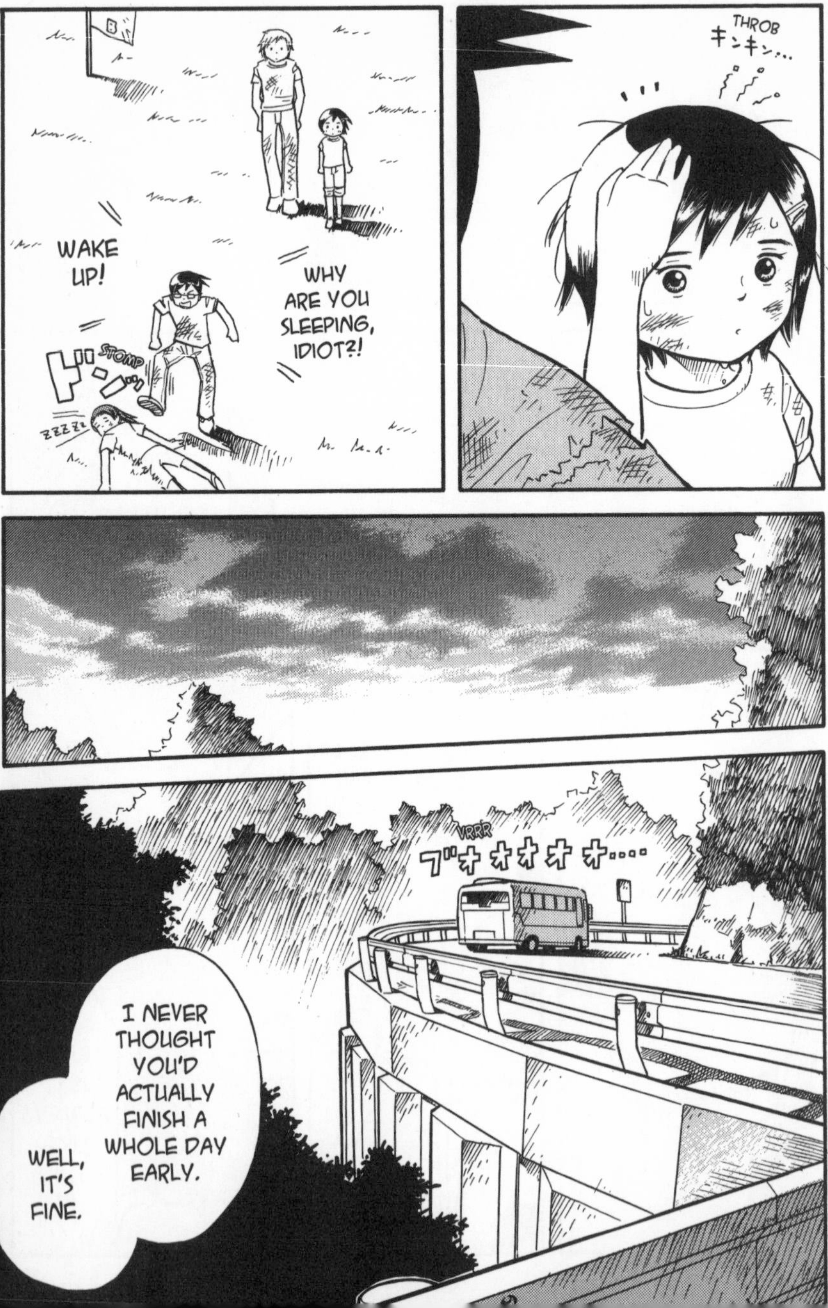
THROB
キンキン…
WHY ARE YOU SLEEPING, IDIOT?!
WAKE UP!
STOMP
ドーン
ZZZZZ
VRRR
ブォオオオオ…
I NEVER THOUGHT YOU'D ACTUALLY FINISH A WHOLE DAY EARLY.
WELL, IT'S FINE.

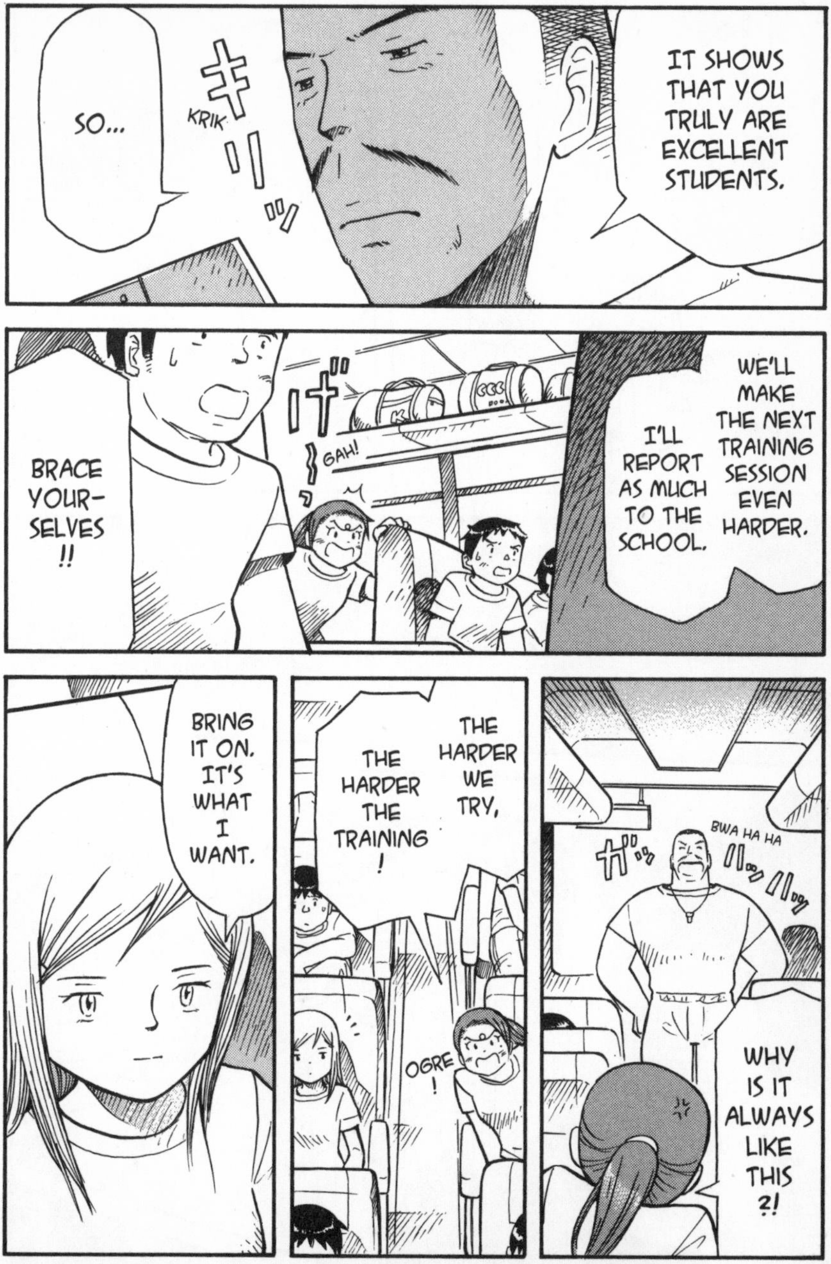
IT SHOWS THAT YOU TRULY ARE EXCELLENT STUDENTS.
KRIK
SO...
WE'LL MAKE THE NEXT TRAINING SESSION EVEN HARDER.
I'LL REPORT AS MUCH TO THE SCHOOL.
GAH!
BRACE YOUR-SELVES!!
BWA HA HA
WHY IS IT ALWAYS LIKE THIS?!
THE HARDER WE TRY,
THE HARDER THE TRAINING!
OGRE!
BRING IT ON. IT'S WHAT I WANT.

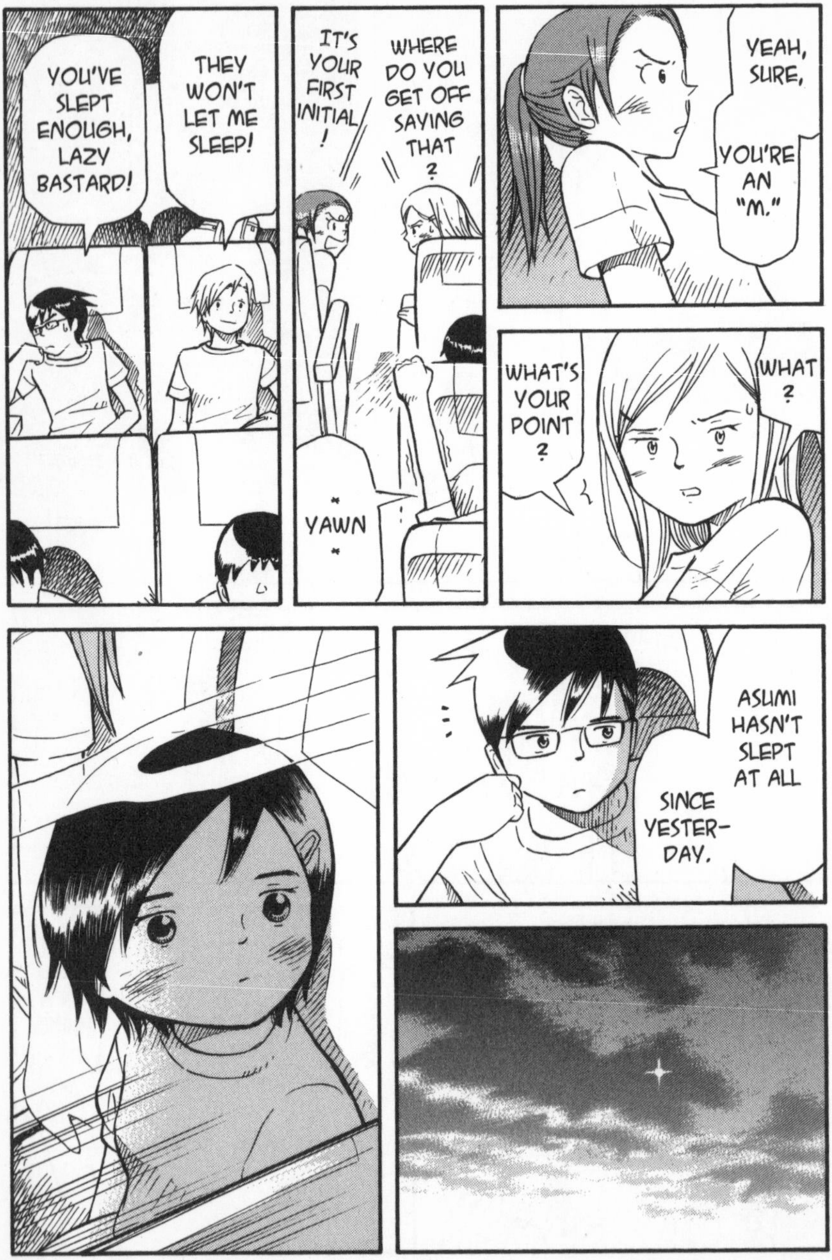
YEAH, SURE,
YOU'RE AN "M."
WHAT?
WHAT'S YOUR POINT?
WHERE DO YOU GET OFF SAYING THAT?
IT'S YOUR FIRST INITIAL!
YAWN
THEY WON'T LET ME SLEEP!
YOU'VE SLEPT ENOUGH, LAZY BASTARD!
ASUMI HASN'T SLEPT AT ALL
SINCE YESTER-DAY.

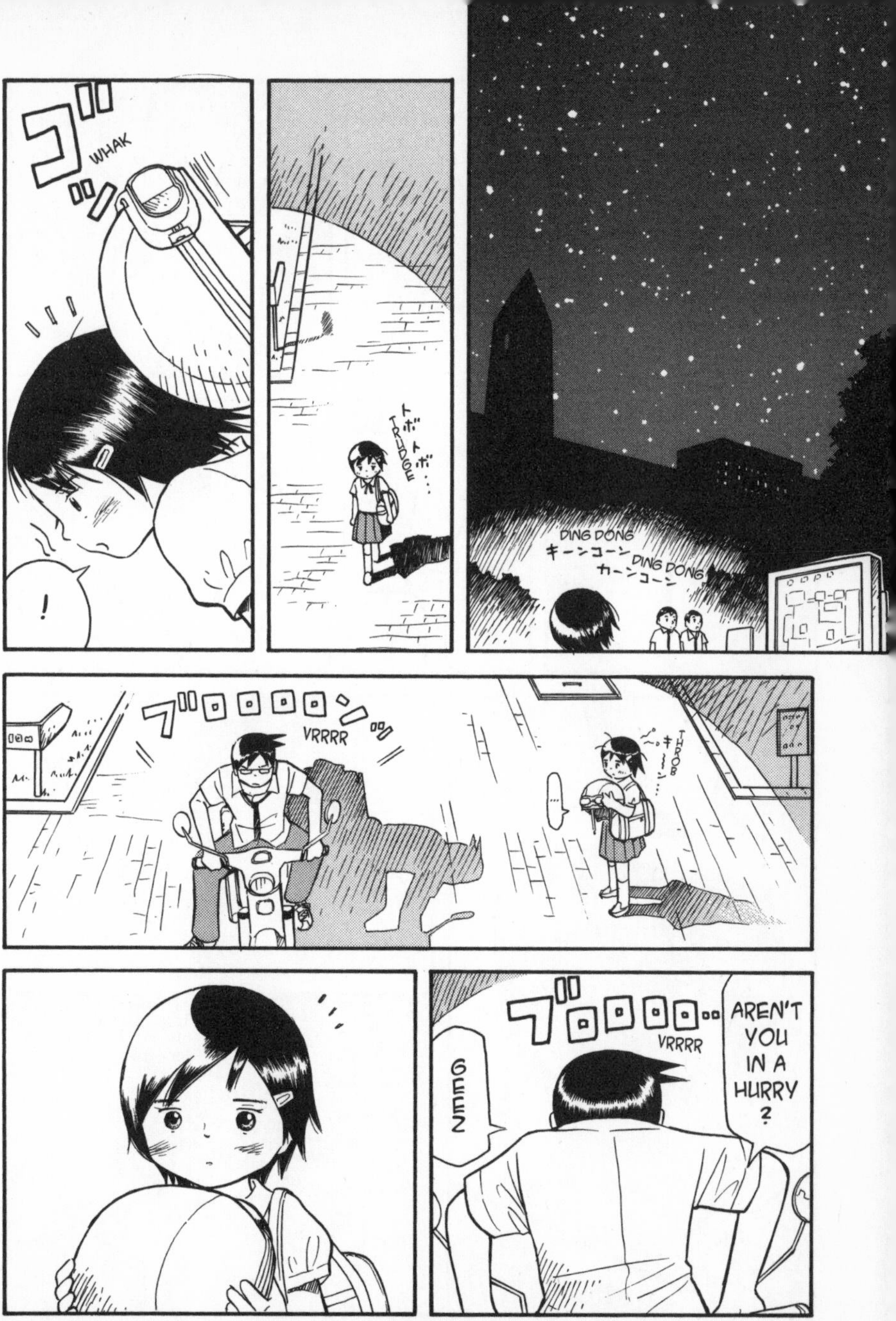
DING DONG
キーンコーン
DING DONG
カーンコーン
トボトボ…
TRUDGE
ゴッ
WHAK
!
ブロロロロロン
VRRRR
…
キーン
THROB
ブロロロロ…
VRRRR
AREN'T YOU IN A HURRY?
GEEZ

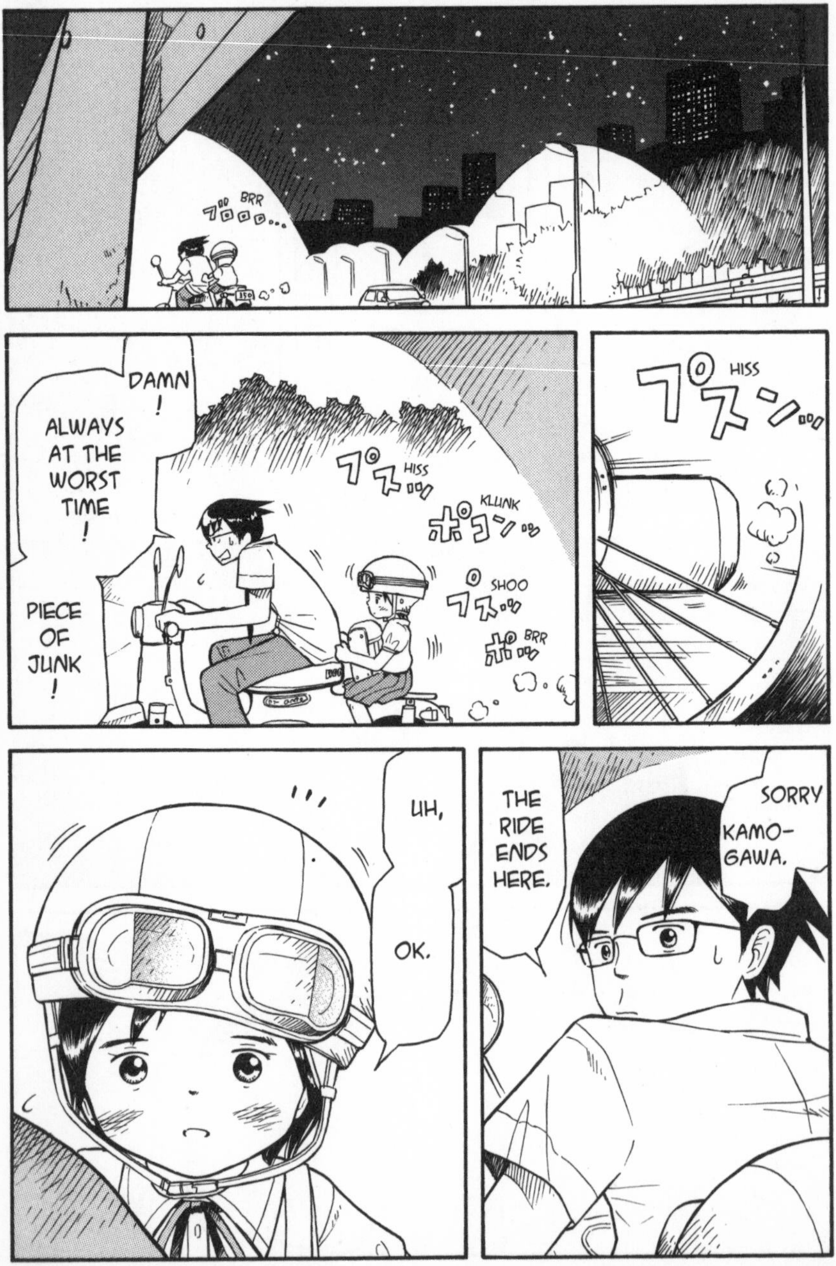
ブロロロ...
BRR
プスン...
HISS
DAMN!
ALWAYS AT THE WORST TIME!
プスッ
HISS
ポコンッ
KLUNK
プスッ
SHOO
ポッ
BRR
PIECE OF JUNK!
SORRY KAMOGAWA.
THE RIDE ENDS HERE.
UH,
OK.

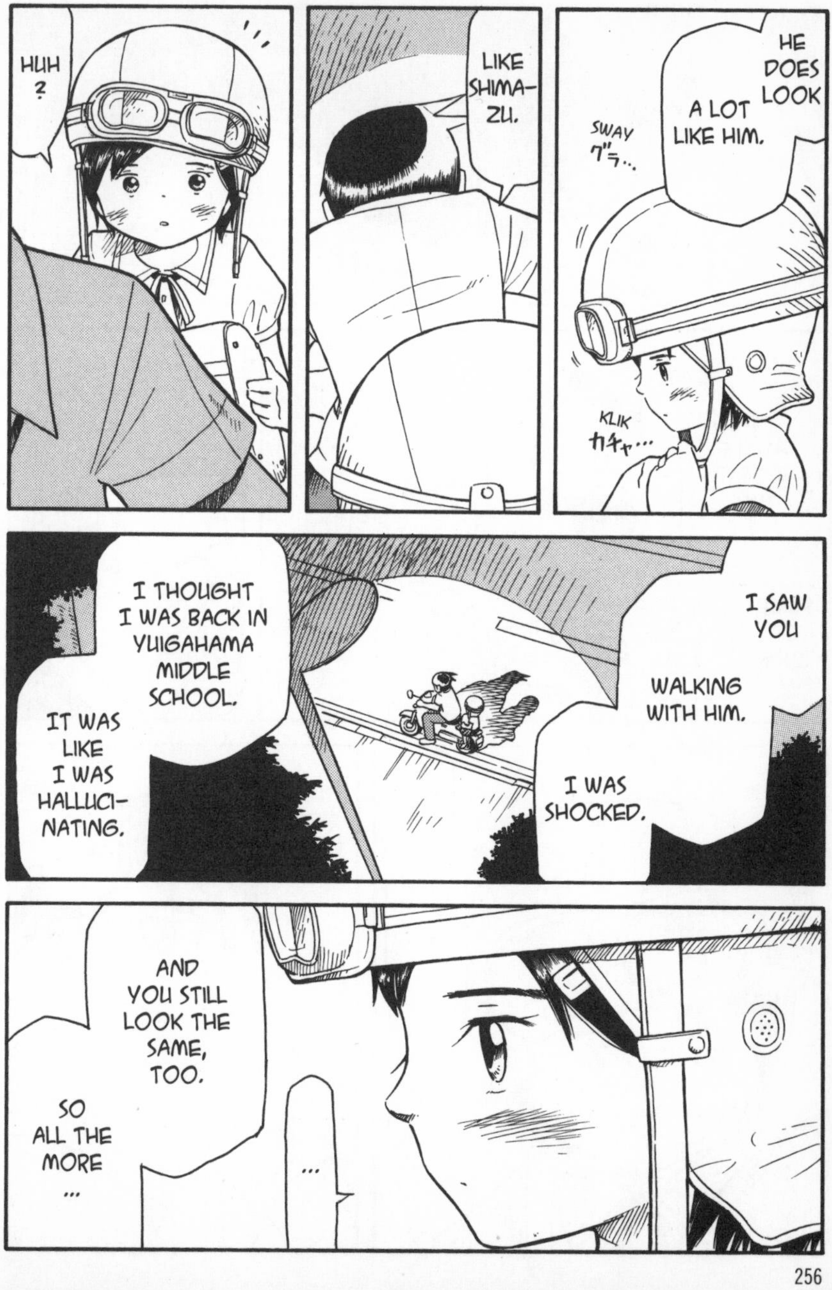
HE DOES LOOK A LOT LIKE HIM.
SWAY
グラ…
KLIK
カチャ…
LIKE SHIMAZU.
HUH?
I SAW YOU
WALKING WITH HIM.
I WAS SHOCKED.
I THOUGHT I WAS BACK IN YUIGAHAMA MIDDLE SCHOOL.
IT WAS LIKE I WAS HALLUCINATING.
AND YOU STILL LOOK THE SAME, TOO.
SO ALL THE MORE ...
...

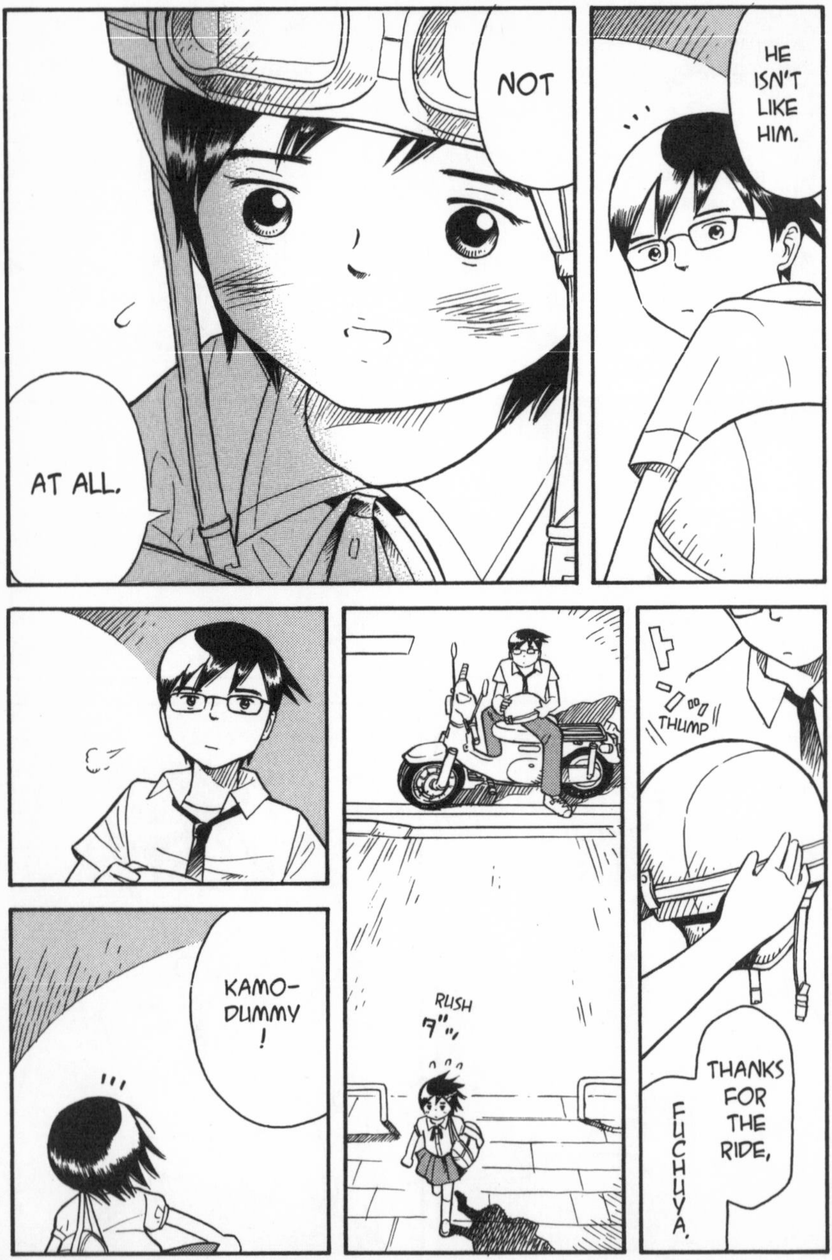

HE ISN'T LIKE HIM.
NOT
AT ALL.
THUMP
THANKS FOR THE RIDE, FUCHUYA.
RUSH
KAMO-DUMMY!

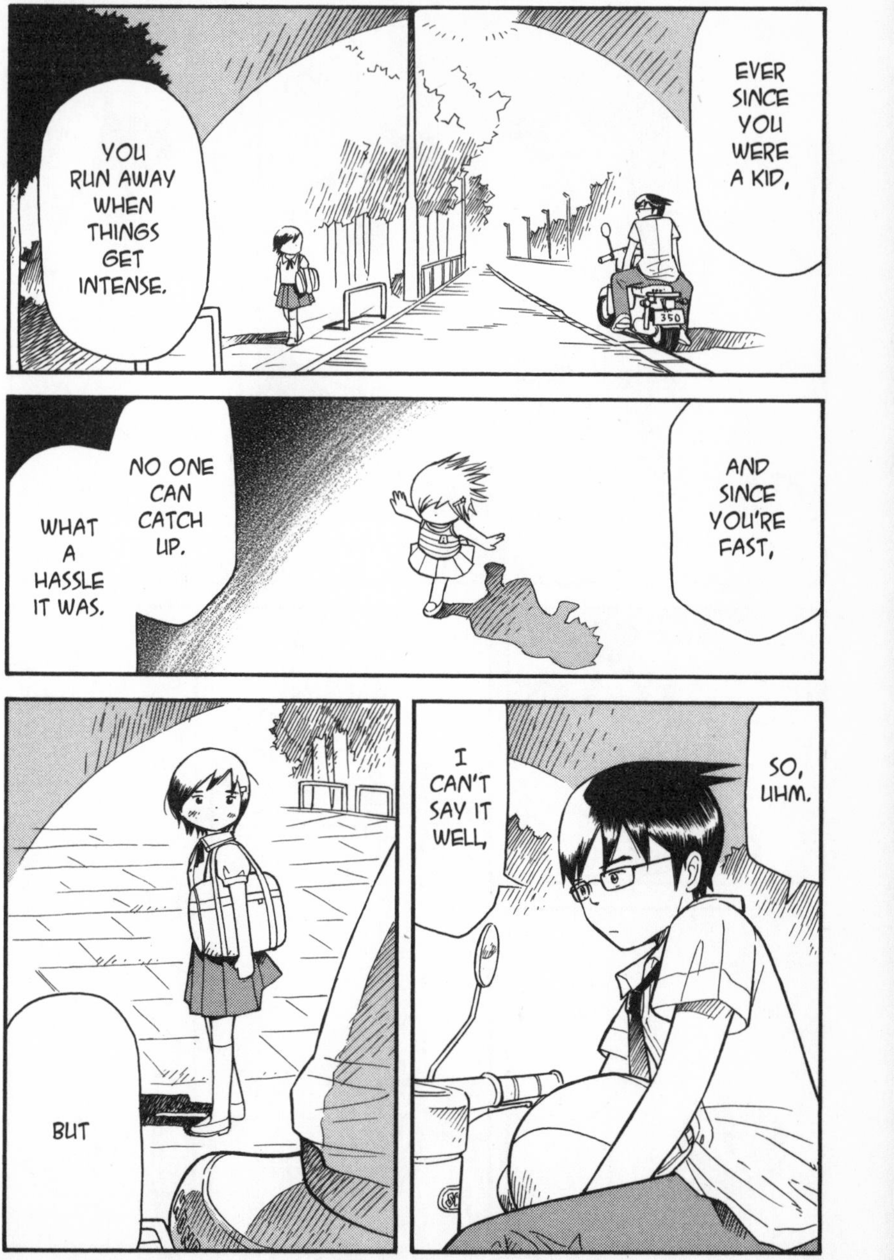
EVER SINCE YOU WERE A KID,
YOU RUN AWAY WHEN THINGS GET INTENSE.
AND SINCE YOU'RE FAST,
NO ONE CAN CATCH UP.
WHAT A HASSLE IT WAS.
SO, UHM.
I CAN'T SAY IT WELL,
BUT

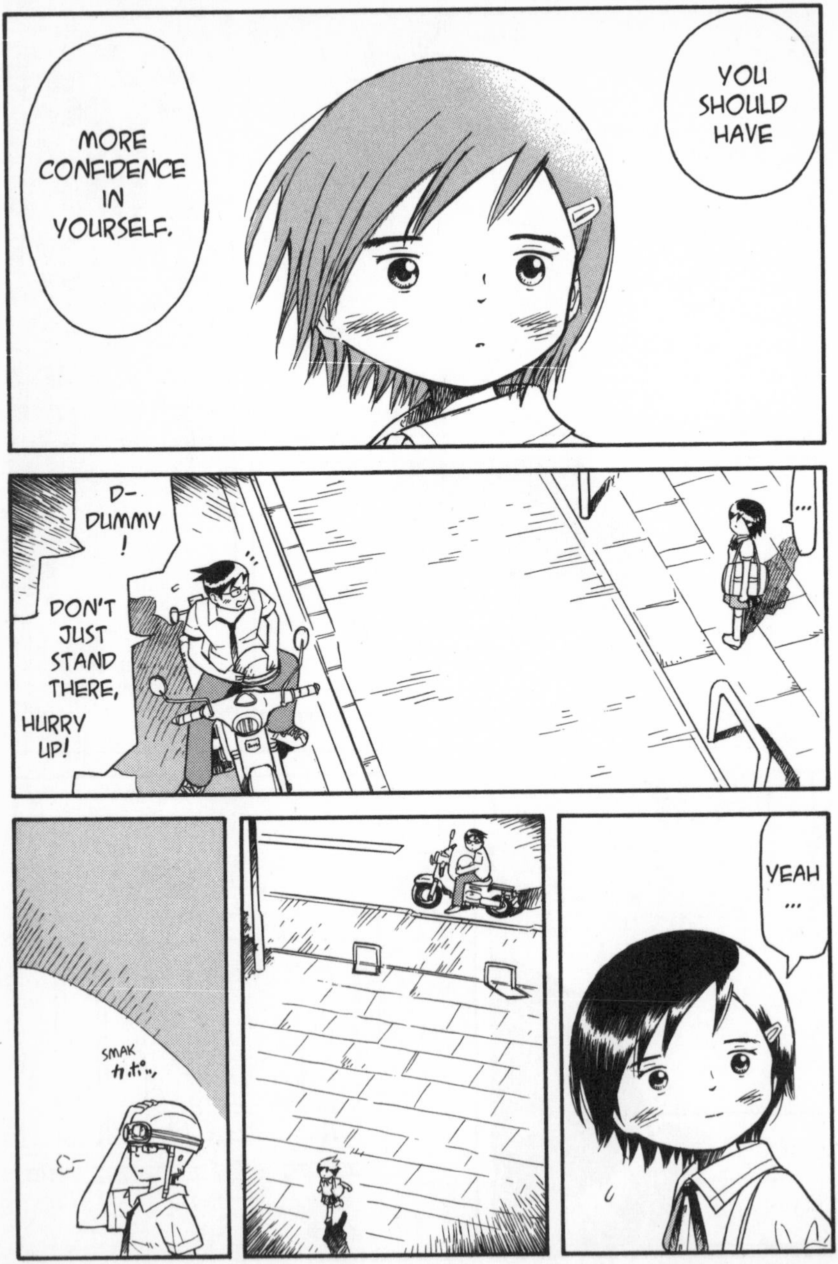
YOU SHOULD HAVE
MORE CONFIDENCE IN YOURSELF.
...
D-DUMMY!
DON'T JUST STAND THERE, HURRY UP!
YEAH ...
SMAK
カポッ

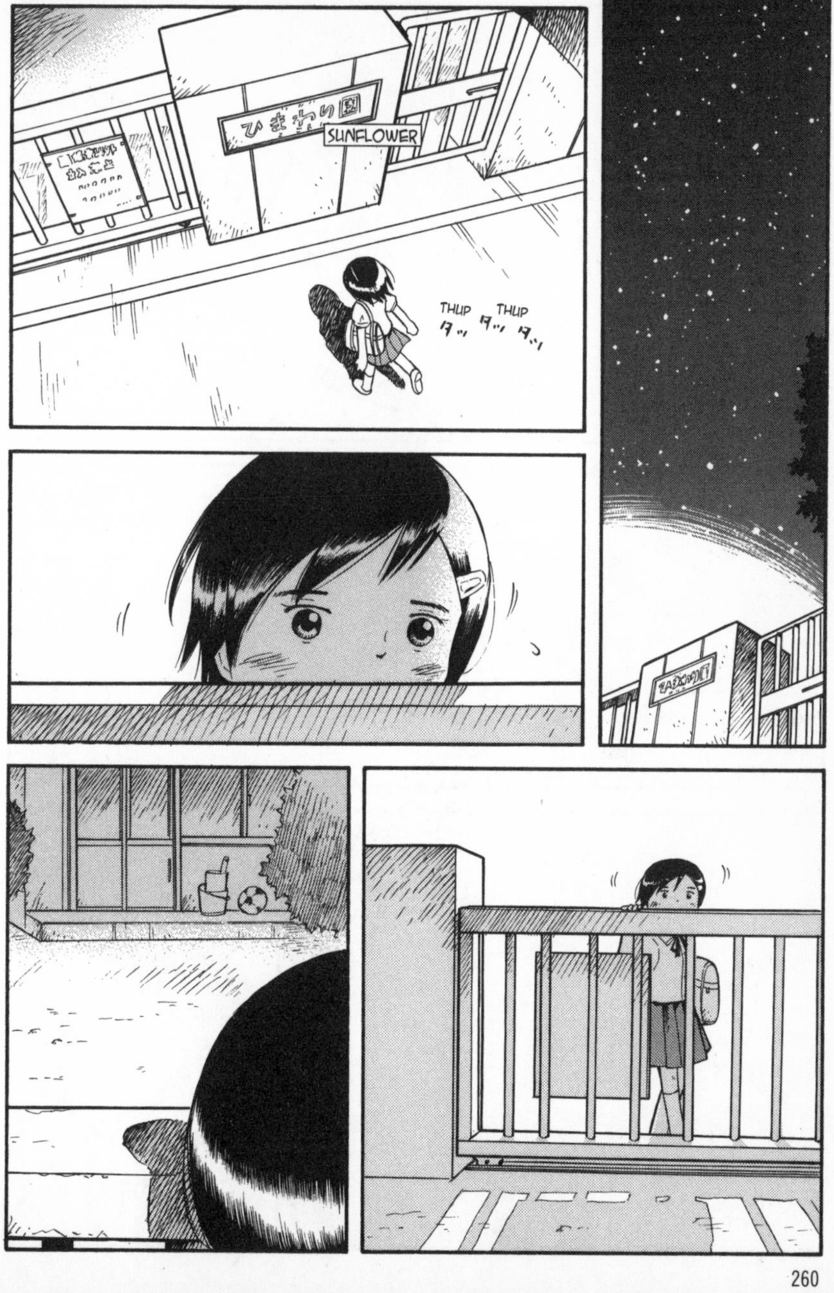
ひまわり園
SUNFLOWER
THUP THUP
タッ タッ タッ

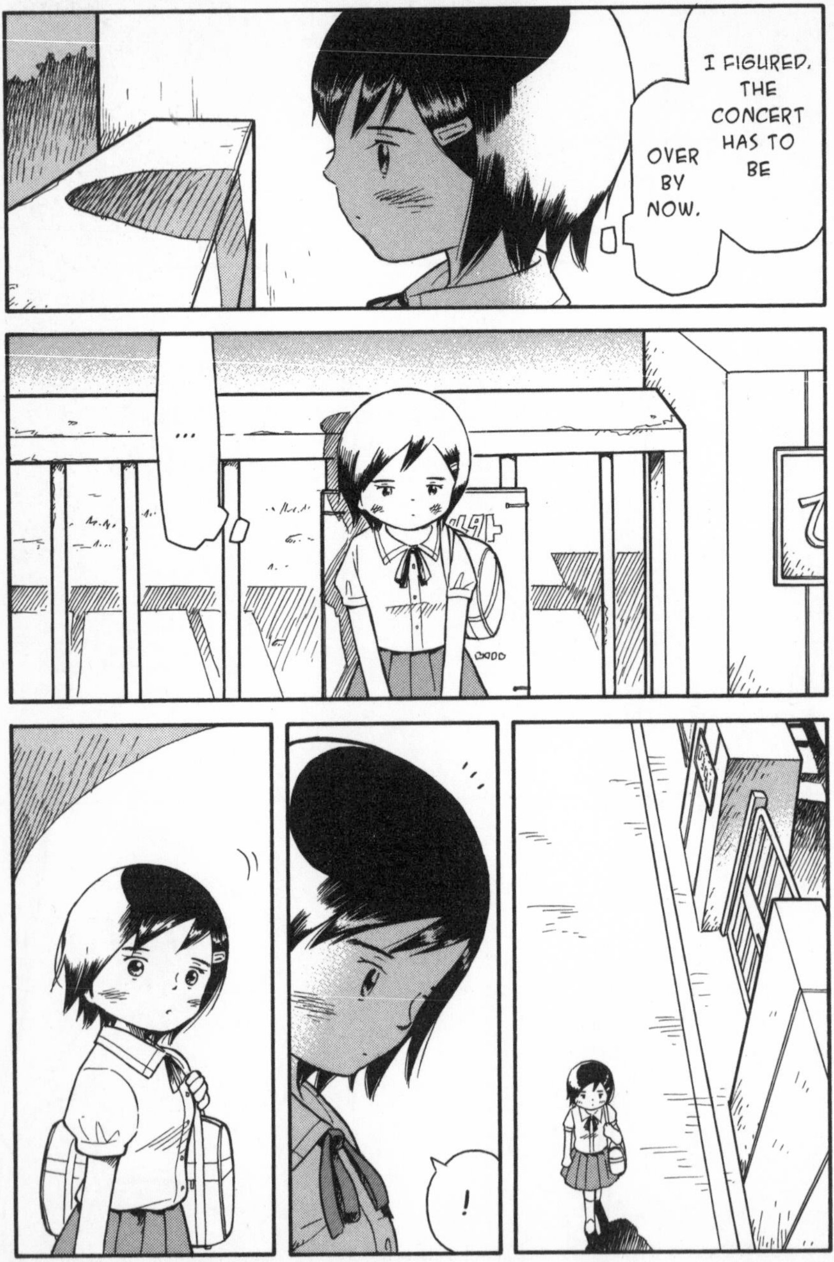
I FIGURED. THE CONCERT HAS TO BE OVER BY NOW.
...
!

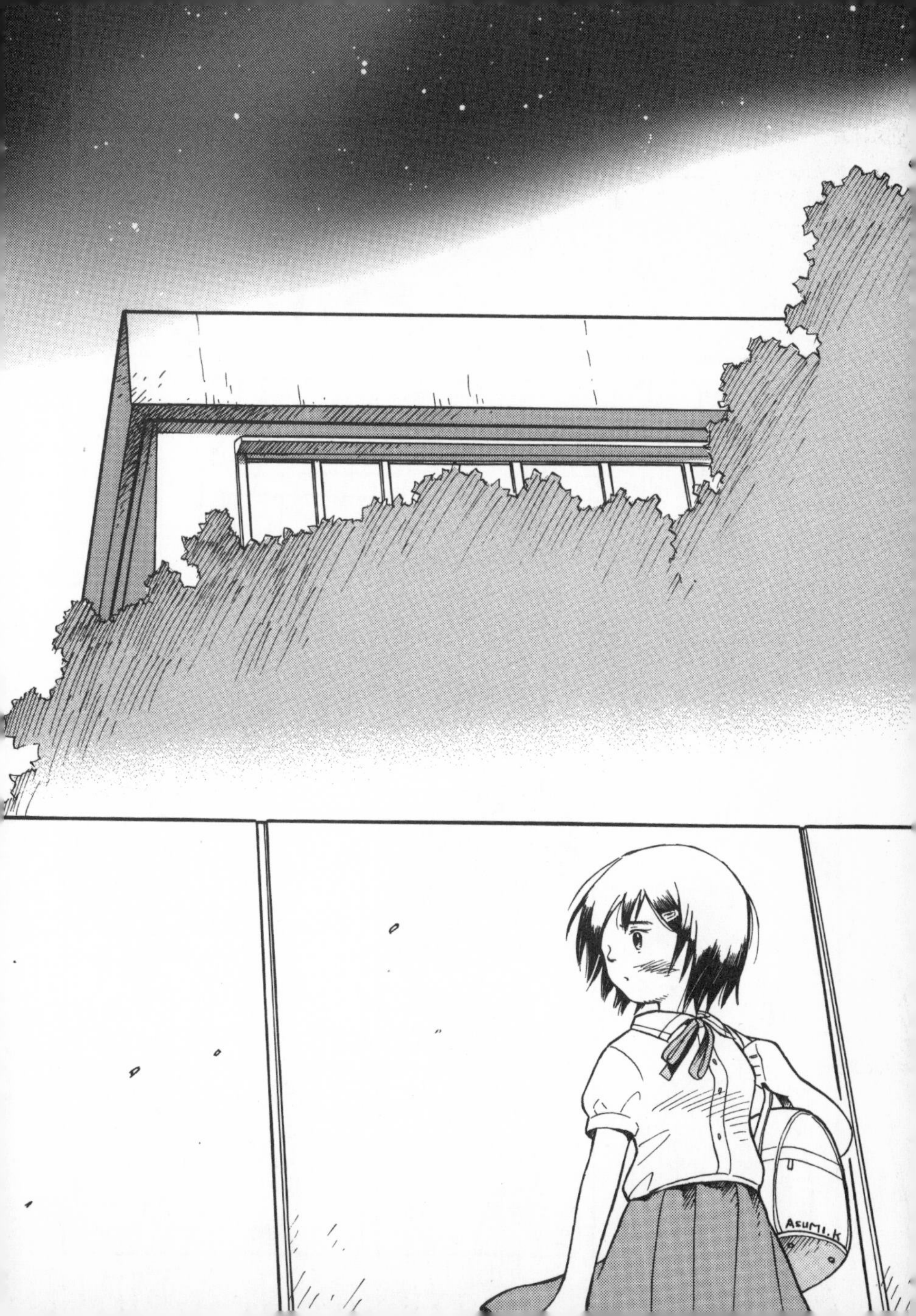
ASUMI.K

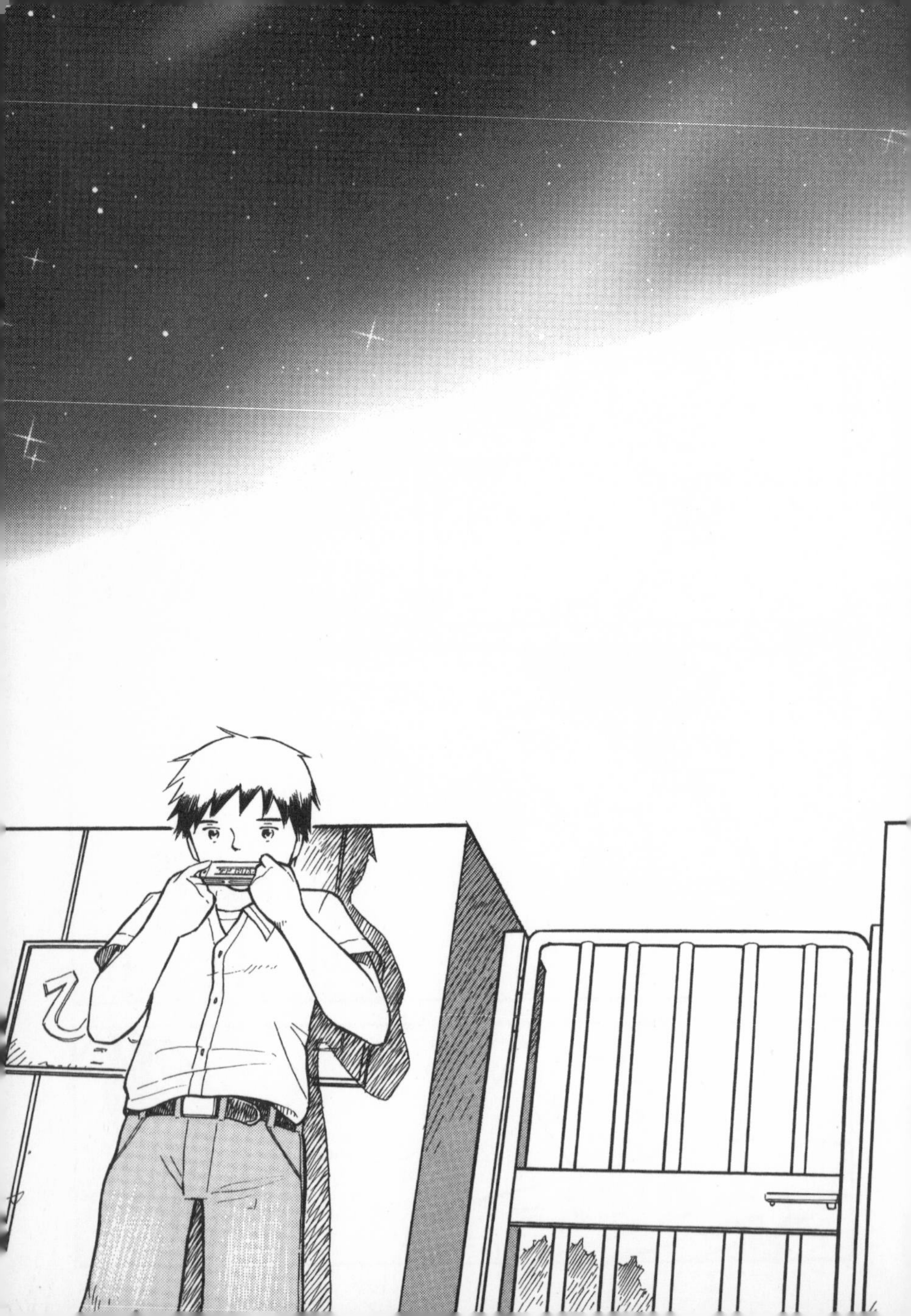

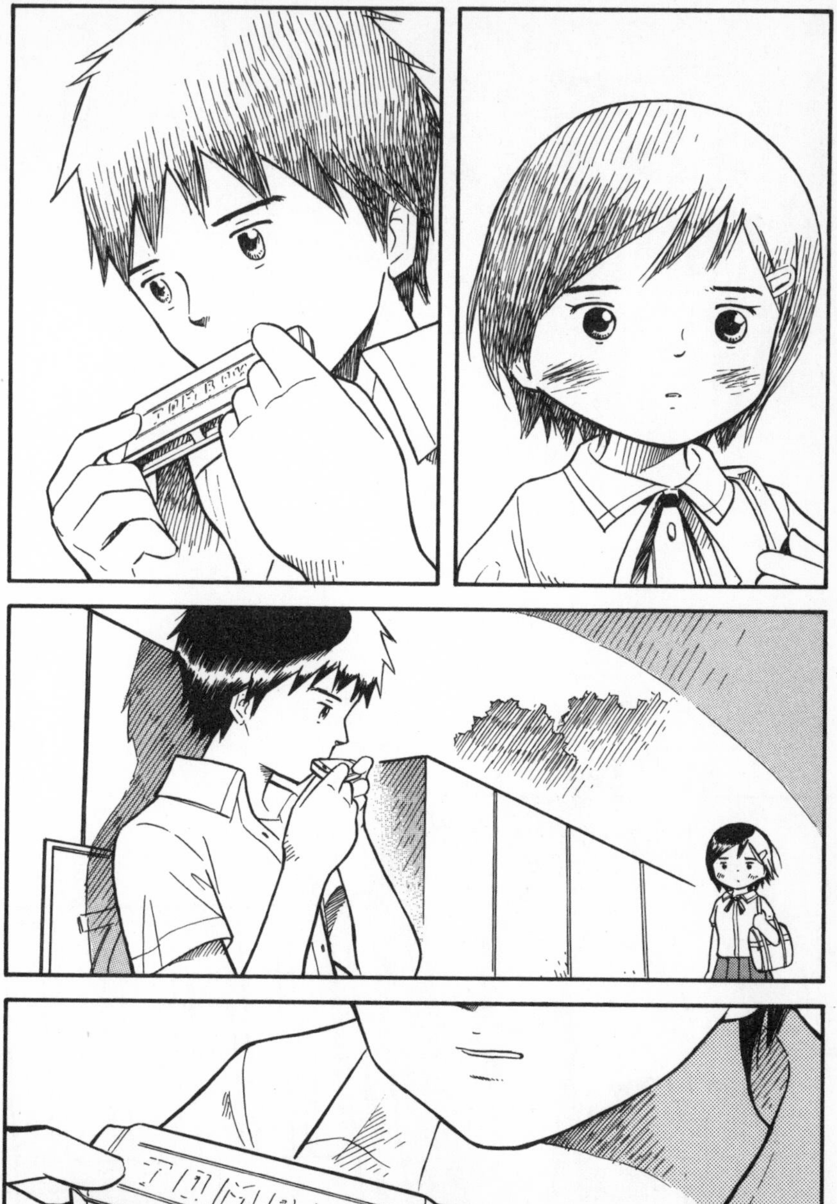

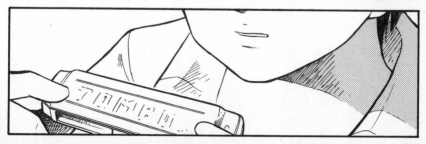

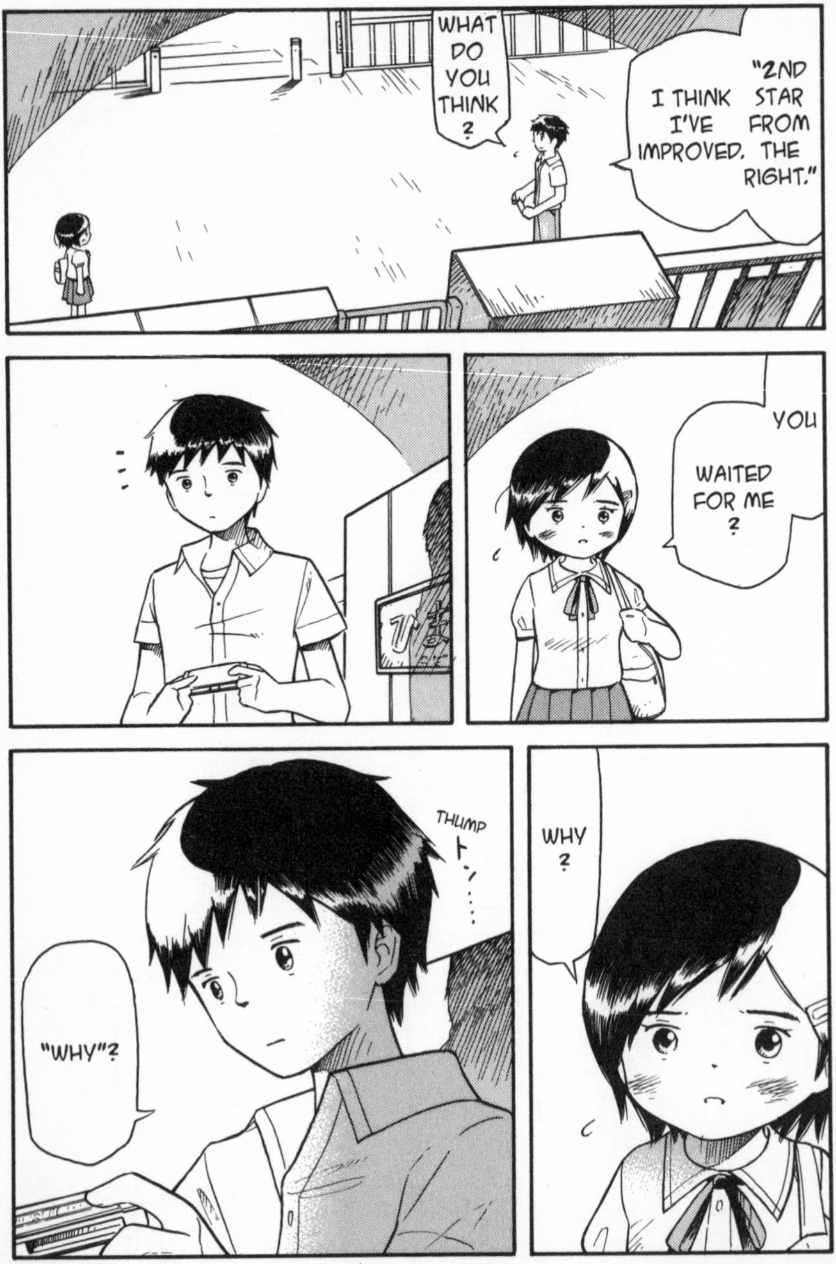
"2ND STAR FROM THE RIGHT."
I THINK I'VE IMPROVED.
WHAT DO YOU THINK?
YOU WAITED FOR ME?
WHY?
THUMP
"WHY"?

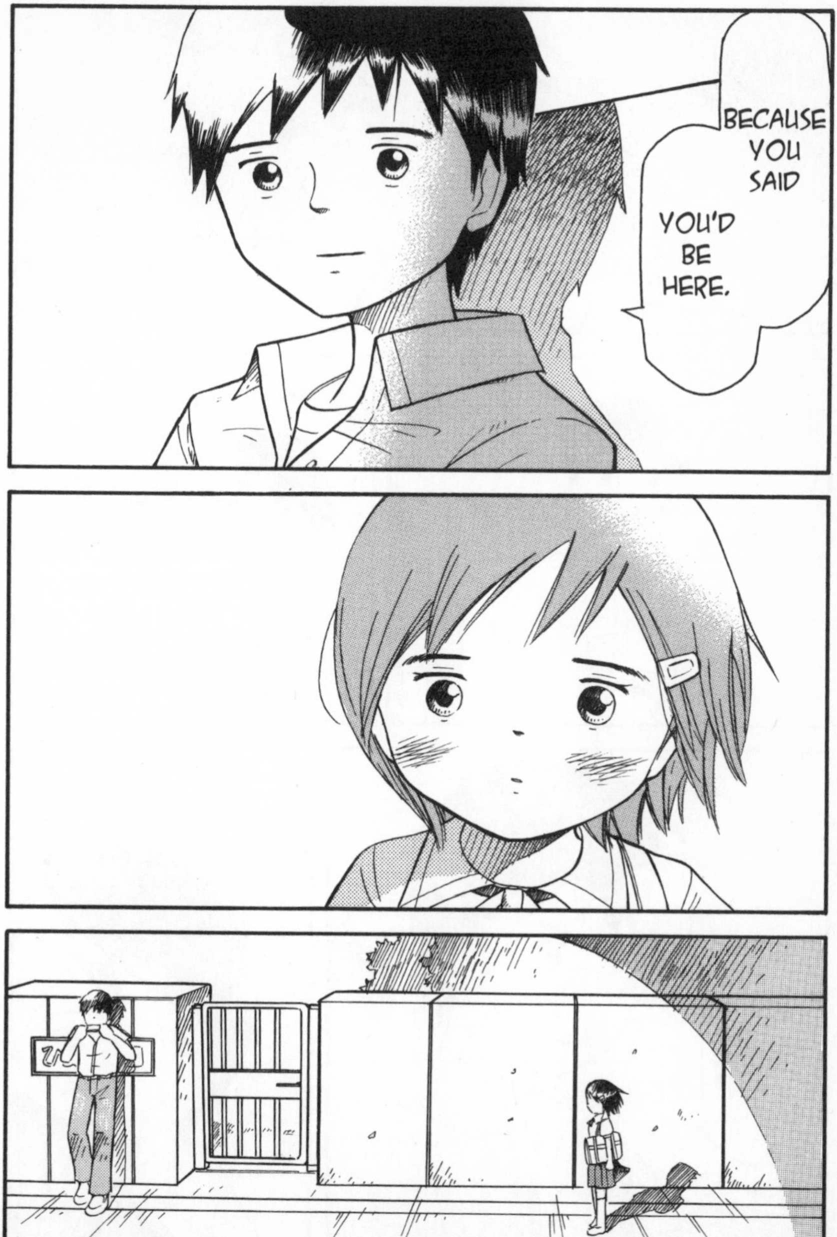
BECAUSE YOU SAID YOU'D BE HERE.

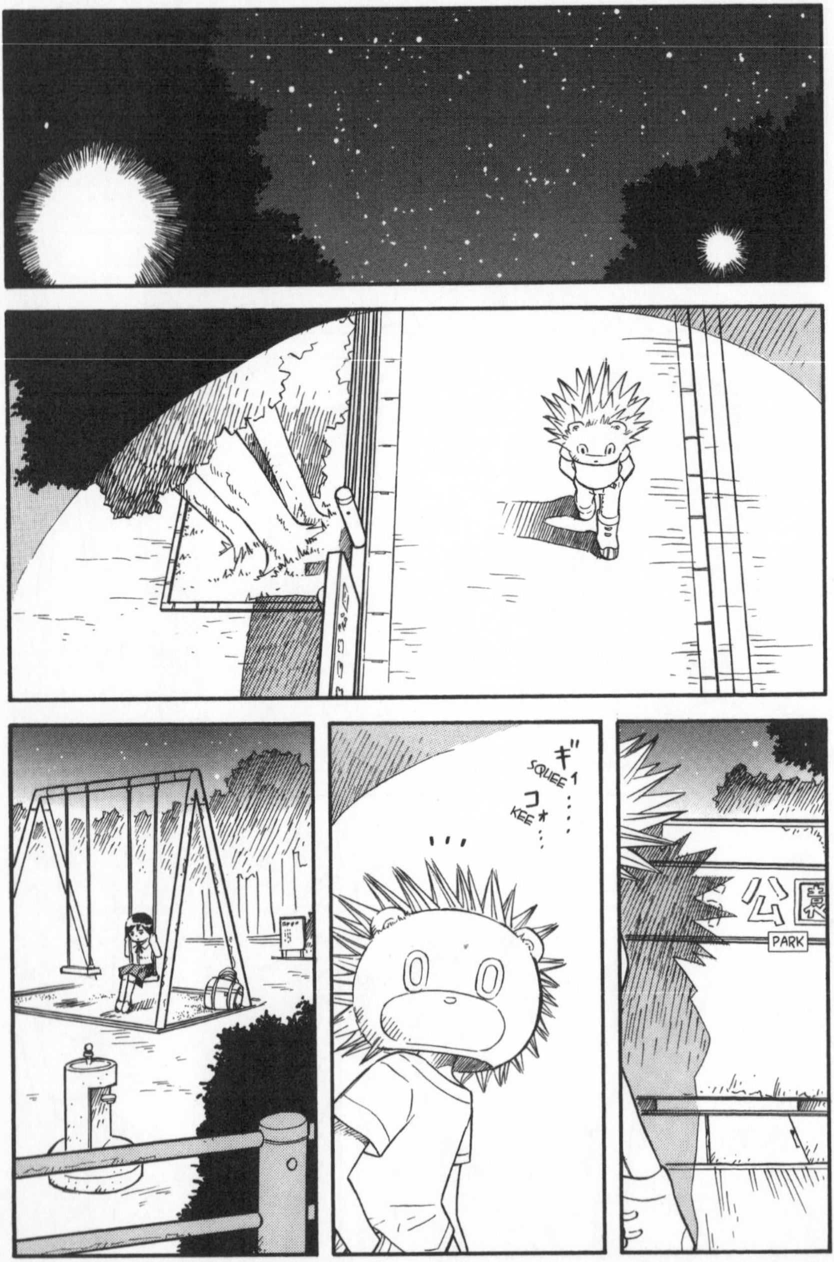
公園
PARK
ギィ…
SQUEE
コォ…
KEE

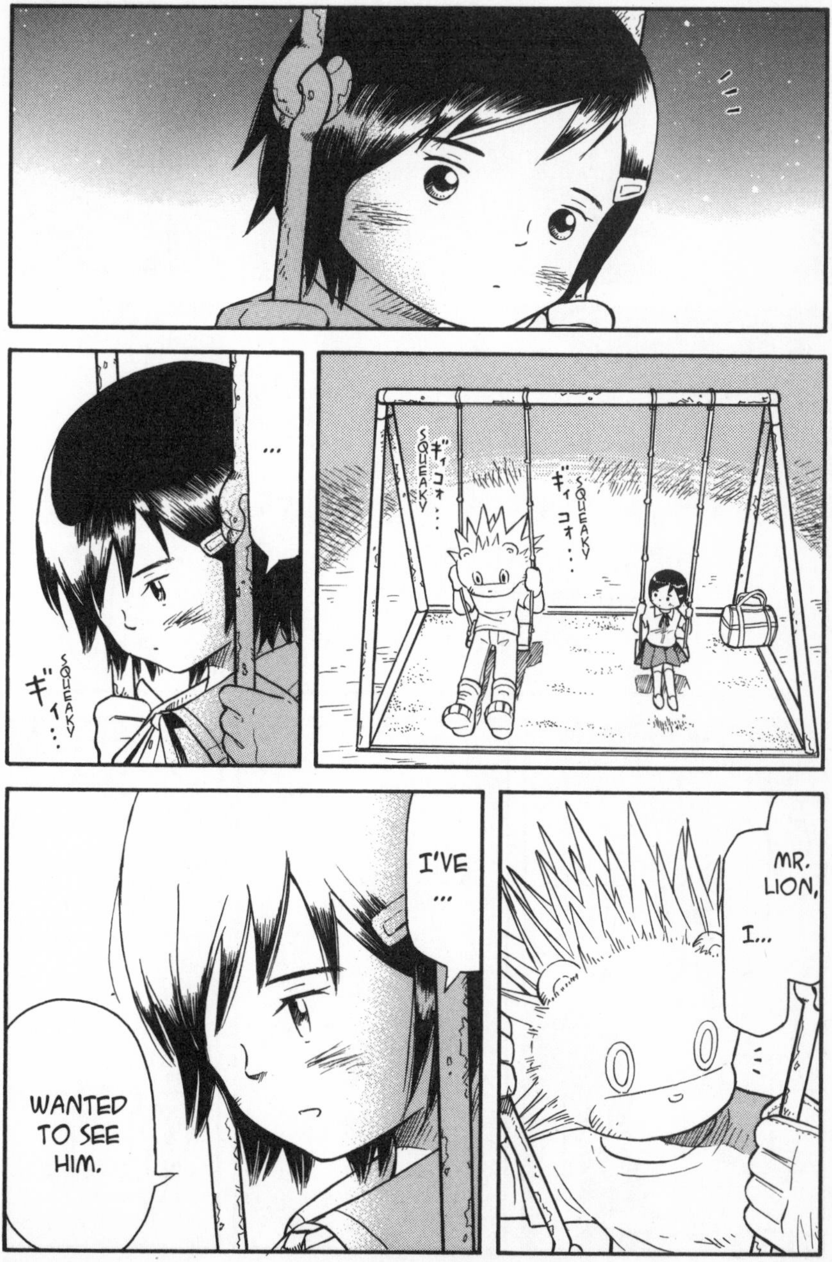
ギィコォ…
SQUEAKY
ギィコォ…
SQUEAKY
…
ギィ…
SQUEAKY
MR. LION,
I…
I'VE …
WANTED TO SEE HIM.

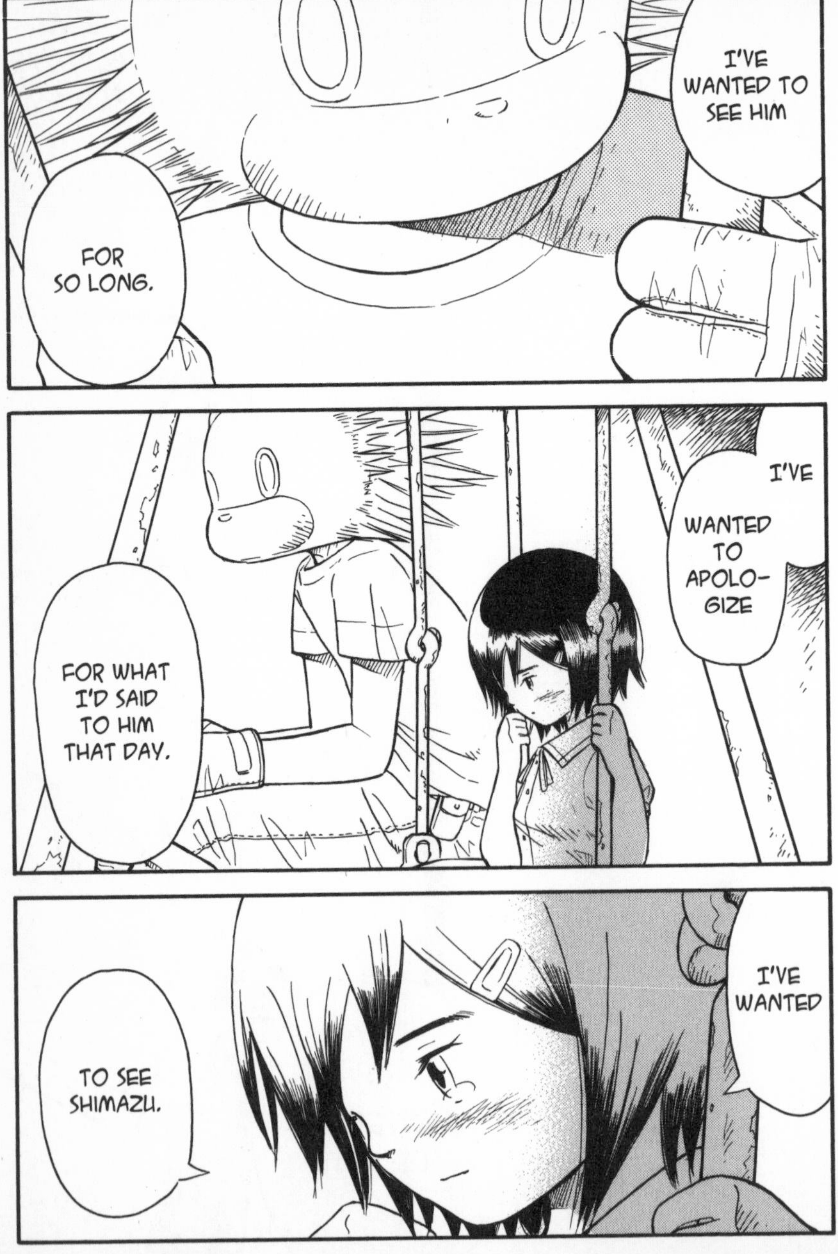
I'VE WANTED TO SEE HIM
FOR SO LONG.
I'VE WANTED TO APOLO-GIZE
FOR WHAT I'D SAID TO HIM THAT DAY.
I'VE WANTED
TO SEE SHIMAZU.

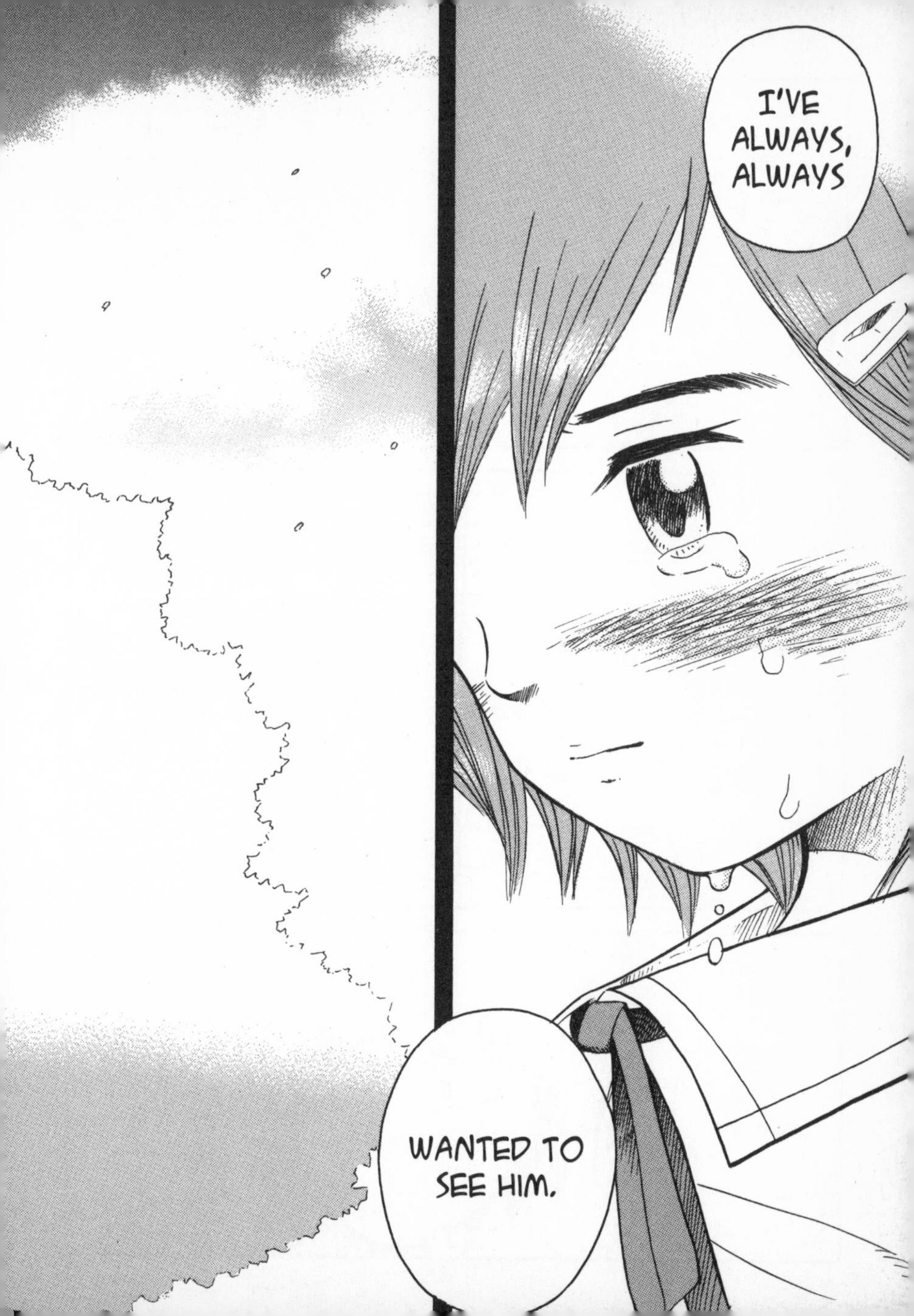
I'VE ALWAYS, ALWAYS
WANTED TO SEE HIM.

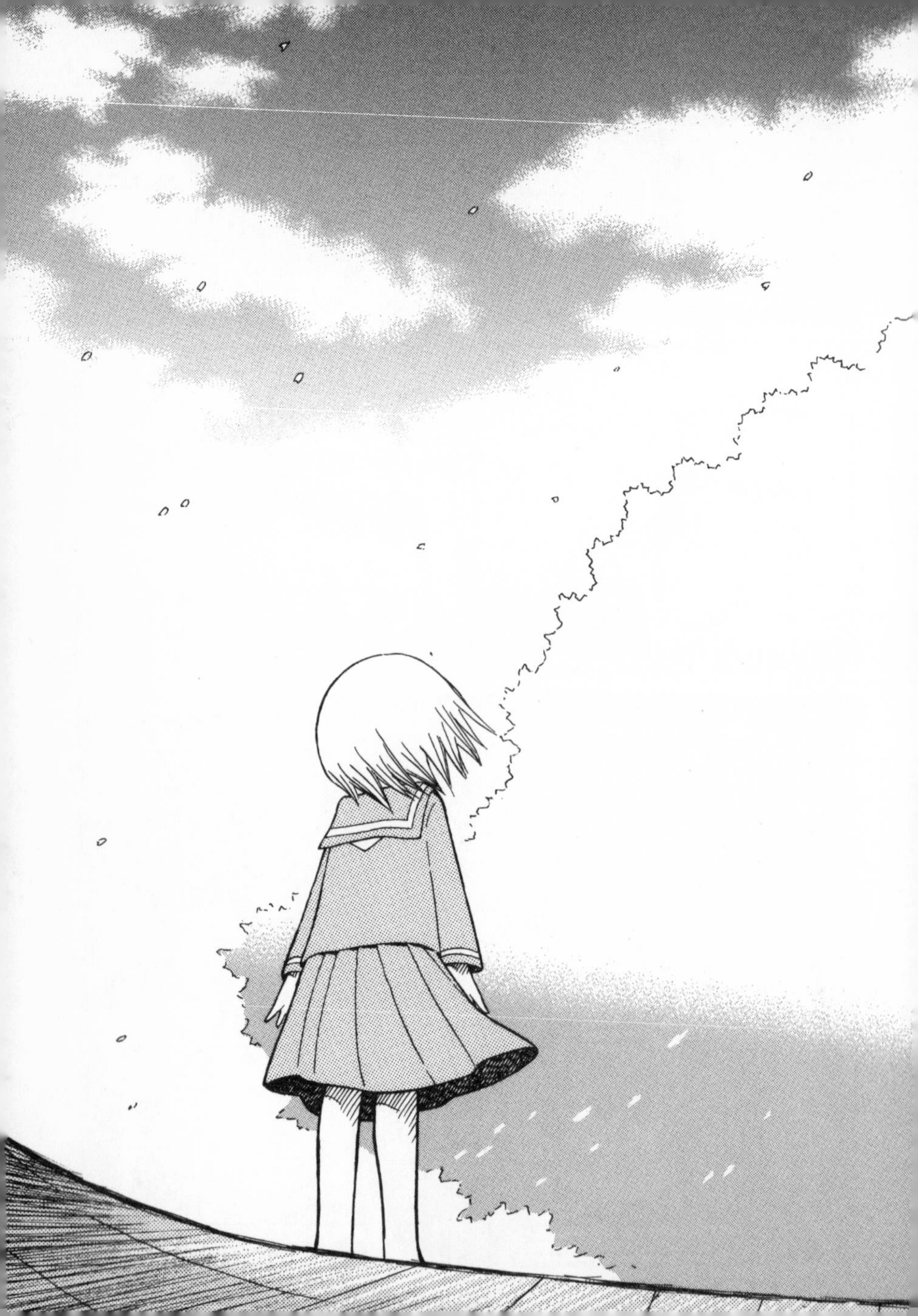

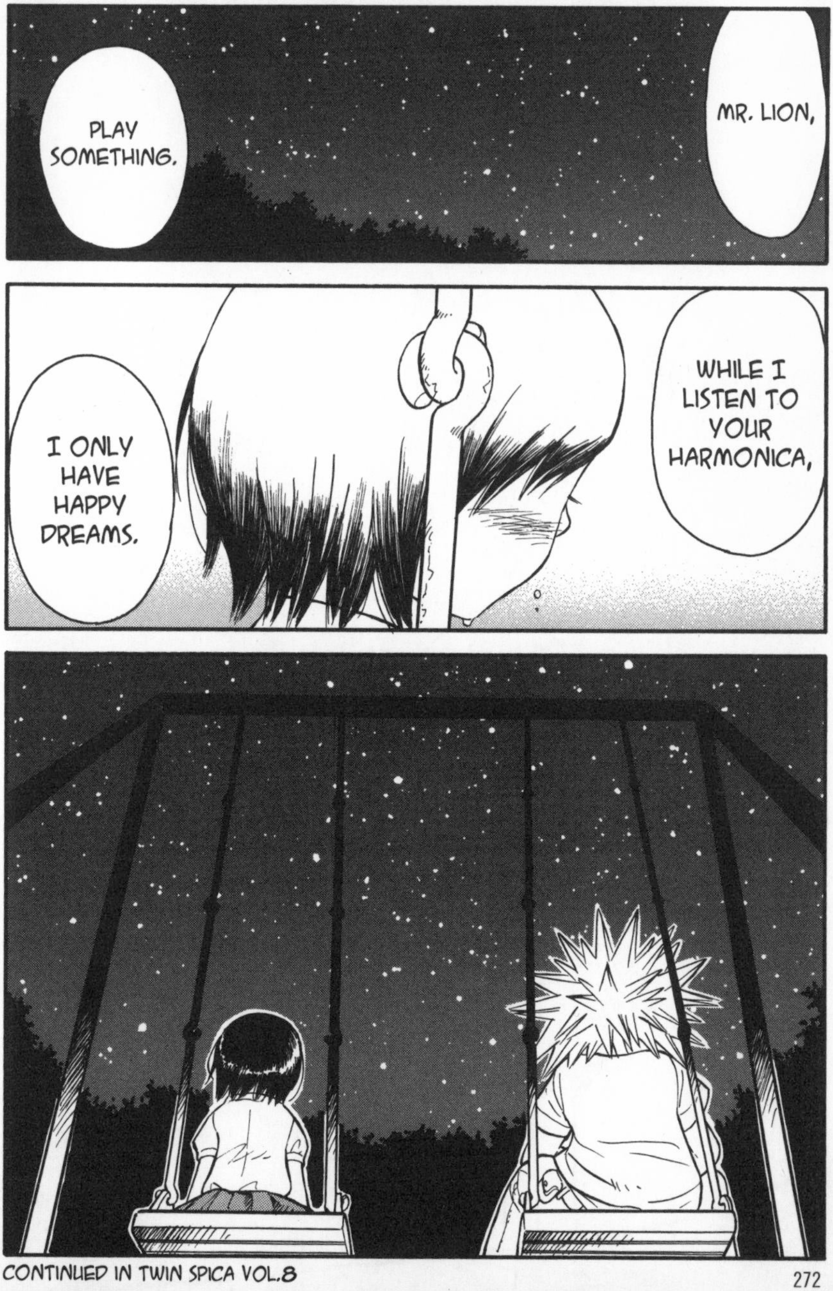
MR. LION,
PLAY SOMETHING.
WHILE I LISTEN TO YOUR HARMONICA,
I ONLY HAVE HAPPY DREAMS.

CONTINUED IN TWIN SPICA VOL.8

ANOTHER SPICA

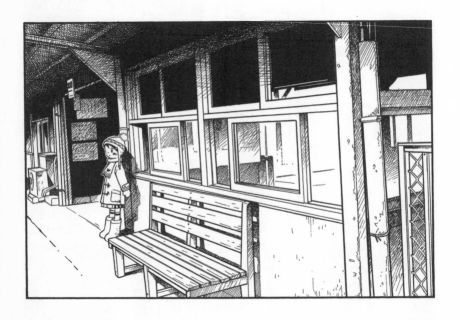

KOU YAGINUMA

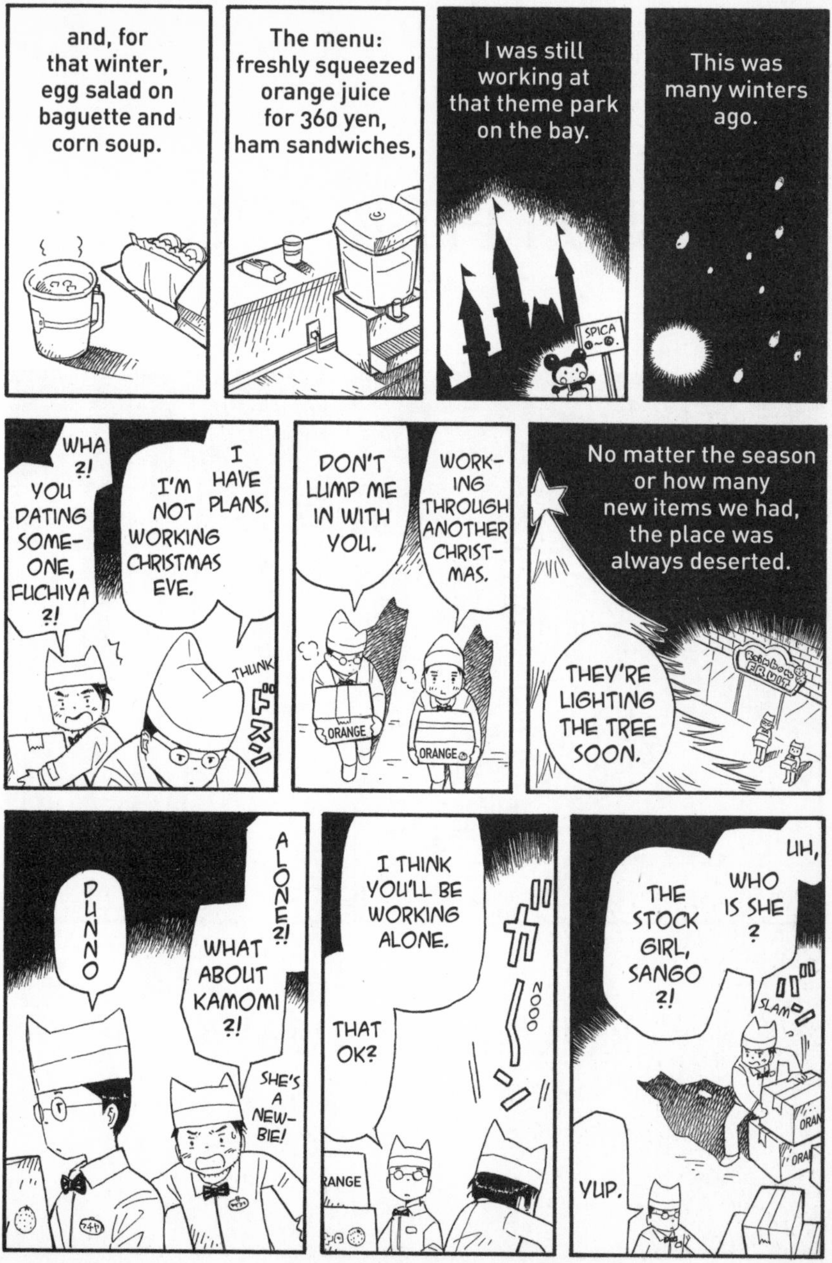
This was many winters ago.
I was still working at that theme park on the bay.
SPICA
The menu: freshly squeezed orange juice for 360 yen, ham sandwiches,
and, for that winter, egg salad on baguette and corn soup.
No matter the season or how many new items we had, the place was always deserted.
THEY'RE LIGHTING THE TREE SOON.
WORKING THROUGH ANOTHER CHRISTMAS.
DON'T LUMP ME IN WITH YOU.
ORANGE
ORANGE
I HAVE PLANS.
I'M NOT WORKING CHRISTMAS EVE.
WHA?!
YOU DATING SOMEONE, FUCHIYA?!
THUNK
UH,
WHO IS SHE?
THE STOCK GIRL, SANGO?!
SLAM
YUP.
I THINK YOU'LL BE WORKING ALONE.
THAT OK?
NOOO
ALONE?!
WHAT ABOUT KAMOMI?!
SHE'S A NEWBIE!
DUNNO

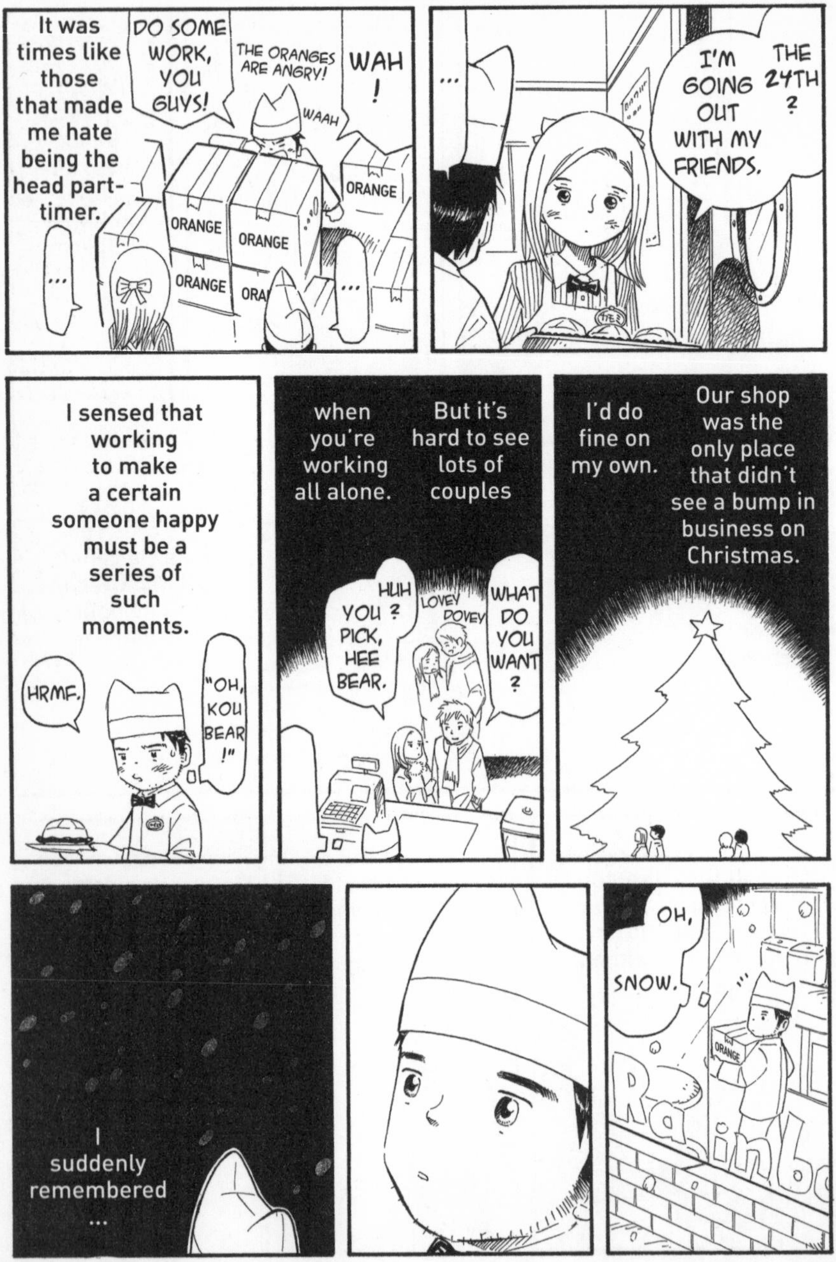
THE 24TH ?
I'M GOING OUT WITH MY FRIENDS.
...
WAH !
THE ORANGES ARE ANGRY!
DO SOME WORK, YOU GUYS!
It was times like those that made me hate being the head part-timer.
WAAH
ORANGE
ORANGE
ORANGE
ORANGE
...
...
Our shop was the only place that didn't see a bump in business on Christmas.
I'd do fine on my own.
But it's hard to see lots of couples
when you're working all alone.
WHAT DO YOU WANT ?
LOVEY DOVEY
HUH ? YOU PICK, HEE BEAR.
I sensed that working to make a certain someone happy must be a series of such moments.
"OH, KOU BEAR !"
HRMF.
OH,
SNOW.
...
ORANGE
I suddenly remembered ...

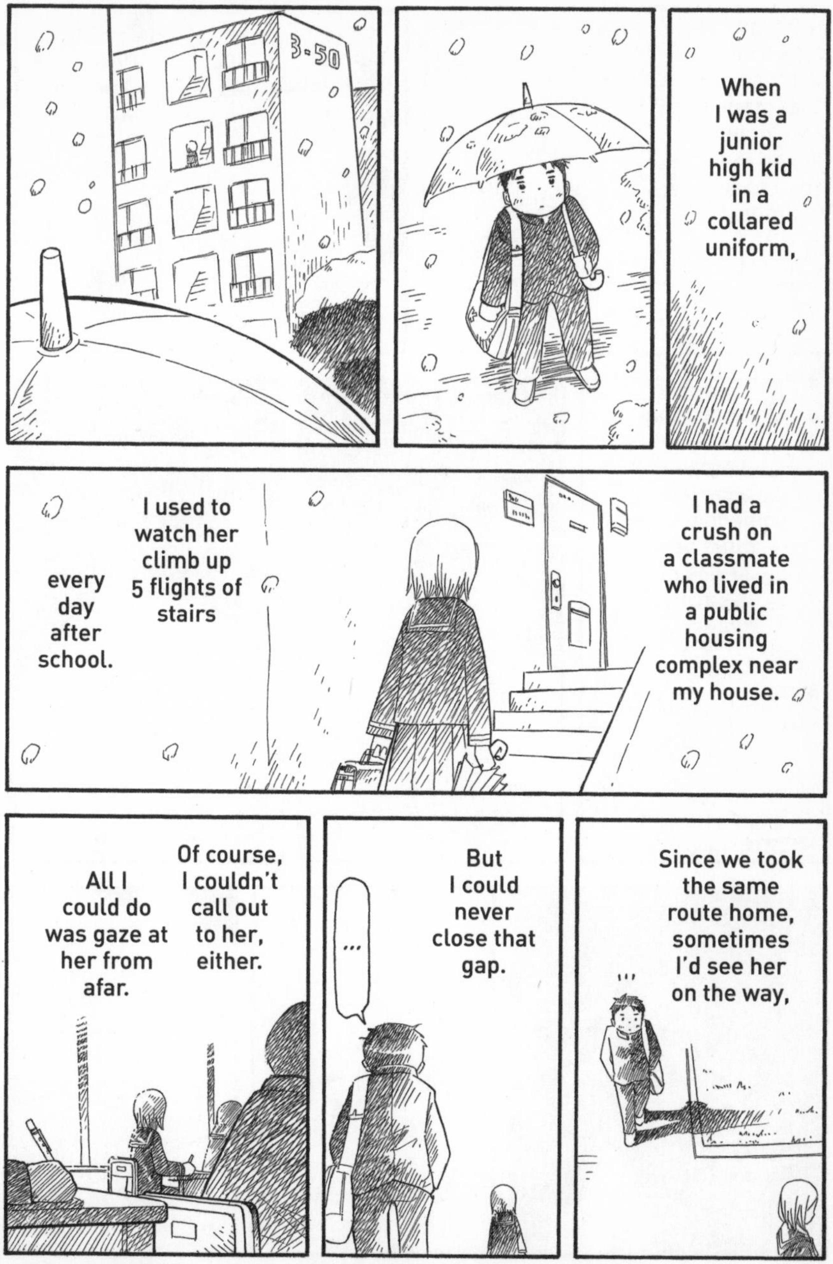
When I was a junior high kid in a collared uniform,
3-50
I had a crush on a classmate who lived in a public housing complex near my house.
I used to watch her climb up 5 flights of stairs
every day after school.
Since we took the same route home, sometimes I'd see her on the way,
...
But I could never close that gap.
...
Of course, I couldn't call out to her, either.
All I could do was gaze at her from afar.

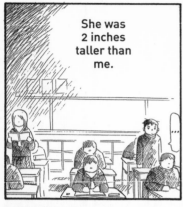

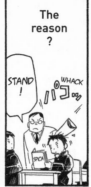

My friends told me to confess my love to her,
but I didn't dare to.
SHAAA
CONFESS!
WHO'RE YOU?!
The reason ?
WHACK
パコッ
STAND !
SPICA
She was 2 inches taller than me.
...
When we lined up according to height,
I was 3rd from the front.
FRONT AND CENTER !
ムキッ
FLEX
WHO'S HE?
She was the very last. I tried to stretch to be taller.
URRR
ぐぐぐぐ…
WHAT'RE YOU DOING ?
480
ヤギヌマ
YAGINUMA
Even my grades didn't reach very high.
HUH, YOU'RE A DIM-WIT.
I spent all night thinking of something I had that she didn't but couldn't find an answer.
NO IDEA.
When I think of it now, it was silly to worry over 2 inches,
but at the time it felt like a huge difference.
I decided I would confess my feelings for her when I grew taller than her.
BASELESS CONFIDENCE + MISGUIDED POSITIVITY
NO,
I WILL GROW !
THAT'LL JUST STRETCH YOUR RIBS.
HUH ?
In the end,
that day never came.

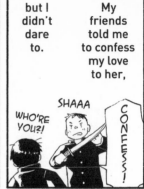

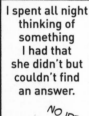

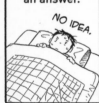

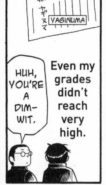

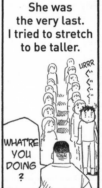

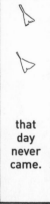

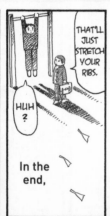

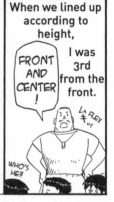

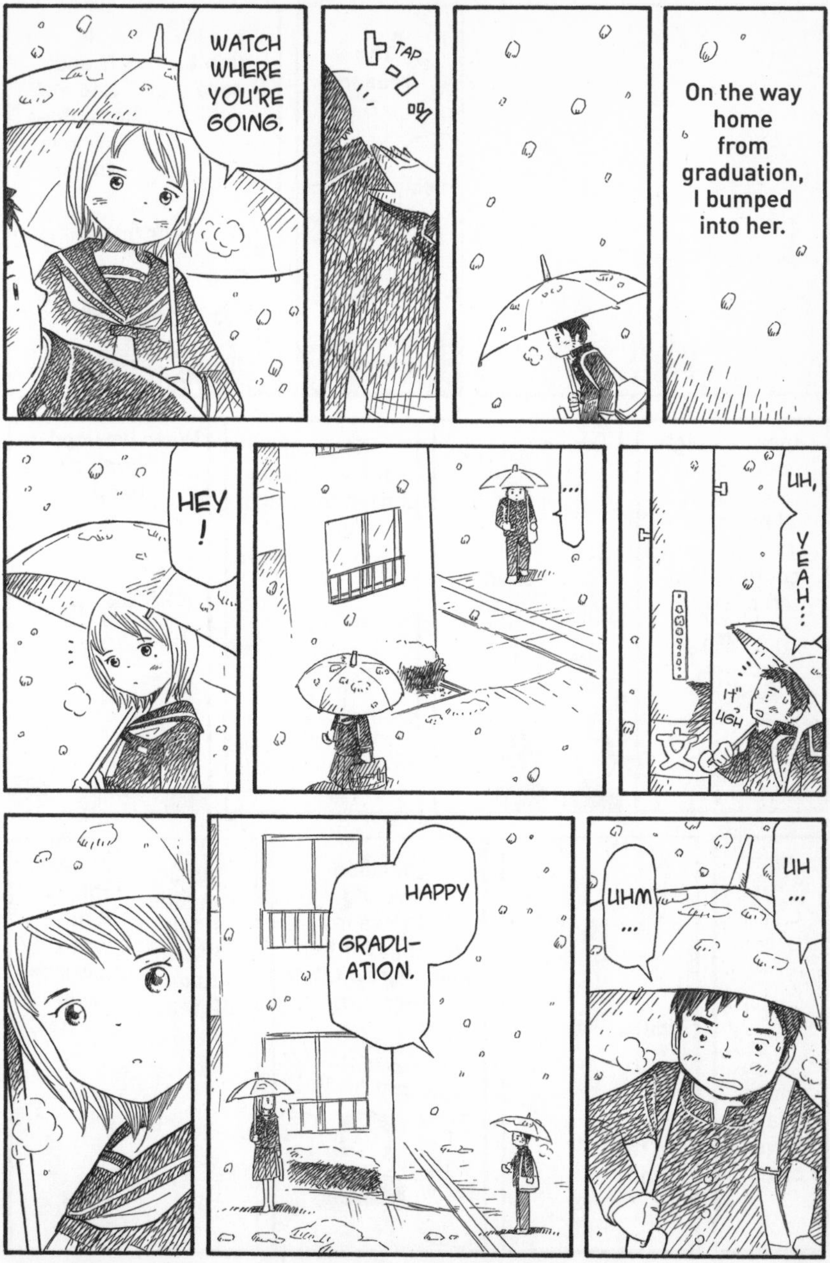
On the way home from graduation, I bumped into her.
TAP
WATCH WHERE YOU'RE GOING.
UH, YEAH...
げ UGH
...
HEY!
UH ...
UHM ...
HAPPY GRADUATION.

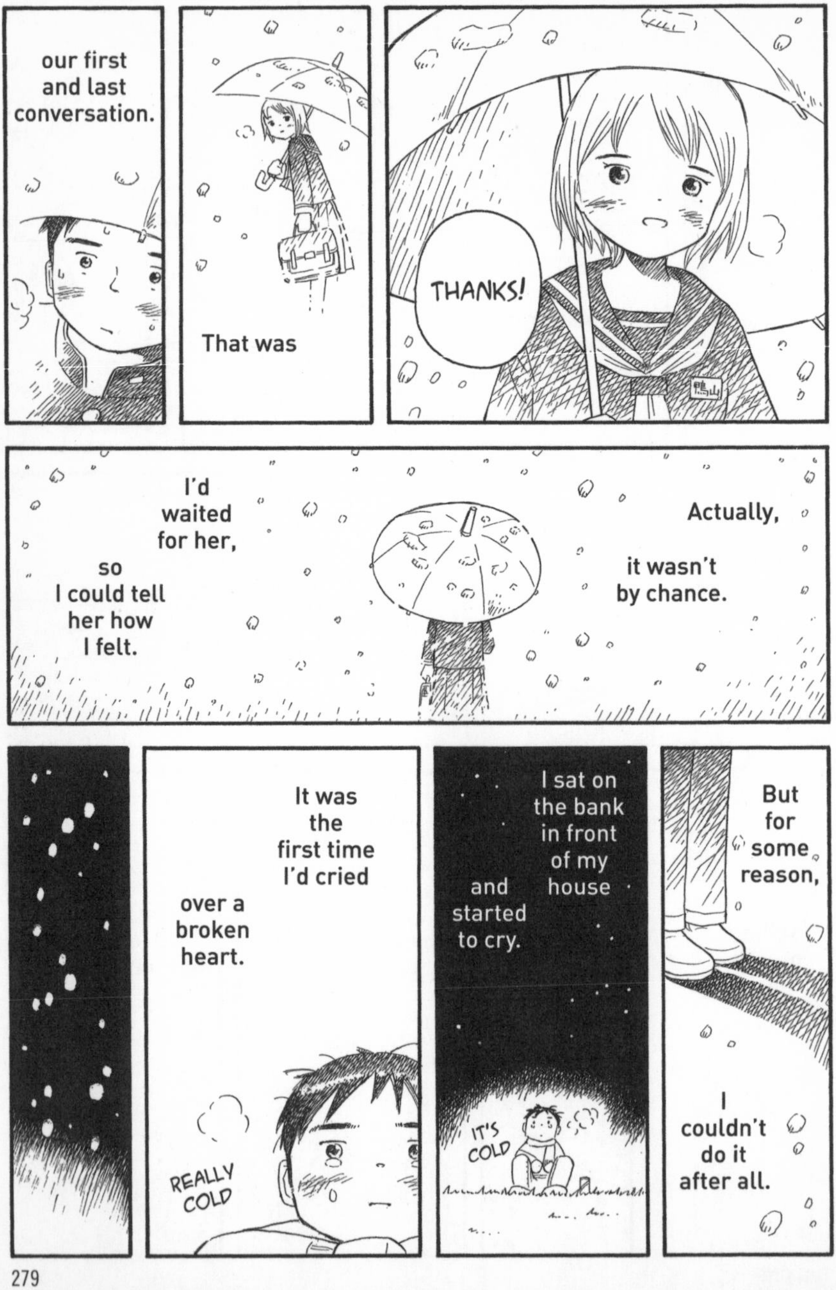
THANKS!
That was
our first and last conversation.
Actually,
it wasn't by chance.
I'd waited for her,
so I could tell her how I felt.
But for some reason,
I couldn't do it after all.
I sat on the bank in front of my house
and started to cry.
IT'S COLD
It was the first time I'd cried
over a broken heart.
REALLY COLD

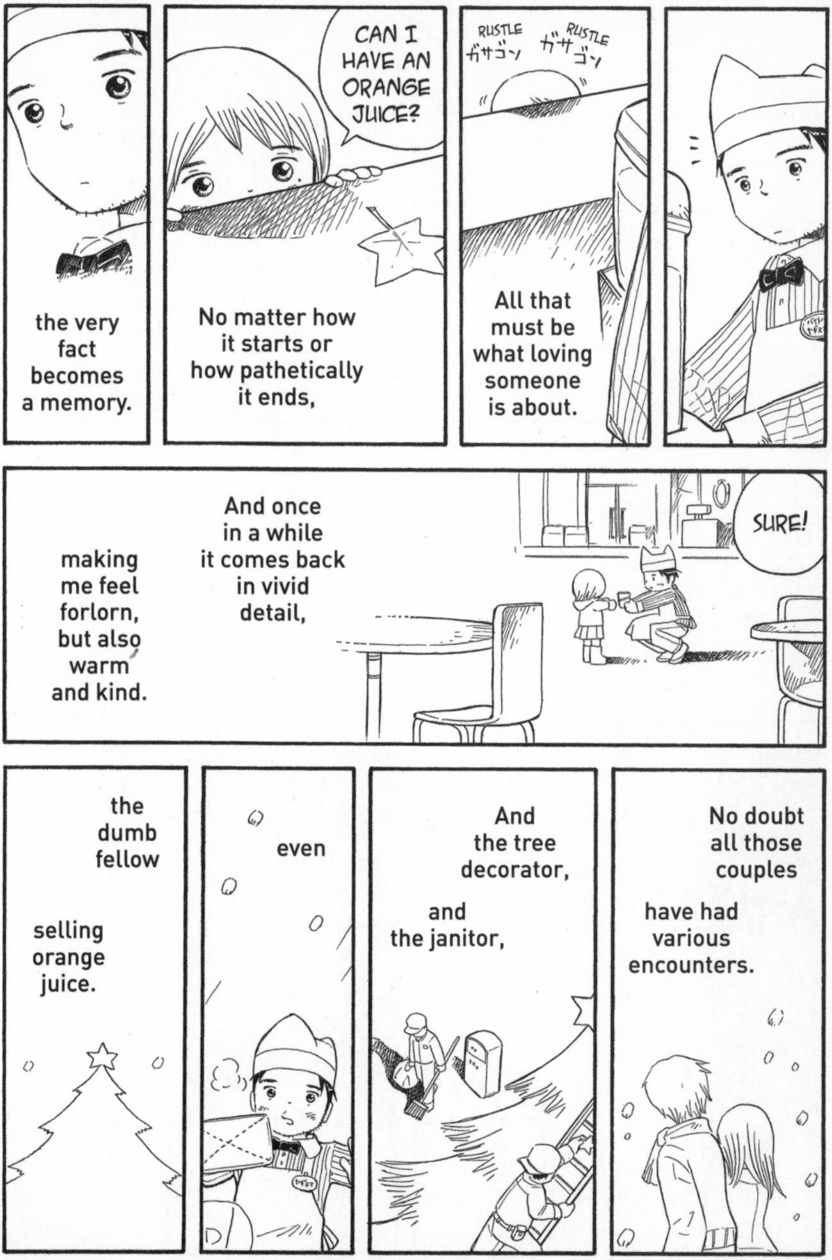
RUSTLE
ガサゴソ
RUSTLE
ガサゴソ
All that must be what loving someone is about.
CAN I HAVE AN ORANGE JUICE?
No matter how it starts or how pathetically it ends,
the very fact becomes a memory.
SURE!
And once in a while it comes back in vivid detail,
making me feel forlorn, but also warm and kind.
No doubt all those couples
have had various encounters.
And the tree decorator,
and the janitor,
even
the dumb fellow
selling orange juice.

THE END

ANOTHER SPICA

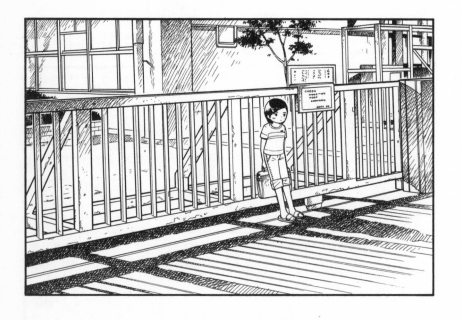

KOU YAGINUMA

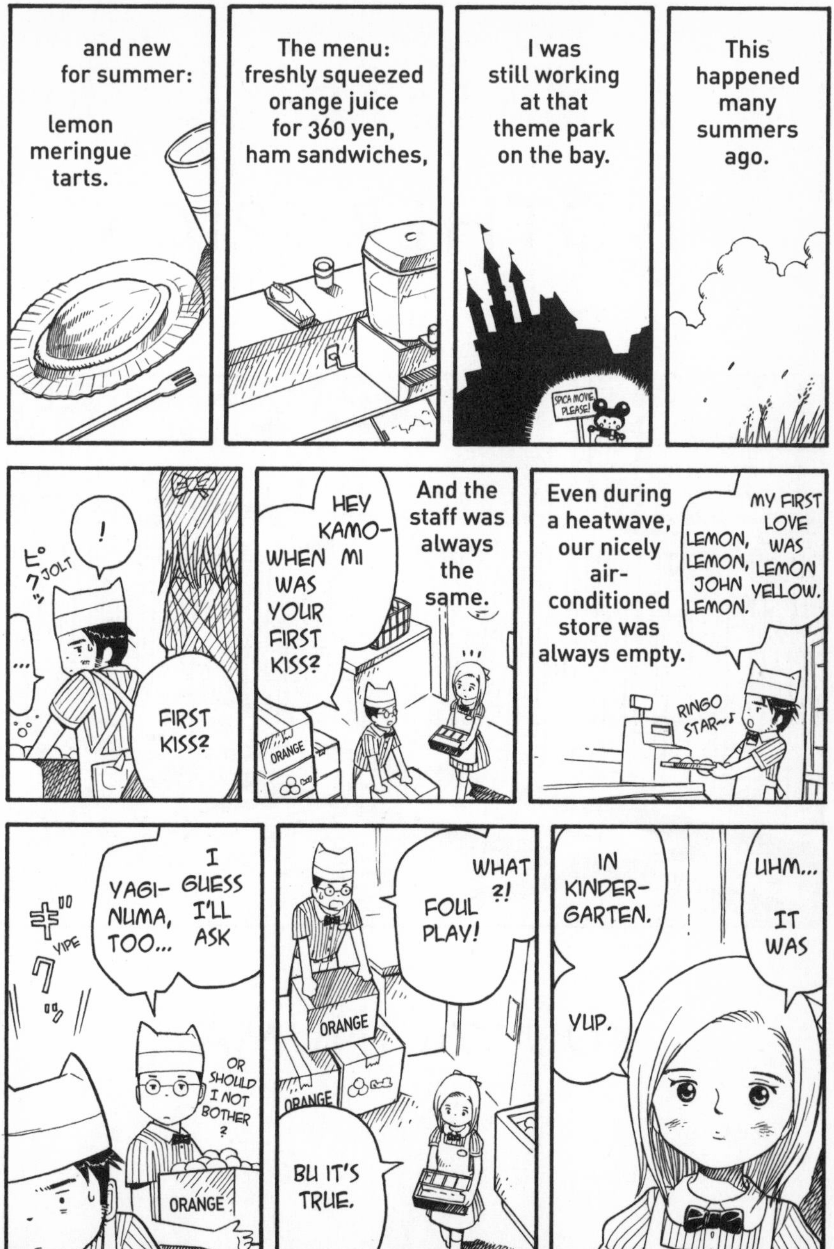
This happened many summers ago.
I was still working at that theme park on the bay.
SPICA MOVIE PLEASE!
The menu: freshly squeezed orange juice for 360 yen, ham sandwiches,
and new for summer:
lemon meringue tarts.
Even during a heatwave, our nicely air-conditioned store was always empty.
MY FIRST LOVE WAS LEMON YELLOW.
LEMON, LEMON, JOHN LEMON.
RINGO STAR~♪
And the staff was always the same.
HEY KAMO-MI WHEN WAS YOUR FIRST KISS?
ORANGE
!
ピクッ JOLT
...
FIRST KISS?
UHM... IT WAS
IN KINDER-GARTEN.
YUP.
WHAT?!
FOUL PLAY!
ORANGE
ORANGE
BU IT'S TRUE.
I GUESS I'LL ASK YAGI-NUMA, TOO...
ギクッ YIPE
OR SHOULD I NOT BOTHER?
ORANGE

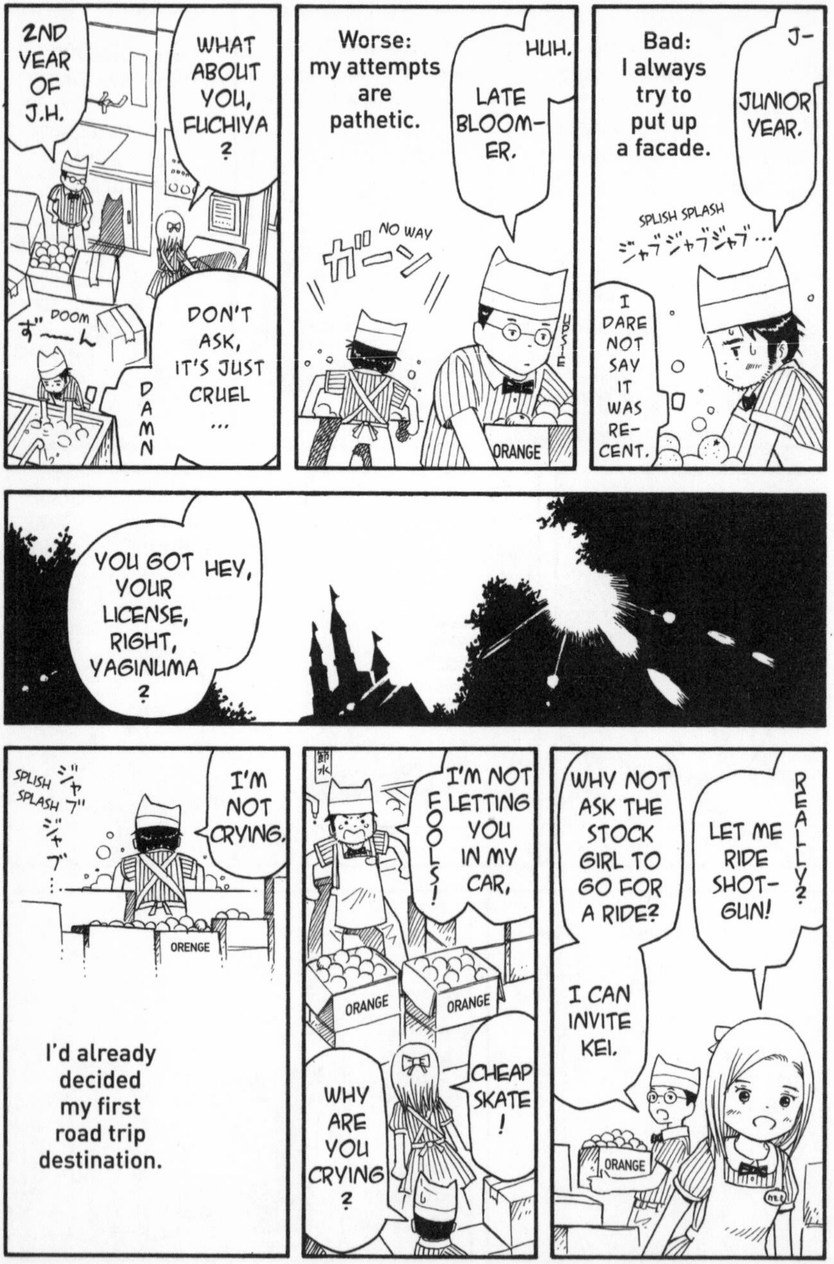
Bad: I always try to put up a facade.
J- JUNIOR YEAR.
SPLISH SPLASH
ジャブジャブジャブ…
I DARE NOT SAY IT WAS RE-CENT.
Worse: my attempts are pathetic.
HUH. LATE BLOOM-ER.
NO WAY
ガーン
ORANGE
WHAT ABOUT YOU, FUCHIYA?
2ND YEAR OF J.H.
DOOM
ずーん
DON'T ASK, IT'S JUST CRUEL...
DAMN
HEY, YOU GOT YOUR LICENSE, RIGHT, YAGINUMA?
REALLY?
LET ME RIDE SHOT-GUN!
WHY NOT ASK THE STOCK GIRL TO GO FOR A RIDE?
I CAN INVITE KEI.
ORANGE
I'M NOT LETTING YOU IN MY CAR,
FOOLS!
ORANGE
ORANGE
CHEAP SKATE!
WHY ARE YOU CRYING?
I'M NOT CRYING.
SPLISH SPLASH
ORENGE
I'd already decided my first road trip destination.

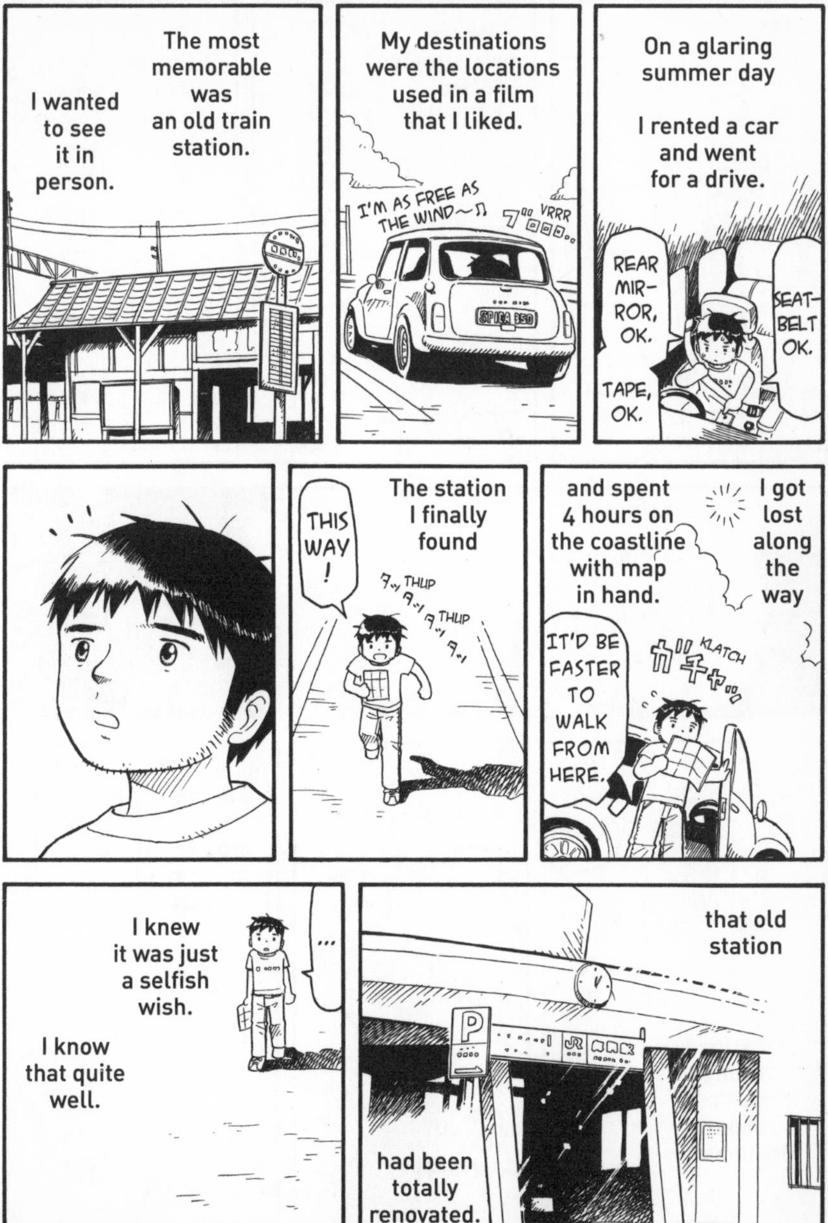
On a glaring summer day
I rented a car and went for a drive.
REAR MIR-ROR, OK.
SEAT-BELT OK.
TAPE, OK.
My destinations were the locations used in a film that I liked.
VRRR
I'M AS FREE AS THE WIND~♫
SPICA 350
The most memorable was an old train station.
I wanted to see it in person.
I got lost along the way
and spent 4 hours on the coastline with map in hand.
KLATCH
IT'D BE FASTER TO WALK FROM HERE.
The station I finally found
THUP
THUP
THIS WAY!
that old station
had been totally renovated.
...
I knew it was just a selfish wish.
I know that quite well.

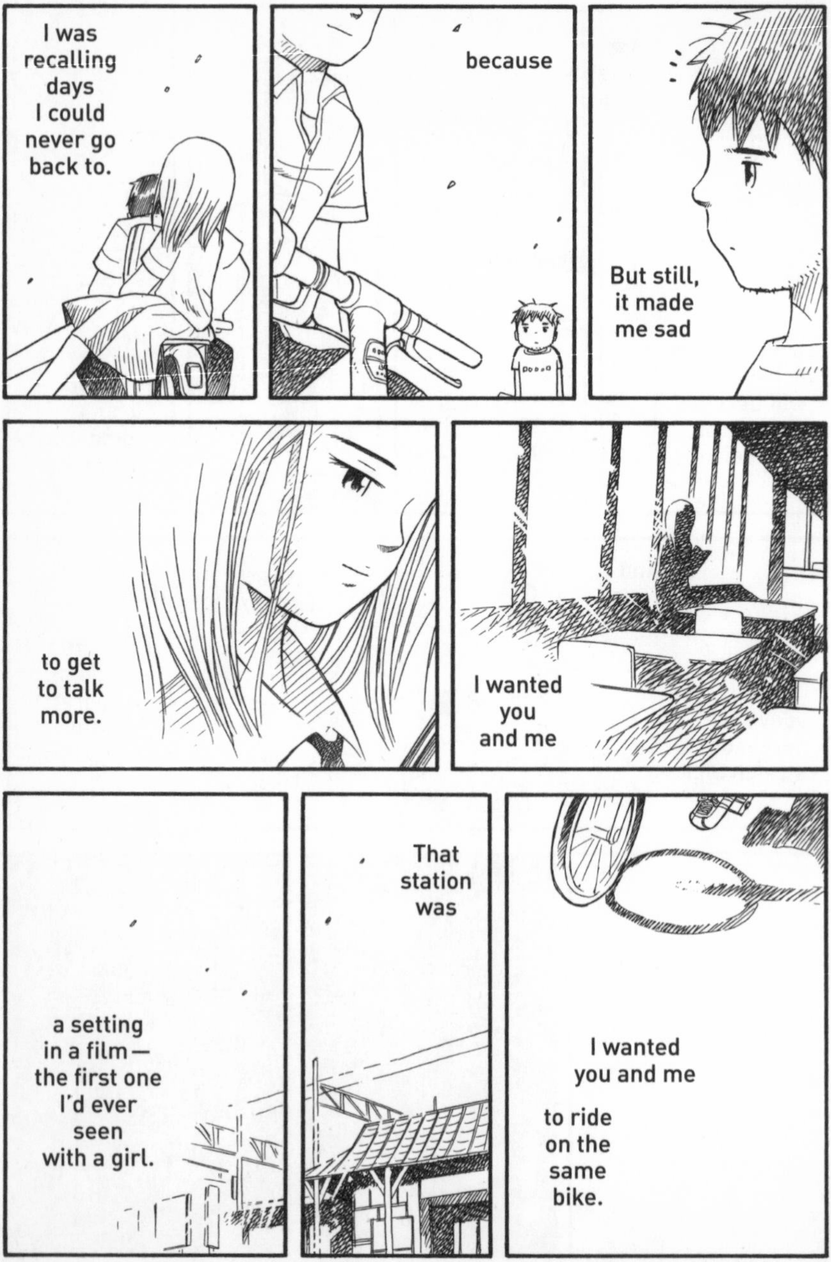
But still, it made me sad
because
I was recalling days I could never go back to.
I wanted you and me
to get to talk more.
I wanted you and me
to ride on the same bike.
That station was
a setting in a film—the first one I'd ever seen with a girl.

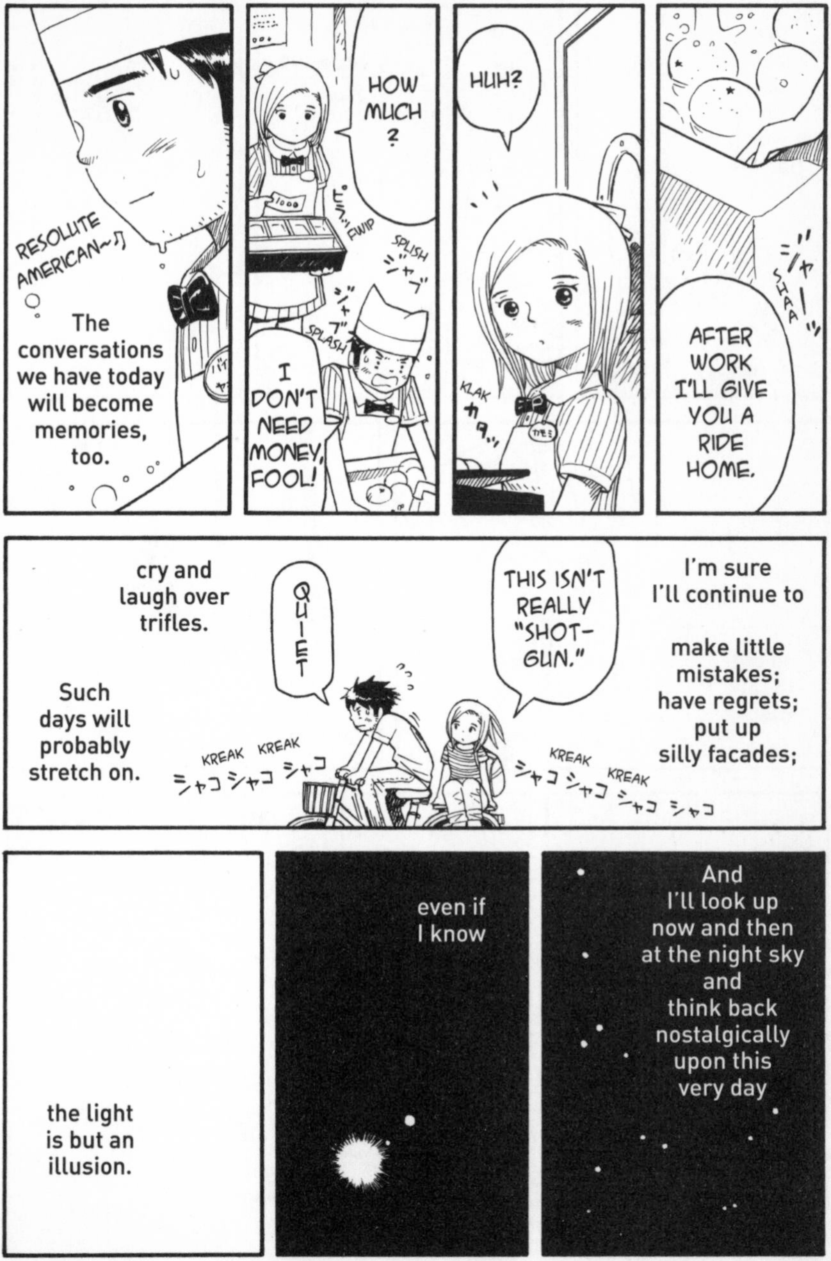
ジャ
SHAA
AFTER WORK I'LL GIVE YOU A RIDE HOME.
HUH?
KLAK
カタッ
HOW MUCH?
ピッ
FWIP
SPLISH
ジャブ
ジャブ
SPLASH
I DON'T NEED MONEY, FOOL!
RESOLUTE AMERICAN~♫
The conversations we have today will become memories, too.
I'm sure I'll continue to
make little mistakes; have regrets; put up silly facades;
THIS ISN'T REALLY "SHOT-GUN."
KREAK KREAK
シャコ シャコ シャコ シャコ
QUIET
cry and laugh over trifles.
KREAK KREAK
シャコ シャコ シャコ
Such days will probably stretch on.
And I'll look up now and then at the night sky and think back nostalgically upon this very day
even if I know
the light is but an illusion.

THE END

Notes on the Translation

P. 13

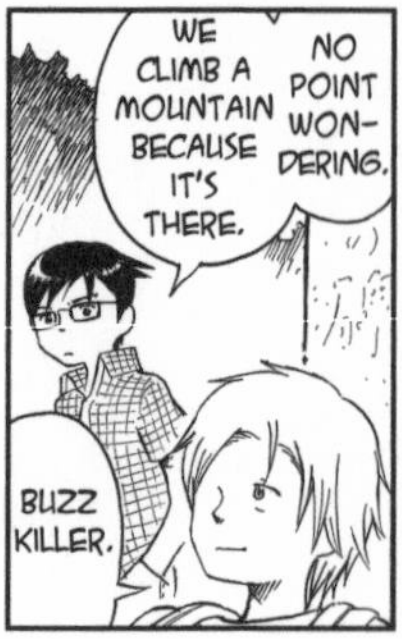
NO POINT WON-DERING.
WE CLIMB A MOUNTAIN BECAUSE IT'S THERE.
BUZZ KILLER.

Asked by a newspaper why he wanted to scale Mt. Everest, the English mountaineer George Mallory (1886-1924) is reported to have answered, "Because it's there." While the exact terse phrasing may not have been Mallory's, his simple rationale has resonated with numerous explorers. A year after his immortal reply, he perished in an expedition on the world's tallest mountain's north face.

P. 14

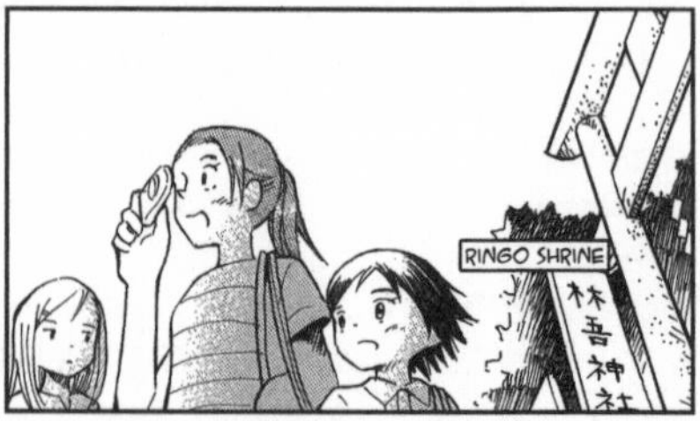
RINGO SHRINE
林吾神社

"Ringo Shrine," too cute to be true, no doubt isn't. Though the second character has been substituted for another with the same phonetic reading, "ringo" means *apple*. Meanwhile, the first character, which means *woods*, is a common enough name for shrines.

P. 186

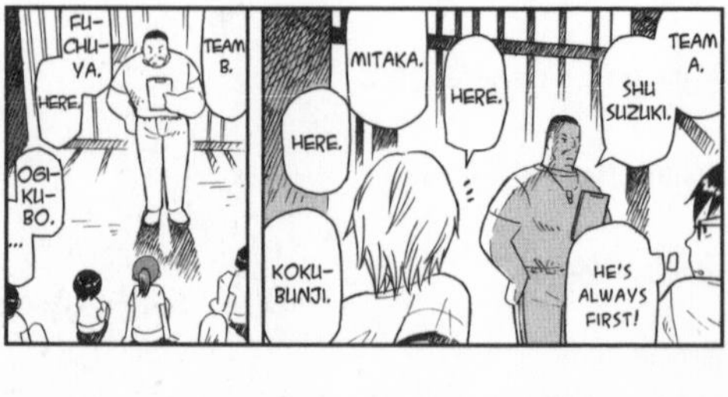
TEAM A.
SHU SUZUKI.
HERE.
MITAKA.
HERE.
KOKU-BUNJI.
HE'S ALWAYS FIRST!
TEAM B.
FU-CHU-YA.
HERE.
OGI-KU-BO.
...

Mitaka, Kokubunji, and Ogikubo are all stations on the Chuo line west of Tokyo. Readers may recall that a string of student names in volume six were taken from stops on the Oume line.

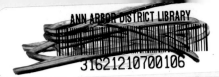

Production - Hiroko Mizuno
             Tomoe Tsutsumi
             Rina Nakayama

Originally published in Japanese as *Futatsu no Supika 7, 8*
by MEDIA FACTORY, Inc., Tokyo 2004, 2005
Futatsu no Supika first serialized in Gekkan Comic Flapper,
MEDIA FACTORY, Inc., 2001-2009

This is a work of fiction.

ISBN: 978-1-935654-12-4

Manufactured in Canada

First Edition

Vertical, Inc.
451 Park Avenue South, 7th Floor
New York, NY 10016
www.vertical-inc.com